Art across Time — Third Edition

Volume III The Sixteenth Century to the Present

Selected material from

VOLUME I: Prehistory to the 14th Century
VOLUME II: The Fourteenth Century to the Present

Laurie Schneider Adams

John Jay College
City University of New York

Boston Burr Ridge, IL Dubuque, IA New York San Francisco St. Louis
Bangkok Bogotá Caracas Lisbon London Madrid
Mexico City Milan New Delhi Seoul Singapore Sydney Taipei Toronto

The McGraw·Hill Companies

ART ACROSS TIME
Volume III The Sixteenth Century to the Present

Selected material from
VOLUME I: Prehistory to the 14th Century
VOLUME II: The Fourteenth Century to the Present

This book is a McGraw-Hill Learning Solutions textbook and contains select material from *Art Across Time, Volume II: The Fourteenth Century to The Present* by Laurie Schneider Adams. Copyright © 2007, 2002, 1999 by Laurie Schneider Adams. Reprinted with permission of the publisher. Many custom published texts are modified versions or adaptations of our best-selling textbooks. Some adaptations are printed in black and white to keep prices at a minimum, while others are in color.

1 2 3 4 5 6 7 8 9 0 QSR QSR 0 9 8 7

ISBN-13: 978-0-07-322728-3
ISBN-10: 0-07-322728-5

Editor: Katherine Kilburg
Production Editor: Carrie Braun
Cover: Photo of Henri de Toulouse-Lautrec's lithograph: *Divan Japonais* (Japanese Settee), 1893. Photo © Fototeca Storica Nazionale / Getty Images
Printer/Binder: Quebecor World

Welcome to the History of Art survey courses at the University of Cincinnati.

About the Program:
Art History is important to students who like art, enjoy learning and wish to become broadly educated. Art historians are experts on the lives and works of artists and designers, and on questions having to do with the forms, traditions, meanings and cultural context of art, architecture and design. They are specialists both in art and history.

The History of Art I: Ancient-Early Medieval is a three credit hour undergraduate course. This course is a survey of art and architecture in the ancient world and medieval Europe until about A.D. 1100. The course number is 23-ARTH-111 the section numbers will vary and the majority of classes will meet in the DAAP Aronoff building.

The History of Art II: Romanesque-Renaissance is a three credit hour undergraduate course. This course is a survey of European art and architecture from about A.D. 1100 to 1600. The course number is 23-ARTH-112 the section numbers will vary and the majority of classes will meet in the DAAP Aronoff building.

The History of Art III: Seventeenth-Twentieth Centuries is a three credit hour undergraduate course. This course is a survey of European and American art and architecture from 1600 to the present. The course number is 23-ARTH-113 the section numbers will vary and the majority of classes will meet in the DAAP Aronoff building.

The following codes are particular to these courses: T – Approved transfer module course; H – University Honors courses available; BoK:DC-p, HP – Breadth of Knowledge with partial Diversity & Culture and Historical Perspective.

Basic Component of General Education
The General Education Program fosters an important intellectual attitude: commitment to and participation in a life of thought and continuous learning. The Program includes three essential parts: a Baccalaureate Competencies (BoK) component, and a Program/Major component.

All first degree baccalaureate students must fulfill all of the requirements of the General Education Program.

The History of Art survey courses are open to majors and non-majors alike. It is our goal to reveal the history of art through contemporary social, political, religious, philosophical and historical trends and events of the given time period. We will look at, discuss, and write about art. The terminology and descriptive components of art are specific to our area of study therefore we will also strive to introduce, explain, use and become comfortable with this terminology. It is also our goal that our command of this terminology will be incorporated into the writing of a quarterly paper. This paper will focus on local art and architecture and its comparison to the works from our text.

The biggest single mistake that a student makes when writing their quarterly art or architecture paper is an improper use of scholarly material. Anytime you write a paper that includes words and/or ideas that are not your own it is imperative that you cite the source in which it came from. Failure to do so implies that you are taking sole credit for all information presented and it is called *plagiarism.* This is a serious offense and should be avoided at all costs. Provided are some examples of citation methods:

MLA Documentation Style

In the MLA format, the sources are documented within the paper. In addition to this in-text style, a Works Cited page must be provided at the end of the paper. This will be alphabetized by the author's last name. The information necessary within the paper is the author's last name accompanied by the page number on which the information is originated. If the author's name is mentioned within the sentence, then a page number will suffice.

Example:

"The stele of Naram-Sin is an impressive image of the king's power, for it proclaims the military, political, and religious authority of Naram-Sim" (Adams, 63).

Adams states that the stele of Naram-Sim carries military, political and religious messages as well as asserts the image of kingly power (63).

Chicago Documentation Style

The Chicago style uses footnotes or endnotes to cite a source. These two methods ultimately serve the same purpose with footnotes appearing at the bottom of each page and endnotes appearing at the end of the paper. In addition to this, a Bibliography must be provided and include both consulted works and cited works. This listing will be alphabetized by the author's last name. The footnote or endnote will consist of publication information, and the page number on which the information originated. If a work is repeated in successive notes, use the Latin abbreviation "Ibid.", and if the page number is different: Ibid., page number.

Example:

"The undisputed architectural masterpiece of Justinian's reign is the basilica of Hagia Sophia in Constantinople; the name in Greek is 'Holy (hagia) Wisdom (Sophia).'"[1]

Adams states that the Hagia Sophia has forty small windows at the base of its dome.[2]

Bibliography

Adams, Laurie Schneider. Art Across Time 3rd Edition, New York, New York: McGraw-Hill Companies, Inc, 2007.

---

1 Adams, Laurie Schneider. *Art Across Time* 3rd edition (New York: McGraw-Hill, 2007), 288.
2 Ibid., 289.

Contents in Brief

Contents

16 Sixteenth-Century Painting and Printmaking in Northern Europe 604

PART FIVE

17 The Baroque Style in Western Europe 626

18 Rococo and the Eighteenth Century 677

PART SIX

19 Neoclassicism: The Late Eighteenth and Early Nineteenth Centuries 702

20 Romanticism: The Late Eighteenth and Early Nineteenth Centuries 721

21 Nineteenth-Century Realism 746

22 Nineteenth-Century Impressionism 772

PART SEVEN

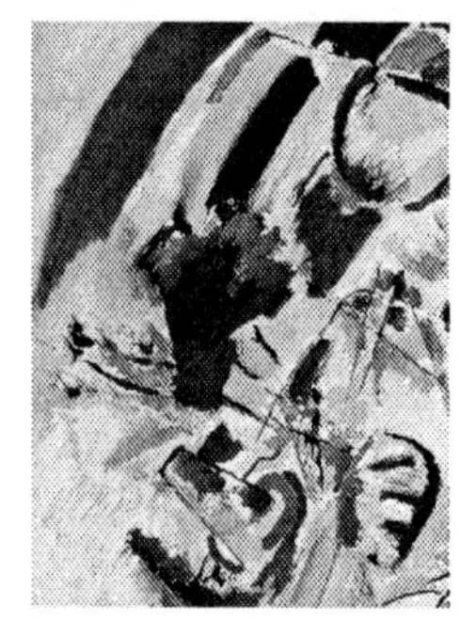

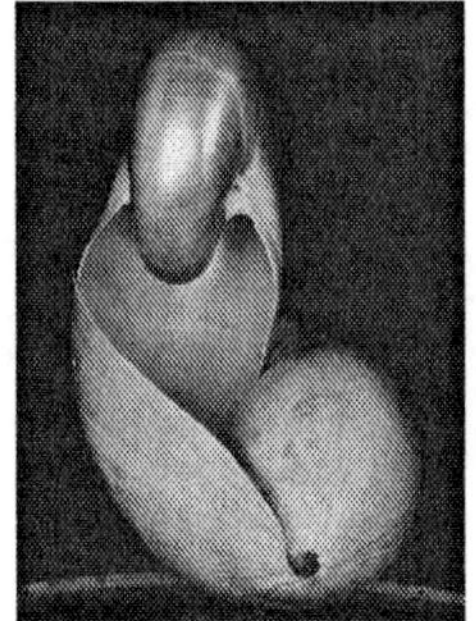

Campbell's
CONDENSED
TOMATO
SOUP

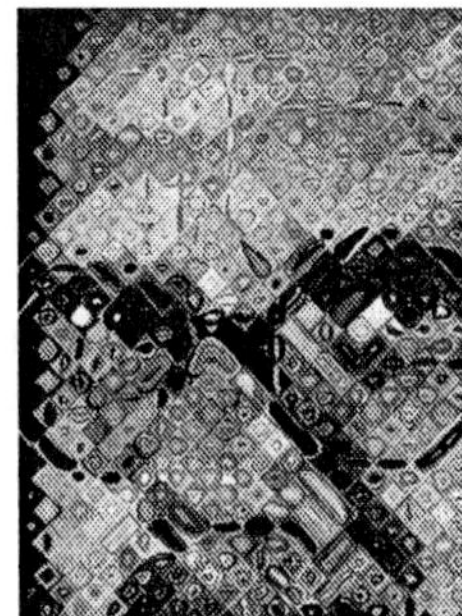

29 Innovation, Continuity, and Globalization 951

Maps

Preface

We are bombarded with images from birth and tend to assume that we understand their meaning. But the paradoxical fact is that, although children read pictures before words, a picture is more complex than a word—hence the proverbial "a picture is worth a thousand words." One aim of *Art across Time* is, therefore, to introduce readers to the complexity of images, while also surveying the history of those images. Context is a particular area of concern, for works of art lose much of their meaning if separated from the time and place in which they were created. Context also includes function, patronage, and the character and talent of the individual artist.

The complexity of the visual arts has led to different approaches to reading images. Throughout the text, therefore, there are discussions of methodology as well as new boxes entitled "Methods of Interpretation," and there is a brief survey of the modern methodologies of art-historical interpretation in the Introduction.

While comprehensive, *Art across Time* avoids an encyclopedic approach to art history and attempts instead a more manageable narrative that is suitable for a one-year survey course. Certain key works and artists are given more attention than in some books, while other works and artists are omitted entirely. An effort is made to present the history of art as a dynamic narrative grounded in scholarship, a narrative that is a dialogue between modern viewers and their past.

"Windows on the World"

Sections entitled "Window on the World" provide an introduction to the art of certain non-Western cultures. They highlight specific periods within cultures, particularly when they are thematically related to, or have significantly influenced, Western art. Some of the Windows—such as Aboriginal rock paintings in the chapter on prehistory and Japanese woodblock prints in the chapter on Impressionism (Chapter 22)—are placed within Western chapters. Others—for example, those dealing with the Indus Valley civilization, Mesoamerica, and the Far East—are placed chronologically between Western chapters. The Windows offer a sense of the range of world art and remind readers that the history of Western art is only one of many art-historical narratives. These narratives reflect the differences, as well as the similarities, between cultures and emphasize the complexity of the visual arts by taking Western readers far afield of their accustomed territory and exposing them to unfamiliar ways of thinking about the arts. As with the European artists of the early twentieth century who collected African and Oceanic sculpture in search of new, non-Classical ways of representing the human figure, so viewers who encounter such works for the first time are encouraged to stretch their own limits of seeing and understanding.

Boxes

Within chapters, readers will find boxes that encapsulate background information necessary for the study of art. These boxes take students aside, without interrupting the flow of the text, to explain media and techniques as well as different philosophies of art from Plato to Marx, Burke to Freud, and Winckelmann to Greenberg. Significant works of literature related to the arts are also covered: epics such as *Gilgamesh,* the *Iliad* and the *Odyssey,* the *Edda,* and *Beowulf,* as well as excerpts of Romantic, Dada, and contemporary poetry. One box shows Beauford Delaney quoting Balzac, an example of a personal artistic genealogy within the broader narrative of art history. Another illustrates the symbolism of color in Roman marble sculptures.

Illustration Program

The illustrations in *Art across Time* are in a consistently large format, which encourages careful looking. All of the paintings are reproduced in color, and the percentage of color is higher than in any other survey text presently on the market. Two shades of black are used for the black-and-white illustrations, resulting in greater tonal density, and all illustrations are printed on a five-color press for optimal quality. Occasionally, more than one view of a sculpture or a building is illustrated to give readers a sense of its three-dimensional reality. This has been increased for the third edition.

A new feature in the illustration program of this edition is the placement of "Connections"—small, repeated images—to show thematic continuity in the arts. Thus, for example, a small figure of Titian's *Venus of Urbino* accompanies Manet's *Olympia.* A similar system is also used for comparative purposes.

Architectural discussions are enhanced with labeled plans, sections, and axonometric diagrams. Diagrams of the Mesopotamian cone mosaic technique, of the Greek lost-wax method, of altarpieces, and of lithography and cantilever have been added. Many of the picture captions include anecdotes or biographical information about the artists; these are intended to encourage readers to identify with painters, sculptors, and architects, and they also provide a sense of the role of artists in society. Maps both define geographical context and indicate changing national boundaries over time.

Other Pedagogical Features

Languages as well as the visual arts have a history, and the etymology of art-historical terms is, therefore, provided. This reinforces the meanings of words and reveals their continuity through time. In the chapter on ancient Greece, transcriptions of terms and proper names are given according to Greek spelling, with certain exceptions in deference to convention: Acropolis, Euclid, Socrates, and Laocoön, all of which would be spelled with a "k" rather than a "c" in Greek. Likewise, Roman names and terms are given according to Latin transcription. The first time an art-historical term appears in the text, it is **boldfaced** to indicate that it is also defined in the glossary at the back of the book.

At the end of each chapter, a chronological time line of the works illustrated is useful for review purposes. This lists contemporaneous developments in other fields as well as cross-cultural artistic developments, and it contains selected images for review.

New to the Third Edition

At the request of reviewers and adopters of the second edition, the text is divided into seven parts. Each two-page part opener incorporates a time line that, in addition to placing key works of art in a chronological continuum, highlights other important developments relevant to the cultural contextualization of art. The part openers have been redesigned for the third edition and now include an introductory paragraph surveying developments covered in each part. The Introduction, formerly Chapter 1, has been updated.

In addition to the numerous text refinements, several substantial changes should be noted. The Window on the World for Mesoamerica has been rewritten, and Georgia Riley de Havenon, a pre-Columbian specialist, has contributed sections on Aztec and Andean art. The coverage of the Renaissance and Gothic periods has been reorganized. With the help of Robert Maxwell of the University of Michigan, Gothic diagrams have been redrawn to improve accuracy and pedagogy. Additional diagrams have been included and the number of color plates has been expanded in the Windows as well as throughout the text.

Finally, the last chapter has been updated to include recent artistic developments—especially globalization.

Supplements

Interactive CD-ROM

Art across Time's Core Concepts in Art CD-ROM, available free to students with every new copy of the textbook in any of its iterations, provides valuable supplemental materials. Below is a brief description and table of contents.

Description Conceived, designed, and written by students for students under the leadership of Bonnie Mitchell (Bowling Green State University), one of the preeminent multimedia designers, *Art across Time's* Core Concepts in Art CD-ROM provides supplemental exercises and information in the areas students experience difficulties.

Contents

- **Elements of Art:** Allows students to interact with the formal elements of art by working through over 70 interactive exercises illustrating line, shape, color, light, dark, and texture.
- **Art Techniques:** Takes students on a tour of art studios. *Art Techniques* illustrates working with a variety of media from bronze pouring, to painting, to video techniques with extensive, narrated video segments.
- **Chapter Resources:** Study resources correlated to each chapter of *Art across Time;* both a review and test preparation. Students will find key terms, chapter summaries, and a self-correcting study quiz to help prepare for in-class tests, midterms, and finals. Also included is an exercise on methodologies that demonstrates the application of different methods to Van Eyck's *Arnolfini Portrait.*
- **Research and the Internet:** Introduces students to the research process from idea generation, to organization, to researching on- and off-line, and includes guidelines for incorporating sources for term papers and bibliographies.
- **Study Skills:** Helps your students adjust to the rigors of college work. The *Study Skills* section of the CD-ROM provides practical advice on how to succeed at college.

Online Learning Center

Recently, the Internet has played an increasing role in college education; *Art across Time* is, therefore, supported by an Online Learning Center <http://www.mhhe.com/artacrosstime> that offers additional resources for students wishing to quiz themselves. They can send the results to their instructor via e-mail, link to additional research topics on the World Wide Web, use the pronunciation guide, follow links to artists, and more.

Student Study Guide

The student study guides are designed as chapter-by-chapter workbooks to accompany *Art across Time.* Perforated pages allow professors to assign exercises to be handed in along with each reading assignment. The exercises include brief essays, fill-in-the-blanks, matching artists with works and works with their sites. In addition, students are asked to identify key figures and define terms.

Finally, slide sets for qualifying adopters and an instructor's manual complete the impressive supplemental support package for *Art across Time.* For more information, please contact your local McGraw-Hill sales representative, or e-mail <art@mcgraw-hill.com>.

Acknowledgments

Many people have been extremely generous with their time and expertise during the preparation of this text. John Adams has helped on all phases of the book's development. Marlene Park was especially helpful during the formative stages of the one-volume text. Others who have offered useful comments and saved me from egregious errors include Steve Arbury, Paul Barolsky, Hugh Baron, James Beck, Allison Coudert, Jack Flam, Sidney Geist, Mona Hadler, Ann Sutherland Harris, Arnold Jacobs, Donna and Carroll Janis, Genevra Kornbluth, Carla Lord, Maria Grazia Pernis, Catherine Roehrig, Elizabeth Simpson, Leo Steinberg, and Rose-Carol Washton Long.

For invaluable assistance with the chapters on antiquity, I am indebted to Larissa Bonfante, Professor of Classics at New York University; Ellen Davis, Associate Professor of Art and Archaeology at Queens College, CUNY; and Oscar White Muscarella of the Department of Ancient Near Eastern Art at the Metropolitan Museum of Art, New York. Carol Lewine, emerita, Queens College, CUNY, lent her expertise to the medieval chapters and Mark Zucker, professor at Louisiana State University, vetted the Renaissance and Baroque chapters.

For assistance with illustrations, I have to thank, among others, ACA Galleries, Margaret Aspinwall, Christo and Jeanne-Claude, Anita Duquette, Michael Findlay, Georgia de Havenon, the Flavin Institute, Duane Hanson, M. Knoedler and Co., Inc., John Perkins, Carroll Janis, Ronald Feldman Gallery, Robert Miller Gallery, Pace Gallery, and Allan Stone Gallery.

For assistance in developing the third edition, I would like to thank Julia Moore and, at McGraw-Hill, Joseph Hanson and Lyn Uhl. April Wells-Hayes and Christina Gimlin shepherded the book through production, and Robin Sand did an excellent job of researching the photographs. The expert editing of Carol Flechner improved the text immeasurably, and the effective layout is due to the finely honed skills of Roberta Flechner. Jeanne Schreiber deserves high praise for the new design of the third edition and the excellent quality of the covers. Thanks also to Linda Toy and Alexis Walker for their expertise and commitment to the quality of the book.

Reviewers

Thanks to our reviewers of the third edition: Roger Aikin, Creighton University; Steve Arbury, Radford University; Peter Barr, Siena Heights College; Vince Bodily, Ricks College; Kelly Dennis, University of Connecticut; Kimberly Francev, University of Arizona; Mitchell Frank, Carleton University; Richard Green, Eastern Arizona College; Pamela Hall, Glendale Community College; Kim Hartswick, George Washington University; LuAnn S. Kanabay, University of Connecticut; Janette Knowles, Ohio Dominican University; Ellen Konowitz, State of Universty of New York at New Paltz; Jane Kyle, University of Portland; Lisa Livingston, Modesto Junior College; David Ludley, Clayton College & State University; Virginia Marquardt, Marist College; Floyd Martin, University of Arkansas-Little Rock; Dr. Andrew Marvick, Southwestern Oklahoma State University; Beth A. Mulvaney, Meredith College; Fr. James Neilson O. Praem, St. Norbert College; Mallory O'Connor, Santa Fe Community College; Michelle Pacansky-Brock, Sierra College; Donald Paoletta, Nebraska Wesleyan University; Kristin Ringelberg, Elon College; Gil Rocha, Richland Community College; Jerry Soneson, University of Northern Iowa; Carolyn Tate, Texas Tech University; Rita Tekippe, State of Universty of West Georgia; Radford Thomas, Radford University; Gavin Townsend, University of Tennessee-Chattannoga; Anne Betty Weinshenker, Montclair State.

Introduction

Why Do We Study the History of Art?

We study the arts and their history because they teach us about our own creative expressions and those of our past. Studying the history of art is one way of exploring human cultures—both ancient and modern—that have not developed written documents. For example, the prevalence of animals in the prehistoric cave paintings of western Europe reveals the importance of animals in those societies. Female figurines with oversized breasts and hips express the wish to reproduce and ensure the survival of the species. Prehistoric structures, whether oriented toward earth or sky, provide insights into the beliefs of early cultures. If such objects had not been preserved, we would know far less about ancient cultures than we now do.

We would also know less about ourselves, for art is a window onto human thought and emotion. For example, van Gogh's self-portraits are explicitly autobiographical. From what is known about his life, he was sustained by his art. In figure **I.1** he depicts himself in front of a painting that we do not see, even though we might suspect that it, too, is a self-portrait. For there are several elements in the painting that assert the artist's presence. Van Gogh's self-image predominates; he holds a set of brushes and a palette of unformed paint composed of the same colors used in the picture. At the center of the palette is an intense orange, the distinctive color of his beard, as well as

The Western Tradition

"Western art" is the product of a group of cultures that have historically been thought of as sharing common traditions. Some of these cultures, such as that of medieval France, developed in the Western Hemisphere, but others, such as that of ancient Babylon (in modern Iraq), did not. Likewise, some cultures that were geographically western, such as that of the Maya (in modern Mexico and Central America), have not traditionally been considered part of the West. This book follows the conventional (Western) usage of the terms *Western* and *non-Western:* the Western world comprises North America and Europe, as well as ancient Egypt and the ancient Near East, while the non-Western world comprises all areas and traditions outside those boundaries. It is important, however, to be aware that these categories are based as much on ideas about culture as on geography.

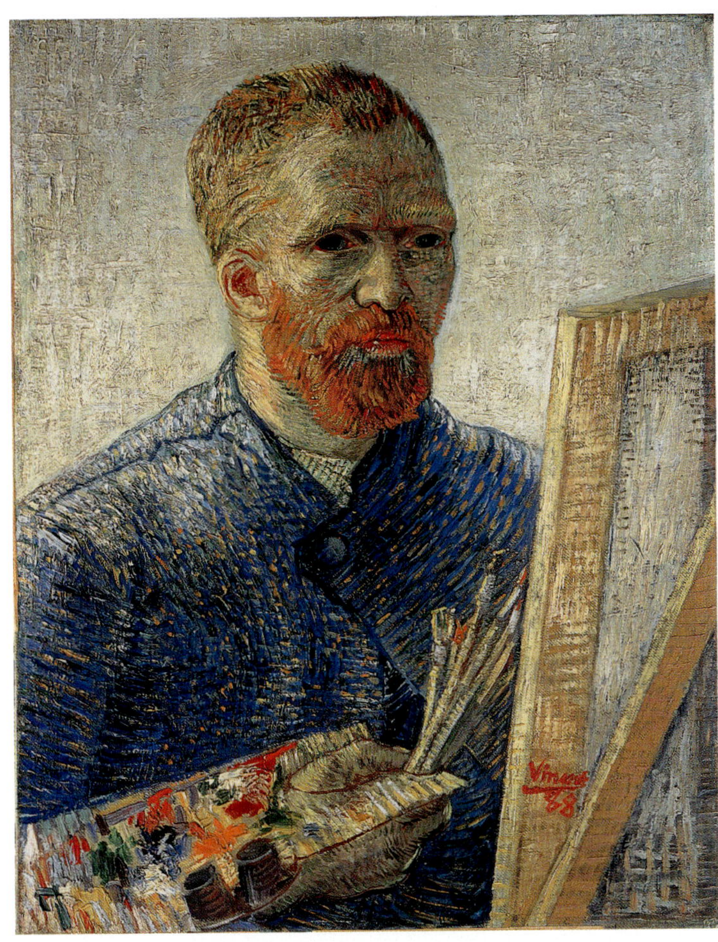

I.1 Vincent van Gogh, *Self-Portrait before his Easel*, 1888. Oil on canvas; 25¾ × 19⅞ in. (65.5 × 50.5 cm). Rijksmuseum, Amsterdam. Vincent van Gogh Foundation.

of his name (Vincent) and the date ('88), with which he simultaneously signs both the painting we see and the painting we do not see.

The arts exemplify the variety of creative expression from one culture to the next. This book surveys the major periods and styles of Western art (see box, p. 1), with certain highlights of non-Western art included to give readers a sense of differences—as well as similarities—between works of art around the world.

In the West, the major visual arts fall into three broad categories: pictures, sculpture, and architecture. Pictures (from the Latin word *pingo,* meaning "I paint") are two-dimensional images (from the Latin *imago,* meaning "likeness"), with height and width, and are usually flat. Pictures are not only paintings, however: they include mosaics, stained glass, tapestries, drawings, prints, and photographs.

Sculptures (from the Latin word *sculpere,* meaning "to carve"), unlike pictures, are three-dimensional: besides height and width, they have depth. Sculptures have traditionally been made of a variety of materials such as stone, metal, wood, and clay. More modern materials include glass, plastics, cloth, string, wire, television monitors, and even animal carcasses.

Architecture, which literally means "high (*archi*) building (*tecture*)," is the most utilitarian of the three categories. Buildings are designed to enclose and order space for specific purposes. They often contain pictures and sculptures as well as other forms of visual art. Some ancient Egyptian tombs, for example, were filled with statues of the deceased. Many churches are decorated with sculptures, paintings, mosaics, and stained-glass windows illustrating the lives of Christ and the saints. And Buddhist caves and temples contain sculptures and paintings representing events in the life of the Buddha.

One powerful motive for making art is the wish to leave behind after death something of value by which to be remembered. The work of art symbolically prolongs the artist's existence. This parallels the pervasive feeling that by having children one is ensuring genealogical continuity into the future. Several artists have made such a connection. In an anecdote about Giotto, the fourteenth-century Italian artist, the poet Dante asks Giotto why his children are so ugly and his paintings so beautiful; Giotto replies that he paints by the light of day but reproduces in the darkness of night. According to his biographers, Michelangelo said that he had no human children because his works were his children. The twentieth-century Swiss artist Paul Klee also referred to his pictures as children and equated artistic genius with procreation. His German contemporary Josef Albers cited this traditional connection between creation and procreation in relation to color: he described a mixed color as the offspring of two original colors, and compared it to a child who combines the genes of two parents.

Related to the role of art as a memorial is the wish to preserve one's likeness after death. Artists are often commissioned to paint **portraits,** or likenesses, of specific people. They also make self-portraits—likenesses of themselves. "Painting makes absent men present and the dead seem alive," wrote Leon Battista Alberti, the fifteenth-century Italian humanist. "I paint to preserve the likeness of men after their death," wrote Albrecht Dürer in sixteenth-century Germany.

See figure 16.11. Albrecht Dürer, *Self-Portrait,* 1500.

The Artistic Impulse

Art is a vital and persistent aspect of human experience. But where does the artistic impulse originate? We can see that it is inborn by observing children, who make pictures, sculptures, and model buildings before learning to read or write. Children trace images in the earth, build snowmen and sand castles, and decorate just about anything—from their own faces to the walls of their houses. All are efforts to impose order on disorder and to create form from formlessness. Although it may be difficult to relate an Egyptian pyramid or a Greek temple to a child's sand castle or toy tower, all express the natural impulse to build.

In the adult world, creating art is a continuation and development of the child's inborn impulse to play. This is clear from the statements of artists themselves: Picasso said that he was unable to learn math because every time he looked at the number 7 he thought he saw an upside-down nose. The self-taught American artist Horace Pippin described his impulse to attach drawings to words when learning to spell.

Chronology

The Christian calendar, traditionally used in the West, is followed throughout this book. Other religions, such as Hinduism, Buddhism, Islam, and Judaism, have different dating systems.

Dates before the birth of Jesus are followed by the letters B.C., an abbreviation for "before Christ." Dates after his birth are denoted by the letters A.D., from the Latin phrase *anno Domini,* meaning "in the year of our Lord." The newer terms B.C.E. ("before the common era," equivalent to B.C.) and C.E. ("common era," equivalent to A.D.) are considered more religiously neutral, but they are less historical. There is no year 0, so A.D. 1 immediately follows 1 B.C. If neither B.C. nor A.D. accompanies a date, A.D. is understood. When dates are approximate or tentative, they are preceded by "c.," an abbreviation for the Latin word *circa,* meaning "around."

See figure 4.27. "Mask of Agamemnon," from Mycenae, c. 1500 B.C.

As early as the Neolithic era (in western Europe c. 6000/4000–2000 B.C. [see box] and the seventh millennium in the Near East), skulls were modeled into faces with plaster, and shells were inserted into the eye sockets. In ancient Egypt, a pharaoh's features were painted on the outside of his mummy case so that his *ka,* or soul, could recognize him. The Mycenaeans made gold death masks of their kings, and the Romans preserved the images of their ancestors by carving marble portraits from wax death masks.

It is not only the features of an individual that are valued as an extension of self after death. A **patron,** someone who commissions (sponsors) works of art, often ordered more monumental tributes. For example, the Egyptian pharaohs spent years planning and overseeing the construction of their pyramids, not only in the belief that such monumental tombs would guarantee their existence in the afterlife, but also as a statement of their power while on earth. In ancient China, the emperor Qin was buried with a "bodyguard" of several thousand life-sized **terra-cotta** statues of warriors, chariots, and horses (fig. **I.2**). Their function was literally to guard his body in the afterlife.

In fifth-century-B.C. Athens, the Parthenon was built to house a colossal sculpture of the patron goddess Athena and, at the same time, to embody the intellectual and creative achievements of Athenian civilization. Over two thousand years later, Louis XIV, king of France, built his magnificent palace at Versailles as a monument to his political power, to his reign, and to the glory of France. And in the same period in India, the Mughal emperor Shah Jahan commissioned the Taj Mahal as a memorial to his wife, Mumtaz Mahal (fig. **I.3**).

See figure 5.48. The Parthenon, Athens, 448–432 B.C.

I.2 Bodyguard of the emperor Qin, terra-cotta warriors, Qin dynasty (221–206 B.C.), in situ. Lintong, Shaanxi Province, China.

I.3 (below) Taj Mahal, Agra, India, 1632–1648.

Why Is Art Valued?

Works of art are valued not only by artists and patrons, but also by entire cultures. In fact, the periods of history that we tend to identify as high points of human achievement are those in which art was most highly valued and encouraged.

During the Gothic era in Europe (c. 1200–1400/1500), a significant part of the economic activity of every cathedral town revolved around the construction of its cathedral, the production of sculpture, and the manufacture of stained-glass windows. In medieval India, the construction of a Hindu temple brought similar economic benefits, the largest temples supporting permanent communities of artists and other temple workers. The fourteenth- and fifteenth-century banking families of Italy spent enormous amounts of money on art to adorn public spaces, churches, chapels, and private palaces.

Today institutions as well as individuals fund works of art, and there is a flourishing art market throughout the world. More people than ever before buy and enjoy art —often as an investment—and the auctioning of art has become an international business. Art theft is also international in scale, and the usual motive is money. Well-known stolen works may be difficult to fence and thus are often held for ransom. The outrage that a community feels when some works of art disappear (or are vandalized) reflects their cultural importance. Various ways in which art is valued are explored below.

Material Value

Works of art may be valued because they are made of a precious material. Gold, for example, was used in Egyptian art to represent divinity and the sun. These associations recur in Christian art, which reserved gold for the background of religious icons (the word **icon** is derived from the Greek word *eikon,* meaning "image") and for halos on divine figures. During the Middle Ages in Europe, ancient Greek bronze statues were not valued for their **aesthetic** character (their beauty), nor for what they might have revealed about Greek culture. Instead, their value lay in the fact that they could be melted down and re-formed into weapons. Through the centuries art objects have been stolen and plundered, in disregard of their cultural, religious, or artistic significance, simply because of the value of their materials. Even the colossal cult statue of Athena in the Parthenon disappeared without a trace, presumably because of the value of the gold and ivory from which it was made.

Intrinsic Value

A work of art may contain valuable material, but that is not the primary basis on which its quality is judged. Its intrinsic value depends largely on the general assessment of the artist who created it and on its own aesthetic character. The *Mona Lisa,* for example, is made of relatively modest materials—paint and wood—but it is a priceless object nonetheless and arguably the Western world's most famous image (see fig. 14.16). Leonardo da Vinci, who painted it around 1503 in Italy, was acknowledged as a genius in his own day, and his work has stood the test of time. The works of van Gogh have also endured, although he was ignored in his lifetime. Intrinsic value is not always apparent; it varies in different times and places, as we can see in the changing assessment of van Gogh's works. "Is it art?" is a familiar question that expresses the difficulty of defining "art" and of recognizing the aesthetic value of an object (see box, p. 5).

See figure 14.16. Leonardo da Vinci, *Mona Lisa,* c. 1503–1505.

Religious Value

One of the traditional ways in which art has been valued is in terms of its religious significance. Paintings and sculptures depicting gods and goddesses make their images accessible. Such buildings as the Mesopotamian **ziggurat** (stepped tower), temples in many cultures, and Christian churches have served as symbolic dwellings of the gods, relating worshipers to their deities. Tombs express the belief in an afterlife. During the European Middle Ages, art often served an educational function. One important way of communicating Bible stories and legends of the saints to a largely illiterate population was through the sculptures, paintings, mosaics, wall hangings, and stained-glass windows in churches. Beyond its didactic (teaching) function, the religious significance of a work of art may be so great that entire groups of people identify with the object.

Nationalistic Value

Works of art have nationalistic value inasmuch as they express the pride and accomplishment of a particular culture. Nationalistic sentiment was a primary aspect of the richly carved triumphal arches of ancient Rome, which were gateways for returning military victors. Today, as in the past, statues of national heroes stand in parks and public squares in cities throughout the world.

Sometimes the nationalistic value of art is related to its religious value. In such cases, rulers take advantage of the patriotism of their subjects to impose a new religious system and to enhance its appeal through the arts. In the fourth century, under the Roman emperor Constantine, art was used to reinforce the establishment of Christianity as

Brancusi's *Bird:* Manufactured Metal or a Work of Art?

A trial held in New York City in 1927 illustrates just how hard it can be to agree on what constitutes "art." Edward Steichen, a prominent American photographer, had purchased a bronze sculpture entitled *Bird in Space* (fig. **I.4**) from the Romanian artist Constantin Brancusi, who was living in France. Steichen imported the sculpture to the United States, whose laws do not require payment of customs duty on original works of art as long as they are declared to customs on entering the country. But when the customs official saw the *Bird,* he balked. It was not art, he said: it was "manufactured metal." Steichen's protests fell on deaf ears. The sculpture was admitted into the United States under the category of "Kitchen Utensils and Hospital Supplies," which meant that Steichen had to pay $600 in import duty.

Later, with the financial backing of Gertrude Vanderbilt Whitney, an American sculptor and patron of the arts, Steichen appealed the ruling of the customs official. The ensuing trial received a great deal of publicity. Witnesses discussed whether the *Bird* was a bird at all, whether the artist could make it a bird by calling it one, whether it could be said to have characteristics of "birdness," and so on. The conservative witnesses refused to accept the work as a bird because it lacked certain biological attributes, such as wings and tail feathers. The more progressive witnesses pointed out that it had birdlike qualities: upward movement and a sense of spatial freedom. The court decided in favor of the plaintiff. The *Bird* was declared a work of art, and Steichen got his money back. In today's market, Brancusi *Birds* would sell for millions of dollars.

I.4 Constantin Brancusi, *Bird in Space,* 1928. Bronze, unique cast; 54 × 8½ × 6½ in. (137.2 × 21.6 × 16.5 cm). Museum of Modern Art, New York. Given anonymously. Brancusi objected to the view of his work as abstract. In a statement published shortly after his death in 1957, he declared: "They are imbeciles who call my work abstract; that which they call abstract is the most realist, because what is real is not the exterior form but the idea, the essence of things."

well as imperial power. Centuries earlier, the Indian emperor Ashoka had commissioned monuments throughout his realm to proclaim his conversion to Buddhism. Both Constantine and Ashoka patronized the arts in the service of revolutionary developments in politics and religion.

See figure 7.40. Arch of Constantine, Rome, c. A.D. 313.

Works of art need not represent national figures or even national or religious themes to have nationalistic value. In 1945, at the end of World War II, the Dutch authorities arrested an art dealer, Hans van Meegeren, for treason. They accused him of having sold a painting by the great seventeenth-century Dutch artist Jan Vermeer to Hermann Goering, the Nazi Reichsmarschall and Hitler's most loyal supporter. When van Meegeren's case went to trial, he lashed out at the court: "Fools!" he cried, "I painted it myself." What he had sold to the Nazis was actually his own forgery, and he proved it by painting another "Vermeer" under supervision while in prison. It would have been treason to sell Vermeer's paintings, which are considered national treasures, to the German enemy.

Another expression of the nationalistic value of art can be seen in recent exhibitions made possible by shifts in world politics. Since 1989, which marked the end of the Cold War between communist Eastern Europe and the West, Russia has been sending works of art from its museums for temporary exhibitions in the United States. In such circumstances, the traveling works become a kind of diplomatic currency, improving relations between nations.

The nationalistic value of certain works of art has frequently made them spoils of war. When ancient Babylon was defeated by the Elamites in c. 1170 B.C., the victors stole the stele of Naram-Sin (see fig. 2.17) and the law code of Hammurabi (see fig. 2.21). In the early nineteenth century, when Napoleon's armies overran Europe, they plundered thousands of works that are now part of the French national art collection in the Musée du Louvre, in Paris.

When the nineteenth-century German archaeologist Heinrich Schliemann excavated ancient Troy, in modern Turkey, he removed a hoard of gold from the site and brought it to Germany. During World War II, the Russians invaded Germany and took the treasure to Russia. They later denied any knowledge of its whereabouts, admitting only in 1994 that they had it. The issue that then arose was who owned the gold—Turkey, Germany, or Russia. The Turks argued that it was theirs by right of origin, the Germans claimed that they had excavated and essentially "discovered" it, and the Russians pointed out that they had been victors in the war (which Germany had started).

The nationalistic value of art can be so great that countries whose works have been taken go to considerable lengths to recover them. Thus, at the end of World War II, the Allied armies assigned a special division to recover the vast numbers of artworks stolen by the Nazis. A United States army task force discovered Hermann Goering's two personal hoards of stolen art in Bavaria, one in a medieval castle and the other in a bomb-proof tunnel in nearby mountains. The task force arrived just in time, for Goering had equipped an "art train" with thermostatic temperature control to take "his" collection to safety. At the Nuremberg war trials, Goering claimed that his intentions had been purely honorable: he was protecting the art from air raids.

Another example of the nationalistic value of art can be seen in the case of the Elgin Marbles. In the early nineteenth century, when Athens was under Turkish rule, Thomas Bruce, seventh earl of Elgin, obtained permission from Turkey to remove sculptures from the Parthenon and other buildings on the Acropolis. At huge personal expense (£75,000), Lord Elgin sent the sculptures by boat to England. The first shipment sank, but the remainder of the works reached their destination in 1816 and the British Museum in London purchased the sculptures for only £35,000. The Elgin Marbles, also known as the Parthenon Marbles, are still in the British Museum, where they are a tourist attraction and are studied by scholars. For years, the Greeks have been pressing for the return of the sculptures, but the British have refused. This kind of situation is a product of historical circumstance. Although Lord Elgin broke no laws and probably saved the sculptures from considerable damage, he is seen by many Greeks as having looted their cultural heritage.

See figure 5.53. Lapith and Centaur, from south metope XXVII of the Parthenon, 5th century B.C.

Modern legislation in some countries is designed to avoid similar problems by restricting or banning the export of national treasures. International cooperation agreements (protocols) attempt to protect cultural property and archaeological heritage worldwide.

Psychological Value

Another symbolic value of art is psychological. Our reactions to art span virtually the entire range of human emotion. They include pleasure, fright, amusement, avoidance, and outrage.

One of the psychological aspects of art is its ability to attract and repel us, and this is not necessarily a function of whether or not we find a particular image aesthetically pleasing. People can become attached to a work of art, as Leonardo was to his *Mona Lisa* (see fig. 14.16). Instead of delivering it to the patron, Leonardo kept the painting until his death. Conversely, one may wish to destroy certain works because they arouse anger. In London in the early twentieth century, a suffragette slashed Velázquez's *Rokeby Venus* (see fig. 17.54) because she was offended by what she considered to be its sexist representation of a woman. During the French Revolution of 1789, mobs protesting the injustices of the royal family destroyed statues and paintings of earlier kings and queens. In 1989 and 1990, when Eastern Europe began to rebel against communism, the protesters tore down statues of their former leaders. In Afghanistan, the fundamentalist Islamic Taliban regime blew up colossal statues of the Buddha because the statues were figurative and thus seen as not conforming to the rules of the Koran (Qu'ran). In so doing, the Taliban breached the UNESCO Convention of 1972 and the Geneva Convention riders of 1977 and 1997. Both forbid the destruction of cultural property. All these examples illustrate intense responses to the symbolic power of art.

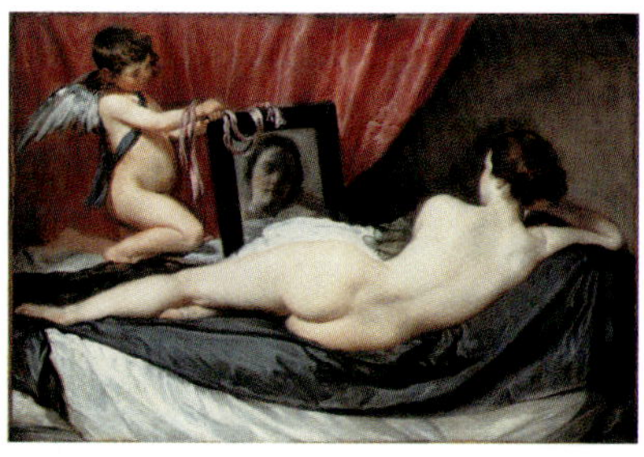

See figure 17.54. Diego Velázquez, *Venus with a Mirror (Rokeby Venus)*, c. 1648.

Art and Illusion

Before considering illusion and the arts, it is necessary to point out that when we think of illusion in connection with an image, we usually assume that the image is true to life, or naturalistic (cf. **naturalism**). This is often, but not always, the case. With certain exceptions, such as some Judaic and Islamic art, Western art was mainly representational until the twentieth century. **Representational,** or **figurative,** art depicts recognizable natural forms or created objects (see p. 24). When the subjects of representational pictures and sculptures are so convincingly portrayed that they may be mistaken for the real thing, they are said to be illusionistic (cf. **illusionism**). Where the artist's purpose is to fool the eye, the effect is described by the French term ***trompe-l'oeil.***

The deceptive nature of pictorial illusion was simply but eloquently stated by the Belgian Surrealist painter René Magritte in *The Betrayal of Images* (see box, p. 7). This work is a convincing (although not a *trompe-l'oeil*) rendition of a pipe. Directly below the image, Magritte reminds the viewer that in fact it is not a pipe at all—*"Ceci n'est pas une pipe"* ("This is not a pipe") is Magritte's explicit message. To the extent that observers are convinced by the image, they have been betrayed. Even though Magritte was right about the illusion falling short of reality, the observer nevertheless enjoys having been fooled.

Images and Words

Artists express themselves through a visual language which has pictorial, sculptural, and architectural, rather than verbal, elements. As a result, no amount of description can replace the direct experience of viewing art. As discussed on pages 18–23, the artist's language consists of formal elements such as line, shape, space, color, light, dark, and so forth, whereas discussion about art is in words. Imagine, for example, if the words in Magritte's *The Betrayal of Images* (fig. **I.5**) read "This is a pipe" *(Ceci est une pipe)* or even only "Pipe," instead of "This is not a pipe" *(Ceci n'est pas une pipe)*. Although we might receive the same meaning of "pipeness" from both the word and the image, our experience of the verbal description would be quite different from our experience of its subject.

I.5 René Magritte, *The Betrayal of Images* ("This is not a pipe"), 1928. Oil on canvas; 23½ × 28½ in. (55.0 × 72.0 cm). Los Angeles County Museum of Art, California.

The pleasure produced by *trompe-l'oeil* images is reflected in many anecdotes, perhaps not literally true but illustrations of underlying truths. For example, the ancient Greek artist Zeuxis was said to have painted grapes so realistically that birds pecked at them. In the Renaissance, a favorite story recounted that the painter Cimabue was so deceived by Giotto's realism that he tried to brush off a fly that Giotto had painted on the nose of a painted figure. The twentieth-century American sculptor Duane Hanson was a master of *trompe-l'oeil.* He used synthetic materials to create statues that look so alive that it is not unusual for people to approach and speak to them.

In these examples of illusion and *trompe-l'oeil,* artists produce only a temporary deception. But such may not always be the case. For instance, the Latin poet Ovid relates the tale of the sculptor Pygmalion, who was not sure whether his own statue was real. Disillusioned by the infidelities of women, Pygmalion turned to art and fashioned a beautiful girl, Galatea, out of ivory. He dressed her and brought her jewels and flowers. He undressed her and took her to bed. During a feast of Venus (the Roman goddess of love and beauty), Pygmalion prayed for a wife as lovely as his *Galatea.* Venus granted his wish by bringing the statue to life.

See figure 29.6. Duane Hanson, *The Cowboy,* 1995.

Artists and Gods

The fine line between reality and illusion, and the fact that gods are said to create reality and artists create illusion, have given rise to traditions equating artists with gods. Both are seen as creators, the former making replicas of nature and the latter making nature itself. Alberti referred to the artist as an *alter deus,* Latin for "other god," and Dürer said that artists create as God did. Leonardo wrote in his *Notebooks* that artists are God's grandsons and that painting, the grandchild of nature, is related to God. Giorgio Vasari, the Italian Renaissance biographer of artists, called Michelangelo "divine," a reflection of the notion of divine inspiration. The nineteenth-century American painter James McNeill Whistler declared that artists are "chosen by the gods."

Artists have been compared with gods, and gods have been represented as artists. In ancient Babylonian texts, God is described as the architect of the world. In the Middle Ages, God is sometimes depicted as an architect drawing the universe with a compass (fig. **I.6**). Legends in the Apocrypha, the unofficial books of the Bible, portray Christ as a sculptor who made clay birds and breathed life into them. Legends such as these are in the tradition of the supreme and omnipotent male artist-as-genius, and they reflect the fact that the original meaning of *genius* was "divinity."

The comparison of artists with gods, especially when artists make lifelike work, has inspired legends of rivalry between these two types of creator. Even when the work itself is not lifelike, the artist may risk incurring divine anger. For example, the Old Testament account of the Tower of Babel illustrates the dangers of building too high and rivaling God by invading the heavens. God reacted by confounding the speech of the builders so that they seemed to each other to be "babbling" incomprehensibly. They scattered across the earth, forming different language groups. In the sixteenth-century painting by the

I.6 *God as Architect (God Drawing the Universe with a Compass)*, from the *Bible moralisée*, Reims, France, fol. Iv, mid-13th century. Illumination; 8⅓ in. (21.2 cm) wide. Österreichische Nationalbibliothek, Vienna.

Flemish artist Pieter Bruegel the Elder (fig. **I.7**), the Tower of Babel seems about to cave in from within, although it does not actually do so. Bruegel's tower is thus a metaphor for the collapsed ambition of the builders. A related story is told by the Roman historian Pliny: the emperor Nero angered the god Jupiter by erecting a colossal statue of himself. Jupiter destroyed the image of the presumptuous mortal with a thunderbolt.

Some legends endow sculptors and painters with the power to create living figures without divine intervention. In Greek mythology, the sculptor Daedalos was reputed to have made lifelike statues that could walk and talk. Prometheus, on the other hand, was not satisfied with merely lifelike works: he wanted to create life itself. Since the ancient Greeks believed that human beings were made of earth (the body) and fire (the soul), Prometheus knew that he needed more than clay to create living figures. He therefore stole fire from the gods, and they punished him with eternal torture.

I.7 Pieter Bruegel the Elder, *The Tower of Babel*, 1563. Tempera on panel; 3 ft. 9 in. × 5 ft. 1 in. (1.14 × 1.55 m). Kunsthistorisches Museum, Vienna.

Art and Identification

Reflections and Shadows: Legends of How Art Began

Belief in the power of images extends beyond the work of human hands. In many societies, not only certain works of art but also reflections and shadows are thought to embody the spirit of an animal or the soul of a person. Ancient traditions trace the origin of image making to drawing a line around a reflected image or shadow. Alberti recalled the myth of Narcissus—a Greek youth who fell in love with his own image in a pool of water—and compared the art of painting to the reflection. The Roman writer Quintilian, on the other hand, identified the first painting as a line traced around a shadow. A Buddhist tradition recounts that the Buddha was unable to find an artist who could paint his portrait. As a last resort, he had an outline drawn around his shadow and filled it in with color himself.

A Greek legend attributes the origin of sculpture to a young woman of Corinth, who traced the shadow of her lover's face cast on the wall by lamplight. Her father, a potter, filled in the outline with clay, which he then **fired** (burned in a kiln). This story became particularly popular during the Romantic period in Europe and has been memorialized in *The Corinthian Maid* (fig. **I.8**) by the English painter Joseph Wright of Derby. Legends such as this indicate that works of art are inspired not only by the impulse to create form, but also by the discovery or recognition of forms that already exist and the wish to capture and preserve them.

Image Magic

People in many cultures believe that harm done to an image of someone will hurt the actual person. In sixteenth-century England, Queen Elizabeth I's advisers summoned a famous astrologer to counteract witchcraft when they discovered a wax effigy of the queen stuck through with pins.

See figure 20.25. George Catlin, *The White Cloud, Head Chief of the Iowas*, 1844–1845. Oil on canvas; 28 × 22⅞ in. (71.1 × 58.1 cm). National Gallery of Art, Washington, D.C.

Sometimes, usually in cultures without strong traditions of figural art, people fear that pictures of themselves may embody—and snatch away—their souls. Many nineteenth-century Native Americans objected to having their portraits painted. One of the outsiders who did paint their portraits was George Catlin, whose memoirs record suspicious and occasionally violent reactions. Even today, with media images permeating so much of the globe, people in remote areas may resist being photographed for fear of losing themselves if their image is taken away. In fact, the very language we use to describe photography reflects this phenomenon: we "take" pictures and "capture" our subjects on film.

I.8 Joseph Wright of Derby, *The Corinthian Maid*, 1782–1784. Oil on canvas; 41⅞ × 51½ in. (1.06 × 1.30 m). National Gallery of Art, Washington, D.C. Paul Mellon Collection.

I.9 James Abbott McNeill Whistler, *Arrangement in Black and Gray (Portrait of the Artist's Mother)*, 1871. Oil on canvas; 4 ft. 9 in. × 5 ft. 4½ in. (1.45 × 1.64 m). Musée d'Orsay, Paris.

Portraits can also create very strong impressions. The nineteenth-century English art critic John Ruskin fell in love with an image on two separate occasions. He became so enamored of the marble tomb effigy of Ilaria del Caretto in Lucca, Italy, that he wrote letters home to his parents describing the statue as if it were a living girl. Later, when Ruskin was in a delusional state, he persuaded the Accademia, a museum in Venice, to lend him a painting of Saint Ursula by the sixteenth-century artist Carpaccio. Ruskin kept it in his room for six months and became convinced that he had been reunited with his former fiancée, a young Irish girl named Rose la Touche, whom he merged in his mind with the painted saint. A less extreme form of the identification of a woman with an image concerns Whistler's famous portrait of his mother (fig. **I.9**). "Yes," he replied when complimented on the picture. "One does like to make one's mummy just as nice as possible."

The ability to identify with images and the sense that a replica may actually contain the soul of what it represents have sometimes led to an avoidance of images. Certain religions prohibit their adherents from making pictures and statues of their god(s) or of human figures in sacred contexts. In Judaism, the making of figurative images is expressly forbidden in the second commandment: "Thou shalt not make unto thee any graven image, or any likeness of any thing that is in heaven above, or that is in the earth beneath, or that is in the water under the earth" (Exodus 20:4). Before receiving these instructions, the Israelites had been worshiping a golden calf, which Moses destroyed when he brought them the Commandments. Years later, the prophet Jeremiah declared both the pointlessness and the dangers of worshiping objects instead of God the Creator.

In Islam, as in Judaism, the human figure is generally avoided in religious art. The founder of Islam, the prophet Muhammad, condemned those who would dare to imitate God's work by making figurative art. As a result, Islamic art developed its characteristic emphasis on complex patterns.

During the Iconoclastic Controversy in the eighth and ninth centuries, Christians argued vehemently over the potential dangers of creating any images of holy figures. Like the Jews, Christians wishing to destroy existing images and to prohibit new ones believed that such works of art would lead to idolatry, or worship of the image itself rather than what it stood for.

A different interpretation of this connection between images and gods can be seen in Hindu beliefs about religious sculpture, which is intensely figurative. Hindu statues are considered available for their associated deities to inhabit. Because they are thought capable of changing their outer appearances in order to become manifest and comprehensible to human worshipers, the gods can enter sculptures that have the appropriate forms. Hindu sculpture is thus conceived of as a sacred vessel for the divine presence.

In the modern era, as societies have become increasingly technological, traditional imagery seems to have lost some of its magic power. But art still engages us. A peaceful **landscape** painting, for example, provides a respite from everyday tensions as we contemplate its rolling hills or distant horizon. A **still life** depicting fruit in a bowl reminds us of the beauty inherent in objects we take for granted. And it remains true that abstract works of art containing no recognizable objects or figures can involve us in the rhythms of their shapes, the movements of their lines, and the moods of their colors. Large public sculptures, many of which are **nonrepresentational,** mark our social spaces and humanize them. Architecture, too, defines and enriches our environment. In addition, contemporary images, many in electronic media, exert power over us in both obvious and subtle ways by drawing on our image-making traditions. Movies and television affect our tastes and aesthetic judgments. Advertising images influence our decisions—what we buy and which candidates we vote for. Computer-based digital art is one of the fastest growing art fields. Such modern media use certain traditional techniques of image making to convey their messages.

See figure W3.10. The Great Stupa at Sanchi, Madhya Pradesh, India, 3rd century B.C.

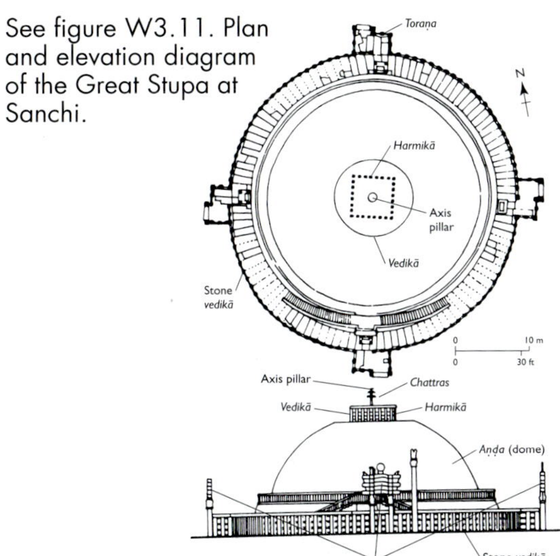

See figure W3.11. Plan and elevation diagram of the Great Stupa at Sanchi.

Architecture

As is true of pictures and sculptures, architecture evokes a response by identification. A building may seem inviting or forbidding, gracious or imposing, depending on how its appearance strikes the viewer. One might think of a country cottage as welcoming and picturesque, or of a haunted house as endowed with the spirits of former inhabitants who inflict mischief on trespassers.

Architecture is more functional, or utilitarian, than pictures and sculptures. Usually the very design of a building conforms to the purpose for which it was built. The criterion for a successful building is not only whether it looks good, but also whether it fulfills its function well. A hospital, for example, may be aesthetically pleasing, but its ultimate test is whether it serves the patients and medical staff adequately. A medieval castle was not only a place to live, it was also a fortress requiring defensive features such as a moat, drawbridge, towers, small windows, and thick, crenellated walls.

Beyond function, the next most important consideration in architecture is its use of space. The scale (size) of buildings and the fact that, with very few exceptions, they can enclose us make our responses to them significantly different from our reactions to pictures or sculptures. Pictures convey only the illusion of space. Sculptures occupy actual, three-dimensional space, although the observer generally remains on the outside of that space looking in.

In the ancient world, many buildings, such as Egyptian pyramids and Greek temples, were intended to be experienced either exclusively or primarily from the outside. But a Buddhist **stupa** had a solid core and, therefore, no interior at all. Its hemispherical shape represented the Buddha's original burial mound, which became a symbol of the cosmos. Worshipers enter the sacred space surrounding a stupa through a gateway marking the transition from the ordinary to the spiritual world. They walk around the perimeter of the stupa in a ritual **circumambulation** that reiterates the Buddha's own spiritual journey. When religious structures do have interiors, access to their inner sanctuaries is frequently restricted. Psychologically as well as aesthetically, therefore, our response to architecture is incomplete until we have experienced it physically. Because such an experience involves time and motion as well as vision, it is particularly challenging to describe architecture through words and pictures.

The experience of architectural space appears in everyday language. We speak of "insiders" and "outsiders," of being "in on" something, and of being "out of it." The significance of "in" and "out" recurs in certain traditional architectural arrangements. In parts of the ancient world, the innermost room of a temple, its sanctuary, was considered the most sacred, the "holy of holies," which only a high priest or priestess could enter. Likewise, an appointment with a VIP is often held in an inner room that is generally closed to the public at large. Access is typically through a series of doors, so that in popular speech we say of people who have influence that they can "open doors."

I.10 Jan van Eyck, *The Virgin in a Church*, c. 1410–1425. Oil on panel; 12¼ × 5½ in. (31.0 × 14.0 cm). Gemäldegalerie, Staatliche Museen, Berlin. It is thought that, given the narrowness of this picture, it may originally have been part of a **diptych**—a work consisting of two panels—in which case the other section is lost.

Our identification with the experience of being inside begins before birth. Unborn children exist in the enclosed space of their mother's womb, where they are provided with protection, nourishment, and warmth. This biological reality has resulted in a traditional association between women and architecture. The inner sanctum of Hindu temples, for example, is called a ***garbha griha,*** meaning "womb chamber." In medieval Christianity, the intuitive relationship between motherhood and architecture gave rise to a popular metaphor equating the Virgin Mary (as mother of Christ) with the Church building. This metaphor is given visual form in Jan van Eyck's fifteenth-century painting *The Virgin in a Church* (fig. **I.10**). Here Mary is enlarged in relation to the architecture, identifying her with the Church as the House of God. Van Eyck portrays an intimacy between the Virgin and Christ that evokes both the natural closeness of mother and child and the spiritual union between the human and the divine.

This union is an important aspect of the sense of space in religious architecture. The vast interior spaces of Gothic cathedrals, for example, are awe-inspiring, making worshipers feel small compared to an all-encompassing God. The upward movement of the interior space, together with the tall towers and spires on either side of the entrance, echo the Christian belief that paradise is up in the heavens. The rounded spaces of certain other places of worship, such as the domed ceilings of some mosques, likewise symbolize the dome of heaven. In a sense, then, these religious buildings stand as a kind of transitional space between earth and sky, between our limited time on earth and beliefs about infinite time, or eternity.

Just as we respond emotionally and physically to the open and closed spaces of architecture, so our metaphors indicate our concern for the structural security of our buildings. "A house of cards" or a "castle in the air" denotes instability and irrational thinking. This notion is reflected in the old joke "Neurotics build castles in the air, and psychotics live in them." Since buildings are constructed from the bottom up, a house built on a "firm foundation" can symbolize stability, rational thinking, forethought, and advance planning. In the initial stages of a building's conception, the architect makes a plan. Called a **ground plan,** or floor plan, it is a detailed drawing of each story of the structure, indicating where walls and other architectural elements are located. Although in everyday speech we use the term *to plan* in a figurative sense, unless the architect constructs a literal and well-thought-out plan, the building, like a weak argument, will not stand up.

Why Do We Collect Art?

In antiquity, art was valued as booty taken from conquered peoples. In ancient Egypt, Babylon, China, and India, looted art was exhibited in temples and palaces to enhance the power of rulers and priests. Even today, the value of art as military booty has not been entirely eliminated. In 1992, when the National Museum in Kabul, Afghanistan, was hit by rockets, looters pillaged the collection. Afghanistan's location made it a crossroads of trade for thousands of years, and this was reflected in unique objects from many different cultures that have now disappeared. Experts believe that some of these thefts were "commissioned" by agents working for unscrupulous collectors.

Ancient cultures have a long history of royal and aristocratic art collecting. In Europe, art collecting for the intrinsic value of the works began in Hellenistic Greece (323–31 B.C.). Romans plundered Greek art and also had a thriving industry copying Greek art, which was collected, especially by emperors. During the Middle Ages, the Christian Church was the main collector of art in Europe.

Interest in collecting ancient art revived in the West during the Renaissance and continued in royal families for several centuries. Some of these royal collections became the basis for major museums—in the late eighteenth century, the Louvre was opened in Paris, and the Russian and British royal collections were opened to the public in the early nineteenth century. By that time more and more private individuals collected art, and since then dealers, auction houses, museums, and the media have further expanded collecting.

Archaeology and Art History

The works of art illustrated in this book are the subject of two academic fields: archaeology and art history. Archaeology (from the Greek words *archaios,* meaning "old" or "beginning," and *logos,* meaning "word") is literally a study of beginnings. The value of such study was expressed by the German author Johann Wolfgang von Goethe in 1819 as follows:

> He who'd know what life's about
> Three millennia must appraise;
> Else he'll go in fear and doubt,
> Unenlightened all his days.[1]

A related sentiment was expressed by Sigmund Freud when he declared that "only a good-for-nothing is not interested in his past."

The primary aim of the archaeologist is the reconstruction of history from the physical remains of past cultures. These remains are not confined to the arts, but can be anything from bone fragments and debris, safety pins and frying pans, to entire water-supply systems of buried cities. Unvandalized graves protected from the elements and hidden from the view of potential plunderers yield some of the best evidence. On occasion, cities such as Pompeii and Herculaneum in southern Italy are discovered relatively intact, providing a remarkable glimpse of the past. In its early days in the nineteenth century, archaeology was largely the province of amateur explorers and collectors of antiquities. There was little or no concern for preserving the cultural or historical context of the finds.

Today archaeology is more scientific and professional, calling on many other disciplines to assist with analyzing its discoveries by material, stylistic type, function, and date, as well as in preserving them (see box, p. 14). Ecology, for example, elucidates aspects of the natural environment, some of which can be used for dating. Statistics indicating population size and growth in a particular culture can clarify its development and longevity. Other fields that contribute to archaeology include chemistry, physics, computer science, linguistics (where there is evidence of writing), sociology, anthropology, and art history.

Art history is the study of the history of the visual arts. It should be distinguished from art appreciation, which is primarily about aesthetics. Philosophers of both the East and the West have discussed the nature of aesthetics since antiquity. While art history has a venerable tradition in China, it did not become an academic discipline in the West until the nineteenth century. Art history in the West has traditionally dealt with the analysis of individual works of art and their grouping into larger categories of style. Art historians recognize that many factors contribute to the production of a work, including its culture (time and place), artist, patron, medium, and function. Art history is used by archaeologists as well as other scholars studying everyday life, religious practices, means of warfare, and so forth. Stylistic analysis of works of art helps archaeologists date layers of cultures and is of great importance to cultural and economic historians in determining patterns of trade.

How Do We Approach Art?

The complexity of images has led to the development of various interpretative approaches. Principal among these so-called methodologies of art-historical analysis are formalism, iconography and iconology, Marxism, feminism, biography and autobiography, semiology, deconstruction, and psychoanalysis. Generally, art historians approach works using some combination of these methods.

The Methodologies of Art

Formalism Chronologically, the earliest codified methodology is **formalism**, which grew out of the nineteenth-century aesthetic of "Art for Art's Sake"—artistic activity as an end in itself. Adherents of pure formalism view works of art independently of their context, function, and content. They respond to the formal elements and to the aesthetic effect that the arrangement of those elements creates. Two philosophers, Plato in ancient Greece and Immanuel Kant in eighteenth-century Germany, can be seen as precursors of formalist methodology. They

The Archaeological Dig

Archaeologists locate buried cultures by observing anomalies in topography such as earth mounds, traces of roads, and the geological disposition of rocks and minerals. Aerial photography is particularly helpful for this purpose. The location chosen for excavation is known as the site. Typically, each site has a director, a trained archaeologist who oversees the excavation. Under the director are various supervisors, staffers, and volunteers. Architectural drawings are made to record the remains of buildings and reconstruct their original plans. Finds are photographed, drawn, catalogued, and analyzed by specialists. A conservator advises on preserving objects. A foreman hires and oversees local workers and attends to necessities such as food, water, and medical supplies.

Archaeological Dating Techniques

The role of archaeology in studying prehistoric periods (i.e., those for which no contemporary written records exist) is crucial. Central to archaeological methods is the establishment of time sequences for events and objects. During the twentieth century a number of techniques have been developed for arriving at the age of ancient objects and the chronology of prehistoric events.

Through **stratigraphy** (the geological study of the layers [strata] of the earth), objects deposited in these layers can be dated. Stratigraphy rests on the principle—known as the Law of Superposition—that, in the absence of external factors, older (earlier) materials in an archaeological deposit are found lower than newer (later) materials. By careful excavation and meticulous record keeping, archaeologists are able to relate objects to each other both vertically (to determine their relative chronology) and horizontally (for clues to cultural patterns within individual periods).

Seriation, another method of fixing relative dates, is based on the reconstruction of changes in style or type that can be observed in archaeological artifacts (e.g., tools, ceramics) over time. For instance, in any group of examples of a particular kind of object, the percentage of the total is small at the start of its production phase, increases as the object becomes popular and widely used, and decreases through its phases of declining popularity and eventual disuse.

Dendrochronology (tree-ring dating) is the study of information contained in the annual growth layers of trees. It was discovered in 1917 that trees in any particular area have identical sequences of wide and narrow rings, each ring corresponding to one year's growth. This natural phenomenon has allowed archaeologists to reconstruct historic and prehistoric ring sequences and to assign accurate dates to prehistoric sites. Dendrochronology is valuable in areas such as North America and Europe, where there is an abundance of wood and charcoal remains, but is of less value where such materials are scarce.

Radiocarbon dating, which was first developed in 1947, provides a method of determining the precise age of carbonized wood and other organic materials such as antler, bone, and shell. Each living organism has a trace of radiocarbon (carbon 14), which begins to decay when death occurs. By measuring the residual carbon 14 content of an object, it is possible to establish, within fairly narrow limits, its actual age.

Archaeometry involves the application of analytical techniques from the physical sciences and engineering to archaeological materials. Its interdisciplinary nature requires close cooperation between the archaeologists and experts in various fields in dating objects. The work of the archaeometrist is facilitated by computer analysis, with its potential for storing vast amounts of data.

believed in an ideal, essential beauty that transcends time and place. Other formalist writers on art did relate changes in artistic style to cultural change. This approach was demonstrated by the Swiss art historian Heinrich Wölfflin, considered one of the founders of modern art history. In his *Principles of Art History,* first published in German in 1915, he demonstrated the respective formal consistency of Renaissance and Baroque styles.

In order to grasp the effect of formal elements, we take as an example Brancusi's *Bird in Space* (see fig. I.4). Imagine how different it would look lying in a horizontal plane. A large part of the effect of the work depends on its verticality. But it also has curved outlines, sleek proportions, and a highly reflective bronze surface. Its golden color might remind one of the sun and thus reinforce the association of birds and sky. Imagine the *Bird* made of another material (Brancusi did make some white marble *Birds*); its aesthetic effect would be very different.

Even more radical an idea: what if the texture of the *Bird* were furry instead of hard and smooth? Consider, for example, the *Fur-covered Cup, Saucer, and Spoon* of 1936 (fig. **I.11**) by the Swiss artist Meret Oppenheim. When we experience the formal qualities of texture in these two sculptures, we respond to the *Bird* from a distance, as if it were suspended in space, as the title indicates. But the *Cup* evokes an immediate tactile response because we think of drinking from it, of touching it to our lips, and its furry texture repels us. At the same time, however, the *Cup* amuses us because of its contradictory nature. Whereas our line of vision soars vertically *with* the *Bird, we* instinctively withdraw *from* the *Cup.*

Iconography and Iconology In contrast to formalism, the **iconographic** method emphasizes content over form in individual works of art. The term itself denotes the "writing" (*graphe* in Greek) of an image (from the Greek

I.11 Meret Oppenheim, *Fur-covered Cup, Saucer, and Spoon (Le Déjeuner en Fourrure)*, 1936. Cup $4\frac{3}{8}$ in. (10.9 cm) diameter; saucer $9\frac{3}{8}$ in. (23.7 cm) diameter; spoon 8 in. (20.2 cm) long; overall height $2\frac{7}{8}$ in. (7.3 cm). Museum of Modern Art, New York.

word *eikon*), and implies that a written text underlies an image. In Bruegel's *Tower of Babel* (see fig. I.7) the biblical text is Genesis 11:6, in which God becomes alarmed at the height of the tower. He fears that the builders will invade his territory and threaten his authority. The iconographic elements of Bruegel's picture include the tower as well as the figures and other objects depicted. The actual tower referred to in the Bible was probably a ziggurat commissioned by King Nebuchadnezzar of ancient Babylon, who is depicted with his royal entourage at the lower left of the picture. He has apparently come to review the progress of the work, which—according to the text—is about to stop. Bruegel shows this by the downward pull at the center of the tower that makes it seem about to cave in. He also refers to God's fear that the tower will reach into the heavens by painting a small, white cloud overlapping the top of the tower. The cloud thus heightens dramatic tension by referring to the divine retribution that will follow. Recognizing the symbolic importance of this iconographic detail significantly enriches our understanding of the work as a whole.

Iconology refers to the interpretation or rationale of a group of works, which is called a **program.** In a Gothic cathedral, for example, an iconographic approach would consider the textual basis for a single statue or scene in a stained-glass window. Iconology, on the other hand, would consider the choice and arrangement of subjects represented in the entire cathedral and explore their interrelationships.

See figure 11.11. West façade of Chartres Cathedral, France, c. 1140–1150.

Marxism The Marxist approach to art history derives from the writings of Karl Marx, the nineteenth-century German social scientist and philosopher whose ideas were developed into the political doctrines of socialism and communism. Marx himself, influenced by the industrial revolution, was interested in the process of making art and its exploitation by the ruling classes. He contrasted the workers (proletariat) who create art with the property-owning classes (the bourgeoisie) who exploit the workers, and believed that this distinction led to the alienation of artists from their own productions. Marxist art historians, and those influenced by Marxism, study the relationship of art to the economic factors (e.g., cost and availability of materials) operating within its social context. They analyze patronage in relation to political and economic systems. Marxists study form and content not for their own sake, but for the social messages they convey and for evidence of the manipulation of art by the ruling class to enhance its own power.

A Marxist reading of the message of Bruegel's *Tower* might associate the builders with the proletariat and God with the bourgeoisie. In between is Nebuchadnezzar, who, because he is a king, is not punished as the workers are. It is they who assume the brunt of God's anger; their language is confounded and they are scattered across the earth, whereas Nebuchadnezzar continues to rule his empire. Bruegel emphasizes the greater importance of Nebuchadnezzar in relation to the workers by his larger size, his upright stance, and his royal following. The workers are not only much smaller, but some kneel before the king.

Feminism Feminist methodology assumes that the making of art, as well as its iconography and its reception by viewers, is influenced by gender. Like Marxists, feminists are opposed to pure formalism on the grounds that it ignores the message conveyed by content. Feminist art historians have pointed out ways in which women have been discriminated against by the male-dominated art world. They have noted, for example, that before the 1970s the leading art-history textbooks did not include female artists. Through their research, they have also done a great deal to establish the importance of women's contributions to art history as both artists and patrons—rescuing significant figures from obscurity as well as broadening our sense of the role of art in society. Feminists take issue with traditional definitions of art and notions of artistic genius, both of which have historically tended to exclude women. The fact that traditionally it has been difficult for women to receive the same training in art as men, due in part to family obligations and the demands of motherhood and partly to social taboos, is an issue that the feminists have done much to illuminate.

Taking the example of this introductory chapter, a feminist might point out that of all the illustrations of works of art only one is by a woman (Meret Oppenheim, see fig. I.11). Furthermore, its subject is related to the woman's traditional role as the maker and server of food in the household. At the same time, the work is a visual joke constructed by a woman that combines female sexuality with eating and drinking. The "household" character of the *Cup* contrasts with the "divine" character of *God as Architect (God Drawing the Universe with a Compass)* (fig. I.6). As depicted in this Introduction, the male figures are gods, kings, soldiers, and workers, whereas female figures (except *The Corinthian Maid,* fig. I.8) are mothers.

Biography and Autobiography Biographical and autobiographical approaches to art history interpret works as expressions of their artists' lives and personalities. These methods have the longest history, beginning with the mythic associations of gods and artists described above. Epic heroes such as Gilgamesh and Aeneas are credited with the architectural activity of building walls and founding cities. The anecdotes of Pliny the Elder about ancient Greek artists have a more historical character, which was revived in fourteenth-century Italy. Vasari's *Lives of the Artists,* written in the sixteenth century, covers artists from the late thirteenth century up to his own time and concludes with his autobiography. From the fifteenth century on, the genre of biography and autobiography of artists has expanded into various literary forms—for example, sonnets (Michelangelo), memoirs (Vigée-Lebrun), journals (Delacroix), letters (van Gogh), and, more recently, films and taped interviews.

The biographical method emphasizes the notion of authorship and can be used to interpret iconography, using the artist's life as an underlying "text." This being said, there are certain standard conventions in artists' biographies and autobiographies that are remarkably consistent and that arise in quite divergent social and historical contexts. These conventions parallel artists with gods, especially in the ability to create illusion. They also include episodes in which an older artist recognizes talent in a child destined to become great, the renunciation of one's art (or even suicide) when confronted with the work of superior artists, sibling rivalry between artists, artists who are rescued from danger by their talent, and women as muses for (male) artists.

Whistler's portrait of his mother (see fig. I.9) obviously has autobiographical meaning. By placing his own etchings on the wall beside her, he relates her dour personality to his black-and-white drawings and etchings, rather than to his more colorful paintings. Vincent van Gogh's *Self-Portrait before His Easel* (1888) in figure I.1 is one of many self-portraits that reflect the artist's inner conflicts through the dynamic tension of line and color. In works such as these, it is possible to apply the biographical method because the artist's identity is known and because he makes aspects of himself manifest in his imagery. When works are entirely anonymous, such as Emperor Qin's "bodyguard" (fig. I.2), biographical readings in terms of the artist(s) are more difficult, although they may sometimes be applied to the patron.

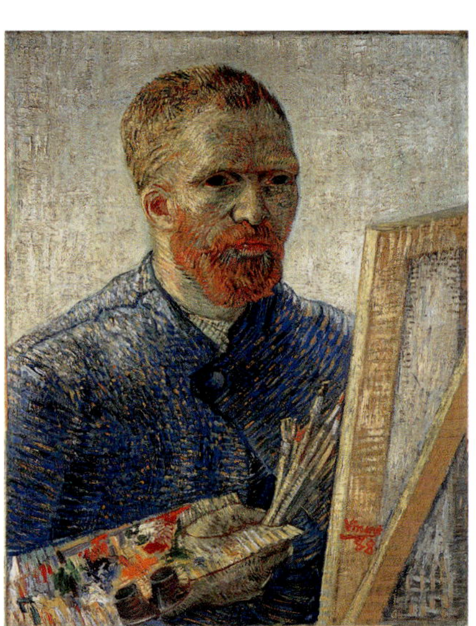

See figure I.1. Vincent van Gogh, *Self-Portrait before His Easel,* 1888.

Semiology Semiology—the science of signs—takes issue with the biographical method and with much of formalism. It has come to include elements of structuralism, poststructuralism, and deconstruction. Structuralism developed from a branch of language study called structural linguistics in the late nineteenth and early twentieth centuries as an attempt to identify universal and meaningful patterns in various cultural expressions. There are several structuralist approaches to art, but in general they diverge from the equation of artists with gods, from the Platonic notion of art as *mimesis* (making exact copies of nature), and from the view that the meaning of a work is conveyed exclusively by its author.

In the structural linguistics of the Swiss scholar Ferdinand de Saussure, a "sign" is composed of "signifier" and "signified." The former is the sound or written element (such as the four letters *p-i-p-e*) and the latter is the concept of what the signifier refers to (in this case, a pipe). A central feature of this theory is that the relation between signifier and signified is entirely arbitrary. Saussure insists on that point specifically to counter the notion that there is an ideal essence of a thing (as stated by Plato and Kant). He is also arguing against the tradition of a "linguistic equivalent." The notion of linguistic equivalents derived from the belief that, in the original language spoken by Adam and Eve, words matched the essence of what they referred to so that signifier and signified were naturally related to each other. Even before Adam and Eve, the logocentric (word-centered) Judaic God had created the world through language: "Let there be light" made light, and "Let there be darkness" made darkness. The New Testament Gospel of John (1:1) takes up this notion again, opening with "In the beginning was the Word."

For certain semioticians, however, some relation between signifier and signified is allowed. These would agree that Magritte's painted pipe is closer to the idea of pipeness than the four letters *p-i-p-e*. But most semioticians prefer to base stylistic categories on signs rather than on formal elements. For example, Magritte's pipe and Oppenheim's cup do not resemble each other formally, and yet both have been related to Dada and Surrealism. Their similarities do not lie in shared formal elements, but rather in their ability to evoke surprise by disrupting expectations. We do not expect to read a denial of the "pipeness" of a convincing image of a pipe written by the very artist who painted it. Nor do we expect fur-covered cups and spoons because the fur interferes with their function. The unexpected—and humorous—qualities of the pipe and the cup could be considered signs of certain twentieth-century developments in imagery. Another element shared by these two works is the twentieth-century primacy of everyday objects, which can also be considered a sign.

See figure I.5. René Magritte, *The Betrayal of Images* ("This is not a pipe"), 1928.

Deconstruction The analytical method known as deconstruction is most often associated with Jacques Derrida, a French poststructuralist philosopher who writes about art and written texts. Derrida's deconstruction opens up meanings rather than fixing them within structural patterns. But he shares with the structuralists the idea that works have no ultimate meanings conferred by their authors.

Derrida's technique for opening up meanings is to question assumptions about works. Whistler's mother (see fig. I.9), for example, seems to be sitting for her portrait, but we have no proof from the painting that she ever did so. Whistler could have painted her from a photograph or from memory, in which case our initial assumption about the circumstances of the work's creation would be incorrect, even though the portrait is a remarkably "truthful" rendering of a puritanical woman.

Derrida also opens up the Western tendency to binary pairing: right/left, positive/negative, male/female, and so forth. He notes that one of a pair evokes its other half and plays on the relationship of presence and absence. Since a pair of parents is a biological given, where, a Derridean might ask, is Whistler's father? In the pairing of father and mother, the present parent evokes the absent parent. There is, in Whistler's painting, no reference to his father, only to himself via the etchings hanging on the wall. The absent father, the present mother, the etchings of the son—the combination invites speculation about their relationships: was the son trying to displace the father? Such psychological considerations lead us to the psychoanalytic methodologies.

See figure I.9. James Abbott McNeill Whistler, *Arrangement in Black and Gray (Portrait of the Artist's Mother)*, 1871.

Psychoanalysis The branch of psychology known as psychoanalysis was originated by the Austrian neurologist Sigmund Freud in the late nineteenth century. Like art history, psychoanalysis deals with imagery, history, and creativity. Like archaeology, it reconstructs the past and interprets its relevance to the present. The imagery examined by psychoanalysts is found in dreams, waking fantasies, jokes, slips of the tongue, and neurotic symptoms, and it reveals the unconscious mind (which, like a buried city, is a repository of the past). In a work of art, personal imagery is reworked into a new form that "speaks" to a cultural audience. It thus becomes part of a history of style (and, for semioticians, of signs).

Psychoanalysis has been applied to art in different ways and according to different theories. In 1910 Freud published the first psychobiography of an artist, in which he explored the personality of Leonardo da Vinci through the artist's iconography and working methods. For Freud, the cornerstone of psychoanalysis was the Oedipus complex, which refers to various aspects of children's relationships to their parents. In the case of a boy, the Oedipus complex includes his wish for a romance with his mother and the elimination of his father. The Oedipus complex of a girl is more complicated because her first love object is her mother and she is expected to grow up and love a man.

As we have seen, the Oedipus complex can be applied to Whistler's painting of his mother. An oedipal reading of that work is enriched by the fact that it contains an underpainting—a preliminary painting covered up by the final painting—of a baby. An oedipal reading of Brancusi's *Bird* would have to consider the artist's relationship to his peasant father, an ignorant and abusive man who would have preferred his son to have been born a girl. In that light, the sculpture has been interpreted as a phallic self-image, declaring its triumph over gravity and outshining the sun. With *Bird in Space,* Brancusi symbolically "defeats" his father and "stands up" for himself as a creator.

According to classical psychoanalysis, works of art are "sublimations of instinct" through which instinctual energy is transformed by work and talent into aesthetic form. The ability to sublimate is one of the main differences between humans and animals, and it is necessary for creative development in any field. Because art is expressive, it reveals aspects of the artist who creates it, of the patron who funds it, and of the culture in which it is produced.

See figure I.4. Constantin Brancusi, *Bird in Space,* 1928.

See figure I.5. René Magritte, *The Betrayal of Images* ("This is not a pipe"), 1928.

See figure I.6. *God as Architect (God Drawing the Universe with a Compass),* mid-13th century.

How Do We Talk about Art?

The visual arts have their own language, and the artist thinks in terms of that language, just as a musician thinks in sounds and a mathematician in numbers. The basic visual vocabulary consists of the so-called **formal elements,** which include line, shape, space, color, light, and dark. When artists combine these elements in a characteristic way, they are said to have a **style.** In order to describe and analyze a work of art, it is helpful to be familiar with the artist's perceptual vocabulary.

Composition

In its broadest sense, the **composition** of a work of art is its overall plan or structure. It denotes the relationship among component parts, and it involves balance and harmony, the relationships of parts to each other and to the whole work, and the effect on the viewer. The composition of a work depends on how the formal elements are arranged and is distinct from the subject matter, content, or theme.

Plane

A **plane** is a flat surface having a direction in space. Brancusi's *Bird* (fig. I.4) rises in a vertical plane, Magritte's *pipe* (fig. I.5) lies in a relatively horizontal plane, and the figure of God in *God as Architect (God Drawing the Universe with a Compass)* (fig. I.6) bends over to create two diagonal planes. Stonehenge (see fig. 1.22) is a building that occupies a circular plane because it is round, whereas the towers of Gothic cathedrals are vertical planes and Greek temples lie in horizontal planes.

A plane can also be thought of as a flat surface. We thus speak of a **picture plane** when referring to the flat surface of a painting or a **plane of relief** when referring to the surface of a relief sculpture (see Chapter 1).

Balance

In a successful composition, the harmonious blending of formal elements creates **balance.** The simplest form of balance is **symmetry,** in which there is an exact correspondence of parts on either side of an axis or dividing line. In other words, the left side of a work is a mirror image of the right side. The Taj Mahal (fig. I.3) is a symmetrical building, meaning that if we draw a line through its center, we will have two equal parts.

Balance can also be achieved by nonequivalent elements. In *God as Architect (God Drawing the Universe with a Compass)* (fig. I.6), the weight of the figure is not evenly distributed on either side of the central axis. But

See figure I.3. Taj Mahal, Agra, India, 1632–1648.

even though the parts are not arranged symmetrically, there is an equilibrium between them that produces an aesthetically satisfying result. This is known as **asymmetrical balance.**

Line

A line is the path traced by a moving point. For the artist, the moving point is the tip of the brush, pen, crayon, or whatever instrument is used to create an image on a surface. In geometry, a line has no width or volume; its only quality is inherent in its location, a straight line being defined as the shortest distance between two points. In the language of art, however, a line can have many qualities, depending on how it is drawn (fig. **I.12**). A vertical line seems to stand stiffly at attention, a horizontal line lies down, and a diagonal seems to be falling over. Zigzags have an aggressive, sharp quality, whereas a wavy line is more graceful and, like a curve, more naturally associated with the outline of the human body. Parallel lines are balanced and harmonious, implying an endless, continuous movement, while perpendicular, converging, and intersecting lines meet and create a sense of force and counterforce. The thin line (a) seems delicate, unassertive, even weak. The thick one (b) seems aggressive, forceful, strong. The undulating line (c) suggests calmness, like the surface of a calm sea, whereas the more irregularly wavy line (d) implies the reverse. The angular line (e) climbs upward like the edge of a rocky mountain. (Westerners understand (e) as going up and (f) as going down, since we read from left to right.)

Expressive Qualities of Line Many of the lines in figure I.12 are familiar from geometry and can, therefore, be described formally. But the formal qualities of line also convey an expressive character because we identify them with our bodies and our experience of nature. By analogy with a straight line being the shortest distance between two points, a person who follows a straight, clear line in thought or action is believed to have a sense of purpose. "Straight" is associated with rightness, honesty, and truth, while "crooked"—whether referring to a line or a person's character—denotes the opposite. We speak of a "line of work," a phrase adopted by the former television program *What's My Line?* When a baseball player hits a line drive, the bat connects firmly with the ball, and a "hardliner" takes a strong position on an issue.

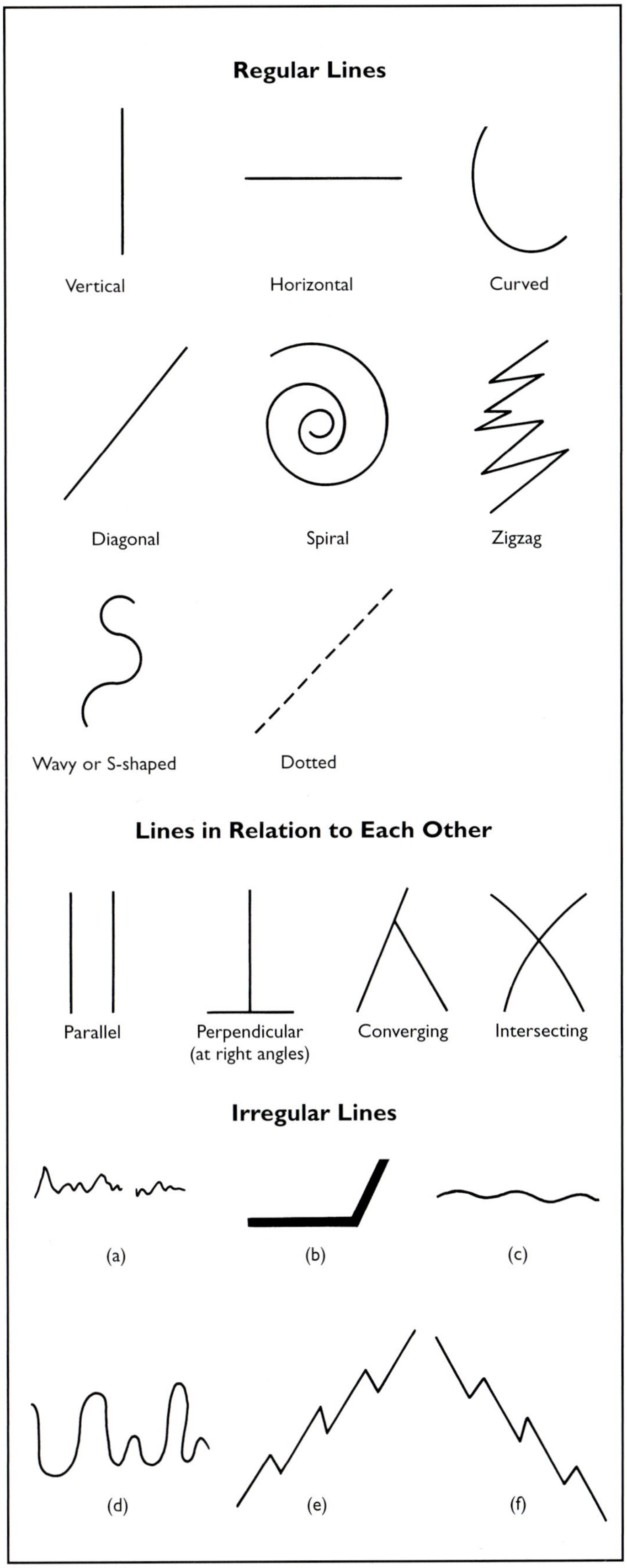

Regular Lines

Vertical
Horizontal
Curved
Diagonal
Spiral
Zigzag
Wavy or S-shaped
Dotted

Lines in Relation to Each Other

Parallel
Perpendicular (at right angles)
Converging
Intersecting

Irregular Lines

(a) (b) (c)
(d) (e) (f)

I.12 Lines.

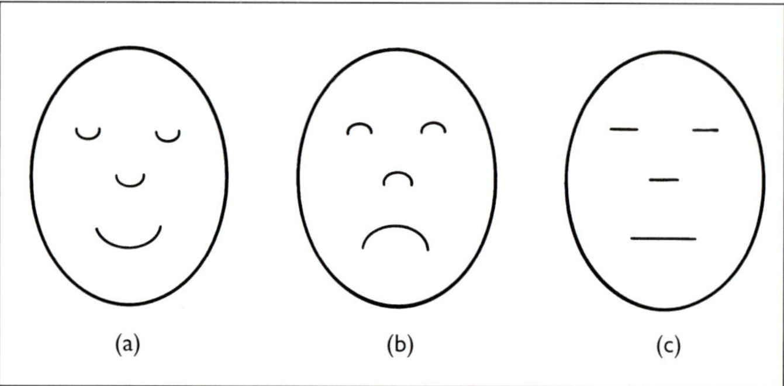

I.13 Lines used to create facial expressions.

It is especially easy to see the expressive impact of lines in the configuration of the face (fig. **I.13**). In (a), the upward curves create a happy face, and the downward curves of (b) create a sad one. These characteristics of upward and downward curves actually correspond to the emotions as expressed in natural physiognomy. And they are reflected in language when we speak of people having "ups and downs" or of events being "uppers" or "downers."

Alexander Calder's (1898–1976) *Cat* (fig. **I.14**) merges the linear quality of the written word with the pictorial quality of what the word represents. The curve of the *c* outlines the face, a dot stands for the eye, and a slight diagonal of white in the curve suggests the mouth. The large *A* comprises the body, feet, and tail, while the tiny *t* completes the word, without interfering with reading the ensemble as a cat. The figure seems to be walking because the left diagonal of the *A* is lower than the right one, and the short horizontals at the base of the *A* suggest feet. Not only is this cat a self-image—*C A* are the artist's initials reversed—but it contradicts the semiotic argument that signifier (*c-a-t*) and signified (the mental image of a cat) have no natural relation to each other.

I.14 Alexander Calder, *Cat*, 1976. 22 × 30 in. (55.9 × 76.2 cm).

The importance of line in the artist's vocabulary is illustrated by an account of two ancient Greek painters, Apelles, who was Alexander the Great's portraitist, and Apelles' contemporary Protogenes. Apelles traveled to Rhodes to see Protogenes' work, but when he arrived at the studio, Protogenes was away. The old woman in charge of the studio asked Apelles to leave his name. Instead, Apelles took up a brush and painted a line of color on a panel prepared for painting. "Say it was this person," Apelles instructed the old woman.

When Protogenes returned and saw the line, he recognized that only Apelles could have painted it so well. In response, Protogenes painted a second, and finer, line on top of Apelles' line. Apelles returned and added a third line of color, leaving no more room on the original line. When Protogenes returned a second time, he admitted defeat and went to look for Apelles.

Protogenes decided to leave the panel to posterity as something for artists to marvel at. Later it was exhibited in Rome, where it impressed viewers for its nearly invisible lines on a large surface. To many artists, the panel seemed a blank space, and for that it was esteemed over other famous works. After his encounter with Protogenes, it was said that Apelles never let a day go by without drawing at least one line. This anecdote was the origin of an ancient proverb, "No day without a line."

Shape

Lines enclosing space create shapes. Shapes are another basic unit, or formal element, used by artists. There are regular and irregular shapes. Regular ones are geometric and have specific names. Irregular shapes are also called "biomorphs," or biomorphic (from the Greek words *bios*, "life," and *morphe*, "shape"), because they seem to move like living, organic matter (fig. **I.15**).

Expressive Qualities of Shape Like lines, shapes can be used by artists to convey ideas and emotions. Open shapes create a greater sense of movement than closed shapes (see fig. I.15). Similarly, we speak of open and closed minds. Open minds allow for a flow of ideas, flexibility, and the willingness to entertain new possibilities; closed minds, in contrast, are not susceptible to new ideas.

Specific shapes can evoke associations with everyday experience. Squares, for example, are symbols of reliability, stability, and symmetry. To call people "foursquare" means that they are forthright and unequivocal, that they confront things "squarely." If something is "all square," a certain equity or evenness is implied; a "square meal" refers to both the amount and content of the food. When the term "brick" is applied to people, it means that they are good-natured and reliable. Too much rectangularity, on the other hand, may imply dullness or monotony—to call someone "a square" suggests overconservatism or conventionality.

The circle has had a special significance for artists since the Neolithic era. In the Roman period, the circle was considered a divine shape and thus most suitable for temples. This view persisted in the Middle Ages and the Renaissance, when the circle was considered to be the ideal church plan—even though such buildings were rarely constructed.

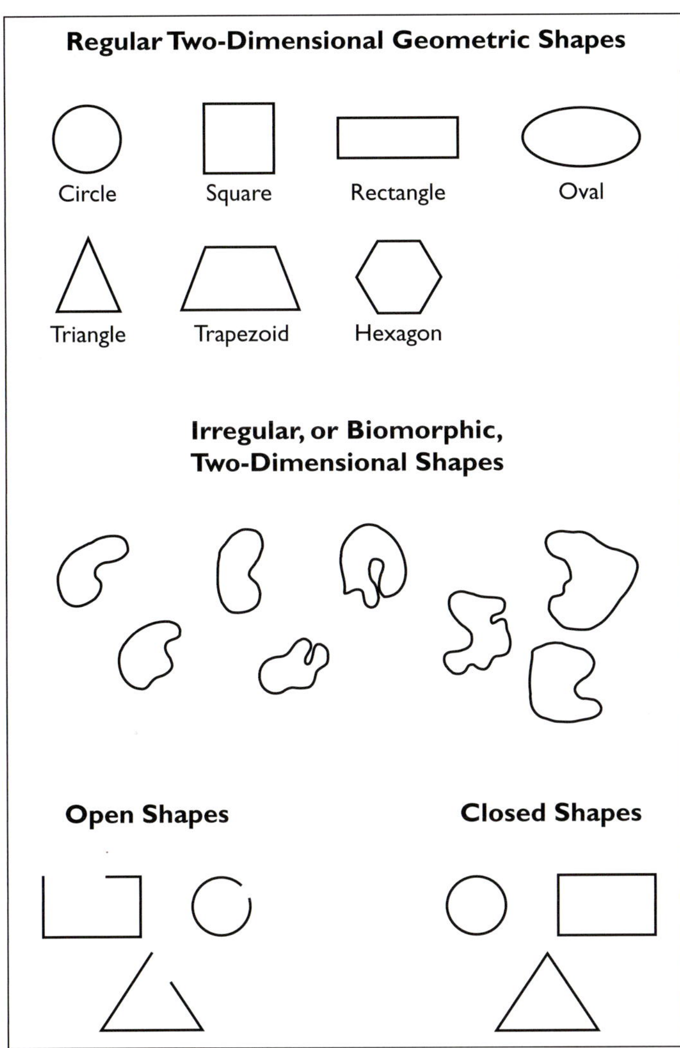

I.15 Shapes.

I.16 Drawing of solid shapes showing hatching and crosshatching. The lines inside the objects create the illusion that they are solid and also suggest that there is a source of light coming from the upper left and shining down on the objects. Such lines are called modeling lines.

Lines are two-dimensional, but the use of **modeling** lines to form **hatching** or **crosshatching** (fig. **I.16**) creates the illusion of mass and volume, making a shape appear three-dimensional. Hatching and crosshatching can also suggest shade or **shading** (the gradual transition from light to dark) on the side of an object that is turned away from a light source.

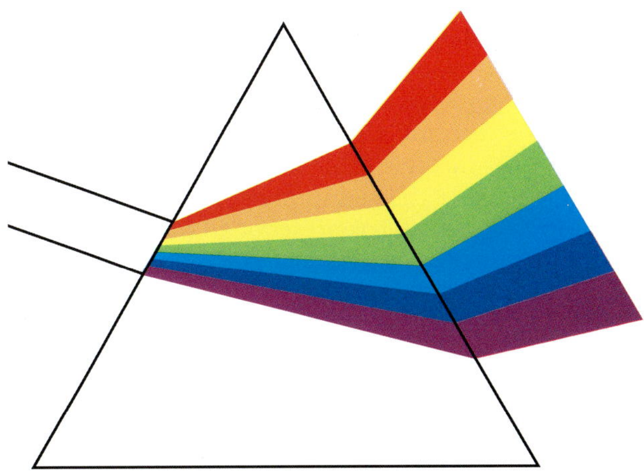

I.17 The visible spectrum has seven principal colors—red, orange, yellow, green, blue, indigo (or blue-violet), and violet—that blend together in a continuum. Beyond the ends is a range of other colors, starting with infrared and ultraviolet, which are invisible to the human eye. If all the colors of the spectrum are recombined, white light is again reproduced.

Light and Color

The technical definition of light is electromagnetic energy of certain wavelengths that, when it strikes the retina of the eye, produces visual sensations. The absence, or opposite, of light is dark.

Rays of light having certain wavelengths create the sensation of color, which can be demonstrated by passing a beam of light through a prism (fig. **I.17**). This breaks the light down into its constituent **hues.** Red, yellow, and blue are the three **primary colors** (hues) because they cannot be produced by mixing any other colors. A combination of two primary colors produces a **secondary color:** yellow and blue make green, red and blue make purple, yellow and red make orange. A **tertiary color** is made by mixing a secondary and a primary color.

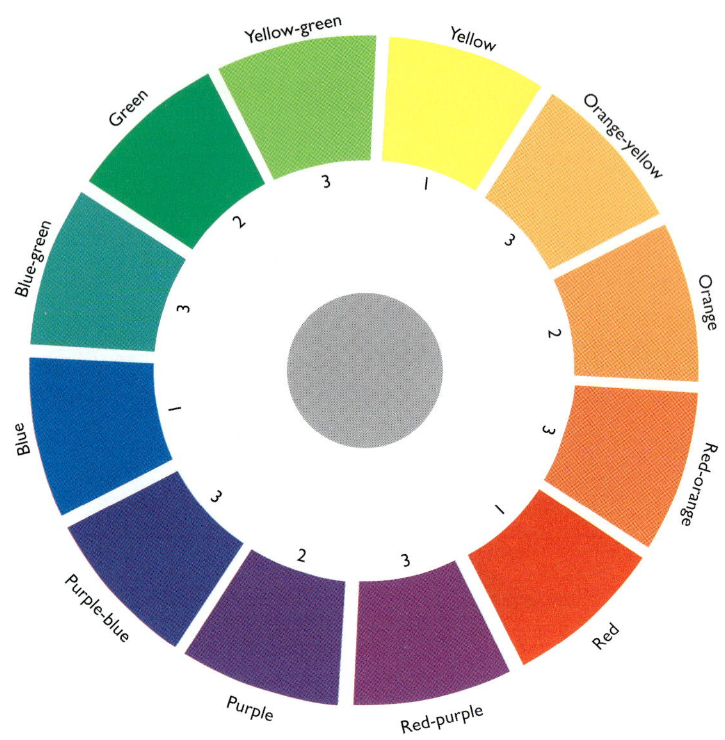

I.18 The color wheel. Note that the three primary colors—red, yellow, and blue—are equally spaced around the circumference. They are separated by their secondary colors. Between each primary color and its two secondary colors are their related tertiaries, giving a total of twelve hues on the rim of the wheel.

The **color wheel** (fig. **I.18**) illustrates the relationships between the various colors. The farther away hues are, the less they have in common and the higher their contrast. Hues directly opposite each other on the wheel (red and green, for example) are the most contrasting and are known as **complementary colors.** They are often juxtaposed when a strong, eye-catching contrast is desired. Mixing two complementary hues, on the other hand, has a neutralizing effect and lessens the intensity of each. This can be seen in figure I.18 as you look across the wheel from red to green. The red's intensity decreases, and the gray circle in the center represents a "standoff" between all the complementary colors.

The relative lightness or darkness of an object is its **value,** which is a function of the amount of light reflected from its surface. Gray is darker in value than white but lighter in value than black. The value scale in figure **I.19** provides an absolute value for different shades.

Value is characteristic of both **achromatic** works of art—those with no color, consisting of black, white, and shades of gray—and **chromatic** ones (from the Greek word *chroma,* meaning "color"). On a scale of color values (fig. **I.20**), yellow reflects a relatively large amount of light, approximately equivalent to "high light" on the neutral scale, whereas blue is equivalent to "high dark." The normal value of each color indicates the amount of light it reflects at its maximum intensity. The addition of white or black would alter its value (i.e., make it lighter or darker) but not its hue. The addition of one color to another would change not only the values of the two colors, but also their hues.

Intensity, which is also called **saturation,** refers to the relative brightness or dullness of a color. Dark red (red mixed with black) is darker in value, but less intense than pink (red mixed with white). There are four methods of changing the intensity of colors. The first is to add white. Adding white to pure red creates light red or pink, which is lighter in value and less intense. If black is added, the result is darker in value and less intense than pure red. If gray of the same value as the red is added, the result is less intense but retains the same value. The fourth way of changing a color's intensity is to add its complementary hue. This makes the mixed color less intense and more neutral than the original.

I.19 This ten-step value scale breaks the various shades from white to black into ten gradations. The choice of ten is arbitrary because there are many more values between pure white and pure black. Nevertheless, it illustrates the principle of value gradations.

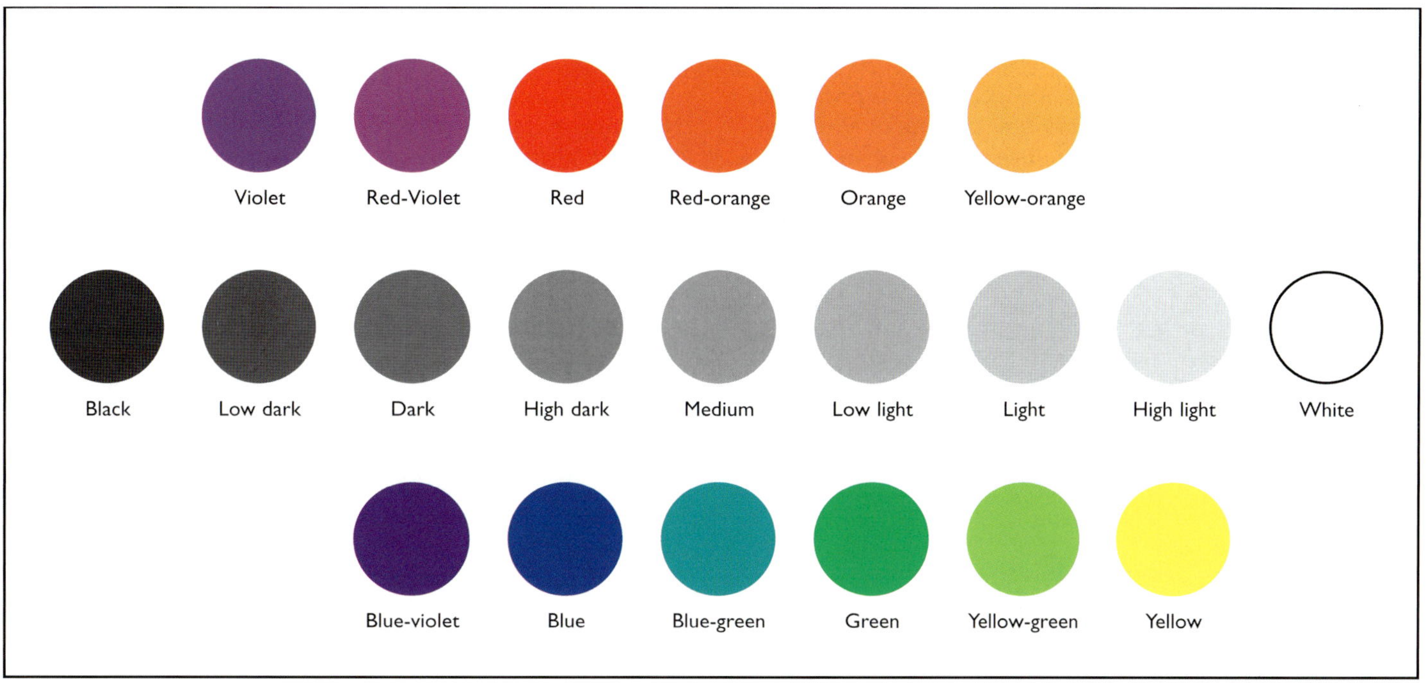

I.20 A color value scale. The central row contains a range of neutrals from white to black; the rows above and below match the twelve colors from the color wheel with the neutrals in terms of the amount of light reflected from each.

Expressive Qualities of Color Just as lines and shapes have expressive qualities, so too do colors. Artists select colors for their effect. Certain ones appear to have intrinsic qualities. Bright or warm colors convey a feeling of gaiety and happiness. Red, orange, and yellow are generally considered warm, perhaps because of their associations with fire and the sun. It has been verified by psychological tests that the color red tends to produce feelings of happiness. Blue and any other hue containing blue—green, violet, blue-green—are considered cool, possibly because of their association with the sky and water. They produce feelings of sadness and pessimism.

Colors can also have symbolic significance and suggest abstract qualities. A single color, such as red, can have multiple meanings. It can symbolize danger, as when one waves a red flag in front of a bull. But to "roll out the red carpet" means to welcome someone in an extravagant way, and we speak of a "red-letter day" when something particularly exciting has occurred. Yellow can be associated with cowardice, white with purity, and purple with luxury, wealth, and royalty. We might call people "green with envy," "purple with rage," or "in a brown study" if they are quietly gloomy.

Texture

Texture is the quality conveyed by the surface feel of an object. This may be an actual surface or a simulated or represented surface. The surface of Oppenheim's *Fur-covered Cup* (see fig. I.11), for example, is actually furry, but the gold of Mary's crown in figure I.10 is simulated. The cup is made of real fur, whereas van Eyck has painted the crown so that it only looks like real gold.

See figure I.11. Meret Oppenheim, *Fur-covered Cup, Saucer, and Spoon (Le Déjeuner en Fourrure)*, 1936.

See figure I.10. Jan van Eyck, *The Virgin in a Church*, c. 1410–1425.

Stylistic Terminology

Subject matter refers to the actual elements represented in a work of art, such as figures and objects or lines and colors. **Content** refers to the themes, values, or ideas in a work of art, as distinct from its form. The following terms are used to describe representational, or figurative, works of art that depict their subject matter so that it is relatively recognizable:

- **naturalistic:** depicting figures and objects more or less as we see them. Often used interchangeably with "realistic."
- **realistic:** depicting figures and objects to resemble their actual appearances, rather than in a distorted or abstract way.
- **illusionistic:** depicting figures, objects, and the space they occupy so convincingly that the appearance of reality is achieved.

Note that an image may be representational without being realistic. Figures **I.21–I.24** are recognizable as images of a cow and are therefore representational, but only figures I.21–I.23 can be considered relatively naturalistic.

If an image is representational but is not especially faithful to its subject, it may be described as

- **idealized:** depicting an object according to an accepted standard of beauty.
- **stylized:** depicting certain features as nonorganic surface elements rather than naturalistically or realistically.
- **romanticized:** depicting its subject in a nostalgic, emotional, fanciful, and/or mysterious way.

I.21 Theo van Doesburg, study 1 for *Composition (The Cow)*, 1916. Pencil on paper; 4⅝ × 6¼ in. (11.7 × 15.9 cm). Museum of Modern Art, New York. Purchase.

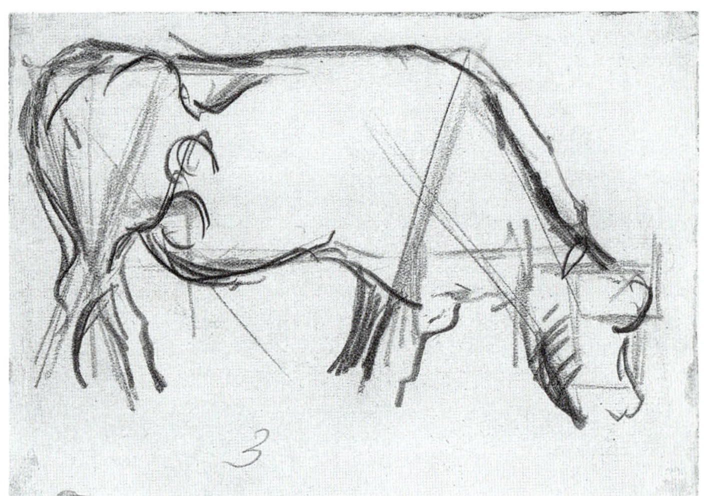

I.22 Theo van Doesburg, study 2 for *Composition (The Cow)*, 1917. Pencil on paper; 4⅝ × 6¼ in. (11.7 × 15.9 cm). Museum of Modern Art, New York. Purchase.

I.23 Theo van Doesburg, study 3 for *Composition (The Cow)*, 1917. Pencil on paper; 4⅝ × 6¼ in. (11.7 × 15.9 cm). Museum of Modern Art, New York. Gift of Nelly van Doesburg.

I.24 Theo van Doesburg, study for *Composition (The Cow)*, c. 1917 (dated 1916). Tempera, oil, and charcoal on paper; 15⅝ × 22¾ in. (39.7 × 57.8 cm). Museum of Modern Art, New York. Purchase.

If the subject matter of a work has little or no relationship to observable reality, it may be called

- **nonrepresentational** or **nonfigurative:** the opposite of representational or figurative, implying that the work does not depict (or claim to depict) real figures or objects.
- **abstract:** describes forms that do not accurately depict real objects. The artist may be attempting to convey the essence of an object rather than its actual appearance. Note that the subject matter may be recognizable (making the work representational), but in a nonnaturalistic form.

The transition from naturalism to geometric abstraction is encapsulated in a series by the early-twentieth-century Dutch artist Theo van Doesburg (figs. I.21–I.25). He gradually changed his drawing of a cow from I.21, which could be called naturalistic, figurative, or representational, to image **I.25,** which is an abstract arrangement of flat squares and rectangles. In I.21 and I.22, the cow's form is recognizable as that of a cow—it is composed of curved outlines and a shaded surface that creates a three-dimensional illusion. In image I.23, the cow form is still recognizable, especially since it follows I.21 and I.22. It is now devoid of curves but still shaded—it has become a series of volumetric (solid, geometric) shapes. Even in image I.24, the general form of the cow is recognizable in terms of squares, rectangles, and triangles, but there is no longer any shading. As a result, each distinct color area is flat. In image I.25, however, the shapes can no longer be related to the original natural form. It is thus a pure abstraction and is also nonfigurative and nonrepresentational.

I.25 Theo van Doesburg, study for *Composition (The Cow)*, c. 1917. Oil on canvas; 14¾ × 25 in. (37.5 × 63.5 cm). Museum of Modern Art, New York. Purchase.

15

Mannerism and the Later Sixteenth Century in Italy

The sixteenth century was a period of intense political and military turmoil from which no Italian artist could remain completely insulated. Charles I of Spain (also Charles V, the Holy Roman emperor) extended his empire to Austria, Germany, the Low Countries, and, finally, Italy. His aggressive tactics culminated in the sack of Rome in 1527. The 1500s were also a period of fundamental religious change. The power of the Catholic Church was challenged, and finally fractured, by the Protestant Reformation (see box).

The counterchallenge, or Counter-Reformation, went far in the opposite direction, and religious orthodoxy was strictly enforced by the Inquisition. Established in 1232 by the emperor Frederick II, the Inquisition was a group of state officials dedicated to identifying, converting, and punishing heretics. Pope Gregory IX (died 1241) appropriated the Inquisition and instituted papal Inquisitors for the same purposes. Their power was increased by Pope Innocent IV (died 1254), who permitted the use of torture to force confessions from the accused.

During the sixteenth century, in the climate of upheaval within the Church and the Protestant challenges to its authority, humanism seemed to pose a greater threat than it had in the fifteenth century. Notions of the primacy of man

The Reformation

By the second decade of the sixteenth century, after more than a thousand years of religious unity under the Roman Catholic Church, western Christendom underwent a revolution known as the Reformation. This led to the emergence in large parts of Europe of the Protestant Church.

During the fifteenth century, the Catholic Church had become increasingly materialistic and corrupt. Particularly offensive was the selling of "indulgences" (a kind of credit against one's sins), which allegedly enabled sinners to buy their way into heaven. In 1517, the German Augustinian monk Martin Luther protested. He nailed to a church door in Wittenberg, Saxony, a manifesto listing ninety-five arguments against indulgences. Luther criticized the basic tenets of the Roman Church. He advocated abolition of the monasteries and restoration of the Bible as the sole source of Christian truth. Luther believed that human salvation depended on individual faith and not on the mediation of the clergy. In 1520, he was excommunicated.

In 1529, the Holy Roman emperor Charles V tried to stamp out dissension among German Catholics. Those who protested were called Protestants. In the course of the next several years, most of north and west Germany became Protestant. England, Scotland, Denmark, Norway, Sweden, the Netherlands, and Switzerland also espoused Protestantism. For the most part, France, Italy, and Spain remained Catholic. By the end of the sixteenth century, about one-fourth of western Europe was Protestant.

King Henry VIII of England had been a steadfast Catholic, but his wish for a male heir led him to ask the pope to annul his marriage to Catherine of Aragon, the first of his six wives. The pope refused, and Henry broke with the pope. In 1534, the Act of Supremacy made Henry, and all future English monarchs, head of the Church of England. In 1536, the fundamental doctrines of Protestantism were codified in John Calvin's *Institutes of the Christian Religion*. His teachings became the basis of Presbyterianism.

The Reformation dealt a decisive blow to the authority of the Roman Catholic Church, and the balance of power in western Europe shifted from religious to secular authorities. As a result, the cultural and educational dominance of the Church waned, particularly in the sciences. In the visual arts, the Reformation had a far greater impact in northern Europe than in Italy or Spain, where the Counter-Reformation had an immense influence on the visual arts. Throughout Europe, however, the Reformation marked the beginning of a progressive decline in Christian imagery in Protestant churches.

were replaced by a harsh view of nature. More emphasis was placed on God's role as judge and on the penalties of sin rather than on the possibility of redemption. Besides splitting Europe into two religious camps, the Reformation and Counter-Reformation (also called the Catholic Reformation) had fundamental effects on art, artists, and patrons.

Mannerism

After the death of Raphael in 1520, new artistic trends began to emerge in Italy. The most significant of these has been called Mannerism. It coexisted with the later styles of Michelangelo and Titian, and remained influential until the end of the sixteenth century.

The term *Mannerism* is ambiguous and has potentially conflicting meanings. Among the several derivations that have been proposed for Mannerism are the Latin word *manus* (meaning "hand"), the French term *manière* (meaning a style or way of doing things), and the Italian *maniera* (an elegant, stylish refinement). In English, too, the term is fraught with possible interpretations. We speak of being "well-mannered" or "mannerly," when we mean that someone behaves according to social convention. "To the manner born" denotes that one is suited by birth to a certain social status. Being "mannered," on the other hand, suggests a stilted, unnatural style of behavior. "Mannerisms," or seemingly uncontrolled gestures, are considered exaggerated or affected. The nature of Mannerism also inspired the term *manneristic,* used in clinical psychology, which means exhibiting bizarre, stylized behavior of an individual nature.

All of these terms apply in some way to the sixteenth-century style called Mannerism. In contrast to the Renaissance interest in studying, imitating, and idealizing nature, Mannerist artists typically took as their models other works of art. The main subject of Mannerism is the human body, which is often elongated, exaggerated, elegant, and arranged in complex, twisted poses. Classical Renaissance symmetry does not apply in Mannerism, which creates a sense of instability in figures and objects. Spaces tend to be compressed and crowded with figures in unlikely or provocative positions, and colors are sometimes jarring. Finally, Classical proportions are rejected, and odd juxtapositions of scale and space often occur.

In contrast to the dominance of papal patronage in the High Renaissance, Mannerism was a style of the courts. It appealed to an elite, sophisticated audience. Mannerist subjects are often difficult to decipher, and their iconography can be highly complex and obscure, except to the initiated. They may also be self-consciously erotic.

Mannerist Painting

Pontormo The sometimes disturbing quality of Mannerism is evident in the work of Jacopo da Pontormo (1494–1557). His *Entombment* of 1525–1528 (fig. **15.1**) was painted for the Church of Santa Felicità in Florence: Jesus has

15.1 Jacopo da Pontormo, *Entombment*, Capponi Chapel, Santa Felicità, Florence, 1525–1528. Oil on panel; 10 ft. 3 in. × 6 ft. 4 in. (3.12 × 1.93 m). The painting was commissioned for the altar, with an *Annunciation* on an adjacent wall. This pairs Christ's Incarnation and Death—the former event heralding his birth and the latter his rebirth. The image of the Entombment on an altar was also a visual reminder of the Eucharist.

been taken down from the Cross, and his contorted body, with gray areas denoting the pallor of death, is being carried to his tomb. Michelangelo's influence can be seen in the sculptural, carved appearance of the drapery—especially that worn by the figure seen from the back at the right—as well as in Jesus's pose (see fig. 14.18). But the ambiguous space, the pink-and-blue palette, and the stony rather than fleshy forms create an entirely different effect.

In an uncanny juxtaposition, the activated forms and agitated poses contrast sharply with the fixed, terror-stricken gazes of the two youths carrying Jesus. Several gazes focus on the more languid figure of Mary (in blue), who seems withdrawn into herself, her relaxed, semiconscious state at odds with the dynamic pose of the woman in front of her. Mary's characterization corresponds to that of her dead son—both are removed from the frenzy of the moment. Likewise, the gray-black sky alludes to the tradition that the sky darkened at Jesus's death. Another uncanny juxtaposition is thus the contrast between the gloomy chromatic setting and the pastel colors of the draperies.

Parmigianino Mannerist virtuosity and artifice is exemplified by the *Self-Portrait in a Convex Mirror* (fig. **15.2**) of Parmigianino (1503–1540). He painted it in 1524 at the age of twenty-one with the intention of dazzling the pope, Clement VII, with his skill. According to Vasari, the artist got the idea from seeing his reflection in a barber shop and decided to "counterfeit everything." The painting does indeed replicate the image in a convex mirror and is, in reality, convex. In the background, Parmigianino's studio appears curved by the mirror's surface. The face is not distorted because of its relation to the picture surface, whereas the hand, which is closer, is enlarged. In these spatial arrangements, Parmigianino has emphasized the hand, making it as important a part of the image as the face. The role of the artist's hand in the artifice is thus an integral part of the picture's iconography (see box).

15.2 Parmigianino, *Self-Portrait in a Convex Mirror,* 1524. Oil on wood; diameter 9⅝ in. (24.4 cm). Kunsthistorisches Museum, Vienna. Il Parmigianino ("The Little Fellow from Parma") was the nickname of Francesco Mazzola, who worked in Parma, Rome, and Bologna. His career was fraught with conflicts and lawsuits, and his interest in pictorial illusionism can be related to his preoccupation with counterfeiting. He was obsessed with alchemy (the science of converting base metal to gold), and eventually he abandoned painting altogether.

John Ashbery on Parmigianino

The artifice of Parmigianino's *Self-Portrait in a Convex Mirror,* and the mirror as a metaphor for self-portraiture and self-revelation, appealed to the imagination of the twentieth-century American poet John Ashbery. The following are excerpts from his poem "Self-Portrait in a Convex Mirror":

As Parmigianino did it, the right hand
Bigger than the head, thrust at the viewer
And swerving easily away, as though to protect
What it advertises . . .
In a movement supporting the face, which swims
Toward and away like the hand
Except that it is in repose. It is what is
Sequestered . . .
Chiefly his reflection, of which the portrait
Is the reflection once removed.
The glass chose to reflect only what he saw
Which was enough for his purpose: his image
Glazed, embalmed, projected at a 180-degree
angle . . .[1]

15.3 Parmigianino, *Madonna and Child with Angels (Madonna of the Long Neck)*, c. 1535. Oil on panel; approx. 7 ft. 1 in. × 4 ft. 4 in. (2.16 × 1.32 m). Galleria degli Uffizi, Florence. Parmigianino's perverse nature is evident in this painting. Its undercurrent of sinister, lascivious eroticism is also consistent with Mannerist tastes. Vasari described him as "unkempt . . . melancholy, and eccentric" at the time of his early death and related that he was, at his own request, buried naked with a cypress cross standing upright on his breast—apparently an expression of his psychotic identification with Christ.

Parmigianino's *Madonna and Child with Angels* (fig. **15.3**), also called the *Madonna of the Long Neck*, illustrates odd spatial juxtapositions and non-Classical proportions typical of Mannerism. The foreground figures are short from the waist up and long from the waist down. The Madonna, in particular, has an elongated neck and tilted head; their movement flows into the spatial twist of the torso and legs, creating a typically Mannerist ***figura serpentinata***. Mary's dress, in contrast to the usual blue and red of earlier periods, is a cool metallic color. The man in the distance unrolling a scroll could be an Old Testament prophet. His position between the Madonna and the unfinished rows of columns is a logical visual link between pagan antiquity and the Christian era. His improbably small size in relation to both the columns and the Madonna, however, is illogical. The visual juxtaposition of Mary's neck with the column may allude to traditional associations between her and a column—both being conceived of as architectural supports. In a Christian context, Mary was seen as both the church building and its structural support.

15.4 Agnolo Bronzino, allegory called *Venus, Cupid, Folly, and Time*, c. 1545. Oil on wood; 5 ft. 1 in. × 4 ft. 8¾ in. (1.55 × 1.44 m). National Gallery, London.

Agnolo Bronzino The allegorical painting of about 1545 by Bronzino (1503–1572), traditionally called *Venus, Cupid, Folly, and Time* (fig. **15.4**), illustrates the Mannerist taste for enigmatic imagery with erotic overtones. The attention paid to silky textures, jewels, and masks is consistent with Bronzino's courtly, aristocratic patronage. There is no consensus on the identification of every figure or even on the overall meaning of this painting. It was apparently commissioned by Cosimo I de' Medici as a gift for Francis I of France. Despite the strictures of the Counter-Reformation as codified by the Council of Trent (see box, p. 588), court patronage clearly delighted in playful and erotic, if somewhat obscure, iconography.

Venus and her son Cupid are easily recognizable as the two figures in the left foreground. Both are nude and bathed in a white light that creates a porcelain skin texture. Cupid fondles his mother's breast and kisses her lips. To the right, a nude *putto* with a lascivious expression on his face dances forward and scatters flowers. All three twist in the Mannerist *serpentinata* pose. But only the *putto's* pose seems consistent with his action. The undulating forms of Venus and Cupid are rendered for their own sakes rather than to serve the logic of the narrative. A more purposeful gesture is that of Time, the old man who angrily draws aside a curtain to reveal the incestuous transgressions of Venus and Cupid. The identity of the remaining figures is less certain. The hag tearing her own hair has been called Envy, and the creature behind the *putto,* with a serpent's tail, reversed right and left hands, and the rear legs of a lion, Fraud.

A more sedate type of Mannerist painting can be seen in Bronzino's portrait of *Eleonora of Toledo and Her Son Don Giovanni* (fig. **15.5**). In contrast to the nudity of the *Venus, Cupid, Folly, and Time,* these figures are very much attired. Indeed, the portrait is as much about clothing and its significance as about the figures wearing them. Bronzino delights in the carefully ordered patterns of velvet and brocade, and the regularity of Eleonora's curved tiara, which is echoed in the double strands of her pearl necklace. The porcelain skin textures of the Venus and Cupid are translated here to the aloof stares of the sitters. Gazing coldly on the world from a lofty social position, Eleonora and her son exemplify the elite sophistication of the court. Whereas the allegorical painting is about revelation and the exposure of perversion, the portrait depicts figures who are restrained and formal.

15.5 Agnolo Bronzino, *Eleonora of Toledo and Her Son Don Giovanni*, 1545–1546. Oil on wood; 3 ft. 8 in. × 3 ft. 1 in. (1.11 × 0.93 m). Galleria degli Uffizi, Florence.

The Counter-Reformation

In response to the Reformation, the Roman Catholic Church mounted the Counter-Reformation and tried to eliminate internal corruption. From 1545 to 1563, the Council of Trent was convened at Trento (Trent, in English) in northern Italy. It denounced Lutheranism and reaffirmed Catholic doctrine. Measures were initiated to improve the education of priests and reassert papal authority beyond Italy. The council established an Inquisition in Rome to identify heretics and bring them to trial.

In its final session, the Council of Trent restated the Roman Church's view that art should be didactic, ethically correct, decent, and accurate in its treatment of religious subjects. Parallels between the Old and New Testaments were to be emphasized, rather than Classical events. The council directed that art should appeal to emotion rather than reason—an implicitly antihumanist stance, which resulted in an increase of miraculous themes. The Roman Inquisition was granted the power to censor works of art that failed to meet the requirements of the council.

In 1573, the Venetian painter Paolo Veronese (1528–1586) was summoned to appear before the Holy Tribunal to defend his monumental painting of the *Last Supper* (fig. **15.6**). The trial transcript, which has been preserved, makes it clear that the Inquisition objected to Veronese's naturalism. The Inquisitors asked Veronese to identify his profession and describe his painting.

"In this Supper," the prosecutor asked, ". . . what is the significance of the man whose nose is bleeding?"

"I intended to represent a servant whose nose was bleeding because of some accident," the artist replied.

The Inquisitor asked about one of the apostles. "He has a toothpick and cleans his teeth," said Veronese.

The Inquisitor also objected to German soldiers eating and drinking on the stairs, and to the jesters and other figures in the picture. Germany, he declared, no doubt thinking of Martin Luther, was "infected with heresy." Veronese was contrite, admitting he had used artistic license. He said that Christ's Last Supper had taken place in the house of a rich man who might be expected to have visitors, servants, and entertainment. The Inquisitor was not impressed.

"Does it seem fitting at the Last Supper of the Lord to paint buffoons, drunkards, Germans, dwarfs, and similar vulgarities?"

"No, milords."[2]

Veronese was given three months to alter his picture. He merely changed its title to *Christ in the House of Levi*.

In Catholic countries, the zeal of the Counter-Reformation led to intolerance, moralizing, and a taste for exaggerated religiosity. Michelangelo came under particular attack. In 1549, a copy of his *Pietà* (see fig. 14.18) was unveiled in Florence. Because of Mary's depiction as an attractive figure, scarcely older than Christ himself, Michelangelo was called an "inventor of filth." In 1545, Pietro Aretino wrote to Michelangelo, criticizing his *Last Judgment* (see fig. 14.27) as suitable for a bath house (*un bagno*) but not for a chapel.

It was against this background of political and religious turmoil that sixteenth-century art developed after 1520. One cannot prove that this directly affected the development of Mannerism. Nevertheless, there is, in that style, an undercurrent of anxiety and tension—beneath the refinement and elegance—that is not inconsistent with the times.

15.6 Paolo Veronese, *Last Supper,* renamed *Christ in the House of Levi,* 1573. Oil on canvas; 18 ft. 3 in. × 42 ft. (5.56 × 12.80 m). Galleria dell'Accademia, Venice. Paolo Caliari was born in Verona, hence his name, Il Veronese. In 1553, he moved to Venice, where, with Titian and Tintoretto, he dominated 16th-century Venetian painting. Although Veronese liked to dress luxuriously—in keeping with the taste for pageantry evident in his paintings—he was known for his piety and financial acumen.

Mannerist Sculpture

Cellini Benvenuto Cellini's elaborate gold and enamel saltcellar (fig. **15.7**) illustrates the iconographic complexity and taste for mythological subject matter that appealed to Mannerist artists and their patrons. Cellini himself gave conflicting accounts of the object's meaning. Perhaps he simply forgot—but the ambiguity is nevertheless consistent with Cellini's ambivalent lifestyle (see box). What is clear is that the two main nude figures represent the bearded Neptune, holding a trident and surrounded by seahorses, next to a ship, and the Earth goddess next to an Ionic triumphal arch. According to Cellini's description of the saltcellar, Neptune's ship was designed to contain the salt, and Earth's arch the pepper. Other figures include personifications of times of day and wind gods. The style and poses of the figures are clearly Mannerist, some appropriated from sculptures by Michelangelo. They are elegantly proportioned and arranged to form spatial twists that result in impossible poses. Both Neptune and Earth lean so far back that in reality they would topple over. The absence of any visible means of support reinforces their uneasy equilibrium, and the movement inherent in their poses and surface patterns is enhanced by the high polish of the gold itself.

Benvenuto Cellini: A Mannerist Lifestyle

Benvenuto Cellini (1500–1571) could be described as a Mannerist personality. Although trained as a goldsmith, he was equally comfortable as a sculptor in marble, an architect, and an author. His celebrated autobiography was written when he was fifty-eight and under house arrest for sodomy. Cellini was restive, moving from place to place, often to avoid lawsuits. He was continually in trouble—he was charged with two murders in Rome in 1529—and had a reputation for violence. His flamboyant lifestyle, which he describes in his autobiography, included overt homosexuality, bisexuality, and episodes of transvestism. In 1558, he took preliminary vows for the priesthood but later renounced them and married the mother of his two children. His autobiography was published posthumously in 1728, and Berlioz based an opera on it.

15.7 Benvenuto Cellini, saltcellar of Francis I, finished 1543. Gold and enamel; 10¼ × 13⅛ in. (26.0 × 33.3 cm). Formerly in the Kunsthistorisches Museum, Vienna. Benvenuto Cellini (1500–1571), a versatile Mannerist artist, made this elaborate saltcellar while working in France as Francis I's court goldsmith. This work was stolen from the museum and, as of this writing, is still missing.

Giambologna Although Mannerism was primarily an Italian style, Jean de Boulogne (1529–1608)—known as Giovanni Bologna, or Giambologna in Italy—was born in Flanders and became a leading Mannerist sculptor. His bronze *Mercury* (fig. **15.8**) of around 1576 shows the increasing importance of open space in Mannerism. The god flies forward, his left foot on a breath of air blown by a wind god beneath it. Mercury stretches upward, opening a variety of spaces bounded by curves and diagonals that enhance the sense of motion. The forms are thin and elongated, and the rippled surface of the bronze creates a pattern of reflected light.

Compared with the bronze *Davids* of Donatello and Verrocchio (see figs. 13.29 and 13.37), the *Mercury* offers multiple viewpoints, for the difference between the front view and the side view is considerable. Not only do we see another aspect of the figure itself, but the spaces around it change. The bronze *Davids* are more of a consistent piece—enclosing rather than opening space, and exhibiting smooth, fleshy surfaces. The content also contributes to the differences between the figures. Whereas the *Davids* are self-satisfied and relaxed after victory, the *Mercury*'s winged cap, sandals, and caduceus identify him as the god of speed. Giambologna has used the expanded formal movement and taste for virtuosity that are characteristic of Mannerism to convey the impression of swiftness and flight.

See figure 13.29. Donatello, *David*, c. 1430–1440.

See figure 13.37. Andrea del Verrocchio, *David*, early 1470s.

15.8a, b Giambologna, *Mercury* (front and side views), c. 1576. Bronze; 24⅛ in. (61.3 cm). Museo Nazionale del Bargello, Florence.

Vasari on Women Artists

In his view of women artists, Vasari was something of a humanist. He included the biography of Madonna Properzia de' Rossi (c. 1490–1530) in his *Lives,* where he has a lot to say about the excellence of women in antiquity. He also names the women of his own day who achieved fame in letters but elaborates further on the women artists.

Properzia de' Rossi was born in Bologna, where she studied drawing. She received a few public commissions and did several marble portrait busts. Payment for sculptures on the façade of San Petronio in Bologna is documented, but it is not certain which are by her hand. Vasari describes a panel of *Joseph and Potiphar's Wife,* which has been attributed to Properzia. He relates the subject directly to the artist's life—for she, like Potiphar's wife, conceived an unrequited passion for a young man.

The scene itself (fig. **15.9**) is quite complex. Potiphar's wife turns to grab Joseph's cloak, and Joseph, who turns to leave, seems to rush from the plane of the relief. Properzia has conveyed the erotic passion of Potiphar's wife—and Joseph's flight from it—by the agitated swirls of drapery and the open, inviting flaps of the tent. The technical skill of this panel is consistent with Vasari's admiration of Properzia's carvings made from peach stones: "They were singular and marvellous to behold."[3]

15.10 Sofonisba Anguissola, *The Artist's Sister Minerva,* c. 1559. Oil on canvas; 33½ × 26 in. (85.1 × 66.0 cm). Milwaukee Art Museum. Gift of the family of Mrs. Fred Vogel, Jr.

15.9 Properzia de' Rossi (attrib.), *Joseph and Potiphar's Wife,* c. 1520. Marble relief panel; 19 ft. ¼ in. × 18 ft. ⅛ in. (5.86 × 5.55 m). Museo di San Petronio, Bologna.

According to Vasari, there were many other women whose talent in drawing and painting equaled Properzia's in carving. Among these was Sofonisba Anguissola (1532/5–1625). Her success brought her to the attention of Philip II of Spain, at whose court she spent many years. She had five sisters who were also artists and was married twice—first to a Sicilian lord and then to a ship's captain.

Sofonisba was an accomplished portrait painter. Her portrait of her sister Minerva (fig. **15.10**) captures a rather wistful expression and emphasizes the textured variation of the dress. She wears coral and gold jewelry, lace, and fur, which, like her features, are delicately rendered. Her pendant depicts the Roman Minerva, goddess of the art of weaving as well as of war and wisdom.

The style of Properzia's relief is well within Renaissance tradition, although there is a Mannerist flavor in the draperies and in the slightly contorted pose of Potiphar's wife. Sofonisba's *Minerva,* however, has affinities with Bronzino's *Eleonora of Toledo* (see fig. 15.5).

Giulio Romano: The Palazzo del Tè

Giulio Romano (1492/9–1546) created in the Palazzo del Tè, in Mantua, a Mannerist environment that combined architectural humor with painted illusionism. He had been Raphael's chief assistant on the Vatican *stanze*, and when Raphael died in 1520, Giulio completed many of his unfinished works. Four years later, Federigo Gonzaga commissioned a villa for a weekend getaway, a place of entertainment and festivity, and a horse farm. From 1525 to 1535, Giulio Romano worked on the project. The plan illustrated in figure **15.11** shows the square courtyard.

In the design of the courtyard façades (fig. **15.12**), Giulio subverted the classical forms recommended by Alberti. The effect is a more animated surface and a disruption of Classical proportions. The **rustication** is heavier, and the bulky Tuscan Doric columns support an architrave that seems too thin for the frieze above it. The central triglyphs push down a section of the architrave, and both drop below their usual level. The bases of the pediments over the blind windows are missing, leaving them unsupported except for stone brackets at the corners. Keystones, the structural function of which is to lock in the voussoirs, seem to pop forward, as if being pushed from behind. In these variations on Classical Orders, Giulio Romano mocks traditional forms of Western architecture—which he nevertheless retains—by slight alterations in placement and proportion.

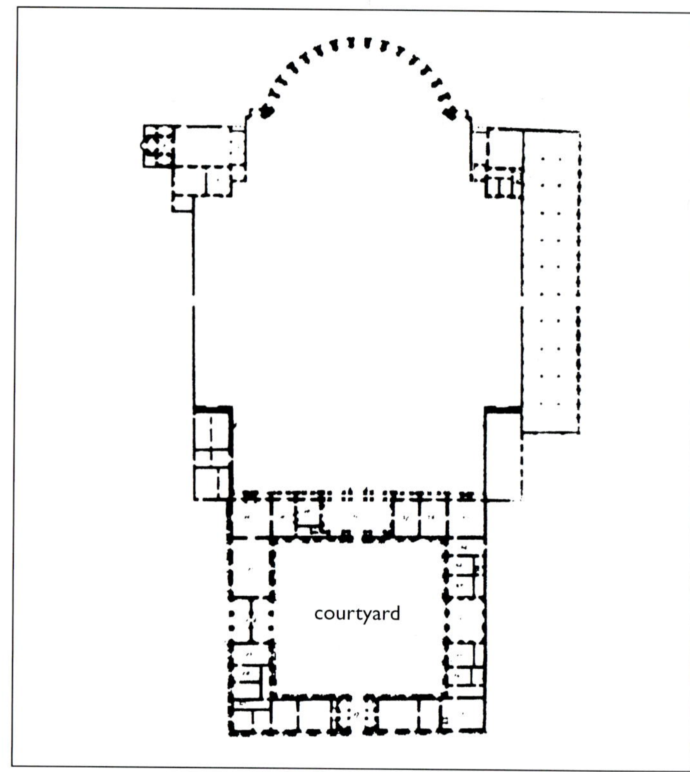

15.11 Giulio Romano, plan of the Palazzo del Tè, Mantua, 1525–1535.

15.12 Giulio Romano, courtyard façade of the Palazzo del Tè, Mantua, 1525–1535.

The most spectacular interior decorations in the Palazzo del Tè are the frescoes in the Sala dei Giganti (Room of the Giants). The ceiling and walls (figs. **15.13** and **15.14**) depict the cataclysmic battle between the Olympian gods and the Titans. The ceiling is a Mannerist version of Mantegna's *oculus* (see fig. 13.54), which was also painted in Mantua under Gonzaga patronage. It is covered with a large scene depicting Jupiter's temple, swirling cloud formations, and monumental, twisting figures. The gods surround Jupiter as he hurls thunderbolts at the Titans laying siege to Mount Olympos. Below, the world itself seems to crumble before Jupiter's fury.

On the walls, colossal Titans cower under collapsing buildings or grasp in vain as columns crack in their arms. As in Mantegna's Camera Picta (see fig. 13.53), the viewer is thrown off balance by the illusionistic blend of real and fictive forms. In the Mannerist conception, however,

See figure 13.54. Mantegna, ceiling *oculus* of the Camera Picta, Mantua, finished 1474.

15.13 Giulio Romano, Sala dei Giganti ceiling, Palazzo del Tè, Mantua, 1530–1532.

15.14 Giulio Romano, Sala dei Giganti wall view showing the *Fall of the Giants*, Palazzo del Tè, Mantua, 1530–1532.

there is an increased turbulence that animates the surface and deepens the space. The humor in all this is contained in the implicit relationship between the meaning of the Titanic mythological battle and Giulio Romano's architectural disruptions on the courtyard façades. Both represent a rebellion against the rules of a previous era and the establishment of a new order. In the myth it is a social and religious order, and in the building an architectural Order. It is no accident, therefore, that Giulio depicts the Titans' fall in architectural terms and that the crumbling structures are Classical.

Counter-Reformation Painting

Tintoretto

The impact of the Council of Trent and the Counter-Reformation on the visual arts is most evident from the second half of the sixteenth century. Tintoretto (1518–1594), for example, a leading Venetian painter and a contemporary of Veronese, painted a *Last Supper* (fig. **15.15**) in 1592–1594 that conformed well to Counter-Reformation requirements. The choice of the moment represented,

15.15 Jacopo Tintoretto, *Last Supper,* 1592–1594. Oil on canvas; 12 ft. × 18 ft. 8 in. (3.66 × 5.69 m). Choir, San Giorgio Maggiore, Venice. Jacopo Robusti (1518–1594) was nicknamed Tintoretto ("Little Dyer" in Italian) because of his father's profession as a wool dyer. He worked for most of his life in Venice and succeeded Titian as official painter to the republic. He was very prolific and employed many assistants, including two sons and a daughter, Marietta (see box).

when Christ demonstrates the symbolic meaning of the bread as his body and the wine as his blood, lends itself to mystical interpretation.

In Tintoretto's *Last Supper,* in contrast to those by Veronese (fig. 15.6) and Leonardo (see fig. 14.13), the picture space is divided diagonally. The table is no longer parallel to the picture plane but recedes into the background, and the figures are not evenly lit from a single direction. The humanist interest in psychology and observation of

The Painter's Daughter

In the seventeenth-century biography of Tintoretto by Carlo Ridolfi, the author includes an account of two of the artist's children, Domenico and Marietta, who were also painters. Both children assisted their father in completing commissions and were well thought of by their contemporaries. Ridolfi reports that Tintoretto trained Marietta and had her instructed in music. She accompanied her father everywhere and dressed as a boy. Because Tintoretto was so attached to her, he arranged for her to marry a local jeweler rather than leave Venice. Her special talent, according to Ridolfi, was portraiture, although he notes that her works have disappeared. Marietta died at age thirty.

Particularly striking, in the light of modern feminist approaches to art history, is Ridolfi's vigorous defense of women artists. Like Vasari, he cites examples of famous women in antiquity as well as in his own day. He condemns the discrimination that kept women untrained and at home. Ridolfi concludes, however, that women will triumph because, in addition to natural talents, they are also armed with beauty.

CONNECTIONS

See figure 14.13. Leonardo da Vinci, *Last Supper,* c. 1495–1498.

Loyola's *Spiritual Exercises*

Saint Ignatius Loyola (1491/5–1556) was born to a noble Spanish family and entered military service as a young man. He was wounded and during his convalescence decided to become a Christian soldier. He renounced the material world, lived the life of a beggar, and underwent numerous mystical experiences. In response to Martin Luther and the Protestant Reformation, Ignatius decided to reform the Church from within. He founded the Society of Jesus, which Pope Paul III sanctioned in 1540, and wrote the *Spiritual Exercises* to instruct his followers in meditation.

Loyola's system was calculated to conquer fears and passions by a form of empathetic identification practiced in advance of an experience. For example, in the meditation on the "Agony of Death," he recommends contemplating four things: (1) the dim light and familiar objects in the death room; (2) the people you leave behind; (3) the disintegration of your own body as death approaches; and (4) devils and angels fighting for your soul. His technique was for potential sufferers to create a mental picture, through which trauma would be experienced in advance, and to prepare themselves for the worst. Contemplate, he writes, the "sound of the clock which measures your last hours . . . your painful labored breathing . . . your face . . . covered with cold sweat."[4] And after death has come, imagine yourself "enclosed in a coffin" and the "open grave where they are laying your body." Contemplate your tombstone, months later, "blackened by time . . . the worms [that] devour the remains of putrid flesh . . . this mass of corruption." And finally, "ask yourself what are health, fortune, friendship of the world, pleasures of the senses, life itself: 'vanity of vanities, all is vanity' (Eccles. 1:2)."

nature has been subordinated to mystical melodrama. To the right of the table, in deep shadow, are servants going about their business, apparently unaware of the significant event taking place. On the left of the table are the apostles, some in exaggerated poses, illuminated by a mystical light that is consistent with official Counter-Reformation requirements. Toward the center of the table, Jesus distributes bread to the apostles. Light radiates from his head so that he is depicted literally as "the light of the world." On the other side of the table, brooding, isolated, and in relative darkness, sits Judas. At the upper right, outlined in glowing light, is a choir of angels.

El Greco

El Greco (Domenikos Theotokopoulos, 1541–1614) was even more directly a painter of the Counter-Reformation. He worked in Spain from 1577 onward, when Counter-Reformation influence was at its strongest. In his paintings virtually all traces of High Renaissance style and Classical subject matter have disappeared. Although he spent time in Titian's workshop, El Greco's style was more affected by the Byzantine influence prevalent in his native Crete and in Venice, to which he moved, than by Titian's humanism. He was more in tune with the mystical fervor and religious zeal that predominated in Catholic Spain (see box).

While still in Italy, El Greco painted *Christ Healing the Blind* (fig. **15.16**), in which Tintoretto's influence is evident in the strong diagonal thrust of the space. As in Tintoretto's *Last Supper,* El

15.16 El Greco, *Christ Healing the Blind,* c. 1577. Oil on canvas; 47¼ × 57½ in. (120.0 × 146.1 cm). Metropolitan Museum of Art, New York. Domenikos Theotokopoulos was born in Crete and was subsequently nicknamed El Greco (Spanish for "The Greek"). Most of his work was executed for the Church rather than the court and has a strongly spiritual quality. Of the leading Mannerist painters, El Greco was the most mystical and was therefore well suited to the fervent religious atmosphere of Counter-Reformation Spain.

15.17 El Greco, *Burial of the Count of Orgaz,* 1586–1588. Oil on canvas; 15 ft. 9 in. × 11 ft. 10 in. (4.80 × 3.61 m). Church of Santo Tomé, Toledo.

Greco's figures are elongated and occupy somewhat exaggerated poses. The intensity of their gestures reinforces the miracle of Christ restoring sight to a blind man. El Greco's characteristic shimmering silver light creates a mystical aura consistent with Counter-Reformation taste. At the same time, however, the classicizing architecture reflects the continuing impact of the Renaissance revival of antiquity.

Once El Greco had settled in Spain, he spent most of his life in the small town of Toledo. There he painted his famous work in the Church of Santo Tomé for the burial chapel of Gonzalo Ruiz, count of Orgaz (fig. **15.17**). The painting, which is over 15 feet high, is divided into two levels—the earthly and the heavenly. Local tradition had it that the count of Orgaz was rewarded for his good works by the appearance of Saints Stephen and Augustine at his funeral. Here, the elderly Bishop Augustine (on our right) and the youthful Saint Stephen (on our left) lift the count into his grave. Lined up behind the burial scene are citizens of Toledo wearing black costumes and somber expressions. A small boy at the lower left, thought to be the artist's son, points us toward the miracle. At the right, the only figure seen in back view wears a luminous white robe and leads us heavenward with his upward gaze.

The scene taking place in heaven shows the count's nearly naked soul before Christ. The Virgin Mary, opposite the count, is clad in her traditional red and blue robes and acts as intercessor—her traditional role. Just behind the Virgin, Saint Peter dangles the keys to the gate of heaven. Receding upward and into the background, the heavenly host seems to swirl weightlessly, illuminated by variations of mystical, translucent light.

Mystic Saints

Saint Teresa of Ávila (1515–1582) and Saint John of the Cross (1542–1591) were full-fledged mystics caught up in Spanish Counter-Reformation zeal. In 1555, at the age of thirty-nine, Teresa converted to the spiritual life while praying to an image of the flagellated Christ. She established the Discalced ("barefoot") communities of Carmelites. In addition to Spain, Teresa had missions in the Middle East and Africa. She was aided in her efforts at spiritual reform by Saint John of the Cross. He, too, joined the Carmelites and wrote poems and a treatise on the journey of the soul from the world of the senses to God.

Saint Teresa wrote *The Way of Perfection* to instruct her nuns and an autobiography, which recounts her visions and mystical experiences.

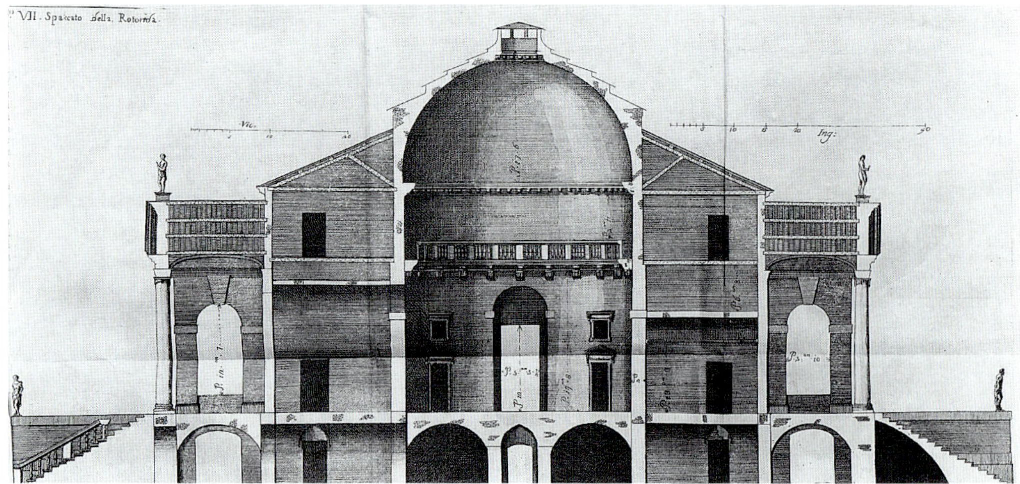

15.18 Section of the Villa Rotonda, Vicenza (from the *I quattro libri dell'architettura,* 1570), 18th-century engraving, Bibliothèque de l'Arsenal, Paris.

Late Sixteenth-Century Architecture

Andrea Palladio

The greatest architect of late sixteenth-century Italy was Andrea Palladio (1508–1580), who synthesized elements of Mannerism with High Renaissance ideals. His use of ancient sources, particularly Vitruvius, was inspired by a humanist education (see box, p. 600).

From 1567 to 1570, Palladio built the Villa Rotonda (figs. **15.18, 15.19,** and **15.20**), near the northern Italian city of Vicenza, for a Venetian cleric. The façade replicates the Classical temple portico—Ionic columns supporting an entablature crowned by a pediment—in the context of domestic architecture. There are four porticos, all in the same style and one on each side of the square plan. In Palladio's view, the Classical entrance endowed the building with an air of dignity and grandeur. The strict symmetry

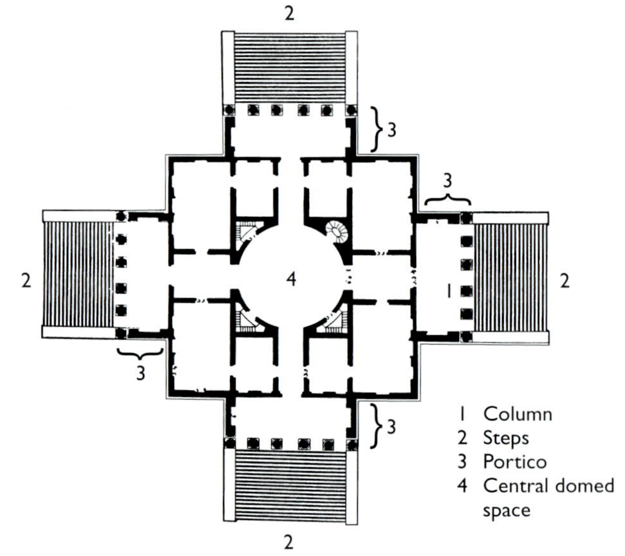

15.19 Plan of the Villa Rotonda, Vicenza.

15.20 Andrea Palladio, Villa Rotonda, Vicenza, begun 1567–1569. Andrea di Pietro della Gondola was renamed Palladio (after Pallas Athena) by Count Trissino, a humanist scholar and poet who supervised his education and career. Palladio is known to have been involved in over 140 building projects, of which no more than about 35 survive. He also published *L'antichità di Roma,* one of the first Italian guidebooks, in 1554.

15.21 Andrea Palladio, San Giorgio Maggiore, Venice, begun 1565.

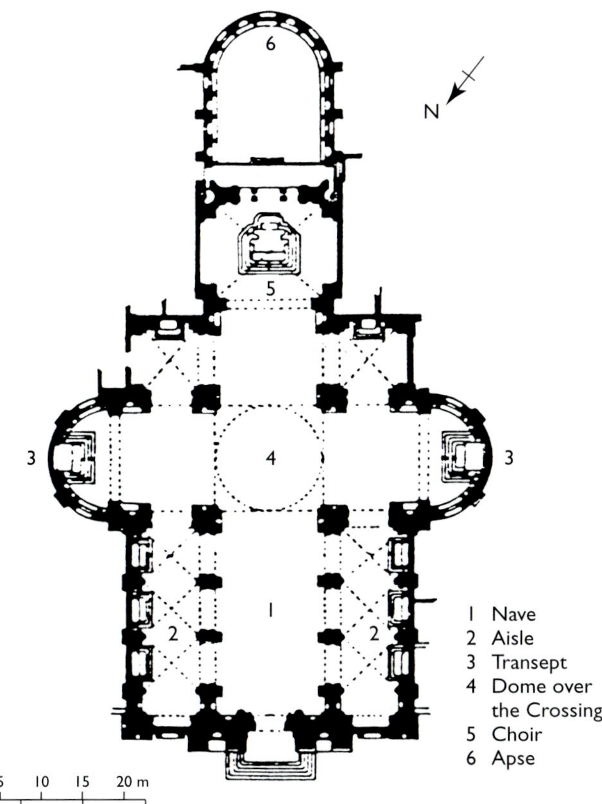

15.22 Plan of San Giorgio Maggiore, Venice.

was both a Classical and a Renaissance characteristic. Such features recalled ancient Rome, where the villa had originated as an architectural type.

The square plan of the Villa Rotonda is typical of Palladio's villas. Passages radiate from a domed central chamber to each of the four exterior porticos. They, in turn, offer views of the surrounding landscape in four different directions. At the sides, each portico is enclosed by a wall pierced by an arch, thereby providing shelter as well as ventilation.

In figure 15.20, some of the classically inspired statues at each angle of the pediments are visible. Others decorate the projecting walls flanking each side of the steps. Since the Villa Rotonda was a purely recreational building, used exclusively for entertaining, it did not have the functional additions found in Palladio's other villas.

From 1570, Palladio worked mainly in Venice, particularly on church design. His Church of San Giorgio Maggiore (figs. **15.21** and **15.22**), begun in 1565 but not completed until 1592, stands on a small island off the Grand Canal. In this building, Palladio solved the problem of relating the façade to an interior with a high central nave and lower side aisles—a problem similar to the one

Palladio's *Four Books of Architecture*

Four Books of Architecture (*I quattro libri dell'architettura*) by Palladio is one of the first Western architectural treatises that deal with the work of its author, in addition to ancient architecture. Palladio studied Roman ruins and published an illustrated edition of Vitruvius in 1556. His own *Four Books*, which were published in 1570, reveal his interest in the Pythagorean philosophy relating musical ratios to the harmony of the universe. In the Renaissance, architectural harmony was also linked with the structures and intervals of music. Palladio illustrated the Classical Orders together with his own plans, elevations, and **cross sections** of buildings, thereby claiming his own place in the genealogy of Western architects. In 1715, the *Four Books* were translated into English. As a result, Palladio had many architectural descendants, including the eighteenth-century English designer Lord Burlington and, in America, Thomas Jefferson.

that Alberti had confronted in the Tempio Malatestiano and Sant'Andrea in Mantua (see figs. 13.31 and 13.33). He did so by superimposing a tall Classical façade with engaged Corinthian columns and a high pediment on a shorter, wider façade with shorter pilasters and a low pediment. The former corresponded to the elevation of the nave and the latter to that of the side aisles. This relationship between the façade and the nave and side aisles unified the exterior and interior of the church in a new way (although Alberti had achieved a similar solution in the later fifteenth century in Florence). They are further unified by the repetition of Corinthian columns along the nave and of the shorter pilasters on the side aisles.

In these solutions, Palladio incorporates Classical elements into religious as well as domestic architecture. Nevertheless, the order and the relationship of the elements are not strictly Classical. It would be difficult to demonstrate that his works are Mannerist, but they share with Mannerism the tendency to juxtapose form and space in a way that is inconsistent with Classical arrangements. For example, Palladio breaks, or interrupts, one pediment in imposing another over it. This feature, called a broken pediment, which Michelangelo used in the Laurentian Library vestibule (see fig. 14.26), became a characteristic aspect of Baroque architecture in the seventeenth century (see Chapter 17). In superimposing larger and smaller façades, as in San Giorgio Maggiore, and in combining a temple portico with a domestic villa, Palladio recalls certain unexpected juxtapositions and combinations found in Mannerist painting.

Palladio was the single most important architect of his generation, and his influence on subsequent generations of Western architects was extensive. His style was revived in England and America in the eighteenth century, and his palaces and villas are still imitated today.

Vignola and Il Gesù

There developed in the late sixteenth century a new conception of church design that would exert a profound influence on the Baroque architecture of the seventeenth century. This was brought about when the Jesuit Order founded by Saint Ignatius decided to build a new mother church, the Church of Il Gesù, for its headquarters in Rome. The powerful Roman cardinal Alessandro Farnese became the patron of the Jesuits in 1565, and he eventually gave the commission for the construction of the church to Giacomo da Vignola (1507–1573). In contrast to the classicizing architecture of Palladio, Vignola's design was intended to reflect Counter-Reformation concerns and to satisfy the requirements of the Council of Trent.

Figure **15.23** shows the plan of the Gesù, based on a Latin cross to accommodate large congregations rather than on the centralized Greek cross preferred in the Renaissance. The transepts are short, and, instead of side

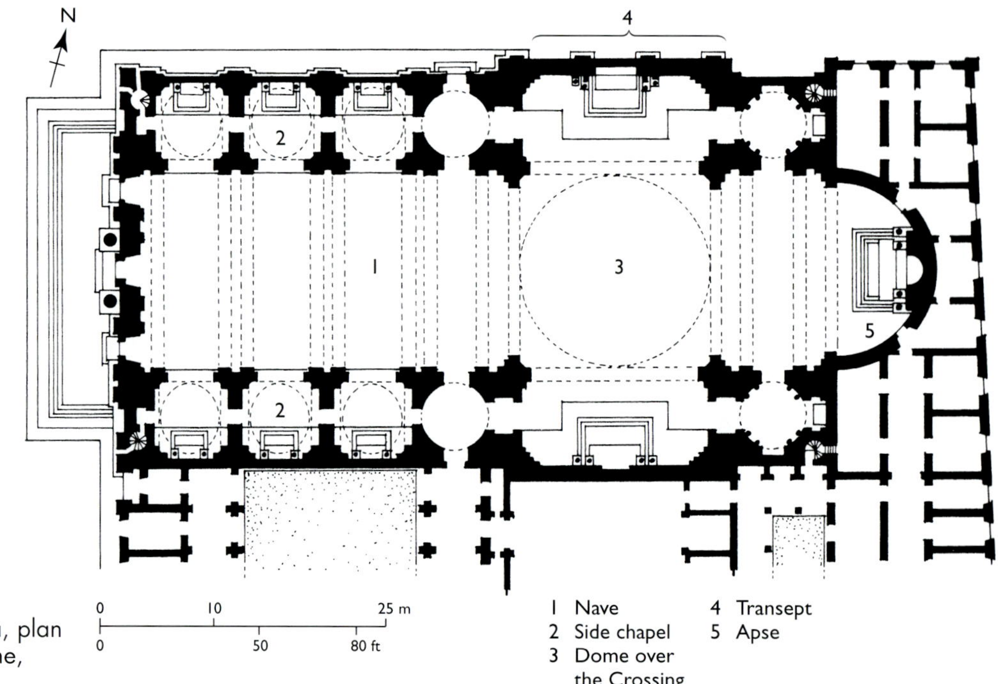

15.23 Giacomo da Vignola, plan of the Church of Il Gesù, Rome, 1565–1573.

aisles to permit circulation around the nave, Vignola designed side chapels for individual prayer. Most of the worshipers were thus channeled into the large, barrel-vaulted nave, and their attention was focused on the priest and the altar. At the same time, the choir was separated from the nave to accentuate the hierarchical distinction between the clergy and the public. Also emphasizing this distinction was the lengthened route from the sacristy, where the priest prepares for Mass, to the altar, where he performs it. This increased the time it took the priest to reach the altar and heightened worshipers' sense of anticipation before the Mass began. Most of the interior light came from the windows of the dome and was thus concentrated on the crossing below, creating a mystical effect of the sort encouraged by the Council of Trent.

Vignola died before completing the Gesù, and the dome and façade were finished by Giacomo della Porta (1532/3–1602) in 1573. Figure **15.24** shows the façade as Vignola

15.24 Engraving of Vignola's design for the façade of the Church of Il Gesù, Rome, late 16th century.

designed it, preserved in a sixteenth-century engraving, and figure **15.25** is the existing façade by della Porta. The façade as conceived by Vignola was influenced by Alberti's architecture and has some similarities to that of Palladio's San Giorgio Maggiore, but the superimposed Greek portico of San Giorgio has been eliminated. Instead of a colossal Order of engaged half columns supported on a large base that overlaps the ground floor and its pediment, the Gesù has two sets of double columns, one on each story. As a result, the Gesù appears to be more imposing and taller than San Giorgio, which was a quality that appealed to the Jesuits.

Vignola originally planned the interior with simplicity in mind, which would have conformed to the style of other early Jesuit churches. But della Porta increased its complexity, integrating sculpture into the wall surface of the façade and adding volutes. He also used two sets of half columns, one set on each level, as well as several pairs of pilasters. The final product was more complex, and had more surface movement and formal animation, than most Renaissance churches. The Gesù was enormously influential. Its complexity would be taken up by Baroque architects and carried by Jesuit missionaries throughout the world.

15.25 Giacomo da Vignola and Giacomo della Porta, façade of the Church of Il Gesù, Rome, c. 1575–1584.

	Style/Period	Works of Art	Cultural/Historical Developments
1520	MANNERISM AND LATE 16TH-CENTURY ITALY 1520–1540	de' Rossi (attrib.), *Joseph and Potiphar's Wife* (**15.9**) Parmigianino, *Self-Portrait in a Convex Mirror* (**15.2**) Pontormo, *Entombment* (**15.1**) Romano, Palazzo del Tè (**15.12–15.14**), Mantua Parmigianino, *Madonna and Child with Angels* (**15.3**)	**Parmigianino, *Self-Portrait***
	1540–1550 **Cellini, saltcellar**	Cellini, saltcellar of Francis I (**15.7**) Bronzino, *Venus, Cupid, Folly, and Time* (**15.4**) Bronzino, *Eleonora of Toledo and Her Son Don Giovanni* (**15.5**) 	Council of Trent introduces Counter-Reformation policies (1545–1563) **El Greco, *Burial of the Count of Orgaz***  **Bronzino, *Eleonora of Toledo and Her Son Don Giovanni***
1550	1550–1570 **Palladio, San Giorgio Maggiore**	Anguissola, *The Artist's Sister Minerva* (**15.10**) Palladio, San Giorgio Maggiore (**15.21**), Venice Palladio, Villa Rotonda (**15.18, 15.20**), Vicenza	Sir Philip Sidney, English poet and soldier (1554–1586) Francis Bacon, English philosopher and statesman (1561–1626) Pierre de Ronsard, *Elegies* (1565) Vasari, *Lives . . .* (1550, 1568)
1600	1570–1600 **Giambologna, *Mercury***	Veronese, *Christ in the House of Levi* (**15.6**) Vignola and della Porta, Church of Il Gesù (**15.24–15.25**), Rome Giambologna, *Mercury* (**15.8**) Tintoretto, *Last Supper* (**15.15**) El Greco, *Christ Healing the Blind* (**15.16**) El Greco, *Burial of the Count of Orgaz* (**15.17**) 	Turkish fleet defeated at Lepanto (1571) Francis Drake starts circumnavigation of world via Cape Horn (1577) Catacombs discovered in Rome (1578) Mary, Queen of Scots, executed (1587) Monteverdi's first book of madrigals (1587) Christopher Marlowe, *Dr. Faustus* (1588) English fleet defeats Spanish Armada (1588) Galileo Galilei, *De Motu,* describing experiments on falling bodies (1590) Edict of Nantes establishes religious toleration (1598) William Shakespeare, *Hamlet* (1600) **Veronese, *Christ in the House of Levi***

16

Sixteenth-Century Painting and Printmaking in Northern Europe

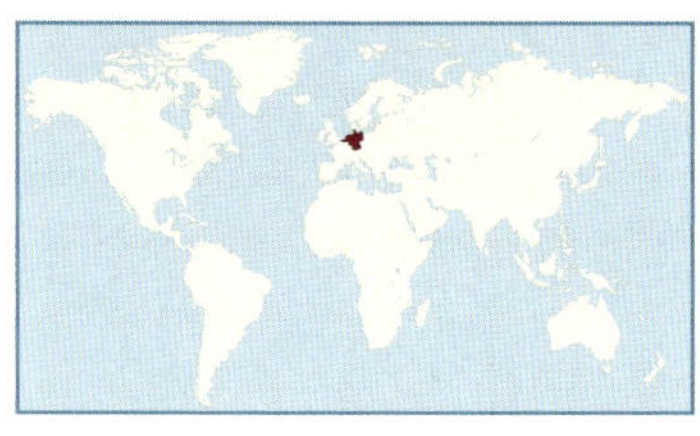

As in the fifteenth century, northern Europe in the sixteenth century underwent many of the same developments as the South did (see map). The most important northern artists were the painters from Germany and the Netherlands, several of whom traveled to Italy and were influenced by Renaissance humanism. Nevertheless, the North was always less comfortable with Classical forms in art than was Italy. The elegant linear qualities, rich colors, and crisp edges of International Gothic forms persist in Netherlandish and German painting. Northern artists were also less interested than the Italians in the subtleties of *chiaroscuro* and modeling, and the textured, painterly qualities of the late Venetian Renaissance do not often appear in the North.

The North produced some of Europe's most distinguished humanists, including the prolific writer and scholar Erasmus of Rotterdam (see box, p. 622, and fig. 16.21). Germany was the home of Martin Luther (see box, p. 605, and fig. 16.20), whose views launched the Protestant Reformation. Humanism, as well as Protestantism, clashed with the Inquisition, and religious strife continued to intensify from the late fifteenth century. The opposition of the Church to both the humanists and the Protestants was often virulent and excessive. One striking expression of the work of the Inquisition was its opposition to alleged witchcraft. In 1487, two German Inquisitors—Heinrich Kramer (d. 1500) and James Sprenger (d. 1494), both of whom were members of the Dominican order—had published *The Witches' Hammer.* In it, they described the characteristics of witches and recommended methods of torture for extracting confessions from them.

In a more humanist vein, northern Europe, like Italy, displayed an interest in artists' biography, which was revived as part of the Classical tradition and was consistent with the rise in the social status of the artist. In 1604, Karel van Mander (1548–1606) of Haarlem, Holland, published *Het Schilderboeck* (*The Painter's Book*), describing the lives of Northern artists. Like Vasari's *Lives,* it has become an important source for the history of Renaissance art.

One of the most prevalent humanist expressions in the North was the proverb. Humanists such as Erasmus collected proverbs, many of which were Classical in origin, as a way of educating people and arousing interest in antiquity. They explained the proverbs, placing them in their historical context, and also showed their relevance to contemporary life. This development was consistent with the Northern tradition of depicting bourgeois **genre** scenes (scenes of everyday life).

Northern and central Europe in the Renaissance.

Luther

Martin Luther (1483–1546), as we have seen, initiated the Protestant Reformation, which divided Europe and broke the monopoly of the Catholic Church. He objected to the practice of selling indulgences and particularly to Johann Tetzel (c. 1465–1519), the Dominican "pardoner." Luther saw Tetzel and the papacy as profiting from the fear and ignorance of his German compatriots. This view was confirmed by Tetzel's "Sermon on Indulgences," in which he compared indulgences to "letters of safe conduct" into heaven and pointed out that each mortal sin was punished by seven years of purgatory. Since people repeatedly commit mortal sins, Tetzel argued, they could save themselves many years of torture by buying indulgences.

Luther's *Ninety-five Theses* included scathing attacks on the principle of buying one's way into heaven. Referring to the financial motives of the Church, thesis number 28 stated, "It is certain that, when the money rattles in the chest, avarice and gain may be increased, but the effect of the intercession of the Church depends on the will of God alone." Number 43 declares, "He who gives to the poor man, or lends to a needy man, does better than if he bought pardons." And number 50, "If the pope were acquainted with the exactions of the preachers of pardons, he would prefer that the basilica of Saint Peter [then being rebuilt] should be burnt to ashes rather than that it should be built up with the skin, flesh, and bones of his sheep."[1]

In these sentiments, Luther essentially refuted the pope's right to speak for God. His zeal for ecclesiastic reform spilled over into the socioeconomic arena. In 1524, following Luther's example, the peasants of southwest Germany rebelled against the increasing demands of the nobility. This time, however, Luther did not sanction the revolt. He published virulent attacks against the peasants on the grounds that the Bible encourages suffering as a means to salvation. According to Luther, the rebels "cause uproar and sacrilegiously rob and pillage monasteries and castles that do not belong to them, for which, like public highwaymen and murderers, they deserve the twofold death of body and soul."[2]

The Netherlands

Hieronymus Bosch

The most important Netherlandish artist at the turn of the sixteenth century was Hieronymus Bosch (c. 1450–1516). Little is known of his artistic development, but he created some of the most original and puzzling imagery in Western art.

The Seven Deadly Sins and the Four Last Things

Corruption in the Catholic Church, which led to the Reformation, and the follies of humanity became popular subjects in the North. Religious and social satire inspired writers and artists, especially in the Netherlands and Germany. In the visual arts, this provided the impetus for iconographic themes containing moral messages. A satirical, moralizing tone is evident in Bosch's *Seven Deadly Sins and the Four Last Things* (fig. **16.1**), which has been dated early in Bosch's career by some scholars and late by others. Some question the attribution to Bosch, but it is generally accepted as either his work or his conception. Painted on a tabletop, it expresses the medieval view that life on earth is a mere reflection, or mirror, of heavenly perfection. God, according to this view, is both the creator and the "eye." He watches, remembers, and in the end punishes or rewards, according to one's merits while on earth.

The large central circle of the painting is a metaphor in which the eye is a mirror. It is a variation on the convex mirror in van Eyck's *Arnolfini Portrait* (see fig. 13.67), which, according to one iconographic reading, reflects the artist and also symbolizes God's presence. In the *Seven Deadly Sins*, the resurrected Christ occupies the center of a dark circle, with rays of light extending from it—a visual metaphor for the pupil in an eye. Inscribed in Latin in Gothic script under the figure of Christ is *Cave cave Dus* [an abbreviation of *Dominus*] *videt* ("Beware beware, the Lord sees").

On the outermost ring of the circle are seven scenes of daily life illustrating the Seven Deadly Sins. They are no longer represented as medieval personifications, but instead are integrated into everyday activities. Superbia (Pride, fig. **16.2**) is represented as a vain, bourgeois woman admiring herself in a mirror. A box of jewels, symbolizing vanity, lies open on the floor. The figure occupies an orderly, middle-class room, decorated with elegant jugs and vases, that reveals pride in her house. Reaching around from behind the chest and holding up the mirror is a devil—a moral warning against self-love and the vanity of appearances.

To the left of Pride is Ira (Anger), shown as a street fight between neighbors, and Invidia (Envy), the next scene to the left, is a verbal quarrel, the acrimony of which is enhanced by barking dogs with bared teeth. The dog on the left gazes at a large bone, while the other glares enviously at him. Neither dog seems interested in the two available bones between them on the ground. Like envious people, the dogs are never satisfied with what they have but only want what the other one has. Avaritia (Avarice) is represented as a rich man taking money from a poor man while bribing a judge. The remaining scenes represent Gula (Gluttony), Accidia (Sloth), and Luxuria (Lust). This combination of Christian moralizing with scenes of daily life infused with humor is characteristic of late Renaissance painting in the Netherlands.

The four corners of the tabletop illustrate the Four Last Things, a reminder of mortality and the rewards or

16.1 Attributed to Hieronymus Bosch, *Seven Deadly Sins and the Four Last Things*, painted tabletop. Oil on wood; 3 ft. 11¼ in. × 4 ft. 11 in. (1.20 × 1.50 m). Museo del Prado, Madrid. None of Bosch's pictures has a documented date. This painting is variously regarded as an early (c. 1475) or a late (1505–1515) work. All that is known of Bosch is that he lived in the small Dutch town of 's-Hertogenbosch (from which his name is derived) and was a member of a religious fraternity, the Brotherhood of Our Lady. He believed in the pervasiveness of sin, usually of a sensual nature, and his works illustrate the torments of hell in vivid detail.

punishments that follow. In the deathbed scene at the upper left, a dying man receives last rites. The angel and devil at the head of the bed wait to see which will take his soul. In the corner, members of his family carry on with their lives, more engaged in the game they are playing than in the deathbed scene. At the upper right, Christ presides over the Last Judgment, and the dead rise from their graves. In the lower right and left, respectively, are heaven, where Saint Peter greets the saved, and a fiery hell. Heaven is an orderly, harmonious court illuminated by divine light. Hell is dark, disordered, and fraught with torture and destruction.

16.2 Attributed to Hieronymus Bosch, *Superbia* (detail of fig. 16.1).

Garden of Earthly Delights The meaning of Bosch's huge, complex, and controversial triptych known as the *Garden of Earthly Delights* (fig. **16.3**), now generally dated about 1510–1515, is more obscure than the images on the painted tabletop. Documents suggest that the *Garden* was a secular commission for the stateroom of the House of Nassau in Brussels, although this is debated by scholars. The work has been interpreted in a number of ways: as a satire on lust, as an alchemical vision, and as a dream-world revealing unconscious impulses. But there are also a number of traditional Christian features in the triptych, which argues for a religious commission, and some scholars identify the primary source of the iconography as the Bible. The Garden of Eden is represented in the left panel. In the foreground, God presents the newly created Eve to a seated Adam. The prickly tree behind Adam is the Tree of Life. In the middle ground, a curious *fons vitae* (fountain of life) stands in a pool of water, and in the background wild animals exist in a state of apparent tameness.

Even in paradise, however, Bosch's taste for biting satire is evident in certain details that prefigure the Fall. In the foreground, for example, a self-satisfied cat strolls off with a dead mouse in its mouth. At the upper right, a lion eats a deer, while a boar pursues a fantastic animal. Ravens, which can symbolize death, perch on the fountain of life, and the owl in the opening of the fountain could denote the nocturnal activities of witches and devils. Eve's role as the primal seductress is clear from Adam's response to her. He is not the traditional languid or sleeping figure of Michelangelo (see fig. 14.23), but is alert and wide awake. He literally "sits up and takes notice" of the creature to whom he is being introduced.

The human figures in the central panel seem engaged in sexual pursuits. The amorous couple enclosed in a transparent globe, a reference to the transience of lust (fig. **16.4**, p. 610), illustrates the proverb "Happiness and glass, how soon they pass." The upper regions of the central panel depict what is sometimes identified as a Tower of Adultresses in a Pool of Lust. It is decorated with horns and filled with cuckolded husbands. Four so-called castles of vanity stand at the pool's edge. In the middle ground, a procession of frenzied human figures mounted on animals endlessly circles a Pool of Youth. The human figures are small in relation to the strange plant and animal forms that populate the picture. Some are enclosed in transparent globular shapes that suggest alchemical vessels. The illogical juxtapositions of scale, together with the strange symbolic details, such as the enlarged strawberries, have led some scholars to think that Bosch is depicting an inner, dreamlike world. Consistent with Christian tradition, however, is the conventional opposition of the era before the Fall on the left and hell on the right. The sinister aura of the central panels suggests moralizing on the artist's part, which may refer to the decadence of humanity that led God to unleash the Flood.

In hell, buildings burn in the distance. The scene is filled with elaborate tortures and dismembered body parts taking on a life of their own. Musical instruments that cause pain rather than pleasure reflect the medieval notion that music is the work of Satan. One figure is crucified on the strings of a harp, and another is tied to a long flute. A seated monster, probably Satan himself, swallows one soul and simultaneously expels another through a transparent globe. Two ears with no head are pierced by an arrow.

16.3 Hieronymus Bosch, *Garden of Earthly Delights,* c. 1510–1515. Triptych: left panel, *Garden of Eden;* center panel, *World before the Flood;* right panel, *Hell.* Oil on wood; left and right panels 7 ft. 2 in. × 3 ft. (2.18 × 0.91 m), center panel 7 ft. 2 in. × 6 ft. 4 in. (2.18 × 1.93 m). Museo del Prado, Madrid.

16.4 Hieronymus Bosch, couple in a transparent globe (detail of fig. 16.3).

16.5 Hieronymus Bosch, monster with an egglike body (detail of fig. 16.3).

At the center of this vision of hell is a monster whose body resembles a broken egg (fig. **16.5**). This might refer to the alchemical egg, which was believed by alchemists, who strove to transmute base metal into gold and silver, to be the source of spiritual rebirth (see box, p. 612). He is supported by tree-trunk legs, each of which stands in a boat. His egglike body is cracked open to reveal a crone by a wine keg and a table of sinners. On his head, the egg man balances a disk with a bagpipe, which is a traditional symbol of lust in Western art. Peering out from under the disk, and seemingly weighed down by it, is an individualized face. Its self-conscious appeal to the observer is a convention of artists' self-portraits. Like the fantastic complexity and tantalizing obscurity of Bosch's images in this work, however, the meaning of the face remains unexplained.

Pieter Bruegel the Elder

The foremost sixteenth-century painter of the Netherlands was Pieter Bruegel the Elder (c. 1525–1569), a follower of Bosch. Early in his career, Bruegel worked in the port city of Antwerp, in modern Belgium, an international center of commerce and finance. Bruegel trained in a printing concern, which accounts for his prolific graphic output. In 1551, he became a master in the painters' guild and the following year departed for Italy. His trip influenced his work considerably, in particular his taste for landscape. While in Italy, he made many drawings of the landscape, especially the Alps and the southern seacoast, but he made no known sketches of the Roman sculpture and architecture that appealed to Italian Renaissance artists. Bruegel's passion for landscape reflects his belief that nature is the source of all life, a notion that can be related to contemporary explorations of the globe and is also derived from Petrarch's humanism.

In his *Landscape with the Fall of Icarus* (fig. **16.6**), Bruegel expresses his love of landscape for its own sake, for much of the picture is dominated by a seascape. Bruegel's vision of humanity in nature is shown by the intense relationship between the peasant pushing his plowshare and the land. The folds of the peasant's tunic repeat the furrows of the plowed earth beneath him, formally uniting him with the land. Below the peasant, a shepherd tends his flock, and a peasant sits by the edge of the sea. The shepherd rests on his crook and gazes up at the sky. In the context of the myth (see caption), it is likely that he is watching the flight of Daedalos, but he does not notice the drowning Icarus. The other two figures are so absorbed in their tasks that they fail to observe the mythical event taking place. Bruegel's philosophy as expressed in this painting conforms to the proverb "No plow stops for a dying man."

To the humanist integration of antiquity with contemporary concerns, Bruegel adds the Christian moralizing tradition of northern Europe. The *Fall of Icarus* demonstrates that it is wiser to till the land than to brave the skies, which was also the message of his *Tower of Babel* (see fig. I.7). There, too, though in a biblical setting, Bruegel depicts the dangers of unrealistic ambition, as the tower seems to crumble and fall like Icarus. For Bruegel, therefore, what the Greeks called *hubris* (a combination of pride and unrealistic ambition) corresponds to the Netherlandish notion of human folly. Folly, in Bruegel's view, turns things upside down, just as Icarus has landed head first with his feet flailing in the air. To avoid such a fall, according to Bruegel's imagery, one is advised to concentrate on work. Even in our own age of air travel and space programs, popular wisdom considers it a virtue and a sign of mental stability to "have one's feet planted firmly on the ground." People who "fly too high" are considered overly ambitious and destined for a fall.

See figure I.7. Pieter Bruegel the Elder, *The Tower of Babel*, 1563.

16.6 Pieter Bruegel the Elder, *Landscape with the Fall of Icarus*, c. 1554–1555. Oil on panel (transferred to canvas); 2 ft. 5 in. × 3 ft. 8⅛ in. (0.74 × 1.12 m). Musées Royaux des Beaux-Arts de Belgique, Brussels. Although famous for his peasant scenes and known as "Peasant Bruegel," Bruegel was a townsman and a humanist. Here he combines the theme of man's unity with landscape with the Classical myth of Icarus. Daedalos, the father of Icarus, fashioned a pair of wings out of feathers held together by wax and warned his son not to fly too near the sun. Icarus disobeyed, the sun melted his wings, and he drowned in the Aegean Sea. In the painting, Icarus can be seen flailing in the water just below the large ship on the right.

Alchemy

Alchemy is the process by which base metals are believed capable of being changed into gold, and it was practiced by several well-known historical figures, including Leonardo da Vinci. The practice of alchemy in both Eastern and Western cultures had symbolic, as well as financial, meanings that are complex and elusive. (The unreal and obsessive qualities of alchemy were satirized by moralists such as Bruegel—see *The Alchemist,* fig. 16.7). Alchemy could symbolize the cosmos and the quest for immortality, the spiritual evolution of the individual, and the recovery of a state of perfection that existed before the Fall of Man. Of the numerous symbolic constructs in alchemy, two of the most prominent are the philosopher's stone and the philosopher's egg. The former makes possible regeneration and spiritual fulfilment, while the latter embodies the source of birth and, therefore, of spiritual rebirth.

Bruegel's 1558 drawing of *The Alchemist* (fig. **16.7**) is another visual parable about the folly of irrational ambition. The alchemist spurns real work and, instead of earning money for his family, tries to make gold from a spurious formula. Bruegel indicates the obsessive nature of alchemy by the alchemist's intense concentration and the lab equipment filling his home. The results of his obsession are evident as his wife and children leave the house to beg. The irony of the family going begging while the father pursues a fantasy of gold contributes to the biting satire of Bruegel's drawing.

In 1559, Bruegel painted *Netherlandish Proverbs* (fig. **16.8**), which is the visual equivalent of Erasmus's *Adagia* (see box, p. 622). It is an outdoor scene filled with about one hundred figures, each of whose activities exemplify a moral principle. But every instance fulfills the proverb in the negative, creating the "world upside down" that stood for Bruegel's view of human folly. The predominant colors are yellows and browns, which are accented throughout by blues and reds—blue denoting cheating and foolishness, and red, sin and arrogance. The painting is also called the *Blue Cloak* from the detail in which a woman in a sinful red dress puts a blue cloak on her foolish husband. The pointed hood is an allusion to the horns of the cuckold.

16.7 Pieter Bruegel the Elder, *The Alchemist,* 1558. Drawing; 12 × 17¾ in. (30.5 × 45.1 cm). Kupferstichkabinett, Staatliche Museen, Berlin. After 1563, according to Karel van Mander's biography of him, Bruegel's mother-in-law insisted he move to Brussels and end the relationship with his mistress in Antwerp. While in Brussels, he received commissions from the city council as well as from private patrons.

The large number of scenes in this painting makes it difficult to discern the individual proverbs in a small reproduction, but we can identify a few of them. At the lower left, a woman carries a bucket of water and a burning fire poker ("to hold fire in one hand and water in the other"). Above her, a man sits on the ground between two stools ("to fall between two stools in the ashes"). In the lower center, a man whose calf has already drowned is filling the well ("to fill the pothole after the calf has drowned"), and roses are scattered around a pig ("to cast roses before swine"). Gossip is represented as two women, one spinning and the other holding the distaff (they literally "spin tales"). Other proverbs illustrated in the picture include "to hold an eel by the tail" (the man at the hut on the water is holding a large eel), "big fish eat little fish" (in the water), "jumping from ox to ass," or "from the frying pan into the fire" (the man by the door of the castle tower), and at the lower left another man "beats his head against a brick wall."

W. H. Auden on Bruegel's *Icarus*

The twentieth-century poet W. H. Auden included a description of Bruegel's *Icarus* in his 1938 poem "Musée des Beaux-Arts" (Museum of Fine Arts):

> In Bruegel's *Icarus*, for instance: how everything turns away
> Quite leisurely from the disaster; the ploughman may
> Have heard the splash, the forsaken cry,
> But for him it was not an important failure; the sun shone
> As it had to on the white legs disappearing into the green
> Water; and the expensive delicate ship that must have seen
> Something amazing, a boy falling out of the sky,
> Had somewhere to get to and sailed calmly on.[3]

16.8 Pieter Bruegel the Elder, *Netherlandish Proverbs,* 1559. Panel; 3 ft. 10 in. × 5 ft. 4½ in. (1.17 × 1.63 m). Staatliche Museen, Berlin.

16.9 Pieter Bruegel the Elder, *Peasant Dance,* c. 1567. Oil on wood; approx. 3 ft. 9 in. × 5 ft. 5 in. (1.14 × 1.65 m). Kunsthistorisches Museum, Vienna. After 1563, according to Karel van Mander's biography of him, Bruegel's mother-in-law insisted he move to Brussels and end the relationship with his mistress in Antwerp. While in Brussels, he received commissions from the city council as well as from private patrons.

Entirely different in mood, but nevertheless moralizing, is Bruegel's *Peasant Dance* (fig. **16.9**) of about 1567, which represents the celebration of a feast day of the church. In contrast to the workaday peasants in the *Fall of Icarus,* these indulge in the enjoyments of dancing, eating, drinking, music-making, and lust. On the right, two peasants "kicking up their heels" seem to dance their way into the picture. The dancers in the background give way to even greater abandon. On the left, the bagpipe is a formal echo of the rotund figures. The slow, deliberate peasants who occupied the landscape near Icarus's fall have become energetic, filled with vitality and rhythm. Their folly, according to Bruegel's iconography, is that they ignore the distant church and the image of the Virgin and Child attached to the tree at the right.

Bruegel lived during the tense years of the Reformation and the Counter-Reformation, which coincided with Spanish rule of the Netherlands. Nothing is known for certain of his political views, but it is clear that he was a humanist. In his art, Bruegel creates a synthesis of Christian genre and Classical imagery, which is at once moralizing and satirical.

Germany

Albrecht Dürer

The German taste for linear quality in painting is especially striking in the work of Albrecht Dürer (1471–1528). He was first apprenticed to his father, who ran a goldsmith's shop. Then he worked under a painter in Nuremberg, which was a center of humanism, and in 1494 and 1505 he traveled to Italy. He absorbed the revival of Classical form and copied Italian Renaissance prints, which he translated into a more rugged, linear Northern style. He also drew the Italian landscape, studied Italian theories of proportion, and read Alberti. Like Piero della Francesca and Leonardo, Dürer wrote a book of advice to artists: the *Four Books of Human Proportion* (*Vier Bücher von menschlichen Proportion*).

Self-Portraits The *Self-Portrait* of 1498 (fig. **16.10**) reveals the influence of Leonardo (see fig. 14.16), whom Dürer greatly admired, in the figure's three-quarter view and the distant landscape. Although set in a three-dimensional cubic space according to the laws of fifteenth-century

16.10 Albrecht Dürer, *Self-Portrait,* 1498. Oil on panel; 20½ × 16 in. (52.1 × 40.6 cm). Museo del Prado, Madrid. Dürer was born in Nuremberg, Germany, to a family of goldsmiths. He was trained as a metalworker and painter, and in his twenties traveled in Italy. Young German artists traditionally spent a *Wanderjahr,* or year of travel, visiting different parts of Europe and studying art. From 1512, as court painter to the Holy Roman emperor, Dürer became the most important figure in the transition from late Gothic to Renaissance style in northern Europe.

CONNECTIONS

See figure 14.16. Leonardo da Vinci, *Mona Lisa,* c. 1503–1505.

The Development of Printmaking

Printmaking is the generic term for a number of processes, of which **engraving** and woodcut are two prime examples. **Prints** are made by pressing a sheet of paper (or other material) against an image-bearing surface (the **print matrix**) to which ink has been applied. When the paper is removed, the image adheres to it but in reverse.

The woodcut had been used in China from the fifth century A.D. for applying patterns to textiles, but was not introduced into Europe until the fourteenth century. First it was used for textile decoration and then for printing on paper. Woodcuts are created by a relief process. First, the artist takes a block of wood sawed parallel to the grain, covers it with a white ground, and draws the image in ink. The background is then carved away, leaving the design area slightly raised. The woodblock is inked, and the ink adheres to the raised image. It is then transferred to damp paper either by hand or with a printing press.

Engraving, which grew out of the goldsmith's art, originated in Germany and northern Italy in the middle of the fifteenth century. It is an intaglio process (from the Italian *intagliare,* "to carve"). The image is incised into a highly polished metal **plate,** usually of copper, with a cutting instrument, or **burin.** The artist then inks the plate and wipes it clean so that ink remains only in the incised grooves. An impression is made on damp paper in a printing press, with sufficient pressure being applied so that the paper picks up the ink.

Both woodcut and engraving have distinctive characteristics. Dürer's engraving in figure 16.13, for example, shows how this technique lends itself to subtle modeling and shading through the use of fine lines. Hatching and crosshatching determine the degree of light and shade in a print. Woodcuts, as in figure 16.12, tend to be more linear, with sharper contrasts between light and dark, and hence more vigorous.

Printmaking is well suited to the production of multiple images. A set of multiples is called an **edition.** Both methods described here can yield several hundred good-quality prints before the original block or plate begins to show signs of wear. Mass production of prints in the sixteenth century made images available, at a lower cost, to a much broader public than before. Printmaking played a vital role in Northern Renaissance culture, particularly in disseminating knowledge, in expanding social consciousness, and in transmitting artistic styles.

perspective and consistently illuminated from the left edge, Dürer's figure is painted with crisp contours that would be unusual in Italy. The attention to patterning in the long curls and in the details of costume also reveal Dürer's interest in line for its own sake. Particularly prominent in this and other works by the artist is his signature monogram—a *D* within an *A*—which is accompanied by an inscription—the artist's statement of his own role in creating the image. Dürer's confident sense of himself is conveyed by his upright posture, firmly clasped hands, and elegant costume; it is also a reflection of the social status he had achieved—or hoped to achieve—in Nuremberg.

In 1500, Dürer painted his most famous self-portrait (fig. **16.11**). He shows himself in a manner reminiscent of the frontal images of Christ and saints in Byzantine icons (see Chapter 8). Dürer has placed himself against a dark background and is depicted with more softened, idealized features than in the earlier example. By eliminating the window and landscape vista, Dürer pushes his figure forward, increasing its direct impact on the viewer. The gesture of the right hand, which seems to be touching the fur lining of the cloak, is a reference both to traditional images of Christ blessing the world and to the notion of the artist's divine creative hand.

16.11 Albrecht Dürer, *Self-Portrait*, 1500. Oil on panel; 26¼ × 19¼ in. (66.7 × 48.9 cm). Alte Pinakothek, Munich. Note the "AD" monogram and the date "1500" to the left of the figure.

Prints Dürer's interest in line is most apparent in his work as a **woodcut** artist and engraver (see box, p. 615).

Around the time of the 1498 *Self-Portrait*, Dürer produced the *Apocalypse*, the first book to be designed and published by a single artist. In it, Dürer included the full text of the book of Revelation in Latin and German editions, which he illustrated. In the *Four Horsemen of the Apocalypse* (fig. **16.12**), the aged and withered figure of Death rides a skeletal horse, trampling a bishop whose head is in the jaws of a monster. Cowering before the horse are figures awaiting destruction. Next to Death, and the most prominent of the four, rides Famine, carrying a scale. War brandishes a sword, which is parallel to the angel above. Plague, riding the background horse, draws his bow (arrow wounds were associated with the sores caused by the plague). Finally, the presence of God as the ultimate motivating force behind the four horsemen is implied by rays of light entering the picture from the upper left corner.

In this image, Dürer took evident delight in the graphic and psychological expressiveness of line. The powerful left to right motion of the horses and their riders is created by

16.12 Albrecht Dürer, *Four Horsemen of the Apocalypse*, c. 1497–1498. Woodcut; 15⅖ × 11 in. (39.2 × 27.9 cm). Metropolitan Museum of Art, New York. Gift of Junius S. Morgan, 1919. This is one of a series of fifteen woodcuts from the late 1490s illustrating the Apocalypse.

The Myth of the Mad Artist

Artists, particularly melancholic artists, have traditionally been considered "different" (from the general population) to the point of madness. Aristotle made the first known connection between melancholy—derived from the Greek words *melas,* meaning "black," and *cholos,* meaning "bile" or "wrath"—and genius. Melancholics were thought to have an excess of black bile (one of the four bodily humors) in their systems, an idea revived in the Renaissance.

Marsilio Ficino believed that melancholics were born under the astrological sign of Saturn, an ancient Roman god known for his moody temperament, and hence shared this particular aspect of Saturn's personality. Consistent with his Neoplatonic philosophy, Ficino combined his astrological theories with Plato's notion that artistic genius is a gift of the gods, who inspire artists with a creative *mania* (Greek for "madness" or "frenzy"). Thus, from the Renaissance onward, artists and other creative people have been thought to be saturnine (in the sense of temperamental), melancholic, and eccentric.

Saturn, who was also identified with Kronos, one of the Greek Titans, was a god of agriculture, which was associated with geometry ("measurement of the earth"). Artists, farmers, and geometricians alike used measuring instruments in their work, as seen in the compass in the hand of Dürer's Melancholy (see fig. 16.13).

The pose of Dürer's uninspired genius echoes those of Raphael's Heraklitos/Michelangelo in the *School of Athens* (see fig. 14.35) and of Michelangelo's *Jeremiah* (see fig. 14.25) on the Sistine Chapel ceiling. But Dürer's engraving is the earliest representation of the *idea* of melancholy as an artistic image in its own right. It influenced the view of the artist as a divinely inspired, melancholic genius who suffers bouts of creative frenzy and gloomy idleness. Both Dürer and Michelangelo identified with that image, which declined in popularity in the seventeenth century but was revived by the nineteenth-century Romantics (see Chapter 20).

their diagonal sweep across the width of the picture. The less forceful, zigzag lines of the cowering figures reveal their panic in the face of the relenting and inevitable advance of the horsemen.

Dürer's copper engraving of *Melencolia* (fig. **16.13**), or Melancholy, signed and dated 1514, is an early example of the tradition of portraying artists as having saturnine, melancholic personalities (see box). The female winged

16.13 Albrecht Dürer, *Melencolia I,* 1514. Engraving; 9½ × 7⁵⁄₁₆ in. (24.3 × 18.6 cm). Metropolitan Museum of Art, New York. Harris Brisbane Dick Fund, 1943.

CONNECTIONS

See figure 14.25. Michelangelo, *Jeremiah,* 1508–1512.

See figure 14.35. Raphael, *Heraklitos/ Michelangelo,* 1509–1511.

genius may represent Dürer, as is suggested by the location of his monogram underneath her bench. She leans on her elbow in the pose of melancholy that had been conventional since antiquity.

Dürer's Melancholy is an idle creator, an unemployed "genius" looking inward for inspiration and not finding it. She is in the grip of obsessive thinking and, therefore, cannot act. Idle tools, including a bell that does not ring, empty scales, and a ladder leading nowhere seem to reflect her state of mind. The winged child conveys a sense of anxiety that could mirror the anxiety felt by the uninspired artist. Other details, such as the hourglass above the genius, refer to the passing of time. In the upper left, a squeaking bat displays a banner with "MELENCOLIA I" written on it. The bat, associated with melancholy because of its isolation in dark places, comes out only at night. By combining the bat with the darkened sky pierced by rays of light, Dürer seems to be making a visual play on the contrasting mental states of black melancholy and the light of inspiration.

Matthias Grünewald

Contemporary with Dürer's engraving of Melancholy is the Isenheim Altarpiece (figs. **16.14** and **16.15**), a monumental polyptych by the German artist Matthias Grünewald (d. 1528). It was commissioned for the hospital chapel of the monastery of Saint Anthony in Isenheim. The hospital specialized in the treatment of skin diseases, particularly ergotism, known as "Saint Anthony's fire." The altarpiece was a form popular in Germany between 1450 and 1525. It typically consisted of a central corpus, or body, containing sculpted figures and was enclosed by doors (wings) painted on the outside and carved in low relief inside. In the Isenheim Altarpiece, it is the base, not the corpus, that contains the sculptures; but sculptured figures of Saints Anthony, Jerome, and Augustine are located in the central corpus behind the *Virgin and Child with Angels*—they are revealed when the two panels of this scene are opened (fig. **16.16**).

The exterior of the doors depicts the *Crucifixion;* its emphasis on physical suffering and the wounds of Jesus was related to healing. This is enhanced by Grünewald's color—the greenish flesh (suggesting gangrene), the gray-black sky, and the rich reds of the drapery that echo the red of Jesus's blood—to accentuate the overwhelming effect of the scene. The Cross is made of two logs tied and nailed together, its arms bowed from Jesus's weight. The Crown of Thorns, a visual echo of the contorted fingers, causes blood to drip from Jesus's scalp, and his loincloth is torn and ragged.

Grünewald's depiction of Jesus has been related to some fourteenth-century mystical writings, notably the *Revelations* of the Swedish saint Bridget. "The crown of thorns," she wrote, "was impressed on his head; it was firmly pushed down covering half his forehead, the blood, gushing forth from the prickling of thorns. . . . The color of death spread through his flesh. . . . His knees . . . contracted. . . . His feet were cramped and twisted. . . . The cramped fingers and arms were stretched out painfully."[4]

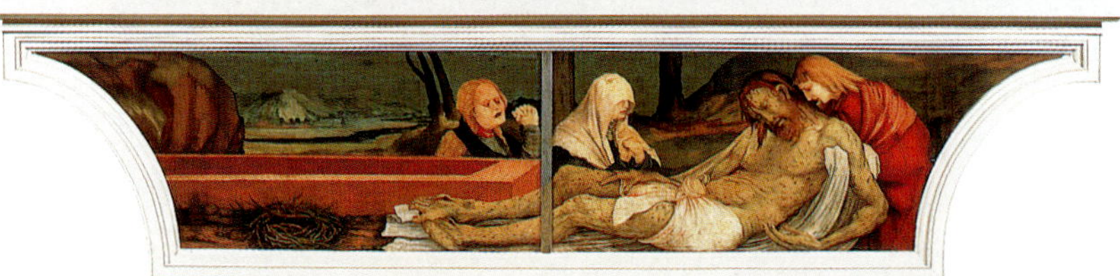

16.14 Matthias Grünewald, *Crucifixion with Saint Sebastian* (left) *and Saint Anthony* (right), and *Lamentation* (below), the Isenheim Altarpiece, closed, c. 1510–1515. Oil on panel (with frame); side panels 8 ft. 2½ in. × 3 ft. ½ in. (2.50 × 0.93 m); central panel 9 ft. 9½ in. × 10 ft. 9 in. (2.98 × 3.28 m); base 2 ft. 5½ in. × 11 ft. 2 in. (0.75 × 3.40 m); Musée d'Unterlinden, Colmar, France.

16.15 Matthias Grünewald, *Annunciation, Virgin and Child with Angels,* and *Resurrection,* the Isenheim Altarpiece, opened, c. 1510–1515.

16.16 Nicholas von Hagenau, central corpus and base of the Isenheim Altarpiece, early 16th century. Polychrome wood sculpture. The corpus sculptures depict Saints Augustine at the left, Jerome at the right with his lion attribute, and Anthony, enthroned in the center. Represented on the base are Jesus and the twelve apostles. Two side panels by Grünewald depicting scenes from Saint Anthony's life are not illustrated.

16.17 Lucas Cranach the Elder, *Judgment of Paris,* 1530. Panel; 13½ × 8¾ in. (34.4 × 22.2 cm). Staatliche Kunsthalle, Karlsruhe, Germany. According to Greek myth, the Trojan prince Paris judged a beauty contest among the goddesses Athena, Hera, and Aphrodite. He awarded the prize of a golden apple to Aphrodite, who had promised him the most beautiful woman in the world (Helen of Troy).

John the Baptist, on our right, points to Jesus. The Latin inscription, written in blood red, which John seems to be speaking, reads: "He must increase and I must decrease." At John's feet, holding a small cross, is the sacrificial Lamb, whose blood drips into a chalice that prefigures the Eucharist. On Jesus's right, Mary Magdalen wrings her hands in anguish. The curve of her arms continues backward toward the swooning Virgin and John the Evangelist supporting her. The darkening sky recalls the biblical account of the sun's eclipse and nature's death at the time of the Crucifixion. On the base of the closed altarpiece, Grünewald has depicted the *Lamentation* against a snowy, alpine background with barren trees, both being natural metaphors of Jesus's death.

The wings of the closed altarpiece depict Saint Anthony, who was associated with healing the sick, on the right; and Saint Sebastian, known as a plague saint because his sores from being shot through with arrows were likened to those of the bubonic plague, on the left. The altarpiece was generally kept in the closed position. Patients prayed before it to atone for their sins and to effect a cure. On Sundays and feast days, however, the altarpiece was opened to reveal an interior transformed by bright colors (see fig. 16.15). In the right panel, Jesus, who has become Christ, attains a new, spiritual plane of existence beyond the pull of gravity. His body, defined by curvilinear forms, floats upward into a fiery orb. Christ as Sun is juxtaposed with the Roman soldiers, whose sinful ignorance causes them to stumble in a rock-filled darkness.

Lucas Cranach the Elder

The German artist Lucas Cranach the Elder (1472–1553) was an admirer of Martin Luther. In his early work, he primarily depicted landscapes, an interest that continued in some of his later mythological pictures. In the *Judgment of Paris* (fig. **16.17**), Cranach sets the Greek myth (see caption) in sixteenth-century Germany, with a Saxon castle on a distant hill. An aged, bearded Hermes presents the three goddesses to Paris. Both male figures wear the armor of Saxon knights. The women pose coquettishly, in a way that is reminiscent of the conventional arrangement of the three Classical Graces—the one in the center is seen from the back, and the others, one on each side, from the front. A comparison of the *Judgment of Paris* with the first-century-A.D. Roman fresco of the *Three Graces* (fig. **16.18**) illustrates the extent to which Cranach has altered the character of the women to suit his patrons at the court of Saxony. The horse to the left of the tree adds a touch of humor, for its gaze is riveted by the unexpected sight of

16.18 *Three Graces,* from Pompeii, 1st century A.D. Fresco. National Archaeological Museum, Naples.

16.19 Lucas Cranach the Elder, *Crucifixion*, 1503. Oil on panel; 54½ × 43 in. (138.4 × 109.2 cm). Alte Pinakothek, Munich.

16.20 Lucas Cranach the Elder, *Martin Luther*, 1533. Panel; 8 × 5¾ in. (20.5 × 14.5 cm). City of Bristol Museum and Art Gallery, England.

the nudes. The horse's raised leg reveals his erotic excitement and contrasts with the relaxed, indifferent pose of Paris, who casually converses with Hermes.

One of Cranach's most important Christian paintings is the large *Crucifixion* of 1503 (fig. **16.19**). As in the *Judgment of Paris,* landscape plays a role in the image and reflects the artist's humanist interest in nature. In both works, the emphasis on linear quality is characteristic of sixteenth-century German painting and shows the influence of Dürer.

Cranach creates the effect of towering figures by showing us the event as if we are looking up at it from below. At the left are the two thieves, one partly hidden from view and the other grotesque in appearance. A more idealized Jesus hangs from the Cross at the right. Mary and John are united in mourning, their agitated gestures repeating Jesus's windblown loincloth and the turbulent sky. Behind them, a dead tree rises, pushing through the green tree and denoting the death of God's son. The responsiveness of nature to human events is both part of Christian tradition—that the sky turned black when Jesus died—and a reflection of Cranach's humanism.

Cranach was best known for his portraits. His portrait of Martin Luther (fig. **16.20**), who was a close friend, is as austere as the *Judgment of Paris* is delicate and decorative. The figure is set against a solid green background, eliminating the sense of a natural context. Luther's dark robe is also unmodulated so that the only three-dimensional form is the head. In the emphasis on the stubble of Luther's beard, Cranach makes his subject seem above the concerns of daily grooming. He is rendered as a man of vision, staring out of the picture with an air of inner resolution.

Hans Holbein the Younger

The last great German painter of the High Renaissance was Hans Holbein the Younger (c. 1497–1543). He combined German linear technique with the fifteenth-century Northern taste for elaborately detailed surface textures and rich color patterns. Perhaps his greatest achievements were his portraits.

Holbein's family came from the southern German city of Augsburg, which, like Antwerp, was a center of

Erasmus of Rotterdam

Desiderius Erasmus of Rotterdam (c. 1466–1536) was a Roman Catholic reformer and one of the greatest Renaissance humanists in northern Europe. The illegitimate son of a priest, Erasmus was ordained in 1492 and then studied Classics in Paris. Among his most important works is *Encomium moriae* (The Praise of Folly) of 1514, in which he satirizes greed, superstition, and the corruption and ignorance of the clergy. He argues that piety depends on spiritual substance rather than on the observance of religious ceremony.

Erasmus's satirical inclinations were well suited to the northern interest in proverbs as a way of revealing human folly. His *Adagia* (Adages), published in 1500, is a compendium of sayings that contain hidden or double meanings. In 1513, he published a satire on Julius II in which the pope is excluded from heaven. Julius announces himself to Saint Peter as "P.M." (meaning *Pontifex Maximus*, or "Highest Priest"), but Saint Peter takes "P.M." to mean *Pestis Maxima*—"the Biggest Plague." Through the personage of Saint Peter, Erasmus objects to Julius II as an arrogant lush tainted by political and military ambition.

Erasmus's knowledge of Classical languages is evident in his publication of the first edition of the New Testament in Greek (1516); he also published a Latin translation of it. He believed that Latin would bridge the gap between divergent cultures and thus be a force for unification.

Erasmus was a moderate in an age of extremism. But his tolerance and reason limited his influence as compared with that of Martin Luther. He opposed the Reformation, fearing the destructive effects of partisan religious strife. Attacked by Catholics and Protestants alike, Erasmus remained committed to reconciliation and unity.

international trade. At the age of eighteen, Holbein traveled to Basel, where he met Erasmus (see box) and painted his portrait (fig. **16.21**). In contrast to the assertive and slightly unkempt character of Cranach's Luther, Holbein's Erasmus is a scholarly gentleman. He is well groomed, neat, and wears a fur-lined coat. Holbein's painting places the figure in a three-dimensional room. Erasmus rests his hands on a book with the Greek inscription "The Labors of Herakles." Erasmus is thus depicted as a man of his own era whose thought was formed by the Renaissance synthesis of Christianity with Classical antiquity. The pilaster with its Classical motifs shows the influence of artists such as Giovanni Bellini and Mantegna.

Holbein left Basel in 1526 and, on the recommendation of Erasmus, sought the patronage of the humanist Sir Thomas More in England. On a second trip in 1532, Holbein became the court painter to Henry VIII. Holbein's *Henry VIII* (fig. **16.22**) of about 1540 portrays the overpowering force of the king's personality. Henry's proverbial bulk dominates the picture as he stares directly out at the observer. In contrast to the *Erasmus,* Henry's forceful character is unrelieved by a three-dimensional background or by objects in the surrounding space. But the fine textures and minute patterns of his costume create a surface luster that is reminiscent of van Eyck; they also appear in areas of the *Erasmus.* Henry's bent right arm is posed so that the elbow is thrust forward,

16.21 Hans Holbein the Younger, *Erasmus of Rotterdam,* c. 1523. Panel; 30 × 20¼ in. (76.2 × 51.4 cm). National Gallery, London.

16.22 Hans Holbein the Younger, *Henry VIII,* c. 1540. Oil on panel; 34¾ × 29½ in. (88.3 × 74.9 cm). Galleria Nazionale d'Arte Antica, Rome.

emphasizing the elaborate sleeves. From the neck down, the king's body forms a rectangle filling the lower two-thirds of the picture. His head seems directly placed on his shoulders, creating a small, almost cubic shape. The hat, by contrast, forms a slightly curved diagonal, echoing the chain across his chest and also softening the monumental force of Henry's body and gesture.

The main source of variety in this picture is in the material quality of the surface patterns. Their richness is calculated to remind viewers of Henry's wealth, just as his pose exudes power, self-confidence, and determination, while his face reflects his intelligence and political acumen. In this image, therefore, Holbein has fused formal character with a specific personality, creating a Henry VIII who is "every inch a king."

After Holbein's death, no major artists emerged in Germany during the sixteenth century. By 1600, the conflicts between Protestant and Catholic, Reformation and Counter-Reformation, mysticism and humanism, though hardly at an end, had at least become familiar. Their effects on art would continue, though to a lesser degree, into the seventeenth century.

	Style/Period	Works of Art	Cultural/Historical Developments
1490	NORTHERN EUROPE 16th century 1490–1500 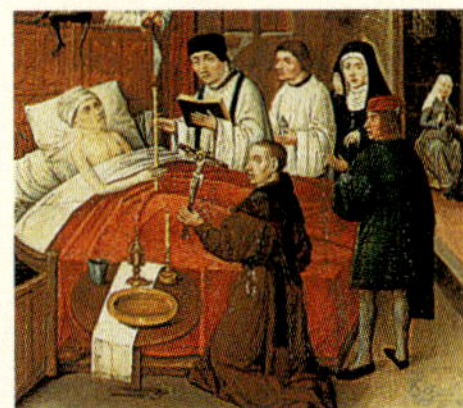 **Bosch, *Seven Deadly Sins and the Four Last Things***	Pompeii fresco (*Three Graces*) (**16.18**), 1st century A.D. Bosch (attrib.), *Seven Deadly Sins and the Four Last Things* (**16.1–16.2**) Dürer, *Four Horsemen of the Apocalypse* (**16.12**) Dürer, *Self-Portrait* (**16.10**), 1498 Dürer, *Self-Portrait* (**16.11**), 1500	Heinrich Kramer and James Sprenger, *The Witches' Hammer* (1487) Sebastian Brant, *Das Narrenschiff* (*The Ship of Fools*) (1494) **Dürer, *Self-Portrait,* 1498** **Dürer, *Self-Portrait,* 1500**
1520	1500–1530  **Bosch, *Garden of Earthly Delights***	Cranach the Elder, *Crucifixion* (**16.19**) Bosch, *Garden of Earthly Delights* (**16.3–16.5**) Grünewald, Isenheim Altarpiece (**16.14–16.15**) von Hagenau, corpus and base of the Isenheim Altarpiece (**16.16**) Dürer, *Melencolia I* (**16.13**) Holbein the Younger, *Erasmus of Rotterdam* (**16.21**)	Erasmus of Rotterdam, *The Praise of Folly* (1514) Martin Luther's *Ninety-five Theses;* beginning of the Reformation (1517) Martin Luther excommunicated (1521) Peasants' Revolt in Germany (1524–1525)
1570	1530–1570  **Holbein the Younger, *Henry VIII***  **Bruegel the Elder, *Netherlandish Proverbs***	Cranach the Elder, *Judgment of Paris* (**16.17**) Cranach the Elder, *Martin Luther* (**16.20**) Holbein the Younger, *Henry VIII* (**16.22**) Bruegel the Elder, *Landscape with the Fall of Icarus* (**16.6**)  **Bruegel, *Landscape with the Fall of Icarus*** Bruegel the Elder, *The Alchemist* (**16.7**) Bruegel the Elder, *Netherlandish Proverbs* (**16.8**) Bruegel the Elder, *Peasant Dance* (**16.9**)	Hans Holbein the Younger becomes court painter to Henry VIII (1532) Henry VIII rejects papal authority, founds Anglican Church (1534) John Calvin, *Institutes of the Christian Religion* (1536) Council of Trent introduces Counter-Reformation policies (1545–1563) Wars of Lutheran versus Catholic princes in Germany; Peace of Augsburg (1555) Elizabeth I queen of England (1558–1603) John Knox founds Presbyterian Church (1560) Protestant Netherlands rebel against Catholic Spain (1568) Karel van Mander, *Het Schilderboeck* (*The Painter's Book*) (1604)  **Cranach the Elder, *Judgment of Paris***

PART FIVE

CHAPTER PREVIEWS

THE BAROQUE STYLE IN WESTERN EUROPE, 17th CENTURY

Age of Absolutism: Louis XIV of France; Philip IV of Spain; Charles I of England
Heliocentrism and advances in science: Kepler; Copernicus; Galileo; Newton
Thirty Years' War (1618–1648)
Treaty of Westphalia (1648)
Dutch East India Company; the rise of capitalism
Charles I of England executed (1649)
Oliver Cromwell (1599–1658)
Witch craze in Europe and New England
Lives of the Artists: Bellori; van Mander, *The Painter's Book*
New Saint Peter's completed
Great Fire of London (1666)
Wren builds Saint Paul's, the first Protestant cathedral, in London
Urban VIII (papacy 1623–1644)
New genres in painting: landscape; *vanitas;* still life
Italian artists: Bernini; Borromini; Caravaggio; Gentileschi; the Carracci; Pietro da Cortona; Gaulli
Flanders: Rubens; van Dyck
Holland: Rembrandt; Hals; Leyster; Vermeer; Ruisdael; Oosterwyck; Etching and drypoint
France: The Louvre
    The Court of Versailles: LeBrun; Tuby; Le Vau; Perrault; Le Nôtre, Hardouin-Mansart
    French Academy founded (1648)
    Poussin: theory of artistic modes
Spain: Velázquez

Mughal Art and the Baroque

ROCOCO AND THE 18th CENTURY

Age of Enlightenment
Science: Priestley; Halley; Leibniz
Music: Vivaldi; Bach; Haydn; Mozart
Literary satire: Voltaire; Swift
Sturm und Drang in Germany: Goethe
The *encyclopédistes*: Diderot
Political philosophers: Locke; Rousseau
Seven Years' War (1756–1763)
American Revolution (1776)
    The U.S. Constitution and the Bill of Rights
French Revolution (1789)
Louis XVI and Marie Antoinette guillotined (1793)
Art patronage moves from Versailles to the Paris salon
Revival styles: Chinoiserie; discovery of Pompeii and Herculaneum
Winckelmann and the beginning of art history
Painters in France: Watteau; Boucher; Fragonard; Rigaud; Vigée-Lebrun; Chardin; Carriera
Painters in England: Wright of Derby; Gainsborough; Hogarth; Kauffmann
Painters in America: Copley; West
German architects: Neumann; Pöppelmann; Zimmermann
Tiepolo in the Kaisersaal
Architects in England: Lord Burlington; Adam; Walpole
Art Theory: Winckelmann; Kant; Hegel

The seventeenth century in western Europe is sometimes called the Age of Absolutism because rulers wanted complete control of their subjects. The most important of these monarchs—Louis XIV of France, Philip IV of Spain, and Charles I of England—used the arts in the service of their political agenda. With Europe now split into Catholic and Protestant countries, the prevailing Baroque style varied according to national tastes. In Protestant Holland, art tended to be more secular than in Catholic countries. New art genres—notably, landscape and still life—evolved in Holland and elsewhere. Trade with India produced cross-cultural motifs, especially under the Mughal dynasty, which, contrary to Islamic tradition, encouraged figurative painting.

The eighteenth century, called both the Age of Reason and the Enlightenment, boasted new discoveries in science, a wealth of musicians—including Bach, Haydn, and Mozart—and political philosophers who challenged the divine right of kings. With the death of Louis XIV, the center of French patronage moved from the court at Versailles to Paris, and the predominant art style became Rococo—a fussy, frivolous version of Baroque with occasional undercurrents of serious satire. The so-called Bourgeois Realism of Chardin emphasized the virtues of everyday hard work. At the end of the eighteenth century, two great revolutions—the American Revolution in 1776 and the French Revolution in 1789—shattered the age-old notion that kings rule by divine right.

17

The Baroque Style in Western Europe

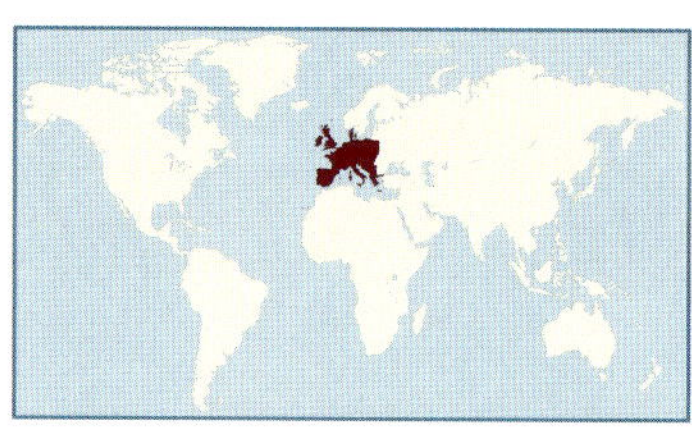

The Baroque style corresponds roughly to the closing years of the sixteenth century, overlapping Mannerism and lasting, in some areas, as late as 1750. Politically, the seventeenth century was a period of crisis and conflict. Religious tensions continued to escalate, while great strides were being made in science. These developments are reflected in the painting, sculpture, and architecture of the time.

Developments in Politics and Science

Although Europe (see map) had rarely been free of war in the sixteenth century, in 1618 the smoldering hostilities between Catholics and Protestants erupted into the Thirty Years War (1618–1648). This was one of the most devastating conflicts in European history. Beginning with a revolt of the Bohemians against Austrian rule, the war spread throughout the entire Continent, involving France, Spain, and many small principalities that were part of the Holy Roman Empire. Aided by the French, the northern Netherlands rebelled against the Catholic domination of Philip II and Philip IV of Spain (both Hapsburg monarchs) and ended forty years of Spanish rule.

When the Treaty of Westphalia was signed in 1648, the war was officially over, although none of the religious differences had been settled. Nevertheless, the principle of national sovereignty was established, and each country controlled its lands and population. A general redistribution of territory also took place, with France receiving most of Alsace, and Sweden annexing provinces on the Baltic Sea. The Netherlands split into Protestant Holland and Catholic Flanders (roughly equivalent to modern Belgium). The authority of the Holy Roman emperor over Germany was severely weakened, and Germany itself was ravaged by mercenaries.

Politically, the seventeenth century is known as the Age of Absolutism because of certain rulers who tried to exercise absolute power over their countries. According to the principle of divine right of kings, rulers derived their authority directly from God. The embodiment of absolute monarchy, Louis XIV of France (reigned 1643–1715), centralized all national authority into his own hands and ruled for fifty-four years.

In England, another absolute monarch, Charles I (reigned 1625–1649), succeeded his father, the first Stuart king, James I. Charles's persecutions of the Puritans (English Calvinists who favored substituting a presbyterian form of church government for the episcopal system) drove them to join with other antiroyalist factions; the English Civil War led to the execution of the king. For eleven years after the death of Charles I, England was a Free Commonwealth under Oliver Cromwell (1599–1658) as Lord Protector. In 1660, Charles's son, Charles II, was restored to the throne.

A reaction to absolutism emerged in the course of the seventeenth century in the first serious study since Plato of the rights of citizens. Political philosophers, notably Thomas Hobbes (1588–1679) and John Locke (1632–1704), argued that government is based on a social contract. Hobbes believed that ultimate power rested with the monarch, whereas Locke maintained that governments derive their authority from the consent of the governed, who may overthrow any ruler threatening their fundamental rights.

The geographic discoveries of the fifteenth century had been spearheaded by navigators from Spain and Portugal. In 1494, these two countries signed the Treaty of Tordesillas, in which they divided up the non-European world between them. Their confidence, however, was misplaced, and by the beginning of the seventeenth century the commercial map of Europe had been redrawn. Venice had declined to the status of a regional market, and the Dutch had overtaken the Hanseatic League (a confederation of north German cities) to become the leading trading nation

Europe during the Baroque period.

of the Western world. For most of the 1600s, Amsterdam was the financial and trade center of Europe, although Seville, in Spain, was also an important port. The English, who had begun to erode the Spanish Empire in the Americas, presented the only serious challenge to the Dutch, for England had the advantage of surplus citizens with which to populate overseas settlements. By the early 1700s, the Dutch had yielded naval superiority to the English, who, together with the French, emerged as the leading colonial and commercial power of Europe.

The period 1600 to 1750 was a time of enormous progress in scientific experimentation and observation. Although religious tensions ran high, with fundamentalism and superstition increasing and executions for heresy and witchcraft multiplying, scientists began to view the universe as a system with natural and predictable laws.

In 1543, Nicolaus Copernicus (1473–1543), a Polish physician and astronomer, had published *De revolutionibus orbium coelestium* (*On the Revolutions of the Heavenly Spheres*), in which he hypothesized that the sun, rather than the earth, was the center of the universe and that the planets revolved around it. This heliocentric theory was confirmed by Johan Kepler (1571–1630), a German mathematician who measured the movement of the five known planets and showed that they orbited the sun in elliptical paths. The Italian astronomer Galileo Galilei (1564–1642) proved that bodies of unequal weight fall with the same speed, impelled by gravity. Galileo also improved the recently invented telescope, which permitted him to see the satellites of the planets and led him to accept the system of Copernicus.

These discoveries flew in the face of Catholic doctrine, which held that the universe was an extension of God's will, that the earth was the center of the universe, and that mankind was central to that system. In 1616 Copernicus's writings were banned by the Church, and in 1633 Galileo was forced by the Inquisition to recant his views. These setbacks notwithstanding, scientific progress was an important feature of the Baroque period. The empirical method, with its emphasis on the direct experience, measurement, and analysis of natural phenomena, culminated in the work of the English natural philosopher Isaac Newton (1642–1727). Newton's laws of motion and theory of gravity (which held that every object in the universe exerts its own gravitational pull) formed the basis of physics until the end of the nineteenth century.

Baroque Style

The term *Baroque* is applied to diverse styles, a fact that highlights the approximate character of art-historical categories. Like Gothic, Baroque was originally a pejorative term. It is a French variant of the Portuguese *barroco,* meaning an irregular, imperfect pearl. The Italians used *barocco* to describe an academic and convoluted medieval style of logic. Although Classical themes and subject matter continued to appeal to artists and their patrons, Baroque painting and sculpture tended to be relatively unrestrained, overtly emotional, and more energetic than earlier styles.

Baroque artists rejected aspects of Mannerist virtuosity and stylization, while absorbing its taste for *chiaroscuro* and theatrical effects. They were more likely than Mannerists to pursue the study of nature directly. As a result, Baroque art achieves a new kind of naturalism that reflects some of the scientific advances of the period. There is also a new taste for dramatic action and violent narratives, and the representation of emotion is given a wide range of expression—a departure from the Renaissance adherence to Classical restraint. Baroque color and light are dramatically contrasted, and surfaces are richly textured. Baroque space is usually asymmetrical and lacks the appearance of controlled linear perspective; sharply diagonal planes generally replace the predominant verticals and horizontals of Renaissance compositions. Landscape, genre, and still life, which had originated as separate, but minor, categories of painting in the sixteenth century, gained new status in the seventeenth. Allegory also takes on a new significance in Baroque art and is no longer found primarily in a biblical context. Portraiture, too, develops in new directions as artists depict character and psychology along with the physical presence of their subjects.

The considerable variety within the Baroque style is partly a function of national and cultural distinctions. Baroque art began in Italy, particularly Rome, whose position as the center of western European art had been established during the High Renaissance by papal patronage and Rome's links with antiquity. At the end of the Baroque period, Paris would emerge as the artistic center of Europe, a position it retained until World War II. Two major Baroque architectural achievements—the completion of Saint Peter's in Rome and the sumptuous court of the French monarch Louis XIV at Versailles—reflect the enormous resources that were devoted to the arts in seventeenth-century Europe.

In Italy, Spain, and Catholic Flanders, the influence of the Counter-Reformation remained strong. In France, the Baroque style had its greatest expression at the court of Versailles. Court patronage also prevailed in Spain and England, whereas in capitalist Holland the art market was primarily, though not entirely, secular.

Architecture

Italy

The rebuilding of Saint Peter's Basilica, which began when Julius II became pope in 1503, was finally completed during the Baroque period. Its interior decoration and spatial design, however, still required attention. Pope Urban VIII (papacy 1623–1644) appointed Gianlorenzo Bernini (1598–1680) to the task, and he remained the official architect of Saint Peter's until his death. One of Bernini's objectives was to reduce the space at the crossing so that worshipers would be drawn to the altar. He achieved this by erecting the bronze **baldacchino** (canopy) (fig. **17.1**) over the high altar above Saint Peter's tomb.

The baldacchino's height is about one-third the distance from the floor of Saint Peter's to the base of its lantern. Although small in relation to the dome, it is the size of a modern nine-story building, and its foundations reach deep into the floor of the old Constantinian basilica.

Four twisted columns, decorated with acanthus scrolls and surmounted by angels, support a bronze valance resembling the tasseled cloth canopy used in religious processions. At the top, a gilded cross stands on an orb. The twisted-column motif did not originate with Bernini. In the fourth century, Constantine was thought to have used spiral columns originally from Solomon's Temple in Jerusalem at Old Saint Peter's. Eight of these columns were incorporated into the pier niches of New Saint Peter's. They are decorated with laurel branches and bees, both of which are devices of the Barberini family, of which Urban VIII was a member. Bernini's columns seem to pulsate as if in response to some internal pressure or tension. The dark bronze, accented with gilt, stands out against the lighter marble of the nave and apse. Such contrasts of light and dark, like the organic quality of the undulating columns, are characteristic of Baroque style.

Visible beyond the baldacchino is the *Cathedra Petri* (Throne of Saint Peter) in the western apse. It is actually a reliquary surrounded at its base by bronze figures of the four doctors of the Church—Saints Augustine and Ambrose (the doctors of the Western Church), and Saints Athanasius and John Chrysostom (the doctors of the Eastern Church). Representatives of Western and Eastern Christendom thus combine to support the Roman pope. Although they appear to be holding up the throne, it is actually cantilevered out from the wall. The illusory support is a metaphor for upholding the spiritual doctrine of faith in the early days of Christianity. Above the throne (actually an early medieval work) the Holy Spirit is framed by a stained-glass window. Because the building is oriented to the west, the window catches the afternoon sun, which reflects from the gilded rods, representing divine light.

In 1656, Bernini began work on the exterior of Saint Peter's. His goal was to provide an impressive approach to the church and, in so doing, to define the Piazza San Pietro.

17.1 Gianlorenzo Bernini, baldacchino, Saint Peter's, Rome, 1624–1633. Gilded bronze; approx. 95 ft. (28.96 m) high. The baldacchino's height is about one-third the distance from the floor of Saint Peter's to the base of its lantern. Although small in relation to the dome, it is the size of a modern nine-story building, and its foundations reach deep into the floor of the old Constantinian basilica.

17.2 Gianlorenzo Bernini, aerial view of the colonnade and piazza of Saint Peter's, Rome, begun 1656. Travertine; longitudinal axis approx. 800 ft. (243.84 m). Copper engraving by Giovanni Piranesi, 1750. Kunstbibliothek, Berlin. The enormous piazza in front of the east façade of Saint Peter's can accommodate over 250,000 people.

The piazza, or public square (fig. **17.2**), is the place where the faithful gather on Christian festivals to hear the pope's message and receive his blessing. Bernini conceived of the piazza as a large open space organized into elliptical and trapezoidal shapes (in contrast to the Renaissance circle and square). He used Classical Orders and combined them with statues of Christian saints.

He divided the piazza into two parts (fig. **17.3**). The first section has the approximate shape of an oval or ellipse, and at its center is an obelisk 83 feet (25.30 m) high, imported from Egypt during the Roman Empire.

A radial pattern converges at the obelisk. The shape and width of the oval—approximately 800 feet (243.84 m)—and the location of a fountain within each of its semicircular sections help to establish a stronger north–south axis. That axis is perpendicular to the direction in which most visitors move—namely, along the east–west axis of the nave and dome.

Around the curved sides of the oval, Bernini designed two colonnades, consisting of 284 travertine columns in the Tuscan Order, each one 39 feet (11.89 m) high. The columns are four deep, and the colonnades end in temple fronts on either side of a large opening. Crowds can thus convene and disperse easily; they are enclosed, but not confined. Bernini wrote that the curved colonnades were like the arms of Mother Church, spread out to embrace the faithful.

The second part of the piazza is a trapezoidal area connecting the oval with the church façade. The trapezoid lies on an upward gradient, and the visitor approaches the portals of Saint Peter's by a series of steps. As a result, the walls defining the north and south sides of the trapezoid become shorter toward the façade. This enhances the verticality of the façade and offsets the horizontal emphasis produced by the incomplete flanking towers. The two sections of the piazza are tied together by an Ionic entablature that extends all the way around the sides of both the oval and the trapezoid, and the entablature is crowned by a balustrade with marble statues of saints. The integration of the architecture with the participating crowds reflects

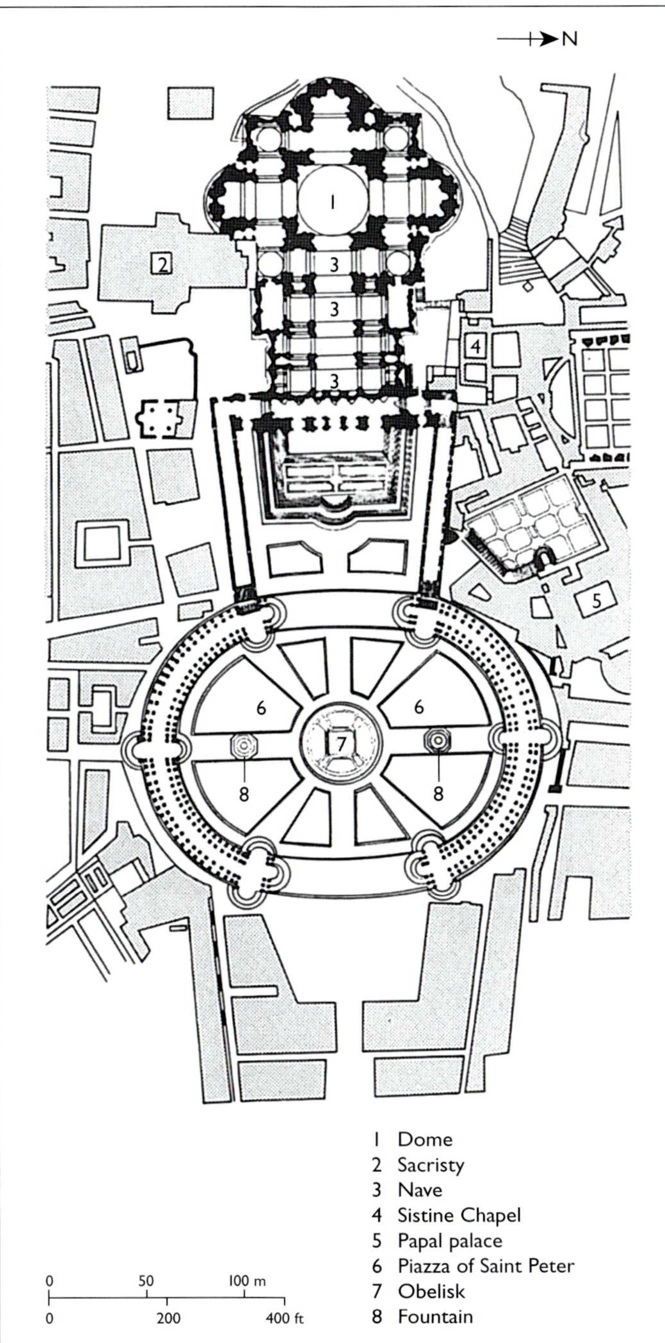

17.3 Plan of Saint Peter's and the piazza, Rome. In the center of the oval, a radial pattern converges at the obelisk. The shape and width of the oval—approx. 800 ft. (244 m)—and the location of a fountain within each of its semicircular sections help to establish a stronger north–south axis. That axis is perpendicular to the direction in which most visitors move: along the east–west axis of the nave and dome.

the theatrical Baroque taste for involving audiences in a created space, in particular a processional space leading to the high altar.

Bernini's greatest professional rival in Rome was Francesco Borromini (1599–1667). They collaborated on the baldacchino, but their interests diverged immediately afterward. Born in Lombardy, Borromini was the son of an architect. In 1621, he moved to Rome and worked under both Maderno and Bernini. Borromini and Bernini were intense rivals of very different temperaments, and Borromini resented living and working in Bernini's shadow. Moody and constantly dissatisfied, he eventually committed suicide. From about 1634 until his death, Borromini worked on the Trinitarian monastery of San Carlo alle Quattro Fontane (Saint Charles of the Four Fountains) in Rome (figs. **17.4, 17.5, 17.6,** and **17.7**), named after the fountains at the four corners of the street intersection. The small monastery church is Borromini's best-known building, and it established his reputation for daring architectural innovation.

The alternation of convexity and concavity in the façade of San Carlo is repeated with variations in the walls. The plan is shaped like a pinched and distended oval. Its main altar and entrance are opposite each other on the short sides of the oval. Side chapels, which seem to be parts of

17.4 Francesco Borromini, San Carlo alle Quattro Fontane, Rome, 1665–1667.

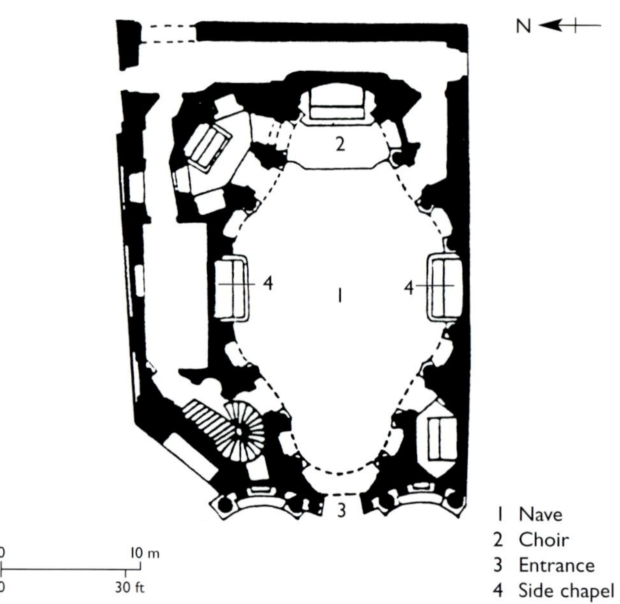

17.5 Francesco Borromini, plan of San Carlo alle Quattro Fontane, Rome, 1638–1641. The plan is shaped like a pinched and distended oval. Its main altar and entrance are opposite each other on the short sides of the oval, and the walls are a series of convexities and concavities. Side chapels, which seem to be parts of smaller ovals, bulge out from the walls.

17.6 Francesco Borromini, view toward the high altar, San Carlo alle Quattro Fontane, Rome, 1638–1641.

smaller ovals, bulge out from the walls. At ground level, there are three bays—alternately concave, convex, and concave. At the upper level, the bays are all concave, although a small **aedicule** (niche) and a balustrade fill the central bay, echoing the convex shape of the level below. Borromini's undulating walls, like the twisted columns of Bernini's baldacchino, are characteristic of the plasticity of Italian Baroque architecture.

Above the door of the church, a statue of Saint Charles stands in a niche, surmounted by a pointed gable. A large painted medallion of the saint, crowned with a gable that echoes the lower one, has been placed above the top level, in alignment with the statue. The corner of the building is beveled and contains one of the four fountains referred to in the name of the church. Above the entablature are pendentives supporting an oval ring at the base of the dome.

The interior view (fig. 17.6) toward the high altar shows the use of large, smooth-shafted Corinthian columns to create a plastic effect in the walls. This is enhanced by the undulating character of the walls as they approach the apse. Surmounting the relatively sharp curve of the apse's entablature is a pediment that seems to be stretching its lower corners outward.

In figure 17.7, we are looking up at the interior of the dome, which expresses the Baroque concern for lightening

17.7 Francesco Borromini, interior dome of San Carlo alle Quattro Fontane, Rome, 1665–1667.

17.8 Francesco Borromini, Collegiate Church of Sant'Ivo della Sapienza, Rome, 1642–1660. In 1632, Borromini was appointed the official architect of Rome University by Pope Urban VIII.

architectural volume. The dome is illuminated on the interior by windows at its base, and contains coffers in the shape of hexagons, octagons, and crosses. At the center of the dome, an oval *oculus* contains a triangle, a geometric symbol of the Trinity and emblem of the Trinitarian Order that commissioned the church. The appearance of increased height, and of actual upward motion, is enhanced by coffers that decrease in size as they approach the center of the dome.

From 1642 to 1660, Borromini worked on the church of Sant'Ivo della Sapienza, which is another product of his original architectural imagination. Its concave façade (fig. **17.8**) blends into the surrounding buildings of Rome University, known at the time as the Sapienza (Wisdom). The crowning features of this church are particularly innovative—for example, the stepped, pyramidal form supporting the lantern, which is surmounted by a spiral ramp leading to a stone laurel wreath. This is decorated with carved flames and supports an iron cage upholding an orb with a cross. The sources of these motifs and their unusual combinations are difficult to identify, but they appear to have been inspired by the ancient Near Eastern ziggurat.

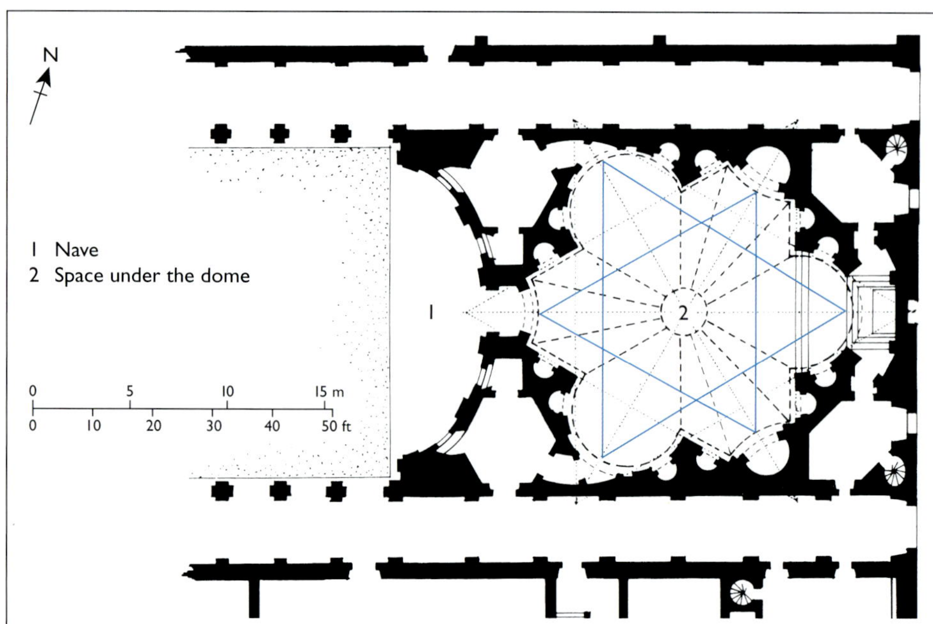

17.9 Francesco Borromini, plan of the Collegiate Church of Sant'Ivo della Sapienza, Rome.

17.10 Francesco Borromini, interior of dome, Collegiate Church of Sant'Ivo della Sapienza, Rome, 1642–1660.

The plan of Sant'Ivo (fig. **17.9**) is formed by two equilateral triangles superimposed to form the shape of a six-pointed star. The center is hexagonal, with a bay at each side. Three of the angles end in semicircular apses, and three in pointed apses. The walls of the latter are convex and seem to push in toward the center of the plan. As a result, there is an organic quality in Borromini's conception that is enhanced by continual tension in the relationship of the walls to the space.

A comparison of the interior view of Sant'Ivo's dome (fig. **17.10**) with that of San Carlo (fig. 17.7) shows the greater complexity of the former. Here the alternation of curves over the semicircular apses with the convex apse walls is clear. The effect is to increase the variation of shapes and spaces, which seem to radiate from the central circle. At San Carlo, on the other hand, the sides of the dome appear to have been pushed inward toward the center to create its oval form. The interior illumination of Sant'Ivo's dome enhances the impression of a large architectural star, which evokes the celestial associations of domed buildings in a new and original way. Being in the form of a Star of David, the dome refers to the typological tradition relating Old Testament kings with Christ, and specifically to Christ's descent from the House of David.

France

French seventeenth-century architecture is elegant, ordered, rational, and restrained, recalling the Classical aesthetic. France rejected the exuberance of Italian Baroque, preferring a strictly **rectilinear** approach to Borromini's curving walls or the open, activated spaces of Bernini. Geometric regularity was also more in keeping with the French political system—absolute monarchy personified by Louis XIV.

Louis ascended the throne in 1643 at the age of five and ruled from 1661, when he came of age, until his death in 1715. His shrewd policies and talented ministers made France the most powerful, and most populous, nation in Europe. His chief minister, Jean-Baptiste Colbert, organized the arts in the service of the monarchy. Their purpose was to glorify Louis's achievements and enhance his power and splendor in the eyes of the world. To this end, the building industry and the crafts guilds were subjected to a central authority. An Academy was established to create a national style that would reflect the glory of France and its king (see box, p. 636).

The first task of Louis and Colbert was to complete the rebuilding of the Louvre (fig. **17.11**) in Paris. Now the city's principal art museum, the Louvre was then a royal palace. Bernini submitted a series of proposals and was summoned to work on the Louvre project. His final proposal was rejected, however, on the grounds that it did not match the existing structure or conform to French taste. The eventual design for the east façade was the work of three men: the painter Charles Le Brun (director of the French Academy), the architect Louis Le Vau, and Claude Perrault, a physician. The restrained, classicizing symmetry of the façade, in contrast to Bernini's plan for a curved wall, occupies a long horizontal plane; it set the style for seventeenth-century French architecture. Paired, two-story columns separate the windows and are linked by a continuous entablature. The flat roof is hidden by a surrounding balustrade, which accents the horizontality of the building. The central pavilion, resembling a Roman temple front, is crowned by a pediment, which is echoed by the small individual pediments above the windows. The main floor rests on a ground floor presented as a **podium.** Its masonry blocks have roughened surfaces and sunken joints.

In 1667, Louis XIV decided to move his court to Versailles, a small town about 15 miles (24 km) southwest of Paris. This involved moving not only the vast royal household, but also the whole apparatus of government. Versailles was the site of a hunting lodge built in 1624 by Louis's father, Louis XIII, and enlarged from 1631 to 1636. His son had visited this modest twenty-room **château** as a child. The lodge was at the center of a radiating landscape design and formed the nucleus of the new palace, which

17.11 Claude Perrault, Louis Le Vau, and Charles Le Brun, east façade of the Louvre, Paris, 1667–1670.

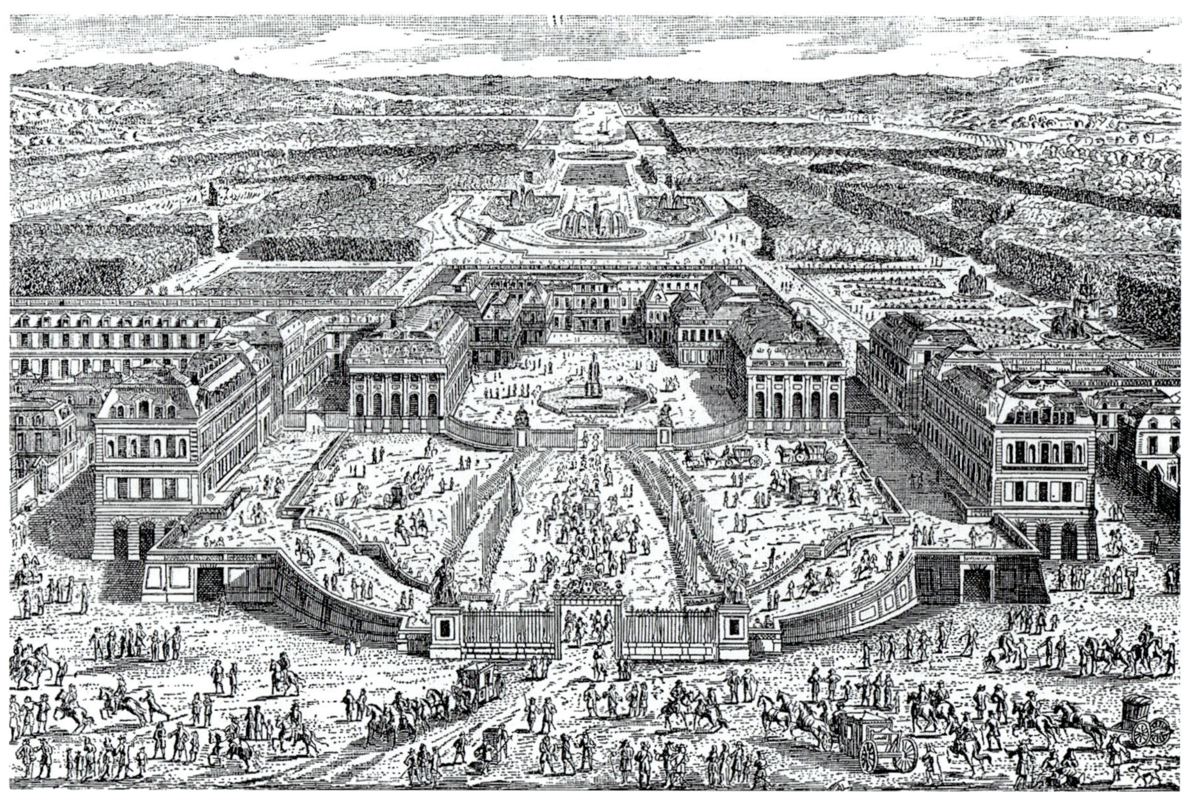

17.12 Aerial view of the park and palace of Versailles, after a 17th-century engraving by G. Pérelle. Versailles was the epitome of the French château (meaning "castle," "mansion," or "country house"), which had been established in the 16th century as the centerpiece of lavish country estates. A small town grew up at the eastern end of the palace, planned in grid formation around three broad boulevards. These radiated out from the palace and funneled visitors into the courtyard, or Court of Honor.

was built under Louis XIV (fig. **17.12**). From 1661 to 1708 the building underwent a series of enlargements, the earlier ones under the direction of Le Brun and Le Vau. The landscape architect André Le Nôtre (1613–1700) designed the elaborate gardens with pools and fountains—typical Baroque features. By 1678, the new palace was large enough for the court to move to Versailles, which then became the seat of government, including the treasury and the diplomatic corps. The palace contained hundreds of rooms and accommodated over 20,000 people. Four thousand servants lived inside the palace and 9,000 soldiers were billeted nearby.

The French Academy (Académie Royale de Peinture et de Sculpture)

Louis XIV extended his notion of the monarch's absolute power to the arts. In 1648, his minister, Jean-Baptiste Colbert, founded the Royal Academy of Painting and Sculpture with a view to manipulating imagery for political advantage. The philosophy and organization of the Academy were as hierarchical as Louis's state. Artists were trained according to the principle that tradition and convention had to be studied and understood. Art students drew from plaster casts and copied the old masters. They were steeped in the history of art and of French culture.

Another issue of philosophical importance to the Academy was the role of nature in the concept of the "ideal." Artists, if properly trained, should be able to produce the ideal in their work. The representation of emotion through physiognomy, expression, and gesture was also discussed at length by Charles Le Brun, who headed the Academy for twenty years. All such considerations were subject to a system of rules, which was derived partly from Platonic and Renaissance theory and partly from the French interest in the creation of an aesthetic order.

The subject matter of art was also organized according to a hierarchy. At the top were the Christian Sacraments, followed by history painting. In these two categories, the philosophy of the Academy supported the religious and political hierarchy imposed by Louis XIV. Next in line were portraiture, genre (scenes of daily life), landscape (with or without animals), and, lowest on the scale, still life.

With all the Academy's emphasis on systems and rules, a number of artistic "quarrels" were prevalent in the seventeenth century. The High Renaissance arguments over the merits of line and color (*disegno* and *colorito*) continued in the Baroque period, now exemplified by Poussin and Rubens. The *Rubénistes* championed color, whereas the *Poussinistes* preferred line. A parallel quarrel between the "Ancients" and "Moderns" arose: this concerned the question of which was the best authority for artists to follow. The Ancients were more traditional and tended to be allied with the proponents of *disegno* and Poussin. Line was considered rational, controlled, and Apollonian. Color, which was allied with Rubens and the Moderns, was emotional, exuberant, and related to Dionysiac expression.

17.13 Charles Le Brun and Jean-Baptiste Tuby, Fountain of Apollo, Versailles, 1668–1670. Gilded metal.

Unprecedented in scale and grandeur, the palace at Versailles was intended to glorify the power of the French monarch—and so was its iconography. The latter was supervised by Le Brun, who portrayed Louis as *Le Roi Soleil* (the Sun King), an appellation designed to bolster his divine right to rule. The unrivaled splendor and life-giving force of the king was proclaimed throughout the lavish interior of the palace.

Located in the pool at one end of the east–west axis of the vast park was an elaborate gilded fountain representing Apollo with his chariot drawn by four horses (fig. **17.13**). Jets of water spraying up from the statues enliven the ensemble and create the impression that the horses are leaping from the pool at dawn to begin their daily course across the sky. On either side of the chariot, four Tritons (sea gods) blow their conches to announce the new day. The four dolphins swimming away from the fountain appear to have been startled by Apollo's sudden emergence from the pool. This is only one of several fountains identifying Louis XIV with the sun god through the use of solar iconography.

A second stage in the construction of Versailles lasted from 1678 to 1688 and included the great Galerie des Glaces (Hall of Mirrors) (fig. **17.14**), which

17.14 Jules Hardouin-Mansart and Charles Le Brun, Galerie des Glaces (Hall of Mirrors), palace of Versailles, c. 1680.

17.15 Gianlorenzo Bernini, *Louis XIV*, 1665. Marble; life-sized. Versailles.

CONNECTIONS

See figure 5.68a. Head of Alexander, from Pergamon, c. 200 B.C.

was added by Jules Hardouin-Mansart. The Galerie has seventeen large arched mirrors, which form a literal wall of glass. They multiplied the sunlight entering the windows opposite and reflected the glittering splendor of Louis and his court. At each end of the Hall of Mirrors are the Salons of War and Peace, decorated with the relevant symbols. Foreign ambassadors were received in the appropriate salon to learn Louis's political intentions.

The reflected sunlight in the Hall of Mirrors was only one of the many solar allusions at Versailles. The Salon d'Apollon, named after Apollo, the sun god, was the throne room. The gardens are laid out along axes that radiate like the sun's rays from a central hub. They are adorned with sculptures, such as those illustrated in figure 17.13, illustrating Apollonian myths.

Above the main entrance, at the center of the palace, was the king's bedroom. Here, Louis enacted his daily ceremonies of *lever* (rising) and *coucher* (going to bed), which, like the garden fountains, identified him directly with the rising and setting sun. Bernini's life-sized marble bust of Louis XIV (fig. **17.15**), which is still in the king's bedroom, contains more subtle allusions to Louis's role as the Sun King. The smooth surface of the face, in contrast to the luxurious curls framing it, suggests the sun radiating as a central force through the clouds. With the sharp turn of Louis's head, as if something has suddenly caught his attention, and his wide-eyed, energetic gaze, the bust is also reminiscent of the Hellenistic type of Alexander the Great (see fig. 5.68) and other royal figures. Bernini creates the impression that Louis is both of this world—as a king and warrior, a worthy successor to Alexander the Great—and destined for apotheosis.

England

Baroque was also the architectural style of seventeenth-century England. Its greatest exponent was Sir Christopher Wren (1632–1723). Following the Great Fire (1666), which destroyed over two-thirds of the old walled city of London, Wren was appointed the King's Surveyor of Works. From 1670 to 1700, he took part in redesigning fifty-one of the churches that had burned down. Wren's priority during this period, however, was Saint Paul's, the first cathedral to be built for the Protestant Church of England.

The longitudinal plan and section (fig. **17.16**) blended elements from several styles. The formal arrangement (although not the style) of the nave, side aisles, and clerestory is based on the Early Christian basilica. The western façade (fig. **17.17**), with its paired columns and central pediment, is reminiscent of the Louvre. Two flanking towers, although similar in conception to Gothic cathedral towers, are more Baroque in their execution. They include round arches and triangular pediments on the two lower stories, while curved walls appear at the bases of the spires. On the two stories of the façade between the towers, like the façade of the Louvre, paired Corinthian columns support an entablature. Both are also crowned by a triangular pediment. The dome, which rises over the crossing and spans both the nave and the aisles, was originally a Renaissance feature.

It took forty years to complete Saint Paul's under Wren's supervision. The result is a successful synthesis of French and Italian Baroque, with elements of Renaissance and Gothic style.

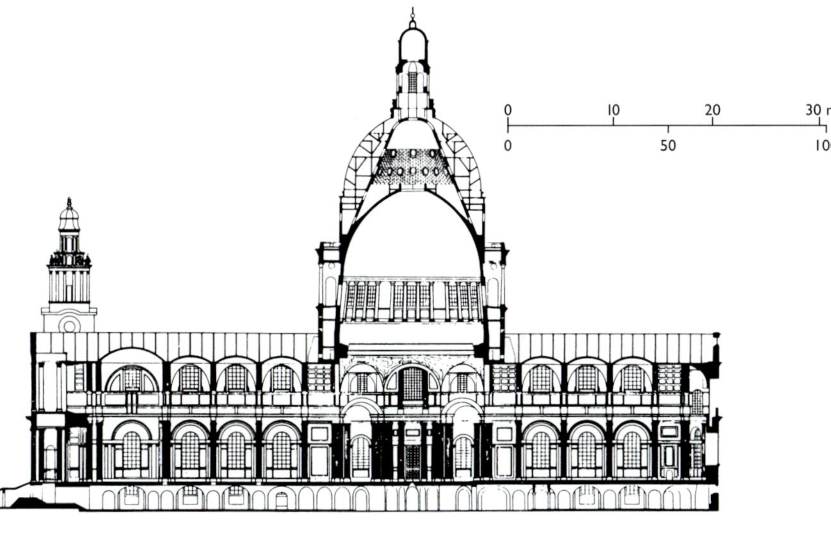

17.16 Longitudinal **section** and plan of Saint Paul's Cathedral, London. An invisible conical brick structure supports the lantern and the lead-faced, wooden framework of the outer dome. Extra support is supplied by flying buttresses, which are masked by the upper parts of the side aisle walls.

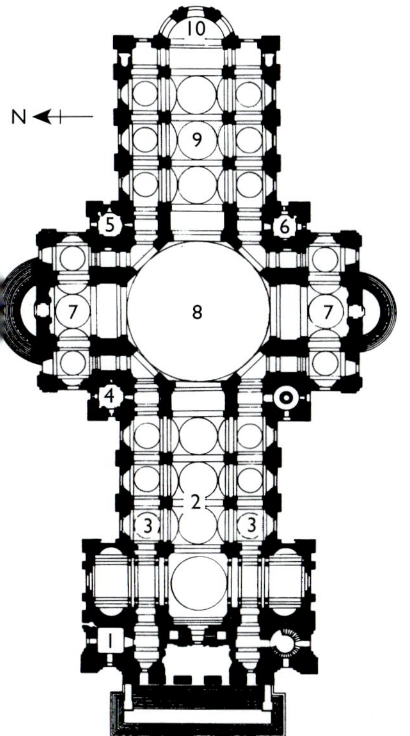

1 Bell tower
2 Nave
3 Aisle
4 Lord Mayor's vestry
5 Minor canons' vestry
6 Dean's vestry
7 Transept
8 Crossing under the dome
9 Choir
10 Jesus Chapel

17.17 Christopher Wren, western façade of Saint Paul's Cathedral, London, 1675–1710. The dome of Saint Paul's is 112 ft. (34.14 m) in diameter and 300 ft. (91.44 m) high, second in size only to Saint Peter's in Rome. Today, the dome continues to dominate the London skyline, but the lower façade is visible only from nearby.

Sculpture: Gianlorenzo Bernini

The most important Baroque sculptor in Rome was Gianlorenzo Bernini. His over-life-sized sculpture *Pluto and Proserpina* (fig. **17.18**) represents the most violent moment in the Greek myth designed to explain the change in seasons—namely, the abduction of Proserpina, daughter of Ceres, the goddess of agriculture. A muscular Pluto, the Roman god of the underworld who wants Proserpina for his wife, grabs hold of her, his fingers convincingly digging into her flesh. She, in turn, pushes Pluto's head away from her as she assumes a version of the Mannerist *figura serpentinata* and squirms to escape his grasp. Here, however, the pose is in the service of a violent narrative moment rather than being a virtuoso Mannerist exercise. Both figures are in strong *contrapposto,* leaning sharply backward at the waist. The flowing hair and beard echo the rippling motion of the body surfaces and reinforce the sense of action. Seated next to Pluto is Cerberus, the three-headed dog who guards the underworld. One head eyes the abduction intently, while another howls behind Proserpina's foot.

Bernini creates erotic tension between Pluto and Proserpina by a combination of pose and gesture characteristic of Baroque style. Although Proserpina struggles against Pluto, she also turns toward him. In pushing away Pluto's head, her fingers curl around a peak of his crown, as he in turn leers amorously at her. The exuberant back-and-forth

17.18a Gianlorenzo Bernini, *Pluto and Proserpina (Rape of Persephone)* (after restoration), front view, 1622. Marble. Galleria Borghese, Rome.

17.18b Gianlorenzo Bernini, *Pluto and Proserpina (Rape of Persephone)*, side view.

motion of the figures echoes the movement of Cerberus's two visible heads. The rhythm of the struggle can be related to the myth itself, for Proserpina is committed to Pluto for one-half of the year (corresponding to fall and winter) and returns to her mother for the other half (spring and summer).

In the Roman myth borrowed from Greece, Pluto's abduction of Proserpina (Persephone in Greek) explained the seasonal changes. When Proserpina's mother, Ceres, went in search of her daughter, vegetation ceased to grow and winter fell. Ceres found Proserpina in Pluto's underworld. Because her daughter had eaten six seeds from Pluto's pomegranate, she was doomed to spend half the year in his domain. During the six months of fall and winter, Ceres mourns and nature dies. Spring and summer return when Proserpina rejoins her mother.

In the life-sized marble sculpture of *David* of 1623 (**fig. 17.19**), all trace of Mannerism has disappeared. Once again Bernini has chosen to represent a narrative moment requiring action. David leans to his right and stretches the sling, while turning his head to look over his shoulder at Goliath. In contrast to Donatello's relaxed and self-satisfied bronze *David* (see fig. 13.29), who has already killed Goliath, and Michelangelo's (see fig. 14.19), who tensely sights his adversary, Bernini's is in the throes of the action.

The vertical plane of the Renaissance *Davids* has become, in the Baroque style, a dynamic diagonal extending from the head to the left foot. That diagonal is countered by the left arm, the twist of the head, and the drapery. In contrast to the *Pluto and Proserpina,* Bernini's *David* is a single figure. Nevertheless, his portrayal assumes the presence of Goliath, thereby expanding the space—psychologically as well as formally—beyond the immediate boundaries of the sculpture. Such spatial extensions are a characteristic, dramatic Baroque technique for involving the spectator in the work.

17.19a Gianlorenzo Bernini, *David,* 1623. Marble; life-sized. Galleria Borghese, Rome. According to Bernini's biographers, Cardinal Maffeo Barberini (elected pope in 1623) held up a mirror so that Bernini could carve the *David*'s face as a self-portrait. Whether true or not, the story is consistent with Bernini's habit of studying his mirror reflection for the purpose of self-portraiture.

17.19b Gianlorenzo Bernini, *David,* side view (after cleaning).

CONNECTIONS

See figure 13.29. Donatello, *David,* c. 1430–1440.

See figure 14.19. Michelangelo, *David,* 1501–1504.

17.20 Gianlorenzo Bernini, Cornaro Chapel, Santa Maria della Vittoria, Rome, 1640s. The Cornaro Chapel illustrates Bernini's skill in integrating the arts in a single project. Here he uses the chapel as if it were a little theater. Directly opposite the worshiper, the altar wall opens onto the dramatic encounter of Saint Teresa and the angel. Joining the worshiper in witnessing the miracle are members of the Cornaro family, who are sculptured in illusionistic balconies on the side walls.

Even more theatrical in character is Bernini's "environmental" approach to the chapel of the Cornaro family (fig. **17.20**) in the church of Santa Maria della Vittoria. This was the funerary chapel of Cardinal Federico Cornaro, who came to Rome from Venice in 1644. The event taking place behind the altar is the *Ecstasy of Saint Teresa* (fig. **17.21**), representing the visionary world of the mystic saint. Life-sized figures occupy a Baroque niche with paired Corinthian columns and a broken pediment over a curved entablature. As in the *David* and *Pluto and Proserpina,* Bernini represents a moment of heightened emotion—in this case the transport of ecstasy. The angel has just pierced Saint Teresa's breast with a spear as he gently pulls aside her drapery. Although Teresa appears elevated from the ground, she is actually supported by a formation of billowing clouds. Leaning back in a long, slowly curving diagonal plane, she closes her eyes and opens her mouth slightly, as if in a trance. Her inner excitement contrasts with the relaxed state of her body and is displaced onto the elaborate, energetic drapery folds, which blend with the clouds. Behind Saint Teresa and the angel are gilded rods, representing rays of divine light. They seem to descend from the infinite realm of heaven and enter the niche behind the altar.

This scene synthesizes the Baroque taste for inner emotion with Counter-Reformation mysticism. Only a sculptor as great as Bernini could combine the powerful religious content of this scene with its erotic implications in a way that would satisfy the Church. Also characteristic of the Baroque style is Bernini's ability to draw the observer into the event, which is reinforced by the theatrical arrange-

17.21 Gianlorenzo Bernini, *Ecstasy of Saint Teresa,* Cornaro Chapel, Santa Maria della Vittoria, Rome, 1645–1652. Marble; 11 ft. 6 in. (3.51 m) high. Saint Teresa was born in Ávila, Spain, in 1515. She was a Carmelite nun who, in her *Life,* described the mystical experience depicted here: "He was not tall, but short, and very beautiful, his face so aflame that he appeared to be one of the highest types of angel who seem to be all afire . . . they do not tell me their names. . . . In his hands I saw a long golden spear and at the end of the iron tip I seemed to see a point of fire. With this he seemed to pierce my heart several times. . . . When he drew it out . . . he left me completely afire with a great love for God . . . so excessive was the sweetness caused me by this intense pain that one can never wish to lose it."[1] Teresa was canonized in 1622.

ment of the chapel itself. Sculptures of the Cornaro family on the side walls occupy an illusionistic architectural space in low relief. Broken pediments and convincing barrel vaults are supported by Ionic columns. Some of the onlookers witness and discuss Saint Teresa's mystical experience like theatergoers watching a play. All except the cardinal were, in fact, deceased at the time of the commission. They represent the earthly, material world of the donor and his family, while two skeletons inlaid on the marble floor (not visible in the illustration) occupy purgatory—one prays for redemption, and the other raises his hands in despair.

Italian Baroque Painting

The two leading painters in Rome at the start of the seventeenth century were Annibale Carracci (1560–1609) and Michelangelo Merisi da Caravaggio (1571–1610). Both had the Church and the nobility as patrons. Carracci turned the late sixteenth-century Mannerist trends back to classicism, while infusing his images with exuberant Baroque drama. Caravaggio pursued a new kind of realism.

Ceiling frescoes in churches and palaces became particularly elaborate in this period, using illusionism to glorify the message of the Catholic Church. Two of the most impressive creators of these were Pietro da Cortona (1596–1669), who painted the ceiling of the Barberini Palace, and Giovanni Battista Gaulli, called Baciccio (1639–1709), who decorated the ceiling of Il Gesù (see figs. 15.23–15.25), both in the grand Baroque manner.

Annibale Carracci

Annibale was the most important member of the Carracci family of artists from the northern Italian city of Bologna (see box, p. 645). In 1597, Cardinal Odoardo Farnese commissioned him to decorate the Grand Gallery of his Roman palace in celebration of the marriage of a Farnese duke. The subject of the frescoes, the loves of the gods (fig. **17.22**), was in keeping with the wedding of an aristocratic Roman family. It also reflects Annibale's attraction to Classical iconography, which he infused with the formal elements of Baroque.

The ceiling is a curved vault, on which Annibale painted monumental imitation caryatid reliefs with picture frames dividing the narrative scenes. The colors are lively and reflect the amorous exuberance of the content. Although the subject matter is mythological, certain motifs such as the male figures seated in strong *contrapposto* are inspired by those in the Sistine ceiling. Implicit in the

17.22 Annibale Carracci, ceiling frescoes in the Grand Gallery, Farnese Palace, Rome, 1597–1601. Altogether there are eleven scenes. Clearly visible in this view is *Polyphemos* in the far lunette and the large ceiling panel of the *Triumph of Bacchus*. The ceiling panel next to this shows an airborne Mercury approaching Paris.

theme of the gods' loves is also a Christian subtext in which divine love is moralized as a unifying force that leads to salvation. Another theme can be seen in the fresco to the left of the one-eyed Cyclops Polyphemos, which represents Venus and her mortal lover Anchises (fig. **17.23**). As the parents of Aeneas, Venus and Anchises refer to the founding of Rome and, by implication, to the antiquity of the Farnese family. They thus link the Farnese Palace and its ecclesiastical patron with the mythological past.

17.23 Annibale Carracci, *Venus and Anchises* (detail of fig. 17.22).

Pietro da Cortona

Pietro da Cortona's *Glorification of the Reign of Urban VIII* of 1633–1639 on the ceiling of the great hall of the Palazzo Barberini also links moralized allegories using mythological figures with the exaltation of the Catholic Church (fig. **17.24**). Vigorous spatial shifts, illusionistic architecture, and variations of pose, color, and light animate and dissolve the surface of the walls and ceiling. The central field of the painted ceiling, in keeping with the traditional association of church ceilings and the heavens, is depicted as the sky. It is defined by an illusionistic, rectangular frame, with corner octagons containing fictive bronze reliefs and simulated sculptures below each corner. The curvilinear billows of the clouds are formal echoes of the twisted, dynamic poses of the figures.

The iconography incorporates the family and achievements of Maffeo Barberini (1568–1644), who was elected Pope Urban VIII. He was a zealous church reformer (Galileo's second condemnation occurred during his papacy), a classicist who published poems in Latin, and Bernini's most powerful patron. At the lower section of the center rectangle (from the point of view illustrated here), the figure in orange draperies holding a scepter personifies Divine Providence. This is reflected in the fact that the whitest light surrounds her head. Her upraised right hand directs the viewer to the figure of Immortality carrying a crown of stars upward toward the Barberini arms.

Above Immortality are three huge bees encircled by a laurel wreath, which is held aloft by Faith, Hope, and Charity. The three bees are Barberini devices that Bernini would later depict in relief on Urban VIII's tomb. There they refer to the sweet odor of sanctity believed to have emanated from his body after death. Their juxtaposition with laurel on the Barberini ceiling links the pope with the grandeur of ancient Rome, while the little *putto* underneath the laurel refers to Urban as a poet. Surmounting the laurel are personifications of Religion with the keys to the Church and the papal tiara.

At the sides of the heavenly realm, but depicted as below it, are mythological subjects connected in some way with the overall themes of the fresco. The side figures are consistently shown in relative darkness, emphasizing their role as precursors, or forerunners, of the Christian faith. Athena, for example, battles the pre-Greek Giants, a scene that was read in the seventeenth century as an allusion to Urban VIII's efforts to eradicate heresy. Below Divine Providence are the three Fates and Saturn (the Roman counterpart of Kronos) devouring his children. This juxtaposition of mythological figures associated with time—the Fates who control the life span of mortals—alludes, by contrast, to the Christian concept of future eternity at the end of time.

Bellori on the Lives of Artists

Giovanni Pietro Bellori's (1613–1696) *Lives* of Annibale and Agostino Carracci are from his *Lives of Modern Painters, Sculptors, and Architects.* This work continues Giorgio Vasari's biographical approach to art and artists. Bellori was appointed Antiquarian of Rome by Pope Clement X and also worked as librarian (in Rome) and art adviser to Queen Christina of Sweden. He wrote the *Lives* from the point of view of a francophile and a classicist. As a result, he approved the classicism of Raphael and Annibale Carracci, as well as of his friend Poussin. Of Caravaggio, however, Bellori was critical. He objected to what he saw as Caravaggio's lack of Classical idealization and to his taste for sometimes unrestrained and unattractive realism.

Bellori was in close contact with Le Brun and the Royal Academy of Painting and Sculpture in Paris, which became affiliated with the French Academy in Rome in 1676. He dedicated the *Lives* to Louis XIV's minister, Colbert, and was made an honorary member of the Royal Academy. His art theory was consistent with the Academy's view that artists should select from nature in order to create the "ideal," which in turn reflected the divine. In this, Bellori drew on Raphael's Platonic description of how to paint a beautiful woman (see p. 564). He praised Carracci for his historical and mythological paintings; just as Giotto had steered the art of painting out of the Byzantine past, according to Bellori, so Annibale Carracci rescued it from the decline of Mannerism. Of Carracci's Farnese frescoes, Bellori wrote: "Altogether the sight leaves a rich measure of its infinite beauty."[2]

17.24 Pietro da Cortona, *Glorification of the Reign of Urban VIII,* 1633–1639. Ceiling fresco. Palazzo Barberini, Rome.

Giovanni Battista Gaulli

One of the most spectacular of the seventeenth-century ceiling paintings in Rome is Giovanni Battista Gaulli's fresco of the *Triumph of the Name of Jesus* in the barrel vault of Il Gesù (fig. **17.25**). The artist had worked with the devoutly Catholic Bernini in Rome and eventually surpassed him in illusionistic effects. Despite Vignola's plan for a simple interior of the Gesù (see fig. 15.23), a new general of the Jesuit order, Padre Giovanni Paolo Oliva, elected in 1664, had a more elaborate program in mind.

In a large oval space framed by architectural features and writhing figures, Gaulli painted the IHS, the first three letters of "Jesus" in Greek, as a dramatic source of formal and spiritual light. The scene resembles a Last Judgment, with the saved rising toward the light of Jesus's name, and the damned, depicted in shadow, plummeting toward the nave below. Worshipers thus appear to be on the same material plane as the sinners, whereas the vault of heaven and of the mother church of the Jesuit Order merge in a blaze of light.

17.25 Giovanni Battista Gaulli, *Triumph of the Name of Jesus*, 1676–1679. Ceiling fresco with stucco figures on the vault of the Church of Il Gesù, Rome.

Michelangelo Merisi da Caravaggio

Michelangelo Merisi was born in the small northern Italian town of Caravaggio, the name by which he is known. When he was thirteen, his father apprenticed him to a painter in Milan. In 1592, Caravaggio moved to Rome, where his propensity for violence repeatedly landed him in trouble. During his relatively short life, and despite the interruptions to his career caused by brushes with the law, Caravaggio worked in an innovative style and used new techniques that influenced painters in Italy, Spain, and northern Europe. In contrast to Annibale Carracci, Caravaggio painted in oil directly on the canvas and made no preliminary drawings. Although Carracci worked in the faster medium of fresco, he did many drawing studies and thus appeared to his contemporaries to be a more deliberate, restrained artist than the flamboyant Caravaggio.

In 1604, Karel van Mander (1548–1606) published *The Painter's Book,* a biography of artists inspired by Vasari (see Chapter 14). He was the first art theoretician in the Netherlands, and he wrote perceptively about Caravaggio. Van Mander admired the artist for his talent and for the fact that he had risen to fame from humble beginnings. His view that Caravaggio studied nature closely and painted realistically reflected the artist's general reputation. Van Mander also shared the theoretical bias—influenced by Neoplatonism—of Giovanni Bellori and the French Academy when he wrote that "one should distinguish the most beautiful of life's beauties and select it." But van Mander also understood the effect of Caravaggio's self-destructive lifestyle on his art:

> He does not study his art constantly, so that after two weeks of work he will sally forth for two months together with his rapier at his side and his servant-boy after him, going from one tennis court to another, always ready to argue or fight, so that he is impossible to get along with. This is totally foreign to art; for Mars and Minerva have never been good friends.[3]

Van Mander's comments are consistent with Caravaggio's artistic style and iconography as well as with his lifestyle. His attention to realism can be seen in his early painting *Boy with a Basket of Fruit* (fig. **17.26**). The convincing rendition of the fruit confirms Caravaggio's close study of nature. Details such as the points of light on the grapes and the veins in the leaves contribute to the realistic effect. The boy stands out against a plain background, which is divided by irregular Baroque illumination. He may be a fruit vendor, but he offers himself as well as the fruit to the observer.

In contrast to the Renaissance view of painting as the natural world made visible through the window of the picture plane, Baroque artists draw the observer into the picture by means other than Brunelleschian linear perspective. In this painting, Caravaggio attracts us through the diagonal planes of the boy's right arm and the tilt of his head. His seductive nature is reinforced by the theatrical quality of his illumination. The fruit, which traditionally has erotic connotations, creates another transition between the observer and the boy. For example, the bright red and yellow peach at the front of the basket is a visual echo of the bare shoulder. Both have a slight cleft, repeated in the boy's chin, as if to suggest that the boy is as edible as the fruit. The wilting leaf at the right, which droops from the basket, is a reference to time. Together with the yellow piece of fruit turning brown at the center of the basket, the leaf calls on the viewer to enjoy life's pleasures—of the palate as well as of the flesh—before they become rotten with age.

17.26 Caravaggio (Michelangelo Merisi), *Boy with a Basket of Fruit,* c. 1594. Oil on canvas; 27½ × 26⅓ in. (69.9 × 66.9 cm). Galleria Borghese, Rome.

Caravaggio's *Medusa* (fig. **17.27**) has the opposite effect: it repels rather than attracts. Painted on a tournament shield, the head exemplifies the artist's fascination with violence and decapitation. With its snaky hair, the head is highlighted against a dark background. Caravaggio thus focuses our attention on the very source of repulsion. The writhing snakes, whose skins reflect light, seem to squirm anxiously in response to the dangers of beheading. Likewise, the face itself looks down, as if at its own severed body, and cries out in horror as fresh blood spurts from the neck.

According to a contemporary source, Caravaggio, like Bernini, studied his own grimacing reflection in a mirror. It was also rumored that he used his own features for Medusa's face. If so, then Caravaggio represented himself as an androgynous, monstrous, mythological female who is simultaneously dead and alive. The transitional state between life and death recurs in some of the artist's other decapitated heads and is also implied in the rotting fruit and wilting leaf of the *Boy with a Basket of Fruit.* In this unusual

17.27 Caravaggio, *Medusa*, c. 1597. Oil on canvas on a wooden shield. Galleria degli Uffizi, Florence. According to a contemporary source, the *Medusa* was commissioned by Cardinal del Monte as a wedding present for the grand duke of Tuscany. It is a play on the Western tradition of putting the *gorgoneion* (the representation of Medusa's head) on shields and armor, recalling the similar decoration on the aegis of the goddess Athena.

iconography, Caravaggio expresses his personal ambivalence, oscillating between male and female, self-destructive criminal and creative artist, life and death, and, as van Mander noted, between the warlike Mars and the wise, creative goddess Minerva.

The oppositions that are characteristic of Caravaggio's iconographic choices—and their relation to the nature of his patronage—can be seen by comparing his *Calling of Saint Matthew* (fig. **17.28**), which was an ecclesiastical commission, with the *Boy with a Basket of Fruit* (fig. 17.26). The *Calling of Saint Matthew* is a good example of Caravaggio's innovative approach to Christian subjects. Following the account in the Gospel, Jesus and an apostle approach a group of older men and youths who are counting money. Among them is Matthew, the tax collector. Jesus points to him with a gesture that is a visual quotation of Michelangelo's *Creation of Adam* (see fig. 14.23) as if to

CONNECTIONS

See Michelangelo, *Hand of God* (detail of fig. 14.23, *Creation of Adam*, c. 1510).

17.28 Caravaggio, *Calling of Saint Matthew,* Contarelli Chapel, San Luigi dei Francesi, Rome, 1599–1600. Oil on canvas; 10 ft. 6¾ in. × 11 ft. 1⅞ in. (3.22 × 3.40 m). Caravaggio's criminal behavior and his acquaintance with Roman street life contributed to the character of this picture. In 1606, Caravaggio fled Rome after killing a man in a dispute over a tennis match. He died in 1610 before news of the pope's pardon reached him.

17.29 Caravaggio, *Conversion of Saint Paul,* 1601. Oil on canvas; 90⅝ in. × 68⅞ in. (2.30 × 1.75 m). Cerasi Chapel, Santa Maria del Popolo, Rome.

say, "Follow me." This parallels Adam's original creation with Matthew's re-creation through Jesus. The coin in Matthew's hatband underlines his preoccupation with money. His own gesture echoes that of Jesus, however, and indicates that his future will be dedicated to Jesus's service.

In the *Calling of Saint Matthew,* Caravaggio's **tenebrism**—the use of sharply contrasting light and dark—enhances the Christian message. Jesus enters the picture from the right, along with a shaft of light penetrating the darkness. Light is ironically juxtaposed with sight in the two figures on the far left. The young man who does not see the savior because he is focusing intently on money is covered in shadow. The old man leaning over him peers through his spectacles. But, in his myopia, he sees only the money and remains oblivious to the significance of the event taking place right beside him.

The significance of light as insight also characterizes Caravaggio's *Conversion of Saint Paul* (fig. **17.29**), commissioned by Pope Clement VIII's treasurer general for his funerary chapel in Santa Maria del Popolo. It depicts the moment described in Acts 9:3–9, when Saul of Tarsus, a Roman Jew who persecuted Christians, fell from his horse on the way to Damascus. A bright light illuminated the sky, blinding Saul. The voice of Christ asked why Saul was persecuting him and instructed him to proceed to Damascus. Saul was blind for three days, when an apostle restored his sight. He then converted to Christianity and became the apostle Paul.

In the painting, Saul has fallen abruptly toward the picture plane, his arms outstretched in an echo of the Crucifixion. Sudden shifts from light to dark enhance the drama of the event as the horse and page stand by without understanding the significance of what is happening.

Artemisia Gentileschi

Caravaggio's unstable lifestyle did not lend itself to maintaining a workshop or employing apprentices. Nevertheless, he had a major influence on Western art. Among his followers, known as the *Caravaggisti*, was Artemisia Gentileschi (1593–1652/3), one of the first women artists in Europe to emerge as a significant personality (see box).

Artemisia's *Judith Slaying Holofernes* (fig. **17.30**), which exhibits the Baroque taste for violence, illustrates an event from the book of Judith in the Old Testament Apocrypha. The Assyrian ruler Nebuchadnezzar has sent his general Holofernes to lay waste the land of Judah. A Hebrew widow of Bethulia, Judith, pretending to be a deserter, goes with her maidservant Abra to the camp of Holofernes and flirts with him. Arranging to spend the evening alone with him, Judith plies him with liquor until he falls into a stupor, and she uses his own sword to cut off his head. She places the head in a bag and returns home; the head is exhibited from the city walls, and the Assyrians disperse. Artemisia depicts the moment at which Judith plunges the blade through Holofernes' neck. The violence of the scene is enhanced by the dramatic, Caravaggesque shifts of light and dark and by the energetic draperies.

With *Judith and Her Maidservant with the Head of Holofernes* (fig. **17.31**), Artemisia continues the apocryphal story. The aftermath of the beheading is calmer but no less fraught with tension. The two women watch intently to make certain that no one has observed them. Artemisia creates a chromatic unity—from the red curtain to Abra's blue and lavender dress to the green pallor of Holofernes' head and Judith's rich yellow—that echoes the women's unity of purpose. A series of curves, in Judith's arms, sword, and the curtain, involves the viewer in the rhythms of the picture. In addition, the intensity of light and color against the darkened background throws the figures into relief and conveys a sense of immediacy that is both formal and a feature of the narrative text.

Women Artists: From Antiquity to the Seventeenth Century

Over the past quarter century, art historians have researched and reevaluated the role of women artists in the West. As a result, women's achievements in the visual arts, and the obstacles they have had to overcome, are much better understood.

Pliny's *Natural History* names five women artists in ancient Greece and Rome, together with their works, although nothing else is known of them. From the Roman period through the end of the fourteenth century, there are relatively few records of any individual artists, men or women. During the Middle Ages, women played a role in the production of embroidery and tapestry—more so in northern Europe than in Italy. They were also active in the illumination of manuscripts, although this was largely confined to the daughters of wealthier families. Until the late thirteenth century, illumination was done by nuns, and a woman needed a dowry to enter a convent.

The bylaws of the Company of Saint Luke, a confraternity of artists in Florence founded in 1361, mention dues to be paid by women members. However, no women's names are found in the Company records. From the fifteenth century onward, beginning in Italy, women artists emerge from obscurity. There is evidence, for example, that a woman submitted a model for the lantern of Brunelleschi's dome over Florence Cathedral, but her name is unknown. Previously, women artists in Italy had usually been nuns, women of education and talent but whose work had been limited through their isolation from the wider artistic community. An exception was Sofonisba Anguissola, who worked for Philip II of Spain. Artemisia Gentileschi was the first woman to join the Company's successor, the Accademia del Disegno (Academy of Design), in 1616.

The elevated status of the artist in the Renaissance was largely the result of a new humanist educational curriculum. For the first time, artists mixed socially with the princes of the Church and the nobility as intellectual equals rather than as artisans and craftsmen. Gradually, the new educational standards were extended, especially among the ruling classes, to women, who were encouraged to engage in a wider range of activities, including poetry, music, and art (in that order). By the sixteenth century, it was generally agreed that the daughters of the middle classes should be educated. Women who wanted to become artists had to be trained in the workshops of established masters; many were daughters, sisters, or wives of artists. The courts of fifteenth- and sixteenth-century Italy produced women who were outstanding cultural patrons, as well as having significant artistic accomplishments in their own right. Nevertheless, attributions are always a problem with women, for works by women were likely to have been delivered under the name of the male head of the workshop.

Despite the advances made by women in the Renaissance, however, practical obstacles remained. Marriage, usually followed by continuous childbearing, interfered with some promising careers. Nevertheless, Artemisia Gentileschi did marry and have children. Women were also barred from drawing from live models, which prevented competition on equal terms with men. Artemisia drew from female models, but familiarity with the male nude was important for monumental works. It is thus no accident that, until recently, women's artistic achievements were generally confined to portraiture and still life.

17.30 Artemisia Gentileschi, *Judith Slaying Holofernes,* c. 1614–1620. Oil on canvas; 6 ft. 6⅓ in. × 5 ft. 4 in. (1.99 × 1.63 m). Galleria degli Uffizi, Florence. Artemisia learned painting from her father, Orazio. In 1611, Orazio hired Agostino Tassi to teach her drawing and perspective. Tassi raped Artemisia and then refused to marry her. When Orazio sued Tassi, Artemisia was tortured with thumbscrews to test her veracity before Tassi was convicted. Undoubtedly affected by this experience, Artemisia is known for her pictures of heroic women and of violent scenes.

17.31 Artemisia Gentileschi, *Judith and Her Maidservant with the Head of Holofernes,* c. 1625. Oil on canvas; 72½ in. × 55¾ in. (1.84 × 1.42 m). Detroit Institute of Arts. Gift of Leslie H. Green.

Baroque Painting in Northern Europe

In Flanders, the Catholic Church was the primary patron of the arts. In Protestant Holland, on the other hand, the development of a bourgeois economy and a free commercial art market resulted in a significant change in the kind of art produced. For the first time, artists were able to support themselves by specializing in a particular category such as portraiture, still life, genre, or landscape. Art dealers sold works to middle-class citizens, who often purchased as much for investment and resale as for aesthetic pleasure.

Peter Paul Rubens

The Flemish artist Peter Paul Rubens (1577–1640) was extremely prolific. He worked for the Church, the nobility, private citizens, and himself. Rubens ran a successful workshop with many apprentices and assistants, and dealt shrewdly in the art market. He undertook important diplomatic missions for the Spanish Netherlands and was also the court painter to the Spanish governors. In the late 1620s, Rubens spent several months in Spain at the court of Philip IV, where he influenced Velázquez (see p. 669).

Rubens's mythological paintings, such as *Venus and Adonis* (fig. **17.32**), celebrate the sensual side of life and seem unaffected by the Counter-Reformation. They also reflect Rubens's Classical education. In this work, Venus tries to prevent her handsome mortal lover Adonis from departing. His hunting dogs wait impatiently as he tries to disengage from the goddess and her son Cupid, who has placed his bow and arrow on the ground and tugs at Adonis's leg. Venus clings to his arm, as he turns to leave. The ambivalence of Adonis's pose, forming a long diagonal, reveals his inner struggle between staying and leaving.

Venus herself forms a counterdiagonal, her fleshy, highlighted body a variation on the traditional reclining nude. In contrast to Classical and Renaissance reclining nudes, Rubens's figure is actively, rather than passively, seductive. Venus's more active role in this scene is consistent both with the particular myth and with the moment represented, in which she attempts to control and dominate her lover. Her proportions have also ventured some distance from those of Classical antiquity, for Rubens has emphasized her generous breasts and rippling, dimpled flesh in a way that is frankly sensuous. It is likely that, for Rubens, such full figures reflected, among other things, the Flemish equation of fleshiness with prosperity.

In the *Straw Hat* (fig. **17.33**), Rubens conveys his taste for lusty women. The figure is Susanna Fourment, the

17.32 Peter Paul Rubens, *Venus and Adonis*, c. 1635. Oil on canvas; 6 ft. 5½ in. × 7 ft. 11¼ in. (1.97 × 2.42 m). Metropolitan Museum of Art, New York. Gift of Harry Payne Bingham, 1937.

17.33 Peter Paul Rubens, *Straw Hat* (Susanna Fourment), c. 1620–1625. Oil on wood; 31⅛ in. × 21½ in. (79.1 × 54.6 cm). National Gallery, London.

artist's future sister-in-law. She peers at the observer from beneath a hat set on a diagonal and adorned with feathers. Her proportions are voluptuous: the snug fit of her dress pushes her breasts upward, and her ring squeezes the flesh of her forefinger. The strong contrasts of white light and rich blacks accentuate the textural differences between the soft flesh and the silky sleeves. Their swirling folds and bulky proportions echo the voluminous clouds, and their blackness is repeated in the dress, eyes, and hat. Such striking shifts of light and dark emphasize the increased planar movement of Baroque painting in comparison with Renaissance style.

In contrast to the *Venus and Adonis,* the central panel of the monumental triptych in Antwerp Cathedral depicting the *Raising of the Cross* (fig. **17.34**) is very much affected by Counter-Reformation concerns. Formally and emotionally, viewers are drawn into the picture, and their identification with Jesus's suffering is powerfully evoked. The composition is based on the sharp diagonal of Jesus and the Cross, their weight accentuated by the muscular figures struggling to elevate them into an upright position. A touch of realism is introduced in the dog barking excitedly at the lower left—Rubens has meticulously depicted the texture of its curly coat.

The image juxtaposes the brute force of the executioners with Jesus's enlightened spirituality. In contrast to the pushing and pulling necessary to raise the Cross, Jesus seems to soar toward heaven, despite the suffering caused by the nails and the Crown of Thorns. His form is the most extended highlight in the painting, which is a reminder of his role as the Light of the World. Fluttering weightlessly over his head are inscriptions in Latin, Greek, and Hebrew proclaiming Jesus "King of the Jews."

17.34 Peter Paul Rubens, *Raising of the Cross,* originally for the Church of Saint Walburgis and now in Antwerp Cathedral, 1609. Oil on wood; 15 ft. 1⅞ in. × 11 ft. 1½ in. (4.62 × 3.39 m).

CONNECTIONS

See figure 7.50. Equestrian statue of Marcus Aurelius, A.D. 164–166.

17.35 Anthony van Dyck, *Charles I on Horseback*, c. 1638. Oil on canvas; 12 ft. × 9 ft. 7 in. (3.66 × 2.92 m). National Gallery, London.

Anthony van Dyck

Rubens's assistant, Anthony van Dyck (1599–1641), was born in Antwerp but reached the height of his career as the court portrait painter to the Stuart king Charles I of England. As such, van Dyck set a standard for portraiture that influenced successive generations of English painters. His portrait of Charles I on horseback (fig. **17.35**) memorializes the ten years when Charles ruled England as an absolute monarch—called the Period of Personal Rule—after he dissolved Parliament in 1629.

Van Dyck depicts Charles in the tradition of equestrian portraiture, exemplified by the bronze *Marcus Aurelius* in Rome (see fig. 7.50). The monumental horse, Charles's shiny armor and baton of rule, and the king surveying the landscape create an image of imperial power. Like Rubens, van Dyck conveys a sense of painterly texture in rendering materials and creates an atmospheric sky. Behind the horse is a page in rich red silk who holds the king's helmet. Charles's melancholy, watery-eyed expression is characteristic of van Dyck's portraits and would later be related to the king's tragic end. Otherwise, there is nothing in the painting to suggest the reality of the political situation in England at the time. The inscription on the plaque attached to the tree reads "Charles I, King of Great Britain." Like the painting itself, the inscription reflects the degree to which Charles was out of touch with the dissatisfied and rebellious mood of his subjects.

Rembrandt van Rijn

Rembrandt van Rijn (1606–1669) was born in Leiden, in Protestant Holland. He quickly became successful and moved to Amsterdam. Unlike Rubens, Rembrandt worked largely for Protestant patrons. However, he ran his own commercial enterprise as free as possible from the influence of patronage, preferring that his works be valued as "Rembrandts" rather than as the products of a contractual agreement. He thus reflected the seventeenth-century rise in Dutch capitalism, which, through the East India Company, had become international in scope (see box, p. 665).

The subject matter of Rembrandt's paintings includes biblical and mythological scenes, landscapes, and portraits. Like Caravaggio, Rembrandt was attracted to the dramatic effects of light and dark, but he used them as much to create the character of his figures as their backgrounds. His *Blinding of Samson* (fig. **17.36**) shows the most dramatic moment in the story told in the book of Judges (16:20–21). The Philistines have pinned down Samson and are chaining his hand as he struggles fiercely. Rembrandt draws the viewer into the picture through the strong, silhouetted diagonals of the man in red who directs his lance at Samson. Leaning over Samson is the armored soldier plunging a dagger into his eye. Delilah, who is thought to be a portrait of Rembrandt's wife Saskia (see fig. 17.40), runs away, carrying the hair that was the source of Samson's strength and the scissors she used to cut it. At the upper right is a figure with a raised sword, who is nevertheless appalled at the blinding, a theme that had enormous significance for Rembrandt. It recurs throughout his work, but this is its most violent expression. As a painter, Rembrandt would have identified with the horror of a man blinded and his right hand immobi-

17.36 Rembrandt van Rijn, *Blinding of Samson* (*Triumph of Delilah*), 1636. Oil on canvas; 6 ft. 8¾ in. × 8 ft. 11 in. (2.05 × 2.72 m). Städelsches Kunstinstitut, Frankfurt.

17.37 Rembrandt van Rijn, *Belshazzar's Feast,* c. 1635. Oil on canvas; 5 ft. 5¾ in. × 6 ft. 9½ in. (1.67 × 2.07 m). National Gallery, London. Rembrandt shared the Baroque interest in naturalism. For his Old Testament scenes, he liked to frequent the Jewish quarter of Amsterdam for inspiration and models.

lized. Here, the sharp contrasts of light and dark emphasize the effect of blindness, and the violence is accentuated by the force of diagonal thrusts that are typically Baroque.

In the Old Testament scene of *Belshazzar's Feast* (fig. **17.37**), Rembrandt emphasizes the mystical light required by the text. Belshazzar, the son of the regent of Babylon in the sixth century B.C., sees a great light on the wall during a feast. Beside the light a hand appears with a cryptic message, which Daniel interprets as "You have been weighed in the balance and found wanting." The same night, Belshazzar is killed, fulfilling the sense of menace that is still popularly associated with "handwriting on the wall."

In Rembrandt's image, Belshazzar rises from the table and turns to face the mysterious light. He spreads out his arms in a sweeping diagonal, displaying the elaborate gold embroidery of his cloak. Light is also concentrated on his face, jewelry, turban, and crown, contrasting these reflections of his material wealth with the illumination of inner fear and awe in the faces of the two figures on Belshazzar's right (our left) and with the light from heaven appearing on the wall. This painting is primarily rendered in warm brown tones, with a prominent color shift in the red-orange of the woman at the lower right corner. She withdraws in fear from the light and spills her drink. In so doing, she helps to draw the observer

17.38 Rembrandt van Rijn, *Militia Company of Captain Frans Banning Cocq* (known as the *Night Watch*), 1642. Oil on canvas; 12 ft. 2 in. × 14 ft. 4 in. (3.71 × 4.37 m). Rijksmuseum, Amsterdam. This was originally located in the headquarters of the Amsterdam Civic Guard. In 1975, a cook who had been fired from the Dutch navy slashed the *Night Watch*. This painting is so identified with the Dutch nation that the sailor believed he was taking revenge on Holland itself.

into the picture plane by virtue of her forceful diagonal movement.

By mid-career, Rembrandt was Amsterdam's most esteemed portrait painter. His *Night Watch* (fig. **17.38**) is a group portrait that depicts a militia company, led by Captain Banning Cocq. The city wall, pierced by an arch in the background, evokes the triumphal arches of ancient Rome; it also reminded viewers that the Dutch had overthrown their Spanish conquerors and were now a free people.

The two men striding into the foreground form a diagonal link between the observer and the company. The captain extends his left hand as if to invite us into the scene. Light falls on to his hand from above and casts a shadow across the yellow jacket of his companion. As a result, the shadow continues the line of the captain's red sash, creating a typical Baroque interplay of light, dark, and color.

The facial features are defined by gradations of light and dark. Each figure is a portrait, mainly of the company members. Included in the crowd is a young woman highlighted in yellow; hanging from her belt is a bird, whose claws were the emblem of the militia. Peering out over the shoulder of the flag bearer is Rembrandt's own face—possibly his most unassuming self-portrait.

Rembrandt painted many portraits and more self-portraits than any other artist before the seventeenth century. Including paintings, etchings, and drawings, he produced at least seventy-five self-portraits, which constitute a visual autobiography. They chronicle Rembrandt's changing fortunes and moods and, above all, his journey through life from youth to old age.

In figure **17.39**, at age thirty-four, Rembrandt is dressed in velvet and fur, resting his arm on a windowsill in the manner of portraits by Raphael and Titian. He looks optimistically out on the world. In the facial shading, Rembrandt creates a sense of inner character visible through the "window" of the eyes, just as the picture itself is a "window" on the figure.

Eight years before the 1640 self-portrait, Rembrandt married the young and wealthy Saskia, whom he adored. Around 1634, he painted her portrait in an impressive large, red feathered hat (fig. **17.40**). Both the hat and the

17.39 Rembrandt van Rijn, *Self-Portrait, Leaning on a Sill* (aged thirty-four), 1640. Oil on canvas; 3 ft. 4⅛ in. × 2 ft. 7½ in. (1.02 × 0.80 m). National Gallery, London.

17.40 Rembrandt van Rijn, *Saskia,* 1634. Oil on panel; 3 ft. 4 in. × 2 ft. 7 in. (99.5 × 78.8 cm). Staatliche Museen Kassel, Gemäldegalerie Alte Meister.

17.41 Rembrandt van Rijn, *Self-Portrait as Saint Paul* (aged fifty-five), 1661. Oil on canvas; 35⅞ × 30⅜ in. (91.1 × 77.2 cm). Rijksmuseum, Amsterdam.

feather form sharp Baroque diagonals, which are repeated in the position of the torso. Rembrandt's taste for rich materials of costume—velvet, brocade, fur, lace, gold, and pearls—is conveyed with an exuberance mitigated only by Saskia's proper demeanor. In this case, the artist's attention to tactile variety, to red tones, and to the subtle lighting playing over surface textures expresses the intensity of his passion for Saskia.

By 1661, after several personal tragedies, including the death of Saskia, Rembrandt is an older and more sorrowful figure (fig. **17.41**). He is no longer the prosperous, bourgeois artist, confident of his future. Now he is a "Saint Paul," humbled and saddened; his pose is less assertive, and he seems weighed down by his own body. Barely visible is the sword, which is Saint Paul's traditional attribute; it emerges in flecks of gold from under his left arm. Rather than endow the saint with a conventional halo, Rembrandt weaves a yellow band into the cloth of his hat, merging light, color, and the paint itself with content in a unique way. The figure looks up from the rather worn pages of an open book, as if shrugging his shoulders at the twists of fate. (Traditionally, Saint Paul is depicted carrying a book.) The slight tilt of the artist's head and the loose brushwork emphasize the sagging cheeks. The raised eyebrows create a pattern of wrinkles on Rembrandt's forehead, and his hair has turned gray. As in the earlier pictures, Rembrandt highlights the face and hand, leaving a darkened surrounding space from which the figure seems to emerge.

17.42 Rembrandt van Rijn, *Self-Portrait in a Cap, Openmouthed and Staring*, 1630. Etching; 2 × 1⅞ in. (5.1 × 4.6 cm). Rijksmuseum, Amsterdam.

17.43 Rembrandt van Rijn, *Self-Portrait, Grimacing*, 1630. Etching; 3¼ × 2⅞ in. (8.3 × 7.2 cm). Kupferstichkabinett, Staatliche Museen, Berlin.

The medium of etching (see box) was suited to Rembrandt's genius for manipulating light and dark. Although etching had been invented in the sixteenth century, it was Rembrandt who perfected the technique during the seventeenth century. The three little self-portrait etchings reproduced here illustrate his use of black and white, or pure dark and pure light, to convey character.

The earliest figure (fig. **17.42**) is the twenty-four-year-old Rembrandt in a cap. His youthful vigor is indicated by the short, wavy lines of hair and the sharp twist of the head. Something seems suddenly to have caught his attention, for his eyes are round with wonder and his mouth is slightly open as if he is about to speak. Figure **17.43,** in which the artist is the same age, shows him grimacing. Like Caravaggio and Bernini, Rembrandt studied his own facial expressions in a mirror, which he used in self-portraits and biblical scenes. The third etching (fig. **17.44**) was executed in 1639, not long before the painted self-portrait in figure 17.39, to which it is related. A well-dressed Rembrandt, his hat perched rakishly on his head, exudes the self-confidence of success. His inner artistic energy seems to shine forth from the illumination of his face.

Etching

Etching, like engraving, is an intaglio method of producing multiple images from a metal (usually copper) plate. In etching, the artist covers the plate with a resinous, acid-resistant substance (the **etching ground**). A pointed metal instrument, or stylus, is then used to scratch through the ground and create an image on the plate. When the plate is dipped in acid, or some other corrosive chemical, the acid eats away the exposed metal. In so doing, it creates grooves where the ground was scratched through by the stylus. The ground is then wiped off, the plate inked, and impressions taken just as in engraving. The result, however, is different. Whereas in engraving the artist pushes the burin to cut into the metal surface, the etching stylus moves more easily through the ground, allowing for more delicate marks and greater freedom of action. The result is a more convincing sense of spontaneity in the image and a blurred, atmospheric quality (see, for example, the sleeves in fig. 17.44).

Rembrandt also used the intaglio **drypoint** method, in which the image is scratched directly on to the plate. "Dry" signifies that acid is not used. The incisions on the plate make metal grooves with raised edges, called the **burr.** When the drypoint plate is inked, the burr collects the ink and produces a soft, rich quality in the darker areas of the image.

In both etching and drypoint, the burin can also be used for emphasis. It is possible to combine the two techniques in one image, as Rembrandt did. It is also possible to make alterations to an etched or engraved plate and then produce additional prints. One can see the artist's changes by studying in order the different **states,** or subsequent versions, of the same image.

17.44 Rembrandt van Rijn, *Self-Portrait, Leaning on a Stone Sill*, 1639. Etching and drypoint, state 2; 8⅛ × 6½ in. (20.5 × 16.4 cm). Rembrandt House Museum, Amsterdam.

Frans Hals

Frans Hals (c. 1581–1666) worked mainly in the Dutch town of Haarlem. Known primarily for his individual and group portraits, he did not have as wide a range of subject matter as Rembrandt. His portraits, such as the *Laughing Cavalier* (fig. **17.45**), convey a sense of exuberance and immediacy, which is enhanced by the sitter's pose, character, and proximity to the picture plane. The cavalier, a courtly soldier, is set at an oblique angle. His left arm forms two diagonals simultaneously leading in and out of the picture space, which are repeated in the torso and the tilted hat. He does not actually laugh, but the upturned curves of his mustache and his direct gaze create that impression. Hals's evident delight in the textural variations of the portrait add to its cheerful effect. The hat is virtually flat in contrast to the ruddy complexion and slightly fleshy face. The intricate lace and embroidery of the costume is interrupted, and relieved, by the broad brushstrokes defining the black silk sash.

Judith Leyster

Judith Leyster (1609–1690) also worked in Haarlem, where she was the only woman elected to the painters' Guild. Her figures, like Hals's *Laughing Cavalier*, are vital and energetic. Her genre painting *The Last Drop* (formerly known as the *Gay Cavalier*) (fig. **17.46**) provides an instructive contrast to the Hals and shows the influence of Caravaggio's tenebrism. In *The Last Drop*, exuberance is created, as in the Hals, by broad, hearty gestures and strong diagonals. This is accentuated by Leyster's dramatic contrasts of light and dark, the flickering candle, and the rich red costume. Whereas Hals's figure is right up against the picture plane, Leyster's two youths are farther back in space. They are less monumental in their impact and do not confront the viewer directly. Instead, the drinker engages us by his absorption in the wine cask, and the smoker by his graceful, dancelike motion. The skeleton and hourglass allude to the passage of time, which was a popular theme in seventeenth-century Dutch art.

17.45 Frans Hals, *Laughing Cavalier*, 1624. Oil on canvas; 33¾ × 27 in. (85.7 × 68.6 cm). Reproduced by permission of the Trustees, The Wallace Collection, London.

17.46 Judith Leyster, *The Last Drop* (*Gay Cavalier*) (after restoration), c. 1628–1629. Oil on canvas; 35⅛ × 29 in. (89.3 × 73.7 cm). Philadelphia Museum of Art (The John G. Johnson Collection). Leyster was the daughter of a brewer in Haarlem. She married a painter of genre scenes and had five children. In 1635, she successfully sued Frans Hals for taking one of her students as his apprentice.

Jan Vermeer

Jan Vermeer (1632–1675) left a very small number of pictures—no more than thirty-five in all. Like Rembrandt, he was a master of light, though in a completely different way. Most of his paintings are interior genre scenes, many with allegorical meanings. His canvases are generally small, and his subjects, as well as their treatment, are intimate.

Vermeer's *Geographer* (fig. **17.47**) reflects both the Dutch interest in exploration and science, and the artist's meticulous depiction of interiors. It shows a scholarly geographer surrounded by maps and charts. The globe above him refers to the exterior world, which is contrasted with the enclosed space of the room. Reinforcing the sense of a vast world are the cropped map on the wall and the gaze of the geographer. He looks toward the window, whose light brightly illuminates his desk. Clearly preoccupied with the outside world, he holds a pair of calipers and rests his hand on a book. His intellectual energy is conveyed by his alertness and the sense that a sudden thought has arrested his movement.

Vermeer's characteristic use of light and color to convey texture is particularly evident in the wooden chest and rumpled tapestry. The areas of glistening, pearl-like light are typical of Vermeer and reflect contemporary advances in microscopic research. (The anatomist and microscopist Anton van Leeuwenhoek was appointed executor of Vermeer's estate.)

17.48 Jan Vermeer, *Lacemaker*, c. 1669–1670. Oil on canvas laid down on wood, $9\frac{5}{8} \times 8\frac{1}{4}$ in. (24.5×21.0 cm). Louvre, Paris.

In the *Lacemaker* (fig. **17.48**) of around 1669–1670, which is typical of his small-scale, intimate interiors, Vermeer depicts a figure totally absorbed in concentrated work. The view of the girl and her threads is a close-up, creating the impression that we share her space. We follow her gaze to the needles and bobbins as her hands work them with determined focus. At the left, the unformed, textured threads hang limply as they wait to be made into lace. Vermeer's characteristic pinpoints of light play over the surfaces, and we can imagine his own intense focus on each dab of paint, just as the lacemaker pores over her threads.

17.47 Jan Vermeer, *Geographer*, c. 1668. Oil on canvas; $20\frac{7}{8} \times 18\frac{1}{4}$ in. (53.0×46.4 cm). Städelsches Kunstinstitut, Frankfurt. Vermeer lived and worked in Delft, Holland. Little is known of his life and career, but it appears that he earned a good income from his paintings. After his death, his works were neglected by critics and collectors until the late 19th century. Today they are among the most highly valued in the world. The signature and date at the upper right are not original.

17.49 Jan Vermeer, *View of Delft* (after restoration), c. 1660–1661. Oil on canvas; 3 ft. 2 in. × 3 ft. 9½ in. (0.97 × 1.16 m). Mauritshuis, The Hague.

The juxtaposition of expansive space and minute detail characterizes Vermeer's *View of Delft* (fig. **17.49**). It is a particularly striking example of the Dutch taste for landscape, and it is unique among his known works. Vermeer has combined an atmospheric sky with houses and water in a way that illustrates his genius for conveying jewel-like areas of light. Despite the large size of the canvas, Vermeer's attention to meticulous detail creates a feeling of intimacy.

The shifting lights and darks of the clouds and the delicately colored buildings are reflected in the water. Standing on the shore in the foreground are a few small human figures, who seem insignificant compared with the vast sky and the implied continuation of the scene beyond the picture's frame. Their staunch verticals anchor the church spires, the towers of the drawbridge, and their reflections. Silvers, blues, and grays alternate in the sky, as yellow sunlight filters through the clouds. The sparkle of the sunlight, as it catches details of the houses or glimmers on the water, shows Vermeer's concern for naturalistic effects and creates a glowing, textured surface motion that was entirely new in Western European art.

17.50 Jacob van Ruisdael, *Extensive Landscape with Ruins*, c. 1670. Oil on canvas; 13⅓ × 15¾ in. (33.9 × 40.0 cm). National Gallery, London.

Jacob van Ruisdael

The landscapes of Jacob van Ruisdael (c. 1628–1682) extend the vistas farther toward the horizon than Vermeer does in the *View of Delft*. Much of Holland's landscape was artificially created by the dikes that hold back the sea. Ruisdael's subjects, therefore, resonate with the very survival of Holland and its economy. His panoramic view in *Extensive Landscape with Ruins* (fig. **17.50**), for example, seems to encompass a vast space, which is expanded by the broad, horizontal sweep of earth, water, and sky. Together, these natural features produce a sense of atmospheric intensity enhanced by the rumbling clouds that menace the calm water and land.

The strong vertical accent provided by the church tower serves to anchor the painting and to emphasize the flatness of the surrounding landscape. It also proclaims the transitional character of religious architecture as it mediates between earth and sky. Painterly atmospheric effects and imagery that shows the smallness of human creations (the church) in relation to the vastness of nature took on a moralizing quality in seventeenth-century Holland. The ruins show the deterioration over time of man-made works, in contrast to the seasonal renewal of nature. In the nineteenth century, these themes are integrated into the Romantic aesthetic (see Chapter 20).

Maria van Oosterwyck

The moralizing trends in Dutch art are perhaps clearest in Baroque ***vanitas*** still lifes. In contrast to the macrocosmic views of Dutch landscape, the still lifes reflect the microcosm. Both illustrate the scientific concerns of northern Europe.

In the *Vanitas Still Life* of Maria van Oosterwyck (fig. **17.51**), each element contains a warning against folly. As such, it is well within the Northern tradition of Erasmus's *Adagia* (see p. 622). Flowers are transient and die —the tulip refers to the economic folly of the Dutch tulip craze, which collapsed in 1637. The skull, the stalk being eaten by a mouse, and the ear of corn are images of transience and decay. An hourglass marks the passage of time, and the astrological globe contrasts the vastness of the universe and the notion that humanity is ruled by the stars with minute creatures such as flies and butterflies. Written texts accompanying the images reinforce their message: *Rekeningh* ("reckoning") alludes to the final accounting at the end of time, and *Self-Stryt* ("self-struggle") to the moral conflicts of the human soul. Visible in the carafe at the left are a window and the artist herself, continuing the Northern interest in reflective surfaces and in asserting the artist's presence in the work.

17.51 Maria van Oosterwyck, *Vanitas Still Life,* 1668. Oil on canvas; 29 × 35 in. (73.7 × 88.9 cm). Kunsthistorisches Museum, Vienna.

The Dutch East India Company: Seventeenth-Century Capitalism

Holland was a small country, not blessed with natural resources and constantly on the defensive against the North Sea. Among its more important industries were commercial fisheries (mainly herring) and the production of linen and other cloths. During the seventeenth century, Dutch fortunes benefited from an expansion in world trade. The East India Company, established in 1602 by a group of Dutch merchants and sea captains, exemplified the capitalist trends of the period.

The purpose of the company was to corner the market in products imported from India. Fleets of Dutch ships brought commodities such as spices, silks, and metals from India to the company's headquarters in the Netherlands. Competitors, principally the English and the Portuguese, were driven out of the market by various stratagems, including setting prices below actual cost. By keeping large stores of goods in warehouses, the Dutch maintained a continuous stock of merchandise and could raise prices when their competitors ran out of supplies. Surplus cargo was occasionally destroyed but, more often, was used to undersell the competition and put rivals out of business. Production was in the hands of Dutch settlers in India, who relied on slave labor. The profits from these enterprises, which were distributed to the shareholders of the company, could be enormous and helped to swell the prosperity of the Dutch merchant class.

By combining their resources and channeling their efforts through the company, the Dutch had secured a monopoly of the spice market (cinnamon, cloves, nutmeg, pepper) by the second half of the seventeenth century as well as a strong position in cotton, porcelain, and silk.

Window on the World Eight

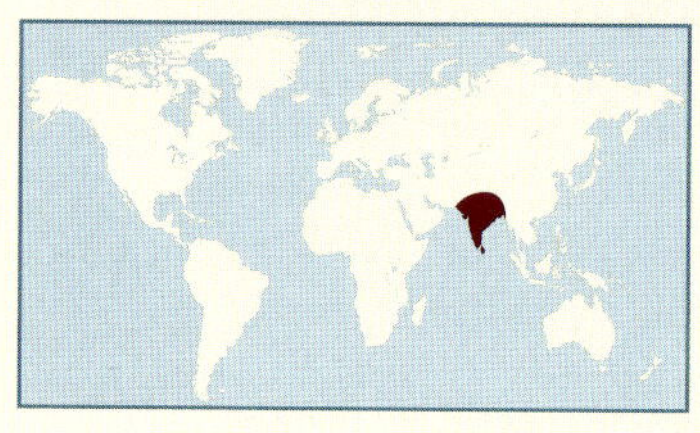

Mughal Art and the Baroque

The sixteenth-century age of exploration led to colonization, missionary activity, and trade with the Americas and the Far East. In Holland, many Chinese and Japanese objects were imported through the Dutch East India Company. Although by and large any real understanding of these distant regions on the part of Europeans was minimal, Eastern motifs began to influence furniture design, and a general taste for the exotic emerged in Europe. These cultural exchanges were most meaningful in contacts with Mughal painters of seventeenth-century India (see map). Rembrandt copied Mughal miniatures, and Rubens drew figures from the Mughal court.

The Mughal school of painting in India was known in Europe largely through the enlightened patronage of three emperors: Akbar (reigned 1555–1603), Jahangir (reigned 1603–1627), and Shah Jehan (reigned 1627–1658). Descended from Genghis Khan, Akbar's Persian grandfather founded the Mughal dynasty in India. He brought with him Persian artists, with whom Akbar studied as a child. Although raised as a Muslim, Akbar did not subscribe to the Islamic prohibition against figurative art. He therefore had Hindu artists working at his court, and they painted in a naturalistic tradition.

Akbar wished to unite Hinduism with Islam and to synthesize both with Christianity. He endorsed the progressive notion that the divine status of a ruler depended on a just and fair administration. His advanced religious views and desire for political unity inspired him to collect European art.

Akbar's European collection influenced Mughal artists, who began to introduce Western perspective into their own work. The **miniature** of *Akbar Viewing a Wild Elephant Captured near Malwa* (fig. **W8.1**) combines Hindu shading, which forms the elephant's bulk, Islamic patterning, and elements of Western perspective. For example, the oblique angle of the castle's middle wall creates a three-dimensional effect. Reinforcing this is the depiction of the ground as convincingly supporting elephants, riders, and trees.

Although orthodox Muslims in India objected to Akbar's patronage of figurative art, his son Jahangir continued to encourage artists to study nature and European painting. In the *Allegorical Representation of the Emperor Jahangir Seated on an Hourglass Throne* (fig. **W8.2**, p. 668), the Baroque interest in the *vanitas* theme of time (the hourglass) is incorporated into an Islamic setting. The border designs, calligraphic

India in the 17th century.

W8.1 Lal and Sanwah, *Akbar Viewing a Wild Elephant Captured near Malwa,* 1600. Gouache on paper; 13⅛ in. (33.4 cm) high. Victoria and Albert Museum, London.

lettering, and elaborate carpet that flattens the space are the result of Persian influence. The figures and hourglass, on the other hand, are rendered three-dimensionally and are shaded. Jahangir, surrounded by a double sun and moon halo, greets four personages, who reveal his international outlook: a Muslim divine with a long white beard, a Muslim prince with a black beard, a European delegate in Western dress, and an artist holding up a picture. Two little angels, copied from a European painting, play by the hourglass. Above and to the left, a Cupid carries a bow and arrow. To the right is another Cupid who covers his eyes—an allusion to the Western notion of blind love.

The masterpiece of Mughal architecture combines Hindu and Islamic features. The Taj Mahal (literally, "Crown of Buildings"; fig. **W8.3**) was commissioned by Jahangir's son, Shah Jehan, as a memorial to his wife, Mumtaz Mahal, who died in 1631. The jewel-like building is located in a garden and approached by four waterways, its ensemble signifying paradise and its four rivers. The mausoleum has a large cusped arch over a deep recess and stands on a podium with four domed minarets, one at each corner. On either side of the mausoleum are two identical structures—a mosque and a secular building. Balancing the large central onion dome, which is a characteristic feature of Mughal architecture, are two smaller *chattris*—the parasol-shaped elements that are derived from the *chattras* on early stupas (see fig. W3.10). The entire structure is perfectly symmetrical, which contributes to its calm, imposing impression. Elaborate curvilinear designs of inlaid semiprecious stones enhance the marble surface of the Taj Mahal.

W8.2 Bichtir, *Allegorical Representation of the Emperor Jahangir Seated on an Hourglass Throne,* early 17th century. Color and gold on paper; 10⅞ in. (27.6 cm) high. Freer Gallery of Art and Arthur M. Sackler Gallery, Smithsonian Institution, Washington, D.C. (42.15V).

CONNECTIONS

See figure W3.10. Great Stupa at Sanchi, India, 3rd century B.C.

W8.3 Taj Mahal, Agra, India, 1634.

Spanish Baroque Painting: Diego Velázquez

The paintings of the leading Baroque artist in seventeenth-century Counter-Reformation Spain, Diego Velázquez (1599–1660), covered a broad spectrum of subject matter. His genius was nurtured by his Classical education, stimulated by his admiration for Titian, and spurred by his competition with Rubens.

Velázquez's *Crucifixion* (fig. **17.52**), probably painted in the 1630s, is thought to have been commissioned for a Benedictine Order of nuns in Madrid. The work would have satisfied the Counter-Reformation view that observers should identify with Jesus's Passion. His illuminated body stands out against a darkened background, which may refer to the tradition that the sky went black at the time of the Crucifixion. The softly textured hair falls forward over Jesus's face, and the curved glow of light surrounding his head is reflected in the crown of thorns. Velázquez's taste for realistic detail is indicated by the blood dripping from Jesus's wounds and the grain and knots of the Cross's wood. The precision of such details recurs in the lettering on the plaque at the top of the Cross. Clearly written in Greek, Hebrew, and Latin is "Jesus of Nazareth, King of the Jews." (See also fig. 17.34, Rubens's *Raising of the Cross*.)

Despite the mystical quality of the light, Jesus is actually supported by the platform beneath his feet. The slight *contrapposto* that results from the weight-bearing right leg and the bent left knee resembles the relaxed Classical pose of Polykleitos's *Spear Bearer* (see fig. 5.27). In thus combining the formal elements of Baroque style with a Classical pose, Velázquez conforms to Counter-Reformation ideology, according to which physical suffering leads to moral repose.

For Philip IV, his most constant patron, Velázquez painted numerous pictures. The equestrian portrait *Philip IV on Horseback* (fig. **17.53**) was commissioned for the Hall of Realms in Philip's Buen Retiro Palace. It was one of several equestrian portraits of Philip and members of his family, which, like van Dyck's *Charles I on Horseback* (see fig. 17.35), served a dynastic as well as a political purpose. Philip's exalted pose is a Baroque version of the mounted Roman emperor, which implicitly connects him to the glory of ancient Rome (see fig. 7.50). Philip controls the horse with apparent ease as he executes a *levade*—a difficult Spanish Riding School maneuver in which the rider uses one hand to control a rearing horse. Despite the skill required for this exercise, Philip remains calm and in control. His upright posture contrasts with the diagonal plane of the horse, the slanting ground below, and the horizontal expanse of the sky. The blues and yellows spreading across the sky, the metal sheen of Philip's armor, and the rendering of the horse are all testimony to Velázquez's remarkable command of color and texture.

In addition to equestrian portraits, Philip's Hall of Realms was decorated with battle scenes intended to project an image of Spain's military superiority. But in the *Surrender of Breda* (fig. **17.54**), Velázquez also depicted Spanish moral superiority by departing from the traditional approach—portraying the domination of the vanquished by the victor. Rather than show Spinola, the victorious general, on horseback, Velázquez places him on the ground and to the right. He is therefore on an equal footing—although his head is higher—with Nassau, the defeated Dutch commander, to the left. In a gesture of friendship and compassion, Spinola restrains Nassau from kneeling. Nevertheless, Velázquez makes clear that the Spaniards are militarily as well as morally superior. The greater number of lances on the Spanish side —the right side—signify military superiority. They are aligned in an orderly formation, and the well-groomed soldiers are elegantly costumed. The Dutch,

17.52 Diego Velázquez, *Crucifixion*, 1630s. Oil on canvas; 8 ft. ⅛ in. × 5 ft. 5 in. (2.48 × 1.69 m). Museo del Prado, Madrid.

17.53 Diego Velázquez, *Philip IV on Horseback,* 1629–1630. Oil on canvas; 9 ft. 10½ in. × 10 ft. 5¼ in. (3.01 × 3.18 m). Museo del Prado, Madrid.

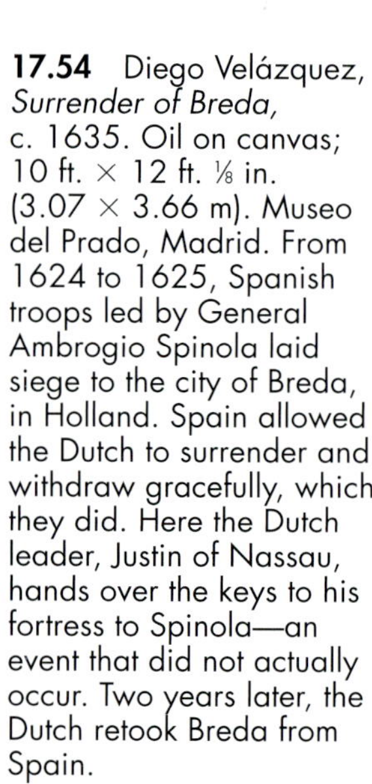

17.54 Diego Velázquez, *Surrender of Breda,* c. 1635. Oil on canvas; 10 ft. × 12 ft. ⅛ in. (3.07 × 3.66 m). Museo del Prado, Madrid. From 1624 to 1625, Spanish troops led by General Ambrogio Spinola laid siege to the city of Breda, in Holland. Spain allowed the Dutch to surrender and withdraw gracefully, which they did. Here the Dutch leader, Justin of Nassau, hands over the keys to his fortress to Spinola—an event that did not actually occur. Two years later, the Dutch retook Breda from Spain.

17.55 Diego Velázquez, *Venus with a Mirror* (*Rokeby Venus*), c. 1648. Oil on canvas; 4 ft. ⅜ in. × 5 ft. 9⅝ in. (1.23 × 1.77 m). National Gallery, London. The existence of this painting demonstrates that it was acceptable, even in Counter-Reformation Spain, to paint the female nude—provided it was for a private patron. Even so, Velázquez has erred on the side of modesty by showing only the face of the model in the mirror. A stricter application of the laws of physics might have shown another part of her body.

in contrast, are disheveled, and their clothing is torn. Behind their weapons, smoke and fire indicate the aftereffects of battle, whereas the landscape beyond the Spanish side is peaceful. Also conveying Spanish power is the monumental form of the partly foreshortened horse from which Spinola has dismounted, and the clean diagonal of the checkered flag.

In contrast to his political pictures, the *Venus with a Mirror* (fig. **17.55**), known as the *Rokeby Venus* after the nineteenth-century family that owned it, was designed for a private patron, probably the marquis of Eliche, who was well known as both a libertine and a collector of Velázquez's works. The painting obscures the identity of the model by turning her away from the viewer and blurring her features in the mirror. Cupid's presence hints at, but does not specifically identify, the amorous content of the scene, which is enhanced by the painterly textures and rich colors. Seen in rear view, the nude is a long series of curves, which are repeated in the grand sweep of the silky curtain. The rarity of the female nude in seventeenth-century Spain makes this painting all the more unusual. It reflects the influence of reclining Venuses by Giorgione (see fig. 14.48) and Titian (see fig. 14.52), which Velázquez probably studied during his two trips to Italy.

Velázquez's unqualified masterpiece is the monumental *Las Meninas* of 1656 (fig. **17.56**). This work is not only a

CONNECTIONS

See figure 14.48. Giorgione, *Sleeping Venus*, c. 1509.

See figure 14.52. Titian, *Venus of Urbino*, c. 1538.

17.56 Diego Velázquez, *Las Meninas* (after cleaning), 1656. Oil on canvas; 10 ft. 7 in. × 9 ft. ½ in. (3.23 × 2.76 m). Museo del Prado, Madrid. Velázquez's personal pride in his own status—as a "divine" artist and member of the royal circle—is evident in his self-confident stance and raised paintbrush. The red cross on his black tunic is the emblem of the Order of Santiago, of which Velázquez became a knight in 1659. Since the painting was completed in 1656, the cross must have been a later addition. Velázquez became court painter to Philip IV early in his career. He followed the humanist leanings of his teacher, Francisco Pacheco, who later became his father-in-law. Like Titian, Velázquez worked for the elevation of painting to the status of a Liberal Art, alongside music and astronomy. In Spain, painting and sculpture were still considered mere crafts because artists worked with their hands.

tribute to the artist's genius as a painter, but it is about the very art of painting. The setting is a vast room in Philip's palace, and the five-year-old infanta, or princess, Margharita, is the focus of the picture. She is attended by her maids (*meninas*) and accompanied by a midget, a dwarf, and a dog. The elaborate costumes of the Spanish court are painted in such a way that the brushstrokes highlight the textures.

Certain forms, such as the infanta and the doorway, are emphasized by light. Other areas of the picture—the paintings on the side wall, for example—are unclear. Most obscure of all is the huge canvas at the left on which Velázquez himself is working. It is seen, like the *Venus with a Mirror*, from the back.

Below the mythological pictures on the back wall, depicting contests between gods and mortals (inevitably won by the gods), is a mirror, which has been the subject of extensive scholarly discussion. King Philip IV and Queen Mariana, the parents of the infanta, are visible in the mirror. Does their image mean that they are actually standing in front of their daughter, that they are the subjects of Velázquez's canvas? Or is this perhaps not a reflection at all, but rather a painted portrait? These are among the questions most often posed about the unusual iconography. We have seen that mirror images occur in paintings for a variety of reasons (see figs. 13.68 and 15.2). The mirror in *Las Meninas* may be intentionally ambiguous, which would be consistent with Baroque taste.

Another issue to which Velázquez almost certainly refers in *Las Meninas* is the status of the art of painting in seventeenth-century Spain. It was not considered a Liberal Art as it was in Italy, but rather a handicraft. By placing himself in royal company, it is likely that Velázquez was arguing for elevating the status of painting as well as that of the artist (see caption).

17.57 Nicolas Poussin, *Assumption of the Virgin*, c. 1626. Oil on canvas; 4 ft. 4⅞ in. × 3 ft. 2⅝ in. (1.34 × 0.98 m). National Gallery, Washington, D.C. Ailsa Mellon Bruce Fund.

French Baroque Painting: Nicolas Poussin

Although Nicolas Poussin (1594–1665) was a French painter, born in Normandy, he lived most of his adult life in Rome. He studied the Italian Renaissance and was drawn to Classical as well as biblical subjects. In his later works, Poussin represents the most Classical phase of the Baroque style, particularly in scenes with ancient Greek and Roman subject matter. By 1624, Poussin was in Rome, working for influential patrons. Ironically, his reputation was at its highest with the French Academy, but he preferred to live in Rome, where his restrained classicizing style was out of tune with the more exuberant Roman Baroque.

In his *Assumption of the Virgin* (fig. **17.57**), Poussin's attraction to antique forms is apparent. Large fluted columns frame the scene asymmetrically, and cherubs drop flowers into a sarcophagus. The Virgin rises in an exuberant swirl of blue drapery, which echoes the cloud formations, as excited cherubs celebrate their joy at her ascent to heaven. The contrast of the carefully arranged white drapery with the dark stone of the sarcophagus continues the zigzag motion of the dark clouds right down to the lower edge of the picture. At the ground, the short diagonal of the drapery invites us into the scene and sends our vision soaring upward with the Virgin.

17.58 Nicolas Poussin, *Dance of Human Life,* c. 1638–1640. Oil on canvas; 2 ft. 8⅝ in. × 3 ft. 8⅝ in. (0.83 × 1.05 m). The Wallace Collection, London.

Poussin's Theory of Artistic Modes

This was one expression of the seventeenth-century French pursuit of an ordered system for conveying emotions in art. It was based on ancient Greek musical theory and Greek modes, from which the modern "keys" of music are derived. Modes were associated with different emotions. The Dorian mode, which was steady, solemn, and severe, corresponded to intellectual gravity and wisdom. The subtle modulations of the Phrygian mode made possible strong and violent effects. The Lydian mode was elegiac, the Hypolydian evoked sweetness and divinity, and the Ionian was cheerful and joyous.

Each mode was considered suited to a particular category of subject. Dorian was for Classical histories, Phrygian for representations of war, Lydian for funerals, Hypolydian for scenes of Paradise, and Ionian for celebrations, dancing, and feasting. Of Poussin's three paintings illustrated in this chapter, the *Assumption* is in the Hypolydian mode, the *Ashes of Phokion* corresponds to the Dorian mode, and the *Dance of Human Life* to the Ionian.

The *Dance of Human Life,* also called *Dance to the Music of Time* (fig. **17.58**), was made for Pope Clement IX (then still a cardinal), who suggested the subject to Poussin. In this painting, Poussin uses mythology in the service of Christian allegory and *vanitas.* Three women and one man in Classical dress join hands and dance in a circle. They represent Luxury, Wealth, Poverty, and Industry—four states of human existence—locked in never-ending circular movement. Time, the old winged man at the right, is the musician. Apollo drives his chariot across the sky, symbolizing the passage from day to night. Leading the chariot is Aurora, the dawn goddess, and following behind are the Horai (the four seasons). The twin heads of Janus—the god of gateways who sees the past and future simultaneously—adorn the top of an antique stele. Two children, one with an hourglass and the other blowing bubbles, are reminders that life is fleeting and insubstantial.

Entirely different in its somber, stoic, and elegiac mood is Poussin's *Ashes of Phokion* (fig. **17.59**). Phokion was a fourth-century-B.C. Athenian politician. Although elected general forty-five times, he consistently opposed the war against Macedon because he believed that Athenian military supremacy had come to an end. As a result, he was

17.59 Nicolas Poussin, *Ashes of Phokion,* 1648. Oil on canvas; 3 ft. 9¾ in. × 5 ft. 9¼ in. (1.16 × 1.76 m). Walker Art Gallery, National Museums Liverpool.

convicted of treason and executed, and his ashes were buried outside the city limits. The Greek author Plutarch included Phokion in his *Lives* as a model of Stoic virtue. Despite Baroque lighting, everything seems ordered and rational, in keeping with the Classical restraint of Poussin's later style. The Classical temple façade is set off by the dark landscape forms, and tiny figures stroll calmly in the clearing between foreground and background. Closest to the picture plane and highlighted by a white headscarf and sleeve is Phokion's widow. Ignored by the other figures, she collects her husband's ashes, evoking the *vanitas* theme of "ashes to ashes, and dust to dust." A related theme is evident in Poussin's combination of buildings from different historical periods. Buildings and nature, he suggests, may last; human beings do not.

	Style/Period	Works of Art	Cultural/Historical Developments
1580	BAROQUE WESTERN EUROPE 1580–1600 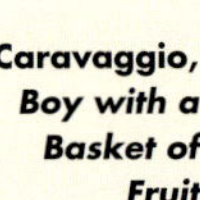  **Caravaggio, *Boy with a Basket of Fruit***	Caravaggio, *Boy with a Basket of Fruit* (**17.26**) Caravaggio, *Medusa* (**17.27**) Annibale Carracci, Farnese ceiling frescoes (**17.22–17.23**) Caravaggio, *Calling of Saint Matthew* (**17.28**)	Death of Saint Teresa of Ávila (1582) English East India Company founded (1600) **Caravaggio, *Calling of Saint Matthew***
1600	1600–1630  **Bernini, *David***	Lal and Sanwah, *Akbar Viewing a Wild Elephant Captured near Malwa* (**W8.1**) Caravaggio, *Conversion of Saint Paul* (**17.29**) Bichtir, *Allegorical Representation of the Emperor Jahangir Seated on an Hourglass Throne* (**W8.2**) Rubens, *Raising of the Cross* (**17.34**) Gentileschi, *Judith Slaying Holofernes* (**17.30**) Rubens, *Straw Hat* (**17.33**) Bernini, *Pluto and Proserpina* (**17.18**) Bernini, *David* (**17.19**) Hals, *Laughing Cavalier* (**17.45**) Bernini, baldacchino, Saint Peter's (**17.1**), Rome Gentileschi, *Judith and Her Maidservant with the Head of Holofernes* (**17.31**) Poussin, *Assumption of the Virgin* (**17.57**) Leyster, *The Last Drop* (**17.46**) Velázquez, *Philip IV on Horseback* (**17.53**)	Dutch East India Company founded (1602) Bodleian Library, Oxford, opened (1602) Cervantes, *Don Quixote* (1605) William Shakespeare, *King Lear* (1605) First permanent English settlement at Jamestown, Virginia (1607) Johan Kepler postulates planetary system (1609) Publication of King James Bible (1611) First use of Manhattan by the Dutch as a fur-trading center (1612) Thirty Years War (1618–1648) Puritans reach New England (1620) Molière (Jean-Baptiste Poquelin), French dramatist (1622–1673) Cardinal Richelieu adviser to Louis XIII of France (1624–1642) William Harvey describes circulation of the blood (1628) Great migration to America begins (1630)
1630	1630–1640  **Rubens, *Raising of the Cross***	Rembrandt, *Self-Portrait in a Cap* (**17.42**) Rembrandt, *Self-Portrait, Grimacing* (**17.43**) Velázquez, *Crucifixion* (**17.52**) da Cortona, *Glorification of the Reign of Urban VIII* (**17.24**) Rembrandt, *Saskia* (**17.40**) Taj Mahal (**W8.3**), Agra Velázquez, *Surrender of Breda* (**17.54**) Rubens, *Venus and Adonis* (**17.32**) Rembrandt, *Belshazzar's Feast* (**17.37**) Rembrandt, *Blinding of Samson* (**17.36**) van Dyck, *Charles I on Horseback* (**17.35**) Poussin, *Dance of Human Life* (**17.58**) Borromini, San Carlo alle Quattro Fontane (**17.4–17.7**), Rome Rembrandt, *Self-Portrait, Leaning on a Stone Sill* (**17.44**)	Galileo forced to recant by the Inquisition (1633) John Donne, *Poems* (1633) Harvard College founded (1636) René Descartes, *Discourse on Method* (1637) Collapse of Dutch tulip market (1637)  **Velázquez, *Surrender of Breda***
1640	1640–1650 	Rembrandt, *Self-Portrait, Leaning on a Sill* (**17.39**) Rembrandt, *Night Watch* (**17.38**) Borromini, Sant'Ivo della Sapienza (**17.8, 17.10**), Rome Bernini, Cornaro Chapel (**17.20–17.21**), Rome Velázquez, *Venus with a Mirror* (**17.55**) Poussin, *Ashes of Phokion* (**17.59**) **Rembrandt, *Self-Portrait***	Louis XIV succeeds to French throne (1643) Battle of Rocroi ends Spanish ascendancy in Europe (1643) Treaty of Westphalia ends Thirty Years War (1648) French Royal Academy founded, Paris (1648) Charles I beheaded; England declared a Commonwealth (1649)
1650 1710	1650–1710  **Vermeer, *View of Delft***	Velázquez, *Las Meninas* (**17.56**) Bernini, piazza of Saint Peter's (**17.2**), Rome Rembrandt, *Self-Portrait as Saint Paul* (**17.41**) Bernini, *Louis XIV* (**17.15**) Vermeer, *View of Delft* (**17.49**) Perrault, Le Vau, and Le Brun, east façade of the Louvre (**17.11**), Paris Le Brun, Le Vau, and Le Nôtre, Versailles (**17.12**) Le Brun and Tuby, Fountain of Apollo (**17.13**), Versailles Oosterwyck, *Vanitas Still Life* (**17.51**) Vermeer, *Geographer* (**17.47**) Vermeer, *Lacemaker* (**17.48**) van Ruisdael, *Extensive Landscape with Ruins* (**17.50**) Wren, Saint Paul's Cathedral (**17.17**), London Gaulli, *Triumph of the Name of Jesus* (**17.25**) Hardouin-Mansart and Le Brun, Hall of Mirrors (**17.14**), Versailles	Thomas Hobbes, *Leviathan*, a defense of absolute monarchy (1651) Oliver Cromwell becomes Lord Protector of England (1653) Restoration of Stuart monarchy in England under Charles II (1662) Plague in London (1665) Great Fire of London (1666) John Milton, *Paradise Lost* (1667) Antonio Vivaldi, Italian composer (1675–1741) Jean Racine, *Phèdre* (1677) John Bunyan, *Pilgrim's Progress* (1678) Versailles becomes residence of French kings (1682) Isaac Newton, *Philosophiae naturalis principia mathematica* (1687) John Locke, *An Essay Concerning Human Understanding* (1690) Witchcraft trials in Salem, Massachusetts (1692)

18

Rococo and the Eighteenth Century

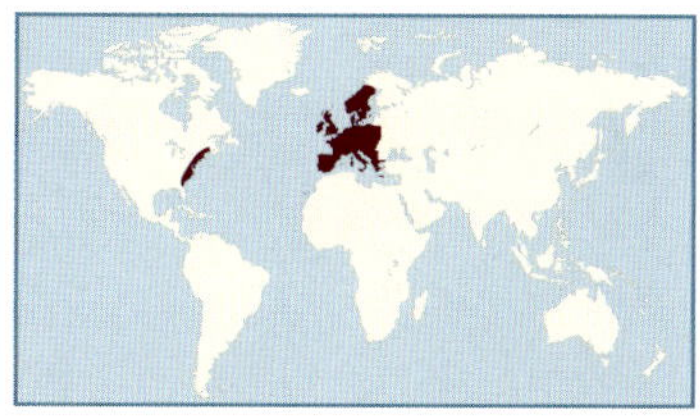

The eighteenth century (see map), particularly its latter half, was a complex patchwork of several different artistic trends. Two of these, the Neoclassical and the Romantic, overlap each other in time and often converge in a single work. They continue into the nineteenth century and are covered more completely in Chapters 19 and 20. The most distinctive eighteenth-century style, which flourished from about 1700 to 1775, is called *Rococo,* a term apparently coined from the French words *rocaille* and *coquille* (meaning, respectively, "rock" and "shell"—formations used to decorate Baroque gardens). Scholars are divided over whether Rococo was an independent style or a refinement of Baroque.

Rococo style is above all an expression of wit and frivolity, although at its best there are more serious, somber, and satirical undercurrents. On the surface, the typical Rococo picture depicts members of the aristocracy gathered in parks and gardens, as Cupids frolic among would-be lovers. Classical gods and goddesses engage in amorous pursuits. The world of Rococo is a world of fantasy and grace, which also includes a taste for the exotic and for satire. One expression of this taste in the eighteenth century was the fad for **chinoiserie.** From about 1720, an interest in Chinese imagery developed in France and England. This included garden design, architectural follies, costumes, and decorative motifs in general. In 1761, Sir William Chambers built a pagoda in Kew Gardens, on the outskirts of London (fig. **18.1**). The fanciful, unlikely appearance of a Chinese pagoda in an English garden appealed to the Rococo aesthetic.

18.1 Sir William Chambers, Pagoda, Kew Gardens, England, 1761. Engraving by William Woollett after J. Kirby, hand-colored by Heath. Victoria and Albert Museum, London.

After the death of Louis XIV in 1715 and a subsequent decline in royal patronage, the center of French taste shifted from the court to the Paris ***hôtel*** (elegant townhouse) and to the salon (see box). The source of patronage also shifted from being the exclusive province of the French aristocracy to include the upper middle class and the bourgeoisie. In other capitals of Europe, especially in Germany, the Rococo style was quickly taken up by rulers and their courts.

Exemplifying the ornate Rococo interior typical of the Paris *hôtel* is the Salon de la Princesse in the Hôtel de Soubise (fig. **18.2**). Animating the lightly colored walls are elaborate gilded relief patterns of floral and plant designs framing blank spaces and mirrors. At the top of each section of the wall, Cupids perch precariously at the edges of the gilded arches. The lively energy of such interiors and their airy, reflective character provided appropriate settings for the witty social interaction of the eighteenth-century salon.

Although Rococo was the primary artistic style of the eighteenth century, Classicism remained a potent force. Excitement over the discovery of the buried Roman cities of Herculaneum (in 1709) and Pompeii (in 1748) fueled the interest in antiquity. The German scholar Johann Winckelmann introduced a historical approach to the study of ancient Greek and Roman art (see box, p. 681). At the same time, Neo-Gothic and Palladian styles developed—the former especially in England, the latter in both England and America. Toward the end of the century, Romanticism arose in opposition to the Classical aesthetic of the European "Academies."

18.2 Germain Boffrand, Salon de la Princesse, Hôtel de Soubise, Paris, c. 1740.

Salons and *Salonnières*

In the eighteenth century, the salon became the center of Parisian society and taste. The typical salon was the creation of a charming, financially comfortable, well-educated, and witty hostess (the *salonnière*) typically in her forties. She provided good food, a well-set table, and music for people of achievement in different fields who visited her *hôtel*. The guests engaged in the art of conversation and in social and intellectual interchange.

In the seventeenth century, the most important salon had been that of Madame de Rambouillet, who wished to exert a "civilizing" influence on society. By the next century, the salon was a fact of Paris social life, and one in which women played the dominant role. Among the *salonnières* were women of significant accomplishments in addition to hostessing. These included writers (Mesdames de La Fayette, de Sévigné, and de Staël, and Mademoiselle de Scudéry), a scientist (Madame du Châtelet), and the painter Élisabeth Vigée-Lebrun.

Political and Cultural Background

In contrast to the apparent frivolity of Rococo, serious advances were taking place in other fields. The world of music could boast Antonio Vivaldi, Johann Sebastian Bach, Franz Joseph Haydn, and Wolfgang Amadeus Mozart. In science, Gottfried Wilhelm Leibniz developed calculus, Joseph Priestley discovered oxygen, and Edmund Halley identified the comet that bears his name. Technological developments, such as mechanized spinning and James Watt's steam engine, laid the foundations for the industrial revolution. Satire, which is a feature of certain Rococo artists, had as its leading literary exponents Jonathan Swift in Ireland and François-Marie Arouet (Voltaire) in France.

Important political changes also occurred in eighteenth-century Europe. Frederick the Great turned Prussia into an aggressive military power, and France and Austria united against him. This new alignment resulted in the Seven Years' War (1756–1763), which was won by the Prussians. England, whose international influence was based largely on the strength of its navy, consolidated its position in the eighteenth century and took the lead in European industrialization. England's position of economic and naval primacy extended to the New World and to India.

Developments in America mirrored the shifts in European power. The North American colonies belonged mainly to England. The exceptions were in the South, in the Louisiana Territory, and in Canada, where the English did not dislodge the French until 1763. Spain controlled the whole of Central and South America (with the exception of Brazil), Mexico, Texas, parts of California, and most of Florida (which it ceded to England in 1763).

Western Europe, c. 1740.

The Age of Enlightenment

The eighteenth century has been called the Age of Enlightenment. This complex concept derives from certain philosophical ideas that were translated into political movements. The rationalism of the French philosopher René Descartes—"Cogito, ergo sum" (I think, therefore I am)—in the previous century continued to appeal to European and American thinkers. In England, John Locke advanced the notion of "empiricism," the belief that all knowledge of matters of fact derives from experience. This became the basis of the scientific method (see box, below). Seventeenth-century improvements in microscopes and telescopes lent credence to Locke's ideas. And in France, Denis Diderot and other *encyclopédistes* classified the various branches of knowledge on a scientific basis. Diderot's pursuit of scientific

Scientific Experiments in the Enlightenment

Joseph Wright (1734–1797) painted two scenes of scientific experimentation. These placed him firmly in the tradition of the Enlightenment and its interest in empirical reasoning. In addition, he was particularly intrigued by the dramatic effects of artificial light, and this led him into industrial workshops and other settings where he could study figures silhouetted against the glow of forges.

In 1768, Wright exhibited *An Experiment on a Bird in the Air Pump* (fig. **18.3**). The experiment in this picture consisted of putting an animal or bird into a glass container that was connected to a pump. The demonstrator then pumped out the air in order to show the effect on the creature. Here the victim is a white cockatoo, which in reality was too valuable a bird to risk; it was probably chosen for its dramatic effect. In the picture, the air has already been pumped out and the bird has fallen to the bottom of the container. The left hand of the demonstrator is raised to the valve of the pump, which, if turned in time, will restore the air flow and save the bird.

On the table stands a large glass jar containing an opaque liquid and what appears to be a skull, silhouetted by a candle standing behind the jar. Both candle and skull are traditional components of a *vanitas* scene—the candle signifying the passage of time, the skull its inevitable result. The man seated in profile to the left of the pump holds a watch, ostensibly to clock the experiment but also as a further reminder that time is passing.

18.3 Joseph Wright, *An Experiment on a Bird in the Air Pump*, 1768. Oil on canvas; 28⅓ × 37¾ in. (72.0 × 95.9 cm). National Gallery, London. Wright was a British portraitist and landscape painter who spent most of his life in Derby, in the heartland of England. He became known as Wright of Derby to distinguish him from other contemporary artists of the same name.

observation carried over into his views on artistic training. In contrast to the study of tradition advocated by the French Academy, Diderot advised art students to leave the studio and observe real life.

In political philosophy, the concept of a secular "social contract" developed. Locke's *Two Treatises on Government,* published in 1690, argued against the divine right of kings. In Locke's view, government was based on a contract between the ruler and the ruled, who have a right to rebel when their freedom is threatened. In 1762, Jean-Jacques Rousseau went a step further in his *Social Contract.* For him, the "contract" was not between people and government, but among the people themselves. The practical and ultimate effect of such reasoning can be seen in Thomas Jefferson's Bill of Rights and the American Constitution. The American Revolution (1775–1783) ended the oppression of the colonies by the British king George III and was followed a few years later by the French Revolution (1789–1799). These two revolutions essentially shattered the time-honored belief throughout most of western Europe in the divine right of kings.

Traditionally, the image of light, associated with the power of the sun, had been used for political ends. In ancient Egypt, the pharaoh was thought of as the sun god Ra on earth, while the entire court of Louis XIV revolved around his self-image as the Sun King. Likewise, throughout the history of Christian art, Christ is paralleled with the sun as the "Light of the World." With the inroads made by non-Christian philosophies and the decline in the influence of the Church following the Reformation, the notion of "light" became increasingly secular. In the eighteenth century, it became associated with a "rational," empirical outlook. The light in En*light*enment referred to the primacy of reason and intellect, in contrast to the unquestioning acceptance of divine power. This bias was profoundly optimistic because it encouraged a spirit of inquiry and a belief in progress and in the human ability to control nature.

While these were the most dominant eighteenth-century views, countercurrents persisted. The prevalence of irony and satire, for example, implied an awareness that darker forces underlay the optimistic view of nature and the surface levity of Rococo. In Germany, the reaction was even more pronounced, particularly in the aesthetic of the so-called *Sturm und Drang* (storm and stress) movement, which was a manifestation of early Romanticism. According to that more pessimistic outlook, nature had ultimate power over reason. As in Johann Wolfgang von Goethe's play *Faust,* human life was seen as a constant—and losing—battle for control over the evil forces of nature.

Art Theory and the Beginnings of Art History

The eighteenth century, particularly the latter half, saw the beginning of modern art theory and art history. The very term *aesthetic* is an eighteenth-century invention.

Johann Joachim Winckelmann (1717–1768) was born in Berlin and became a librarian near Dresden. There he met artists and visited museums. In the 1760s, he moved to Rome, where he was appointed superintendent of antiquities and oversaw excavations at Herculaneum and Pompeii. Based on his publication in 1764 of *The History of Ancient Art,* Winckelmann has been called the father of art history because he believed that style was determined by culture. He thus expanded the study of art beyond the more biographical approach of Vasari and the Classical tradition, and beyond the philosophical views of Plato and Aristotle. Beauty, for Winckelmann, was a matter of intuition and spirit, and the height of aesthetic beauty had been attained by Greece in the fifth and fourth centuries B.C. Roman art, he said, was derivative of Greek art, which was noble, restrained, and ideal. The Renaissance, in his view, was a revival not of Roman, but of Greek, art. Winckelmann classified ancient art into four phases: Archaic, Phidian, the fourth century B.C., and the period from the third century B.C. through the fall of the Roman Empire. These categories became a model for later art-historical divisions.

A different approach to art theory was espoused by the German philosopher Immanuel Kant (1724–1804). In 1790, he published his *Critique of Judgment,* in which he advanced the notion of aesthetic assessment of, and response to, both nature and art. Beauty, for Kant, resided in the interplay between the viewer and what was viewed. Kant thus accorded to the aesthetic response a significant and independent role in human experience.

In the early decades of the nineteenth century, G. W. F. Hegel (1770–1831) combined elements of Winckelmann and Kant in his theoretical lectures. He addressed the spiritual connection between art and religion, and also identified the historical evolution of style. This evolution, according to Hegel, was inevitable and could be perceived and understood in retrospect. Artistic expression for Hegel symbolized an idea and therefore had a more rational underpinning than in Kant's system. Hegel's belief that art revealed its culture and was a historical artifact conformed to Winckelmann's ideas, but Hegel's historical stages differed. The first, Symbolic, stage was pre-Classical and included ancient Egypt. In the second stage, the fifth- and fourth-century-B.C. Greeks produced the Classical ideal, in which the soul is revealed by the formal perfection of the body. The third and last stage was Hegel's own Romantic period, in which the spiritual and the religious converged.

18.4 Antoine Watteau, *Pilgrimage to Cythera,* 1717. Oil on canvas; 4 ft. 3 in. × 6 ft. 4¼ in. (1.30 × 1.94 m). Louvre, Paris. This was Watteau's presentation painting for admission to the French Academy. Not only was he accepted, but the Academy added the category *fêtes galantes* to its hierarchy of genres. Watteau died of tuberculosis at age thirty-seven.

Rococo Painting

Antoine Watteau

The leading Rococo painter, Antoine Watteau (1684–1721), was born in Flanders but spent most of his professional life in France. He worked in the painterly, colorist tradition of his compatriot Rubens, whose interest in voluptuous nudes and richly textured materials he shared. Nevertheless, the thin, graceful proportions of Watteau's figures as well as his subject matter are more consistent with Rococo style. He is best known for his *fêtes galantes,* paintings of festive gatherings in which elegant aristocrats relax in outdoor settings.

The best known of Watteau's works is the *Pilgrimage to Cythera* (fig. **18.4**), depicting a group of amorous couples who have journeyed to the island of Venus. At the right, her statue is draped with flowers, denoting love and fertility. Her presence in stone marks the enduring character of the Classical tradition, in contrast to the frivolity and transience of the trysting lovers. The emphasis on silk textures that reflect light and the powder-pink Cupids frolicking in the sky are typical of Rococo. As the lovers prepare to depart the magical island, they descend toward the scallop-shell boat at the left; the colors of their costumes become dulled as they begin their return to the world of reality.

The more wistful side of Watteau can be seen in his undated *Gilles* (fig. **18.5**), the sad Harlequin. The actor, in this case a comic lover, wears his costume but does not perform. His pose is frontal, and his arms hang limply at his sides. His melancholy expression betrays his mood, which is at odds with the silk costume and pink ribbons on his

18.5 Antoine Watteau, *Gilles,* undated. Oil on canvas; 6 ft. ⅝ in. × 4 ft. 10¾ in. (1.84 × 1.49 m). Louvre, Paris.

18.6 François Boucher, *Venus Consoling Love,* 1751. Oil on canvas; 3 ft. 6⅛ in. × 2 ft. 9⅜ in. (1.07 × 0.85 m). National Gallery, Washington, D.C. (Chester Dale Collection). It was also during 1751 that Madame de Pompadour, Louis XV's mistress, moved to the north wing of Versailles and lived there until her death. Throughout her tenure at court, Boucher was her favorite artist.

shoes. Presently between roles, this actor is "all dressed up with nowhere to go." The blue-gray sky echoes the figure's mood, as do the sunset-colored clouds. End of day, which is indicated by the sunset, corresponds to the sense that Gilles is at a loss about what to do next. His lonely isolation is accentuated by the four figures around him, who seem engaged in animated conversation.

François Boucher

François Boucher's (1703–1770) "Rubenist" brand of Rococo is evident in the playful *Venus Consoling Love* (fig. **18.6**), which is devoid of Watteau's undercurrent of irony and melancholy. A powder-pink Venus, in a lightly erotic pose, tries to console a pouting, flustered Cupid, whose arrow-filled quiver hangs from his shoulder. Reclining on Venus's couch and watching from the trees are two more Cupids, whose intent gazes draw the viewer toward the central characters. The two white doves—"love birds"—echo the amorous text of this scene. The predominance of pinks, the curly blond heads of the Cupids, and the silky, feathery textures contribute to the cheerful, material richness of Boucher's work.

Jean-Honoré Fragonard

The last significant Rococo painter was Jean-Honoré Fragonard (1732–1806). In *The Swing* (fig. **18.7**), he enlivens nearly the entire picture plane with frilly patterns. The lacy ruffles in the dress of the girl swinging are repeated in the illuminated leaves, the twisting branches, and the scalloped edges of the fluffy clouds.

At the right of the painting, an elderly cleric pushes the swing, while a voyeuristic suitor hides in the bushes and peers under the girl's skirt. His hat and her shoe are sexual references in this context—the former a phallic symbol and the latter a

18.7 Jean-Honoré Fragonard, *The Swing,* 1766. Oil on canvas; 35 × 32 in. (88.9 × 81.3 cm). Wallace Collection, London. *The Swing* was commissioned by the Baron de Saint-Julien, who specified that Fragonard should paint his (the baron's) mistress on the swing, with himself as her observer. Fragonard emphasizes the erotic associations of "swinging" by highlighting the shimmering texture and swirling curves of the dress. Swinging has some of the same connotations today—compare the "swinging sixties."

vaginal one. They complement the setting: an enclosed yet open garden, where amorous games are played. The stone statues also deepen the erotic implications of the scene. On the left, Cupid calls for secrecy and silence by putting his finger to his lips. Between the swing and the old man, two additional Cupids cling to a dolphin. Like Watteau, Fragonard uses Classical imagery to provide a serious underpinning of frivolous erotic themes.

Royal Portraiture

Hyacinthe Rigaud A comparison of the late Baroque, large-scale portrait of *Louis XIV* (fig. **18.8**) by the French artist Hyacinthe Rigaud (1659–1743) with two other royal portraits of the later eighteenth century reflects different artistic trends. Rigaud's Louis XIV stands majestically in an elaborate costume of ermine and blue velvet with gold fleurs-de-lis signifying French royalty. Louis's silk stockings show off his shapely legs, while his high-heeled shoes (which he designed himself) compensate for his short stature. He is framed by the folds of a rich red silk curtain and surrounded by the accoutrements of kingship and power—a scepter and sword. The column, with the classicizing relief on its podium, is an echo of Louis himself and associates his personal iconography with the Classical past. It is also an architectural metaphor for Louis's role as the structure and support of France itself. Rigaud's figure is very much a king, not surprisingly the monarch who declared "L'état, c'est moi" ("I am the state"), thus merging his personal identity with that of France.

18.8 Hyacinthe Rigaud, *Louis XIV*, 1701. Oil on canvas; 9 ft. 2 in. × 7 ft. 10¾ in. (2.79 × 2.41 m). Louvre, Paris.

18.9 Rosalba Carriera, *Louis XV*, 1721. Pastel on paper; 18½ × 15¾ in. (47.0 × 40.0 cm). Museum of Fine Arts, Boston. Rosalba's father was a government official, her mother worked as a lacemaker, and her grandfather was a painter. She never married and devoted herself to her two sisters, to whom she taught art. Rosalba was enormously successful as a portrait painter to 18th-century European royalty.

Pastel

Pastels are chalky crayons made of compressed pigments bound with water and a gum substance. Artists using pastels build up color as they would in a painting. The colors are usually pale, but the higher the proportion of pigment chalk, the deeper the tone. The pastels are applied to pastel paper, which is fibrous and therefore allows the color to adhere to the surface.

Pastels had been used for centuries for drawing studies in red, black, and white, but from the fifteenth century artists began to draw in a wider range of colors. Works in pastel, as they were made in the eighteenth century, are called paintings rather than drawings because they are not as linear; they increased the speed with which a painting could be made and permitted a luminous surface texture that appealed to Rococo tastes. Rosalba Carriera was instrumental in the growing popularity of pastels.

Rosalba Carriera Rosalba Carriera (1675–1757) was born in Venice and worked mainly in Italy and France as a portraitist. Her success won her election to the French Academy. In 1721, she painted a portrait of the ten-year-old King Louis XV, son of Louis XIV (fig. **18.9**). By this time, the Sun King had been dead for six years, a regency had been established, and the court had moved to Paris. There, Rosalba's reputation for quick, flattering portraits earned her extensive aristocratic patronage. In the portrait of Louis XV, the shimmering pastel (see box) quality of the costume, with its prominent gold medal, matches the soft curls of the powdered wig. Compared to the stately portrait of his father, Louis XV seems vapid and devoid of a distinctive personality. This impression is probably a combination of Rosalba's efforts to flatter and Louis XV's own ineffectual character.

Élisabeth Vigée-Lebrun The other major eighteenth-century portrait painter to the aristocracy in France was Élisabeth Vigée-Lebrun (1755–1842). She painted several portraits of Marie Antoinette, the Austrian-born queen of Louis XVI. Like Rosalba Carriera, Vigée-Lebrun befriended monarchs and their families, and benefited from their patronage. In figure **18.10**, Vigée-Lebrun depicts Marie Antoinette wearing an elaborate ruffled silk gown, an ostrich-feathered headdress, and a powdered wig. Her reputation for aloofness is suggested by her gaze, which is directed to the left, away from the viewer. She seems oblivious to the social, political, and economic unrest among her subjects that would erupt the following year, culminating in the French Revolution (see box).

Prelude to the French Revolution

Louis XV died in 1774. Both he and his successor, Louis XVI, were ineffectual rulers. For political reasons, Louis XVI helped the American colonies in their fight against the British king, George III. He encountered internal economic problems when, in 1787, the French nobility and the Church refused to pay taxes. This marked the beginning of an aristocratic revolt against absolute monarchy in France and, with the American example before them, led to the demand for a written constitution. In 1789, on July 14 (now known as "Bastille Day"), angry crowds stormed the Bastille (a prison in Paris). The common people generally supported France's National Constituent Assembly; composed of members of the middle class as well as of the nobility, it backed the idea of a constitution.

Four major developments culminated in the revolution. In 1789, the Assembly abolished the feudal system and imposed a tax on certain aristocratic privileges. The Declaration of the Rights of Man and the Citizen guaranteed new freedoms: the press, speech, religion, equality before the law, the right to own property, and a graduated income tax. By 1791, a new constitution had been introduced. It asserted that legitimate government authority rested with the Assembly; the king had the power of veto but could only use it to delay a decision, not to nullify it. Finally, the clergy was declared subject to civil law, which angered the pope, whom Louis XVI supported.

In June 1791, Louis and Marie Antoinette fled with their children. They were captured at Varennes, not far from the French–German border. A year and a half later, in January 1793, the king and queen of France were executed, two of the thousands of victims of the guillotine.

Surrounding the queen are accoutrements of French royalty. A huge column at the left alludes to the state, and the bust of Louis XVI on the ledge at the right is a reminder of his power. Like the queen, he appears aloof, literally elevated and thus of higher status than she. The room itself is filled with signs of wealth—the red velvet chair with a gilded frame, and the vase of roses and jeweled crown on the table.

18.10 Élisabeth Vigée-Lebrun, *Marie Antoinette*, 1778–1779. Oil on canvas; 9 ft. × 6 ft. 4 in. (2.73 × 1.94 m). Kunsthistorisches Museum, Vienna. The large scale of the painting is typical of the portraits of Marie Antoinette and reflects the power of her position as queen of France.

18.11 Thomas Gainsborough, *Mrs. Richard Brinsley Sheridan*, 1785–1787. Oil on canvas; 7 ft. 2½ in. × 5 ft. ½ in. (2.20 × 1.54 m). National Gallery of Art, Washington, D.C. (Andrew W. Mellon Collection). Gainsborough's patrons included the British royalty and aristocracy, but he also painted portraits of his musical and theatrical friends and their families. Mrs. Sheridan was the wife of Richard Brinsley Sheridan, author of the satirical comedies *The Rivals* and *School for Scandal*.

Thomas Gainsborough

Nature and portraiture, which predominated in French Rococo, were also an important aspect of the style in England. Thomas Gainsborough (1727–1788), who was influenced by van Dyck and best known for his full-length portraits, liked to set his figures in landscape. In his *Mrs. Richard Brinsley Sheridan* (fig. **18.11**), for example, the sitter assumes a slightly self-conscious, prim pose and gazes out of the picture. The shiny, silky textures of her dress and the light filtering through the background trees recall the materials and garden settings of French Rococo. Here, however, the amorous frivolity has been subdued. Mrs. Sheridan is at once enclosed by nature and distinct from it. She is sedate, aristocratic, and surrounded by a landscape as apparently controlled as she is.

William Hogarth

A different expression of British Rococo is found in the witty satire of William Hogarth (1697–1764). Influenced in part by Flemish and Dutch genre paintings, he satirized contemporary manners and social conventions. His series of six paintings entitled *Marriage à la Mode* from the 1740s pokes fun at hypocritical commitments to the marriage contract. The second scene of the series (fig. **18.12**) is illustrated here. The husband, a young aristocrat, has returned home exhausted from carousing. An excited dog sniffs the woman's hat still in the husband's pocket, drawing the viewer's attention to his master's sexual exploits. A black mark on the side of the man's neck indicates that he has already contracted syphilis.

18.12 William Hogarth, *Marriage à la Mode II*, c. 1743. Oil on canvas. National Gallery, London.

The wife, meanwhile, seems to have indulged in some impropriety of her own. As she leans back, a fallen chair in the foreground suggests that someone, perhaps her music teacher, has just made a speedy exit. The architecture reflects the Neoclassical Palladian style of eighteenth-century England, but Rococo details fill the interior. The frills on the clothing, for example, echo the French version of the style. The elaborate chandelier and the wall designs are characteristic of Rococo fussiness. On the mantelpiece, the bric-a-brac of chinoiserie reflects the eighteenth-century interest in Far Eastern exotic objects, as well as referring to a frivolous lifestyle. They are contrasted with the august pictures of saints in the next room.

The device of paintings within paintings performs the same function as the stone statues in the Watteau and Fragonard discussed above. Paintings of saints line a wall of the background room, isolated from the living, who ignore them. Cupid, on the other hand, blows the bagpipes, which, as in Bruegel's *Peasant Dance* (see fig. 16.9), signify lust. The dangers of sexual excess are underscored in the Hogarth by placing Cupid among ruins, foreshadowing the inevitable ruin of the marriage. As in French Rococo, Hogarth uses traditional figures from Classical antiquity for the purpose of playful, but telling, satirical warnings. Also like French Rococo, which typically represents aristocrats, Hogarth's pictures deal with identifiable social and professional classes. But they lack the air of theatrical fantasy that pervades French examples of the style.

Hogarth's satirical imagery included comments on taste and fraud in the art world. In 1761, he produced the etching *Time Smoking a Picture* (fig. **18.13**), in which the motif of a picture within a picture plays a central role. An aged Father Time literally "smokes" a painting in order to make it seem older than it is. He sits on a broken plaster cast, which denotes Hogarth's preference for modern art rather than for old-master paintings (see caption). Time's scythe cuts through the canvas, the top frame of which is inscribed in Greek: "Time is not a clever craftsman, for he makes everything more obscure." At the left, the jar marked "VARNISH" refers to the technique of varnishing pictures to age them artificially. The purpose of Time's activity is to increase the value of the painting, as is indicated by the phrase at the lower right: "As Statues moulder into Worth." Hogarth depicts Time as a fraudulent art dealer, more interested in profit than in paintings and willing to destroy art in order to make money.

18.13 William Hogarth, *Time Smoking a Picture*, 1761. Etching and mezzotint; 8 × 6 11/16 in. (20.3 × 17.3 cm). Guildhall Art Gallery, London. Hogarth's father was a teacher, from whom his son learned Latin and Greek. He also opened a Latin-speaking coffeehouse that went bankrupt. As a result, he spent three years in debtor's prison until Parliament passed an act freeing all debtors. This experience contributed to the artist's fierce opposition to social injustice and hypocrisy. In 1752, Hogarth published his views on art in *Analysis of Beauty*, which, like the etching, states his anti-Academic position. In the couplet at the bottom of the print, he urges people to look at nature and to themselves, rather than to the plaster casts of traditional art schools, for "what to feel."

Rococo Architecture

Several divergent architectural trends can be identified in the eighteenth century, but the most original new style was Rococo. In architecture, as in painting, Rococo emerged from late Baroque Classicism, which it both elaborated and refined. In northern Italy and central Europe, Baroque had been the preferred style for palaces and hunting lodges. Particularly in the countries along the Danube—Austria, Bohemia, and southern Germany—a distinct regional style developed, which was a blend of Italian Baroque and French Rococo.

Balthasar Neumann

A leading exponent of this movement was the German architect Balthasar Neumann (1687–1753). He created one of the most ornate Rococo buildings, the Residenz (fig. **18.14**), or Episcopal Palace, in Würzburg, Bavaria, in southwest Germany. Begun in 1719 and completed in 1753, the Residenz was an enormous edifice built for the hereditary prince-bishops of the Schönborn family. It was designed around a large entrance court, and the side wings, reminiscent of the plan at Versailles, had interior courtyards of their own. Although elements of the Classical Orders remain in the columns and pilasters on the façade of the Würzburg Residenz, the spaces in the pediments are largely filled with elaborate curvilinear designs.

The main feature of the interior of the Residenz is its magnificent staircase, which ascends to a first landing. It then divides, reverses direction, and rises to the upper level (fig. **18.15**). The hall containing the staircase is the largest room—nearly 100 by 60 feet (30.48 by 18.29 meters)—in the Residenz. The banister and balustrade are decorated with statues and stone *kraters,* while Cupids lounge on the entablatures over the doorways. Each door is framed by large, triple Corinthian pilasters, which support another entablature that continues around the entire room. The

18.14 Balthasar Neumann, the Residenz, Würzburg, Germany, 1719–1753.

18.15 Staircase of the Residenz showing the ceiling fresco of Giovanni Battista Tiepolo, Würzburg, Germany, 1752–1753.

ceiling fresco was painted by the Italian Rococo artist Giovanni Battista Tiepolo (1696–1770) and is believed to be the largest in the world. Its portrayal of Apollo and the prince-bishop, the seasons, the zodiac, and the continents of Africa, America, Asia, and Europe is a grand statement of the far-reaching influence of the Schönborns.

The Kaisersaal (Imperial Room) of the Residenz is a two-story octagonal chamber. Painted in white, gold, and pastel colors, it rises to a vaulted oval ceiling pierced by oval windows. The frescoes are by Tiepolo. Engaged Corinthian columns with gilt capitals and bases and the entablature above them are made of **stucco** (fine plaster) painted to resemble marble. The edges of the windows and other architectural features are traced with delicate, thin **moldings,** like designs made of spun sugar. The white surfaces of the vault are covered with ornament. Most striking of all are the giant, illusionistic gilded curtains that are drawn apart by a pair of white Cupids to reveal the *Investiture of Bishop Harold* (fig. **18.16**). Other *trompe l'oeil* devices blur the boundary between the actual ceiling and the exterior space. A dog sits on top of a column, and other figures appear to be half in and half out of the picture frame. Such playful illusions, combined with ornate decoration, are characteristic of Rococo painted spaces.

18.16 Giovanni Battista Tiepolo, *Investiture of Bishop Harold,* detail of the ceiling frescoes in the Kaisersaal, the Residenz, Würzburg, Germany, 1751–1752. Born and trained in Venice, by the 1730s Tiepolo had established himself throughout northern Italy as a master of monumental fresco decoration. He was known for his technical skill, command of perspective, and fondness for illusionistic architecture. He spent three years in Würzburg decorating the Residenz, and in 1762 he was invited to Spain by Charles II to work on the royal palace.

Matthäus Daniel Pöppelmann

One of the best examples of German Rococo architecture is the Zwinger, built in Dresden in 1711–1722 (fig. **18.17**). The Zwinger (German for "enclosure," or "courtyard") is a series of galleries and pavilions commissioned by Augustus the Strong, king of Poland and elector of Saxony. Arranged around an enclosed courtyard, it serves as an open-air theater for tournaments and other spectacles. The section illustrated here is the Wallpavillon, one of the pavilions situated at the corners of the courtyard, to which it is connected by glass-covered arcades. All of these structures were designed to provide shelter for the spectators. The architect, Matthäus Daniel Pöppelmann (1662–1736), claimed that his design was based on Vitruvian proportions. He even included elements that are Classical in origin, such as the statue of Hercules with the world on his shoulders—a reference to Augustus—at the top, and satyrs emerging from the bunched pilasters. But the Classical elements are freely rearranged so that the overall intricate effect is far from Classical in spirit. So elaborate, in fact, is the surface decoration that the wall seems to dissolve into ornate detail.

18.17 Matthäus Daniel Pöppelmann, Wallpavillon, the Zwinger, Dresden, Germany, 1711–1722. Pöppelmann was trained as a sculptor but became court architect to Augustus the Strong, elector of Saxony and king of Poland. Augustus sent Pöppelmann to Rome, Vienna, Paris, and Versailles (the capitals of Rococo taste) to gather ideas for his palace in Dresden. Finally, only the Zwinger was built. It was gutted during World War II but has been accurately reconstructed.

Dominikus Zimmermann

Rococo church architecture is illustrated by Dominikus Zimmermann's Wieskirche, or "Church of the Meadow" (figs. **18.18** and **18.19**). It is a pilgrimage church near Oberammergau in the foothills of the Bavarian Alps. From the plan, it is clear that Zimmermann was influenced by Borromini's elliptical architectural shapes. The exterior is relatively plain, but the interior is typical of German Rococo church interiors, which were designed to give visitors a sense of spiritual loftiness and a glimpse of heaven. The nave is mainly white, and the decoration (including the elaborate pulpit at the left) is largely gold, though there are accents of pink throughout. As one approaches the **chancel**, the colors deepen. Gilt and brown predominate, but the columns flanking the altar are of pink marble, whereas the statues and other decorations are white. The decoration of the ceiling is entirely Rococo in that it merges the painted surfaces with the architecture through ornate illusionism.

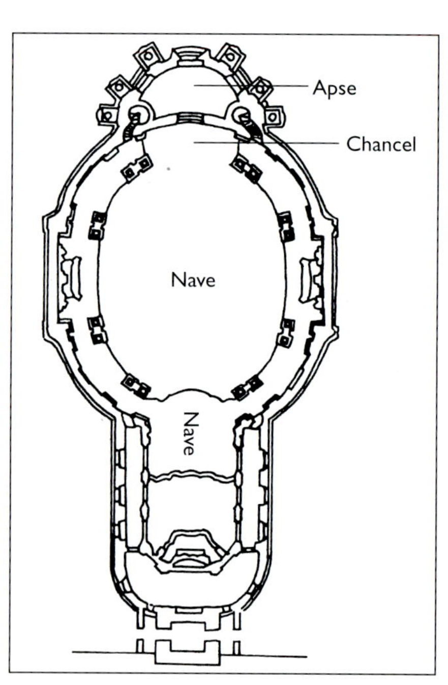

18.18 Plan of the Wieskirche.

18.19 Dominikus Zimmermann, Wieskirche, Bavaria, 1745–1754. The nave is a Rococo development of Borromini's oval church plans in Baroque Rome. The Wieskirche's longitudinal axis is emphasized by the deep, oblong chancel. Eight freestanding pairs of columns with shadow edges (square corners or ridges that accentuate light and shadow) support the ceiling. The ambulatory, which continues the side aisles, lies outside the columns.

CONNECTIONS

See figure 15.20. Andrea Palladio, Villa Rotonda, begun 1567–1569.

18.20 Richard Boyle (Earl of Burlington), Chiswick House, near London, begun 1725. Lord Burlington was one of a powerful coterie of Whigs and supporters of the House of Hanover (George I and his family). He took a grand tour of Europe in 1714 to 1715 and returned to Italy in 1719 to revisit Palladio's buildings. On his return to England, he became an accomplished architect in the tradition of Palladio.

Architectural Revivals

Palladian Style: Lord Burlington and Robert Adam

In England, the Baroque style—and especially Rococo, with all its frills—was rejected in the eighteenth century in favor of renewed interest in the ordered, classicizing appearance of Palladian architecture. Palladio's *Four Books of Architecture* (see Chapter 15) was published in an English translation in 1715 and exerted widespread influence. An early example of English Palladian style is Chiswick House (figs. **18.20** and **18.21**) on the southwestern outskirts of London, which Lord Burlington (1695–1753) began in 1725 as a library and place of entertainment.

Burlington based Chiswick House loosely on Palladio's Villa Rotonda (see fig. 15.20), although it is on a smaller scale and there are some significant differences in the plans (figs. 18.21 and 15.19). Unlike the Villa Rotonda, Chiswick House did not need four porticos. Instead, it has

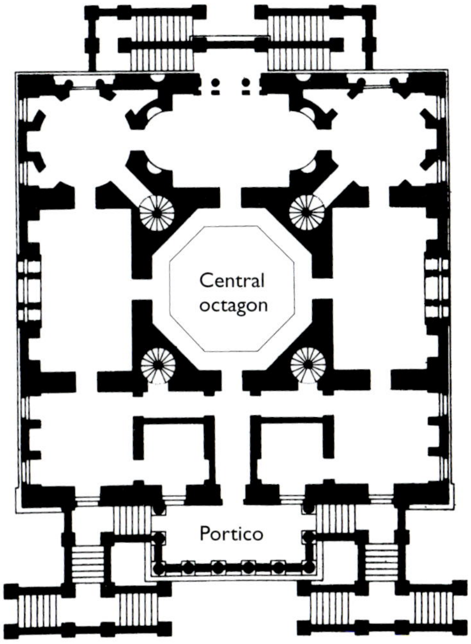

Central octagon

Portico

18.21 Plan of Chiswick House.

CONNECTIONS

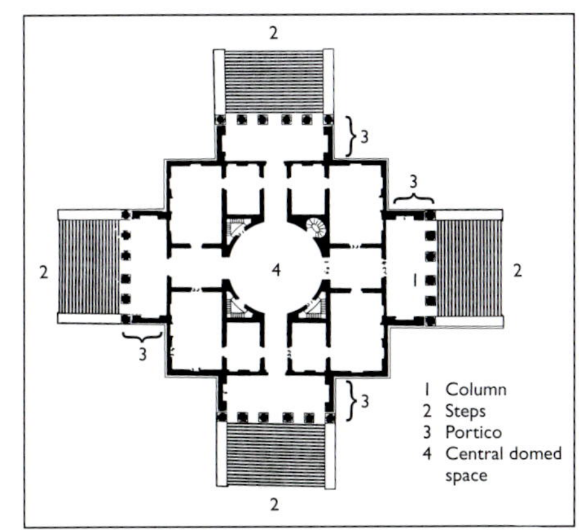

See figure 15.19. Plan of the Villa Rotonda.

18.22 Robert Adam, fireplace niche, Osterley Park House, Middlesex, England, begun 1761. The ornamentation—including pilasters, entablature, moldings, relief over the fireplace, coffered semidome, and sculptures in the smaller niches—was all based on Classical precedents.

one, which is approached by lateral double staircases on each side. The arrangement of the rooms around a central octagon rather than a circle is also different, and the columns are Corinthian rather than Ionic, as in the Villa Rotonda. There are no gable sculptures, and the roof is decorated on each side by a row of obelisks, which function as chimney flues. The dome is shallower than that of the Villa Rotonda and rests on an octagonal drum, allowing more light into the central chamber. Despite such differences, however, the proportions and spirit of Chiswick are unmistakably Palladian.

Another leader of the Classical revival in Britain, particularly in the field of interior design, was Robert Adam (1728–1792). Interest in Classical antiquity had been heightened by the excavations at Herculaneum and Pompeii. Discoveries from these sites provided the first concrete examples of imperial Roman domestic architecture since the eruption of Mount Vesuvius in A.D. 79. Publications on Classical archaeology followed. Not only was Adam influenced by these, but he was himself an enthusiastic amateur archaeologist. He had traveled to Rome and made drawings of the ruins, which informed much of his own work. In a fireplace niche in the entrance hall of Osterley Park House near London (fig. **18.22**), which Adam began to remodel in 1761, he re-created the atmosphere of a Roman villa. Although there is still an element of Rococo delicacy, especially in the pastel color schemes of certain rooms, it is now a much more austere setting. The principal characteristics of this later style are axial symmetry and geometrical regularity, both of which reflect the Classical revival.

Gothic Revival: Horace Walpole

Contemporary with German Rococo architecture and the Palladian movement was a renewed interest in Gothic style. The revival of Gothic—which never completely died out in England—began around 1750. It must be seen in relation to the late eighteenth-century Romantic movement, which is discussed in Chapter 20.

In its most general form, Romanticism rejected established beliefs, styles, and tastes—particularly the Classical ideals of clarity and perfection of form. It fostered the dominance of imagination over reason. At the same time, however, to the extent that it evoked the Classical past, Romanticism shared certain aspects of the Neoclassical style.

One of the earliest non-Classical manifestations of Romanticism in England was the use (from the 1740s) of imitation Gothic ruins and other medievally inspired objects in garden design. This was followed by the more radical activity of Horace Walpole (1717–1797), a prominent figure in politics and the arts. Walpole and a group of friends spent over twenty-five years enlarging and "gothicizing" a small villa in Twickenham, just outside London. The result, renamed Strawberry Hill (fig. **18.23**), was widely admired at the time. It is a large, sprawling structure, without the the soaring grandeur of traditional Gothic buildings. Nevertheless, Strawberry Hill is an interesting combination of Gothic features, including battlements, buttresses, and tracery. There are turrets on the outside and vaulting in the interior. Strawberry Hill also reflected the serious nostalgia with which the British viewed the Middle Ages, associated with a lost sense of community.

18.23 Horace Walpole, Strawberry Hill, Twickenham, near London, 1749–1777. Like his father, Sir Robert Walpole, a Whig prime minister of England, Horace Walpole also sat in Parliament as a Whig. His novel *The Castle of Otranto* started a fashion for Gothic tales of terror. Walpole's prolific correspondence is a valuable record of 18th-century manners and tastes, and, through it, he elevated letter writing to an art form.

European Painting

Bourgeois Realism: Jean-Baptiste-Siméon Chardin

The *encyclopédiste* Diderot praised Jean-Baptiste-Siméon Chardin (1699–1779) as a realist painter. In contrast to the fashionable, aristocratic elegance of his Rococo contemporaries, Chardin's subjects, especially still life and genre, are influenced by Netherlandish painting.

La Fontaine (fig. **18.24**) illustrates the artist's interest in household work. Simple tasks are raised above the level of the ordinary by the conviction and intense concentration of the figures. Work, rather than play—as in Rococo—is Chardin's subject. In the very application of paint to canvas, Chardin conveys his own focus and intensity. The large copper vat at the center of *La Fontaine,* for example, is painted with thick, almost **impasto,** brushstrokes, creating the impression of a shiny metal surface. The wooden bucket, the tiled floor, and the draperies hanging at the left reflect Chardin's attention to the rustic textures of country kitchens. The woman in the foreground carries out her chores with determination and wears plain household attire, in contrast to Rococo silks and laces. In the background, another woman talks to a little girl, as if to instill in her the "bourgeois" values of work. These figures gaze neither at one another nor at the observer. Unlike the flirtatious character and fanciful settings of Rococo, in which time is spent primarily in leisure pursuits, Chardin's scenes extol the moral virtues of work and study in everyday surroundings.

18.24 Jean-Baptiste-Siméon Chardin, *La Fontaine,* first exhibited 1733. Oil on canvas; 15 × 16½ in. (38.1 × 41.9 cm). National Museum, Stockholm.

18.25 Jean-Baptiste-Siméon Chardin, *Pipe and Jug*, undated. Oil on canvas; 12½ × 16½ in. (31.7 × 41.9 cm). Louvre, Paris.

Chardin's still lifes, such as *Pipe and Jug* (fig. **18.25**), eliminate human figures, while assuring the observer of their presence. Chardin also endows his objects with distinctive shapes and textures. The objects seem to have been arranged by an absent person who might return at any moment. The box is a sturdy container, solid and reliable like the woman in *La Fontaine*. It seems as if it has just been opened and the pipe casually propped against it until its owner comes back. A prominent white jug, illuminated from the window at the left, presides over the smaller objects. It dominates the space—like a woman with her hand on her hip. The thick impasto of the jug contrasts with the shiny surfaces of the smaller, more delicate, and less imposing objects. As in *La Fontaine*, Chardin's focused attention and the visible care lavished on the application of the paint herald the nineteenth-century still lifes of Manet and Cézanne (see Chapters 22 and 23).

Neoclassicism: Angelica Kauffmann

Angelica Kauffmann (1741–1807) was a child prodigy who became one of the most important and prolific Neoclassical painters. Her *Cornelia Pointing to Her Children as Her Treasures* (fig. **18.26**) illustrates the late eighteenth-century interest in Classical form and content as well as the degree to which different styles can overlap each other within the same period. Although the content is Classical, the mood is Romantic.

Cornelia was the daughter of the Republican-minded Roman leader Scipio Africanus. Her husband, Tiberius Sempronius Gracchus, was a distinguished Roman official known for his fairness. In this painting, Kauffmann depicts an event that took place in second-century-B.C. Rome, when Cornelia received a visit from a friend. Her friend is shown with an open jewelry box on her lap, displaying a necklace. When she asks to see Cornelia's jewels, her hostess points to her sons—the Gracchi (sons of Gracchus). They, in turn, grew up to be respected politicians, a reflection of their honorable parents. In the first century A.D., the Gracchi became the subject of a well-known biography by the moral philosopher Plutarch, according to whom the Romans honored Cornelia with a statue inscribed "Cornelia, mother of the Gracchi."

Kauffmann's painting is Neoclassical in subject, the figures wear costumes inspired by ancient Rome, and the profiles are reminiscent of Classical busts. But the pronounced gestures and the textured lighting that leaves areas hidden in shadow have a Romantic flavor. At the same time, such details as the jewels and the way they are handled reveal a taste for Rococo fussiness.

18.26 Angelica Kauffmann, *Cornelia Pointing to Her Children as Her Treasures*, 1785. Oil on canvas; 80 × 50 in. (203.2 × 127.0 cm). Virginia Museum of Fine Arts, Richmond. The Adolph D. and Wilkins C. Williams Fund. Kauffmann was born in Switzerland and studied art in Italy. Although a member of the Accademia di San Luca in Rome from 1765, as a woman she was barred from figure drawing. She also worked in England, where she was influenced by Reynolds, and became a founding member of the Royal Academy of Art. She married a man who pretended to be a Swedish count but turned out to be a bigamist. In 1781, she married a Venetian artist and returned to Italy, where her career continued to prosper.

American Painting

John Singleton Copley

In North America (see map), artists of the late eighteenth century were affected by European styles. John Singleton Copley (1738–1815) was a leading painter of the Colonial period. He did not sympathize with the American Revolution and in 1775 emigrated to England, where, under the influence of European Rococo, his work became more ornate.

Before his departure, Copley painted a portrait of Paul Revere (fig. **18.27**), which is typical of his earlier, more realist style. Despite the apparent simplicity of the picture, however, there are elements of Baroque and Rococo. The figure looks directly out of the picture, inviting the viewer into his space, as Baroque figures do. The way in which the sharply focused, illuminated figure is set against a dark background is reminiscent of Baroque portraiture and the tenebrism of Caravaggio. Likewise, the attention to surface shine (the silver teapot and highly polished tabletop with engraving tools) occurs frequently in both Baroque and Rococo. In contrast to those styles, however—and particularly to the latter—Copley's Paul Revere is not idealized; he wears a simple shirt and a plain vest. His solid, squarish bulk is emphasized, and the weight of his head is indicated by his stern expression and the thumb pushing up against his jaw.

18.27 John Singleton Copley, *Paul Revere*, c. 1768–1770. Oil on canvas; 35 × 28½ in. (88.9 × 72.3 cm). Courtesy, Museum of Fine Arts, Boston (Gift of Joseph W., William B., and Edward H. R. Revere). Copley grew up in Boston, the son of Irish emigrants. He was trained by his stepfather, an engraver of mezzotint portraits, and then became a portrait painter.

North American settlements in the 18th century.

Benjamin West

Benjamin West (1738–1820), another important late-eighteenth-century American artist, came from a Pennsylvania Quaker family and began painting at the age of six. Like Copley, West settled in England, where he became known for his pictures of Classical and historical subjects. In 1772, he was appointed history painter to King George III and was president of the Royal Academy from 1792 to 1805 and from 1807 to 1820. Many young American artists visiting London, including Copley, trained at his studio.

In the *Death of General Wolfe* (fig. **18.28**), West caused consternation among conservatives by his choice of contemporary, rather than Neoclassical, dress. King George III was not alone in feeling that modern dress was vulgar. It was generally thought that West's figures should have worn togas so that the picture would convey a universal message. But despite such criticism, the work was enormously popular. Its nostalgic appeal to the past became characteristic of nineteenth-century Romanticism. Although West rejected Classical costume, his training in the Classical tradition is evident. The American Indian in the foreground assumes the traditional pose of mourning. At the same time, however, the use of light and the melodramatic gestures are reminiscent of the Baroque style.

In eighteenth-century America, as in Europe, different trends in artistic style persisted alongside the Palladian movement, the Gothic Revival, and the beginnings of Romantic and Realist developments. By the end of the eighteenth century, Rococo was a style of the past. The Neoclassical, Romantic, and Realist movements would at various times emerge to dominate nineteenth-century taste.

18.28 Benjamin West, *Death of General Wolfe,* c. 1770. Oil on canvas; 4 ft. 11½ in. × 7 ft. ¼ in. (1.51 × 2.13 m). National Gallery of Canada, Ottawa (Gift of the 2nd Duke of Westminster, 1918). James Wolfe, the subject of this painting, was the young general who led the British troops to victory over a much larger French force in Quebec in 1759. His success obliged France to concede Canada to England. At the decisive moment of battle, Wolfe was wounded and died in the arms of his officers.

	Style/Period	Works of Art	Cultural/Historical Developments
1700	ROCOCO AND THE 18TH CENTURY 1700–1740  **Watteau, *Gilles***	Rigaud, *Louis XIV* (**18.8**) Pöppelmann, the Zwinger (**18.17**), Dresden Watteau, *Pilgrimage to Cythera* (**18.4**) Watteau, *Gilles* (**18.5**) Neumann, Residenz (**18.14**), Würzburg Boyle, Chiswick House (**18.20**), near London Chardin, *La Fontaine* (**18.24**) Chardin, *Pipe and Jug* (**18.25**)  **Chardin, *Pipe and Jug***	Peter the Great founds Saint Petersburg (1703) Union of England and Scotland as Great Britain (1707) Alexander Pope, *Rape of the Lock* (1712) Death of Louis XIV of France (1715) Daniel Defoe, *Robinson Crusoe* (1719) Spain occupies Texas (1720–1722) South Sea Bubble (English speculative craze) bursts (1720) Johann Sebastian Bach, Brandenburg Concertos (1721) Establishment of cabinet government in England; Robert Walpole first prime minister (1721) Regular postal service established between London and New York (1721) Jonathan Swift, *Gulliver's Travels* (1726) John Gay, *The Beggar's Opera* (1728) Methodist movement founded by John and Charles Wesley (1730) Discovery of Herculaneum and Pompeii (1738–1748) David Hume, *A Treatise of Human Nature* (1739)
1740	1740–1760  **Hôtel de Soubise**	Hôtel de Soubise (**18.2**), Paris Hogarth, *Marriage à la Mode II* (**18.12**) Zimmermann, Wieskirche (**18.19**), Bavaria Walpole, Strawberry Hill (**18.23**), Twickenham Boucher, *Venus Consoling Love* (**18.6**) Carriera, *Louis XV* (**18.9**) Tiepolo, Residenz frescoes (**18.15–18.16**) **Hogarth, *Marriage à la Mode II***	George Frederick Handel, *Messiah* (1741) Benjamin Franklin invents the lightning conductor (1752) Samuel Johnson begins *Dictionary of the English Language* (1755) Voltaire, *Candide* (1759)
1760	1760–1770  **Copley, *Paul Revere***	Adam, Osterley Park House (**18.22**), Middlesex Hogarth, *Time Smoking a Picture* (**18.13**) Chambers, *Pagoda* (**18.1**), Kew Gardens Fragonard, *The Swing* (**18.7**) Wright, *An Experiment on a Bird in the Air Pump* (**18.3**) Copley, *Paul Revere* (**18.27**) West, *Death of General Wolfe* (**18.28**)  **Walpole, Strawberry Hill**	Jean-Jacques Rousseau, *Social Contract* (1762) Spain cedes Florida to England (1763) England defeats France at the Battle of Quebec and gains control of Canada (1763) Wolfgang Amadeus Mozart writes his first symphony (1764) Johann Winckelmann, *The History of Ancient Art* (1764) James Watt invents the steam engine (1769) Captain James Cook lands at Botany Bay, Australia (1770)  **Boyle, Chiswick House**
1770	1770–1800  **Vigée-Lebrun, *Marie Antoinette***	Vigée-Lebrun, *Marie Antoinette* (**18.10**) Kauffmann, *Cornelia Pointing to Her Children as Her Treasures* (**18.26**) Gainsborough, *Mrs. Richard Brinsley Sheridan* (**18.11**) 	Denis Diderot completes his encyclopedia (1772) Boston Tea Party in protest against tea duty (1773) American Declaration of Independence (1776) Adam Smith, *Wealth of Nations* (1776) Lavoisier proves that air is composed mainly of oxygen and nitrogen (1777) Richard Brinsley Sheridan, *The School for Scandal* (1777) Immanuel Kant, *Critique of Pure Reason* (1781) Beginning of the French Revolution (1789) William Blake, *Songs of Innocence* (1789) Execution of Louis XVI and Marie Antoinette (1793) Eli Whitney invents the cotton gin (1793) Edward Jenner introduces vaccination against smallpox (1796) Napoleon Bonaparte appointed first consul of France (1799) **Kauffmann, *Cornelia Pointing to Her Children as Her Treasures***
1800			

PART SIX

19 Neoclassicism: The Late Eighteenth and Early Nineteenth Centuries

20 Romanticism: The Late Eighteenth and Early Nineteenth Centuries

21 Nineteenth-Century Realism

22 Nineteenth-Century Impressionism

Window on the World Nine: Japanese Woodblock Prints

23 Post-Impressionism and the Late Nineteenth Century

Window on the World Ten: Gauguin and Oceania

CHAPTER PREVIEWS

NEOCLASSICISM: THE LATE 18th AND EARLY 19th CENTURIES

Revolutionary fervor in France
Napoleon becomes emperor of France (1804)
 Imperial patronage: Arc de Triomphe; Vendôme column
Battle of Waterloo (1815)
Painters in France: David; Benoist; Ingres
Sculptors in France: Canova; Houdon
United States Constitution (1787)
American artists: Trumbull; Greenough
 Thomas Jefferson (architect and statesman): Third U.S. president
 Federal style: Richmond, Virginia, Capitol building; Monticello; University of Virginia

ROMANTICISM: THE LATE 18th AND EARLY 19th CENTURIES

Music and poetry; architectural revival styles
Burke on the Sublime (1757)
Artists
 England: Blake; Constable; Turner
 France: Rude; Géricault; Delacroix
 Germany: Friedrich
 Spain: Goya
American Transcendentalism: Emerson; Thoreau
Painters in the United States: Cole; Bingham; Bierstadt; Catlin; Hicks

19th-CENTURY REALISM

Industrial Revolution
Communist Manifesto (1848)
Authors: Dickens; Balzac; Flaubert; Zola
American Civil War (1861–1865)
Emancipation Proclamation (1863)
Development of photography: Daguerre; Niepce; Talbot; Nadar; Cameron; Brady
Expansion of lithography
Painters
 France: Millet; Bonheur; Courbet; Daumier; Manet
 Pre-Raphaelites in England: Rossetti; Millais
 United States: Eakins; Tanner
Architecture: Crystal Palace; Brooklyn Bridge; Eiffel Tower; Statue of Liberty; skyscrapers

19th-CENTURY IMPRESSIONISM

Second Empire in France; urban renewal of Paris
Cult of Bohemia; Paris Opera; optical realism
French artists: Manet; Renoir; Degas; Morisot; Monet; Pissarro; Rodin
Artists quote art: Delaney on Rodin's *Balzac*
American artists: Cassatt; Muybridge; Homer; Sargent; Whistler

Japanese Woodblock Prints of the Edo Period

POST-IMPRESSIONISM AND THE LATE 19th CENTURY

Posters, advertisements; Toulouse-Lautrec
Cézanne's "constructive brushstroke"
Seurat's Pointillism
van Gogh; Gauguin
The Symbolist movement: Moreau; Munch
Aestheticism: Wilde; Beardsley
Art Nouveau: Horta; Guimard
Vienna Secession: Klimt
Freud, *The Interpretation of Dreams* (1899)
Rousseau, *The Dream* (1910)

Gauguin and Oceania

The arts in nineteenth-century Europe and America are characterized by a parade of styles that reflect the context of their time. Paris, still the center of the Western art world, was the origin of the major nineteenth-century styles. Neoclassicism, because of its associations to the Greek and Roman republics, had been a style of revolution in the late eighteenth century. But under Napoleon, who crowned himself emperor of France in 1804, it became an imperial style. In the United States, Neoclassicism was called the Federal style, notably in the architecture of Thomas Jefferson.

The Romantics fought tyranny and colonialism, longed for past and exotic locales, and were fired by poetic imagination—all of which is expressed in their art. Realists strove to represent everyday life and to depict the broad panorama of society. Impressionists and Post-Impressionists, on the other hand, focused on the material of art, using prominent brushstrokes to convey the way we actually see—which they called "optical realism." They shared with the artists of Japanese woodblock prints of the Edo period a taste for scenes of entertainment and leisure, and a formal interest in patterns, silhouettes, and cropped viewpoints. Exhibitions of non-Western art in Europe inspired artists to study works from the Far East and Oceania. At the end of the century, the Symbolist movement in art, music, and theater reflected the late nineteenth-century interest in psychology, dreams, and the unconscious mind.

19

Neoclassicism: The Late Eighteenth and Early Nineteenth Centuries

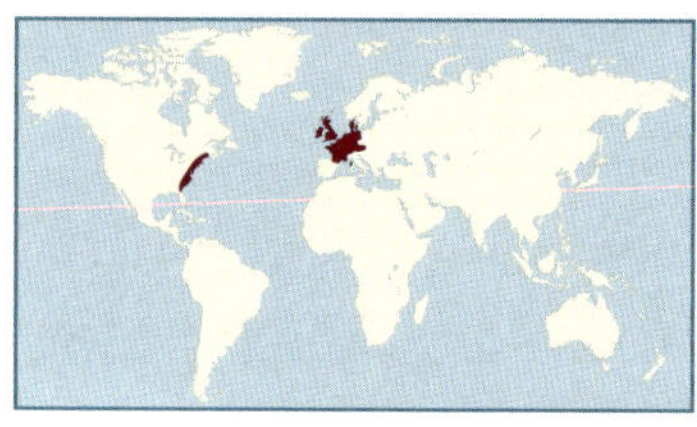

During the late eighteenth and early nineteenth centuries in western Europe, several styles competed for primacy. Paris had become the undisputed center of the Western art world, but Rome was still a significant artistic force. In France, the "True Style," later called the Neoclassical style, was a reaction against the levity of Rococo. French Baroque, especially under Louis XIV, had had a pronounced Classical flavor; from it evolved the Neoclassical style, which was adopted by the leaders of the French Revolution. Neoclassical then became the style most closely associated with the revolutionary movements of the period (see box). But with Napoleon's rise to power, Neoclassicism became an imperial style.

Chronology of the French Revolution and the Reign of Napoleon

1789	The storming of the Bastille prison in Paris, followed by the Reign of Terror. Many associated with the *ancien régime* ("old regime") and the hereditary monarchy are killed.
1793	Louis XVI and his wife, Marie Antoinette, are beheaded by the guillotine.
1795–99	The *Directoire* (Directory)—rule by the middle class.
1799	Napoleon becomes first consul.
1803	The Napoleonic law code is issued.
1804	Napoleon is crowned emperor.
1806	Napoleon launches a building campaign in Paris with the intention of creating a new Rome. He takes Julius Caesar, who was also a consul before becoming dictator, as his model. Like Caesar, Napoleon adopts the eagle for his military emblem and the laurel wreath for his crown.
1812	Napoleon attacks Russia but is forced to retreat.
1814	Napoleon abdicates. The monarchy is restored under Louis XVIII.
1815	Napoleon is defeated in the Battle of Waterloo after returning from Elba. The Congress of Vienna establishes the borders of European countries, which last until World War I (1914–1918).
1821	Napoleon dies in exile.

The Neoclassical Style in France

The contrast between Rococo and Neoclassical style can be illustrated by comparing two sculptures depicting an embrace, both derived from Classical mythology. The terracotta *Nymph and Satyr Carousing* (fig. **19.1**) by Clodion (1738–1814) exemplifies the amorous frivolity of Rococo, whereas the *Cupid and Psyche* (fig. **19.2**) of Antonio Canova (1757–1822) displays the sweeping grandeur of Neoclassical.

In the Clodion, a lusty satyr (see box, p. 703) leans backward, drawing a nude bacchante toward him. She pours wine into his mouth while embracing him and straddling his thigh. The satyr's excitement is revealed by his raised right leg, which echoes the bacchante's left leg. The figures seem prevented from toppling over only by the satyr's hand resting on the rock. Twisted poses and diagonal planes animate and open the space, pointing outward from the core of the statue. The surface motion created by the satyr's rippling muscles and the rough textures of his shaggy hair underline the orgiastic nature of the encounter.

19.1 Clodion (Claude Michel), *Nymph and Satyr Carousing*, c. 1780–90. Terra-cotta; 23¼ in. (59.1 cm) high. Metropolitan Museum of Art, New York, Bequest of Benjamin Altman, 1913 (14.40.687).

Satyrs and Bacchantes

In Greek mythology, satyrs are woodland creatures, part man and part goat, that symbolize male lust. Satyr plays, in which satyrs made fun of human tragedies, were performed in Classical Greece and became the basis of satire in Western literature. The bacchantes were priestesses of Dionysos, the Greek god of wine. The term *bacchante* is related to the Roman wine god, Bacchus, and a *bacchanal* is an orgiastic, drunken party.

19.2 Antonio Canova, *Cupid and Psyche*, 1787–1793. Marble; 5 ft. 1 in. (1.55 m) high. Louvre, Paris. The tragic character of the myth of Cupid and Psyche is more suited than satyrs and bacchantes to the Neoclassical aesthetic. Their romance was fated to end if Psyche should see Cupid. Unable to restrain her curiosity, Psyche did look at her lover and so lost him.

The Napoleonic empire, 1812.

Canova's *Cupid and Psyche* portrays an embrace of another kind. Its subject is the ill-fated romance between Cupid and Psyche. It is a tale that contains the seeds of tragedy, and so this sculpture rises above the frivolous anonymity of the Clodion. The Canova is reminiscent of Classical ballet, with its smooth surfaces, broad poses, and gestures encompassing and enclosing a space beyond the embrace itself. Cupid leans over, his wings spreading out in an eloquent V-shape. Their formal upward motion suggests the rising of the soul and the lofty nature of true love. Psyche lies back in a pose that recalls the traditional reclining nude, and curves her arms about Cupid's head in a gesture that is at once open and closed. It is the tragic grandeur of Canova's sculpture that allies it with the Neoclassical style, in contrast to the "satirical" Rococo revelry of Clodion.

Art in the Service of the State: Jacques-Louis David

The political aspects of the Neoclassical style derived from its associations with heroic subject matter, formal clarity, and the impression of stability and solidity. It also contained implicit references to Athenian democracy and the Roman Republic. In artistic terms, the Neoclassical style was a reaction against Rococo. However, the political preoccupations of the Neoclassical style arose directly from the questioning stance that had characterized eighteenth-century Enlightenment thought. Increasing popular resentment of the abuses of the monarchy was a logical development of the Enlightenment, which championed the rights of the individual. After the French Revolution, Napoleon Bonaparte adopted the Neoclassical style to sustain

19.3 Jacques-Louis David, *Oath of the Horatii,* 1784–1785. Oil on canvas; approx. 11 ft. × 14 ft. (3.35 × 4.27 m). Louvre, Paris. Although the event is not described in Classical sources, the story of the Horatii was known from a tragedy by Pierre Corneille, the 17th-century French dramatist. Rome and Alba Longa had agreed to settle their differences by "triple" combat between two sets of triplets—the Horatii of Rome and the Curiatii of Alba—rather than by all-out war.

his political image—first as general and consul, and later as emperor.

The leading Neoclassical painter, Jacques-Louis David (1748–1825), appealed to the republican sentiments associated with Classical antiquity. His *Oath of the Horatii* (fig. **19.3**), first exhibited in 1785, illustrates an event from Roman tradition in which honor and self-sacrifice prevailed (see caption). The figures wear Roman dress, and the scene takes place in a Roman architectural setting, before three round arches resting on a type of Doric column. Framed by the center arch, Horatius raises his sons' three swords, on which they swear an oath of allegiance to Rome. Within a rectangular space composed of clear verticals and horizontals, and subdued by muted color, the gestures of the soldiers are vigorous, determined, and somewhat theatrical. They express a fervor that links Roman patriotism of the past to the contemporary passions of the French—first for reform and later for revolution. The women and children, in contrast, collapse at the right in a series of fluid, rhythmic curves, which reflect the view that they are more emotional. They include the sisters of the Horatii, one of whom is engaged to an enemy combatant and is overcome by her tragic destiny. In the shadows, the wife of Horatius comforts her grandchildren.

The painting was commissioned by Louis XVI as part of a program aimed at the moral improvement of France. Although the modern viewer tends to see it as a piece of overtly revolutionary propaganda, the ideals embodied in Neoclassical painting were in fact appealing to both the royalist supporters of the king and their republican opponents. The irony of the political subtext was apparently lost on Louis's minister for the arts, who approved the painting.

In the *Death of Socrates* (fig. **19.4**), painted in 1787, David used a subject from Greek history to exemplify individual heroism and self-sacrifice in the service of intellectual freedom. The Athenians objected to Socrates' teaching and condemned him for corrupting the youth. He was offered a choice of exile or death but, as recorded by Plato in *The Apology,* refused to abandon his principles and chose to die. David portrays the last moments of Socrates, who

19.4 Jacques-Louis David, *Death of Socrates,* 1787. Oil on canvas; 4 ft. 3 in. × 6 ft. 5¼ in. (1.29 × 1.96 m). Metropolitan Museum of Art, New York (Wolfe Fund, 1931, Catherine Lorillard Wolfe Collection).

— **CONNECTIO**

See figure 14.37 *Plato,* detail of Raphael, *School of Athens,* 1509–1511.

continues teaching to the very end. One disciple turns away as he hands him the goblet of poison hemlock. Others, wearing Classical dress, gather at the right and listen intently to Socrates' words.

The architecture of the prison, with its round arch, is depicted with the same clarity and boxlike construction as the *Oath of the Horatii.* Not only is the subject drawn from antiquity, but the specific gesture of Socrates—his hand raised and his finger pointing upward as if toward a higher truth—is a visual quotation from Raphael's Plato in the *School of Athens* (see fig. 14.35). The high moral tone of David's *Oath of the Horatii* and the *Death of Socrates,* the former patriotic and the latter intellectual, made them exemplary images for a France on the verge of revolution. In 1789, two years after David painted the *Death of Socrates,* angry mobs in Paris stormed the Bastille and ignited the Revolution.

In the *Death of Marat* (fig. **19.5**), commissioned during the Reign of Terror, David used the principles of the Neoclassical style in the service of contemporary political events (see caption). Both David and Marat were members of the Jacobin

19.5 Jacques-Louis David, *Death of Marat,* 1793. Oil on canvas; approx. 5 ft. 3 in. × 4 ft. 1 in. (1.60 × 1.25 m). Musées Royaux des Beaux-Arts de Belgique, Brussels. On July 13, 1793, Marat was stabbed in his bathtub by Charlotte Corday, a supporter of the conservative Girondin group. Inscribed on the crate supporting Marat's inkwell, pen, and papers is a combined personal and political message. David dedicated the painting "À Marat, David" (To Marat, from David) and dated it "L'An Deux" (The Year Two), the second year of the French revolutionary calendar.

movement, a group of revolutionary extremists and the patrons of David's painting. David himself was elected to the National Convention and voted to send Louis XVI to the guillotine. When Robespierre, the minister who presided over the Reign of Terror, fell, David was imprisoned twice. But he regained favor under Napoleon, who appointed him his imperial painter and granted him a barony. After Napoleon's exile, David left France and died in Brussels in 1825.

The painting, which is set in a clear cubic space, like the *Horatii* and the *Socrates,* depicts a recent, rather than a Classical, event. David's *Marat* has affinities with Christian images of the dead Christ, which emphasizes Marat's role as a political martyr. The influence of Caravaggio's tenebrism can be seen in the darkened background, from which the figure of Marat emerges into light. In both form and content, therefore, David's *Marat* represents intellectual and political enlightenment.

David has idealized Marat in Classical fashion, for his body was in fact ravaged by a skin disease. He found relief from this by soaking in the bath. At the same time, however, the stab wound is visible, and the red bath water has stained the sheet. Marat has placed a writing surface over the tub, and he holds the letter sent by his killer, which reads: *"Il suffit que je sois bien malheureuse pour avoir droit à votre bienveillance,"* meaning "I just have to be unhappy to merit your goodwill."

Marat was the victim of a deceitful woman, and David displays her deceit for all the world to see as political propaganda. The knife that Charlotte Corday has dropped on the floor beside the tub is contrasted ironically with the quill pen still in Marat's limp hand. The instrument of violence and death is thus opposed to the pen, which is associated in this picture with revolutionary political writing. That Marat the revolutionary was stabbed by a member of a more conservative party enhances the tragic irony of David's picture.

Napoleon and the Arts

From 1799, David created images for his new patron, Napoleon Bonaparte, who was first consul of France (see map). His *Napoleon at Saint Bernard Pass* of 1800 (fig. **19.6**), which depicts Napoleon crossing the Alps, is clearly in the tradition of Roman equestrian portraits. Napoleon wears full military regalia and sits proudly astride a splendid rearing white charger. The textures of his uniform and the horse trappings are rendered in precise detail. The wind blows at their backs, whipping forward the horse's tail and mane. Napoleon points ahead, toward the peak of the mountain, and simultaneously looks down at the viewer. His dramatic gesture and the horse's pose are intimations of early Romanticism. David's glorification of his patron is evident from the fact that on this occasion Napoleon actually rode a mule.

David's Neoclassicism is used here in the interests of the new political regime in France. Napoleon's charger

19.6 Jacques-Louis David, *Napoleon at Saint Bernard Pass*, 1800. Oil on canvas; 8 ft. × 7 ft. 7 in. (2.44 × 2.31 m). Musée National du Château de Versailles.

19.7 Jean-François-Thérèse Chalgrin et al., Arc de Triomphe, Paris, 1806–1836. 164 ft. (49.99 m) high.

CONNECTIONS

See figure 7.38. Arch of Titus, A.D. 81.

looms up and dominates the picture, in contrast to the distant soldiers, who struggle with their cannons and are obscured by the misty sky. David relates Napoleon to his illustrious imperial predecessors by the inscriptions "KAROLUS MAGNUS" (Charlemagne) and "ANNIBAL" (Hannibal) carved in stone under "BONAPARTE" in the left foreground.

When Napoleon was crowned emperor in 1804, he set about commissioning monuments throughout Paris with a view to re-creating the grandeur of imperial Rome. To commemorate his military successes, he conceived the idea of constructing an Arc de Triomphe (Arch of Triumph) (fig. **19.7**) that would be based on the triumphal arches of ancient Rome. From these, the architect adopted the relief sculptures on the upper piers, the decorative cornices, and the row of metopes and triglyphs below the upper cornice. There were no columns or pilasters on the Arc de Triomphe, and the design was elaborated later by adding sculptures to the lower parts of the piers. The arch was commissioned in 1806 but only completed in 1836, twenty-one years after Napoleon's defeat at Waterloo in 1815 (he was exiled to the island of Saint Helena the following year). At 164 feet (49.99 m) high, it was the largest arch ever built; it stands at a busy intersection in the Place Charles de Gaulle (formerly named the Place de l'Étoile).

19.8 Charles Percier and Pierre F. L. Fontaine, Place Vendôme column, Paris, 1810. Marble with bronze spiral frieze.

Napoleon also commissioned a monumental freestanding Doric column of marble, surmounted by a statue of himself, for the Place Vendôme in Paris (fig. **19.8**). Decorated with spiral reliefs depicting events from his campaign of 1805, it was directly inspired by Trajan's Column in Rome (see fig. 7.34). The bronze from which the frieze was made had been melted down from the captured artillery of the Austrian and Prussian armies. In the column, as in the Arc de Triomphe, Napoleon expressed his view that architecture and sculpture inspired by ancient Rome would

CONNECTIONS

See figure 7.34. Trajan's Column, dedicated A.D. 113.

enhance both his claim to the throne of France and his image as heir of the Roman emperors.

With a similar purpose in mind, Napoleon brought the sculptor Canova to Paris from Rome and in 1808 commissioned him to carve a life-sized marble sculpture of his sister Pauline (fig. **19.9**). Pauline's proportions are Classical, and she is nude from the waist up. Although she lounges on an Empire-style divan, her pose recalls that of the traditional reclining Venus.

Marie-Guillemine Benoist Napoleon also enlisted the services of Marie-Guillemine Benoist (1768–1826), who painted several portraits of him. Benoist was the daughter of a government official. She studied with Vigée-Lebrun and began her career as a portraitist in pastel. Later she studied with David and in 1791 exhibited two history paintings. When she married a royalist, her career declined, and she was in constant danger under the Reign of Terror. Napoleon awarded her an annual pension.

David's influence is apparent in Benoist's *Portrait of a Negress* of 1800 (fig. **19.10**). Like Canova's *Pauline*, the figure is partly nude from the waist up and is in the tradition of the reclining nude female. She combines aspects of Classicism and Romanticism, reflecting the overlap of the two styles in the late eighteenth and early nineteenth centuries. The figure stands out against a plain background, and the dark brown skin contrasts sharply with the classicizing white drapery. At the same time, Benoist has increased the figure's exotic, Romantic character by adding the turban and the gold earring. But the clear edges, the smooth texture of the paint, and the Neoclassical drapery accentuate the unexpected impact made by a black woman in a conventional European tradition.

19.10 Marie-Guillemine Benoist, *Portrait of a Negress*, 1800. Oil on canvas; 31⅝ in. × 25⅝ in. (80.3 × 65.1 cm). Louvre, Paris.

19.9 Antonio Canova, *Maria Paolina Borghese as Venus*, 1808. Marble; 5 ft. 2⅞ in. × 6 ft. 6¾ in. (1.60 × 2.00 m), including divan. Borghese Gallery, Rome.

19.11 Jean-Auguste-Dominique Ingres, *Madame Rivière,* 1805. Oil on canvas; 3 ft. 9 in. × 3 ft. (1.16 × 0.90 m). Louvre, Paris.

Jean-Auguste-Dominique Ingres

The career of another of David's students who worked for Napoleon, Jean-Auguste-Dominique Ingres (1780–1867), also embodies the interplay of Neoclassicism and Romanticism. There are already hints of Romantic taste for the exotic in Benoist's *Negress,* but Ingres' work also retains traces of Mannerist elegance. His portrait of *Madame Rivière* (fig. **19.11**), painted in 1805, continues the tradition of formal clarity, interest in rich detail, and smooth texture that he learned in David's studio. Placed in an oval frame, Madame Rivière reclines on velvet cushions, which are draped with an elaborately patterned shawl. Its blues echo the velvet, while a slightly diaphanous white veil flutters from behind her head. Her black, piercing eyes repeat the curls, which are derived from Ingres' study of Greek vase painting. The soft shading of her flesh is consistent with the soft material textures and her relaxed, somewhat languid pose. Despite the Classical allusions of the figure, she is clothed in the garb of early nineteenth-century French aristocracy.

19.12 Jean-Auguste-Dominique Ingres, *Napoleon Enthroned,* 1806. Oil on canvas; 8 ft. 8 in. × 5 ft. 5¼ in. (2.59 × 1.55 m). Musée de l'Armée, Paris.

METHODS OF INTERPRETATION

Napoleon's Political Iconography

In 1804, just fifteen years after the outbreak of the French Revolution, Napoleon Bonaparte declared himself emperor of France. He enacted several important social and educational reforms and agreed with the pope that Catholicism would be the country's official religion. Above all, however, Napoleon wanted France (and especially himself) to dominate the world. By 1810, he controlled the entire west coast of Europe. He also became one of the world's greatest art plunderers. Like the conquering rulers of antiquity, Napoleon looted the national treasures of his defeated enemies and used them to found the Napoleonic Museum. He combined the plundered works with the royal collection already in the Louvre, creating a magnificent display of European art from ancient Greece and Rome to his own era.

Napoleon's military genius notwithstanding, his personal grandiosity destroyed him. He made a number of political misjudgments and military blunders that eventually caused his downfall. Indeed, the name of his last battle, fought in Belgium on June 18, 1815, has become synonymous with defeat—the Battle of Waterloo.

In 1806, two years after Napoleon became emperor, the portrait in figure **19.12,** which was commissioned by the French legislature, was exhibited at the Salon. It depicts Napoleon as a deified Roman emperor in all his imperial splendor, recalling the fussiness of Rococo and the exaggeration of Mannerism. On the other hand, the clarity and precision of the details are characteristic of Neoclassical style. Everywhere, the brushstrokes are submerged to enhance the illusion of texture. Ingres' smooth, highly finished surfaces were characteristic of Academic painting rather than of Romanticism (see Chapter 20), which stressed the material quality of the media. Ingres' fondness for rich textures is expressed in the red velvet (red was the color of Roman emperors), ermine, and gold, all of which finally overwhelm the emperor. Napoleon is shown in a way that is reminiscent of the frontal depiction of Christ and the saints in Byzantine icons, as well as the Roman emperors. Ingres thus characterizes Napoleon as a ruler imbued with the power of imperial Rome and sanctioned by God.

As the "head" of the state body, it is significant that the only visible part of Napoleon's body is the head. For the rest, he is covered in signs of wealth, kingship, and divinity; he is dressed in ermine, red velvet, silk, lace, and gold and silver. A number of iconographic elements allude to antiquity—the laurel crown was awarded to Greek athletes victorious in the Olympic Games and to Renaissance poets in imitation of ancient Roman literary ceremonies. The eagles, which signified the divine status of the Roman emperor and were emblems of the Roman legions, adorn the capitals of the columns on either side of the throne and the carpet beneath the throne. Our gaze, in fact, enters the picture at the lower step and follows the eagle upward to the enthroned Napoleon. We thus literally "look up to" the emperor, signaling his domination over us as viewers as he dominated nineteenth-century Europe. By raising up Napoleon, the artist disguises the ruler's small stature, just as short leading men in Hollywood are filmed at angles or on hidden platforms that make them appear tall.

In addition to Christ and the Roman emperors, Ingres' Napoleon is associated with French kings and with Charlemagne (who also allied himself with the Classical tradition). In his right hand Napoleon extends the scepter of Charlemagne, and his left holds the staff surmounted by the ivory hand of justice, signifying kingship in the French Middle Ages. Formally, the diagonals of the staffs create an asymmetrical, open triangle so that each of the top two angles are accentuated by a hand—Napoleon's own right hand to the viewer's left and the ivory hand that makes the Christian gesture of blessing to the viewer's right. Reinforcing Napoleon's association with Christian divinity is the broad, haloesque curve made by the back of the throne, which frames his head. In this image, therefore, Ingres has combined the political connotations of Roman imperial power with the divine imagery of Christian tradition.

Oedipus

The myth of Oedipus is given its definitive literary form in Sophokles' play *Oidipos Tyrannos* (*Oedipus the King*). Oedipus' father, King Laios of Thebes, had been warned by an oracle that his son would kill him. He therefore drove a stake through his son's foot and left him to die on a mountain. A shepherd couple discovered Oedipus and raised him as their own son. Later, Oedipus learned from the oracle that he was destined to kill his father and marry his mother. To avoid this fate, Oedipus left home. Nearing the city of Thebes, he came to a fork in the road where he encountered a man who refused to let him pass. Oedipus killed the man and continued on his way. He met the Sphinx on the outskirts of Thebes and solved her riddle: "What walks on four legs in the morning, two legs in the afternoon, and three legs in the evening?" The answer: "Man." (As a baby, he crawls on all fours; then he walks on two legs; and finally he walks with a cane.) The prominent foot in the lower left corner of Ingres' painting refers both to the name *Oedipus* (which means "swollen foot" in Greek) and to the riddle's emphasis on walking.

The Thebans rejoiced at the destruction of the Sphinx and gave their widowed queen, Jocasta, to Oedipus in marriage. Years later, as king of Thebes and the father of four children by Jocasta, Oedipus is told that he is the cause of a plague ravaging the city. On learning that he has committed patricide and incest—for Laios was the man at the crossroads and Jocasta his mother—Oedipus blinds himself.

This myth has been taken up in various forms by artists and writers ever since. In the early twentieth century, Sigmund Freud named the Oedipus complex after it, believing it to be the core of child development and the nucleus of every neurosis.

19.13 Jean-Auguste-Dominique Ingres, *Oedipus and the Sphinx,* 1808. Oil on canvas; 6 ft. 2⅜ in. × 4 ft. 8⅝ in. (1.89 × 1.44 m). Louvre, Paris.

Drawing on Greek mythology, Ingres painted an *Oedipus and the Sphinx* (fig. **19.13**) in 1808. Oedipus (see box) is shown solving the riddle of the Sphinx as a frightened Theban rushes off toward the Greek city in the background. Oedipus' head, particularly his profile, recalls Greek statuary, but his muscular torso is a departure from the Classical ideal. The bones and the foot in the lower left corner, which are the remains of the Sphinx's victims, and the Sphinx herself are also unclassical because they impart a disturbing sense of mystery. Ingres thus combines themes and motifs from Classical antiquity with certain characteristics that heralded the nineteenth-century Romantic movement.

It was in his "odalisques" that Ingres achieved his most successful synthesis of Neoclassical clarity, rich, aristocratic textures, and a Romantic taste for the exotic. (An odalisque is a harem girl, from *oda,* meaning a room in a Turkish harem.) Ingres' *Grande Odalisque* (fig. **19.14**), exhibited in 1814 (the year of Napoleon's abdication), is the

19.14 Jean-Auguste-Dominique Ingres, *Grande Odalisque,* 1814. Oil on canvas; approx. 2 ft. 11¼ in. × 5 ft. 4¾ in. (0.89 × 1.65 m). Louvre, Paris.

CONNECTIONS

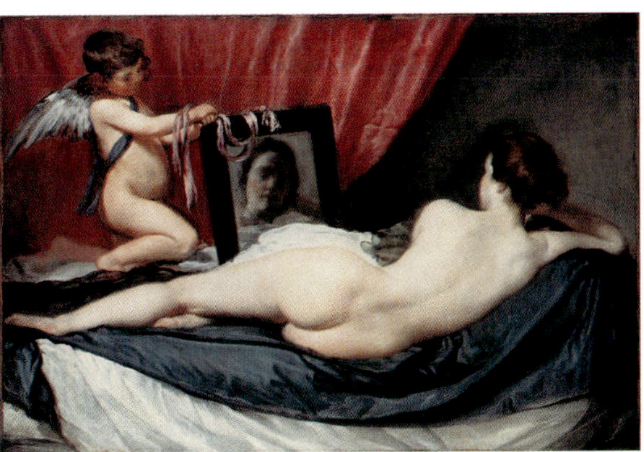

See figure 17.54. Diego Velázquez, *Venus with a Mirror (Rokeby Venus),* c. 1648.

best example. The idealized, reclining nude is seen from the back, as is Velázquez's *Venus with a Mirror* (see fig. 17.55). But here the figure turns to gaze at the observer. In contrast to the painterliness that obscures Velázquez's Venus, Ingres' nude has precise edges and a clear form. At the same time, however, the odalisque remains aloof and somewhat distant by comparison with the Baroque Venus. She is removed from everyday contemporary French experience by an exotic setting filled with illusionistic textures—the silk curtain and sheets, the peacock feathers of the fan, the fur bed covering, the headdress, and the hookah (a Turkish pipe in which the smoke is cooled by passing through water). The *Grande Odalisque* illustrates Ingres' love of clarity, which he associated with line—hence his Academic motto: "Drawing is the probity of art." Nevertheless, he, more than the purely Neoclassical David, was attracted to the Romantic elements of sensuality and color.

Developments in America

The American Revolution preceded the French Revolution by only a few years. As in France, the intent of the American Revolution was liberation from monarchy. But the additional factor of throwing off the yoke of a foreign ruler made the Revolution in America somewhat different from its French counterpart. Once liberated from the British throne, which was then occupied by King George III, America abandoned monarchy completely. The system designed by Jefferson and the other framers of the Constitution resulted in a smoother transition of power than in France and a more stable form of government.

In America, the Revolution not only signified a political break with its colonial origins, it also marked a departure from the pre-Revolutionary "Colonial Georgian" style, named after the British king. Just as republican Rome was the political model to which the newly independent colonies aspired, so Roman architecture was more closely imitated in the early period of independence. Since this period (c. 1780–1810) coincided with the establishment of many United States government institutions, the style is referred to as the Federal style.

Chronology of the American Campaign for Independence

1776 Declaration of Independence. The colonies declare independence from Britain, marking the beginning of the American Revolution.

1787 The Constitution of the United States is signed.

1789 George Washington is inaugurated as the first president of the United States.

1790 Washington, D.C., is founded as the nation's capital.

1801 Thomas Jefferson is inaugurated as the third president of the United States.

The Architecture of Thomas Jefferson

No single American embodied the principles of Neoclassicism more than Thomas Jefferson (1743–1826). In 1789, the leading French sculptor, Jean-Antoine Houdon (1741–1828), carved a marble portrait bust of Jefferson (fig. **19.15**) during his stay in France as United States minister to that country (1785–1789). Houdon captured an air of kindly self-

The United States during Jefferson's presidency, c. 1803.

19.15 Jean-Antoine Houdon, *Bust of Thomas Jefferson, frontal view,* 1789. White marble on white marble base; 21½ in. (54.6 cm) high. Museum of Fine Arts, Boston, George Nixon Black Fund (inv. 34.129). Jefferson was a member of the Continental Congress of 1775–1776 and was principally responsible for drafting the Declaration of Independence. He was governor of Virginia 1779–1781, U.S. minister in France 1785–1789, secretary of state under George Washington 1789–1793, vice president 1796–1801, and president 1801–1809.

confidence and suggested his sitter's profound intellect. The indentation by the side of Jefferson's jutting chin, his smile, and the slight furrow of his brow convey the impression of a composed, thoughtful individual. The portrait bust itself was a type derived from ancient Rome and therefore further reflects the Neoclassical tastes of both Houdon and Jefferson.

Jefferson's views on contemporary architecture also reveal his Classical education and humanist outlook. Although Jefferson was a native of Virginia, which was then the wealthiest and most populous of the states (see map), he disliked the houses of Virginia and wrote that they were "very rarely constructed of stone and brick. . . . It is impossible to devise things more ugly, uncomfortable, and happily more perishable." He described the buildings of colonial Williamsburg, which he knew from his student days at the College of William and Mary, as "rude, misshapen piles, which, but that they have roofs, would be taken for brick-kilns."[1] In addition to his other accomplishments, Jefferson studied Classical and Palladian architectural theory, and owned the first copy in America of Palladio's *Four Books on Architecture.* His work as an architect produced three of the finest Neoclassical buildings in America.

Jefferson began the construction of his own home, Monticello (Italian for "Little Mountain"), in 1769 (fig. **19.16**). It is located on a hilltop outside Charlottesville, Virginia. Jefferson designed Monticello himself and, despite frequent absences, supervised its construction over a period of more than forty years. The house was planned and built in two stages. At first (1769–1784) it was designed as a building with a double portico, two stories high. On the east façade, a second-story Ionic Order was to be superimposed on a ground-floor Doric, a concept that Jefferson borrowed from Palladio, but it was never executed.

In 1789, Jefferson returned to America with new plans for enlarging and remodeling Monticello, which he began to put into effect in 1794, soon after his resignation as secretary of state. Since Palladio's most admired designs had a single story, Jefferson decided that he too wanted a house that would appear to be one story. The final result was a building that seemed to have only one high-ceilinged floor. In fact, however, the entablature and balustrade conceal a second and a third floor, both containing bedrooms. The windows for these rooms are near floor level, and on the east façade they look from the outside like the top sashes of the ground-floor windows.

19.16 Thomas Jefferson, Monticello, near Charlottesville, Virginia, 1769–1784 (rebuilt 1794–1809).

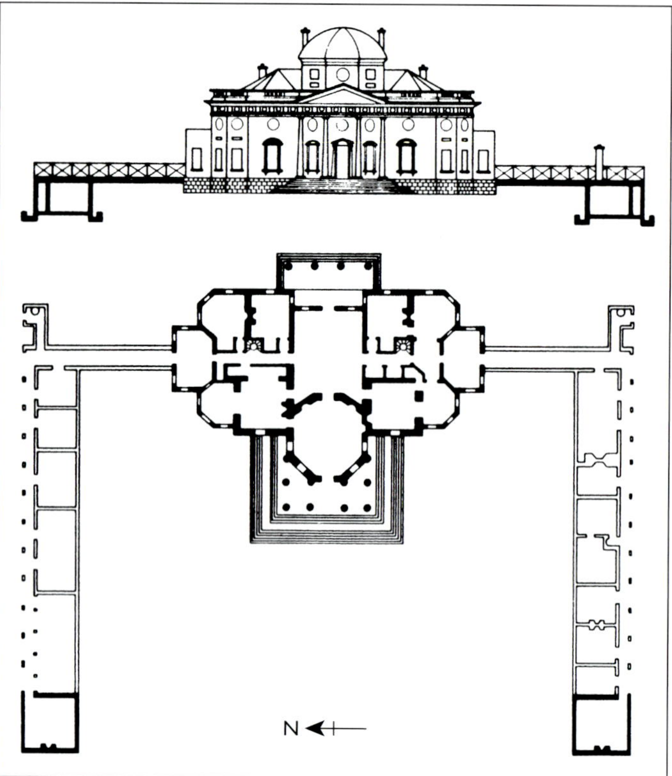

19.17 Plan and elevation of Monticello. (From W. Blaser.)

The remodeling of the ground floor can be seen from the plan (fig. **19.17**), where the shaded areas represent the old floor plan. The new plan, which is more than twice the size of the old, includes a large entrance hall with a gallery, a suite of rooms (bedroom, library, and study) on the south side of the house for Jefferson's personal use, and a corresponding set of public rooms on the north side. The house itself is connected to two small pavilions by a wooden boardwalk. Located underneath the boardwalk and below the level of the lawn were the service areas of the house—the kitchen, cellar, icehouse, stables, and so forth. The symmetry of these side extensions, or "dependencies" as they were called, is another feature that Jefferson borrowed from Palladio's country estates. Jefferson's design for Monticello, in particular the dome and the two entrances, was also influenced by that of Chiswick House (see fig. 18.20).

Monticello's individual rooms, its dome, and central drum are octagons, which was a favorite shape of Jefferson's. The octagon tended to broaden the corners of a building and expand the interior spaces. Roman influence is evident in the dome and east portico, which is colonnaded in the Doric Order. Just as republican Rome represented Jefferson's political ideal, so Monticello fulfilled the Classical ideal that he found lacking in the previous domestic architecture of colonial America.

While in France, Jefferson had become familiar with the elegant Paris *hôtels* and French Neoclassical architecture. He visited the ruins of Roman Gaul and saw the so-called Maison Carrée at Nîmes in southern France. This was a small, well-preserved Roman temple, similar to the Temple of Portunus (see fig. 7.23). Jefferson used it as the model for a new State Capitol of Virginia in Richmond. Figure **19.18** shows the projecting Ionic portico, surmounted by a Classical pediment.

19.18 Thomas Jefferson, State Capitol, Richmond, Virginia, 1785–1789.

CONNECTIONS

See figure 7.23. Temple of Portunus, late 2nd century B.C.

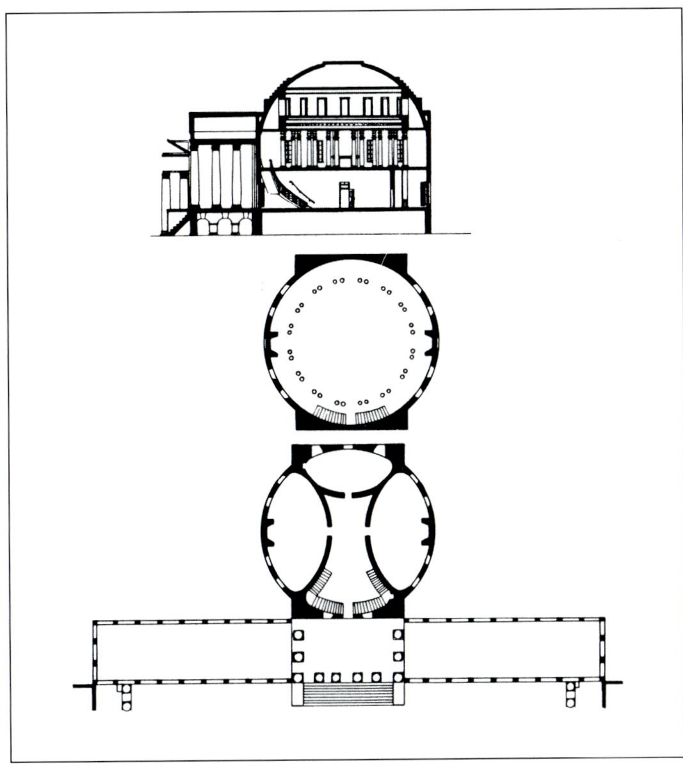

19.19 Thomas Jefferson, plan and section of the Rotunda, University of Virginia, Charlottesville. (From W. Blaser.)

The pride and joy of Jefferson's later years was the University of Virginia, the first state-supported educational establishment, located just a few miles from Monticello. Its centerpiece is the Rotunda (figs. **19.19** and **19.20**), originally the library. Although its proportions are somewhat taller, its inspiration is the Pantheon in Rome (see fig. 7.27). Among the purely Jeffersonian features are an entablature encircling the building and two layers of windows (pedimented on the ground floor, plain on the second).

On either side of the Rotunda, framing the central lawn, are two symmetrical rows of low, colonnaded buildings, which were (and still are) student quarters. These link a series of pavilions, built in the form of Roman temples. Each pavilion faithfully reproduces an architectural order according to a Classical prototype. The pavilions also housed the academic departments, with classrooms on the ground floor and living quarters for the professors on the upper floor.

19.20 Thomas Jefferson, Rotunda, University of Virginia, Charlottesville, 1817–1826. Jefferson was the first rector of the university and described himself on his tombstone as "Father of the University." Both the curriculum and the architectural conception were a tribute to Jeffersonian humanist principles. In the quality of its individual parts and the harmony of the whole environment, Jefferson's "academical village," as he called it, is a masterpiece of the Federal style.

CONNECTIONS

See figure 7.27. The Pantheon, A.D. 117–125.

John Trumbull's *Declaration of Independence*

In 1817, President James Madison commissioned John Trumbull to paint four pictures illustrating American independence; they were to hang in the Rotunda of the Capitol building in Washington, D.C. One of these was the *Declaration of Independence* (fig. **19.21**). The Declaration was a product of Enlightenment philosophy and of the belief that reason could impose an intelligent order on human society. According to Trumbull's autobiography, he was given advice on the composition by Jefferson himself.

All the signers are present in the painting, in which the solemn dignity of the occasion is portrayed. Formally, it is a construction of rectangular space, with simple doors and an unadorned Doric frieze. The furniture is austere, and the figures wear plain, contemporary American dress. Contrasting with the overall austerity are the sweeping—and slightly more colorful—diagonals of the flags and the drum on the far wall. These refer to the battles that had made it possible to achieve the aims of the Declaration. Visually, the flags unite the long diagonal of mostly seated figures at the left with the central group in front of the desk and the seated figures at the right. The tallest figure, distinguished by a long red vest, is Jefferson. He hands a copy of the Declaration to John Hancock of Massachusetts. Standing to Jefferson's left is the stocky Benjamin Franklin of Pennsylvania, and at the left in the foreground is John Adams of Massachusetts. Between Adams and Jefferson are Roger Sherman of Connecticut and Robert Livingston of New York.

19.21 John Trumbull, *Declaration of Independence*, 1818. Oil on canvas; 12 × 18 ft. (3.66 × 5.49 m). U.S. Capitol Rotunda, Washington, D.C. Trumbull came from a Calvinist family of Connecticut. He fought in the Revolution and was educated at Harvard. In 1780, he went to London and studied with Benjamin West, who influenced his history paintings. He also painted many portraits.

Greenough's *George Washington*

Shortly after the University of Virginia was completed, the United States Congress decided to erect a statue to commemorate George Washington in a grand manner. In 1832, the commission was given to Horatio Greenough (1805–1852), America's first professional sculptor, then living in Italy. The colossal marble statue that he produced (fig. **19.22**) was inspired by Phidias's Early Classical sculpture of Zeus in the temple at Olympia (see fig. 5.36). Although this work, one of the Seven Wonders of the ancient world, was lost, it was known from ancient descriptions and from representations on coins. Figure **19.23** shows a nineteenth-century illustration based on the original statue of Zeus by Phidias at Olympia.

The imposing presence, monumental scale, and grand gestures of the *Washington* also have a Romantic quality. Nude from the waist up, the figure points upward in the manner of David's Socrates (see fig. 19.4) and Raphael's Plato (see fig. 14.36). The statue embodies the various aspects of Washington—man of action, political philosopher, ruler, and general. A frontal pose and imposing presence, combined with a lion throne, create the impression of a powerful leader. Unfortunately, the statue did not reach America until 1841, by which time tastes had changed. The Neoclassical style was no longer in fashion, and the statue was criticized for its partial nudity. It was placed outside the Capitol building in Washington, D.C., where it began to erode; today it sits unceremoniously inside the rotunda of the National Museum of American Art, part of the Smithsonian Institution.

In the United States, as in western Europe, the purity of Neoclassicism gave way to Romanticism. In its own way, the Romantic movement, like the Neoclassical, had political, cultural, and literary significance, much of which is reflected in the visual arts.

19.22 Horatio Greenough, *George Washington,* 1832–1841. Marble; 11 ft. 4 in. × 8 ft. 6 in. × 6 ft. 10 in. (3.45 × 2.59 × 2.08 m). National Museum of American Art, Smithsonian Institution, Washington, D.C.

19.23 Antoine Chrysostome Quatremère de Quincy, *Reconstruction of Zeus at Olympia,* frontispiece to *Le Jupiter Olympien,* 1815.

	Style/Period	Works of Art	Cultural/Historical Developments
1730	NEOCLASSICAL 1730–1800  **Jefferson, Monticello**	Jefferson, Monticello (**19.16**), Charlottesville Clodion, *Intoxication of Wine* (**19.1**) David, *Oath of the Horatii* (**19.3**) Jefferson, State Capitol, Richmond (**19.18**) Canova, *Cupid and Psyche* (**19.2**) David, *Death of Socrates* (**19.4**) Houdon, *Thomas Jefferson* (**19.15**) David, *Death of Marat* (**19.5**) 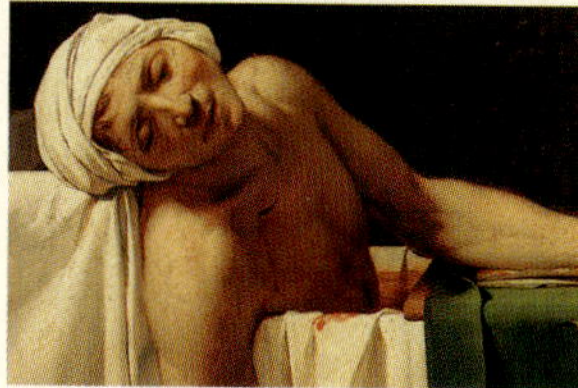 **David, *Death of Marat***	Lord Burlington promotes Neoclassical architecture in England (1725–1750) James Watt perfects the steam engine (1775) American Declaration of Independence (1776) American Revolutionary War (1776–1784) Edward Gibbon, *Decline and Fall of the Roman Empire* (1776–1788) French Revolution begins (1789) Thomas Paine, *Rights of Man* (1790) Wolfgang Amadeus Mozart, *Magic Flute* (1790) **Benoist, *Portrait of a Negress***
1800	1800–1810 	Benoist, *Portrait of a Negress* (**19.10**) David, *Napoleon at Saint Bernard Pass* (**19.6**) Ingres, *Madame Rivière* (**19.11**) Ingres, *Napoleon Enthroned* (**19.12**) Chalgrin et al., Arc de Triomphe (**19.7**), Paris Canova, *Maria Paolina Borghese as Venus* (**19.9**) Ingres, *Oedipus and the Sphinx* (**19.13**) Percier and Fontaine, Place Vendôme column (**19.8**), Paris **David, *Napoleon at Saint Bernard Pass***	Thomas Jefferson negotiates Louisiana Purchase (1803) Expedition to the Pacific Coast by Lewis and Clark (1803–1806) Napoleon proclaimed emperor of France (1804) Ludwig van Beethoven, the Eroica Symphony (1804) Lord Nelson defeats French fleet at Trafalgar (1805)  **Canova, *Maria Paolina Borghese as Venus***
1810 1840	1810–1840  **Jefferson, Rotunda, University of Virginia**	Ingres, *Grande Odalisque* (**19.14**) Quatremère de Quincy, *Reconstruction of Zeus at Olympia* (**19.23**) Jefferson, Rotunda, University of Virginia (**19.20**), Charlottesville Trumbull, *Declaration of Independence* (**19.21**) Greenough, *George Washington* (**19.22**) 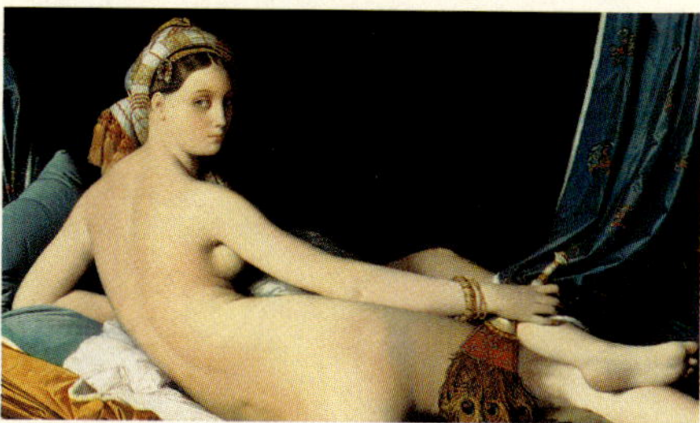 **Ingres, *Grande Odalisque***	Johann Wolfgang von Goethe, *Faust* (1808–1832) Napoleon retreats from Russia (1812) Lord Elgin brings sculptures from the Parthenon to England (1812) Jane Austen, *Pride and Prejudice* (1813) Stephenson's first steam locomotive (1814) Congress of Vienna (1814–1815) Napoleon defeated at Waterloo; exiled to Saint Helena (1815) University of Virginia founded by Thomas Jefferson (1817) Greece declares independence from Turkey (1822) James Fenimore Cooper, *Last of the Mohicans* (1826) Alexandre Dumas, *Three Musketeers* (1828) July Revolution; Louis-Philippe king of France (1830) Stendhal, *The Red and the Black* (1830) Alfred Lord Tennyson, "The Lady of Shalott" (1832) Honoré de Balzac, *Comédie Humaine* (1832–1850) Charles Dickens, *Oliver Twist* (1838)

20

Romanticism: The Late Eighteenth and Early Nineteenth Centuries

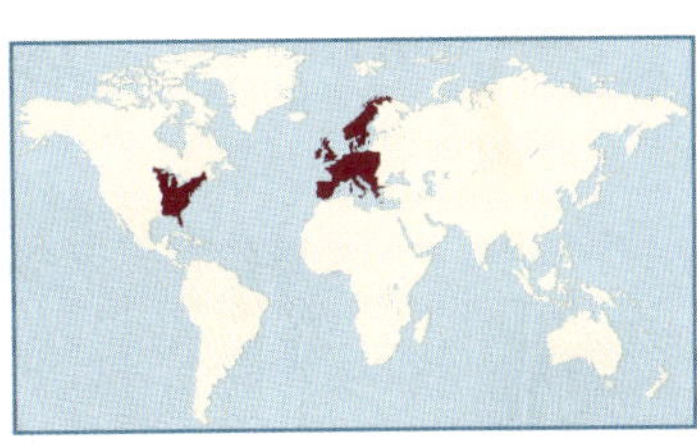

The Romantic Movement

The Romantic movement, like Neoclassicism, swept through western Europe and the United States. The term *Romantic* is derived from the Romance languages (French, Italian, Spanish, Portuguese, and Romanian) and from the medieval tales of chivalry and adventure written in those languages, such as the *Chanson de Roland* (Song of Roland). Romantic literature shares with the so-called "Gothic" novels and poems by English writers of the late eighteenth and early nineteenth centuries a haunting nostalgia for the past. The Romantic aesthetic of "long ago" and "far away" is conveyed in works with locales and settings that indicate the passage of time, such as ruined buildings and broken sculptures. To the extent that Neoclassicism expresses a nostalgia for antiquity, it too may be said to have a "Romantic" quality.

Whereas Neoclassicism has its roots in antiquity, the origins of Romanticism are found in the eighteenth century, especially in the work of the French philosopher Jean-Jacques Rousseau (see box). The effect of the Romantic movement on early nineteenth-century culture is evident not only in the visual arts, but also in politics, social philosophy, music, and literature (see box, p. 722).

It is impossible to assign precise dates to the Romantic movement. Historians generally agree, however, that the *Lyrical Ballads* of Wordsworth and Coleridge, which were published in 1798, are a seminal work, that the July Revolution of 1830 in France (see box) marks the high point in Romantic influence on politics, and that by 1848 enthusiasm for Romanticism was in decline.

Romanticism comprised a wide range of subject matter, which offered more thematic possibilities than Neoclassicism. In contrast to the Neoclassical virtues of order and clarity, the Romantics believed in emotional expression and sentiment. Instead of encouraging heroism on behalf of an

Chronology of Events in France

1814	Napoleon abdicates, and the Bourbon monarchy is restored under Louis XVIII (the Restoration).
1824	Charles X becomes king of France.
1830	The July Revolution. The Bourbons are overthrown and Louis-Philippe becomes "citizen-king" with limited powers. More citizens are given the right to vote for the legislature.
1848	The February Revolution. Louis-Philippe is overthrown, and the Second Republic begins. Napoleon's nephew, Louis-Napoleon, is elected president.
1852	Louis-Napoleon is proclaimed emperor (Napoleon III); the Second Empire begins.
1870	Louis-Napoleon abdicates following France's defeat in the Franco-Prussian War; the Third Republic begins.

Rousseau on the Return to Nature

Jean-Jacques Rousseau (1712–1778) was a leading eighteenth-century French philosopher. His writings inspired the French Revolution and also provided the philosophical underpinning of the Romantic movement. The artists and writers who subscribed to Rousseau's views are known as the "Romantics." Rousseau advocated a "return to nature." He believed in the concept of the "noble savage"—that humanity was born to live harmoniously with nature, free from vice, but had been corrupted by civilization and progress. Such ideas led to the political belief that the people themselves should rule. In his literary fiction, Rousseau created elaborate descriptions of natural beauty that were consistent with the Romantic aesthetic.

Romanticism in Music and Poetry

The various strains of Romanticism that are evident in the visual arts are also found in nineteenth-century music and poetry. In Romantic music, the expression of mood and feeling takes precedence over form and structure. Its antithesis is classical music, in which classical form and proportion predominate over emotional expression.

Romantic music was often based on literary themes, and literary or geographical references evoked various moods. Some of Hector Berlioz's overtures, for example, are based on Sir Walter Scott's historical novels, which are set in the Middle Ages. Felix Mendelssohn's "Italian" and "Scottish" Symphonies are based on the composer's travels in Italy and Scotland. The Polish mazurkas of Frédéric Chopin and the Hungarian rhapsodies of Franz Liszt reflect the strong nationalistic strains of Romanticism. In opera, the emotional and nationalistic intensity of the Romantic movement found its fullest expression in the works of Richard Wagner.

In English poetry, the leaders of Romanticism were William Wordsworth (1770–1850) and Samuel Taylor Coleridge (1772–1834). In 1798, they jointly published a collection of poems, *Lyrical Ballads,* the introduction to which served as a manifesto for the English Romantics.

Wordsworth's "The Solitary Reaper" conveys a sense of the melancholy oneness of humanity with an all-encompassing nature. The reaper is alone in a vast expanse of land when seen by the poet:

Behold her, single in the field,
Yon solitary Highland Lass!
Reaping and singing by herself;
Stop here, or gently pass!
Alone she cuts and binds the grain,
And sings a melancholy strain;
O listen! for the Vale profound
Is overflowing with the sound. (stanza I)

Other English poets of the Romantic movement included Lord Byron (1788–1824), Percy Bysshe Shelley (1792–1822), and John Keats (1795–1821). Byron's nostalgic yearning for ancient Greece is evident in much of his poetry:

The isles of Greece, the isles of Greece!
Where burning Sappho loved and sung,
Where grew the arts of war and peace,
Where Delos rose, and Phoebus sprung!
Eternal summer gilds them yet,
But all, except their sun, is set.
("Don Juan" III, lxxxvi)

Shelley's "Ozymandias" conveys the attraction of exotic locales and explores our ability to communicate with the past through time-worn artifacts:

I met a traveller from an antique land
Who said: "Two vast and trunkless legs of stone
Stand in the desert . . ."
And on the pedestal these words appear:
"My name is Ozymandias, king of kings:
Look on my works, ye Mighty, and despair!"
Nothing beside remains. Round the decay
Of that colossal wreck, boundless and bare,
The lone and level sands stretch far away.
(lines 1–3, 9–14)

In 1819, Shelley visited the Uffizi Gallery in Florence, where he saw a painting of Medusa's head, then attributed to Leonardo da Vinci. The head lies on the ground, crawling with lizards, insects, and snakes. Shelley's poem expresses the Romantic taste for the macabre, the appeal of death, and the theme of the aloof, unattainable woman:

It lieth, gazing on the midnight sky,
Upon the cloudy mountain-peak supine;
Below, far lands are seen tremblingly;
Its horror and its beauty are divine.
("On the Medusa of Leonardo da Vinci in the
Florentine Gallery," lines 1–4)

The aloof and unattainable woman, seen by the Romantics as cold and deathlike but nevertheless fascinating, is celebrated with a medieval flavor in Keats's "La Belle Dame sans Merci":

I saw pale kings and princes too,
Pale warriors, death-pale were they all;
They cried—"La Belle Dame sans Merci
Hath thee in thrall!" (lines 37–40)

abstract ideal in the Neoclassical manner, the Romantics were often partisan supporters of contemporary causes, such as the individual's struggle against the abuses of the state.

In addition to their nostalgia for the past and idealistic participation in current events, the Romantics were interested in the mind as the site of mysterious, unexplained, and possibly dangerous phenomena. For the first time in Western art, dreams and nightmares were depicted as internal events, with their source in the individual imagination, rather than as external, supernatural happenings. States of mind, including insanity, began to interest artists, whose studies anticipated Freud's theories of psychoanalysis at the end of the nineteenth century and the development of modern psychology in the twentieth.

Architecture

In architecture, the Romantic movement was marked by revivals of historical styles. The Gothic Revival had begun in the late eighteenth century with such buildings as Horace Walpole's Strawberry Hill (see fig. 18.23). Likewise, the Neoclassicism of Jefferson was a revival of ancient Greek and Roman forms, which were ideologically appropriate for a newly founded democracy.

The first important nineteenth-century public buildings in the Gothic style were the new Houses of Parliament in London (fig. **20.1**). These were constructed from 1836 to 1870 to replace the old palace of Westminster, which had been destroyed by fire in 1834 (see fig. 20.21). There was

20.1 Sir Charles Barry and Augustus W. N. Pugin, Houses of Parliament, London, 1836–1870.

CONNECTIONS

See figure 11.28. West façade, Amiens Cathedral, 1220–1269.

20.2 Richard Upjohn, Trinity Church, New York, 1841–1852.

considerable debate over whether the new Houses should be in the Classical or the Gothic style. In the end, Gothic prevailed because it was regarded as both the national and the more Christian style. In addition, it would be a reminder that the parliamentary system of government had been established in the Middle Ages.

A competition held for this commission was won by Sir Charles Barry (1795–1860), one of the most established English architects. His collaborator, Augustus Pugin (1812–1852), was responsible for the decoration and details. A Catholic convert and almost a cult figure in early Victorian England, Pugin was the most vocal crusader for the Gothic style; he proclaimed its moral and religious superiority as the "only correct expression of the faith, wants, and climate" of England. In his book *Contrasts,* Pugin discusses architecture as a reflection of society; and in *The True Principles of Pointed or Christian Architecture,* he writes that architecture should be judged by the highest standards of Christian morality.

The new Houses of Parliament have Gothic decoration and fixtures but retain formal symmetry. (The overall result reportedly disappointed Pugin, who thought it too "Greek.") Despite the strong vertical accent of the Victoria Tower in the southwest corner and the clock tower of Big Ben at the north, the Houses of Parliament lack the soaring quality of Gothic cathedrals (see fig. 11.28). Instead, when seen from a distance, they give an impression of low horizontality.

Architects in America as well as Europe were influenced by the Gothic Revival. Richard Upjohn (1802–1878), an English immigrant to America, built over forty Gothic Revival churches. He is best known for Trinity Church, which he built in the pure Perpendicular Gothic style, at the intersection of Wall Street and Broadway in New York City (fig. **20.2**). Its vaulting is of plaster, and the rest of the construction is stone. The deep chancel and elevated altar reflected the liturgical views of the High Church Anglican (Episcopalian) movement, to which Upjohn belonged. Trinity Church served a wealthy, urban parish, but Upjohn also designed churches built entirely of timber for poorer, rural

CONNECTIONS

See figure I.3. Taj Mahal, 1632–1648.

communities. *Upjohn's Rural Architecture,* published in 1852, was an illustrated handbook for the construction of inexpensive churches, chapels, and houses. These were largely of wood and provided the origin of the term *carpenter's Gothic.*

The Romantic vision of the Far East as a distant, exotic locale also became a source for nineteenth-century architecture. The Royal Pavilion (fig. **20.3**) in Brighton, a fashionable English seaside resort, was constructed for the prince regent by John Nash (1752–1835) in the Indian Gothic style (see fig. I.3). A mixture of minarets and onion domes, borrowed from Islamic architecture, covers a cast-iron framework. The Royal Pavilion echoes the Eastern forms that attracted Coleridge, whose "Kubla Khan" incorporates the exotic sounds of faraway places and suggests the typically Romantic taste for endless time and infinite space:

In Xanadu did Kubla Khan
A stately pleasure-dome decree;
Where Alph, the sacred river, ran
Through caverns measureless to man
Down to a sunless sea. (lines 1–5)

20.3 John Nash, Royal Pavilion, Brighton, England, 1815–1818. Nash had to leave London because of bankruptcy in 1793. By the end of the decade, his affairs were in order, and he returned to become a member of the prince regent's circle. He then made a fortune in real estate, especially from the development of Regent's Park and Regent Street, named after the title of his royal patron.

Sculpture

Romantic sculptors were generally less prominent than poets, painters, and architects. One sculpture inspired by Romantic ideals is François Rude's (1784–1855) stone relief of 1833–1836 (fig. **20.4**). Originally entitled the *Departure of the Volunteers of 1792,* it is known as *La Marseillaise* and was one of four reliefs added to the Arc de Triomphe in Paris (see fig. 19.7).

The relief shows a group of volunteers answering the call to arms in defense of France against foreign enemies. They seem caught up in the "romance" of their enthusiasm as the rhythmic energy of their motion echoes the imaginary beat of military music (see caption). Rude's soldiers range from youths to old men, who are either nude or equipped with Classical armor. But unlike the stoic imagery of Neoclassical patriotism (see Chapter 19), Rude's volunteers seem carried away by the force of the crowd. Vigorously striding above the volunteers and driving them on is an allegory of Liberty. She is a nineteenth-century revolutionary version of the traditional winged Victory (cf. fig. 5.70).

20.4 François Rude, *Departure of the Volunteers of 1792* (*La Marseillaise*), 1833–1836. Limestone; approx. 42 ft. (12.80 m) high. Arc de Triomphe, Paris. The "Marseillaise," the French national anthem, was composed in 1792 by the army officer Claude-Joseph Rouget de Lisle. Volunteers from the port of Marseille, who led the storming of the Tuilleries, brought the song to Paris.

Painting in Europe

William Blake

There was a strong Christian strain in Romanticism. This was associated with the longing for a form of religious mysticism, which, from the Reformation onward, had been on the wane in western Europe. This longing can be seen in the work of the English visionary artist and poet William Blake (1757–1827).

From 1793 to 1796, Blake illuminated a group of *Prophetic Books* dealing with visionary biblical themes. His watercolor and gouache (see box) *God Creating the Universe* (fig. **20.5**), also called the *Ancient of Days,* shows God organizing the world with a compass (cf. fig. I.6).

In this image, Blake's God is almost entirely enclosed in a circle. The light extending from each side of his hand forms the arms of a compass. The precision of the circle and triangle contrasts with the looser painting of clouds and light, and the frenetic quality of God's long, white hair, blown sideways by the wind. Blake's nostalgic combination of medieval iconography and a Michelangelo-style God with a revival of mysticism is characteristic of the Romantic movement. His passionate yearning for a past (and largely imaginary) form of Christianity appears in his poems as well as in his pictures. It is exemplified by the opening lines of his hymn "Jerusalem":

And did those feet in ancient time
  Walk upon England's mountains green?
And was the holy Lamb of God
  On England's pleasant pastures seen?

20.5 William Blake, *God Creating the Universe (Ancient of Days)*, frontispiece of *Europe: A Prophecy,* 1794. Metal relief etching, hand-colored with watercolor and gouache; 12¼ × 9½ in. (31.1 × 24.1 cm). British Museum, London. Blake was an engraver, painter, and poet whose work was little known until about a century after his death.

CONNECTIONS

See figure 5.70. *Winged Nike (Winged Victory)*, c. 190 B.C.

See figure I.6. *God as Architect (God Drawing the Universe with a Compass)*, mid-13th century.

Watercolor

In **watercolor,** powdered pigments are mixed with water, often with gum arabic used as a binder and drying agent. Watercolor is transparent, and so one color overlaid on another can create a **wash** effect. The most common **ground** for watercolor is paper. Because the medium is transparent, the natural color of the paper also contributes to the image.

Watercolor had been known in China as early as the third century A.D. but was only occasionally used in Europe before the late eighteenth and early nineteenth centuries. At that point, it became popular, particularly with English artists such as Constable and Turner, for landscape paintings on a small scale. In the second half of the nineteenth century, watercolor also became popular among American artists. It was favored by those who preferred to paint directly from nature rather than in a studio and needed a more portable, quickly drying medium.

Gouache is a watercolor paint that, when dry, becomes opaque. It is commonly used on its own or in combination with transparent watercolor.

Théodore Géricault

Although Théodore Géricault (1791–1824) died at the age of thirty-three, his work was crucial to the development of Romantic painting, especially in France. His *Mounted Officer of the Imperial Guard* (fig. **20.6**), painted in 1812, when Géricault was only twenty-one, shows the early expression of his prodigious talent. It is a tour de force illustrating the Romantic theme of man against nature. The officer turns sharply as he tries to control the rearing charger, on which he depends for his life. The turbulent sky and the indications of battle in the distance enhance the dramatic effect of the scene. A comparison of this work with David's *Napoleon at Saint Bernard Pass* (see fig. 19.6), which also glorifies equestrian courage, shows the difference between the idealized clarity of Neoclassicism and the energetic textures of Romanticism.

Géricault's interest in human psychology is evident in his studies of the insane, which he executed from 1822 to 1823. In these works, he captured the mental disturbance of his subjects through pose and physiognomy. In the *Madwoman with a Mania of Envy* (fig. **20.7**), for example, the figure hunches forward and stares suspiciously off to the left, as if afraid of some potential menace. The raising of one eyebrow and the lowering of the other, combined with the slight shift in the planes of her face, indicate the wariness of paranoia.

Géricault's loose brushstrokes create the textures of the woman's face, which is accentuated by light and framed by the ruffle of her cap. By the conscious organization of light, color, and the visibility of his brushwork, Géricault unifies the composition both formally and psychologically. The sweeping, light brown curve below the collar echoes the more tightly drawn curve of the mouth. Reds around the eyes and mouth are repeated in the collar, and the white of the cap ruffle recurs in the small triangle of the white undergarment. The untied cap laces and the few disheveled strands of her hair are a subtle metaphor for the woman's emotional state, as if she is "coming apart" and "unraveling" physically as well as mentally.

Géricault was a man of paradoxes—a fashionable society figure, but a political and social liberal who was active in exposing injustice. The subject of this portrait, which is also known as *L'Hyène de la Salpêtrière* (*The Hyena of the*

See figure 19.6. Jacques-Louis David, *Napoleon at Saint Bernard Pass,* 1800.

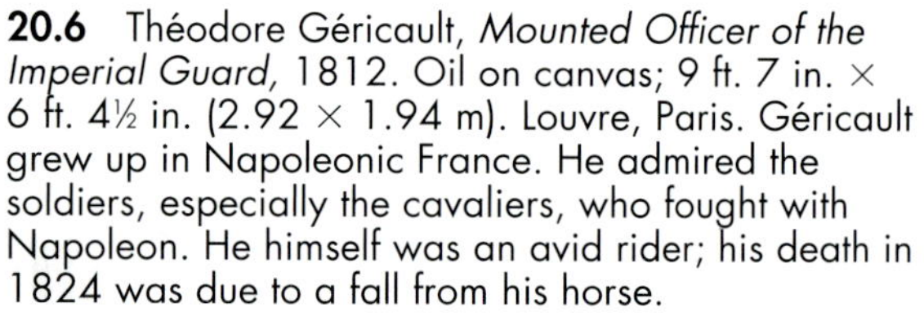

20.6 Théodore Géricault, *Mounted Officer of the Imperial Guard,* 1812. Oil on canvas; 9 ft. 7 in. × 6 ft. 4½ in. (2.92 × 1.94 m). Louvre, Paris. Géricault grew up in Napoleonic France. He admired the soldiers, especially the cavaliers, who fought with Napoleon. He himself was an avid rider; his death in 1824 was due to a fall from his horse.

20.7 Théodore Géricault, *Madwoman with a Mania of Envy*, 1822–1823. Oil on canvas; $28\frac{3}{8} \times 22\frac{4}{5}$ in. (72.3×58.3 cm). Musée des Beaux-Arts, Lyons.

Salpêtrière), was a child murderess. La Salpêtrière was a mental hospital in Paris where Freud studied under the celebrated neurologist Jean-Martin Charcot and learned that hypnosis could temporarily relieve the symptoms of hysteria.

Géricault's commitment to social justice is reflected in his acknowledged masterpiece, the *Raft of the "Medusa"* (fig. **20.8**), which he began in 1818 and exhibited at the Salon (see box, p. 728) the following year. This picture

20.8 Théodore Géricault, *Raft of the "Medusa,"* 1819. Oil on canvas; 16 ft. × 23 ft. 6 in. (4.88 × 7.16 m). Louvre, Paris.

The Salon

The Salon refers to the official art exhibitions sponsored by the French authorities. The term is derived from the Salon d'Apollon in the Louvre Palace. It was here, in 1667, that Louis XIV sponsored an exhibition of works by members of the Académie Royale de Peinture et de Sculpture (Royal Academy of Painting and Sculpture). From 1737, the Salon was an annual event, and in 1748 selection by jury was introduced. Throughout the eighteenth century, the Salons were the only important exhibitions at which works of art could be shown. This made acceptance by the Salon jury crucial to an artist's career.

During the eighteenth century, the influence of the Salon was largely beneficial and progressive. By the nineteenth century, however, despite the fact that during the Revolution the Salon was officially opened to all French artists, it was in effect controlled by Academicians, whose conservative taste resisted innovation.

commemorates a contemporary disaster at sea rather than a heroic example of Neoclassical patriotism. On July 2, 1816, the French frigate *Medusa* hit a reef off the west coast of Africa. The captain and senior officers boarded six lifeboats, saving themselves and some of the passengers. The 149 remaining passengers and crew were crammed onto a wooden raft, which the captain cut loose from a lifeboat. During the thirteen-day voyage that followed, the raft became a floating hell of death, disease, mutiny, starvation, and cannibalism. Only 15 people survived.

The episode became a national scandal when it was discovered that the ship's captain owed his appointment to his monarchist sympathies rather than to merit. Furthermore, the French government had tried to cover up the worst details of the incident. It was not until the ship's surgeon, one of the survivors from the raft, published an account of the disaster that the full extent of the tragedy became known. Géricault took up the cause of the victims against social injustice and translated it into a struggle of humanity against the elements.

The writhing forms, which are reminiscent of Michelangelo's Sistine Chapel figures from the *Flood,* echo the turbulence of sea and sky. In the foreground, a father mourns his dead son. Other corpses hang over the edge of the raft, while in the background, to the right, frantic survivors wave hopefully at a distant ship. The raft itself tilts upward on the swell of a wave, and the sail billows in the wind. As a result, the viewer looks down on the raft, directly confronting the corpses. The gaze gradually moves upward, following the diagonals of the central figures, and finally reaches the waving drapery of the man standing upright. In this painting, Géricault incorporates the Romantic taste for adventure and individual freedom into an actual event in which victims of injustice fight to survive the primal forces of nature. The mood of this painting is evoked by lines from "The Rime of the Ancient Mariner" by Coleridge, the English Romantic poet: "I looked upon the rotting deck, and there the dead men lay." To ensure authenticity, Géricault spoke with survivors and made studies of the dead and dying in morgues and hospitals before executing the final painting.

Eugène Delacroix

The most prominent figure in French Romantic painting was Eugène Delacroix (1798–1863), who outlived Géricault by nearly forty years. Delacroix was rumored to be the illegitimate son of the French statesman Charles Talleyrand (whom he resembled physically), but he was brought up in the family of a French government official. His celebrated *Journal,* which reveals his talent for writing, is a useful source of information on the social context of his life as well as on his philosophy of art.

In painting, Delacroix stood for color just as Ingres, his contemporary and rival, championed line. In this theoretical opposition, Delacroix and Ingres transformed the traditional aesthetic quarrel between *colorito* and *disegno,* the Rubenists and the Poussinists, the Moderns and the Ancients, into Romanticism versus Classicism. Delacroix's paintings are characterized by broad sweeps of color, lively patterns, and energetic figural groups. His thick brushstrokes, like Géricault's, contribute to the character of the image as well as to the surface textures of the canvas. They are in direct contrast to the precise edges and smooth surfaces of Neoclassical painting. Just as in literature Delacroix's contemporary, Victor Hugo (see box, p. 729), broke with the classically inspired rules of seventeenth-century French drama, so Delacroix continued and developed Géricault's taste for emotional expression, a wider range of textures, and freer outlines.

In an early work, the *Bark of Dante* (fig. **20.9**), exhibited in 1822, Delacroix reflects the Romantic revival of interest in Dante's *Inferno*. Dante and his guide, Virgil, are in the lake around the infernal city of Dis, the burning towers of which are visible in the background. The bark lists precariously as the damned souls rise up from the turbulent water to grasp hold of its sides. At the left, a terrified soul bites into the wooden rim of the boat. Dante reveals his own terror by raising his right hand in alarm to maintain his balance. In contrast, the figure of Virgil, clad in a heavy robe and a Classical laurel wreath, is calm. Leaning over and rendered in back view is Charon, the boatman of Hades.

20.9 Eugène Delacroix, *Bark of Dante,* 1822. Oil on canvas; 6 ft. 2⅞ in. × 8 ft. ⅞ in. (1.88 × 2.46 m). Louvre, Paris.

Victor Hugo

Victor Hugo (1802–1885), a prolific author of novels, plays, and poems, led the French Romantic movement in literature, especially in the 1820s and 1830s. Since his father was a general in Napoleon's army, his family was on close terms with the emperor. This gave Hugo an overview of French society, which he chronicled in his novels. He equated artistic freedom with political and social freedom, and championed all three. His novel *Les Misérables* deals with social injustice, and his poem "Written after July 1830"—like Delacroix's *Liberty*—supported the July 1830 Revolution:

> Too long by tyrant hand restrain'd,
> Too long in slavery enchain'd,
> Paris awoke—and in his breast,
> Each his ideas at once confest:
> "Vainly may despots not essay
> To lead a mighty race astray;
> True to themselves, the French shall bring
> Such treason home unto the king."

Hugo also defended the cause of Greek emancipation from Turkey, which is the subject of Delacroix's *Massacre at Chios*. His play *Hernani,* performed in 1830, led to a quarrel between conservative "Classicists," who favored order, rules, and restraint, and the proponents of a more "Romantic" emotional style. Like the other Romantics, Victor Hugo was drawn to subjective expression and to exotic, nostalgic, and melancholic themes.

20.10 Eugène Delacroix, *Massacre at Chios,* 1822–1824. Oil on canvas; 13 ft. 10 in. × 11 ft. 7 in. (4.22 × 3.53 m). Louvre, Paris.

In the *Massacre at Chios* (fig. **20.10**) of 1822–1824, Delacroix satisfied the Romantic interest in distant places and political freedom. In this, he shared the views of Byron (see p. 722), who died in 1824 fighting for Greek independence from Turkey. Delacroix enlists the viewer's sympathy for Greece by showing the suffering and death of its people in the foreground. They are individualized and thus elicit identification with their plight. At the same time, Delacroix has concentrated attention on the details of their exotic dress. Two Turks—one holding a gun and the other on a rearing horse—threaten the Greeks, while scenes of burning villages and massacre are depicted in the distance.

20.11 Eugène Delacroix, *Death of Sardanapalus*, 1827–1828. Oil on canvas; 12 ft. 11½ in. × 16 ft. 3 in. (3.95 × 4.95 m). Louvre, Paris. When the painting was exhibited at the Salon in February 1828, it was widely criticized. Delacroix was unable to sell it until 1845, and then the buyer was an English collector. The Louvre purchased the work in 1921.

The enormous *Death of Sardanapalus* (fig. **20.11**), inspired by Byron's play of the same subject, also reflects Delacroix's affinities with the poet. Both Byron and Delacroix portray the Assyrian king as a meditative figure in the midst of violence and debauchery. In the play, Sardanapalus accepts that his empire has fallen because his officials betrayed him, and he kills himself on a pyre with his favorite Ionian concubine, Myrrha. Delacroix's figure reclines on a large bed with a rich red covering that accentuates the sensuality of the scene and echoes the multiple reds throughout the painting. The opulence associated with the East is shown in the jewels and objects of gold strewn on the floor, and in the exotic costumes. Only Sardanapalus and Myrrha, lying at the king's feet, are calm. They are surrounded by vignettes of murderous rage and helpless victims. At the lower left, a black man pulls a fallen horse decked out in elaborate trappings, and at the upper right the city is engulfed in smoke.

Delacroix's *Liberty Leading the People* (fig. **20.12**), executed in 1830, applies Romantic principles to the revolutionary ideal. In contrast to Rude's *Marseillaise* (see fig. 20.4), whose figures are shown in side view, Delacroix's rebels march directly toward the viewer. Delacroix "romanticizes" the uprising by implying that the populace has spontaneously taken up arms, united in yearning for liberty (see caption). The figures emerge from a haze of smoke—a symbol of France's political emergence from the shackles of tyranny to enlightened republicanism. Visible in the distance is the Paris skyline with the towers of Notre-Dame Cathedral. From here the rebels will fly the tricolor (the red, white, and blue French flag).

As in the *Raft of the "Medusa,"* Delacroix's corpses lie in contorted poses in the foreground. The diagonal of the kneeling boy leads upward to Liberty, whose raised hand, holding the flag aloft, forms the apex of a pyramidal composition. Her Greek profile and bare breasts recall ancient statuary, while her towering form and costume confirm her allegorical role. By incorporating antiquity into his figure of Liberty, Delacroix makes a nostalgic, "Romantic" appeal to republican sentiment. Among Liberty's followers are representatives of different social classes, who are united by their common cause. In their determined march forward, they trample the corpses beneath them. They are willing to die themselves, secure in the knowledge that others will arise to take their place.

A colorist in the tradition of Rubens, Delacroix integrates color with the painting's message. In an image that is primarily composed of brown tones and blacks, the colors that appear most vividly on the flag are repeated with more or less intensity throughout the picture. Whites are more freely distributed. In the sky, reds and blues are muted. Denser blues are repeated in the stocking of the fallen man at the left and the shirt of the kneeling boy. His scarf and belt, like the small ribbon of the corpse at the right, are

20.12 Eugène Delacroix, *Liberty Leading the People*, 1830. Oil on canvas; 8 ft. 6 in. × 10 ft. 7 in. (2.59 × 3.23 m). Louvre, Paris. This painting refers to the July 1830 uprising against the Bourbon king Charles X, which led to his abdication. Louis-Philippe, the "citizen-king," was installed in his place, though his powers were strictly limited.

20.13 Eugène Delacroix, *Women of Algiers,* 1834. Oil on canvas; 5 ft. 10⅞ in. × 7 ft. 6⅛ in. (1.80 × 2.29 m). Louvre, Paris.

accents of red. In echoing the colors of the flag, which is at once a symbol of Liberty and of French republicanism, Delacroix paints a political manifesto.

In 1832, Delacroix traveled to North Africa, where he visited a harem and became fascinated by the lively patterns of Moorish costume and interior decor. The exotic, Moorish character of the region appealed to his Romantic taste. Although he continued to paint scenes of violence, including battles and animal hunts, he was also attracted by more tranquil scenes. A comparison of the *Women of Algiers* (fig. **20.13**) of 1834 with Ingres' *Grande Odalisque* (fig. 19.14) highlights Delacroix's rejection of the precise edges and smooth surface texture of Neoclassicism. He combines the relaxed, languorous poses of the harem women with the formal motion of surface design. Throughout the picture plane, the arabesques of Islamic lettering are reflected in pose and gesture, as well as in the designs themselves. The figures are redolent of the exotic, perfumed, and probably drugged harem atmosphere, whereas Ingres' odalisque is alert and clear. In contrast to the three seated harem girls, the black African woman at the right seems in full possession of her faculties. She turns in a dancelike motion, as if something has caught her attention. The figure at the far left is a Moorish version of the traditional reclining nude, which is at odds with the pictorial principles of Ingres' odalisque.

See figure 19.14. Jean-Auguste-Dominique Ingres, *Grande Odalisque,* 1814.

Francisco de Goya y Lucientes

The leading Spanish painter of the late eighteenth and early nineteenth centuries, Francisco de Goya (1746–1828), was attracted by several Romantic themes. His compelling images reflect his remarkable psychological insights, and many also display his support for the causes of intellectual and political freedom. He studied Rembrandt and Velázquez both for their painterly techniques and for their penetrating character studies. Goya's affinity for Rembrandt's etchings is evident in his own prolific work in that medium.

In 1799, Goya published *Los Caprichos* (The Caprices), a series of etchings combined with the new medium of aquatint (see box). In this series, he depicts psychological phenomena, often juxtaposing them with an educational or social message. In plate 3 (fig. **20.14**), for example, the title of which may be translated as "The Bogeyman Is Coming," Goya illustrates the nighttime fears of childhood. The mother's gaze is riveted on the unseen face of the bogeyman, and her children cringe in fear. Their terrified expressions, contrasted with the anonymity of the apparition, accentuate the uncanny character of the bogeyman. Goya takes full advantage of the dramatic possibilities of the blacks and whites characteristic of the medium. The bogeyman's sharply contrasting light and dark—his "dark side" turned toward the children, whose white faces and black features accentuate their terror—is a metaphor for his two-sided nature. An inscription on the plate confirms Goya's enlightened view of child development, consistent with the philosophy of Jean-Jacques Rousseau, which was unusual in a country still haunted by the shadow of the Inquisition.

The *Witches' Sabbath* (fig. **20.15**) of 1798–1799 satirizes the irrational belief in witchcraft by exaggerating the primitive quality of such thinking. Goya implicitly attacks the Inquisition, which opposed the principles of the Enlightenment. He depicts the widespread fantasy that witches were old, ugly, deformed women who sucked the blood of children and fed infants to Satan. His witches form a circle around a devil in the guise of a goat, and one witch offers him a bloodless, skeletal infant. The lascivious implications of the goat and the bacchanalian grape leaves on his horns refer to popular notions of the witches' sabbath as an orgiastic, cannibalistic ritual.

Aquatint

Although etching was not new to the nineteenth century, its use in combination with **aquatint** was. In aquatint, the artist covers the spaces between etched lines with a layer of **rosin** (a form of powdered resin). This partially protects against the effects of the acid bath. Since the rosin is porous, the acid can penetrate to the metal, but the artist controls the acid's effect on the plate by treating the plate with varnish. This technique expands the range of grainy tones in finished prints. Aquatint thus combines the principles of engraving with the effects of a watercolor or wash drawing.

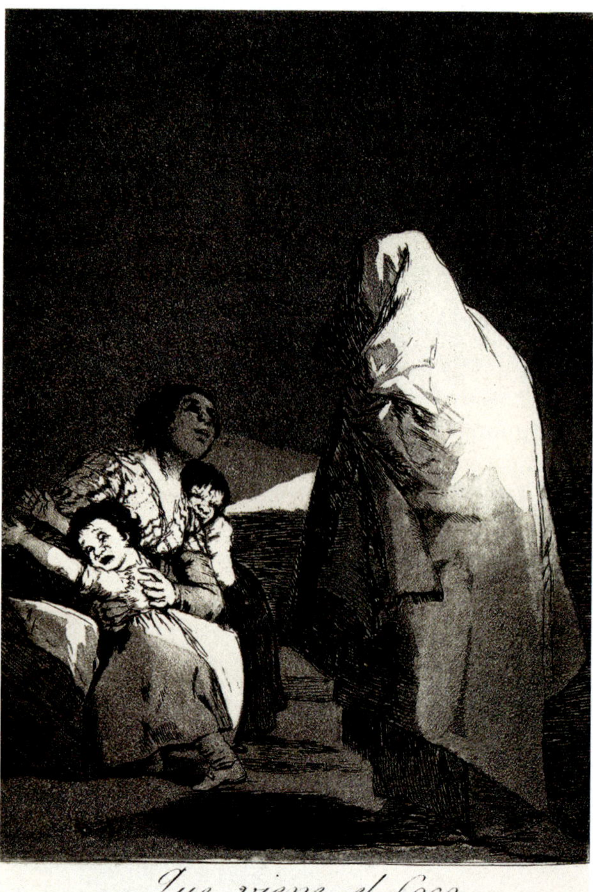

20.14 Francisco de Goya y Lucientes, *Los Caprichos*, plate 3, published 1799. Etching and aquatint. Inscribed on the plate (but not visible here) is Goya's warning against instilling needless fears into children: "Bad education. To bring up a child to fear a Bogeyman more than his own father is to make him afraid of something that does not exist."

20.15 Francisco de Goya y Lucientes, *Witches' Sabbath*, 1798–1799. Oil on canvas; 17¼ × 12¼ in. (43.8 × 31.1 cm). Museo Lázaro Galdiano, Madrid.

In 1786, Charles III of Spain appointed Goya court painter, and his successor, Charles IV, promoted the artist to the position of principal painter. In his monumental portrait of the *Family of Charles IV* of 1800 (fig. **20.16**), Goya left a record of three generations of Spanish royalty. The pompous poses, glittering costumes, and blank stares highlight the unappealing character of the royal family. Such grandiose self-display conforms to the setting—the palace picture gallery—that had served the political image of Spanish royalty for centuries.

Goya's irony is enhanced by the insertion of his self-portrait at the left. In a quotation from Velázquez's *Las Meninas* (see fig. 17.56), Goya faces a large canvas of which only part of the back is visible to the observer. In contrast to the dynamic poses of Velázquez's picture, however, Goya's are stiff, rather like stuffed dolls. Instead of being drawn into the space of the picture as in *Las Meninas*, Goya's space comes to an abrupt halt in the shallow depth of the hall. The family of Charles IV is arrayed in a horizontal plane and seems to compete for visibility, like a group posing for a photograph. Whereas Velázquez stands proudly among his royal "peers," displaying his palette and brush for all to see, Goya portrays himself as diffidently fading into the background.

20.16 Francisco de Goya y Lucientes, *Family of Charles IV*, 1800. Oil on canvas; 9 ft. 2 in. × 11 ft. (2.79 × 3.35 m). Prado, Madrid.

In his images of war Goya champions Enlightenment views of individual freedom against political oppression. In the *Executions of the Third of May, 1808* (fig. **20.17**) he dramatically juxtaposes the visible faces of the victims with the covered faces of the executioners. This painting depicts the aftermath of events that occurred on May 2 and 3, 1808. Two Spanish rebels had fired on fifteen French soldiers from Napoleon's army. In response, the French troops rounded up and executed close to a thousand inhabitants of Madrid and other Spanish towns. Six years later, after the French had been ousted, the liberal government of Spain commissioned a pair of paintings, of which this is one, to commemorate the atrocity.

The firing squad is an anonymous, but deadly, force, whose regular, repeated rhythms and dark mass contrast with the highlighted, disorderly victims. The emotional poses and gestures, accentuated by thick brushstrokes, and the stress on individual reactions to the "blind," brute force of the firing squad are characteristic of Goya's Romanticism. The raised arms of the central, illuminated victim about to be shot recall the death of Jesus. His pose and gesture, in turn, are repeated by the foremost corpse. The lessons of Jesus's Crucifixion, Goya seems to be saying, are still unlearned. By mingling reds and browns in this section of the picture, Goya creates the impression that blood is flowing into the earth. Somewhat muted by the night sky, a church rises in the background and towers over the scene.

When he was in his seventies, Goya painted a series of so-called "black paintings." Since they were not commissioned, these late pictures reveal some of the artist's most intimate preoccupations. *Chronos Devouring One of His Children* (fig. **20.18**), of about 1820–1822, is a disturbing indictment of man's bestial nature.

According to Greek mythology, Chronos devoured his children to thwart the prophecy that they would overthrow him. But the children were gods and therefore immortal. They survived to fulfill their destiny and became the twelve Olympians. Goya's Chronos, on the other hand, crushes the child like a flimsy doll and tears away its arms

20.17 Francisco de Goya y Lucientes, *Executions of the Third of May, 1808*, 1814. Oil on canvas; 8 ft. 9 in. × 11 ft. 4 in. (2.67 × 3.45 m). Prado, Madrid.

20.18 Francisco de Goya y Lucientes, *Chronos Devouring One of His Children,* c. 1820–1822. Wall painting in oil detached on canvas; 4 ft. 9⅞ in. × 2 ft. 8⅝ in. (1.47 × 0.83 m). Prado, Madrid.

and head. His savagery is accented by the red of the blood outlining the upper torso and flowing across his hands.

Chronos stares wildly out of the picture, his gaping mouth tearing off a piece of the child's body. Goya depicts the Titan as a crazed, wide-eyed cannibal who is barely contained by the picture space. The loose brushstrokes, especially in the long hair and body, reinforce his bestial nature. In this frenzied, un-Classical image of a father devouring his child, Goya combines several themes that preoccupied him throughout his life. In particular, as in the "Bogeyman," he deals with the image of a terrifying father who destroys his vulnerable children, psychologically in the former and physically in the *Chronos.* Goya confronts humanity with an example of its "blackest," most primitive forms of behavior—infanticide and cannibalism. It is ironic that Goya's most anti-Classical image should ultimately project a humanistic message.

Burke on the Aesthetic of the Sublime

In 1757, the British philosopher Edmund Burke (1729–1797) published *A Philosophical Enquiry into the Origin of Our Ideas of the Sublime and Beautiful.* Certain artists and writers of the late eighteenth and early nineteenth centuries took up his views on the sublime, which reflect the ambivalent character of the Romantic aesthetic. According to Burke, the passions and the irrational exert a powerful, awesome force on people. These, he believed, explain the subjective reaction to art. Burke's aesthetic system describes the "irrational" attraction to fear, pain, ugliness, loss, hatred, and death (all of which comprise the notion of the sublime) on the one hand, and to beauty, pleasure, joy, and love on the other. (Some one hundred and fifty years later, Freud would show the co-existence of these oppositions in the unconscious and relate their dynamics to child development. Freud's essay of 1919 entitled "The Uncanny," which is his only work on aesthetics, has affinities with both the writing of Burke and the psychological paintings of Goya.) Pain and danger, according to Burke, "are the most powerful" passions. Life and health, in contrast, make less of an impression on people.

A summation of Burke's aesthetic is reflected in Shelley's "Medusa," whose "horror and . . . beauty are divine." Of the paintings illustrated in this chapter, several can be related to Burke's ideas. Revolutionary zeal that elevates the passions to new heights appears in Rude's *Marseillaise* and Delacroix's *Liberty Leading the People.* Géricault's *Madwoman* and Goya's *Chronos* evoke the terror of being killed or devoured by one's parents. Irrational fears are aroused in Goya's *Los Caprichos,* plate 3, and *Witches' Sabbath.* And nature, as in Friedrich's *Two Men Contemplating the Moon* (see fig. 20.19), has a quality of beauty, but it also threatens to envelop and submerge humanity with its infinite vastness. Friedrich's two men gazing at the moon evoke Burke's view that "terror is in all cases whatsoever, either more openly or latently, the ruling principle of the sublime."[1]

Germany: Caspar David Friedrich

Romantic themes often focused on the longing to return to nature and on the insignificance of the individual in relation to nature's vastness. The varying moods of nature were seen as a reflection of states of mind. Such themes led to an expansion of landscape painting in the nineteenth century. Romantic landscape often evoked a sense of the sublime (see box, p. 737), which included an uncanny quality of terror.

In Germany (see box), the poetic landscapes of Caspar David Friedrich (1774–1840) express these Romantic trends. His *Two Men Contemplating the Moon* (fig. **20.19**) exemplifies the merging of human form and mood with nature. The scene is barren, and the vastness of the landscape is suggested by its implied continuation beyond the borders of the picture. The two men have no identity other than their relationship to the landscape and their medieval dress, which reflects Romantic nostalgia for the past. Their forms are pure silhouettes and provide vertical accents cutting through the horizon line. As a result, they seem transitory and ghostly in contrast to the permanence of nature, which contributes to the sense of awe and the sublime.

German *Sturm und Drang*

In Germany, the *Sturm und Drang* (Storm and Stress) movement of the late eighteenth century marked an early phase of Romanticism. A reaction against the domination of French Classical taste, it was a literary movement that exalted individualism and nature. It placed emotion, instinct, and originality above rational and scientific thought. As young men, the playwrights Johann Wolfgang von Goethe (1749–1832), whose *Faust* was illustrated by Delacroix, and Johann Christoph Friedrich von Schiller (1759–1805) were among its principal exponents. Another major figure was Johann Gottfried von Herder (1744–1803), an influential critic who "rediscovered" ancient German literature. His views reflected the nationalist strain of German Romanticism. For Herder, the virtues of natural feeling and emotion prized by the Romantics resided in old German folk songs and sagas, rather than in Greek and Roman antiquity or in French Classicism.

20.19 Caspar David Friedrich, *Two Men Contemplating the Moon*, 1819. Oil on canvas; 13¾ × 17½ in. (35.0 × 44.5 cm). Gemäldegalerie Neue Meister, Staatliche Kunstsammlungen, Dresden.

England: John Constable and Joseph Mallord William Turner

In England, the two greatest Romantic landscape painters, John Constable (1776–1837) and Joseph Mallord William Turner (1775–1851), approached their subjects quite differently. Whereas Constable's images are clear and tend to focus on the details of English country life, Turner's are apt to become swept up in the paint.

In Constable's *Salisbury Cathedral from the Bishop's Garden* (fig. **20.20**), for example, cows graze in the foreground, while couples stroll calmly along pathways. The cathedral is framed by trees that repeat the verticality of its spire. Nostalgia for the past is evident in the juxtaposition of the day-to-day activities of the present with the Gothic cathedral. Humanity, like the cathedral, is at one with nature, and there is no hint of the industrialization that in reality was encroaching on the pastoral landscape of nineteenth-century England. Echoing the atmosphere of this painting are the poems of Wordsworth, who wanted to break away from eighteenth-century literary forms and return to nature, to a "humble and rustic life." In "Tintern Abbey," Wordsworth evokes the Romantic sense of the sublime that is achieved by oneness with nature:

> . . . And I have felt
> A presence that disturbs me with the joy
> Of elevated thoughts; a sense sublime
> Of something far more deeply interfused,
> Whose dwelling is the light of setting suns,
> And the round ocean and the living air,
> And the blue sky, and in the mind of man . . .
> (lines 93–99)

20.20 John Constable, *Salisbury Cathedral from the Bishop's Garden,* 1820. Oil on canvas; 2 ft. 10⅝ in. × 3 ft. 8 in. (0.91 × 1.12 m). Metropolitan Museum of Art, New York (Bequest of Mary Stillman Harkness, 1950). (See also figs. 11.45–11.47.)

20.21 Joseph Mallord William Turner, *Burning of the Houses of Lords and Commons, October 16, 1834,* 1835. Oil on canvas; 3 ft. ¼ in. × 4 ft. ½ in. (0.92 × 1.23 m). Cleveland Museum of Art (Bequest of John L. Severance, 42.647).

In contrast to the calm landscapes of Constable, Turner's approach to Romanticism is characterized by dynamic, sweeping brushstrokes and vivid colors that blur the forms. His *Burning of the Houses of Lords and Commons* (fig. **20.21**) is a whirlwind of flame, water, and sky, structured mainly by the dark diagonal pier at the lower right, the bridge, and the barely visible towers of Parliament across the Thames. The painting is based on an actual fire of 1834. Turner spent the entire night sketching the scene. After the fire, the new Houses of Parliament (still standing today) were built in the Gothic Revival style (see fig. 20.1), which was inspired by Romantic nostalgia for a medieval Christian past.

The luminous reds, yellows, and oranges of the fire dominate the sky and are reflected in the water below. In this work, architectural structure is in the process of dissolution, enveloped by the blazing lights and colors of the fire. The forces of nature let loose and their destruction of man-made structures are the primary theme of this painting. In Constable, on the other hand, nature is under control and in harmony with human creations.

Painting in the United States

In the United States as well as Europe, the Romantic movement infiltrated both art and literature (see box). The landscape of different parts of the country inspired artists, individually and in groups, to produce works that were often monumental in size and breathtaking in effect.

Thomas Cole

One such painting is *The Oxbow* (fig. **20.22**) by Thomas Cole (1801–1848), which depicts a bend in the Connecticut River, near Northampton. (*Oxbow* is the term used to describe the crescent-shaped, almost circular, course of a river caused by its meandering.) One is struck by the abrupt contrast between the two sides of the painting. On the left is wilderness, where two blasted trees in the foreground bear witness to the power of the elements. A thunderstorm, an example of nature's dramatic, changing moods characteristic of the Romantic aesthetic, is passing over. The direction of the rain indicates that the storm is moving away to the left and that it has already passed the farmland at the right, which now lies serene and sunlit. A landscape of neatly arranged fields, dotted with haystacks, sheep, and other signs of cultivation, extends into the distance. Boats ply the river, and plumes of smoke rise from farmhouses. Barely visible in the foreground, just right of center, is a single figure, the artist at work before his easel. On a jutting rock are his umbrella and folding stool and, leaning against them, a portfolio with the name T. Cole on its cover. Both artist and viewer have a panoramic view from the top of the mountain, a feature that became typical of the Hudson River school of painting, of which Cole was the acknowledged leader.

It was Cole's habit to journey on foot through the northeastern states, making pencil sketches of the landscape. He

20.22 Thomas Cole, *View from Mount Holyoke, Northampton, Massachusetts, after a Thunderstorm* (*The Oxbow*), 1836. Oil on canvas; 4 ft. 3½ in. × 6 ft. 4 in. (1.31 × 1.93 m). Metropolitan Museum of Art, New York (Gift of Mrs. Russell Sage, 1908). Cole was born in England and emigrated to America with his family at the age of seventeen. In 1825, his work came to the attention of John Trumbull (see Chapter 19), then president of the American Academy, who is quoted as saying: "This youth has done at once, and without instruction, what I cannot do after fifty years' practice." This story, whether anecdotal or not, places Cole squarely in the tradition of other "boy wonders" such as Giotto and Picasso.

American Romantic Writers

Nineteenth-century America produced many important Romantic works of literature. The historical adventures of James Fenimore Cooper (1789–1851), particularly *The Last of the Mohicans* (1826), extol Native Americans as examples of the "noble savage." The supernatural poems and tales of Edgar Allan Poe (1809–1849) contain uncanny portrayals of death and terror. Likewise, the Gothic novels and short stories of Nathaniel Hawthorne (1804–1864) create a haunted, medieval atmosphere in which supernatural phenomena abound. In *Tales of the Alhambra*, Washington Irving (1783–1859) evokes the mysterious atmosphere and exoticism of Islamic Spain.

A characteristic American Romantic philosophy emerged in the Transcendentalism of Ralph Waldo Emerson (1803–1882) and Henry David Thoreau (1817–1862), a doctrine that stressed the presence of God within the human soul as a source of truth and a moral guide. After a trip to England (where he met Coleridge and Wordsworth), Emerson became a spokesman for Romantic individualism, which he expressed in poems and essays. A more personal form of natural philosophy can be seen in Thoreau's experimental return to nature. He lived alone for two years in a hut at the edge of Walden Pond in Massachusetts and recorded his experience in *Walden; or, Life in the Woods* (1854).

would then develop them into finished paintings during the winter, and this was the case with *The Oxbow*. It is likely that Cole never actually witnessed the storm in the way he depicts it, and that there is a large element of the artist's imagination at work. If so, why did Cole choose this particular image? An untitled poem that he wrote in January 1835, a year before he completed *The Oxbow*, begins as follows:

I sigh not for a stormless clime,
Where drowsy quiet ever dwells,
Where purling waters changeless chime
Through soft and green unwinter'd dells—

For storms bring beauty in their train;
The hills that roar'd beneath the blast,
The woods that welter'd in the rain
Rejoice, whene'er the tempest's past.

Cole's affinity for storms has been interpreted by some scholars as a metaphor for his inner life, symbolic of some unresolved conflict or of inner peace following a period of stress. It is also possible to see the painting as an allegory of civilization (the right) versus savagery (the left), which is certainly consistent with Cole's own outlook. For although he made his reputation primarily as a landscape artist, Cole always aspired to a "higher style of landscape," a mode of painting having moral or religious significance.

George Bingham

In the latter half of the eighteenth century, most rural communities consisted of clusters of largely self-sufficient family-owned farms. Over the next fifty years, population growth and the increasing demand for new land made it hard for this system to survive. The building of canals and railroads commercialized the farm sector and stimulated competition between regions, all vying to sell the same crops to the same markets. Cole's country, the Hudson Valley and the Catskills, faced new competition from the Midwest and the Great Lakes. Agriculture became subject to the laws of the marketplace, vulnerable to changes in prices, government policies, and credit conditions. Some farmers prospered, while those who were unable to adjust to the changes became marginalized by progress. Many immigrants, who had come to America in search of opportunity, never rose above the bottom rung of the economic ladder.

This darker side of American rural life is illustrated in the *Squatters* (fig. **20.23**) by George Caleb Bingham (1811–1879), who combined a career in Missouri politics with a vocation as a painter. His image of a poor rural family outside a log cabin reminds us that there were many agricultural workers who, unable to compete in a market economy and having perhaps lost their land through overmortgaging, led a hand-to-mouth existence as tenants, wage laborers, or squatters.

20.23 George Caleb Bingham, *Squatters*, 1850. Oil on canvas; 25 × 30 in. (63.5 × 76.2 cm). Museum of Fine Arts, Boston (Bequest of Henry L. Shattuck in memory of Ralph W. Gray).

Albert Bierstadt

The interest in American landscape pushed west from the Hudson River and inspired paintings of panoramic spaces with spectacular views of nature. Variations of light play over mountains, trees, and lakes, the colors softening and changing with the time of day. This emphasis on light led to the term **luminism**, an example of which can be seen in Albert Bierstadt's (1830–1902) *Sunrise, Yosemite Valley* (fig. **20.24**).

Bierstadt was born in Germany but raised in Massachusetts. He combined the German taste for Romanticism with an enthusiasm for the American West. In 1859, Bierstadt traveled west with European landscape painters in mind and an ambition to create a new vision in America. In *Sunrise, Yosemite Valley,* his rich yellow lighting is gradually transformed into muted grays as it moves left. The still lake is a mirror of change as it captures the fleeting sensations of nature. As with Friedrich (see fig. 20.19), Bierstadt emphasizes nature's vastness compared with humanity's smallness.

20.24 Albert Bierstadt, *Sunrise, Yosemite Valley,* n.d. Oil on canvas; 36½ × 52½ in. (92.7 × 133.4 cm). Amon Carter Museum, Fort Worth.

20.25 George Catlin, *The White Cloud, Head Chief of the Iowas*, 1844–1845. Oil on canvas; 28 × 22⅞ in. (71.1 × 58.1 cm). © 1998 Board of Trustees, National Gallery of Art, Washington, D.C., Paul Mellon Collection.

George Catlin

Although westward expansion in the nineteenth century caused conflict with the native population, it also led artists and authors to depict Native Americans—often in a Romantic light. The artist and ethnographer George Catlin (1796–1872), for example, created a visual and literary record of Native American life. He observed the Native American sense of oneness with nature, which, as with the European Romantics and American landscape painters, was seen as imbued with powerful spiritual forces.

In figure **20.25**, *The White Cloud, Head Chief of the Iowas,* Catlin shows the chief in full ritual dress, including feathers, war paint, animal skins, and a bear-claw necklace. The upright posture of White Cloud signifies the cultural pride of Native Americans, while his stoic, slightly worried expression suggests concern for his people.

Folk Art: Edward Hicks

Another view of nature in nineteenth-century American painting can be found in folk art. Typically, folk artists are not academically trained; their forms are usually flattened, their proportions are unnatural, and their imagery is without reference to the Classical tradition. As a result, their works tend to have a spontaneous quality that can be refreshing, compared with the more "finished" appearance of works by artists who have had formal training.

One example of this genre that embodies the Romantic ideal of a return to nature is the *Peaceable Kingdom* (fig. **20.26**) by Edward Hicks (1780–1849), who during his lifetime was celebrated more as a Quaker preacher than as an artist. Hicks based this painting on a passage from the book of Isaiah (11:6–9): "The wolf also shall dwell with the lamb, and the leopard shall lie down with the kid; and the calf and the young lion and the fatling together; and a little child shall lead them. . . ." Rather than being drawn into a vast space, the viewer experiences an immediate confrontation with the image, especially the wild cats. Its impact is enhanced by the close-up view of wild animals coexisting peacefully with humans. Their careful, almost staged arrangement and immobile frontality endow them with a static quality. The *Peaceable Kingdom* merges the natural landscape with a utopian ideal related to the notion of a Garden of Eden. The background scene, also utopian, is a visual quotation of a scene in Benjamin West's *Penn's Treaty with the Indians.* In contrast to the capricious, dangerous, and constantly changing eruptions of nature that are captured in the work of Turner, Cole, and Bierstadt, Hicks's image seems frozen in time.

20.26 Edward Hicks, *Peaceable Kingdom*, c. 1834. Oil on canvas; 29⅜ × 35½ in. (74.8 × 90.2 cm). National Gallery of Art, Washington, D.C. (Gift of Edgar William and Bernice Chrysler Garbisch).

	Style/Period	Works of Art	Cultural/Historical Developments
1790	ROMANTICISM 1790–1800	Blake, *Ancient of Days* (**20.5**) Goya, *Witches' Sabbath* (**20.15**) Goya, *Los Caprichos* (**20.14**)	Samuel Taylor Coleridge, *Kubla Khan* (1797) Wordsworth and Coleridge, *Lyrical Ballads* (1798) Romantic literary movement (1798–1850)
1800	1800–1820  **Friedrich, *Two Men Contemplating the Moon***	Goya, *Family of Charles IV* (**20.16**) Géricault, *Mounted Officer of the Imperial Guard* (**20.6**) Goya, *Executions of the Third of May, 1808* (**20.17**) Nash, Royal Pavilion (**20.3**), Brighton Géricault, *Raft of the "Medusa"* (**20.8**) Friedrich, *Two Men Contemplating the Moon* (**20.19**)  **Nash, Royal Pavilion**	French army under Napoleon occupies Spain (1808) John Keats, *Endymion* (1818) Lord Byron, *Don Juan* (1819)  **Géricault, *Mounted Officer of the Imperial Guard***
1820	1820–1830  **Goya, *Chronos Devouring One of His Children***	Goya, *Chronos Devouring One of His Children* (**20.18**) Constable, *Salisbury Cathedral from the Bishop's Garden* (**20.20**) Delacroix, *Bark of Dante* (**20.9**) Géricault, *Madwoman with a Mania of Envy* (**20.7**) Delacroix, *Massacre at Chios* (**20.10**) Delacroix, *Death of Sardanapalus* (**20.11**)  **Constable, *Salisbury Cathedral from the Bishop's Garden***	Percy Bysshe Shelley, "Adonais" (1821) Walter Scott, Waverley novels (1821–1825) Ludwig van Beethoven, Choral Symphony (1824) John James Audubon, *Birds of America* (1827)  **Delacroix, *Death of Sardanapalus***
1830	1830–1840  **Turner, *Burning of the Houses of Lords and Commons***	Delacroix, *Liberty Leading the People* (**20.12**) Rude, *La Marseillaise* (**20.4**) Hicks, *Peaceable Kingdom* (**20.26**) Delacroix, *Women of Algiers* (**20.13**) Turner, *Burning of the Houses of Lords and Commons* (**20.21**) Barry and Pugin, Houses of Parliament (**20.1**), London Cole, *The Oxbow* (**20.22**)  **Delacroix, *Liberty Leading the People***	Charles Darwin begins *Beagle* voyage (1831) Hector Berlioz, *Symphonie fantastique* (1832) End of slavery in British Empire (1834) William Wordsworth, *Poems* (1835) Victoria, queen of England (1837–1901)  **Catlin, *The White Cloud, Head Chief of the Iowas***
1840 1850	1840–1850 	Upjohn, Trinity Church (**20.2**), New York Catlin, *The White Cloud, Head Chief of the Iowas* (**20.25**) Bingham, *Squatters* (**20.23**) Bierstadt, *Sunrise, Yosemite Valley* (**20.24**) **Bierstadt, *Sunrise, Yosemite Valley***	John Ruskin, *Modern Painters I* (1843) Edgar Allen Poe, *The Raven and Other Poems* (1845) Irish famine leads to mass emigration (1845) Richard Wagner, *Tannhäuser* (1845) Pre-Raphaelite Brotherhood founded in England (1848) California gold rush begins (1848) John Ruskin, *Seven Lamps of Architecture* (1849) Nathaniel Hawthorne, *The Scarlet Letter* (1850)

21

Nineteenth-Century Realism

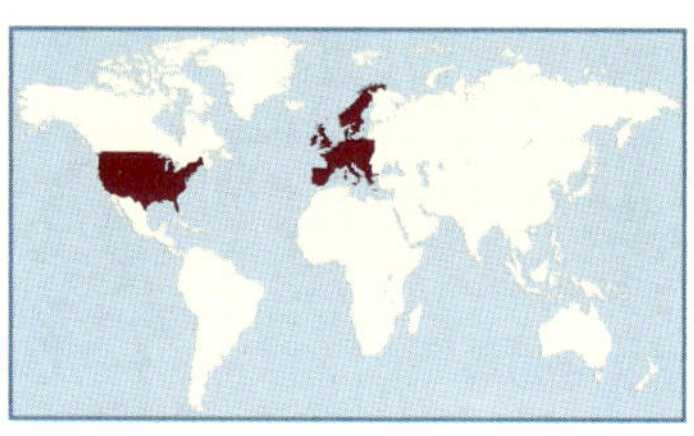

Cultural and Political Context

The nineteenth century was an age of revolutions—economic, social, and political—and these, like contemporary ideas about human rights, can be traced to the eighteenth-century Enlightenment. Resulting conflicts between different classes of society were often implicit in works of art—usually depicted from the viewpoint of those rebelling against political oppression.

A major force in polarizing social classes was the industrial revolution, which began in England, transforming the economies, first of western Europe (see map), then of the United States and other parts of the world, from an agricultural to a primarily industrial base. The process of industrialization continued at breakneck speed. Inventions such as the steam engine and new materials such as iron and steel made manufacturing possible. The iron industry was transformed by the substitution of coke for charcoal in the smelting process. The greater availability of iron as a building material, in addition to its strength and resistance to fire, made it preferable to wood. By the third quarter of the nineteenth century, new processes led to the manufacture of inexpensive steel (an alloy of low-carbon iron and other metals), which by 1875 had begun to replace iron in the building and industrial sectors.

Factories were established, mainly in urban areas, and people moved to the cities in search of work. New social class divisions arose between factory owners and workers. Demands for individual freedom and citizens' rights were accompanied in many European countries by social and political movements for workers' rights. In 1848 Karl Marx and Friedrich Engels (see box) published the most influential of all political tracts on behalf of workers—the *Communist Manifesto*. The same year, the first convention for women's rights was held in New York.

Marx and Engels: The *Communist Manifesto*

The political theory of communism was set out by Karl Marx (1818–1883) and Friedrich Engels (1820–1895) in the *Communist Manifesto*, published in England in 1848.

Marxism views history as a struggle to master the laws of nature and apply them to humanity. The *Manifesto* outlines the stages of human evolution, from primitive society to feudalism and to capitalism, each phase being superseded by a higher one.

Marxists believed that bourgeois society had reached a period of decline; it was now time for the working class (or "proletariat") to seize power from the capitalist class and organize society in the interests of the majority. The next stage would be socialism under the rule of the working-class majority ("dictatorship of the proletariat"). This, in turn, would be followed by true communism, in which the guiding principle "from each according to his ability, to each according to his needs" would be realized. Part analysis, part rhetoric, the *Manifesto* ends: "The proletarians have nothing to lose but their chains. They have a world to win. Working men of all countries, unite!"

Marx wrote very little about art, but he did discuss it briefly in his *Introduction to the Critique of Political Economy* (1857–1858). He believed that art is linked to its cultural context and thus should not be regarded in a purely aesthetic light. His primary interest was in the relationship of art production to the proletarian base of society, and its exploitation by the superstructure (the bourgeoisie). For Marx, the arts were part of the superstructure, which comprises the patrons of art, while the artists were "workers." As a result, he argued, artists, like other members of the working class, had become alienated from their own productions. His view of the class struggle has led to various so-called "Marxist" theories of art history in which art is interpreted in an economic context.

Industrialized Europe in the 19th century.

English and French literature of the nineteenth century is imbued with the currents of reform inspired by a new social consciousness. Novelists such as Charles Dickens, Honoré de Balzac, Gustave Flaubert, and Émile Zola described the broad panorama of society as well as the psychological motivations of their characters (see box, p. 749). In science, the observation of nature led to new theories about the human species and its origin. In 1859 the naturalist Charles Darwin (1809–1882) published *On the Origin of Species by Means of Natural Selection,* written after a five-year sea voyage aboard the *Beagle*.

Newspapers and magazines reported scientific discoveries and also carried **cartoons** and **caricatures** satirizing political leaders, the professions, actors, and artists. The proliferation of newspapers reflected the expanding communications technology, and advances in printing and photography made articles and images ever more accessible to a wider public. Inventions such as the telegraph (1837) and telephone (1876) increased the speed with which messages and news could be delivered. Travel was also accelerated; the first passenger railroad, powered by steam, went into service in 1830.

Paralleling the more general social changes in the nineteenth century was the change in the social and economic structure of the art world that had begun in the previous century. Crafts were replaced by manufactured goods. Guilds were no longer important to an artist's training, status, or economic well-being. A new figure on the art scene was the critic, whose opinions, published in newspapers and journals, influenced buyers. Patronage became mainly the province of dealers, museums, and private collectors. Both the art gallery and the museum as they exist today originated in the nineteenth century.

In the visual arts, the style that corresponded best to the new social awareness is Realism. The term was coined in 1840, although the style appeared well before that date. The primary concerns of the Realist movement in art were direct observation of society and nature, as well as political and social satire.

French Realism

Jean-François Millet

The *Gleaners* (fig. **21.1**), by Jean-François Millet (1814–1875), illustrates the transition between Romanticism and Realism in painting. The heroic depiction of the three peasants in the foreground and their focus on their tasks recall the Romantic sense of "oneness with nature." Two peasants in particular are monumentalized by their foreshortened forms, which convey a sense of powerful energy. Contrasted with the laborers gleaning the remains of the harvest is the prosperous farm in the background. The emphasis on class distinctions—the hard physical labor of the poor as opposed to the comfortable lifestyle of the wealthy—is characteristic of Realism. In addition to social observation, Millet uses light to highlight economic differences—the farm is illuminated in a golden glow of sunlight, whereas the three foreground figures and the earth from which they glean are in shadow.

Rosa Bonheur

Another approach to nature in which Realism and Romanticism are combined is found in the work of Rosa Bonheur (1822–1899). Her painting *Horse Fair* (fig. **21.2**) shows her close study of the anatomy and movement of horses galloping, rearing, and parading. Consistent with the Realist interest in scientific observation, Bonheur dissected animals from butcher shops and slaughterhouses; she also visited horse fairs such as this one and cattle markets. In addition to the Realist qualities of the *Horse Fair,* the thundering energy of the horses and the efforts of their grooms to keep the animals under control have a Romantic character. Likewise, the turbulent sky echoes the dramatic (and Romantic) dynamism of the struggle between humanity and the untamed forces of nature.

Rosa Bonheur regularly exhibited in the Salons of the 1840s and achieved international renown as an animal painter. In 1894, she was named the first woman artist of the Legion of Honor. Her father was a landscape painter

21.1 Jean-François Millet, *Gleaners,* 1857. Oil on canvas; approx. 2 ft. 9 in. × 3 ft. 8 in. (0.84 × 1.12 m). Musée d'Orsay, Paris. Because of their powerful paintings of rural labor, Millet and his contemporary Courbet were suspected of harboring anarchist views. Both were members of the Barbizon school, a group of French artists who settled in the village of that name in the Fontainebleau Forest. They painted directly from nature, producing landscapes tinged with nostalgia for the countryside, which was receding before the advance of the industrial revolution.

21.2 Rosa Bonheur, *Horse Fair,* 1853. Oil on canvas; 8 ft. ¼ in. × 16 ft. 7½ in. (2.44 × 5.07 m). Metropolitan Museum of Art, New York (Gift of Cornelius Vanderbilt, 1887).

and a Saint-Simon socialist who favored women's rights and believed in a future female Messiah. Bonheur made a point of imitating the dress and behavior of men and lived only with women. In order to wear men's clothes in Paris—they were especially practical when she made sketches in slaughterhouses—she had to have a police permit, which was renewable every six months. The *Horse Fair* toured England and was privately exhibited in Windsor Castle at the behest of Queen Victoria. In 1887, Cornelius Vanderbilt donated it to the Metropolitan Museum of Art. When Buffalo Bill took his Wild West show to France, he brought Bonheur a gift of two mustangs from Wyoming.

Realism in Literature

The current of Realism and its related "-ism," Naturalism, flows through nineteenth-century literature, science, and art. In England, Charles Dickens (1812–1870) described the dismal conditions of lower-class life. He drew on direct observation and personal experience, for as a boy he had worked in a factory while his father was in debtors' prison. In *Hard Times,* published in 1854, Dickens condemns the purely utilitarian emphasis on industry as abusive and lacking in creative imagination.

In France, Honoré de Balzac (1799–1850) wrote eighty novels comprising the *Comédie humaine* (Human Comedy)—a sweeping panorama of nineteenth-century French life. The novelists Gustave Flaubert (1821–1880) and Émile Zola (1840–1902) also focused on society and personality. In 1857, Flaubert published *Madame Bovary,* the story of the unfaithful wife of a French country doctor. The description of her suicide by arsenic poisoning is a classic example of naturalistic observation. Zola's *Thérèse Raquin* (1871) details a particular state of mind—namely, remorse—while his *Nana,* the story of a prostitute, has broader social connotations. Zola not only championed a Realist approach to the arts; he was also a staunch defender of political and social justice.

Charles Baudelaire (1821–1867) published his first book of verse, *Les Fleurs du mal* (The Flowers of Evil), in 1857. Both he and the printer were fined and censored for endangering French morals, a condemnation that was not lifted until 1949. He was obsessed with the beauty of evil and decadence, but he was also a Realist in depicting the specific details of perversion.

Realist theater can be found throughout nineteenth-century Europe. In France, Alexandre Dumas the Younger's (1824–1895) novel *La Dame aux Camélias* (1849) was turned into a play. Its description of Camille's death from tuberculosis has become a classic. In Norway, Henrik Ibsen (1828–1906) carefully detailed the psychological motives of his characters. In England, George Bernard Shaw (1856–1950) portrayed both the inevitability and the absurdity of class distinctions.

Gustave Courbet

The painter most directly associated with Realism was Gustave Courbet (1819–1877), who believed that artists could accurately represent only their own experience. He rejected historical painting and the Romantic depiction of exotic locales and revivals of the past. Although Courbet had studied the history of art, he claimed to have drawn from it only a greater sense of himself and his own experience. In 1861, he wrote that art could not be taught. One needed individual inspiration, he believed, fueled by study and observation. Courbet's Realist approach to his subject matter is expressed in the statement in his manifesto: "Show me an angel and I'll paint one."

In the *Stone Breakers* of 1849 (fig. **21.3**), Courbet reveals the impact of socialist ideas on his iconography. It depicts two workers, one breaking up stones with a hammer and the other lifting a heavy rock. Like Millet's *Gleaners,* these figures evoke the romantic nostalgia for a simple existence but also show the mindless, repetitive character of physical labor born of poverty. The figures in both the *Gleaners* and the *Stone Breakers* are rendered anonymously—their faces are lost in shadow—which allies them with a class of work rather than accentuating their human individuality.

A similar emphasis on repetitive sameness as an aspect of French society can be seen in Courbet's enormous frieze-like *Burial at Ornans* (fig. **21.4**). Turning to his native town of Ornans, Courbet depicted the local bourgeoisie attending a funeral. At the right, female mourners in black attract the gaze of the dog in the foreground. A circle formed by male relatives, a group of beadles (local officials) in red, and a priest frames the newly dug grave. Churchmen occupy the far left. The long horizontal of figures is interrupted only by the vertical crucifix penetrating the somber sky. The dark colors that predominate are varied only by the red costume of the beadles and the blue stocking on the man by the dog.

This intensely Catholic group, its compact arrangement, and its minimal variety reflect the monotonous reality of life in rural nineteenth-century France. It is also possible that by equalizing his figures through the use of isocephaly, Courbet was making a revolutionary political statement in favor of egalitarianism. When the *Burial* was first exhibited in 1850, critics found it boring. They also objected to monumentalizing such an everyday occurrence.

Courbet's huge and complex *Interior of My Studio: A Real Allegory Summing Up Seven Years of My Life as an Artist from 1848 to 1855* (fig. **21.5**) can be considered a "manifesto" in its own right. The seven-year period in the title begins with the February Revolution of 1848 and the proclamation of the Second Republic. Over this period, Courbet struggled to free himself from the style of his Romantic predecessors. He wanted to embark on a new artistic phase in which his subject matter would reflect the reality of French society.

21.3 Gustave Courbet, *Stone Breakers,* 1849. Oil on canvas; 5 ft. 3 in. × 8 ft. 6 in. (1.60 × 2.59 m). Whereabouts unknown since World War II.

21.4 Gustave Courbet, *Burial at Ornans,* 1849. Oil on canvas; 10 ft. 4 in. × 21 ft. 11 in. (3.15 × 6.68 m). Musée d'Orsay, Paris.

21.5 Gustave Courbet, *Interior of My Studio: A Real Allegory Summing Up Seven Years of My Life as an Artist from 1848 to 1855,* 1855. Oil on canvas; 11 ft. 10 in. × 19 ft. 7¾ in. (3.61 × 5.99 m). Musée d'Orsay, Paris.

The *Studio* depicts Courbet's broad view of society on the one hand and his relationship to the art of painting on the other. In his own words, the painting showed "society at its best, its worse, and its average" ("la société dans son haut, dans son bas, dans son milieu"). While working on the *Studio,* Courbet described the figures on the right as his friends—workers and art collectors.

The thirty figures portrayed cover the spectrum of society, from the intelligentsia to the lower classes. The group on the left are anonymous working-class types. They consist mainly of country folk and include laborers, an old soldier with a begging bag, a Jew, a peddler, a fairground strongman, a clown, and a woman sprawled on the ground, suckling a child. On the floor are the paraphernalia of Romanticism—a dagger, a guitar, a plumed hat. A skull rests on a newspaper, symbolizing the death of journalism. Behind the easel, as if invisible to the artist, is an academic sculpture of a nude male.

On the right, and more brightly illuminated, are portraits of friends, members of Courbet's artistic and literary coterie, an art collector and his fashionable wife, and a pair of lovers. Many of these are recognizable, including Courbet's patron, J. L. Alfred Bruyas, who financed the Realist exhibition (see below). Seated at the far right and reading a book is the poet Charles Baudelaire, who was a champion of Realism at the time. Echoing Baudelaire's absorption in his book is a boy lying on the floor sketching; he has been interpreted as an allusion to Courbet as a child as well as to the ideal of freedom in learning.

The central group illustrates Courbet's conception of himself as an artist and of his place in the history of western European painting. Having come from a provincial background, Courbet identifies the group on the left with his past. Those on the right refer to his present and future role in the sophisticated world of Parisian society. He himself is at work on a rural landscape, characteristically building up the paint with brushes and a **palette knife** in order to create the material textures of "reality." He displays the unformed paint by tilting his **palette** toward the observer, while also extending his arm to place a daub of paint on the landscape. In this gesture, he has appropriated the creative hand of Michelangelo's God in the *Creation of Adam* (see fig. 14.24). As such, Courbet shows himself in the act of observing nature and then re-creating it with his brush and colors. The creative hand of the artist, echoing an ancient tradition, is a metaphor for the creating hand of God.

Courbet also had in mind Velázquez's *Las Meninas* (see fig. 17.56) and Goya's *Family of Charles IV* (see fig. 20.16), in which the artist paints in royal company. Whereas Velázquez and Goya place themselves in the same room as the royal family but off to one side, Courbet places himself at the center of the picture within the spectrum of society, midway between the workers and the intellectual elite. In contrast to his Spanish predecessors, whose canvases are unseen by the viewer, Courbet the artist is "enthroned" before his picture, which we can see.

A nude woman inspires the painter-king. She is a kind of artistic "power behind the throne," or muse. In this role, she fulfills Courbet's stated relationship to earlier art—that is, he studies and absorbs it but then transforms it according to his inspiration in the "real," present world. The further significance in the woman's placement behind Courbet is that the artist "turns his back" on her, rejecting the Academic tradition embodied by the Classical nude.

A small boy stands at Courbet's knee and stares raptly at his work, perhaps personifying the untrained, childlike admiration that Courbet hoped to arouse in his public. The boy has no socks and wears *sabots* (clogs) to indicate his rural origin. To the boy's right is a white cat that seems to be playing with the nude's falling drapery. But it turns its head and looks up at Courbet, recalling the sixteenth-century saying "A cat may look at a king." The adage as represented here is a subtle combination of Courbet's egalitarian "socialism" and his self-portrait as an artist-king.

The *Studio* was offered to the International Exhibition of 1855 but was rejected by the jury. Courbet rented an exhibition space nearby, where he hung forty of his own paintings—the first one-man show in the history of art. The sign over the entrance read "Realism, G. Courbet." The public ignored the show, and most critics derided it. Courbet took the picture back to his studio and exhibited it only twice more. It remained unsold until after his death.

Honoré Daumier

Honoré Daumier (1808–1879), one of the most direct portrayers of social injustice, has been called both a Romantic and a Realist. In this chapter, he is discussed in the context of Realism. A comparison of his *Third-Class Carriage* (fig. **21.6**) with *Interior of a First-Class Carriage* (fig. **21.7**) illustrates his attention to Realist concerns. In both works, Daumier's characteristically dark, sketchy outlines and textured surfaces make the viewer aware of his media. In both, a section of society seems to have been framed unawares. Strong contrasts of light and dark, notably in the silhouetted top hats, create clear edges, in opposition to the looser brushwork elsewhere.

Lower-class figures crowd together in a dark, confined space. The three drably dressed passengers in the foreground slump slightly on a hard, wooden bench. They seem resigned to their station in life and turn inward, as if to retreat from harsh economic reality. Their psychological isolation defends them from the crowded conditions in which they live. The very setting, the interior of a railroad car, exemplifies the new industrial subject matter of nineteenth-century painting.

Four well-dressed and comfortably seated passengers occupy the first-class car. One woman looks out of the window, as if alert to the landscape and not destined for a life of crowded confinement. The elegant dress and upright, neatly arranged poses of all these figures reveal their higher social position, compared with the rough dress and peasant-like proportions of their counterparts in third class.

Although Daumier had painted for much of his life, he was not recognized as a painter before his first one-man

21.6 Honoré Daumier, *Third-Class Carriage,* c. 1862. Oil on canvas; 25¾ × 35½ in. (65.4 × 90.2 cm). Metropolitan Museum of Art, New York (Bequest of Mrs. H. O. Havemeyer, 1929).

21.7 Honoré Daumier, *Interior of a First-Class Carriage,* 1864. Crayon and watercolor; 8¹⁄₁₆ × 11¾ in. (20.5 × 29.9 cm). Walters Art Museum, Baltimore.

Lithography

A lithograph, literally a "stone (*lith*) writing or drawing (*graph*)," is a print technique first used at the end of the eighteenth century in France. In the nineteenth century, lithography became the most widely used print medium for illustrating books, periodicals, and newspapers, and for reproducing posters.

To create a lithograph (fig. **21.8**), the artist makes a picture with a grease crayon on a limestone surface. Alternatively, a pen or brush is used to apply ink to the stone. Since limestone is porous, it "holds" the image. The artist then adds water, which adheres only to the nongreased areas of the stone because the greasy texture of the image repels the moisture. The entire stone is rolled with a greasy ink that sticks only to the image. When a layer of damp paper is placed over the stone and both are pressed together, the image is transferred from the stone to the paper, thereby creating the lithograph. This original print can then be reproduced relatively cheaply and quickly, making it suitable for mass distribution. Since the stone does not wear out in the printing process, a large number of impressions can be taken from it.

In transfer lithography, a variant used by Daumier, the artist draws the image on paper and fixes it to the stone before printing. This retains the texture of the paper in the print and is more convenient for mass production.

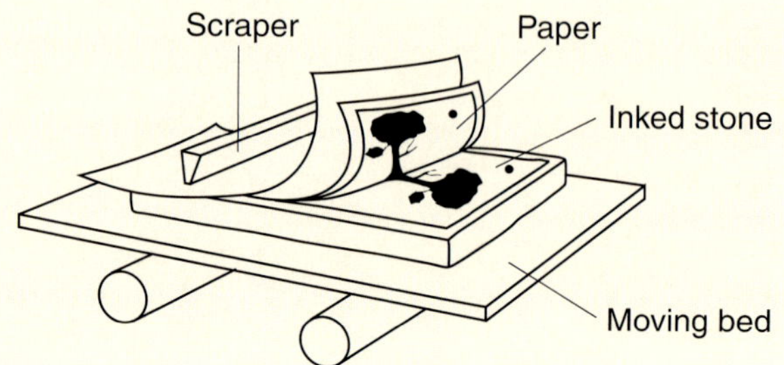

21.8 Creating a lithograph.

show at the age of seventy. He earned his living by selling satirical drawings and cartoons to the Paris press and reproducing them in large numbers by **lithography** (see box). His works usually appeared in *La Caricature,* a weekly paper founded in 1830 and suppressed by the government in 1835, and *La Charivari,* a daily paper started in 1832. Daumier satirized the corruption of political life, the legal system, judges, lawyers, doctors, businessmen, actors, bourgeois hypocrisy, and the king (see box, p. 755).

In 1834, *La Caricature* published Daumier's protest against censorship entitled the *Freedom of the Press: Don't Meddle with It* (fig. **21.9**). The foreground figure in working-class dress is Daumier's hero. He stands firm, with clenched fists and a set, determined jaw. Behind him "Freedom of the Press" is inscribed like raised type on a rocky terrain. He is flanked in the background by two groups of three social and political types, who are the targets of Daumier's caricature. On the left, members of the bourgeoisie feebly brandish an umbrella. On the right, the dethroned and crownless figure of Charles X receives ineffectual aid from two other monarchs in a configuration that recalls West's *Death of General Wolfe* (see fig. 18.28).

So great was the impact of Daumier's caricatures that in 1835 France passed a law limiting freedom of the press to verbal rather than pictorial expression. The French authorities apparently felt that drawings were more apt to incite rebellion than words. Such laws, which are reminiscent of the ninth-century Iconoclastic Controversy (see Chapter 8), are another reflection of the power of images. Clearly, the nineteenth-century French censors felt more threatened by pictures than by the proverbial "thousand words."

21.9 Honoré Daumier, *Freedom of the Press: Don't Meddle with It (Ne Vous y Frottez Pas),* 1834. Lithograph; 12 × 17 in. (30.5 × 43.2 cm). Private collection, France. The implication of this image is that the power of the press is ultimately greater than that of a king. Daumier's depiction of dress according to class distinctions is characteristic of 19th-century Realist social observation.

Daumier and Satire

Gargantua, a good-natured giant in French folklore, became the main character in the classic work by Rabelais (c. 1494–1553) on monastic and educational reform, *La Vie très horrifique du grand Gargantua* (*The Very Horrific Life of the Great Gargantua*). Rabelais's Gargantua is a gigantic prince with an enormous appetite. (The root word *garg* is related to *gargle* and *gorge,* which is French for "throat." In Greek, the word *gargar* means "a lot" or "heaps," and in English one who loves to eat is sometimes referred to as having a "gargantuan" appetite.)

In Daumier's print (fig. **21.10**), a gigantic Louis-Philippe, the French king (reigned 1830–1848), is seated on a throne before a starving crowd. A poverty-stricken woman tries to feed her infant, while a man in rags is forced to drop his last few coins into a basket. The coins are then carried up a ramp and fed to the king. Underneath the ramp, a crowd of greedy but well-dressed figures grasps at falling coins. A group in front of the Chamber of Deputies, the French parliament, applauds Louis-Philippe. The message of this caricature is clear: a never-satisfied king exploits his subjects and grows fat at their expense. Daumier explicitly identified Louis-Philippe as Gargantua in the title of the print. In 1832, Daumier, along with his publisher and printer, was charged with inciting contempt and hatred for the French government and with insulting the person of the king. He was sentenced to six months in jail and fined one hundred francs.

21.10 Honoré Daumier, *Louis-Philippe as Gargantua,* 1831. Lithograph; 8⅜ × 12 in. (21.4 × 30.5 cm). Private collection, Paris.

Photography

Another method of creating multiple images—and one that struggled to become an art form in its own right in the nineteenth century—was photography. It achieved great popularity, and its potential use for both portraiture and journalism was widely recognized. Many painters were also photographers, and, from the nineteenth century to the present, the mutual influence of photography and painting has grown steadily.

At first, photography was primarily a medium of portraiture. As such, it served several purposes. One of its most commercial successes was the *carte de visite* (calling card) bearing the likeness of the sender. Heads of state, such as Queen Victoria and Napoleon III, soon realized the potential of photography for political imagery. Eventually, photography would be used to identify criminals, to capture the physiognomy, gestures, and postures of the insane, to record cultural groups and monuments throughout the world, and to document social conditions of all kinds.

Photography means literally "drawing with light" (from the Greek words *phos,* meaning "light," and *graphe,* meaning "drawing" or "writing"). The basic principles may have been known in China as early as the fifth century B.C.,

21.11 Diagram of a camera obscura. Here the camera obscura has been reduced to a large box. Light reflected from the object (**1**) enters the camera through the lens (**2**) and is reflected by the mirror (**3**) onto the glass ground (**4**), where it is traced onto paper by the artist/photographer.

but the first recorded account of the **camera obscura** (fig. **21.11**), literally a "dark room," is by Leonardo da Vinci. He described how, when light is admitted through a small hole into a darkened room, an inverted image appears on the opposite wall or on any surface (for example, a piece of paper) interposed between the wall and the opening. In the early seventeenth century, the astronomer Johan Kepler devised a portable camera obscura, resembling a tent. It has since been refined and reduced to create the modern camera, the operation of which matches the principles of the original "dark room."

From the eighteenth century, discoveries in photochemistry accelerated the development of modern photography. It was found that silver salts, for example, were sensitive to light and that an image could, therefore, be made with light on a surface coated with silver. In the 1820s, a Frenchman, Joseph-Nicéphore Niepce (1765–1833), discovered a way to make the image remain on the surface. This process was called **fixing** the image; however, the need for a long exposure time (eight hours) made it impractical. The *View from His Window at Gras* (fig. **21.12**) was made with an eight-hour exposure time and is the only surviving example of Niepce's efforts to fix an image from nature.

In the late 1830s another Frenchman, Louis Daguerre (1789–1851), discovered a procedure that reduced the exposure time to fifteen minutes. He inserted a copper plate coated with silver and chemicals into a camera obscura and focused through a lens onto a subject. The plate was then placed in a chemical solution (or "bath"), which "fixed" the image. Daguerre's photographs, called **daguerreotypes**, could not be reproduced, and each one was, therefore, unique. The final image reversed the real subject, however, and also contained a glare from the reflected light. In 1839, the French state purchased Daguerre's process and made the technical details public. The daguerreotype in figure **21.13** shows the sense of immediacy that was possible to achieve in portrait photography.

Improvements and refinements quickly followed. Contemporaneously with the development of the daguerreotype, the English photographer William Henry Fox Talbot (1800–1877) invented negative film, which permitted multiple prints. The negative also solved the problem of Daguerre's reversed print image: since the negative was reversed, reprinting the negative onto light-sensitive paper reversed the image back again. By 1858, a shortened exposure time made it possible to capture motion in a still picture.

During the twentieth century, color photography developed. Still photography inspired the invention of "movies," first in black and white and then in color. Today, photography and the cinema have achieved the status of art forms in their own right.

From its inception, photography has influenced artists. Italian Renaissance artists used the camera obscura to study perspective. Later artists, possibly including Vermeer, are thought to have used it to enhance their treatment of light. In the mid-nineteenth century, artists such as Ingres and Delacroix used photographs to reduce the sitting time for portraits. Eakins was an expert photographer who used photographic experiments to clarify the nature of locomotion.

Black-and-white photography has an abstract character quite distinct from painting, which, like nature, usually has color. The black-and-white photograph creates an image with tonal ranges of gray rather than line or color. Certain photographic genres, such as the close-up, the candid shot, and the aerial view, have influenced painting considerably.

21.12 Joseph-Nicéphore Niepce, *View from His Window at Gras*, 1826. Heliograph. Harry Ransom Humanities Research Center, The University of Texas at Austin, Gernsheim Collection.

21.13 Unknown photographer, daguerreotype, c. 1845.

France: Nadar

In France, the photographic portraits taken by the novelist and caricaturist Gaspard-Félix Tournachon, known as Nadar (1820–1910), were particularly insightful. In 1853, he opened a studio, which was frequented by the celebrities of his generation. In contrast to most of his contemporaries, Nadar photographed his sitters against a plain, dark backdrop, focusing attention solely on the subjects themselves. His portrait of Sarah Bernhardt (fig. **21.14**), the renowned French actress, illustrates the subtle gradations of light and dark that are possible in black-and-white photography. Nadar has captured Bernhardt in a pensive mood. Her piercing eyes stare at nothing in particular but seem capable of deep penetration.

In addition to portraiture, Nadar was a pioneer of aerial photography. He took the first pictures from a balloon in 1856, which demonstrated the potential of photography for creating panoramic vistas and new viewpoints. Nadar then built his own balloon, one of the largest in the world, which he named *Le Géant* (The Giant). In 1870, when France declared war on Prussia, Nadar helped organize the Paris balloon service for military observation.

From 1850, a new "quarrel" arose in the French art world over the status of photography. "Is it ART?" became a controversial issue, with the "Nays," arguing that its mechanical technology made it an automatic, rather than an artistic, process. Because the artist's hand did not create the image directly, it was not "ART." Many adherents of this point of view, however, approved of using photography for commerce, industry, journalism, and science. The exhibition of photography also became an issue, which was exemplified by the International Exhibition of 1855 in Paris. On the one hand, photography was brought before a wide public, and its advantages were recognized. But on the other hand, because it was not shown in the Palais des Beaux-Arts (Palace of Fine Arts), photography was allied with industry and science rather than with the arts. In 1859, the French Photographic Society negotiated an exhibition scheduled at the same time, and in the same building, as the Salon, but the two exhibitions were held in separate areas of the building.

In the 1860s, several books were published that argued that photography should be accorded artistic status. To

21.14 Gaspard-Félix Tournachon (Nadar), *Sarah Bernhardt*, c. 1864. Photograph from a collodion negative. Bibliothèque Nationale, Paris. In 1854, Nadar published *Le Panthéon Nadar*, a collection of his best works. The portrait of Bernhardt (at age fifteen) emphasizes her delicate features and quiet pose, in contrast to the large, voluminous, tasseled drapery folds.

21.15 Honoré Daumier, *Nadar Elevating Photography to the Height of Art,* 1862. Lithograph; 10¾ × 8¾ in. (27.2 × 22.2 cm).

some extent, this debate continues even today. Its irony can be seen in the light of the sixteenth- and seventeenth-century quarrels—in Venice and Spain, respectively—over the status of painting as a Liberal Art. In those instances, because the artist's hand *did* create the work, it was considered a craft and not an art. With photography, the *absence* of the hand is used as an argument against artistic status.

This ongoing quarrel did not escape Daumier's penchant for satire. In 1862, he executed the caricature entitled *Nadar Elevating Photography to the Height of Art* (fig. **21.15**), showing Nadar inside *Le Géant,* photographing the rooftops of Paris. Each roof is inscribed with the word "PHOTOGRAPHIE." Daumier emphasizes Nadar's precarious position by a series of sharp diagonals—from his hat to his camera, which is parallel to his legs, and the line of his back which repeats the basket and rim of the balloon. The force of the wind is indicated by the flying drapery, flowing hair, and hat about to be blown away. Height, in this image, is satirically equated with the lofty aspirations of photography to the status of "ART."

England: Julia Margaret Cameron

In England, the amateur portrait photographer Julia Margaret Cameron (1815–1879) insisted on the aesthetic qualities of her work and avoided the professionalism of studio photography. She manipulated techniques in order to achieve certain effects, preferring blurred edges and a dreamy atmosphere to precise outlines. Her 1867 portrait of Mrs. Herbert Duckworth (fig. **21.16**) illustrates these preferences. The softness of the face and collar, which emerge gradually from the darkness, seem literally "painted in light." Cameron conceived of photography almost with reverence, as a means to elicit the inner character of a talented sitter. She described this in her autobiography, *Annals of My Glass House,* as follows: "When I have had such men before my camera, my whole soul has endeavored to do its duty towards them in recording faithfully the greatness of the inner as well as the features of the outer man. The photograph thus taken has been almost the embodiment of a prayer."[1]

21.16 Julia Margaret Cameron, *Mrs. Herbert Duckworth,* 1867. Photograph. National Museum of Photography, Film and Television/Science and Society Picture Library. Mrs. Duckworth, later Mrs. Leslie Stephen, was the mother of the English author Virginia Woolf. She was also Cameron's niece, reflecting the photographer's preference for using members of her family as subjects.

America: Mathew Brady

In the United States, the photographs of Mathew Brady (c. 1822–1896) combine portraiture with on-the-spot journalistic reportage. His "Cooper Union" portrait of Lincoln (fig. **21.17**) was taken February 27, 1860 at the Tenth Street Gallery in New York City. Lincoln had just delivered his Cooper Union Speech to members of the Young Men's Republican Club.

Brady depicts the president as a thoughtful, determined man. Lincoln's straightforward stare, as if gazing firmly down on the viewer, creates a very different impression from the dreamy, introspective characters of Nadar's *Sarah Bernhardt* and Cameron's *Mrs. Herbert Duckworth*. Lincoln stands before a column, which is both a studio "prop" and an architectural allusion. To foster the union of North and South, Lincoln cited the biblical metaphor "A house divided against itself cannot stand." His hand rests on a pile of books, evoking his profound commitment to literature and intellectual truth. Of the one hundred or so known photographs of Lincoln, more than one-third were taken by Brady.

21.18 Mathew B. Brady, *Robert E. Lee*, 1865. Photograph. Library of Congress, Washington, D.C.

In April 1865, Brady photographed the Confederate general Robert E. Lee (fig. **21.18**). He portrayed the formally dressed and neatly groomed Lee as proud and dignified, despite defeat. Only a few creases in his clothing and under his eyes betray the years of suffering he has witnessed. His house in Richmond, like Lee himself, is shown still standing at the end of the war—he is framed by the rectangle of his back door. The elegant, upholstered chair, half out of the picture plane, is a memento of the passing civilization for which he fought.

21.17 Mathew B. Brady, *Lincoln "Cooper Union" Portrait*, 1860. Photograph. Library of Congress, Washington, D.C.

21.19 Studio of Mathew B. Brady, *Ruins of Gallego Flour Mills, Richmond,* 1863–1865. Albumen-silver print from a glass negative; 6 × 8³⁄₁₆ in. (15.2 × 20.8 cm). Museum of Modern Art, New York (purchase). When the Civil War broke out in 1861, Brady organized a group of cameramen into a "photographic corps" to record the events of the war. The project was a great artistic and historical success but proved a financial disaster for Brady.

Differing from the varied tones that characterize the Lincoln and Lee portraits are the sharp contrasts of the *Ruins of Gallego Flour Mills, Richmond* (fig. **21.19**). The remains of the flour mills, burned when the Union army drove Confederate troops from Richmond, Virginia, stand—like the portrait of Robert E. Lee—as testimony to a dying civilization. The dark architectural skeleton, arranged as a stark horizontal, is silhouetted against a light sky with only a few intervening grays.

English Realism: The Pre-Raphaelites

An altogether different current of Realism developed in England with the Pre-Raphaelite Brotherhood, founded in 1848. It was the conception of three young London painters—William Holman Hunt (1827–1910), Dante Gabriel Rossetti (1828–1882), and John Everett Millais (1829–1896)—and soon grew to include others. The three founders called themselves Pre-Raphaelites because of their belief that the aim of artists since (and including) Raphael had been to achieve beauty through idealization. They considered this aesthetic artificial and sentimental, rather than natural and sincere. They, therefore, decided that their own inspiration would be drawn from the "truthful" crafts tradition that predated Raphael. In thus looking to the past, the Pre-Raphaelite movement also had a Romantic quality.

Although the Pre-Raphaelites followed Turner's ideal of truth to nature, their pictorial style is quite distinct from his. In contrast to the Impressionistic quality of Turner's work, in which forms often dissolve into the paint, Pre-Raphaelite paintings have clear edges, smooth surfaces, and precise patterns. Whereas Turner's color tended to be pastel, Pre-Raphaelite color is pure and vivid, and its subject matter is wide-ranging. It includes portraiture and contemporary, mythological, medieval, and Christian themes.

Dante Gabriel Rossetti

Rossetti's *Ecce Ancilla Domini* ("Behold the Handmaid of the Lord"), also called *The Annunciation* (fig. **21.20**), was exhibited in 1850. It infuses youthful emotional tension into the traditional religious scene. The Virgin, who was modeled on the artist's sister, is sullen and withdrawn. She cringes on her bed as a tall, thin, weightless, and somewhat effete Gabriel floats into her room with yellow flames at his feet. Rossetti represents the Virgin according to his idea of her "truth"—that is, as a frightened adolescent in a sexually equivocal situation. He combines her inner disturbance with an oddly mystical atmosphere, accentuated by the conventional lilies, halos, candle, and open window. Rossetti also depicts the nineteenth-century awareness of conflict between external appearance and internal, psychic reality.

21.20 Dante Gabriel Rossetti, *Ecce Ancilla Domini* (*The Annunciation*), 1850. Oil on canvas; 28½ × 16½ in. (72.4 × 41.9 cm). Tate Gallery, London.

John Everett Millais

One of the most glaring examples of the nineteenth-century conflict between social propriety and hidden emotional turmoil is Millais' portrait of John Ruskin (fig. **21.21**). While the artist was working on the picture in 1854, he fell in love with Ruskin's wife, Euphemia (Effie) Gray. Although Ruskin had been an ardent suitor, he was a disappointment as a husband; in 1855, the Ruskins' marriage was annulled on grounds of nonconsummation. Effie literally escaped from Ruskin, married Millais, and subsequently had six children.

In his five-volume *Modern Painters,* a work of art criticism that he wrote in defense of Turner, Ruskin had advocated truth to nature. Millais' portrait is partly a tribute to Ruskin's vision of nature, which is evident in the landscape. The intricate details of rock formations and leaves reflect Ruskin's passion for geology and botany as well as the Pre-Raphaelite attention to meticulous detail. Ruskin stands calmly, the quintessential picture of a Victorian gentleman in control of himself and his surroundings. His ruddy complexion and pale blue eyes are set against the darker background, while his black clothing contrasts with the light foreground rocks and the whites, yellows, and light blues of the water. He carries a walking stick, which suggests that he had climbed to the edge of the waterfall and stopped to contemplate nature. Ruskin's outward calm, in contrast to the rushing water, is an ironic and tragic image of England's greatest living art critic. Despite his genius for describing works of art and his extraordinary writings on many other subjects, Ruskin tried to conceal his emotional conflicts and repeated bouts of psychosis throughout his life.

John Ruskin (1819–1900), the son of a wealthy sherry merchant, grew up in a materially pampered but psychologically isolated and abusive home. When he went to Oxford University, his mother went too. The sadistic character of his upbringing is described in his autobiography, *Praeterita* (From the Past). In 1843, at the age of twenty-four, Ruskin published the first volume of *Modern Painters.* In 1849, he published *The Seven Lamps of Architecture* and in 1851 *The Stones of Venice.* These books established his reputation as the leading English art critic of his generation. In the 1860s, he wrote on economic and social matters, defending aesthetic, humanitarian, and environmental values against free-market capitalism. In 1885, because of declining mental health, Ruskin had to resign his Slade Professorship at Oxford and retire to his family home in Coniston, in the Lake District. Throughout his life, he kept detailed diaries, some of which describe his psychotic episodes, including his dreams and hallucinations.

21.21 John Everett Millais, *John Ruskin,* 1854. Oil on canvas; 31 × 26¾ in. (78.7 × 67.9 cm). Collection of Lady Gibson.

American Realist Painting

Thomas Eakins

One of the landmarks of Realist painting in America was the *Gross Clinic* (fig. **21.22**) by Thomas Eakins (1844–1916). It depicts a team of doctors led by Dr. Samuel D. Gross, an eminent surgeon and professor at the Jefferson Medical College in Philadelphia. They are performing an operation dressed in street clothes, as was the custom in the nineteenth century. Dr. Gross holds a scalpel and comments on the operation to the audience in the amphitheater.

Eakins uses atmospheric perspective and highlights the surgical procedure. In his choice of subject as well as his lighting, Eakins echoes Rembrandt, who had painted a well-known scene of a doctor dissecting a cadaver. Here, however, the patient is alive, and a female relative, probably his mother, sits at the left and hides her face. In addition to using light to highlight the surgery, Eakins endows it with symbolic meaning. The illumination on Gross's forehead and hand accentuates his "enlightened" mind and his manual skill.

In the early 1870s, Eakins had painted several scenes of rowing, a sport he greatly enjoyed. *John Biglen in a Single Scull* (fig. **21.23**) is one of a series showing the well-known rower with his oars poised above the water. Eakins's watercolors are deliberately executed and were exhibited as finished pictures. This example juxtaposes the calm, undisturbed water and the rower's tension as he awaits the signal to begin. The contrast is reinforced by the horizontals of the water, the horizon, and the body of the scull set against the diagonals of Biglen's outstretched arms, curved back, bent knees, and the long oar.

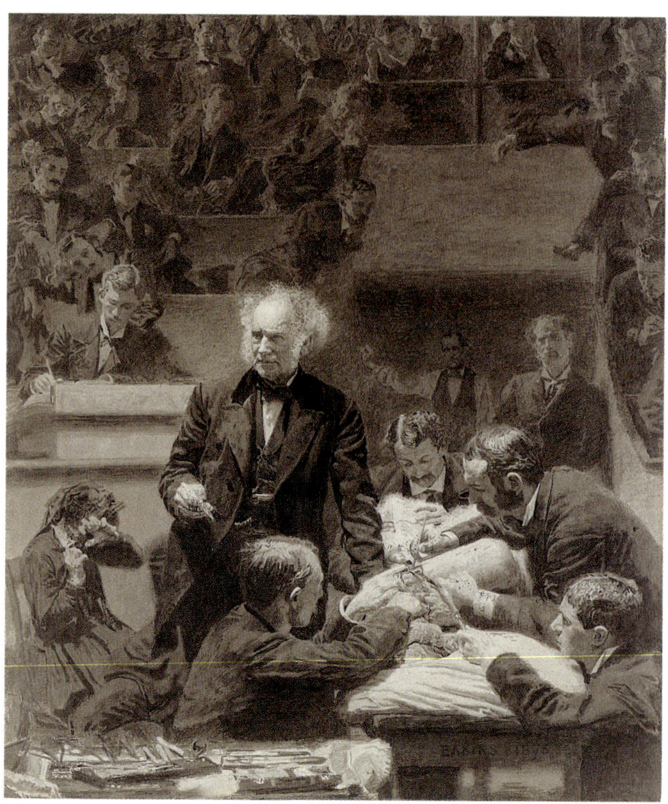

21.22 Thomas Cowperthwait Eakins, *Gross Clinic*, 1875–1876. India ink and watercolor on cardboard; $23\frac{3}{4} \times 19\frac{1}{4}$ in. (60.4×49.1 cm). Metropolitan Museum of Art, New York (Rogers Fund, 1923). As an art teacher, Eakins emphasized the study of anatomy, dissection, and scientific perspective. He clashed with the authorities of the Pennsylvania Academy over his policy that women art students draw from the nude.

21.23 Thomas Cowperthwait Eakins, *John Biglen in a Single Scull*, 1873. Watercolor on off-white wove paper; $19\frac{5}{16} \times 24\frac{7}{8}$ in. (49.2×63.2 cm). Metropolitan Museum of Art, New York (Fletcher Fund, 1924).

Henry Ossawa Tanner

Eakins's student Henry Ossawa Tanner (1859–1937) moved to Paris, where he was the first African American to exhibit at the Paris Salon. Under Eakins's influence, he painted Realist scenes of African-American life in the United States. Later he used his religious faith to express what he believed were the universal emotions—the essential reality—in biblical stories. In that approach, Tanner can be compared with certain of the Pre-Raphaelites. He traveled to the Middle East in January 1897 and absorbed the atmosphere that would provide settings for his biblical pictures.

The next year, Tanner exhibited his *Annunciation* (fig. **21.24**) at the Salon. He shows Mary having just awakened and sitting up in bed. She tilts her head to stare at the appearance of a gold rectangle of light, which signifies a divine presence. The attention to realistic details, such as Mary's dress, the stone floor, and Near Eastern rug, is combined—as in Rossetti's *Ecce Ancilla Domini*—with mystical qualities of light. Tanner shares with Rossetti the depiction of Mary's inner reality as an apprehensive participant in a miraculous event.

21.24 Henry Ossawa Tanner, *Annunciation*, 1898. Oil on canvas; 4 ft. 9 in. × 5 ft. 11½ in. (1.45 × 1.82 m). Philadelphia Museum of Art (W. P. Wilstach Collection). Tanner's mother was born a slave and remained so until her father was given his freedom. She moved to Pittsburgh, attended school, and eventually married the Reverend Benjamin Tucker Tanner, who became a bishop. Tanner's parents admired the abolitionist John Brown; they gave their son the middle name Ossawa after Osawatomie, Kansas, where John Brown killed several vigilantes who were fighting to preserve slavery.

French Realism in the 1860s

Édouard Manet's *Déjeuner sur l'Herbe*

The work of Édouard Manet (1832–1883) in Paris formed a transition from Realism to Impressionism (which is the subject of the next chapter). By and large, Manet's paintings of the 1860s are consistent with the principles of Realism, whereas in the 1870s and early 1880s he adopted a more Impressionist style.

In 1863, Manet shocked the French public by exhibiting *Le Déjeuner sur l'Herbe* (*Luncheon on the Grass*) (fig. **21.25**). It is not a Realist painting in the social or political sense of Daumier, but it is a statement in favor of the artist's individual freedom and challenges the viewer on several grounds. The shock value of a nude woman casually lunching in public with two fully dressed men, which was an affront to the propriety of the time, was accentuated by the recognizability of the figures. The nude, Manet's model Victorine Meurend, stares directly at the viewer. The two men are Manet's brother Gustave and his future brother-in-law, Ferdinand Leenhoff. In the background, a lightly clad woman wades in a stream.

Although Manet's *Déjeuner* contains several art-historical references to well-known Renaissance pictures, in particular to Giorgione's *Fête Champêtre* (see fig. 14.51), they have been transformed in a way that was unacceptable to the nineteenth-century French public. The figures were not sufficiently Classical, or even close enough to their Renaissance prototypes, to pass muster with the prevailing taste. Certain details such as the bottom of Victorine's bare foot and the unidealized rolls of fat around her waist aroused the hostility of the critics. The seemingly cavalier application of paint also annoyed viewers, with one complaining, "I see fingers without bones and heads without skulls. I see sideburns painted like two strips of black cloth glued on the cheeks."

CONNECTIONS

See figure 14.49. Giorgione, *Fête Champêtre,* c. 1510.

21.25 Édouard Manet, *Le Déjeuner sur l'Herbe,* 1863. Oil on canvas; 7 × 9 ft. (2.13 × 2.69 m). Musée d'Orsay, Paris. The visual impact of the painting is partly the result of the shallow perspective. Rather than creating the illusion of a distant space, Manet, like Courbet and Eakins, builds up areas of color so that the forms seem to advance toward the viewer. The final effect of this technique is a direct confrontation between viewer and image, allowing little of the relief, or "breathing space," that comes with distance.

Manet's *Olympia*

Manet created an even more direct visual impact in the *Olympia* (fig. **21.26**), which also caused a scandal when first exhibited in 1865. Here, again, Manet is inspired by the past—most obviously by Giorgione's *Sleeping Venus* (see fig. 14.48) and Titian's *Venus of Urbino* (see fig. 14.52). But whereas the Italian Renaissance nudes are psychologically "distanced" from the viewer's everyday experience by their designation as Classical deities, Manet's figure (the same Victorine who posed for the *Déjeuner*) was widely assumed to represent a prostitute. As such, she raised the specter of venereal disease, which was rampant in Paris at the time. The reference to "Olympia" in such a context only served to accentuate the contrast between the social "reality" of nineteenth-century Paris and the more comfortably removed Classical ideal. Titian had also relieved the viewer's confrontation with his Venus by spatial recession. In the *Olympia,* however, the back wall of the room approaches the picture plane, separated from it only by the bed and the black servant. Olympia is harshly illuminated, in contrast to the soft light and gradual, sensual shading of Titian's Venus. Furthermore, she shows none of the traditional signs of modesty, but instead stares boldly at the viewer.

In 1863, the Salon rejected the *Déjeuner* but two years later accepted the *Olympia.* It is impossible to overestimate not only the depth of feeling that surrounded the decisions of the Salon juries, but also the hostile criticism that generally greeted **avant-garde** (modernist) works. The subsequent outcry following the rejection of over 4,000 canvases by the Salon jury prompted Napoleon III to authorize a special exhibition, the "Salon des Refusés," for the rejected works. Among the "rejected" were Manet, Camille Pissarro, Paul Cézanne (only one of whose works was ever shown in an official Salon during his lifetime), and James Abbott McNeill Whistler—all of whom subsequently gained international recognition.

Manet's *Olympia* caused dissension even among the ranks of the Realists. It offended Courbet, who pronounced it "as flat as a playing card."

CONNECTIONS

See figure 14.50. Giorgione, *Sleeping Venus,* c. 1509.

See figure 14.52. Titian, *Venus of Urbino,* c. 1538.

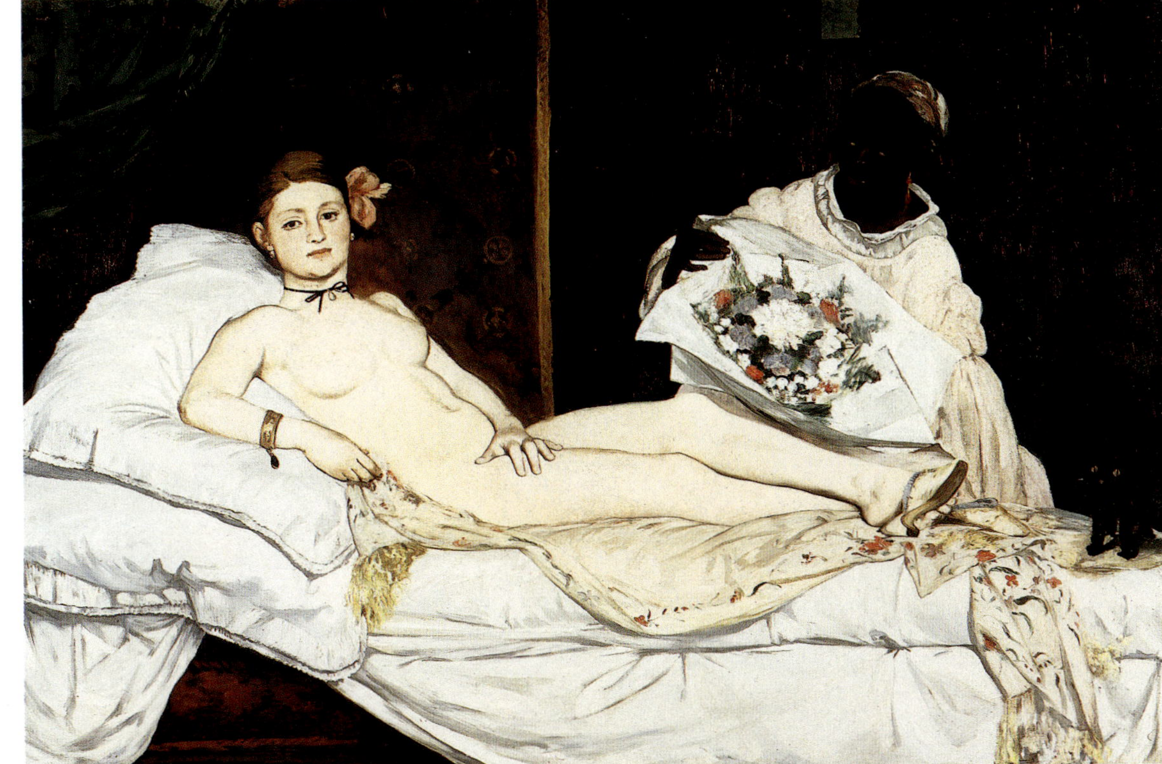

21.26 Édouard Manet, *Olympia,* 1865. Oil on canvas; 4 ft. 3 in. × 6 ft. 3 in. (1.30 × 1.91 m). Musée d'Orsay, Paris. Olympia is naked rather than nude, an impression emphasized by her bony, unclassical proportions. The sheets are slightly rumpled, suggesting sexual activity. The flowers that her maid delivers have clearly been sent by a client. Olympia's shoes may refer to "streetwalking," and the alert black cat is a symbol of sexuality, no doubt because of the popular reputation of the alley cat. The term *cathouse* is commonly used for a brothel.

Architecture and Sculpture

By and large, nineteenth-century architects were not quick to adopt iron and steel, both of which had been recently developed, as building materials. At first, they did not regard them as suitable for such use. The first major project making extensive use of iron was considered a utilitarian structure rather than a work of art.

Joseph Paxton: The Crystal Palace

In 1851, the Great Exhibition of the Works of Industry of All Nations was held in London. This was the first in a series of Universal, or International, Expositions ("Expos") and World's Fairs that continues to this day. Architects were invited to submit designs for a building in Hyde Park to house the exhibition.

When Joseph Paxton submitted his proposal, 245 designs had already been received and rejected. Paxton had started his career as a landscape gardener and had built large conservatories and greenhouses of iron and glass. Not only was his proposal less expensive than the other designs, but it could be completed within the nine-month deadline. The design was subdivided into a limited number of components and subcontracted out. The individual components were thus "prefabricated"—made in advance and assembled on the site. Because of its extensive use of glass, the structure was dubbed the Crystal Palace (fig. **21.27**).

There were many advantages to this construction method. Above all, prefabrication meant that the structure could be treated as a temporary one. After the exhibition had ended, the building was taken apart and reassembled on a site in the south of London. But one alleged advantage of iron and glass—that they were fireproof—proved to be illusory. In 1936, the Crystal Palace was destroyed in a fire, the framework buckling and collapsing in the intense heat.

21.27 Joseph Paxton, Crystal Palace, London, 1850–1851. Cast iron, wrought iron, and glass. Engraving (R. P. Cuff after W. B. Brounger). Victoria and Albert Museum, London. The Crystal Palace was 1,850 feet (563.88 m) long (perhaps an architect's pun on the year in which it was built) and 400 feet (121.92 m) wide. It covered an area of 18 acres (7.3 ha), enclosed 33 million cubic feet (934,000 m^3) of space (the largest enclosed space up to that time), and contained more than 10,000 exhibits of technology and handicrafts from all over the world.

Bridges: The Roeblings

The industrializing countries, particularly the United States with its great distances, needed better systems of transportation to keep up with the advances in communication and commerce. Rivers and ravines had to be crossed by roads and railroads, and this led to new developments in nineteenth-century bridge construction. Until the 1850s, bridges had been designed according to the **truss** method of construction, which utilized short components joined together to form a longer, rigid framework. Wooden truss bridges used by the Romans to cross the river Danube, for example, are illustrated on Trajan's Column (see fig. 7.34). By the 1840s, metal began to replace wood as the preferred material for such bridges.

The principle of the **suspension bridge** had been known for centuries, from the bridges of twisted ropes or vines that had been used to cross ravines in Asia and South America. The superior span and height of the suspension bridge were appropriate for deep chasms or wide stretches of navigable water. Modern suspension bridges were built from the early 1800s using iron chains, but by the middle of the century engineers had begun to see the advantages of using flexible cable made of steel wire.

The greatest American bridge builders of the nineteenth century were John A. Roebling (1806–1869) and his son, W. A. Roebling (1837–1926), who were responsible for the Brooklyn Bridge (fig. **21.28**). Two massive towers of granite were constructed at either end of the bridge. They were linked by four huge parallel cables, each containing over 5,000 strands of steel wire. The steel, which was spun on the site, supported the roadways and pedestrian walkways. It was the first time that steel had been used for this purpose. Ironically, however, in deference to architectural tradition, the pointed arches in the masonry marked a return to Gothic forms.

21.28 John A. and W. A. Roebling, Brooklyn Bridge, New York, 1869–1883. Stone piers with steel cables; 1,595 ft. (486.16 m) span. This suspension bridge spanned the East River to connect Manhattan (New York City) and Brooklyn. Like the Crystal Palace, the Brooklyn Bridge was regarded as a work of engineering rather than of architecture.

The Statue of Liberty

Shortly after the American Civil War, a French intellectual, Édouard de Laboulaye, thought of presenting the United States with a monument to commemorate French assistance to America in the Revolutionary War. For the next ten years, funds were raised from France by public subscription, and the monument was constructed from 1875 to 1884.

Originally called *Liberty Enlightening the World* but popularly known as the Statue of Liberty, the monument is a massive statue (fig. **21.29**) of a classically clothed woman raising the torch of liberty. In her left hand, she holds a tablet bearing the starting date of the American Revolution, July 4, 1776. She stands in a traditional *contrapposto* pose and looks slightly to her right. The statue's weight (225 tons) and height (151 ft. 6 in. [46.18 m]) and the fact that it was destined for a site where it would be constantly exposed to strong winds required the skills of a sculptor and a structural engineer.

The sculptor was Auguste Bartholdi (1834–1904), who was influenced by colossal Egyptian sculptures and had established himself in France as a sculptor on a massive scale. He fashioned the statue by hammering thin copper sheets into the required shape and then attaching them with iron straps to a supporting framework. The frame (fig. **21.30**) was built of steel and wrought iron by Alexandre-Gustave Eiffel (1832–1923).

In 1885, the completed statue was disassembled and shipped to America. It was reassembled on Bedloe's Island (later renamed Liberty Island), which guards the entrance to New York Harbor. The pedestal on which the statue stands, approximately the same height as the statue, was financed by the American public. The statue's proximity to Ellis Island, the most important entry port to America, made it one of the first sights greeting millions of immigrants. As such, its very conception is consistent with the nineteenth-century theme of struggle for social, political, and artistic freedom. It has become an icon of liberty, symbolizing opportunity for Americans and non-Americans alike.

21.29 Auguste Bartholdi and Alexandre-Gustave Eiffel, Statue of Liberty, New York, 1875–1884. Copper plate on a steel and wrought-iron framework; 151 ft. 6 in. (46.18 m) high.

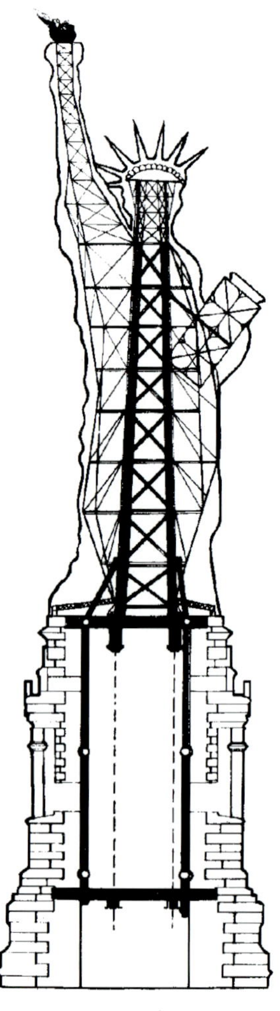

21.30 Alexandre-Gustave Eiffel, diagram of the construction of the Statue of Liberty.

The Eiffel Tower

Like the Crystal Palace, the Eiffel Tower in Paris (fig. **21.31**) was built as a temporary structure. It was designed as a landmark for the Universal Exposition of 1889, celebrating the centenary of the French Revolution. From the third and highest platform of the tower, visitors could enjoy a spectacular panorama of Paris, covering a radius of about 50 miles (80.5 km).

Named for its designer, Alexandre-Gustave Eiffel, the tower was a metal-truss construction on a base of reinforced concrete. Through the curves of the elevation and the four semicircular curves of the base—all executed in open-lattice wrought iron—Eiffel transformed an engineering feat into an elegant architectural monument. An unusual feature of the tower was the design of its elevators (by the American Elisha Otis), which at the lowest level had to ascend in a curve.

The Eiffel Tower was so controversial that a petition demanding its demolition was circulated. When the exposition ended in 1909, the tower was saved because of its value as a radio antenna. Its original height, before the addition of a television mast, was twice that of the dome of Saint Peter's or the Great Pyramid at Giza. Until the Empire State Building was built in New York in 1932, the Eiffel Tower was the highest man-made structure in the world.

21.31 Alexandre-Gustave Eiffel, Eiffel Tower, Paris, 1887–1889. Wrought-iron superstructure on a reinforced concrete base; 984 ft. (299.92 m) high, 1,052 ft. (320.65 m) including television mast.

21.32 Louis Sullivan, Wainwright Building, St. Louis, Missouri, 1890–1891.

Origins of the Skyscraper: Louis Sullivan

By the second half of the nineteenth century, a new type of construction was needed to make more economical use of land. One of the drawbacks of masonry or brick construction is that the higher the building, the thicker the supporting walls have to be at the base. This increases the cost of materials, the overall weight of the structure, and the area that it occupies. The new materials of structural steel and concrete reinforced with steel wire or mesh were stronger than the traditional materials. Their **tensile strength** (ability to withstand longitudinal stress) was also much greater, allowing flexibility in reaction to wind and other pressures. The power-driven electric elevator was another necessity for high-rise construction. All of the ingredients for the skyscraper were now in place. Skyscrapers could be used as apartment houses, office buildings, multistory factories, department stores, auditoriums, and other facilities for mass entertainment.

The Wainwright Building in St. Louis (fig. **21.32**), a nine-story office building built in 1890–1891, is one of the finest examples of early high-rise building. It is based on the **steel frame** method of construction, in which steel girders are joined horizontally and vertically to form a grid. The framework is strong enough for the outer and inner walls to be suspended from it without themselves performing any supporting function. Architectural features that had been used since Classical antiquity and the Gothic era—post and lintel, arch, vault, buttress—were now functionally superfluous.

The architect, Louis Sullivan (1856–1924), used a Classical motif to stress the verticality of the building and to disguise the fact that it was basically a rectangular block with nine similar horizontals superimposed on one another. He treated the first and second floors as a horizontal base. The next seven floors were punctuated vertically by transforming the wall areas between the windows into slender pilasters (every second one corresponding to a vertical steel beam), extending from the third to the ninth floor. The top floor, which contained the water tanks, elevator plant, and other functional units, was made into an overhanging cornice, with small circular windows blending into the ornamental reliefs. The Renaissance impression of the building is heightened by the brick, red granite, and terra-cotta facing. Although the Wainwright Building is not tall by contemporary standards, Sullivan's use of Classical features makes it seem taller than it actually is.

Sullivan believed that the form of a building should correspond to its purpose—"form follows function." In his view, a "properly designed building" should reflect the reason for which it was built, and this should be obvious to even a casual observer. This philosophy of architecture is embodied in the Wainwright Building.

	Style/Period	Works of Art	Cultural/Historical Developments
1830	REALISM 1830–1850  **Brady, *Lincoln "Cooper Union" Portrait***	Niepce, *View from His Window at Gras* (**21.12**) Daumier, *Louis-Philippe as Gargantua* (**21.10**) Daumier, *Freedom of the Press* (**21.9**) Anonymous, daguerreotype (**21.13**) Courbet, *Burial at Ornans* (**21.4**) Courbet, *Stone Breakers* (**21.3**)	John Ruskin, first volume of *Modern Painters* (1843) John Stuart Mill, *Principles of Political Economy* (1848) Karl Marx and Friedrich Engels, *Communist Manifesto* (1848) Alexandre Dumas the Younger, *La Dame aux Camélias* (1849) **Daumier, *Louis-Philippe as Gargantua***
1850	1850–1860  **Courbet, *Interior of My Studio***	Rossetti, *The Annunciation* (**21.20**) Paxton, Crystal Palace (**21.27**), London Bonheur, *Horse Fair* (**21.2**) Millais, *John Ruskin* (**21.21**) Courbet, *Interior of My Studio* (**21.5**) Millet, *Gleaners* (**21.1**)  **Millet, *Gleaners***	Herman Melville, *Moby-Dick* (1851) Harriet Beecher Stowe, *Uncle Tom's Cabin* (1851) Crimean War (1853–1856) Haussmann begins reconstruction of Paris boulevards (1853) Henry David Thoreau, *Walden* (1854) Walt Whitman, *Leaves of Grass* (1855) Gustave Flaubert, *Madame Bovary* (1857) Charles Baudelaire, *Les Fleurs du mal* (1857) First transatlantic cable laid (1858–1866) Charles Darwin, *On the Origin of Species* (1859)
1860	1860–1870  **Manet, *Le Déjeuner sur l'Herbe*** **Cameron, *Mrs. Herbert Duckworth***	Brady, *Lincoln "Cooper Union" Portrait* (**21.17**) Daumier, *Nadar Elevating Photography to the Height of Art* (**21.15**) Daumier, *Third-Class Carriage* (**21.6**) Brady, *Ruins of Gallego Flour Mills, Richmond* (**21.19**) Manet, *Le Déjeuner sur l'Herbe* (**21.25**) Daumier, *Interior of a First-Class Carriage* (**21.7**) Nadar, *Sarah Bernhardt* (**21.14**) Manet, *Olympia* (**21.26**) Brady, *Robert E. Lee* (**21.18**) Cameron, *Mrs. Herbert Duckworth* (**21.16**) Roebling, Brooklyn Bridge (**21.28**), New York 	William Morris founds Arts and Crafts movement in England (1860s) Charles Dickens, *Great Expectations* (1861) American Civil War (1861–1865) Victor Hugo, *Les Misérables* (1862) Le Salon des Refusés, Paris (1863) Leo Tolstoy, *War and Peace* (1864–1869) Assassination of Abraham Lincoln (1865) Lewis Carroll, *Alice's Adventures in Wonderland* (1865) Gregor Mendel formulates laws of genetics (1865) Fyodor Dostoevsky, *Crime and Punishment* (1866) Russia sells Alaska to the U.S.A. (1867) Louisa M. Alcott, *Little Women* (1868) Opening of Suez Canal (1869) U.S. transcontinental railroad completed (1869) **Studio of Brady, *Ruins of Gallego Flour Mills, Richmond***
1870  1900	1870–1900 	Eakins, *John Biglen in a Single Scull* (**21.23**) Eakins, *Gross Clinic* (**21.22**) Bartholdi and Eiffel, Statue of Liberty (**21.29**), New York Eiffel, Eiffel Tower (**21.31**), Paris Sullivan, Wainwright Building (**21.32**), St. Louis Tanner, *Annunciation* (**21.24**) **Roebling, Brooklyn Bridge**	Franco-Prussian War; Bismarck becomes chancellor of Germany (1870–1871) Heinrich Schliemann begins excavations at Troy (1870) Émile Zola, *Thérèse Raquin* (1871) Samuel Butler, *Erewhon* (1872) Thomas Hardy, *Far from the Madding Crowd* (1874) **Bartholdi and Eiffel, Statue of Liberty**

22

Nineteenth-Century Impressionism

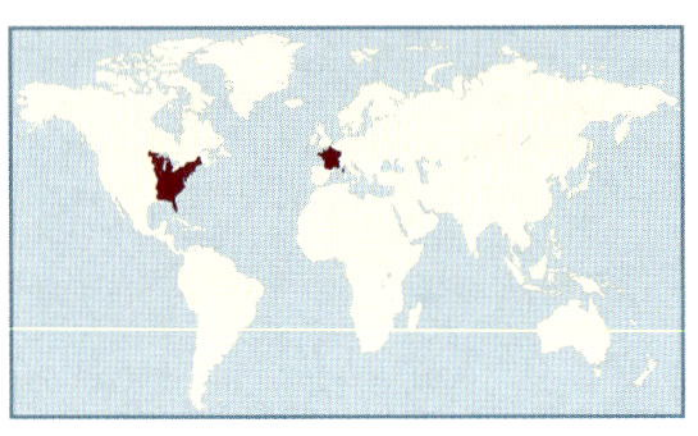

The Impressionist style evolved in Paris in the 1860s and continued into the early twentieth century. Unlike Realism, Impressionism rarely responded to political events. The devastating effects of France's defeat in the Franco-Prussian War in 1871, for example, had virtually no impact on Impressionist imagery. Impressionist painters preferred genre subjects, especially scenes of leisure activities, entertainment, and landscape, and Impressionism was more influenced by Japanese prints (see Window 9, pp. 776–781) and new developments in photography than by politics.

Despite the changing focus of its content, Impressionism was in some ways a logical development of Realism. But Impressionists were more concerned with optical than with social realism. In their preoccupation with political commentary, the Realists had emphasized social observation, whereas the Impressionists were interested in the natural properties of light. They studied changes in light and color caused by weather conditions, times of day, and seasons, making shadows and reflections important features of their iconography. Impressionists also studied the effects of interior, artificial lighting, such as theater spotlights and café lanterns. Nevertheless, these formal concerns did not entirely eliminate the interest in observing society and in the changes brought about by growing industrialization; subject matter included canals and barges, factories with smoking chimneys, and railway stations.

Although many Impressionist artists came from bourgeois families, they liked to exchange ideas in more bohemian surroundings, notably the Café Guerbois in the Montmartre district of Paris, where Manet, Degas, and their circle congregated. Because their paintings were initially, and vociferously, rejected by the French Academy as well as by the French public, the Impressionists became a group apart. They mounted eight exhibitions of their own work between 1874 and 1886, the first of which was held at the studio of Nadar. Ironically, despite the contemporary rejection of Impressionism, it had a greater international impact in the long run than previous styles that France readily accepted.

Urban Renewal during the Second Empire

In 1852, after a coup the previous year, Napoleon Bonaparte's nephew, Napoleon III, had himself proclaimed ruler of the Second Empire. For political as well as aesthetic reasons, he decided to modernize Paris. He wanted the city to be the center of European culture, adapting industrial developments to improve the lifestyle of the general population. New housing would eliminate slums, and wide boulevards would replace the old, narrow, medieval streets. Modern amenities such as drainage and sewer systems, clean water supplies, bridges, lamplighting along the streets, outdoor fountains, and public parks would instill renewed civic pride in the Parisians. The emperor believed that these renovations would discourage revolutionary activity and prevent uprisings of the kind that swept Europe in 1848. With this in mind, in 1853 Napoleon III commissioned Baron Georges-Eugène Haussmann (1809–1891) to plan and supervise the new urban design.

Baron Georges-Eugène Haussmann

Haussmann was inspired by the Baroque grandeur of Bernini's square of Saint Peter's (see fig. 17.2) and the layout of Versailles (see fig. 17.12). His plan was to focus on important buildings, on which the boulevards converged (or from which they radiated). Figure **22.1** shows the Place de l'Étoile (Square of the Star) with the Arc de Triomphe (cf. fig. 19.7) at the center of a traffic circle. This design facilitated the movement of vehicles and crowds, while also emphasizing the political significance of the triumphal arch.

22.1 Aerial view of the Place de l'Étoile, Paris, seen from the west. From the Place de l'Étoile, the Avenue des Champs-Élysées leads eastward to the Jardin des Tuileries and, beyond that, to the Louvre.

22.2 Jean-Louis-Charles Garnier, south façade of the Opéra, Paris, 1862–1875.

Jean-Louis-Charles Garnier

One of the architects hired to work on the renovation was Jean-Louis-Charles Garnier (1825–1898). He created the greatest of the new buildings, the Paris Opéra, from 1862 to 1875. The façade (fig. **22.2**) is Baroque in conception, reflecting the opulence of Second Empire taste as well as the fact that opera itself is a Baroque genre.

The plan (fig. **22.3**) shows Garnier's organization of the entrances, which corresponded to the social rank of the audience. The emperor would have had a private entrance accessible by a ramp, had he not fallen from power before its completion. Everyone else was divided according to whether they arrived by carriage (at the side entrance) or on foot (through the main entrance), and whether they already had tickets or intended to buy them at the box office.

Entrance for those arriving by carriage

N

Entrance for those arriving on foot

Stage

Emperor's entrance

22.3 Plan of the Opéra, Paris.

The interior view of the Grand Staircase (fig. **22.4**) exemplifies the character of this neo-Baroque splendor, with its colossal Ionic columns, the broken pediment at the head of the stairs, the upper-story balustrade surmounted by undulating arches broken by female heads, and the ornate frescoes on the ceiling. Like the Galerie des Glaces at Versailles (see fig. 17.14), mirrors adorned the Opéra walls. This feature, together with the vast open space around the stairway, created a "stage" on which the operagoers circulated. Seeing and being seen, as much as the performance itself, enhanced the excitement of attending the opera.

22.4 Grand Staircase of the Opéra, Paris. Engraving, 1880.

Window on the World Nine

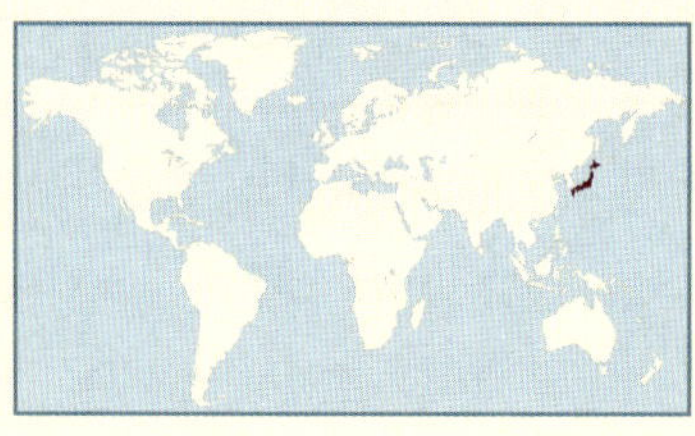

Japanese Woodblock Prints

From 1853 to 1854, Commodore Matthew Perry, a United States naval officer, led an expedition that forced Japan (see map) to end its policy of isolation. This opened up trade with the Far East and set the stage for cultural exchange. In the Paris Universal Exposition of 1867, many Japanese woodblock prints were on view. As a result, *japonisme,* the French term for the Japanese aesthetic, became popular in fashionable Parisian circles. Japanese prints exerted considerable influence on Impressionist painters in France, the United States, and elsewhere.

Woodblock printing had begun in China in the fourth century A.D. In the sixth century, Buddhist missionaries brought the technique to Japan. At first, it was used for printing words, but in the sixteenth century artists began to make woodblock images illustrating texts. Originally the images were black and white, but in the seventeenth century color was introduced. In order to create a woodblock print in color, the artist makes a separate block for each color and prints each block individually. The raised portions differ in each block and correspond to a different color in the final print. It is important, therefore, that the outlines of each block correspond exactly, so that there is no unplanned overlapping or empty space between forms.

Japan in the 19th century.

The prints that most influenced the Impressionist painters were made during the Edo period (1600–1868). In the seventeenth century, Edo (the former name of Tokyo) became an urban center of feudalism in Japan. It was also the primary residence of the emperor, whose power was nearly absolute. Nevertheless, a merchant class developed that produced the main patrons of literature and the visual arts. Woodblock prints provided multiple images, which could be sold to a wide audience. As a result, publishers commissioned artists to prepare preliminary designs and then supervised the engraving, printing, and sale of the final works.

Japanese art students were apprenticed to master artists, just as in western Europe during the Renaissance. The signatures on the prints reflect this system, for the artist had a chosen name (or *go*) as well as an apprentice name. The former was framed by a cartouche (cf. fig. 3.4), whereas the latter was usually unframed and placed at the bottom of the page. A publisher's mark might also be stamped on the print. At the top of the page are the titles of the individual texts, or series of texts, that are illustrated. If the subject is an actor, his name or role is sometimes added.

From 1790 to 1874, the Japanese government made several unsuccessful attempts to censor certain types of imagery —especially erotica—so there is sometimes an official seal and a date printed on the page. The standard dimensions (*oban*) of a woodblock print were 15 by 10½ inches (38.1 × 26.7 cm). Smaller works were reduced proportionally, and subjects requiring larger sizes or several episodes were printed, like polyptychs, in attached sections.

Ukiyo-e

The golden age of Japanese woodblock was the Ukiyo-e school of painting, which was founded around the middle of the seventeenth century. It lasted until the end of the Edo period in 1868. The term *ukiyo-e* means "floating world" and refers to the transience of material existence. The most popular subjects were theater, dance, and erotica, ranging from depictions of various kinds of female services to portraits of high-class courtesans. Respectable, middle-class women performing daily tasks were also depicted, but mythological and historical scenes were less popular, and landscape was used only as background until the nineteenth century. Both the stylistic techniques used in woodblock prints and their subject matter—leisure genre scenes, entertainment, courtesans, landscape and cityscape, aerial views, and so forth—have affinities with French Impressionism.

W9.1 Utagawa Kunisada, *The Actor Seki Sanjuro in the Role of Kiogoku Takumi*, 1860. Woodblock print with *gauffrage* (blind printing) and burnishing. Private collection.

Utagawa Kunisada

The actor in figure **W9.1** by Utagawa Kunisada (1786–1865) is shown in a close-up view. The monumental impact of the print is created by the broad forms that seem barely contained by the frame. The actor's stylized expression—its exaggerated, masklike quality—conforms to the stylization of kabuki theater. Kabuki is a type of Japanese theater derived from sixteenth-century songs and dances that were originally performed by women and later exclusively by men. The typical kabuki play lasts many hours and has many parts. There is a great deal of action in the plot, actors change costume on stage, and props are numerous. Costumes are elaborate, poses and gestures are stylized, and the actors' voices are trained according to strictly defined systems of modulation. Music and sound effects are created by a banjo, drums, bells, and clappers. The triptych (fig. **W9.2**) of around 1835 shows an episode from a kabuki play. The figures assume stylized, contorted, *contrapposto* poses that constrict and monumentalize their space. At the same time, the elaborate patterning of the costumes carries the observer's gaze across the picture plane and accentuates the flatness of the surface.

W9.2 Utagawa Kunisada, *Scene from Sukeroku*, c. 1835. Woodblock print; 8½ × 22½ in. (21.6 × 57.2 cm). Victoria and Albert Museum, London.

Utagawa Toyokuni

Utagawa Toyokuni's (1769–1825) actor portrait (fig. **W9.3**) shows Onoe Matsusuke as a villain. Its lively color and expressive character were qualities that contributed to Toyokuni's reputation as the best artist of his generation. In this work, the figure's full body is represented, but the face, despite its small size, is the focus of attention. The picture plane is dominated by the geometry of the costume, from which the villain's face emerges. The downward curve of his mouth and long, pointed nose accentuate his villainous intent. This, in turn, is reinforced by the upward sweep of his sword's sheath, which repeats the curved eyebrows and headdress. Both Kunisada's and Toyokuni's actor portraits convey an intensity of pose, gesture, and grimace that is typical of kabuki.

Kitagawa Utamaro

The Ukiyo-e images of beautiful women (*bijin*) reflect a new expressiveness of mood and personality. The late eighteenth-century example by Kitagawa Utamaro (1753–1806) illustrated here (fig. **W9.4**) is from a series entitled *Ten Facial Types of Women.* It reveals some of the differences between Western and Japanese portraiture. At first glance, the stylization of the *Young Woman with Blackened Teeth Examining Her Features in a Mirror* appears to eliminate the specificity of Western portraits. The depiction of the features recurs in many of Utamaro's female portraits: the brushed eyebrows form two raised curves, thin oval eyes contain a black pupil, the nose is purely linear, and the small lips are slightly parted. A sense of three-dimensional space is created by contours almost entirely without shading. As in Kunisada's *Actor,* it is by the foreshortening of the forms and the arrangement of curved outlines—especially of the drapery folds—that Utamaro conveys the illusion of depth. The flat background was originally coated with powdered mica, most of which has since worn away. Its shine made the figure stand out, enhancing its three-dimensional quality and creating a reflective, mirrorlike surface.

Two aspects of this print can be related to the prevailing concerns of Impressionism. The intimate, close-up view, in which one sees the woman during a private moment of self-absorption, became an Impressionist theme. She is unaware of being observed, for she is locked in the gaze of her own reflection. The flat blackness of the mirror repeats the other blacks—hair, pupils, teeth, and the official stamps and signatures

W9.3 Utagawa Toyokuni, *Portrait of the Actor Onoe Matsusuke as the Villain Kudo Suketsune,* 1800. Woodblock print; 14⅝ × 9⅝ in. (37.2 × 24.6 cm). Victoria and Albert Museum, London.

W9.4 Kitagawa Utamaro, *Young Woman with Blackened Teeth Examining Her Features in a Mirror,* from the series *Ten Facial Types of Women,* c. 1792–1793. Woodblock print; 14⅔ × 9⅔ in. (37.3 × 24.6 cm). British Museum, London.

in the upper right. Silhouettes of this kind appealed to the Impressionist taste for the effects of black-and-white photography. Furthermore, the back of the mirror—its form as well as its black tone—makes us aware of our exclusion from the intimate interchange between the woman and her reflection. This, too, is characteristic of certain Impressionist works. But it is also a device familiar to us from Velázquez's *Las Meninas* (see fig. 17.56) and Goya's *Family of Charles IV* (see fig. 20.16), where, in both cases, we are prevented from seeing the canvases within the paintings.

Keisei Eisen

The print of the *Oiran on Parade* (fig. **W9.5**) by Utamaro's pupil Keisei Eisen (1790–1848) illustrates a different type of *bijin*. This is one of Edo's high-ranking courtesans, and she is decked out in full regalia for public viewing. Her lofty position is reflected by her height, her massive proportions, and the attention to the design of her costume. Two birds embroidered on the kimono echo the woman herself: the bird at the left repeats the kimono's lower curve, and the other echoes her strutting posture. Utamaro's influence is evident in the depiction of the face and the unmodeled, empty background, but not in the abundance of patterning. This feature, the repetition of orange and blue, and the subject itself are related to the chromatic unity of Impressionism. The Prussian blue, which is used here, was a recent import from the West and attests the contacts between the East and Europe even before 1853.

W9.5 Keisei Eisen, *Oiran on Parade*, c. 1830. Woodblock print; 29 × 9¾ in. (73.7 × 24.8 cm). An *oiran* is the highest ranking Japanese courtesan. Victoria and Albert Museum, London.

W9.6 Utagawa Kuniyoshi, *Tairano Koremochi Waking Up from a Drunken Sleep*, 1843. Woodblock print. Private collection.

Utagawa Kuniyoshi

Tairano Koremochi Waking Up from a Drunken Sleep (fig. **W9.6**) by Utagawa Kuniyoshi (1797–1861) illustrates a scene from the *Tale of Genji*, an epic Japanese romance of the eleventh century attributed to the aristocratic Lady Murasaki Shikibu. It chronicles the life of its hero, Genji, and continues into the generation of his grandchildren. In this episode, a man sees a woman reflected in a *sake* cup as a demon. In contrast to the portraits, this print has a sense of place. Scattered leaves and the *sake* cup appear to be on the ground, and the tree branch identifies the outdoor setting. The detailed attention to the layers of patterned drapery corresponds to the elaborate descriptions of sartorial minutiae that characterize the *Tale of Genji*.

W9.7 Katsushika Hokusai, *Great Wave of Kanagawa,* from the series *Thirty-six Views of Mount Fuji,* 1831. Woodblock print; 9⅞ × 14⅝ in. (25.1 × 37.1 cm). Victoria and Albert Museum, London.

Katsushika Hokusai

The two greatest woodblock artists who accorded a prominent role to landscape were Katsushika Hokusai (1760–1849) and Utagawa Hiroshige (1797–1858). Hokusai's *Great Wave of Kanagawa* (fig. **W9.7**) is from a series entitled *Thirty-six Views of Mount Fuji.* Such series of scenes, in particular different views of the same place or similar views of the same place at different times of day and in different seasons, were also taken up by the Impressionists. The use of Prussian blue in this print enhances the wave's naturalism, but it is the dramatic rise of the wave and its nearness to the picture plane that create its impressive effect. It is a convincing portrayal of the rhythmic power of a swelling wave, even though the wave's flat, patternistic quality seems to arrest its movement. In the distance, the sacred Mount Fuji is small and insignificant by comparison. When the Impressionists first saw this print in the late nineteenth century, they were astounded by it. According to Debussy, this image inspired his famous composition *La Mer* (*The Sea*).

Hokusai's *Horsetail Gatherer* (fig. **W9.8**) of about 1840 uses landscape to create an atmosphere of stillness. As in the *Great Wave,* the artist depicts the scene from a bird's-eye view. It is from a Noh play, another type of Japanese theater. In contrast to Kabuki, Noh plays are austere, usually consisting of one main actor conveying a specific emotion. Hokusai's print shows an old man searching the woods and mountains for his lost child. In the print, the moon moves from behind the distant trees, as if to light the man's way. But although it is nighttime, the landscape is brightly illuminated. Its stillness is broken only by the flowing water under the bridge. The curves of the stream form a sharp contrast to the smooth, glasslike water on which two ducks have settled. Their peacefulness highlights the man's anxious search, which, in turn, is echoed in the rushing stream beneath him.

W9.8 Katsushika Hokusai, *Horsetail Gatherer,* c. 1840. Woodblock print; 19$\frac{1}{16}$ × 9 in. (49.8 × 22.9 cm). Musee des Arts Asiatiques-Guimet, Paris.

W9.9 Utagawa Hiroshige, *Travelers in the Snow at Oi*, late 1830s. Woodblock print; 10¼ × 14½ in. (26.0 × 36.8 cm). British Museum, London.

Utagawa Hiroshige

Travel, which became a popular subject in nineteenth-century France—for example, Daumier's *Third-Class* and *First-Class Carriage* (see figs. 21.6 and 21.7)—is also depicted in Japanese woodblock prints. Hiroshige produced several travel series, which established his reputation. *Travelers in the Snow at Oi* (fig. **W9.9**) is from the *Sixty-nine Stations of the Kisokaida* of the late 1830s. Hiroshige, like the Impressionists, Bruegel, and other artists, conveys a sense of the season. The abundance of white, the heads bowed and arms folded to ward off the falling snow, express the coldness of winter. This impression is enhanced by the minimal color, the stark geometric quality of the round hats, and the predominance of flattened forms.

Hiroshige's last series was entitled *One Hundred Views of Edo*. The *Saruwaka-cho Theater* of 1856 (fig. **W9.10**) shows a busy theater street at night. It is rendered in linear perspective, with the moon causing the figures to cast gray shadows. At the left, theater touts are trying to lure customers. The sense of a busy street, seen from an elevated vantage point, appeals to the same aesthetic as Renoir's *Pont-Neuf* (see fig. 22.21) and Pissarro's *Place du Théâtre Français* (see fig. 22.22). It reflects the fact that just as the Impressionists were influenced by Japanese prints, so some of the Japanese artists, notably Hiroshige, were influenced by Western art.

W9.10 Utagawa Hiroshige, *Saruwaka-cho Theater*, 1856. Woodblock print; 14⅛ × 9¾ in. (35.9 × 24.8 cm). Whitworth Art Gallery, University of Manchester.

Painting

Édouard Manet

At first, Manet remained separate from the core of Impressionist painters, who were his contemporaries. He did not adopt their interest in bright color and the study of light until the 1870s. From around 1866, he was championed by the novelist Émile Zola, who wrote art criticism for the Paris weekly *L'Événement*. Zola argued in favor of Manet's challenge to Academic taste on the grounds that artists should be free to pursue their own aesthetic inclinations.

Manet's *Zola* When Manet exhibited his portrait of Zola (fig. **22.5**) in 1868, it was not popular. As with the *Olympia* (see fig. 21.26), Manet's figure of Zola occupies a narrow space and is close to the picture plane. Even at this early date, the *Zola* reveals elements that would become characteristic of Impressionism. The figure's studied casualness, for example, and the close-up viewpoint create the impression of an unposed snapshot. Zola's manuscripts are piled in front of his books so that his review of Manet's work is visible. The textured paint, in contrast to Neoclassical clarity of edge and smoothness of surface, shows sympathy with the Impressionist aesthetic. At the left is a Japanese screen; its pattern of white flowers is repeated in the gold upholstery nails on the chair and reflects the influence of ***japonisme*** on nineteenth-century painting.

In addition to the Japanese screen, Manet uses the device of pictures within pictures as a kind of visual autobiography, showing the sources for Zola's portrait. A reproduction of Manet's *Olympia* overlaps an etching by Goya of Velázquez's *The Drinkers* and a Japanese print of a wrestler. Goya's assimilation of Velázquez reflects Manet's affinity for Spanish art. Velázquez had, at times, painted in strong contrasts of light and dark, while Goya's late series of black paintings appealed to Manet's early interest in black tones. *Olympia*'s placement on top of reproductions of Manet's predecessors accentuates the fact that Manet is the more "modern," in the sense of "recent," artist. The Japanese print is only slightly overlapped by the *Olympia,* indicating its contemporariness. Both the print and the *Olympia* make use of flattened form and areas of dark silhouettes—characteristics that recur in the *Zola*.

22.5 Édouard Manet, *Zola,* exhibited 1868. Oil on canvas; 57 × 45 in. (144.8 × 114.3 cm). Louvre, Paris.

CONNECTIONS

See figure 21.26. Édouard Manet, *Olympia,* 1865.

Manet's *A Bar at the Folies-Bergère* Manet's *A Bar at the Folies-Bergère* (fig. **22.6**) of 1881–1882 depicts the figure close to the picture plane and reveals the artist's adoption of Impressionist color, light, and brushwork. By the device of the mirror, Manet simultaneously maintains a narrow space and also expands it. The mirror reflects the back of the barmaid, her customer, and the interior of the music hall, which is both in front of her and behind the viewer.

The bright oranges in the glass bowl are the strongest color accent in the picture. The bowl, like the green and brown bottles, is a reflective surface. Daubs of white paint on these objects create the impression of sparkling light. In contrast, the round lightbulbs on the reflected pilasters seem flat because there is no tonal variation. Absorbing the light, on the other hand, is the smoke that rises from the audience, blocking out part of the pilaster's edge and obstructing our view. This detail exemplifies the Impressionist observation of the effect of atmospheric pollution—a feature of the industrial era—on light, color, and form.

A third kind of light can be seen in the chandeliers, the blurred outlines of which create a sense of movement. The depiction of blurring is one aspect of Impressionism that can be related to photography as well as to the ways in which we see. When a photographic subject moves, a blur results. In Manet's painting, the figures reflected in the mirror are blurred, indicating that the members of the audience are milling around.

The formal opposite of blurred edges—the silhouette—is also an important feature of Impressionism. In its purest form, a silhouette is a flat, precisely outlined image, black on white or vice versa, as in the black ribbon around the barmaid's neck. Other, more muted silhouettes occur in the contrast of the round lightbulbs and the brown pilasters, the gold champagne foil against the dark green bottles, or the woman with the white blouse and yellow gloves in the audience. Such juxtapositions, whether of pure black and white or of less contrasting lights and darks, also occur in certain Realist pictures, notably those by Daumier. They reflect the contrasts that are possible in black-and-white photography.

The impression that the image is one section of a larger scene—a "slice of life," or cropped view—is another characteristic of Impressionism that is related to photography.

22.6 Édouard Manet, *A Bar at the Folies-Bergère,* 1881–1882. Oil on canvas; 3 ft. 1½ in. × 4 ft. 3 in. (0.95 × 1.30 m). The Samuel Courtauld Trust, Courtauld Institute of Art Gallery, London. The Folies-Bergère is a Paris music hall, which opened in 1869. Today it is a tourist attraction, offering lavish spectacles featuring a great deal of nudity. In Manet's day, its program consisted of light opera, pantomime, and similar forms of entertainment.

METHODS OF INTERPRETATION

Manet's *A Bar at the Folies-Bergère*

Manet's last important painting has been the subject of extensive study and has been analyzed using several different methodological approaches.[1] As a painter of nineteenth-century contemporary life, Manet wanted to capture the fleeting visual impressions of modernity and represent them as we see them. In this work, he achieves that aim, but he also imbues it with many layers of meaning.

If we consider the **formal** structure of the *Bar,* we note that Manet has divided the picture into a series of long horizontals (the bar, the mirror, and the barrier in front of the audience reflected in the mirror) and shorter verticals (the barmaid, the bottles, the piers, the legs of a trapeze artist, and the man at the far right reflected in the mirror). Despite the emphasis on formal structure, however, the picture is not framed in the traditional sense but, rather, seems to be a piece of a scene that continues above, below, and to the sides of the picture. This "piece of a scene" is the artist's view of "modern life" in Paris.

Iconographically, the subject of the picture is relatively clear. Manet shows us a marble bar attended by a seemingly bored barmaid. She is immobile, as are the bar and the objects on it, whereas most of the action takes place in the mirror's reflection. There we see that a man is approaching the barmaid, whose reflection shows that she is leaning forward on a diagonal toward the viewer. We also see the audience, crowds entering at the back, lights, smoke, and the legs of the trapeze artist. On the surface, therefore, this seems to be a straightforward depiction of nineteenth-century entertainment in context.

In any great painting, however, there must be more than mere illustration to meet the eye. **Feminist** art historians have noted that the barmaid has the quality of a commodity—like the drinks she is selling. In addition, the prominent flowers in the glass vase echo those on her lace collar, her gold bracelet repeats the gold foil of the champagne bottles, the marble countertop is painted in the same black and white as her dress, and the ripe orange fruit in the bowl appears ready to eat. To the degree that these objects signify (in the **semiotic** sense), or symbolize (in the **psychoanalytic** sense), the woman, they connote her role as a commodity to be sexually consumed (for money—in the **Marxist** sense), in the fleeting world of entertainment. In any case, the woman's bored expression implies a sense of humdrum repetition, as if all this has happened many times before.

The barmaid is the object of a double gaze, the gaze being a feature of the psychoanalytic method of interpretation. She is being looked at by us as viewers and by the man inside the picture at the right. The question as to whether he is propositioning her or merely ordering a drink is left open by the artist. In the former instance, we would be witnessing a kind of preliminary to a primal scene, which children experience as both fleeting and riveting. This ambivalent reaction of the child is precisely what Manet has captured in the *Bar,* where objects and figures are both static and in flux. Manet also shows this formally by juxtaposing clear edges that stabilize the image and blurred forms created by prominent Impressionist brushstrokes. The brushstrokes, in a semiotic analysis, might be taken as signs that are unrelated to what is represented—just as words are composed of letters that do not correspond to our mental image of what they refer to. Taken as a whole, however, the *Bar* adds up to one of the major works of the late nineteenth century, and its power to evoke various interpretive approaches is a reflection of its visual and conceptual depth.

In Manet's painting, the customer is cut by the frame, as is the trapeze artist, whose legs and feet are visible at the upper left. The marble surface of the bar is also cut and appears to continue indefinitely to the right and left of the observer.

In addition to the many formal innovations of Impressionism in Manet's *Bar,* the iconography of the painting is also significant. Its structural fragmentation corresponds to the mood of the barmaid. In contrast to the visible energy in the audience, the barmaid stares dully into space. Her immobility is accentuated by the clarity and sharp focus of her edges compared with those of the audience. Nor does she seem interested in the male customer approaching at the right. There the viewpoint shifts, and the two figures are seen as if from an angle, whereas the barmaid and the mirror are seen from the front.

This image has evoked art-historical interpretation from several methodological viewpoints. As a social comment, Manet makes a distinction between the monotony of serving at a bar and the bourgeoisie enjoying leisure time. This effect continues the concerns of Courbet and the Realists (see box).

22.7 Pierre-Auguste Renoir, *Moulin de la Galette,* 1876. Oil on canvas; 4 ft. 3½ in. × 5 ft. 9 in. (1.31 × 1.75 m). Musée d'Orsay, Paris.

Pierre-Auguste Renoir

Renoir's *Moulin de la Galette* (fig. **22.7**) depicts a "slice of life," a scene of leisure set outdoors in the courtyard of a Montmartre dance hall. In the foreground, a group of men and women gather around a table where their half-filled glasses reflect light. They are separated from the dancers by the strong diagonal of the bench, which blocks off a triangular space at the lower right. The dancers comprise the background, along with the lamps and the windmill. Animating the scene are shifting shadows that create patterns of lights and darks. Characteristic of Renoir, even in this relatively early picture, is the soft, velvety texture of his brushstrokes.

Hilaire-Germain-Edgar Degas

Absinthe (fig. **22.8**), painted by Hilaire-Germain-Edgar Degas (1834–1917) in 1876, also represents a "slice of life," the boundaries of which are determined by the seemingly arbitrary placement of the frame. The zigzag construction of the composition creates a slanted viewpoint, like that of a candid photograph. It is as if the photographer had taken the picture without aligning the camera with the space being photographed. The two figures are "stoned"—the white liqueur in the woman's glass is absinthe—and, like Manet's barmaid, stare fixedly at nothing in particular. The poses and gestures convey emotional isolation and physical inertia.

Degas depicted another type of immobility in his painting of the American Impressionist Mary Cassatt in the Louvre (fig. **22.9**). As in *Absinthe,* Degas uses the device of a tilted floor to create a candid impression—itself a play on the gaze. Here, it is the sight of a painting that immobilizes the figure, rather than an alcoholic stupor. Both Cassatt and the woman on the right, possibly her sister, are riveted by the sight of an "impressionistic" picture. The seated figure looks up from her open book as her focus is preempted by the image. Finally, Degas draws in the observer, who, in looking at *his* picture, also watches the painted viewers gazing at a painting.

In his ballet pictures, Degas expresses a wide range of movement. His dancers rest, stretch, exercise, and perform. The *Dancing Lesson* (fig. **22.10**) of 1883–1885, which, like *Absinthe,* is set at an oblique angle, shows a series of ballerinas in various poses and stages of motion or rest. Illuminating the interior and backlighting the figures is

22.8 Hilaire-Germain-Edgar Degas, *Absinthe,* 1876. Oil on canvas; 36¼ × 26¾ in. (92.1 × 67.9 cm). Musée d'Orsay, Paris. Degas, the son of a wealthy Parisian banker, joined the Impressionist circle around 1865 and exhibited in seven of their eight exhibitions between 1874 and 1886.

22.9 Hilaire-Germain-Edgar Degas, *Visit to a Museum,* c. 1885. Oil on canvas; 36⅛ × 26¾ in. (91.8 × 68.0 cm). Gift of Mr. and Mrs. John McAndrew. Courtesy, Museum of Fine Arts, Boston.

22.10 Hilaire-Germain-Edgar Degas, *Dancing Lesson,* 1883–1885. Oil on canvas; 15½ × 34¾ in. (39.4 × 88.4 cm). Sterling & Francine Clark Art Institute, Williamstown, Massachusetts. Degas is well known for his ballet pictures. He sketched ballerinas from the wings of the theater and in ballet studios such as this one. His interest in depicting forms moving through space led him to paint horseraces, acrobats, and other entertainers.

22.11 Hilaire-Germain-Edgar Degas, *At the Races*, 1886–1887. Oil on canvas; 26 × 31⅞ in. (66.0 × 81.0 cm). Musée d'Orsay, Paris.

outdoor light, which enters the rehearsal room through three windows. The dancers are unified by the repeated blue of their costumes, each accented by a different color. Blue, yellow, and reddish orange—the three main colors of the costumes—are assembled in the open fan held by the central girl. The repetition of colors throughout the composition creates a chromatic unity that is a characteristic innovation of the Impressionist style. It also reflects the flat color patterns that are typical of Japanese woodblock prints.

In *At the Races* (fig. **22.11**), Degas' figures are in a state of restlessness before the event. At the right, three mounted jockeys wearing shiny silk vests face in different directions as if impatient for the race to begin. Patches of color that blur the waiting crowd enhance the sense of restless expectation. The woman in the carriage and the man in the top hat also prepare for the race. At the left, a single horse gallops into the picture plane as his jockey reins him in. The arrested movement of the galloping horse draws attention to the distant train. In this detail, Degas refers to the contrast between mechanized and natural movement and to the changing modes of transportation created by the industrial revolution.

Degas was a devoted amateur photographer, and his passion for depicting forms moving through space can be related to his photographic interests. Other nineteenth-century photographers also explored the nature of motion. In 1878, for example, the British-born American photographer Eadweard Muybridge (1830–1904) recorded for the first time the actual movements of a galloping horse (fig. **22.12**). To do so, he set up along the side of a racetrack twelve cameras, the shutters of which were triggered as the horses passed. Muybridge discovered that all four feet are off the ground only when they are directly underneath the horse (as in the second and third frames), and not when they are stretched out, as in Degas' galloping horses, or in the prehistoric running bulls from Lascaux (see fig. 1.12).

See figure 1.12. Hall of Running Bulls, Lascaux, Dordogne, France, c. 15,000–13,000 B.C.

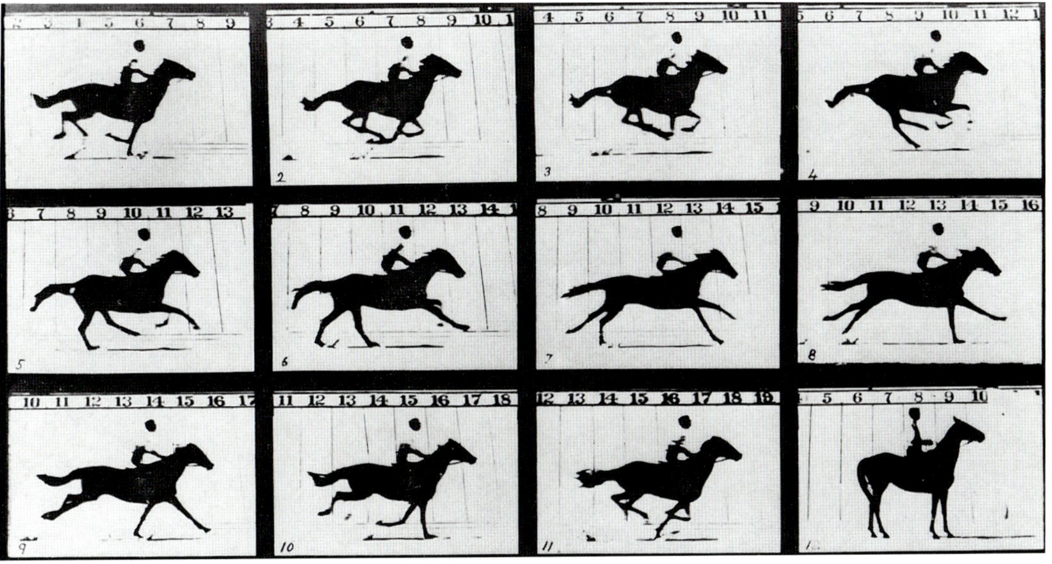

22.12 Eadweard Muybridge, *Galloping Horse*, 1878. Albumen print. Eadweard Muybridge Collection, Kingston Museum, Kingston upon Thames.

22.13 Mary Cassatt, *Boating Party*, 1893–1894. Oil on canvas; 2 ft. 11½ in. × 3 ft. 10⅛ in. (0.90 × 1.17 m). National Gallery of Art, Washington, D.C. (Chester Dale Collection). Cassatt came from a well-to-do Pennsylvania family. For most of her career, she lived in France, where she exhibited with the Impressionists and was a close friend of Degas. She fostered American interest in the Impressionists by urging her relatives and friends—particularly the Havemeyer family—to buy their paintings at a time when the works were unpopular.

Mary Cassatt

In the *Boating Party* (fig. **22.13**) of 1893–1894, Mary Cassatt (1845–1926) uses the Impressionist "close-up," another pictorial device inspired by photography. She combines it with a slanting viewpoint to emphasize the intimacy between mother and child. The rower, on the other hand, is depicted in back view as a strong silhouette. More individualized are the mother and child, who gaze at the rower and are contrasted with his anonymity. Cassatt intensifies the tension among the three figures by flattening the space and foreshortening both child and rower. The compact forms create an image of powerful monumentality. Cassatt's bold planes of color, sharp outlines, and compressed spaces, as well as the *obi* (wide sash) worn by the rower, exemplify the influence of Japanese woodblocks on the Impressionist painters.

A different kind of intimacy characterizes Cassatt's *Letter* (fig. **22.14**). It contains a single figure, whose relationship to another person is implied by the letter. She hunches forward, concentrating on sealing the envelope and oblivious to being observed. Her apprehensive air is given formal expression in the agitated surface designs. The observer looks in on a private moment, just as when viewing Utamaro's *Young Woman with Blackened Teeth* (see fig. W9.4). Cassatt's skill as a printmaker reinforced her affinity for Japanese woodblocks, the flat patterns of which recur in the *Letter*.

22.14 Mary Cassatt, *Letter*, 1891. Etching and aquatint; 17 × 11⅞ in. (43.2 × 30.2 cm). Philadelphia Museum of Art (Louis E. Stern Collection).

Berthe Morisot

As in the work of Cassatt, Berthe Morisot's (1841–1895) *The Cradle* of 1873 (fig. **22.15**) explores the theme of intimacy through a close-up viewpoint. Morisot does not, however, use oblique spatial shifts. Instead, she sets her figures on a horizontal surface within a rectangular composition. Curves and diagonals reinforce the interaction between mother and child. For example, the mother's left arm connects her face with the baby's arm, which is bent back behind her head. The line of the mother's gaze, intently focused on the baby, is repeated by the diagonal curtain. On the left, the mother's right arm curves toward the picture plane and is counteracted by the slow curve of the cradle-covering from top right to lower left. The baby's left arm also curves, so that the unity of mother and child is here indicated by a series of formal repetitions in which both participate.

The loose brushwork, for which Morisot and her Impressionist colleagues were often criticized, is particularly apparent in the lighter areas of the painting. The translucent muslin invites the viewer to "look through" the material at the infant. Looking is also implied by the window and curtain, although in fact nothing is visible through the window. In these lighter areas, as in the edges of the mother's dress, individual white brushstrokes seem to catch the available light and reflect it. Contrasting with the whites are dark, silhouetted areas such as the wall, chair, and the ribbon around the mother's neck. A transitional area is provided by the mother's dress, which, though dark, contains light highlights that create a shiny surface texture.

22.15 Berthe Morisot, *The Cradle*, 1873. Oil on canvas; 22½ × 18½ in. (57.2 × 47.0 cm). Louvre, Paris. Morisot was one of five sisters, all of whom learned to paint. She married Eugène Manet, the brother of the artist, and had one daughter, whom she frequently used as a model in her paintings.

Claude Monet

The work of Claude Monet (1840–1926), more than any other nineteenth-century artist, embodied the technical principles of Impressionism. He was above all a painter of landscape who studied light and color with great intensity. In contrast to the Academic artists, Monet did much of his painting outdoors, in the presence of natural landscape, rather than in the studio. As a result, he and the Impressionists were sometimes called *plein air* ("open air") painters.

The term *Impressionism* is derived from one critic's negative view of Monet's *Impression: Sunrise* (fig. **22.16**), which was painted in 1872 and exhibited two years later. The critic declared Monet's picture and others like it "Impressionisms." By that he meant that the paint was sketchily applied and the work unfinished in appearance. In fact, however, Monet was striving for the transient effects of shifts in nature. He used the technique of "broken color" to show that the clear circle of orange sun is separated into individual brushstrokes when reflected in the water. The same is true of the black, silhouetted boat. Both reflections are composed of horizontal daubs of paint to convey the leisurely motion of the water and blurred forms that we would actually see.

22.16 Claude Monet, *Impression: Sunrise,* 1872. Oil on canvas; 1 ft. 7½ in. × 2 ft. 1½ in. (49.5 × 64.8 cm). Musée Marmottan, Paris.

From the 1860s, early in his career, Monet worked with a wide range of color. A comparison of an early and a late work by Monet illustrates the development of the Impressionist style. The *Garden at Sainte-Adresse* (fig. **22.17**) of about 1866–1867 is a leisure genre scene. In the distance, sailboats and steamships hint at the industrial revolution and the changing times. The *Bassin des Nymphéas,* or

22.17 Claude Monet, *Garden at Sainte-Adresse,* c. 1866–1867. Oil on canvas; 3 ft. 2⅝ in. × 4 ft. 3⅛ in. (0.98 × 1.30 m). Metropolitan Museum of Art, New York. In his youth, Monet lived at Le Havre, a port town on the Normandy coast. It was here that he first became familiar with rapid changes in light and weather. In 1874, he exhibited in the show that launched the Impressionist movement. Until the 1880s, his work was poorly received, and he lived in extreme poverty.

22.18 Claude Monet, *Bassin des Nymphéas (Water-Lily Pond)*, 1904. Oil on canvas; 34½ × 35¾ in. (87.6 × 90.8 cm). Denver Art Museum. In 1883, Monet moved to Giverny, a village about 50 miles (80 km) west of Paris, where he spent his later years. He built a water garden that inspired numerous "waterscape" paintings, including this one and a series of large water-lily murals.

Water-Lily Pond, of 1904 (fig. **22.18**) illustrates Monet's style nearly forty years later.

Both pictures reflect Monet's concern with the direct observation of nature, and both are the result of his habit of painting outdoors with nature itself as his "model." The Impressionist technique of "broken color" breaks up color into light and dark and creates the illusion that the water is moving. In the *Water-Lily Pond,* the lack of motion is indicated by the more vertical arrangement of the broken colors—greens, blues, yellows, and purples—that comprise the water's surface. Monet's method here reflects the way light strikes the eye—in patterns of color rather than in the relatively sharp focus of the *Terrace*. In the *Water-Lily Pond,* the observer's point of view is the same as in the *Terrace,* but the field of vision is much narrower.

These paintings illustrate Monet's fidelity to optical experience through the depiction of colored shadows and reflections. In the *Terrace,* shadows on the pavement are dark gray, and creases in the flags are darker tones of their actual colors—red, yellow, and blue. Likewise, the reflection in the water of the large dark-gray sailboat is composed of more densely distributed dark-green brushstrokes than the rest of the water. In the *Water-Lily Pond,* the reflected foliage is transformed into relatively formless patches of color. Without the lily pads and the shore, there would be no recognizable objects at all and no way for viewers to orient themselves in relation to the picture's space.

Although even in late Impressionism there is never a complete absence of recognizable content, the comparison of these two pictures indicates a progressive dissolution of painted edges. The brushstrokes and the paint begin to assume an unprecedented prominence. As a result, instead of accepting a canvas as a convincing representation of reality, the viewer is forced to take account of the technique and medium in experiencing the picture. This is consistent with Monet's recommendation that artists focus on

22.19 Claude Monet, *Rouen Cathedral, West Façade, Sunlight,* 1894. Oil on canvas; 39½ × 26 in. (1.00 × 0.66 m). National Gallery of Art, Washington, D.C. (Chester Dale Collection).

the color, form, and light of an object rather than its iconography. Monet emphasized the essence of a painted object as an abstract form and not as a replica of the thing itself. A painted "tree," he said, is not a tree at all, but a vertical accent on a flat surface.

In studying the natural effects of light and color on surfaces, Monet painted several series of pictures representing a single locale under different atmospheric conditions. In 1895, he exhibited eighteen canvases of Rouen Cathedral. A comparison of *Rouen Cathedral, West Façade, Sunlight* of 1894 (fig. **22.19**) with the version in figure **22.20** shows the changes in the façade according to the time of day. In both paintings, the myriad details of a Gothic cathedral (see fig. 11.32) dissolve into light and shadow, which are indicated by individual patches of color. The blue sky in figure 22.19 results in a cream-colored façade, the dark areas of which repeat the sky-blue combined with yellows and oranges. In figure 22.20, on the other hand, the gray, early-morning sky casts a lavender hue on the light sections of the façade, while darker blues and purples fall on the shaded areas. A slight yellow glow from the sun pervades the sky and is visible on the tower. Here, as in the *Water-Lily Pond,* viewers are made aware of the medium as much as of the subject matter. They are also reminded that our normal vision lacks sharp focus.

See figure 11.32. West façade, Reims Cathedral, France, begun 1211.

22.20 Claude Monet, *Rouen Cathedral, the Portal and the Tower of Albane, the Morning,* 1894. Oil on canvas; 42 × 29 in. (1.07 × 0.74 m). Fondation Beyeler, Riehen/Basel.

Views of Paris: Renoir and Pissarro

In Renoir's *Pont-Neuf* (fig. **22.21**) of 1872, the influence of photography can be seen in the somewhat elevated vantage point. The rhythms of the city, which became a favorite Impressionist subject, are indicated by the variety of human activity. The scene is a "slice" of a city street, but Renoir also presents a condensed panorama of different social classes. Mothers stroll with children, youths lean against the side of the bridge, some people carry bundles and push carts, and others walk their dogs or ride in carriages. Soldiers and policemen are among the crowd. At the far side of the bridge, the familiar buildings of the Left Bank are visible. Because the sky is blue, the forms—like the day—are relatively clear, and figures cast dark shadows on the pavement. Their patterns, as well as the general view of a busy street, are reminiscent of Hiroshige's *Saruwaka-cho Theater* (see fig. W9.10). Hiroshige's print, in turn, reflects the influence of Western one-point perspective.

22.21 Pierre-Auguste Renoir, *Pont-Neuf,* 1872. Oil on canvas; 29⅝ × 36⅞ in. (75.2 × 93.7 cm). National Gallery of Art, Washington, D.C. (Ailsa Mellon Bruce Collection).

The viewpoint of Camille Pissarro's (1830–1903) *Place du Théâtre Français* of 1898 (fig. **22.22**) is higher than that of Renoir's *Pont-Neuf.* In contrast to the Renoir, this picture represents a rainy day, and the figures are in softer focus, which blurs their forms. Also blurred is the façade of the Paris Opéra at the end of the long Boulevard de l'Opéra. Both are rendered as patches of color and create dark accents against the lighter pavement. The effect of the gray sky is to drain the color from the street and dull it. At the same time, however, the street's surface is enlivened by visible brushstrokes and reflective shadows. Such Impressionist cityscapes offered artists an opportunity to explore the effects of outdoor light on the color and textures of the city. They also record the momentary and fugitive aspects of Haussmann's boulevards in ways that even photographs could not.

22.22 Camille Pissarro, *Place du Théâtre Français,* 1898. Oil on canvas; 29 × 36 in. (73.7 × 91.4 cm). Minneapolis Institute of Arts (William Hood Dunwoody Fund).

French Sculpture

Hilaire-Germain-Edgar Degas

The term *Impressionism* is more applicable to painting than to sculpture. Degas exhibited only one sculpture in his lifetime, and most remained as wax models until his death. About half of these were cast in bronze in the 1920s. Degas' *Fourth Position Front, on the Left Leg* (fig. **22.23**), which was probably modeled during the 1880s, illustrates his ability to capture motion in space in sculpture as well as in painting. The dancer seems as if she is about to spring up and twist around to her right.

Since Degas apparently did not intend to cast such wax figures, they may be considered as preliminary studies for his paintings. As such, they provide a glimpse into his working methods. The textured surface of this bronze, which retains evidence of the medium, recalls the prominence of Impressionist brushstrokes. The observer is made aware of the dynamic modeling process just as the dancer herself shows the process of "working out" her movements in preparation for the finished performance.

22.23 Hilaire-Germain-Edgar Degas, *Fourth Position Front, on the Left Leg*, c. 1880s. Bronze; 16 in. (40.6 cm) high. Musée d'Orsay, Paris.

Auguste Rodin

The acknowledged giant of nineteenth-century sculpture was Auguste Rodin (1840–1917). His influence on twentieth-century sculpture parallels the impact of the Impressionists on the development of painting. Like Degas, Rodin built up forms in clay or wax before **casting** them. His characteristic medium was bronze, but he also made casts of plaster. *The Thinker* of 1879–1889 (fig. **22.24**) reveals the influence of Italian Renaissance sculpture on Rodin's conception of the monumental human figure. The work actually evolved from Rodin's original plan to represent Dante. Its introspective power and large, muscular body, reminiscent of Michelangelo's *Jeremiah* (see fig. 14.25) and Dürer's *Melencolia* (see fig. 16.13), are created by the figure's formal tension and sense of contained energy. Both the *Jeremiah* and *Melencolia* are meditative figures—Jeremiah the Old Testament prophet who "sees" the future, and the idle melancholic genius of Dürer—who have affinities with Rodin's introspective, immobilized *Thinker*.

In 1891, Zola asked Rodin to take over a commission from the French Society of Men of Letters for a monumental statue of the French novelist Honoré de Balzac. Rodin spent the last seven years of his life on the work, which was not cast until after his death. He called it the sum of his whole life. A comparison of the plaster and bronze versions of Rodin's *Balzac* (figs. **22.25** and **22.26**) demonstrates his interest in conveying the dynamic, experimental *process* of making sculpture, rather than in the finished work. In the plaster statue, the great novelist looms upward like a ghostly specter wrapped in a white robe. The bronze is less spectral, but more reflective. In both versions, the nature of the medium defines the surface texture of the work. The rough, unfinished plaster surface recalls the unpolished and unfinished marble sculptures of Michelangelo. In the bronze, the reflecting light activates the surface and energizes it.

Both statues have the Impressionist quality of revealing the surface texture of an artist's material and also

22.24 Auguste Rodin, *The Thinker*, (¾ view), 1881. Bronze; 23 in. (58 cm) high. Musee Rodin, Paris.

CONNECTIONS

See figure 14.25. Michelangelo, *Jeremiah*, 1510.

See figure 16.13. Albrecht Dürer, *Melencolia I*, 1514.

convey an impression of raw power and primal thrust that is characteristic of Rodin. Their surface motion creates a blurred effect similar to the prominence of Impressionist brushwork and mirrors Balzac's dynamic spirit. The figure seems to be in an unfinished state—a not-quite-human character in transition between unformed and formed. Since Balzac's literary output was prodigious, his representation as a monumental, creative power is consistent with the timeless energy of his own work.

In 1898, when the plaster version of the *Balzac* was first exhibited, the public disliked it, and so did the Society of Men of Letters that had commissioned it. Rodin never cast the work in bronze, and it is not known whether he ever intended to do so.

22.25 (left) Auguste Rodin, *Balzac,* 1892–1897. Plaster; 9 ft. 10 in. (3.00 m) high. Musée Rodin, Paris.

22.26 (right) Auguste Rodin, *Monument to Balzac,* 1898 (cast 1954). Bronze; 9 ft. 3 in. × 48¼ in. × 41 in. (281.9 × 122.5 × 104.2 cm). Sculpture Garden, Museum of Modern Art, New York.

22.25, 22.26 Rodin's revolutionary methods of working included the use of nonprofessional models in nontraditional poses. Apart from portrait busts, Rodin was the first major sculptor to create work consisting of less than the whole body—a headless torso, for example.

Artists Quote Art: Beauford Delaney on Rodin

In the 1960s, Beauford Delaney (1901–1979), the African-American artist living in Paris, painted a small tribute to Rodin entitled *Balzac by Rodin* (fig. **22.27**), in which he transported the statue from the Boulevard Raspail to an anonymous landscape setting. He has retained the looming, gigantic aspect of Rodin's sculpture, its sense of process, and the green hue of aged bronze. But he has endowed the work with his own unique white light, which, according to the American author James Baldwin, "held the power to illuminate, even to redeem and reconcile and heal."[2] Henry Miller described Delaney's picture as "saturated with color and light."[3] White light fills the areas of the *Balzac* that in reality are darkened, thus reversing the relationship of light and dark on a sculptured surface. The entire sky is white, except for the blue patch over the *Balzac*'s head, a reversal of the expected, for the blue becomes cloud-like and the naturally blue sky is whitened.

22.27 Beauford Delaney, *Balzac by Rodin,* 1960s. Oil on canvas; 24 × 19½ in. (61.0 × 49.5 cm), whereabouts unknown. Beauford Delaney was the son of a minister in Knoxville, Tennessee. He studied art and went to New York in 1929 at the end of the Harlem Renaissance. In 1954, he moved to Paris, where he painted portraits of the French playwright Jean Genet and the American novelists Henry Miller, James Baldwin, and James Jones.

American Painting at the Turn of the Century

Several important late nineteenth-century American artists correspond chronologically to the French Impressionists. Some, such as Cassatt, lived as expatriates in Europe and worked in the Impressionist style. Others stayed in America and continued in a more Realist vein.

Winslow Homer

Winslow Homer (1836–1910) visited Paris before the heyday of Impressionism, and his work can be regarded as transitional between Realism and Impressionism. In *Breezing Up* (fig. **22.28**) of 1873–1876, Homer's interest in the American identity of his subjects and their place in society is evident. At the same time, however, he has clearly been influenced by the Impressionist interest in weather conditions and their effect on light and color. The sea, churned up by the wind, is rendered as broken color with visible brushstrokes. By tilting the boat in the foreground, Homer creates a slanted "floor" that is related to Degas' compositional technique. The interruption of the diagonal sail by the frame, the oblique viewpoint, and the sailors' apparent indifference to the observer suggest a fleeting moment captured by the camera.

22.28 Winslow Homer, *Breezing Up (A Fair Wind)*, 1873–1876. Oil on canvas; 24⅛ × 38⅛ in. (61.5 × 96.8 cm). National Gallery of Art, Washington, D.C. (Gift of the W. L. and May T. Mellon Foundation). Homer, a largely self-taught artist from Boston, worked as a magazine illustrator. At the outbreak of the Civil War, he was sent by *Harper's Weekly* to do drawings at the front. After the war, he spent a year in France. From 1873, he worked in watercolor, which became as important a medium for him as oil.

John Singer Sargent

John Singer Sargent (1856–1925), who lived in Paris in the early 1880s, espoused Impressionism wholeheartedly. But even though Sargent is sometimes considered an Impressionist, he did not allow form to dissolve into light, as did the French Impressionists. After his death, and with the advent of modernism, Sargent was dismissed as a painter of elegant, superficial portraits that emphasized the rich materials worn by his society patrons. But the *Daughters of Edward Darley Boit* (fig. **22.29**), exhibited in the Salon of 1883, reveals the inner tensions of four young sisters, despite their comfortable lifestyle.

The girls occupy a fashionable room decorated with large Chinese vases and a Chinese rug. The mirror, which recalls Velázquez's *Las Meninas* (see fig. 17.56), complicates the spatial relationships within the picture, while the oblique view locates the figures above the observer. The cropped rug and vase produce a version of the Impressionist "slice of life," and the subjects seem frozen in time. Three gaze at the viewer, and one leans introspectively against a vase. Two are close together and two, echoing the vases, are apart. The spaces separating the figures convey psychological tension and create the impression of an internal subtext. Enhancing the psychological effect of the work is the fact that as the girls become older, they are more in shadow.

22.29 John Singer Sargent, *Daughters of Edward Darley Boit,* 1882. Oil on canvas; 7 ft. 3 in. × 7 ft. 3 in. (2.21 × 2.21 m). Courtesy Museum of Fine Arts, Boston (Gift of Mary Louisa Boit, Florence D. Boit, Jane Hubbard Boit, and Julia Overing Boit, in memory of their father, Edward Darley Boit).

"Art for Art's Sake"

In Paris, widespread public and critical condemnation made it difficult for the Impressionists to sell their work. In London as well, there were aesthetic quarrels. One of these erupted into the celebrated libel trial between the American painter James Abbott McNeill Whistler (1834–1903) and the English art critic John Ruskin. In 1877, Ruskin published a scathing review of Whistler's *Nocturne in Black and Gold (The Falling Rocket)* (fig. **22.30**), painted some two years previously. The picture was on view at London's Grosvenor Gallery, and it threw Ruskin into a rage. He accused Whistler of flinging "a pot of paint . . . in the public's face." Whistler himself, Ruskin added, was a "coxcomb," guilty of "Cockney impudence" and "wilful imposture."

Whistler sued Ruskin for libel, and the case went to trial in November 1878. Ruskin, who was in the throes of a psychotic breakdown, could not appear in court, but his views

22.30 James Abbott McNeill Whistler, *Nocturne in Black and Gold* (*The Falling Rocket*), c. 1875. Oil on oak panel; 23⅝ × 18½ in. (60.0 × 47.0 cm). Detroit Institute of Arts (Gift of Dexter M. Ferry, Jr.). Whistler, born in Lowell, Massachusetts, moved with his family to Russia, where his father designed the Moscow–Saint Petersburg railroad. He set up art studios in Paris and London, finally settling in Chelsea. The author of *The Gentle Art of Making Enemies,* Whistler was known for his distinctive personality and biting wit. He dressed as a dandy, wearing pink ribbons on his tight, patent-leather shoes and carrying two umbrellas in defiance of the inclement London weather.

were presented by his attorney. According to Ruskin, Whistler's picture was outrageously overpriced at 200 guineas, quickly and sloppily executed, technically "unfinished," and devoid of recognizable form. Several of Whistler's other paintings were introduced as exhibits and declared equally "unfinished." In particular, the defense pointed out, Whistler did not paint like Titian, whose works *were* "finished." Ruskin also objected to Whistler's musical titles (in this case *Nocturne*) as pandering to the contemporary fad for the incomprehensible. The paintings were not, he insisted, serious works of art. In his opening statement, the attorney general, acting for Ruskin, had this to say about musical titles:

> In the present mania for art it had become a kind of fashion among some people to admire the incomprehensible, to look upon the fantastic conceits of an artist like Mr. Whistler, his "nocturnes," "symphonies," "arrangements," and "harmonies," with delight and admiration; but the fact was that such productions were not worthy of the name of great works of art. This was not a mania that should be encouraged; and if that was the view of Mr. Ruskin, he had a right as an art critic to fearlessly express it to the public.

On cross-examination, Whistler was questioned about his subject matter:

> "What is the subject of the *Nocturne in Black and Gold*?"
> "It is a night piece," Whistler replied, "and represents the fireworks at Cremorne."
> "Not a view of Cremorne?"
> "If it were a view of Cremorne, it would certainly bring about nothing but disappointment on the part of the beholders. It is an artistic arrangement. . . . It is as impossible for me to explain to you the beauty of that picture as it would be for a musician to explain to you the beauty of a harmony in a particular piece of music if you have no ear for music."

Ironically, Ruskin had once used his critical genius to further the public reception of Turner, himself a rather "Impressionistic" artist. Equally ironic, Whistler was quite capable of producing clear and precise images, as he did in his etchings as well as in some of his portraits. The famous portrait of Whistler's mother (see fig. I.9), which also has a combined musical and artistic title—*Arrangement in Gray and Black*—is a remarkable psychological portrait and also satisfies Ruskin's requirement that a painting appear "finished." It conveys her dour, puritanical character, reflected in the assertion by one of Whistler's friends that she lived on the top floor of his London house in order to be closer to God.

Whistler's two stylistic tendencies—linear and atmospheric—mirrored his psychological conflicts as well as the traditional quarrels between *disegno* and *colorito*, the *Poussinistes* and the *Rubénistes*, Classical art and modernism. In the Impressionist period, the Academy stood for traditional "clarity" and opposed the atmospheric effects of works by Whistler and Debussy. Whistler internalized these quarrels according to his own struggle between male and female forces within himself. He wrote that "Color is vice. . . . When controlled by a firm hand, well-guided by her master, Drawing, Color is then like a splendid woman with a mate worthy of her . . . the most magnificent mistress possible. But when united with uncertainty, with a weak drawing . . . , Color becomes a bold whore, makes fun of her little fellow, isn't it so?"[4]

See figure I.9. James Abbott McNeill Whistler, *Arrangement in Black and Gray (Portrait of the Artist's Mother)*, 1871.

In court, Whistler countered Ruskin's position by stating what was essentially the formalist "art for art's sake" view of art—namely, that art does not necessarily serve a utilitarian purpose. Although designated a painting of fireworks on the Thames, Whistler's *Nocturne* was actually a study in light, color, and form. The atmospheric effects of the cloudy night sky are contrasted with gold spots of light from the exploded rocket. When questioned about the identity of the black patch in the lower right corner, Whistler replied that it was a vertical, placed there for purely formal reasons. In that response, he echoed Monet's view that a painted "tree" is not a tree, but a vertical daub of paint. On the subject of money, Whistler testified that he had spent only a day and a half painting the *Nocturne* but was charging for a lifetime of experience.

The jury followed the judge's instructions and decided in Whistler's favor but awarded him only a farthing in damages. When it was over, the trial was extensively ridiculed in the English and American press. A *New York Times* critic complained (December 15, 1878) that "the world has been much afflicted of late with these slapdash productions of the paint-pot." In his view, musical titles were "exasperating nomenclature," and the "shadowy and unseen presences" of modern art were confusing. "Ordinary men and women in a state of health," he concluded, "prefer to have their pictures made for them." The London *Times* suggested that Whistler might take his "brush" to Ruskin's "pen" and paint a caricature of Ruskin as an "arrangement in black and white." The tragic irony of this notion is that when, at the end of his life, Ruskin descended into his final madness, he went around muttering "everything black . . . everything white."

The trial was also the subject of the cartoon in figure **22.31**, which appeared in the English humorous magazine *Punch* on December 7, 1878. In it, the judge holds up a giant farthing, which he offers to Whistler, who has a large ear on top of his head—his "ear for musical titles." Whistler stands on flute legs, referring not only to his musical titles, but also to his father, whose nickname was "Pipes" since he was an accomplished amateur flautist. At the right, the balloon over the jury reads: "No symphony [for "sympathy"] with the defendant."

Below the jury, Ruskin is represented as an "Old Pelican in the Art Wilderness," his head bowed as if in shame at having lost the case. The box in front of the judge reads "Damages" and has a slot large enough to accommodate the farthing. Slithering along the floor are two serpents emerging from the bottomless pit of court costs. In fact, Whistler was bankrupted by the trial and was forced to sell his house in Chelsea. A fellow artist called the bankruptcy petition an "arrangement in black and white." Nearly seventy years after the trial, *Art Digest* reported that the Detroit Institute of Arts paid $12,000 for the infamous "pot of paint."

The significance of this absurd trial is its function as a window on aesthetic conflict in the late nineteenth century. It also proves the adage that one cannot legislate taste. Whistler later called the trial a conflict between the "brush" and the "pen." It exemplified the rise of the critic as a potent force in the nineteenth-century art world. Although Ruskin had shown foresight when dealing with his own innovative contemporaries—notably Turner and the Pre-Raphaelites, whose causes he had championed—he did not have the same vision about the younger generation of artists. And he was not alone. The French public also failed to recognize the merits of avant-garde nineteenth-century art, and, as a result, many important French paintings were bought by foreign collectors and are now in collections outside France.

We have seen that the history of Western art is fraught with aesthetic quarrels, but passions rose to new heights during the latter half of the nineteenth century. For the first time, the material of art became a subject of art, and content yielded to style. More than anything else, it was the dissolution of form that seems to have caused the most intense critical outrage. But this was the very trend that would prove to have the most lasting impact on the development of Western art.

22.31 *Whistler versus Ruskin: An Appeal to the Law,* from *Punch,* December 7, 1878, p. 254.

	Style/Period	Works of Art	Cultural/Historical Developments
1790 1800	 **Hiroshige, *Saruwaka-cho Theater***	Utamaro, *Young Woman with Blackened Teeth Examining Her Features in a Mirror* (**W9.4**) Toyokuni, *Portrait of the Actor Onoe Matsusuke as the Villain Kudo Suketsune* (**W9.3**) Eisen, *Oiran on Parade* (**W9.5**) Hokusai, *Great Wave of Kanagawa* (**W9.7**) Kunisada, *Scene from Sukeroku* (**W9.2**) Hiroshige, *Travelers in the Snow at Oi* (**W9.9**) Hokusai, *Horsetail Gatherer* (**W9.8**) Kuniyoshi, *Tairano Koremochi Waking Up from a Drunken Sleep* (**W9.6**) Hiroshige, *Saruwaka-cho Theater* (**W9.10**) Kunisada, *The Actor Seki Sanjuro in the Role of Kiogoku Takumi* (**W9.1**)	Edo period (1600–1868) Ukiyo-e school of painting Restoration of Meiji dynasty in Japan (1868)  **Manet, *A Bar at the Folies-Bergère***  **Manet, *Zola***
1860	IMPRESSIONISM 1860–1920	Garnier, Opéra (**22.2–22.4**), Paris Monet, *Terrace at Sainte-Adresse* (**22.17**) Manet, *Zola* (**22.5**)	
1870	1870–1880 **Muybridge, *Galloping Horse***	Monet, *Impression: Sunrise* (**22.16**) Renoir, *Pont-Neuf* (**22.21**) Morisot, *The Cradle* (**22.15**) Whistler, *Nocturne in Black and Gold* (**22.30**) Homer, *Breezing Up* (**22.28**) Degas, *Absinthe* (**22.8**) Renoir, *Moulin de la Galette* (**22.7**) Muybridge, *Galloping Horse* (**22.12**) *Whistler versus Ruskin* (**22.31**) Rodin, *The Thinker* (**22.24**)	Richard Wagner, *Die Walküre* (1870) Giuseppe Verdi, *Aïda* (1871) First Impressionist art exhibition in Paris (1874) Mark Twain, *Adventures of Tom Sawyer* (1875) Georges Bizet, *Carmen* (1875) Alexander Graham Bell invents the telephone (1876) Pyotr Ilich Tchaikovsky, *Swan Lake* ballet (1876) U.S. National Baseball League founded (1876) First lawn-tennis championship played at Wimbledon (1877) Henrik Ibsen, *Doll's House* (1879) Thomas Edison invents the phonograph and electric light bulb (1879–1880)
1880	1880–1890  **Hiroshige, *Travelers in the Snow at Oi*** **Degas, *At the Races***	Degas, *Fourth Position Front, on the Left Leg* (**22.23**) Manet, *A Bar at the Folies-Bergère* (**22.6**) Sargent, *Daughters of Edward Darley Boit* (**22.29**) Degas, *Dancing Lesson* (**22.10**) Degas, *Visit to a Museum* (**22.9**) Degas, *At the Races* (**22.11**) 	European colonization of Africa begins (1880s) Louis Pasteur discovers a chicken cholera vaccine (1880) Andrew Carnegie develops first large steel furnace (1880) Fyodor Dostoevsky, *Brothers Karamazov* (1880) Henry James, *Washington Square* (1881) Johannes Brahms, *Academic Festival Overture* (1881) Brooklyn Bridge opened to traffic (1883) Friedrich Wilhelm Nietzsche, *Thus Spake Zarathustra* (1883) First steam turbine engine invented (1884) Gilbert and Sullivan, *The Mikado* (1885) Walter Pater, *Marius the Epicurean* (1885) American Federation of Labor founded (1886) Robert Louis Stevenson, *Dr. Jekyll and Mr. Hyde* (1886) Karl Marx, *Das Kapital* published in English (1886) Arthur Conan Doyle, *A Study in Scarlet* (1887) John Dunlop invents the pneumatic tire (1888) Nicolai Rimsky-Korsakov, *Scheherazade* (1888) George Eastman develops Kodak box camera (1888)
1890	1890–1900  **Monet, *Rouen Cathedral***	Cassatt, *Letter* (**22.14**) Rodin, *Balzac* (**22.25–22.26**) Cassatt, *Boating Party* (**22.13**) Monet, *Rouen Cathedral, West Façade, Sunlight* (**22.19**) Monet, *Rouen Cathedral, the Portal and the Tower of Albane, the Morning* (**22.20**) Pissarro, *Place du Théâtre Français* (**22.22**)  **Pissarro, *Place du Théâtre Français***	James G. Frazer, *Golden Bough* (1890–1915) Sergei Rachmaninoff, Piano Concerto No. 1 (1891) George Bernard Shaw, *Mrs. Warren's Profession* (1892) F. H. Bradley, *Appearance and Reality* (1893) Antonín Dvořák, *New World Symphony* (1893) Beginning of the Dreyfus Affair in France (1894) Jean Sibelius, *Finlandia* (1894) Rudyard Kipling, *Jungle Books* (1894–1895) Discovery of X-rays by Wilhelm Roentgen (1895) Oscar Wilde, *The Importance of Being Ernest* (1895) H. G. Wells, *The Invisible Man* (1897) Edmond Rostand, *Cyrano de Bergerac* (1897) Edward Elgar, *Enigma Variations* (1899) Ernest Rutherford discovers alpha and beta rays in radioactive atoms (1899) Boxer Rebellion in China against Western interests (1899–1900)
1900  1920	1900–1920	Monet, *Water-Lily Pond* (**22.18**)	 **Monet, *Water-Lily Pond***

23

Post-Impressionism and the Late Nineteenth Century

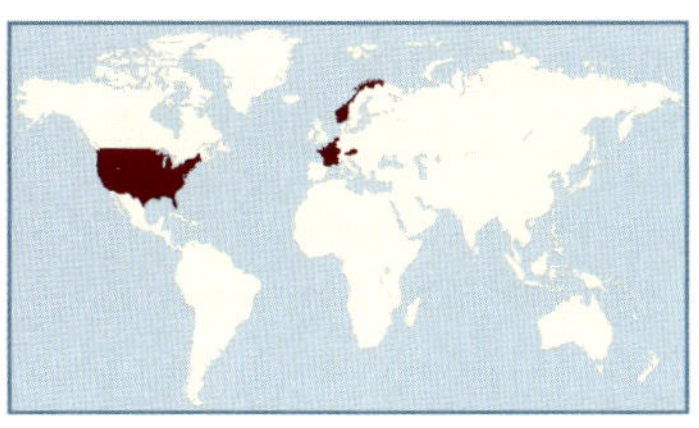

Post-Impressionism, meaning "After Impressionism," is the term used to designate the work of a group of important late nineteenth-century painters. Although their styles are quite diverse, they are united by the fact that nearly all were influenced by Impressionism. Like the Impressionists, the Post-Impressionists were drawn to bright color and visible, distinctive brushstrokes. Despite the prominent brushwork, however, Post-Impressionist forms do not dissolve into the medium as they do in the late works of Monet. The edges in Post-Impressionist works, whether outlined or defined by sharp color separations, are usually relatively clear.

Within Post-Impressionism, two important trends evolved. These are exemplified on the one hand by Cézanne and Seurat, who reassert a strong sense of formal structure and, on the other, by Gauguin and van Gogh, who explore emotional content. Both trends set the stage for the major directions of early twentieth-century art. Certain Post-Impressionist artists were also influenced by the late nineteenth-century Symbolist movement (see p. 818).

Post-Impressionist Painting

Henri de Toulouse-Lautrec

Henri de Toulouse-Lautrec (1864–1901), who was inspired by Degas, based his most characteristic imagery on Parisian nightlife. He frequented dance halls, nightclubs, cafés, and bordellos in search of subject matter. Loose, sketchy brushwork contained within clearly defined color areas contributes to a sense of dynamic motion in his paintings. In the *Quadrille at the Moulin Rouge* (fig. **23.1**), the woman facing the viewer exudes an air of determined, barely contained energy about to erupt in dance. Her stance is the opening position of a quadrille and a challenge to the other figures. Like Degas, Toulouse-Lautrec favored partial, oblique views

23.1 Henri de Toulouse-Lautrec, *Quadrille at the Moulin Rouge*, 1892. Oil on cardboard; 31⅓ × 31½ in. (79.6 × 80.01 cm). National Gallery of Art, Washington, D.C. (Chester Dale Collection). The Moulin Rouge was (and still is) a popular music hall in Montmartre. It was here, in the artisticand entertainment center of Paris, that Toulouse-Lautrec lived and worked. He was descended from the counts of Toulouse, and, although his family disapproved of his lifestyle, his wealth saved him from the poverty suffered by many artists of his generation. He died at age thirty-seven from the effects of alcoholism.

23.2 Henri de Toulouse-Lautrec, *La Goulue at the Moulin Rouge,* 1891. Poster, color lithograph; 6 ft. 3 in. × 3 ft. 10 in. (1.9 × 1.17 m). The Metropolitan Museum of Art, Harris Brisbane Dick Fund. At fifteen, two accidents left Toulouse-Lautrec with permanently stunted legs. Perhaps because of this, dancers had a particular attraction for him. La Goulue was one of the professional dancers who, along with singers, circus performers, and prostitutes, were among his favorite subjects.

that suggest photographic cropping. He was also, like Degas, influenced by Japanese prints, using strong silhouettes to offset the more textured areas of his painted surfaces.

In contrast to the textured surfaces of his paintings, Toulouse-Lautrec's lithograph posters consist of flat, unmodeled areas of color. The poster—which Lautrec popularized at the end of the nineteenth century—was not only an art form. Like the print techniques used by the Realists for social and political ends, posters such as *La Goulue at the Moulin Rouge* (fig. **23.2**) disseminated information. Because the purpose of a poster is to advertise an event, words convey part of the message. In *La Goulue,* the letters are integrated with the composition by repetition of the lines and colors of the printed text within the image. The blacks of "BAL" (Dance) and "LA GOULUE" recur in the silhouetted background crowd and the stockings of the dancer. The flat red-orange of "MOULIN ROUGE" is echoed in the dress. And the thin, dark lines of "TOUS LES SOIRS" (Every Evening) are repeated in the floorboards and the outlines of the figures.

Paul Cézanne

The Post-Impressionist who was to have the most powerful impact on the development of Western painting was Paul Cézanne (1839–1906). He, more than any artist before him, transformed paint into a visible structure. Cézanne's early pictures were predominantly black and obsessed with erotic or violent themes. The *Temptation of Saint Anthony* (fig. **23.3**) of about 1870 depicts an erotic theme that preoccupied Cézanne for many years. Related to a book of the same title by Zola, whom Cézanne had known since childhood, the painting shows the hermit saint at the

23.3 Paul Cézanne, *Temptation of Saint Anthony,* c. 1870. Oil on canvas; 22⅖ × 30 in. (56.9 × 76.2 cm). The Foundation E. G. Buhrle Collection, Zürich.

upper left. He recoils from a nude exposing herself to him. The two figures at the right have an androgynous quality but appear to be male. The seated figure broods in the manner of Dürer's *Melencolia I* (see fig. 16.13), while also reclining in a traditional female pose. The ambivalence of the standing figure lies in the fact that his gaze is riveted to the kneeling woman, while he turns as if to escape the sexual dangers that she represents. The erotic conflicts dramatized in this *Temptation* are Cézanne's own, and they are characteristic of his early imagery.

Cézanne's *Self-Portrait* (fig. **23.4**) of around 1872 depicts a man of intense vitality. Although the colors are dark, the background landscape conveys Impressionist ideas. The thickly applied paint accentuates each brushstroke—short and determined—like the bricks of an architectural structure. The arched eyebrows frame diamond-shaped eye sockets, and the curved brushstrokes of the hair and beard create an impression of wavy, slightly unruly motion.

23.4 Paul Cézanne, *Self-Portrait*, c. 1872. Oil on canvas; 25¼ × 20½ in. (64.1 × 52.1 cm). Musée d'Orsay, Paris. Cézanne was born and lived most of his life in Provence, in the south of France. He studied law before becoming a painter. In 1869, he began living with Hortense Fiquet, by whom he had a son in 1872. They married in 1886, the year his father died.

Cézanne exhibited with the Impressionists in 1873 and 1877, and, under the influence of Pissarro, his palette became brighter and his subject matter more restricted. In *Still Life with Apples* (fig. **23.5**) of c. 1875–1877, painted at the height of his Impressionist period, Cézanne subordinates narrative to form. He condenses the rich thematic associations of the apple in Western imagery with a new, structured abstraction. Cézanne's punning assertion that he wanted to "astonish Paris with an apple" (see box, p. 806) is nowhere more evident than in this work. Seven brightly colored apples are placed on a slightly darker surface. Each is a sphere, outlined in black and built up with patches of color—reds, greens, yellows, and oranges—like the many facets of a crystal. Light and dark, as well as color, are created by the arrangement of the brushstrokes in rectangular shapes. The structural quality of the apples seems to echo Cézanne's assertion that the natural world can be "reduced to a cone, a sphere, and a cylinder."

The apples are endowed with a life of their own. Each seems to be jockeying for position, as if it has not quite settled in relation to its neighbors. The shifting, animated quality of these apples creates dynamic tension, as does the crystalline structure of the brushstrokes. Nor is it entirely clear just what the apples are resting on, for the unidentified surface beneath them also shifts. As a result, the very space of the picture is ambiguous, and the image has an abstract, iconic power.

23.5 Paul Cézanne, *Still Life with Apples*, c. 1875–1877. Oil on canvas; 7½ × 10¾ in. (19.1 × 27.3 cm). By kind permission of the Provost and Fellows of King's College, Cambridge, England (Keynes Collection).

23.6 Paul Cézanne, *Great Bathers,* 1898–1905. Oil on canvas; 6 ft. 10 in. × 8 ft. 3 in. (2.08 × 2.52 m). Philadelphia Museum of Art (W. P. Wilstach Collection).

An Apple a Day . . .

Since its portrayal as the "forbidden fruit" in the Garden of Eden, the apple has had a prominent place in the Western imagination. The traditional associations of the apple with health ("an apple a day keeps the doctor away") and love ("the apple of one's eye") are still apparent in popular expressions. In Greek mythology, one of the Labors of Herakles (the Roman Hercules) required that he steal the golden apples of the Hesperides. The role of the golden apple in the Trojan War was illustrated in the sixteenth century by Cranach, who depicted Paris, the Trojan prince, judging the beauty contest between Hera, Athena, and Aphrodite (see fig. 16.17).

Cézanne's pun condenses the Paris of Greek myth with Paris, the capital city of France. In astonishing "Paris" (in the latter sense), Cézanne wins the beauty contest and becomes a Hercules among painters.

In 1887, Cézanne's active involvement with the Impressionists in Paris ended, and he returned to his native Provence in the south of France. Having integrated Impressionism with his own objectives, he now focused most of his energy on the pursuit of a new pictorial approach. In the *Great Bathers* (fig. **23.6**), painted toward the end of his life, Cézanne achieved a remarkable synthesis of a traditional subject with his innovative technique of spatial construction.

As in *Still Life with Apples,* there is no readily identifiable narrative in the *Great Bathers.* A group of nude women occupies the foreground, blending with the landscape through pose and similarity of construction, rather than through Impressionist dissolution of form. They correspond to the base of a towering pyramidal arrangement, which is carried upward by the arching trees. Two smaller figures visible across a river repeat the distant verticals.

Cézanne's new conception of space is evident in the relationship of the sky and trees. He depicts air and space, as

23.7 Paul Cézanne, *Mont Sainte-Victoire*, c. 1900. Oil on canvas; 30¾ × 39 in. (78.1 × 99.1 cm). Hermitage, Saint Petersburg.

well as solid form, as a "construction." Through his technique of organizing the brushstrokes into rectangular shapes, his surfaces, such as the sky, become multifaceted patchworks of shifting color. In certain areas—the tree on the left, for example—patches of sky overlap the solid forms. This results in spatial ambiguity and in the abandonment of the traditional distinctions between foreground and background.

In *Mont Sainte-Victoire* of c. 1900 (fig. **23.7**), Cézanne returned to a subject that had preoccupied him for years. His personal identification with the mountain is indicated by the anthropomorphism of the rich green tree in the right foreground—possibly a self-image. The landscape itself is a multifaceted patchwork of shifting color—greens, oranges, and blues. Geometry pervades the picture, not only in the cubic character of the brushstrokes but also in the trapezoidal mountain, the rectangular house in the middle ground, and the structured curve of the foreground road. Through Cézanne's faceted, crystalline forms, a breakdown and a restructuring of Western spatial conventions are achieved. This was a revolution made possible by the Post-Impressionist synthesis of prominent brushstrokes and clear edges.

Georges Seurat

In his own brand of Post-Impressionism, short-lived though it was, Georges Seurat (1859–1891) combined Cézanne's interest in volume and structure with Impressionist subject matter. His most famous painting, *Sunday Afternoon on the Island of La Grande Jatte* (fig. **23.8**), monumentalizes a scene of leisure by filling the space with solid, rigid, iconic forms. Human figures, animals, and trees are frozen in time and space. Motion is created formally, by contrasts of color, silhouettes, and repetition, rather than by the figures.

Seurat's attention to detail is apparent from the many studies he made in preparation for the final painting. The little monkey, for example, which stands by the woman at the right, was the subject of several studies. The drawing in figure **23.9** shows a monkey in a different pose from that in the painting. It is also quickly drawn rather than being built up with dots. Here the texture of the paper surface contributes to the tactile coat of the animal. It has a light edge and face, with the inner form darkened to show contour. Endowed with a sense of inherent energy, this monkey seems tense and alert.

Seurat has been called a Neo-Impressionist and a Pointillist after his process of building up color through dots, or points, of pure color; Seurat himself called this technique "divisionism." In contrast to Cézanne's outlined forms, Seurat's are separated from each other by the grouping of dots according to their color. In the detail of the girl holding the spray of flowers (fig. **23.10**), the individual dots are quite clear.

Seurat's divisionism was based on two relatively new theories of color. The first was that placing two colors side by side intensified the hues of each. There is in *La Grande Jatte* a shimmering quality in the areas of light and bright color, which tends to support this theory. The other theory, which is only partly confirmed by experience, asserted that the eye causes contiguous dots to merge into their combined color. Blue dots next to yellow dots, according to this theory, would merge and be perceived as vivid green. If the painting is viewed from a distance or through half-closed eyes, this may be true. It is certainly not true if the viewer examines the picture closely, as the illustration of the detail confirms. True or not, such theories are characteristic of the search by nineteenth-century artists for new approaches to light and color, based on scientific analysis.

23.8 Georges Seurat, *Sunday Afternoon on the Island of La Grande Jatte,* 1884–1886. Oil on canvas; 6 ft. 9 in. × 10 ft. ⅜ in. (2.08 × 3.08 m). Art Institute of Chicago (Helen Birch Bartlett Memorial Collection). La Grande Jatte is an island in the river Seine that was popular with Parisians for weekend outings. Seurat's painstaking and systematic technique reflected his scientific approach to painting. For two years, he made many small outdoor studies before painting the large final canvas of *La Grande Jatte* in his studio. In 1886, it was unveiled for the last Impressionist Exhibition.

23.9 Georges Seurat, *Monkey,* 1884. Conté crayon; 7 × 9¼ in. (17.7 × 23.7 cm). Metropolitan Museum of Art, New York (Bequest of Miss Adelaide Milton de Groot, 1967).

23.10 Detail of fig. 23.8.

Vincent van Gogh

Vincent van Gogh (1853–1890), the greatest Dutch artist since the Baroque period, devoted only the last ten years of his short life to painting. He began with a dark palette and subjects that reflected a social consciousness reminiscent of nineteenth-century Realism. The *Potato Eaters* (fig. **23.11**) of 1885 exemplifies van Gogh's empathy with the poverty of the coal miners he knew in the Borinage region of southern Belgium. It shows four family members gathered around a crude wooden table; their meal consists only of potatoes and coffee. In the foreground, a girl rendered in back view is silhouetted against the rising steam. The rather heavy, ponderous character of all the figures is enhanced by a thick, impasto paint texture.

More than many artists, van Gogh painted unequivocally autobiographical scenes. His signature, "Vincent," on the back of the chair in the left corner of the *Potato Eaters,* indicates his identification with the young man. Tension created by his personal sense of isolation pervades the painting. Although united by their spatial proximity, none of these figures communicates with anyone. The dark interior is warmed solely by the light above the table, which, given van Gogh's strict religious upbringing, might refer to the presence of God in the miners' humble house.

The following year, 1886, van Gogh moved to Paris, where his brother Theo worked as an art dealer. Under the influence of French Impressionism, van Gogh's paintings became explosions of light and color.

Van Gogh's most penetrating exercise in self-portraiture was his correspondence with his younger brother, Theodorus van Gogh, known as Theo. The letters chronicle Vincent's life of poverty and despair, his efforts to find his life's calling, his tortured relationships with women, and his bouts of madness.

Van Gogh's father was a clergyman in Zundert, Holland. His mother was depressed by the death of her first son, after whom Vincent was named, and who was born on the same day as the second Vincent. Van Gogh grew up with the grave of his older brother, which was located near the family house, a constant presence. At first, he aspired to follow his father as a minister in the Dutch Reformed Church, but his religious zeal alarmed the authorities, and he was not ordained. He also worked in his uncle's art dealership (Goupil) in Brussels and London, and taught school in England. He was a prodigious reader, fluent in English and French as well as in Dutch.

Although van Gogh did not decide to be a painter until about 1884, he had—like most artists—begun drawing as a child. Once he settled on his career, he became dependent on Theo for money and emotional support. Virtually every letter details his expenditures on art supplies and complains about the cost of living. Often he went without food in order to paint. His letters describe his efforts to learn to draw, to capture a likeness, and his views on art and artists, particularly Delacroix.

After two years in Paris, van Gogh moved to Arles, in the south of France. There he hoped to found a society of artists who would live and work communally. Gauguin joined him, but these two difficult personalities were destined not to co-exist for long. When van Gogh cut off his earlobe in a fit of jealous despair and was hospitalized, Gauguin left. Van Gogh then suffered several episodes of mental breakdown, and on July 27, 1890, he shot himself, dying two days later. Six months after Vincent's death Theo also died.

23.11 Vincent van Gogh, *Potato Eaters,* 1885. Oil on canvas; 2 ft. 8¼ in. × 3 ft. 9 in. (0.82 × 1.14 m). Amsterdam, Van Gogh Museum (Vincent van Gogh Foundation).

Van Gogh's clinical diagnosis has never been satisfactorily identified. Theories abound, however, and they range from epilepsy to childhood depression to lead poisoning from paint fumes. Unable to sell his pictures during his lifetime, van Gogh's legacy of paintings went to Theo and then to Theo's son, also named Vincent. The young Vincent bequeathed the bulk of the collection to Holland, and most are now permanently exhibited in the Vincent van Gogh Museum in Amsterdam.

Van Gogh's interest in Japanese woodblock prints was consistent with certain features of Impressionism. While living in Paris, he began to collect such prints, which he had known and admired previously. He wrote to Theo from Antwerp that he had decorated his room with "a number of little Japanese prints." Once in Paris, he encountered the new fashion for *japonisme* and its impact on the Impressionists.

His *Japonaiserie: Bridge in the Rain* (*after Hiroshige*), for example, is a copy of Hiroshige's *Sudden Shower at Ohashi Bridge at Ataka* (figs. **23.12** and **23.13**). Both works share certain formal and iconographic interests with the French Impressionists. The pictures are divided by strong diagonals—the bridge and the shoreline—into asymmetrical trapezoids. Reminiscent of the candid-camera effect of Degas' *Absinthe* (see fig. 22.8), the resulting tilt is stabilized by the silhouetted verticals of the piers supporting the bridge. Hiroshige's portrayal of rain is echoed in the Impressionist studies of weather conditions—for example, Pissarro's *Place du Théâtre Français* (see fig. 22.22). The darkened sky and the huddled figures, which are small and anonymous, are consistent with van Gogh's frequent bouts of depression. Finally, the people in Hiroshige's print are arranged in two pairs and two single figures. A lone boatman, working against the current, drives his boat up the river. Such contrasts between pairs and solitary figures were a continuous theme in van Gogh's work. It reflected his personal struggle with isolation and his unsuccessful attempts to form a lasting relationship with a woman. It also evoked his close—"paired"—relationship with Theo.

23.12 Vincent van Gogh, *Japonaiserie: Bridge in the Rain* (*after Hiroshige*), 1887. Oil on canvas; 28¾ × 21¼ in. (73.0 × 54.0 cm). Amsterdam, Van Gogh Museum (Vincent van Gogh Foundation).

23.13 Utagawa Hiroshige, *Sudden Shower at Ohashi Bridge at Ataka*, from the series *One Hundred Views of Edo*, 1857. Woodblock print; 14⅛ × 9¾ in. (35.9 × 24.8 cm). The Brooklyn Museum of Art.

23.14 Vincent van Gogh, *Bedroom at Arles*, 1889. Oil on canvas; 28⅜ × 35⅜ in. (72.1 × 89.9 cm). Musée d'Orsay, Paris.

In 1888, van Gogh moved from Paris to Arles, in the south of France. The following year he painted the famous *Bedroom at Arles* (fig. **23.14**), which is pervaded by isolation and tension. Figures who do not communicate are replaced by an absence of figures. The artist's existence, rather than the artist himself, is indicated by furnishings and clothing. Only the portraits on the wall, one of which is a self-portrait, contain human figures. Like the figures on Hiroshige's bridge, the portraits are arranged as a pair and are juxtaposed with a single landscape over the clothes rack. Likewise, two pillows lie side by side on a single bed. There are two chairs, but they are separated from each other. The same is true of the doors. There are two bottles on the table, and a double window next to a single mirror. Van Gogh's *Bedroom* is thus a psychological self-portrait that records his efforts to achieve a fulfilling relationship with a woman and his failure to do so.

The tension is reinforced by the color, particularly the intense hue of the red coverlet, which is the only pure color in the painting. In October 1888, Vincent sent Theo a sketch of the *Bedroom* (fig. **23.15**) in order to give him an idea of his work:

> I have a new idea in my head and here is a sketch of it. . . . This time it's simply my bedroom, only here color is to do everything, and giving by its simplification a grander style of things, it is to be suggestive here of rest, or of sleep in general. In a word, looking at the picture ought to rest the brain, or rather the imagination.[1]

The sketch was also accompanied by van Gogh's description of the color and mood of the actual painting:

> The walls are pale violet. The floor is of red tiles. The wood of the bed and chairs is the yellow of fresh butter, the sheets and pillows very light greenish citron. The coverlet scarlet. The window green. The toilet table orange, the basin blue. The doors lilac. And that is all—there is nothing in this room with its closed shutters.[2]

23.15 Vincent van Gogh, sketch for *Bedroom at Arles*, 1888. Pen and ink on squared paper; 5¼ × 8⅓ in. (13.3 × 21.1 cm). Amsterdam, Van Gogh Museum (Vincent van Gogh Foundation).

23.16 Vincent van Gogh, *Wheat Field with Reaper*, 1889. Oil on canvas; 29¼ × 36¼ in. (74.3 × 92.1 cm). Amsterdam, Van Gogh Museum (Vincent van Gogh Foundation). Van Gogh described the "all yellow, terribly thickly painted" figure as Death, who reaps humanity like a wheat field. The yellow symbolically derives its power from the sun, which is the painting's source of light. Here it determines the color of the entire picture, and its intensity seems to "heat" the scene.

Van Gogh shared the Impressionist passion for landscape. His *Wheat Field with Reaper* (fig. **23.16**) illustrates his genius for vibrant color. The frenzied curves of wheat—actually formed with individual brushstrokes—repeat the curve of the reaper's scythe. But, despite the impressive power of van Gogh's brushwork, his forms never dissolve completely. The areas of color are maintained as distinct shapes, and the power of the color exceeds that of Impressionism.

In *Starry Night* (fig. **23.17**), van Gogh has depicted an unforgettable image of a nighttime landscape. Here line becomes color in the energetic curves spiraling across the sky. Their movement from left to right is counteracted by hills cascading in the opposite direction. Stabilizing the animated surface are the verticals of the two foreground cypress trees and the church spire. The church itself, as well as the small village, has been identified as van Gogh's memory of Dutch villages, merged here with the French landscape of Provence. Because he painted *Starry Night* while in a mental asylum, it has been seen as the reflection of a disturbed mind. Nothing, however, could be further from the truth, for van Gogh's characteristic control of formal elements, technical skill, and intellectual clarity radiate from every inch of the canvas.

23.17 Vincent van Gogh, *Starry Night*, 1889. Oil on canvas; 28¾ × 36½. (73.0 × 92.7 cm). Museum of Modern Art, New York.

See figure 17.42.
Rembrandt van Rijn,
Self-Portrait in a Cap, Openmouthed and Staring, 1630.

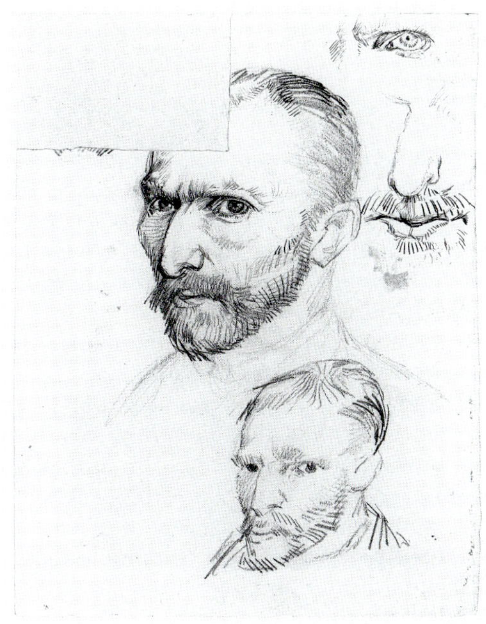

23.18 (right) Vincent van Gogh, studies for *Self-Portrait,* 1889. Pencil and pen drawing; 12⅝ × 9½ in. (32.1 × 24.1 cm). Amsterdam, Van Gogh Museum (Vincent van Gogh Foundation).

Like Rembrandt (see figs. 17.40 and 17.41), whom he studied in his native Holland, van Gogh painted many self-portraits (see fig. I.1). His drawings show that he observed his own features as intensely as he did the world around him. The sheet in figure **23.18** depicts different views of his head, which are related to the *Self-Portrait* in figure **23.19.** The structural quality of the head is emphasized by the firm outlines and gradual shading. Whereas Rembrandt created physiognomy primarily by variations in lightness and darkness, van Gogh did so with color. Aside from the yellows and oranges of the face and hair, the *Self-Portrait* is very nearly monochromatic. The main color is a pale blue-green, varying from light to dark in accordance with the individual brushstrokes. The jacket remains distinct from its background by its darkened color and outline.

Although the figure itself is immobile, like the town and landscape in *Starry Night,* the pronounced spiraling, wavy brushstrokes undulate over the surface of the picture. Yellow—the color associated with death in *Wheat Field with Reaper*—predominates in the depiction of van Gogh's head and is a component of both the orange and the blue-green. The piercing gaze is also achieved through color, for the whites of the eyes are not white at all, but rather the same blue-green as the background. As a result, the viewer has the impression of looking through van Gogh's skull at eyes set far back inside his head.

See figure 17.41.
Rembrandt van Rijn, *Self-Portrait as Saint Paul,* 1661.

23.19 (right) Vincent van Gogh, *Self-Portrait,* 1889. Oil on canvas; 25½ × 21¼ in. (64.8 × 54.0 cm). Musée d'Orsay, Paris.

Paul Gauguin

Compared to the dynamic character of van Gogh's painted surfaces, Paul Gauguin's (1848–1903) brushstrokes are smooth. Although his colors are bright, they are arranged as flat shapes, usually outlined in black. The surfaces of his pictures seem soft and smooth in contrast to the energetic rhythms of van Gogh's thick brushstrokes.

Gauguin began his career under the aegis of the Impressionists—he exhibited with them from 1879 to 1886—and then went on to explore new approaches to style. In *The Yellow Christ* (fig. **23.20**) of 1889, Gauguin identifies with the Symbolist movement and a group of painters referred to as the Nabis, meaning "prophets." He locates the Crucifixion in a Breton landscape and depicts Christ in flattened yellows. Three women in local costume encircle the Cross—a reference to traditional Christian symbolism in which the circle signifies the Church. In fact, the women of Brittany often prayed at large stone crosses in the countryside. The juxtaposition of the Crucifixion with the late nineteenth-century landscape of northern France is a temporal and spatial condensation that is characteristic of the dreamworld depicted by the Symbolists. It is also intended to convey the hallucinatory aspects of prayer, indicating that through meditating on the scene of the Crucifixion the Breton women conjured up an image of the event.

23.20 Paul Gauguin, *The Yellow Christ*, 1889. Oil on canvas; 36¼ × 28⅞ in. (92.1 × 73.3 cm). Albright-Knox Art Gallery, Buffalo, New York.

23.21 Paul Gauguin, *Self-Portrait with Halo*, 1889. Oil on wood; 31⅓ × 20¼ in. (79.5 × 51.4 cm). National Gallery of Art, Washington, D.C. (Chester Dale Collection). In 1873, Gauguin married a Danish piano teacher, with whom he led a middle-class life and had five children. In 1882, he became a full-time painter and deserted his family. After a turbulent year with van Gogh in Arles in the south of France, Gauguin returned in 1889 to Brittany, where he was influenced by the Symbolists, and his work assumed a spiritual, self-consciously symbolic quality.

In *Self-Portrait with Halo* (fig. **23.21**) of the same year, a pair of apples is suspended behind Gauguin's head. They, like the serpent rising through his hand, allude to the Fall of Man. The flat, curved plant stems in the foreground repeat the motion of the serpent, the outline of Gauguin's lock of hair, and the painting's date and signature. The clear division of the picture plane into red and yellow indicates the artist's divided sense of himself; his head is caught between the two colors, implying that his soul wavers between the polarities of good and evil. Gauguin combines Symbolist color with traditional motifs to convey this struggle. He is at once the tempted and the tempter, a saint and a sinner, an angel and a devil. An important feature of the *Self-Portrait* is Gauguin's contrast between himself as a physical body and the red and yellow areas of the picture plane. His hand and face, as well as the apples, are modeled three-dimensionally, whereas the red and yellow are flat. These methods by which the artist depicted animate and inanimate objects continued to be used throughout his career.

23.22 Paul Gauguin, *Nevermore,* 1897. Oil on canvas; 1 ft. 11⅞ in. × 3 ft. 9⅝ in. (0.61 × 1.16 m). The Samuel Courtauld Trust, Courtauld Institute of Art Gallery, London. Although Gauguin's style changed little after he left France, Polynesian life and culture became the subjects of his work. Gradually, poverty, alcoholism, and syphilis undermined his health, and he died at age fifty-five after at least one suicide attempt.

In 1891, Gauguin sold thirty paintings to finance a trip to Tahiti. Apart from an eighteen-month stay in France in 1895–1896, he spent the rest of his life in the South Sea Islands. In his Tahitian paintings, Gauguin synthesized the Symbolist taste for dreams and myth with native subjects and traditional Western themes. *Nevermore* (fig. **23.22**), for example, depicts a Tahitian version of the reclining nude. The brightly colored patterns and silhouettes indicate the influence both of Japanese prints and of native designs. They enliven the composition and contrast with the immobility of the figures.

Gauguin has infused the traditional reclining nude with a sense of danger and suspicion. She evidently knows of the danger since she rolls her eyes as if aware of the two women talking in the background. The title of the picture, spelled out in the upper left corner, echoes the refrain of Edgar Allan Poe's "The Raven," which Gauguin knew from Baudelaire's translation:

Once upon a midnight dreary, while I pondered, weak and weary,
Over many a quaint and curious volume of forgotten lore—
While I nodded, nearly napping, suddenly there came a tapping,
As of someone gently rapping, rapping at my chamber door.
"Tis some visitor," I muttered, "tapping at my chamber door—
Only this and nothing more." . . .
"Prophet!" said I, "thing of evil! prophet still, if bird or devil!—
Whether Tempter sent, or whether tempest tossed thee here ashore,
Desolate yet all undaunted, on this desert land enchanted—
On this home by Horror haunted—tell me truly, I implore—
Is there—is there balm in Gilead?—tell me—tell me, I implore!"
Quoth the Raven, "Nevermore."

In Gauguin's painting, the raven stands on a shelf between the title and the whispering women, and stares at the nude. The juxtaposition of the raven, the nude, and the talking women hints at a silent, but sinister, communication. In this combination of Tahitian imagery and Western themes, self-consciously imbued with a psychic dimension, Gauguin merges his personal brand of Post-Impressionism with a Symbolist quality.

Window on the World Ten

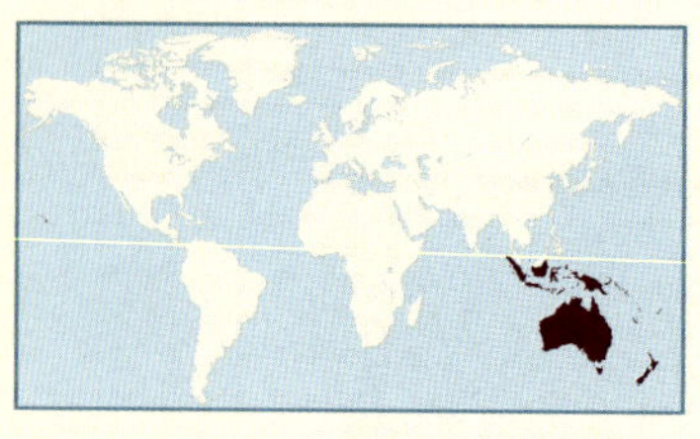

Gauguin and Oceania

Following the eighteenth-century Enlightenment, there developed a new interest in Oceania, which includes Polynesia, Melanesia, Micronesia, and New Guinea (see map). The possibility that humans existed there in the utopian state of nature posited by Jean-Jacques Rousseau intrigued western Europe. Between 1768 and 1778, Captain Cook made three voyages to the South Seas. Collectors began to focus on Oceanic objects that had been brought back by explorers. Descriptions and drawings of the native populations, their artifacts, dwellings, costumes, and even their tattoos achieved a certain popularity in Europe.

In 1872, Sarah Bernhardt was given a drawing of the monumental statues on Easter Island, imposing stone figures with huge heads and blocklike features. They date from the fifth to the seventeenth century A.D. and are the most impressive Oceanic sculptures (fig. **W10.1**). Their frontal poses and impassive gazes endow them with a fascinating, timeless quality. Some mark burials, but their primary purpose was to embody the divine power of a deceased ruler. As such, they can be related to ancestor cults throughout the world, such as the Cambodian cult of the sun king at Angkor (see Window 6).

By the latter half of the nineteenth century, after the fashion for *japonisme* had been established, ethnology museums became more numerous and

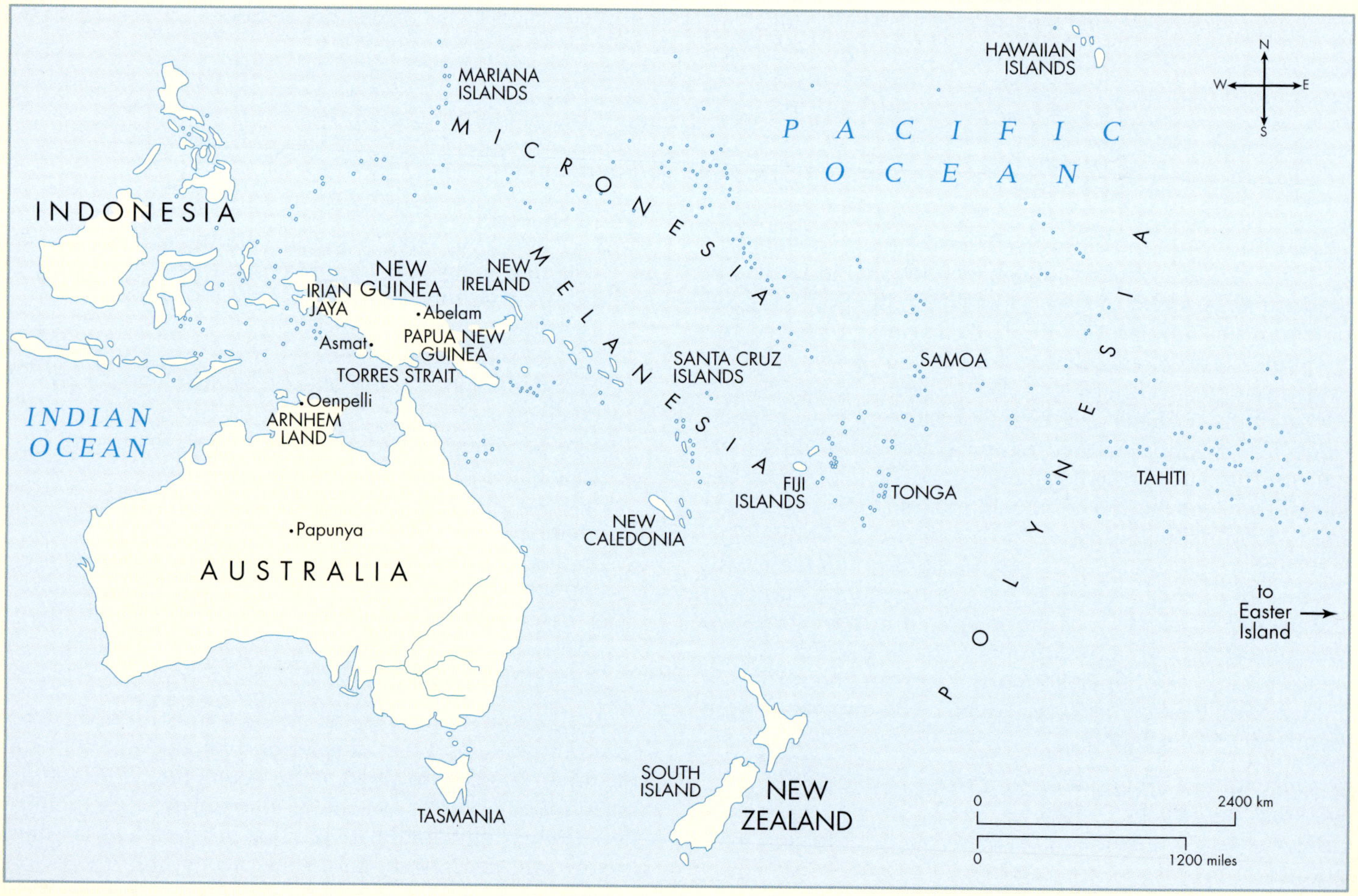

Oceania.

W10.1 Stone heads, Easter Island, 5th–17th centuries.

began to mount exhibits of Oceanic art. This development was encouraged by French colonial expansion in Africa and the Far East (especially Indochina) in the 1880s. In 1882, the Musée d'Ethnographie (Musée de l'Homme) opened in Paris, and the arts of Polynesia were well represented. In an effort to provide "context," the Universal Exposition of 1889 exhibited Oceanic objects in reconstructed village settings.

Gauguin was one of the first major artists to become interested in Oceanic culture and to collect its art and artifacts. The European fantasy of a "noble savage" appealed to him, and in 1891 he gave the following account of his intention to live and work in Tahiti:

> I am leaving in order to have peace and quiet, to be rid of the influence of civilization. I only want to do simple, very simple art, and to be able to do that, I have to immerse myself in virgin nature, see no one but savages, live their life, with no other thought in mind but to render, the way a child would, the concepts formed in my brain and to do this with the aid of nothing but the primitive means of art, the only means that are good and true.[3]

For Gauguin, Tahiti had many complex associations. It was one aspect of the ambivalent self he depicted in the *Self-Portrait* of 1889. He saw Tahiti as a new Eden, an island paradise, where nature took precedence over the corrupt, industrial, "civilized" West, and he described his trip as a return to the "childhood of mankind." The South Seas also fueled the eclectic character of his art. For he never renounced the Western tradition, in which he was deeply immersed. His affinity with late nineteenth-century European abstraction is evident in his reply to a question about his "red dogs" and "pink skies":

> It's music, if you like! I borrow some subject or other from life or from nature as a pretext, I arrange lines and colors so as to obtain symphonies, harmonies that do not represent a thing that is real, in the vulgar sense of the word, and do not directly express any idea, but are supposed to make you think the way music is supposed to make you think, unaided by ideas or images, simply through the mysterious affinities that exist between our brains and such arrangements of colors and lines.[4]

W10.2 Paul Gauguin, *Idol with the Seashell*, c. 1893. Wood; 10⅝ in. (27.0 cm) high. Musée d'Orsay, Paris.

Gauguin was a prodigious synthesizer of different artistic traditions, including those of western Europe, Japanese woodblock, and the sculpture of Egypt, Oceania, Indonesia, and the Far East. For example, he combined Oceanic mythology with Christian and Buddhist iconography. In the *Idol with the Seashell* (fig. **W10.2**) of about 1893, the figure represents Taaroa, who was worshiped on Easter Island as the divine creative force of the universe. The prominent teeth, made of inlaid bone, carry cannibalistic implications. But the idol occupies a traditional pose of Buddha, and the rounded, polished shell is reminiscent of the Christian halo. In such works as this, Gauguin helped to correct the popular misunderstanding of the tribal arts as primitive in the sense of regressive. For him, the incorporation of various non-Western forms and motifs into Western art expanded intellectual as well as aesthetic experience.

The Symbolist Movement

Symbolism was particularly strong in France and Belgium in the late nineteenth century. It began as a literary movement, emphasizing internal psychological phenomena rather than objective descriptions of nature.

The English word *symbol* comes from the Greek word *sumbolon,* meaning "token." It originally referred to a sign that had been divided in two and could be identified because the two halves fitted together. A symbol thus signifies the matching part or other half. It is something that stands for something else. Symbols derive from myth, folklore, allegory, and dreams. The Symbolists believed that, by focusing on dreams, it was possible to rise above the here and now of a specific time and place, and arrive at what is universal. It is no coincidence that the Symbolist movement in art and literature was contemporary with advances in psychology and psychoanalysis.

In literature, the poets' "Symbolist Manifesto" of 1886 rejected Zola's Naturalism in favor of the Idea and the Self. The French poets Charles Baudelaire, Stéphane Mallarmé, and Paul Verlaine became cult figures for the Symbolists, as did the American author Edgar Allan Poe and the Swedish philosopher Emanuel Swedenborg. Their literature of decadence, disintegration, and the macabre shares many qualities with Symbolist painting. An erotic subtext, often containing perverse overtones, pervades and haunts the imagery.

The Symbolists rejected both the social consciousness of Realism and the Impressionist interest in nature and the outdoors. They were attracted instead by the internal world of the imagination and by images that portrayed the irrational aspects of the human mind. Their interest can be related to Goya's Romantic preoccupation with dream and fantasy and Géricault's studies of the insane. They were drawn to mythological subject matter because of its affinity with dreaming, but their rendition of myth was neither heroic in character nor Classical in style. Rather, it was disturbed and poetic, and contained more than a hint of perversity.

Gustave Moreau

Gustave Moreau (1826–1898) was the leading artist of the Symbolist movement in France. His *Orpheus* (fig. **23.23**) depicts an imaginary scene from the Greek myth of the musician who was killed and torn limb from limb by maenads—frenzied female followers of Dionysos. Here, a young woman dressed in rich fabrics gazes down at the severed head of Orpheus as it lies across his lyre. Both she and the head are somewhat idealized, and there is a sense of languid passivity in their expressions, enhanced by the soft yellow light. The idyllic episode at the top of the craggy mountain on the left together with the peaceful quality of Orpheus and the woman belie the violence that has preceded the present moment.

23.23 Gustave Moreau, *Orpheus,* 1865. Oil on canvas; 5 ft. 1 in. × 3 ft. 3½ in. (1.5 × 1.0 m). Musée d'Orsay, Paris. This painting was shown in the Paris Universal Exposition of 1867. The two turtles in the lower right corner, an apparently anomalous feature, may refer to the legend that Orpheus made his lyre by stringing a hollow tortoiseshell. To a public that knew the story of Orpheus, this painting must have seemed macabre indeed.

23.24 Gustave Moreau, *Galatea,* 1880–1881. Oil on panel; 33½ × 26⅓ in. (85.1 × 66.9 cm). Musee d'Orsay, Paris.

In *Galatea* (fig. **23.24**), Moreau reverses the relationship of observer to observed. In *Orpheus,* the woman gazes at the severed head of a man, whereas in the *Galatea* the male, who is the Cyclops Polyphemos (see Chapter 4), gazes at the woman—in this case, Galatea—through the large single eye in the middle of his forehead. He holds the stone with which he has killed her human lover, Acis, because of his primitive longing for her. Like the woman in the *Orpheus,* the very idealization of the Cyclops is sinister, for it is at odds with his bestial nature. Both scenes depict tales of unrequited love and passion turned to murder, and both are pervaded by a disturbing calm. As in the *Orpheus,* an eerie, unreal light transports the *Galatea* into the realm of the imagination: the Cyclops is bathed in orange light, and Galatea is illuminated by white light. There is no rational explanation for the discrepant illumination. Galatea reclines on a bed of mysterious, translucent flowers, and her pose recalls the traditional reclining nude, which enhances the impression of her vulnerability.

A comparison of Moreau's *Orpheus* and *Galatea* with other works discussed in this chapter makes it clear that, while the ideas of the Symbolists influenced certain Post-Impressionists, the Symbolist style did not.

Edvard Munch

The Norwegian artist Edvard Munch (1863–1944) went in 1889 to Paris, where he came into contact with Impressionism and Post-Impressionism. The combination of Symbolist content with Post-Impressionism was particularly well suited to Munch's character. His mental suffering, like van Gogh's, was so openly acknowledged in his imagery and statements that it is unavoidable in considering his work. His pictures conform to Symbolist theory in that they depict states of mind, emotions, or ideas rather than observable physical reality. The style in which Munch's mental states are expressed, however, is Post-Impressionist in its expressive distortions of form and its use of nonlocal color.

In his best-known painting, *The Scream* (fig. **23.25**) of 1893, Munch displaces his sense of disintegration onto a figure crossing the bridge over Oslo's Christianafjord. The bright colors—reds, oranges, and yellows—intensify the sunset, with darker blues and pinks defining the water. Both sky and water seem caught up in an endless swirl that echoes the artist's anguish. In contrast to the pedestrians at the far end of the bridge, Munch stops to face the picture plane, simultaneously screaming and holding his ears. The action of blocking out the sound pushes in the sides of his face so that his head resembles a skull and repeats the landscape curves. Munch described the experience depicted in this painting as follows: "I felt as though a scream went through nature—I thought I heard a scream—I painted this picture—painted the clouds like real blood. The colors were screaming."[5] He thus joins the scream of nature as his form echoes the waving motion of the landscape.

23.25 Edvard Munch, *The Scream*, 1893. Oil, pastel, and casein on cardboard; 35¾ × 29 in. (90.8 × 73.7 cm). National Gallery, Oslo. In 1892, Munch received electric shock treatment for depression and lived thereafter in almost total seclusion. Anxiety is one of Munch's favorite themes, along with death, illness, despair, and other forms of suffering.

In *The Voice* (fig. **23.26**), painted the same year as *The Scream*, Munch's figure merges with the landscape by repeating the vertical tree trunks. In contrast to the fluid curves and warm colors of *The Scream*, *The Voice* is painted in cool colors, and the forms have sharp edges, varied mainly by the gradual slope of the shoreline, a few details of foliage, and the small white boat visible between the trees. The figure conveys a sense of rigid tension, suggesting that the sound of a voice has terrorized her into immobility. Her form is eerily echoed by the yellow moon and its odd, vertical reflection in the water, which Munch repeated in several compositions.

Munch also evokes the folklore associated with the moon, which, as we saw in Friedrich's *Two Men Contemplating the Moon* (fig. 20.19), is imbued with mysticism and magic. *The Voice* was the first of a series called *Love* that became part of Munch's *Frieze of Life*, a loosely organized frieze composed of his paintings—including *The Scream*—arranged to demonstrate his philosophy that art reflects life.

23.26 Edvard Munch, *The Voice*, 1893. Oil on canvas; 34½ × 42½ in. (87.5 × 108 cm). Museum of Fine Arts, Boston.

Fin de Siècle Developments

The last decade of the nineteenth century witnessed the emergence of several related styles. All signaled a reaction against the revival styles of the earlier part of the century. This period, and a few years on either side of it, is referred to as *fin de siècle* ("end of century").

Aestheticism

The principal tenet of Aestheticism was that the sole justification of art is its intrinsic beauty. This notion derived from the philosophy of Immanuel Kant, who believed that aesthetics should be independent of morality and utility. In France, this became the popular *l'art pour art* ("art for art's sake") movement. In England, Whistler had championed this view of art in his lawsuit against Ruskin.

The playwright Oscar Wilde (1854–1900) was also a spokesman for the Aesthetic movement in England. His writings and lifestyle alternately amused and shocked polite society, and in 1895 he was sentenced to prison for homosexual offenses. Aubrey Beardsley (1872–1898), the leading illustrator of the decade, created what he called "embellishments" of Wilde's play *Salomé*. (In the Gospel of Matthew 14:1–12, Salomé's mother, Herodias, persuades her daughter to charm King Herod with her dancing and then to demand the head of John the Baptist as her reward.) Figure **23.27** shows Beardsley's portrayal of Salomé fondling John's severed head. The legend below reads: "J'AI BAISÉ TA BOUCHE IOKANAAN/J'AI BAISÉ TA BOUCHE" (I have kissed your mouth, Jokanaan, I have kissed your mouth). John's Medusa-like hair hangs limply, whereas Salomé's stands on end. Echoing this contrast at the bottom of the drawing is an open, erect flower beside a drooping bud. The blood from John's neck drips into a dark pool.

Beardsley's use of strong blacks, his emphasis on the unnatural and the macabre, and his taste for sexual metaphors with decadent overtones are characteristic of the *fin de siècle* aesthetic. So, too, are the ambiguous features of Salomé and John. Both have an androgynous quality and, were it not clear from the context, it would be difficult to say which was male and which female. This is also a projection of Beardsley himself, for although he was not overtly bisexual, as Wilde was, there is evidence that he engaged in cross-dressing.

Conservative critics denounced Beardsley's work for its decadence. Those who believed that art without morality has no value railed at his thinly disguised eroticism. After the trial and conviction of Oscar Wilde, a general revulsion against Aestheticism set in. Nevertheless, in focusing on the formal, aesthetic qualities of art, the movement was partially successful in establishing the independence of art from ethical considerations.

23.27 Aubrey Beardsley, *Salomé with the Head of John the Baptist*, 1893. Pen drawing; 11 × 6 in. (27.9 × 15.2 cm). Princeton University Library.

Art Nouveau

Art Nouveau ("New Art") was an ornamental style composed of curvilinear, organic forms that was a European-wide response against industrialization and the prevalence of the machine. In France it was known as the *Style Moderne*, or "Modern Style," in Germany as the *Jugendstil* ("Youthful Style"), and in Italy as the *Stile Liberty* (after Liberty of London, a store that imported Art Nouveau fabrics). The style is characterized by sinuous, asymmetrical, linear patterns that mainly influenced architecture and the decorative arts—especially glass, furniture, jewelry, and wrought-iron work.

23.28 Victor Horta, staircase of the Maison Tassel, Brussels, 1892.

23.29 Hector Guimard, entrance to a Métro station, Paris, 1900

From 1892 to 1893 the Belgian architect Victor Horta (1861–1947) designed a house for the Tassel family of Brussels. His patron, Professor Tassel, typified the new generation that wanted to express its opposition to the tastes of the older aristocracy. Figure **23.28** shows the staircase of the house, which reflects the undulating, organic lines of Art Nouveau. They resemble the natural forms of plant stalks, tendrils, vinescrolls, insect wings, and peacock tails. Here, the ornamental ironwork corresponds to the designs painted on the adjoining wall.

Figure **23.29** illustrates the entrance to a Métropolitain (Métro) subway station in Paris. It was designed in 1900 by Hector Guimard (1867–1942) from prefabricated glass and metal. The tall, thin, curvilinear lampposts on either side of the entrance recall certain plant stalks and flowers, and seem to stand on tiptoe. Also reminiscent of floral designs is the elegant ironwork railing that surrounds the opening in the sidewalk. Even the lettering of the sign—"METROPOLITAIN"—corresponds to the sinuous, linear style of Art Nouveau.

The Vienna Secession

Fin de siècle Vienna, the capital of the Austro-Hungarian Empire, was a city of contradictions. The Hapsburg monarchy persisted amid the growth of a liberal bourgeoisie. Technology advanced against a backdrop of conservative nationalism. And Sigmund Freud was formulating a theory of the mind that exploded entrenched philosophical and religious traditions of western Europe.

The resistance to change in Viennese society was nowhere more evident than in its attitude to contemporary art. The visual arts were dominated by two institutions—the Akademie der Bildenden Künste and the Künstlerhausgenossenschaft. The former was Vienna's teaching academy, the latter a private society that owned the city's only exhibition space. Both were conservative and in control of all exhibitions in Vienna, as well as of Austrian exhibits abroad.

In 1897, a group of artists broke away and formed the independent Vereinigung Bildender Künstler Österreichs (Secession), known as the "Vienna Secession." This group did not champion any one artistic style, even though the *Jugendstil* was strongly represented. Rather, its purpose was to provide a forum for diverse styles which shared the rejection of Academic naturalism. The leader of the Secession and its first president was Gustav Klimt (1862–1918), an established painter in the Academic tradition.

Within eighteen months of its formation, the Secession held two successful exhibitions and built its own exhibition hall. Klimt designed the poster (fig. **23.30**) and the cover of the catalogue for the first exhibition. The poster shows a scene derived from Greek mythology—a vigorous Theseus about to plunge his sword into the Minotaur. This symbolizes youth (Theseus) heroically destroying the oppressive forces of conservatism (the Minotaur). Athena, armed as if to defend the wisdom of artistic rebellion, stands at the far right. She is rendered in profile, holding up the Gorgon shield which faces the viewer.

23.30 Gustav Klimt, *Ver Sacrum*, depicting Theseus and the Minotaur, c. 1898. Poster for the first Secession exhibition. Historisches Museum der Stadt, Vienna.

In 1894, Klimt was commissioned to paint a series of allegorical murals for the University of Vienna. Their completion was long delayed, and when Klimt produced the first, full-sized version of one of these, it was clear that his style had radically changed. Because of public criticism, he never completed the project. Klimt's mature style is evident in the *Kiss* (fig. **23.31**) of 1908, in which the kneeling, silhouetted forms of a man and a woman—possibly the artist and his mistress—blend into the design. Aside from their heads and limbs, the figures are submerged by the lively, gold surface patterns.

The remainder of this text surveys the major styles of twentieth-century art, which derive from certain nineteenth-century developments. Realism had introduced a new social consciousness into the visual arts, and Impressionism had made artists and viewers alike aware of the potential, expressive power of the medium. Post-Impressionists explored various ways in which individual brushstrokes could enhance and construct images, even to the point where paint intruded on the subject. At the same time, Symbolism took up the Romantic interest in giving visual form to states of mind. The nineteenth century ended with an artist in whose work both the medium and the imagination were combined as new subjects in Western art.

23.31 Gustav Klimt, *Kiss,* 1908. Oil on canvas; 5 ft. 10⅞ in. × 5 ft. 10⅞ in. (1.8 × 1.8 m). Österreichische Galerie, Vienna.

Henri Rousseau

Although Henri Rousseau (1844–1910) worked largely during the latter part of the nineteenth century, his impact on Western art history must be seen in the context of the first half of the twentieth century. He has been called a naive painter because he had no formal training and spent most of his working life as a customs inspector near Paris—hence his nickname "Le Douanier" (Customs Officer). He painted in his spare time, exhibited at the Salon des Indépendants, and in 1885 retired from his job to become a full-time painter. At first mocked by the critics, Rousseau was later much admired. In 1908, Pablo Picasso (see Chapter 24) held a banquet in his honor at his Montmartre studio.

Rousseau's last great work, *The Dream* (fig. **23.32**), was painted in 1910 shortly before his death and eleven years

CONNECTIONS

See figure 14.52. Titian, *Venus of Urbino*, c. 1538.

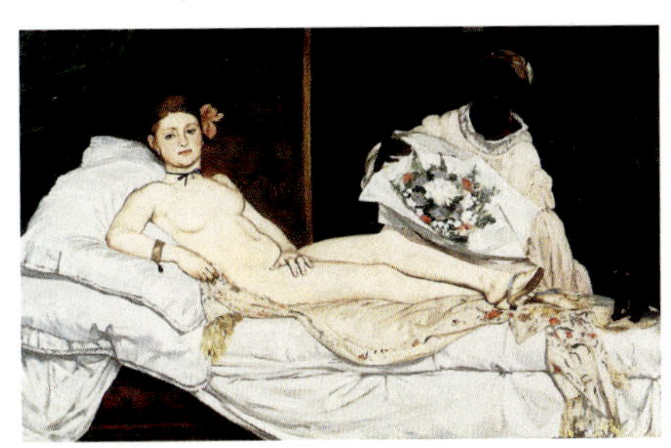

See figure 21.26. Édouard Manet, *Olympia*, 1865.

23.32 Henri Rousseau, *The Dream*, 1910. Oil on canvas; 6 ft. 8½ in. × 9 ft. 9½ in. (2.05 × 2.99 m). Museum of Modern Art, New York (Gift of Nelson A. Rockefeller).

The Mechanisms of Dreaming

In 1899, Sigmund Freud published *The Interpretation of Dreams.* Although initially only a few copies were sold, its impact on Western thought has been enormous. As defined by Freud, there are four mechanisms of dreaming:

1. *Representability* means that an idea or a feeling can be changed into a picture. The dream picture is an unconscious regression from words to images, whereas works of art are consciously produced.
2. *Condensation* merges two or more elements into a new, disguised form. In Rousseau's *The Dream,* the jungle is condensed with a European sitting room, and day is condensed with night.
3. *Displacement* means moving an element from its usual setting to another place. The dark musician in *The Dream* is an example, for nonhuman features have been displaced onto him. Displacement can result in condensation. Geographical condensation in Rousseau's picture is achieved by displacing the couch into the jungle.
4. *Symbolization* is the process of symbol making. A symbol is something that stands for something else. In *The Dream,* the flowers, fruit, serpent, musician, jungle setting, and nude may be interpreted as symbols of the dreamer's sexual fantasies.

after the publication of Freud's *The Interpretation of Dreams* (see box). The painting shows a nude, reclining but alert, who has been transported on a Victorian couch to a jungle setting, complete with wild animals and abundant flowers and foliage. Emerging from the jungle depths is a dark gray creature, clothed and upright, who is simultaneously animal and human and plays a musical instrument. The bizarre gray of its face and skin contrasts with the bright jungle colors. The daytime sky is at odds with the normal time for dreaming, which is night.

When asked about the unlikely juxtaposition of the couch with the jungle in *The Dream,* Rousseau provided two different answers. In the first, he said that the woman is the dreamer; she is sleeping on the couch, and both have been transported to the jungle. In the second, he said that the couch was there simply because of its red color. The following inscription by Rousseau was posthumously published in the French journal *Soirées de Paris* on January 15, 1914:

In a beautiful dream
Yadwigha gently sleeps
Heard the sounds of a pipe
Played by a sympathetic charmer
While the moon reflects
On the rivers and the verdant trees
The serpents attend
The gay tunes of the instrument.

In one sense, *The Dream* can be regarded as a synthesis of the two main trends in western European art at the turn of the century. For lack of better terminology, these trends may be described as "subjectivity" (one of the primary characteristics of Romanticism and Symbolism) and "objectivity" (the ideal aspired to by the Realists and Impressionists.) In *The Dream,* Rousseau merges the visionary world of dream and imagination with a detailed depiction of reality. To this end, he made a careful study of leaves and flowers, although their very "reality" in this painting has an eerie quality. However, *The Dream* is remarkably consistent with Freud's account of the mechanisms of dreaming and, as such, looks forward to twentieth-century Surrealism (see Chapter 26). Rousseau's image merges the dream (the picture) with the dreamer (the nude). Its precise, clear edges serve to contain the wild character of the jungle, which represents the primitive forces revealed in dreams.

	Style/Period	Works of Art	Cultural/Historical Developments
		Stone heads, Easter Island (**W10.1**)	 **Stone heads, Easter Island**
1850	POST-IMPRESSIONISM AND THE LATE NINETEENTH CENTURY 1850–1880	Hiroshige, *Sudden Shower at Ohashi Bridge at Ataka* (**23.13**) Moreau, *Orpheus* (**23.23**) Cézanne, *Temptation of Saint Anthony* (**23.3**) Cézanne, *Self-Portrait* (**23.4**) Cézanne, *Still Life with Apples* (**23.5**)	
1880	1880–1890  **Cézanne, *Still Life with Apples***	Moreau, *Galatea* (**23.24**) Seurat, *Sunday Afternoon on the Island of La Grande Jatte* (**23.8, 23.10**) Seurat, *Monkey* (**23.9**) van Gogh, *Potato Eaters* (**23.11**) van Gogh, *Japonaiserie: Bridge in the Rain* (**23.12**) van Gogh, *Bedroom at Arles* (**23.14–23.15**) van Gogh, *Self-Portrait* studies (**23.18**) van Gogh, *Self-Portrait* (**23.19**) van Gogh, *Starry Night* (**23.17**) van Gogh, *Wheat Field with Reaper* (**23.16**) Gauguin, *The Yellow Christ* (**23.20**) Gauguin, *Self-Portrait with Halo* (**23.21**)	 **van Gogh, *Self-Portrait***
1890	1890–1900 **Gauguin, *Nevermore***	Toulouse-Lautrec, *La Goulue at the Moulin Rouge* (**23.2**) Toulouse-Lautrec, *Quadrille at the Moulin Rouge* (**23.1**) Horta, staircase of the Maison Tassel (**23.28**), Brussels Gauguin, *Idol with the Seashell* (**W10.2**) Munch, *The Scream* (**23.25**) Munch, *The Voice* (**23.26**) Beardsley, *Salomé with the Head of John the Baptist* (**23.27**) Gauguin, *Nevermore* (**23.22**) Klimt, *Ver Sacrum* poster (**23.30**) Cézanne, *Great Bathers* (**23.6**)  **Cézanne, *Mont Sainte-Victoire***	Rudolf Diesel patents internal combustion engine (1892) Emergence of Art Nouveau in Europe (1893) Cinematograph invented (1894) Sino-Japanese War; the Japanese victorious (1894–1895) Wireless telegraphy invented by Guglielmo Marconi (1895) Richard Strauss, *Till Eulenspiegel's Merry Pranks* (1895) Giacomo Puccini, *La Bohème* (1896) The Curies discover radium (1898) Boer War; the English defeat the South Africans (1899–1902) Sigmund Freud, *The Interpretation of Dreams* (1899)  **Munch, *The Scream***
1900 1910	1900–1910  **Rousseau, *The Dream***	Cézanne, *Mont Sainte-Victoire* (**23.7**) Guimard, entrance to a Métro Station (**23.29**), Paris Klimt, *Kiss* (**23.31**) Rousseau, *The Dream* (**23.32**)  	Anton Chekhov, *Uncle Vanya* (1900) Joseph Conrad, *Lord Jim* (1900) Theodore Dreiser, *Sister Carrie* (1900) Max Planck formulates quantum theory (1900) Discovery of Minoan culture in Crete (1900–1909) Wright brothers' first flight in a powered airplane (1903) G. E. Moore, *Principia Ethica* (1903) Jack London, *The Call of the Wild* (1903) Anton Chekhov, *The Cherry Orchard* (1904) James Barrie, *Peter Pan* (1904) Giacomo Puccini, *Madama Butterfly* (1904) Edith Wharton, *The House of Mirth* (1905) Emmeline Pankhurst launches suffragette movement (1906) William James, *Pragmatism* (1907) Lord Baden-Powell founds the Boy Scouts (1907) E. M. Forster, *A Room with a View* (1908) Ford Motor Company produces first Model T car (1908) **Guimard, entrance to a Métro Station**

PART SEVEN

CHAPTER PREVIEWS

TURN OF THE CENTURY

Worringer: *Abstraction and Empathy* (1908); *The Historical Development of Modern Art* (1911)
Wöfflin: *The Principles of Art History* (1915)
Technology advances; Russian Revolution (1917)
Picasso's Blue Period; Matisse's Fauvism
Expressionism in Germany
The Bridge: Kirchner; Nolde
The Blue Rider: Kandinsky; Marc
Kollwitz
Matisse after Fauvism; collage

African Art and the European Avant-Garde

CUBISM, FUTURISM, AND RELATED STYLES

Picasso's Rose Period; *Les Demoiselles d'Avignon* (1907)
Analytic Cubism: Picasso; Braque
Collage and assemblage; Synthetic Cubism
Picasso's Surrealism; Futurism (Boccioni)
Artists influenced by Cubism: Léger; Mondrian; Duchamp; Brancusi; Davis; Douglas
The 1913 Armory Show, New York; Harlem Renaissance
Russia: Malevich's Suprematism
Architecture: the Bauhaus (Gropius); International Style (Le Corbusier, van der Rohe); Prairie Style (Frank Lloyd Wright)

DADA, SURREALISM, FANTASY, AND THE UNITED STATES BETWEEN THE WARS

World War I (1914–1918); Dada in Zurich
Duchamp's Ready-Mades; Breton's *Surrealist Manifesto*
European painters: de Chirico; Klee; Dalí; Miró; Magritte; Ernst

Hopi Kachinas
The Hopi pueblo

Sculptors: Giacometti; Moore; Calder (mobiles)
American painters: Wood; Lawrence; Hopper; Dove; O'Keeffe; Pelton; Moses; Pippin
Photographers: Man Ray; Van Der Zee; Evans; Lange; Weston; Stieglitz
Mexico: Rivera; Kahlo

ABSTRACT EXPRESSIONISM

World War II (1939–1945)
Hofmann and Albers
Abstract Expressionism: Gorky; Pollock; de Kooning; Kline; Frankenthaler
Navajo Sand Painting
Color Field: Rothko; Reinhardt; Stella; Kelly
Sculptors: Noguchi; Smith; Nevelson
West Coast Abstraction: Diebenkorn
European Figuration: Dubuffet; Bacon

POP, OP, MINIMALISM, AND CONCEPTUALISM

Happenings (1960s)
Pop Art: Hamilton; Johns; Rauschenberg; Warhol; Lichtenstein; Lindner; Kitaj; Wesselmann; Thiebaud; Oldenburg; Segal; Marisol; de Saint-Phalle; Op Art: Riley
Minimalism: Judd; Flavin; Martin; Hesse; Conceptualism: Kosuth

INNOVATION, CONTINUITY, AND GLOBALIZATION

Controversy in the United States: government funding for the arts; Serrano; Mapplethorpe
Performance : Gilbert and George; Anderson; Nauman
Return to Realism: Close; Hanson; Estes; Mueck
Installation: Holzer; Barney
Fuller (geodesic dome); Breuer (Whitney Museum)
Post-Modern architecture: Moore and Hersey; Graves; Pei; Rogers
Environmental art: Smithson; Holt; the Christos; Goldsworthy
Feminism: Chicago; Smith; Lin; Sherman; Rothenberg
Graffiti-inspired painting: Basquiat
Video: Paik; Viola; Neshat

The twentieth century witnessed a proliferation of styles, resulting in part from rapid global communication. Early in the century, the innovations of Matisse, Kandinsky, and Picasso revolutionized the approach to the picture plane. These three, like many avant-garde artists, sought to break the hold of the Classical tradition on Western consciousness. To this end, they studied the non-Classical forms of African and other non-Western art. But because Europe was shattered by two world wars, many artists by the end of World War II had emigrated to New York, which supplanted Paris as the art center of the Western world.

Newness became an end in itself, leading to such innovative styles as Dada and Surrealism, Cubism and Futurism, Abstract Expressionism and Pop Art, Minimalism and Conceptualism, Photo-Realism and others. Before 1917, Moscow had been a center of the avant-garde, along with Dresden and Munich. But totalitarianism in Russia and Germany considered modernism subversive. In the United States, the influx of European artists, combined with the young generation of Americans, enriched the visual arts. There had also been a rise in the cultural contributions of black artists, writers, and philosophers that formed the Harlem Renaissance. In addition, new media were explored—plastics, manufactured objects, and video—that opened up new artistic possibilities. In the early years of the twenty-first century, these trends continued, and the arts increasingly reflected the cross-cultural character of globalization.

24

Turn of the Century: Early Picasso, Fauvism, Expressionism, and Matisse

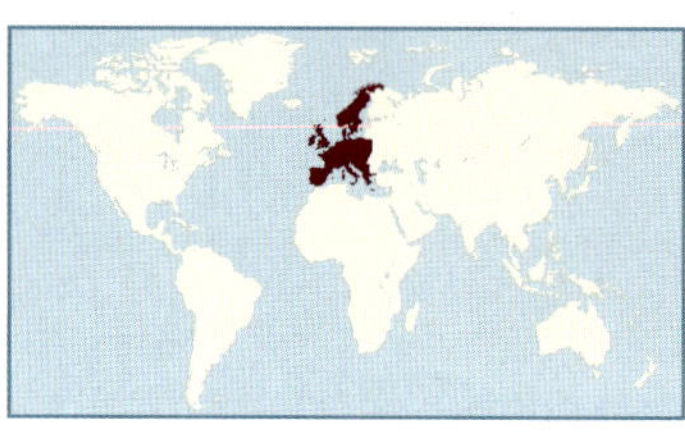

Western history is traditionally divided into centuries, and historians tend to see significance in the "turn of a century." Given the span of human history from the Paleolithic era, in which the first known works of art were produced, a century represents a small, almost infinitesimal, fragment of time. Nevertheless, as we consider historical events that are closer to our own era, their significance seems to increase and time itself to expand. Although we measure the prehistoric era by millennia and later periods by centuries, we tend to measure our own century by decades—or less. Our perception of time depends upon its relation to ourselves.

From the perspective of the end of the twentieth century and the beginning of a new millennium, we can see that rapid changes occurred in many fields. Technological advances set in motion by the industrial revolution speeded up communication and travel to an unprecedented degree. Electric lights have been used from the 1890s, radios from 1895, cars from the early 1900s, televisions and computers from the 1950s, and the Internet from the 1980s. The Wright brothers flew the first airplane at Kitty Hawk in 1903. Sixty-six years later, in 1969, the United States put the first man on the moon. Great strides were made in medicine; Albert Einstein formulated the theory of relativity, and Freud founded the psychoanalytic movement.

In politics, too, major changes took place. Lenin led the Russian Revolution in 1917; by 1991 the Soviet Union was dissolved. World War I (1914–1918) decimated a generation of European men. Following the Great Depression of 1929, Europe witnessed the rise of Hitler and National Socialism, which culminated in World War II (1939–1945). The end of that war ushered in the anxieties of the nuclear age and new concerns about the future of the environment.

In the arts, there were rapid changes in styles, which often merged into one another. For the purposes of this text, the twentieth century is divided by the marker of World War II. Up to that point, Paris had been the undisputed center of the Western art world. As Gertrude Stein (see p. 850) said, "Paris was where the twentieth century was." Paris exerted a strong pull on artists, who studied in its art schools, and on collectors and critics, who toured its studios, galleries, and museums. After the war, and partly because of it, many artists—indeed, entire schools of artists—were forced to flee Europe .

In 1900, many works by Impressionist and Post-Impressionist artists were shown at the World's Fair—the International Exposition—in Paris. These styles had emphasized the primacy of the medium. Building on this innovation, twentieth-century artists expanded into new areas, influenced in part by non-Western cultures. The nineteenth century had developed a taste for *japonisme* as a result of the influence of Japanese woodblock prints. In the early twentieth century, there was a growing interest in African art, the geometric abstraction of which appealed to artists, collectors, and critics.

Just as the Impressionists expanded subject matter by increasing the range of social classes depicted by Neoclassicism, twentieth-century artists developed a new iconography that included everyday objects. They also began to use new materials, such as plastics, which resulted from advances in technology. New techniques for making art were developed, especially in the second half of the century. Technological developments also encouraged new directions in architecture.

The very idea of "newness" became one of the tenets of modernism. The so-called avant-garde (literally, the "vanguard," who were leaders of artistic change) became a prominent force in Western art. Striving for avant-garde status contributed to the rapidity with which styles changed in the twentieth century.

Picasso's Blue Period

In painting, two figures dominated the first half of the twentieth century: the Spanish artist Pablo Picasso (1881–1973) and the French artist Henri Matisse (1869–1954). Both made sculptures but were primarily painters. In contrast to the experience of the Impressionists and Post-Impressionists, the genius of Picasso and Matisse was recognized relatively early in their careers. Their paths crossed at the Paris apartment of Gertrude Stein, who held regular gatherings of artists and intellectuals from Europe and the United States.

Picasso and Matisse began their careers in the nineteenth century under the influence of Impressionism, Post-Impressionism, and Symbolism. They soon branched out —Picasso earlier than Matisse—and spearheaded the avant-garde, although their styles were quite distinct. Matisse began and ended as a colorist, with important evolutions along the way. Picasso, on the other hand, shifted from one style to another, often working in more than one mode at the same time (see Chapter 25). His first major style was Symbolist; it is referred to as his Blue Period.

Picasso's Blue Period lasted from approximately 1901 to 1904. Consistent with the Symbolist aesthetic, his "Blue" paintings depict a mood or state of mind—in this case, melancholy and pessimism. The predominance of blue as the mood-creating element reflects the liberation of color that had been effected by nineteenth-century Post-Impressionism.

Picasso emphasizes the somber quality of the *Old Guitarist* (fig. **24.1**) by the all-pervasive blue color and the shimmering, silver light (see box). The musician's long, thin, bony form, tattered clothes, and downward curves convey dejection. His inward focus enhances the impression that he is listening intently, absorbed in his music, and also indicates that he is blind. The elongated forms and flickering silver light hark back to the spirituality of El Greco.

24.1 Pablo Picasso, *Old Guitarist,* 1903. Oil on panel; 4 ft. ⅗ in. × 2 ft. 8½ in. (1.23 × 0.83 m). Art Institute of Chicago (Helen Birch Bartlett Memorial Collection). Picasso was born in Málaga on the south coast of Spain. His father, José Ruíz Blasco, was an art teacher devoted to furthering his son's career. (Picasso took his mother's family name.) From 1901 to 1904, Picasso moved among Paris, Barcelona, and Madrid, settling permanently in Paris in 1904. The subjects of Picasso's Blue Period were primarily the poor and unfortunate.

Wallace Stevens: "The Man with the Blue Guitar"

The Symbolist quality of Picasso's *Old Guitarist* appealed to the American poet Wallace Stevens (1879–1955), who wrote "The Man with the Blue Guitar" in 1937 in response to it:[1]

The man bent over his guitar,
A shearsman of sorts. The day was green.

They said, "You have a blue guitar,
You do not play things as they are."

The man replied, "Things as they are
Are changed upon the blue guitar."

And they said then, "But play, you must,
A tune beyond us, yet ourselves,

A tune upon the blue guitar
Of things exactly as they are." [Stanza I]

And the color, the overcast blue
Of the air, in which the blue guitar

Is a form, described but difficult,
And I am merely a shadow hunched

Above the arrowy, still strings,
The maker of a thing yet to be made;

The color like a thought that grows
Out of a mood, the tragic robe

Of the actor, half his gesture, half
His speech, the dress of his meaning, silk

Sodden with his melancholy words,
The weather of his stage, himself. [Stanza IX]

Is this picture of Picasso's, this "hoard
Of destructions," a picture of ourselves,

Now, an image of our society?
Do I sit, deformed, a naked egg,

Catching at Good-bye, harvest moon,
Without seeing the harvest or the moon?

Things as they are have been destroyed.
Have I? Am I a man that is dead

At a table on which the food is cold?
Is my thought a memory, not alive?

Is the spot on the floor, there, wine or blood
And whichever it may be, is it mine? [Stanza XV]

Window on the World Eleven

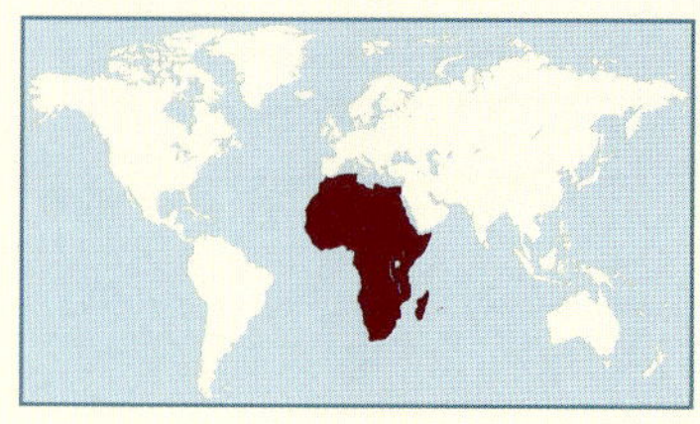

African Art and the European Avant-Garde

With the increasing number of ethnological museums at the end of the nineteenth century, non-Western art was becoming an aesthetic force in Europe. Against the background of nineteenth-century *japonisme*, the influence of Oceanic art, revivals of interest in Egyptian and Iberian art, and the spatial revolution of Cézanne, the early twentieth-century avant-garde was receptive to new formal ideas. One of the major sources for these was the growing interest in African art.

From about 1906, leading European artists began to notice African works in museums and shops, to discuss them with each other, and to collect them. Artists also traveled outside of Europe more than they had in the past. Despite this geographic and intellectual expansion, the early twentieth-century approach to the visual arts led to certain misconceptions about African art. First, Africa is a huge continent (see map), comprising many different cultures, each with its own artistic history. The time span of African art is as vast as that of Europe, ranging from the Stone Age to the present. Second, the understanding of African art is complicated by certain essential differences between it and other non-Western styles. Unlike Far Eastern art, there is virtually no narrative in African art. African artists did not conceive of their objects as set in a time and space in the way that Western artists had. As a result, much African art has a timeless quality, which was one of the sources of its appeal to the West.

The Fang of Gabon, for example, associate large heads with infancy, an age that was believed to be in a state of greater harmony with ancestors. According to the Fang, adults lose contact with the power wielded by deceased ancestors and with their own infantile past. The example illustrated here (fig. **W11.1**) was placed on a reliquary chest.

Africa.

W11.1 Male ancestor statue, eyema-o-byeri, Gabon, northern Fang, Ndoumou substyle. Light brown polished wood; 17¼ in. (43.8 cm) high. Musée Barbier-Mueller, Geneva.

Its legs are broken off, but it was originally in a seated position. Note the combination of a rounded childlike head with the more elongated proportions of an adult.

Another interpretation of such works is that they symbolize the desire for children. Clearly, African sculptures combining childlike with adult features condense time. In so doing, they seem timeless because they are essentially out of the chronological sequence of time as people experience it.

Most surviving African art is sculpture, which can be understood only in its cultural context. The cave paintings and glyptic arts of Africa were little known to nineteenth- and early twentieth-century European artists, who only rarely had contact with African architecture. The range of African sculpture is reflected by the formal, cultural, and iconographic variety of the works illustrated here.

Ife

Figure **W11.2** is from the city of Ife, founded around A.D. 800 to 900 in southwestern Nigeria. Its surviving art dates from the twelfth and thirteenth centuries A.D. and shows currents of naturalism as well as stylization. This copper mask is a convincing likeness, with a sense of soft flesh around the cheeks and lips, a firm bone structure beneath the nose, organic ears, and a broad, curved forehead. The hair, mustache, and beard were attached through holes, which are still visible. The only significantly stylized feature is the outline around the eye. This work shows the Ife skill in modeling, as well as in metal-casting technology. It is believed to have been used in royal burials and was probably worn during funerary ceremonies. There can be little question, however, that it has the quality of a portrait—possibly of a king.

Baule

The Baule figure from the Ivory Coast (fig. **W11.3**) typifies the African sculptures whose abstraction appealed to the Western avant-garde in the early twentieth century. Some scholars identify this as an ancestor, and others argue that it represents so-called otherworld people who are ideal mates for the Baule. Its surface is smooth and polished, with relief patterns of scarification on the face, neck, and torso. The hair is made of finely incised parallel lines. A mechanical effect is created by the abrupt, nonorganic planar shifts that contrast with Classical proportions (cf. fig. 5.27). Such objects offered non-Western artists new ways of approaching the human figure. At the same time, however, the proportions of African sculpture have meanings that vary from culture to culture.

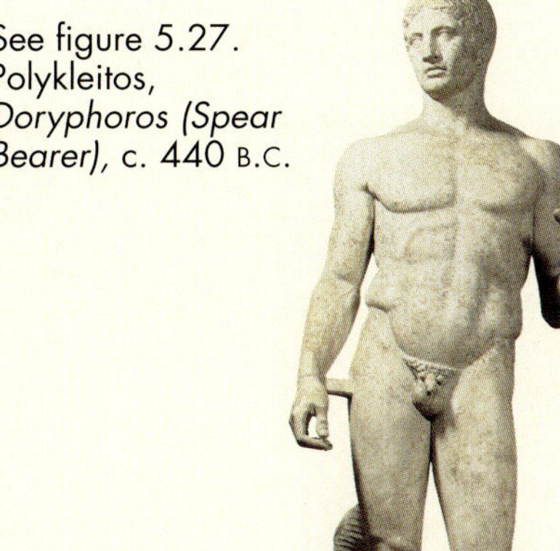

See figure 5.27. Polykleitos, *Doryphoros (Spear Bearer)*, c. 440 B.C.

W11.3 Baule ancestor, Ivory Coast. Wood; 20½ in. (52.1 cm) high. British Museum, London.

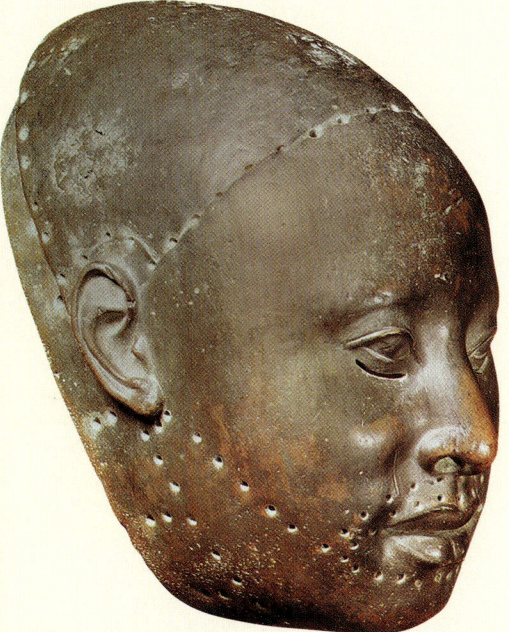

W11.2 Copper mask, Ife, Nigeria, 12th–13th century. 13 in. (33.0 cm) high. Life Museum, Lagos.

Bakota

The Bakota of Gabon made a distinctive type of figure, which was generally of wood covered with metal sheets of brass or copper (fig. **W11.4**). Their flat geometry struck the European avant-garde as particularly expressive. The oval face, identified as such by the lunette-shape eyes and pyramidal nose, is surmounted by a geometric headdress. The neck is cylindrical and the body abstracted to form a diamond shape framing empty space. It is clear that both the Bakota and the Baule figures would have appealed aesthetically to a generation of Western artists on the verge of Cubism. But here, again, the African figure is admired out of context. The actual function of the Bakota statue was to cover a reliquary containing ancestral bones. Ironically, therefore, traditional works within one society (in this case, an African society) became inspirational for artists breaking with tradition in another society (that of western Europe).

W11.4 Bakota figure, Gabon. Wood covered with brass sheeting; 26 in. (66.0 cm) high. British Museum, London.

Benin

Around the turn of the century, the art of Benin, a small kingdom to the west of modern Nigeria, attracted the art world's attention. Benin culture had been known since the fifteenth century, when the Portuguese infiltrated the area, sending missionaries, fighting as mercenaries in the Benin armies, and introducing guns to the local population. As traders, the Portuguese were interested in cloth, ivory, pepper, gold, and slaves. Their presence on Benin soil is known from contemporary accounts and also from bronze Benin sculptures representing Portuguese soldiers. Two centuries later, the Dutch also began trading in Benin. In 1897, a group of British officials went to Benin City during the annual festival honoring royal ancestors. The officials were killed, and Britain sent in a force known as the "Punitive Expedition," which set the city on fire. The metal and ivory objects that survived were taken to England. Some were sold to the British Museum, others to the Berlin Museum of Folk Art. Several ended up in private collections.

W11.5 Bronze Oba head, Benin, mid-19th century. 20⅛ in. (51.1 cm) high. British Museum, London. In 1927, Picasso acquired one of the Oba heads for his personal collection of African art.

The bronze head in figure **W11.5** represents the Oba, or divine king, of Benin. He controls the fate of his subjects through the spiritual power conferred on him by his divine ancestors. According to Benin tradition, which is transmitted orally, the former, celestial kings of Benin had failed their subjects, who sought a new ruler. They turned to the Oni, who ruled the neighboring Ife culture, and he sent his son, Oranmiyan, to Benin. There, Oranmiyan became the father of Eweka I by a local princess. The present Oba is the direct descendant of Eweka I and the undisputed ruler of Benin. He combines the power of earth and sky, and is both feared and loved by his people.

Heads of kings comprise a major iconographic category in Benin art. They reflect the importance of the Oba as a patron and the fact that most Benin art is connected to the court. The example illustrated here is cast in bronze, a technique introduced in the late 1300s. Multiple strands of coral beads covering the neck and chin are indications of wealth and status. The crown is decorated on either side with curved features, which were introduced in the nineteenth century. Such works were placed on ancestral altars—in this instance as a stand for an ivory tusk.

In the sixteenth century, from the period of Oba Esigie's reign, the Benin queen mother was accorded special status. Esigie's mother, Idia, was honored for her role in helping her son achieve victory in the Tgala war. According to oral tradition, Idia was a skillful military tactician who was able to communicate with the spirit world. Her position is reflected in the production of heads cast in brass for altars in the queen mother's home and in the palace (fig. **W11.6**). The high polish of the brass, the beaded strands around the neck, and the beaded crown adorning the so-called chicken's beak hair style are signs of her importance.

All the African figures described here have ritual, spiritual, or royal significance. Each belongs to a distinctive group of people. They also vary in their degree of stylization, abstraction, and naturalism. But together they illustrate some of the qualities that inspired the Western avant-garde. The following quotations from European artists discussed in this text express the liberating effect of their encounter with African sculpture:

W11.6 Head for an altar dedicated to the Benin queen mother. Bronze; 20 in. (50.8 cm) high. Ethologisches Museum, Staatliche Museen zu Berlin.

Kirchner (1910) (on the Benin bronzes in the Dresden Ethnology Museum): "A change and a delight."[2]

Nolde (1912): "Why is it that we artists love to see the unsophisticated artifacts of the primitives?"

"It is a sign of our times that every piece of pottery or dress or jewelry, every tool for living has to start with a blueprint—Primitive people begin making things with their fingers, with material in their hands. Their work expresses the pleasure of making. What we enjoy, probably, is the intense and often grotesque expression of energy, of life."[3]

Kandinsky (statement published 1930): "the shattering impression made on me by Negro art, which I saw in [1907] in the Ethnographic Museum in Berlin."[4]

Marc (1911): "I was finally caught up, astonished and shocked, by the carvings of the Cameroon people, carvings which can perhaps be surpassed only by the sublime works of the Incas. I find it so self-evident that we should seek the rebirth of our artistic feeling in this cold dawn of artistic intelligence, rather than in cultures that have already gone through a thousand-year cycle like the Japanese or the Italian Renaissance."[5]

Matisse (on African sculptures in a shop on the rue de Rennes in Paris; interview recorded in 1941): "I was astonished to see how they were conceived from the point of view of sculptural language; how it was close to the Egyptians . . . compared to European sculpture, which always took its point of departure from musculature and started from the description of the object, these Negro statues were made in terms of their material, according to invented planes and proportions."[6]

Picasso (on African masks): "For me the [tribal] masks were not just sculptures, they were magical objects . . . intercessors . . . against everything—against unknown, threatening spirits. . . . They were weapons—to keep people from being ruled by spirits, to help free themselves. . . . If we give a form to these spirits, we become free."[7]

Braque: "Negro masks opened a new horizon for me."[8]

Henri Matisse and Fauvism

In 1905, a new generation of artists exhibited their paintings in Paris at the Salon d'Automne. Bright, vivid colors seemed to burst from their canvases and dominate the exhibition space. Forms were built purely from color, and vigorous patterns and unusual color combinations created startling effects. To a large extent, they were derived from Gauguin's Symbolist use of color. The critic Louis Vauxcelles noticed one traditional work in the room and reportedly exclaimed, "Donatello parmi les fauves!" ("Donatello among the wild beasts!"), because the color and movement of the paintings reminded him of the jungle. His term stuck, and the style of those pictures is still referred to as "Fauve."

Vauxcelles's observation of a single traditional sculpture juxtaposed with the works of the young artists exhibiting in 1905 signaled the latest skirmish in the traditional western European dispute over the primacy of line versus color. Although there was plenty of "line" in Fauve painting, it was the brilliant, nonnaturalistic color and emotional exuberance that struck viewers. In contrast, Classical restraint and harmony, which were associated with line, appeared more controlled and, by implication, more civilized.

The leading artist of the Fauve group in France was Henri Matisse. His *Notre-Dame in the Late Afternoon* of 1902 (fig. **24.2**) depicts urban spaces as flat planes of color. Although the shapes are clearly defined, as in Post-Impressionism, and the paint texture is visible, Matisse has eliminated detail in favor of the predominance of color. Human figures are silhouettes, and the façade of Notre-Dame contains no reference to the Gothic surface variations on the actual building. Whereas the *Rouen Cathedrals* of Monet (see figs. 22.19 and 22.20) had subordinated Gothic detail (see fig. 11.28) to shifts of light and dark, Matisse's cathedral is reduced to a shape of color. But the color—lavender—combines the blues and pinks that are present throughout the picture. As a result, the cathedral assumes a position of power, for not only does it dominate the scene by its imposing height, but it unifies the view of modern Paris through color—just as it had once been the social, economic, religious, and artistic focal point of the medieval town.

24.2 Henri Matisse, *Notre-Dame in the Late Afternoon*, 1902. Oil on canvas; 28½ × 21½ in. (72.4 × 54.6 cm). Albright-Knox Art Gallery, Buffalo, New York (Gift of Seymour H. Knox).

CONNECTIONS

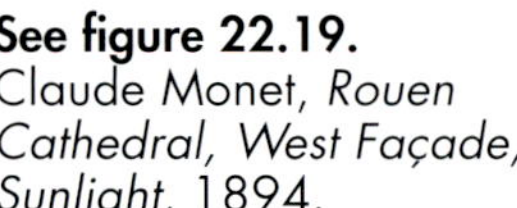

See figure 22.19.
Claude Monet, *Rouen Cathedral, West Façade, Sunlight*, 1894.

See figure 11.28.
West façade, Amiens Cathedral, 1220–1269.

24.3 Henri Matisse, *Madame Matisse (The Green Line)*, 1905. Oil on canvas; 16 × 12¾ in. (40.6 × 32.4 cm). Statens Museum for Kunst, Copenhagen. Matisse was born in northern France. He reportedly decided to become a painter when his mother gave him a set of **crayons** while he was recuperating from surgery.

Three years later, Matisse painted a portrait of his wife in the new style (fig. **24.3**). Here, Madame Matisse is a construction in color—a concept that Matisse had learned from Cézanne. He subtitled the work *The Green Line,* which refers to the line, beginning at the top of the forehead and continuing down the nose, that divides the face into a subdued ocher on the left and pink on the right. Throughout the picture plane, shading, modeling, and perspective are subordinate to color, which creates the features. The dark blue hair, which lacks organic quality because of its flatness, seems to perch on the head. This inorganic relation of head to hair, like the absence of modeling—for example, in the flat planes of the ears—reveals the influence of African masks on Matisse's style.

The background of *The Green Line* is identified only as color. To the right of Madame Matisse (our left) are two tones of red, clearly separated above her ear. At the opposite side, the background is green. Variations on these reds and greens recur in the face, creating a chromatic unity between figure and background.

In Matisse's *Woman with the Hat* (fig. **24.4**), as in *The Green Line* (fig. 24.3), color has again taken the lead, supported by shading, modeling, and perspective. Again, patches of color identify the background—greens, yellows, blues, and oranges to the left of the figure and mainly green and yellow to the right—variations of which appear in the face, thus unifying the work. The painting caused a scandal in the Paris art world for its unconventional use of color. But when purchased by Michael Stein, Gertrude's brother, the painting's reputation was saved. From that point on, Matisse's prices began to rise.

24.4 Henri Matisse, *Woman with the Hat,* 1905. Oil on canvas; 2 ft. 7¾ in. × 1 ft. 11½ in. (80.7 × 60.0 cm). San Francisco Museum of Modern Art, bequest of Elise S. Hass.

Expressionism

In Germany, the artists who, like the Fauves, were most interested in the expressive possibilities of color—as derived from Post-Impressionism—were called Expressionists. They formed groups that outlasted the Fauves in France and styles that persisted until the outbreak of World War I in 1914. Expressionism, like Fauvism, used color to create mood and emotion (see box) but differed from Fauvism in its greater concern with the emotional properties of color. Expressionism was also less concerned than the Fauves with the formal and structural composition of color.

The Bridge (*Die Brücke*)

In 1905, the year of the Fauve exhibition in Paris, four German architecture students in Dresden formed *Die Brücke* (The Bridge). Joined the following year by two others, this group of artists continued to work together until 1913. The name was inspired by the artists' intention to create a "bridge," or link, between their own art and modern revolutionary ideas, and between what was traditional and what was new in art. They modernized both the spiritual abstraction of medieval art and the geometric aesthetic of African and Oceanic art by integrating them with the mechanical forms of the city. Expressionist color was typically brilliant and exuberant and further energized by harsh, angular shapes.

24.6 Ernst Ludwig Kirchner, *Five Women in the Street*, 1913. Oil on canvas; 3 ft. 10½ in. × 2 ft. 11½ in. (1.18 × 0.90 m). Ludwig Museum, Cologne/Rheinisches Bildarchiv, Cologne.

Ernst Ludwig Kirchner The most important founding artist of *Die Brücke* was Ernst Ludwig Kirchner (1880–1938), who had been trained as an architect before becoming a painter. He had been inspired by the *Jugendstil* of the Vienna Secession as well as by Munch, van Gogh, and non-Western art. *The Street* of 1907 (fig. **24.5**), for example, combines Expressionist color with undulating forms reminiscent of Munch. The flat color areas, on the other hand, can be related to Fauvism.

24.5 Ernst Ludwig Kirchner, *The Street*, 1907. Oil on canvas; 4 ft. 11¼ in. × 6 ft. 6⅞ in. (1.51 × 2.00 m). Museum of Modern Art, New York.

A comparison with a later street scene by Kirchner—*Five Women in the Street* of 1913 (fig. **24.6**)—reflects certain stylistic shifts (in this case, toward Cubism) of the period. The dreamlike quality of the earlier picture and its pure, primary hues ally it with nineteenth-century Symbolism and Post-Impressionism. In the later picture, the color is subdued and limited, which shows the influence of Analytic Cubism (see p. 852). The predominance of dulled greens creates a uniformity that accentuates the impersonal character of the women. Kirchner captures the anxious, frenetic pace of urban life through angular, elongated figures occupying a shifting perspective. His training in architecture is evident in the tectonic forms of the women. Their high-heeled shoes, for example, create two-dimensional geometric silhouettes against a lighter space, and their fur ruffs form crescents. The distinctions between light and dark in the dresses are crisply defined, creating a sense of solid, crystalline structure rather than of soft material.

Emil Nolde Another artist associated with German Expressionism, Emil Nolde (1867–1956), spent only a year as a member of The Bridge. His early pictures depicted religious themes infused with a visionary mood. After spending the year 1899 to 1900 in Paris, Nolde increased his range of color. In addition to the influence of nineteenth-century French styles, his work shows very clearly that non-Western art provided him with a significant source of inspiration.

His *Still Life with Masks* of 1911 (fig. **24.7**) combines bright color with thickly applied paint to achieve intense, dynamic effects. The upside-down pink mask and the adjacent yellow one were inspired by northern European carnivals. But the red mask at the far left is based on Nolde's own drawing of an Oceanic canoe prow (fig. **24.8**). The yellow skull at the lower right is also derived from non-Western prototypes—in this case, a shrunken head from Brazil, of which Nolde made sketches. African examples probably inspired the green mask at the upper right, but the combination of a green surface with red outlining the features is an Expressionist use of color. Nolde's non-Western imagery served to express qualities that were finally more in tune with Expressionism than with the cultural or artistic intentions of the non-Western art he studied.

24.7 Emil Nolde, *Still Life with Masks,* 1911. Oil on canvas; 28¾ × 30½ in. (73.0 × 77.5 cm). Nelson-Atkins Museum of Art, Kansas City.

24.8 Emil Nolde, drawing of an Oceanic canoe prow, for left-hand mask in fig. 24.7, 1911. Pencil drawing; 11⅞ × 7⅛ in. (30.2 × 18.1 cm). Stiftung Seebüll Ada und Emil Nolde.

Art History and Aesthetics in Early Twentieth-Century Munich

Two important figures in the Munich art world, Heinrich Wölfflin (1864–1945) and Wilhelm Worringer (1881–1965), were particularly influential. Wölfflin lectured on art history, whereas Worringer's aesthetic theories supported the Expressionist movement.

Wölfflin's most important work, which is still read by art students—*The Principles of Art History*—was first published in German in 1915. He devised a system of determining style by an analysis of its formal elements. Renaissance and Classical styles, for example, were distinguished from Baroque by five pairs of opposing characteristics. The classicizing Renaissance style was, according to Wölfflin, linear, whereas Baroque was painterly. Renaissance planes were constructed according to the verticals and horizontals of linear perspective, while Baroque planes receded diagonally. Space tended to be open in Baroque and closed in Renaissance. Elements were multiple and clarity was absolute in the Renaissance style. In Baroque, elements were unified and clarity was relative.

What united Wölfflin with Worringer was a mutual emphasis on the viewer's experience of works of art. But whereas Wölfflin focused on past styles, Worringer championed the avant-garde—notably, the German Expressionists. In 1908, Worringer published his dissertation *Abstraktion und Einfühlung* (*Abstraction and Empathy*); this argued for new forms of expression and was widely read by the young artists of Worringer's generation. Three years later, in *The Historical Development of Modern Art,* Worringer replied to criticism leveled at the Expressionists, defending them against charges reminiscent of those brought against Whistler and the French Impressionists. Expressionist paintings were accused of being decadent, self-indulgent, without form, finish, or depth. Worringer countered by pointing out the limitations of adherence to naturalism. He called for accessibility to new influences as a way of expanding artistic consciousness. Such infusions, particularly from non-European cultures, Worringer believed, would offer a new route to the spiritual core of creativity.

The Blue Rider (*Der Blaue Reiter*)

Another German Expressionist group more drawn to nonfigurative abstraction than members of The Bridge was *Der Blaue Reiter* (The Blue Rider), established in Munich in 1911. The name of the group, derived from the visionary language of the book of Revelation (cf. the Four Horsemen of the Apocalypse), was inspired by the millennium and the notion that Moscow would be the new center of the world from 1900—as Rome had once been. *Blue Rider* referred to the emblem of the city of Moscow showing Saint George (the "Rider") killing the dragon.

Vassily Kandinsky The Russian artist Vassily Kandinsky (1866–1944) was among the first to eliminate recognizable objects from his paintings. He identified with the Blue Rider as the artist who would ride into the future of a spiritual nonfigurative and mystical art; for him, the color blue signified the masculine aspect of spirituality (cf. fig. 24.11). At the age of thirty, Kandinsky left Moscow, where he was a law student, and went to Munich to study painting. There he was a founder of the Neue Künstler Vereinigung (New Artists' Association), or NKV, the aim of which was rebellion against tradition. A few artists split from the NKV to form the Blue Rider.

For Kandinsky, art was a matter of using rhythmic lines, colors, and shapes rather than narrative. Like Whistler, Kandinsky gave his works musical titles to express their abstract qualities. By eliminating references to material reality, Kandinsky followed the Blue Rider's avoidance of the mundane in order to communicate the spiritual in art. Titles such as *Improvisation* evoked the dynamic spontaneity of creative activity, while the *Compositions* emphasized the organized abstraction of his lines, shapes, and colors.

In 1912, Kandinsky published *Concerning the Spiritual in Art,* in which he explained his philosophy—he argued that music was intimately related to art. He was by temperament drawn to religious and philosophical thinking imbued with strains of mysticism and the occult, which can be related to a millenarian spirit of the Blue Rider emblem. And he believed that art had a spiritual quality because it was the product of the artist's spirituality. The work of art, in turn, reflected this through the musical harmony of form and color.

Panel for Edwin R. Campbell No. 4 (formerly *Painting No. 201, Winter*) of 1914 (fig. **24.9**) was one of four in a series representing the seasons—this one being winter. In it Kandinsky creates a swirling, curvilinear motion within which there are varied lines and shapes. Lines range from thick to thin, color patches from plain to spotty, and hues from solid to blended. The most striking color is red, which is set off against yellows and softer blues and greens. The strongest accents are blacks, while the sense of winter is suggested primarily by the whites, which occur in pure form and also blend with the colors. Blues become light blues, and reds become pinks, creating an illusion of coldness that is readily associated with winter.

Later, in the 1920s, despite stylistic changes inspired by his association with the Moscow avant-garde, Kandinsky continued to pursue the notion of the spiritual in art. He did so by endowing delicate geometric shapes with a dynamic spatial tension. This is evident in *Several Circles, No. 323* (fig. **24.10**), in which translucent circles float in a swirling space. Some of the circles are isolated, others barely touch the edge of adjacent circles, while a few appear to skim over one another, their geometric purity contrasting with the textured background. Kandinsky's image has an "otherworldly" quality, evoking both the minutiae of the invisible molecular world and the vast distances of a solar system occupied by orbiting moons and planets.

24.9 Vassily Kandinsky, *Panel for Edwin R. Campbell No. 4* (formerly *Painting No. 201, Winter*), 1914. Oil on canvas; 5 ft. 4¼ in. × 4 ft. ¼ in. (1.63 × 1.24 m). Museum of Modern Art, New York (Nelson A. Rockefeller Fund, by exchange).

24.10 Vassily Kandinsky, *Several Circles, No. 323,* 1926. Oil on canvas; 55⅛ × 55⅛ in. (140.0 × 140.0 cm). Guggenheim Museum, New York.

24.11 Franz Marc, *Large Blue Horses*, 1911. Oil on canvas; 3 ft. 5⅝ in. × 5 ft. 11 5/16 in. (1.06 × 1.81 m). Walker Art Center, Minneapolis (Gift of the T. B. Walker Foundation, Gilbert Walker Fund, 1942). Marc shared Kandinsky's spiritual attitude toward the formal qualities of painting, especially color. He thought of blue as masculine, yellow as having the calm sensuality of a woman, and red as aggressive. Mixed colors were endowed with additional forms of emotional iconography.

Franz Marc The other major Blue Rider artist was Franz Marc (1880–1916), who joined Kandinsky in editing the *Blue Rider Yearbook* of 1912. This contained discussions of Picasso and Matisse, The Bridge, The Blue Rider itself, and the new interest in expanding aesthetic experience through contact with non-Western art. In contrast to Kandinsky, however, Marc did not entirely eliminate recognizable objects from his work, except in preliminary drawings made shortly before his premature death.

Marc's *Large Blue Horses* of 1911 (fig. **24.11**) combines geometry with rich color. As Gauguin described his "red dogs" and "pink skies" (see Chapter 23), Marc's animals and their setting can be considered in the abstract terms of musical composition. They are an arrangement in blue, foreshortened forms, which harmonize with the curvilinear, brightly colored landscape. Marc's use of animals reflects his belief that they are better suited than humans to the expression of cosmological ideas. The two gray curves representing slender tree trunks serve as structural anchors. They also create a sense of confinement, which compresses the space and enhances the monumentality of Marc's horses.

The Blue Rider, in contrast to The Bridge, was international in scope and had a greater influence on Western art. In particular, Kandinsky's nonfigurative imagery, which was among the first of its kind, was part of a revolutionary development that would remain an important current in twentieth-century art. Neither Matisse nor Picasso, despite all their innovations, ever completely renounced references to nature and other recognizable forms.

Käthe Kollwitz

Although Käthe Kollwitz (1867–1945) was not a formal member of any artistic group, her *Whetting the Scythe* of 1905 (fig. **24.12**) conveys the direct emotional confrontation characteristic of Expressionism. Her harsh textures and the preponderance of rich blacks enhance her typically depressive themes. The gnarled figure concentrating intently on her task is rendered in close-up, which accentuates the detailed depiction of her wrinkled hands and aged, slightly wary expression. In the background, the cruciform arrangement of blacks reinforces the morbid associations of the image. The presence of the scythe, an attribute of the Grim Reaper, or Death, conforms to the woman's rather sinister quality. She is a version of van Gogh's Post-Impressionist *Wheat Field with Reaper* (see fig. 23.16) and Wordsworth's Romantic "Solitary Reaper."

24.12 Käthe Kollwitz, *Whetting the Scythe*, 1905. Soft-ground eighth-state etching; 11 11/16 × 11 11/16 in. (29.7 × 29.7 cm). British Museum, London. Despite being financially comfortable herself, Kollwitz's imagery brings the viewer into contact with the emotional and material struggles of the working classes. This print is from a series published in 1904 to commemorate Germany's 16th-century peasant rebellion.

Matisse after Fauvism

Although Fauvism was short-lived, its impact, like that of Expressionism, was a basis for twentieth-century abstraction. Matisse reportedly said that "Fauvism is not everything, but it is the beginning of everything."

As Matisse developed, he was influenced by abstraction without embracing it completely. His sense of musical rhythm translated into line creates energetic, curvilinear biomorphic form. On the other hand, the shapes and spaces of Matisse that are determined primarily by color and only secondarily by line can be more static and geometric. These two tendencies—fluid line and flat color—create a dynamic tension that persists throughout his career.

Harmony in Red

In *Harmony in Red* of 1908–1909 (fig. **24.13**), Matisse goes beyond the thick, constructive brushstrokes and unusual color juxtapositions of his Fauve period. The subject of the painting, a woman placing a fruit bowl on a table, seems secondary to its formal arrangement. Within the room, the sense of perspective has been minimized because the table and wall are of the same red. The demarcation between them is indicated not by a constructed illusion of space, but by a dark outline and by the bright still-life arrangements on the surface of the table. The perspective is confined to the chair at the left and the window frame behind it. But, despite the flattening of the form by minimal modeling, Matisse endows the woman and the still-life objects with a sense of volume.

The landscape, visible through the open window, relieves the confined quality of the interior view. It is related to the interior by the repetition of energetic black curves, which Matisse referred to as his "arabesques." The inside curves create branchlike forms that animate the table and wall, while those outside form branches and tree trunks. Smaller arabesques define the flower stems and the outline of the woman's hair.

The title *Harmony in Red* reinforces the musical abstraction of Matisse's picture. It refers to the predominant color, the flat planes of which "harmonize" the wall and table into a shared space. Matisse builds a second, more animated "movement" in the fluid arabesques harmonizing interior with exterior. Finally, the bright patches on the woman, the still-life objects, and the floral designs create a more staccato rhythm composed of individual accented forms. Matisse's ability to harmonize these different formal modes within a static pictorial space synthesizes three artistic currents: the Post-Impressionist liberation of color, the Symbolist creation of mood, and the twentieth-century trend toward abstraction.

24.13 Henri Matisse, *Harmony in Red,* 1908–1909. Oil on canvas; 5 ft. 11 in. × 8 ft. 1 in. (1.80 × 2.46 m). State Hermitage Museum, St. Petersburg.

Dance I

In *Dance I* of 1909 (fig. **24.14**), it is the figures, rather than the arabesques, that dance. The black outlines define the dancers, who twist and turn, jump and stretch. Their rhythmic, circular motion has been compared to dancers on the surface of a Greek vase. Although the blue and green background is composed of flat color, Matisse creates a three-dimensional illusion in the dancers. This is enhanced by the warm pinks that make the dancers appear to advance, as the cool background colors recede. Although the individual movements of the dancers vary, together they form a harmonious continuum.

24.14 Henri Matisse, *Dance I*, 1909. Oil on canvas; 8 ft. 6½ in. × 12 ft. 9½ in. (2.60 × 3.90 m). Museum of Modern Art, New York (Gift of Nelson A. Rockefeller in honor of Alfred H. Barr, Jr.).

Piano Lesson

Another painting with a musical subject reflects changes in Matisse's style over the next decade. The *Piano Lesson* of 1916 (fig. **24.15**) has an autobiographical subtext. It is about the conflict between musical discipline and ambition on the one hand and erotic pleasure on the other. In contrast to the earlier paintings, the *Piano Lesson* is constructed geometrically from rectangular and trapezoidal shapes that indicate Matisse's willingness to experiment with Cubist form. The seated woman at the right, for example, who could be the boy's mother or teacher, is a rectangular structure with ovals defining her blank face. She is elevated, as if on a throne, implicitly commanding the boy to practice. The boy stares fixedly at his music. His right eye is blocked out by a gray trapezoid that echoes the shape in the window and the metronome.

To the left of the gray window section is a rich green trapezoid. In the lower left corner, a figurine lounges in a seductive pose reminiscent of Titian's *Venus of Urbino* (see fig. 14.52); it is also a quotation of an earlier sculpture by Matisse. The outlines of the figure echo the arabesques in the music stand and the grillwork in the window. Although the boy is boxed in by the rectangle, which he shares with the "enthroned" woman, he is also related to the figurine through their shared tones of orange-brown. Although prevented from "seeing" her by the gray shape over his right eye, he seems to have her literally "on his mind" by virtue of the color of his hair. The same orange-brown is repeated in the illuminated candle, which is positioned between the boy and the figurine. The candle, which can have erotic implications, also denotes the passage of time.

The opposition of the notion of woman as disciplinarian and as seductress is evident in the formal structure of the painting, as well as in its iconographic details. The rectilinear organization of the space, like the metronome, corresponds to the "lofty" woman in its sense of ordered logic and measured time. (She is based on an earlier portrait of the wife of a Cubist critic and can thus be linked with the geometry of Cubism in content as well as form.)

Inscribed across the center bar of the music stand is the word "PLEYEL" in reverse. This is a reference to the manufacturer of the piano as well as to the Salle Pleyel, the most distinguished concert hall of Paris. It, therefore, combines the present practice of the ambitious young musician with a future that his mother or teacher wishes for him. The *Piano Lesson* can be read as a metaphor for Matisse's relationship to the art of painting. It combines the rules of practice, technique, order, and logic with controlled energy. The role of female inspiration, echoed by the separate implications of metronome and candle, is divided between the two women. In a way, therefore, this picture is to Matisse what the *Studio* (see fig. 21.5) was to Courbet —a psychological "manifesto" of the painter's art.

CONNECTIONS

See figure 14.52. Titian, *Venus of Urbino*, c. 1538.

24.15 Henri Matisse, *Piano Lesson*, 1916. Oil on canvas; 8 ft. ½ in. × 6 ft. 11¾ in. (2.45 × 2.13 m). Museum of Modern Art, New York (Mrs. Simon Guggenheim Fund).

24.16 Henri Matisse, *Jeannette V*, 1916. Bronze; 23 × 7¾ × 11½ in. (58.4 × 19.7 × 29.3 cm). Art Gallery of Ontario, Toronto.

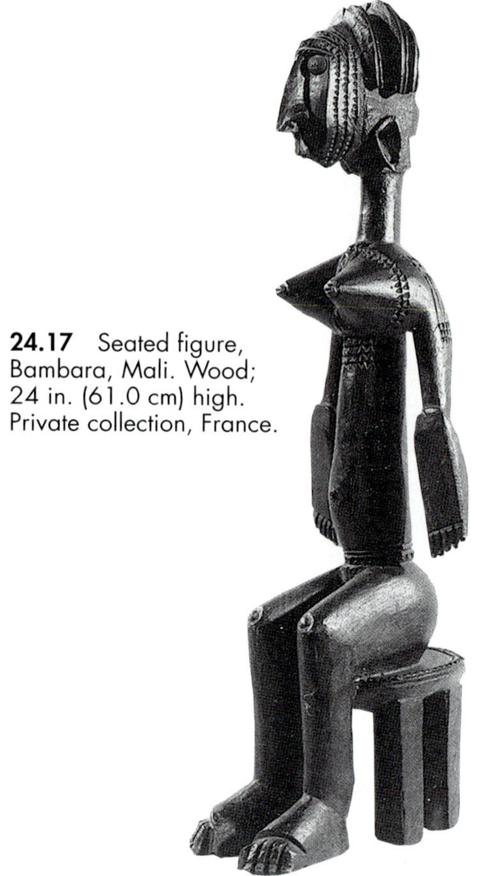

24.17 Seated figure, Bambara, Mali. Wood; 24 in. (61.0 cm) high. Private collection, France.

Jeannette V

The geometric qualities of the *Piano Lesson* recur in a sculpture of the same year that reflects the influence of African art. *Jeannette V* (fig. **24.16**) is a bronze bust organized more according to geometry than to nature; it is the last of a series of heads begun in 1909 that move toward increasingly simplified abstraction. The hair is divided into shifting forms, one of which merges into the long nose, and the neck and body are arranged in three zigzag planes. This work shares an aggressive, angular quality with the seated Bambara figure from Mali (fig. **24.17**) that Matisse owned at the time. In both, there is an emphasis on pointed forms and a vigorous self-assertiveness.

Later Works

Matisse later became interested in the lively, Moorish patterns of North Africa. He traveled to Morocco for the first time in 1906 and painted European models in Moorish settings. In *Decorative Figure in an Oriental Setting* of 1925 (fig. **24.18**), Matisse placed a monumental odalisque in a space crowded with colorful linear energy. The woman, by contrast, is massive and blocklike. She retains some of the geometry of his earlier figures, with her cylindrical neck, circular breasts, triangular side, and rectangular thigh.

The solidity of her form anchors the picture, which is otherwise filled with the motion of elaborate patterns. The curved drapery creates a transition from the still, restful pose of the odalisque to the tilting floor and profusely animated designs of the carpet, wall, and flowerpot. Orange arabesques frame the blue shapes on the wall—a particularly vivid chromatic juxtaposition because blue and orange are opposites on the color wheel (see fig. I.18). The blues are further enlivened by the flowers in their midst, especially by the intense reds. The extent to which Matisse's style has departed from the Classical tradition—while also maintaining its themes—can be seen by comparing his "decorative figure" with the Neoclassical *Grande Odalisque* of Ingres (see fig. 19.14).

During the last decade of his life, Matisse gave up painting, partly because of cancer. Instead, he grappled with the problem of creating a three-dimensional illusion from absolutely flat forms. His medium was *découpage* (cutout),

CONNECTIONS

See figure 19.14. Jean-Auguste-Dominique Ingres, *Grande Odalisque*, 1814.

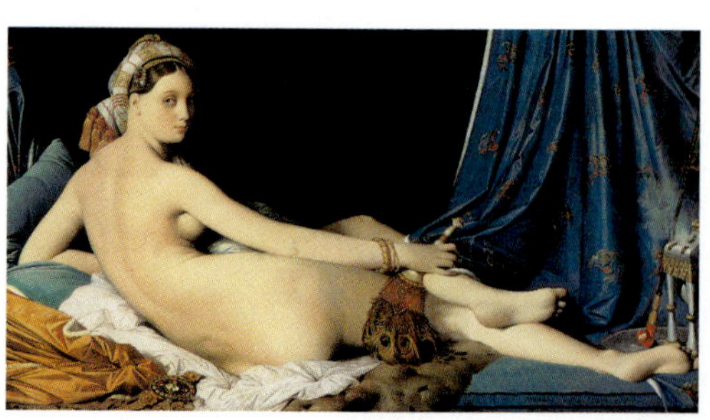

creating an image by pasting pieces of colored paper onto a flat surface. An early series of cutouts, entitled *Jazz,* indicates Matisse's continuing interest in synthesizing musical with pictorial elements. His cutout of *Icarus* of 1947 (fig. **24.19**), from the *Jazz* series, combines a subject from Greek mythology with modern style and technique. By curving the edges and expanding or narrowing the forms, Matisse gives the silhouetted Icarus (see Bruegel's *Landscape with the Fall of Icarus,* fig. 16.6) the illusion of volume. His outstretched, winglike arms and tilting head create the impression that, though he is falling through space, he is not plummeting down to the sea, but floating gracefully in slow motion.

Entirely different in character are the zigzagging bright yellow stars that surround Icarus. Their points shoot off in various directions, and their vivid color is far more energetic than the languid figure of Icarus. There are thus two musical "movements" in this cutout—the slower, curvilinear motion of Icarus and the rapid, angular motion of the stars. Adagio and staccato are combined against the deep, resonant blue sky.

The drive toward new techniques and media for image making, which is evident in Matisse's cutouts, will be seen to characterize many of the innovations of twentieth-century art.

24.18 (above) Henri Matisse, *Decorative Figure in an Oriental Setting,* 1925. Oil on canvas; 51⅛ × 38½ in. (129.8 × 97.8 cm). Museum of Modern Art, Paris.

24.19 Henri Matisse, *Icarus,* plate 8 from *Jazz.* Paris, E. Tériade, 1947. Pochoir, printed in color, each double page 16⅝ × 25⅝ in. (42.2 × 65.1 cm). Museum of Modern Art, New York (Louis E. Stern Collection). The *Jazz* series is composed of individual book-size cutouts printed in book form to accompany Matisse's own text.

	Style/Period	Works of Art	Cultural/Historical Developments
	TURN OF THE CENTURY Benin Oba head	Ife copper mask (**W11.2**) Benin Oba head (**W11.5**) Fang reliquary statue (**W11.1**) Baule figure (**W11.3**) Bakota figure (**W11.4**) Bambara seated figure (**24.17**) Benin head for the altar of the queen mother (**W11.6**)	 **Bakota figure**  **Benin head**
1900	1900–1910  ***Picasso, Old Guitarist***	Matisse, *Notre-Dame in the Late Afternoon* (**24.2**) Picasso, *Old Guitarist* (**24.1**) Matisse, *Madame Matisse* (**24.3**) Matisse, *Woman with the Hat* (**24.4**) Kollwitz, *Whetting the Scythe* (**24.12**) Kirchner, *The Street* (**24.5**) Matisse, *Harmony in Red* (**24.13**) Matisse, *Dance I* (**24.14**)  ***Matisse, Harmony in Red***	Theodore Roosevelt president of the U.S.A. (1901–1909) Foundation of Nobel prizes (1901) August Strindberg, *The Dance of Death* (1901) The hormone adrenalin first isolated (1901) First oil wells drilled in Persia (1901) Maxim Gorky, *Lower Depths* (1902) Anton Chekhov, *Three Sisters* (1902) Aswan Dam opened (1902) Albert Einstein, *Special Theory of Relativity* (1905) Alfred Stieglitz opens the 291 Art Gallery (1905) *Die Brücke* formed in Dresden (1905) Upton Sinclair, *The Jungle* (1906) Ivan Pavlov's study of conditioned reflexes (1907)
1910	1910–1920  ***Marc, Large Blue Horses***	Nolde, *Still Life with Masks* (**24.7**) Nolde, drawing of an Oceanic canoe prow (**24.8**) Marc, *Large Blue Horses* (**24.11**) Kirchner, *Five Women in the Street* (**24.6**) Kandinsky, *Painting No. 201* (**24.9**) Matisse, *Jeannette V* (**24.16**) Matisse, *Piano Lesson* (**24.15**)  ***Kandinsky, Painting No. 201***	Igor Stravinsky, *The Firebird* (1910) *Der Blaue Reiter* formed in Munich (1911) Frederick Delius, *On Hearing the First Cuckoo in Spring* (1912) *Titanic* sinks on maiden voyage (1912) Thomas Mann, *Death in Venice* (1913) First World War (1914–1918) W. Somerset Maugham, *Of Human Bondage* (1915) Ford Madox Ford, *The Good Soldier* (1915) Bolshevik Revolution in Russia (1917) League of Nations established (1919) ***Kandinsky, Several Circles, No. 323*** 
1920 1930	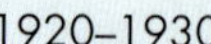1920–1930  ***Matisse, Icarus***	Matisse, *Decorative Figure in an Oriental Setting* (**24.18**) Kandinsky, *Several Circles, No. 323* (**24.10**) Matisse, *Icarus* (**24.19**)	Roaring Twenties, age of prosperity and cultural innovation in America (1920–1929) The Jazz Age (1920s)

25

Cubism, Futurism, and Related Twentieth-Century Styles

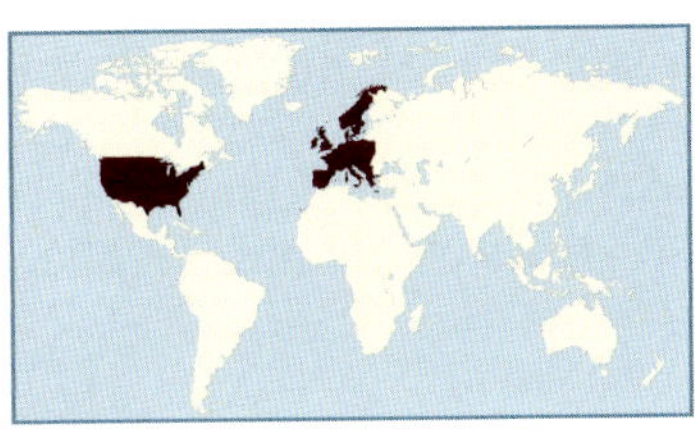

The most influential style of the early twentieth century was Cubism, which, like Fauvism, developed in Paris. Cubism was essentially a revolution in the artist's approach to space, both on the flat surface of the picture and in sculpture. The nonnaturalistic Fauve can be seen as synthesizing nineteenth-century Impressionism, Post-Impressionism, and Symbolism. Cubism, however, together with the nonfigurative innovations of Expressionism, soon became the wave of the artistic future.

The main European impetus for Cubism came from Cézanne's new spatial organization, in which he built up images from constructions of color. Other decisive currents of influence came from so-called "primitive," or tribal, and Iberian art. These offered European artists unfamiliar, non-Classical ways to represent the human figure.

Cubism

Precursors

Picasso's 1906 portrait of Gertrude Stein (fig. **25.1**; see box, p. 850) is executed in the dark red hues that mark the end of his Rose Period, which followed the Blue Period discussed in Chapter 24. The emphasis on color is consistent with contemporary Fauve interests, but a comparison with the *Old Guitarist* of the Blue Period (see fig. 24.1) indicates that more than color has changed. In the *Gertrude Stein,* new spatial and planar shifts occur that herald the beginning of the development of Cubism.

Gertrude Stein's right arm and hand are organically shaded and contoured. Her left hand, however, is flatter, and her arm looks as if it were constructed of cardboard. Picasso reportedly needed over eighty sittings to finish the picture, the main stumbling block being the face. In the final result, Gertrude Stein stares impassively, as if from

25.1 Pablo Picasso, *Gertrude Stein,* 1906. Oil on canvas; 39⅜ × 32 in. (100.0 × 81.3 cm). Metropolitan Museum of Art, New York (Bequest of Gertrude Stein, 1947). In 1909, Gertrude Stein wrote *Prose Portraits,* the literary parallel of Analytic Cubism. Her unpunctuated cinematic repetition reads like free association. The following is from her *Portrait* of Picasso. "One whom some were certainly following was one working and certain was one bringing something out of himself then and was one who had been all his living had been one having something coming out of him. . . . This one was one who was working."[1]

Gertrude Stein

Gertrude Stein (1874–1946) was an expatriate American art collector and writer. She moved to Paris in 1903, after studying psychology at Radcliffe and medicine at Johns Hopkins. Her Paris apartment became a salon for the leading intellectuals of the post–World War I era, whom she dubbed the "lost generation." Her most popular book, *The Autobiography of Alice B. Toklas* (Stein's companion), is actually her own autobiography.

Stein and her two brothers were among the earliest collectors of paintings by avant-garde artists. History has vindicated her judgment, for she left an art collection worth millions of dollars. Ernest Hemingway, in *A Moveable Feast,* wrote that he had been mistaken not to heed Stein's advice to buy Picassos instead of clothes.

behind a mask. The hair does not grow organically from the scalp, and the ears are flat. The sharp separations between light and dark at the eyebrows, the black outlines around the eyes, and the disparity in the size of the eyes detract from the impression of a flesh-and-blood face.

Even more like masks are the faces in Picasso's pivotal picture *Les Demoiselles d'Avignon* (*The Women of Avignon*) of 1907 (fig. **25.2**). With this representation of five nudes and a still life, Picasso launched a spatial revolution. The subject itself was hardly new, and Picasso had adapted traditional poses from earlier periods of Western art. On the far left, for example, the standing figure nearly replicates the pose of ancient Egyptian kings (see Chapter 3). The left leg is forward, the right arm is extended downward, and the fist is clenched. Also borrowed from Egypt is the pictorial convention of rendering the face in profile and the eye in front view. Picasso's two central figures, whose arms stretch behind their heads, are based on traditional poses of Venus. Of all the figures, the faces of the seated and standing nudes on the far right are most obviously based on African prototypes. The wooden mask from the Congo in figure **25.3**, for example, shares an elongated, geometric quality with the face of the standing figure at the right. Here, Picasso has abandoned *chiaroscuro* in favor of the Fauve preference for bold strokes of color. The nose resembles the long, curved, solid wedge of the mask's nose.

In the Mbuya (sickness) mask from Zaire (fig. **25.4**), the natural facial configuration is disrupted. Similarly, the face of Picasso's seated figure defies nature as well as the Classical ideal. In both faces, the nose curves to one side, while

25.2 Pablo Picasso, *Les Demoiselles d'Avignon,* Paris, June–July 1907. Oil on canvas; 8 ft. × 7 ft. 8 in. (2.44 × 2.34 m). Museum of Modern Art, New York (acquired through the Lillie P. Bliss Bequest). This painting was named for a bordello in the Carrer d'Avinyo (Avignon Street), Barcelona's red-light district. Earlier versions contained a seated sailor and a medical student carrying a skull. Both were aspects of Picasso himself. By removing them from the final painting, Picasso shifted from a personal narrative to a more powerful mythic image.

25.3 Mask from the Etoumbi region, People's Republic of the Congo. Wood; 14 in. (35.6 cm) high. Musée Barbier-Müller, Geneva.

25.4 Mbuya (sickness) mask, Pende, Zaire. Painted wood, fiber, and cloth; 10½ in. (26.6 cm) high. Musée Royal de l'Afrique Centrale, Tervuren, Belgium.

the mouth shifts to the other. In the two central nudes as well, the features have been not only simplified, but also distorted, so that one eye is slightly above another, the nose is no longer directly above the mouth, and the ears are asymmetrical. Still more radical is the depiction of the body of the seated figure, the so-called "squatter." She looks toward the picture plane while simultaneously turning her body in the opposite direction so that her face and back are visible at the same time. In this figure, Picasso has broken from tradition by abandoning the single vantage point of the observer in favor of multiple vantage points along the lines pioneered by Cézanne. The so-called simultaneous view was to become an important visual effect of Cubism.

The figures in the *Demoiselles* are fragmented into solid geometric constructions, with sharp edges and angles. They interact spatially with the background shapes, blurring the distinction between foreground and background, as Cézanne had done. Such distortion of the human figure is particularly startling because it assaults our bodily identity. Light as well as form is fragmented into multiple sources so that the observer's point of view is constantly shifting. Because of its revolutionary approach to space and its psychological power, the *Demoiselles* represented the greatest expressive challenge to the traditional Classical ideal of beauty and harmony since the Middle Ages.

Guillaume Apollinaire and Marie Laurencin

Guillaume Apollinaire, the Symbolist poet and critic, was one of the most outspoken advocates of Cubism, particularly that of Picasso. "A man like Picasso," he wrote in 1912, "studies an object as a surgeon dissects a cadaver." According to Apollinaire, modern painters "still look at nature, [but] no longer imitate it. . . . Real resemblance no longer has any importance, since everything is sacrificed by the artist to truth. . . . Thus we are moving towards an entirely new art which will stand . . . as music stands to literature. It will be pure painting, just as music is pure literature."[2]

Figure **25.5** by Marie Laurencin (1885–1956) shows Apollinaire seated with Picasso (on the left) and his dog Frika, Picasso's mistress Fernande Olivier, and the artist herself on the right. Laurencin typically painted in flat planes of pastel blues, pinks, and grays. Here, Picasso's abrupt profile and frontal eye recall his own use of that distortion, which he had found in Egyptian painting. Fernande's face is divided by color into two planes, reminiscent of Cubist construction. Laurencin depicts her self-portrait with the neck characteristically curving sharply into the face, an arrangement that is repeated in the positioning of her left arm and hand.

Laurencin and Apollinaire were inseparable companions for about five years, from 1909 to 1914. She was accused of being a superficial artist and intellectually inferior until Gertrude Stein bought this painting. The affinities of Laurencin's work with Cubism are evident in this picture as well as in some of her designs for stage sets. She also illustrated Poe's "The Raven" (see p. 815), which reveals her admiration for Symbolist poetry. In fact, it was partly through her encouragement that Apollinaire wrote in a Symbolist style.

25.5 Marie Laurencin, *Group of Artists*, 1908. Oil on canvas; 27½ × 31⅞ in. (64.8 × 81.0 cm). The Baltimore Museum of Art. The Cone Collection, formed by Dr. Claribel Cone and Miss Etta Cone. BMA 1950.215.

Analytic Cubism: Pablo Picasso and Georges Braque

In 1907, Picasso met the French painter Georges Braque (1882–1963), who had studied the works of Cézanne and been overwhelmed by the *Demoiselles*. Braque is reported to have declared, when he first saw the *Demoiselles*, that looking at it was like drinking kerosene. For several years, in the Montmartre quarter of Paris, Braque worked so closely with Picasso that it can be difficult to distinguish their Analytic Cubist pictures. Braque's *Violin and Pitcher* of 1909–1910 (fig. **25.6**) is very much like Picasso's works of that time and will serve as an example of the style.

25.6 Georges Braque, *Violin and Pitcher*, 1909–1910. Oil on canvas; 3 ft. 10 in. × 2 ft. 4¾ in. (1.17 × 0.73 m). Öffentliche Kunstsammlung Basel, Kunstmuseum (Gift of Dr. H. C. Raoul La Roche, 1952). Braque was born in Argenteuil, France, and moved to Paris in 1900. There he joined the Fauves and established a collaborative friendship with Picasso. They worked closely together until World War I and were jointly responsible for the development of Cubism. In 1908, on seeing a painting by Braque, Matisse reportedly remarked that it had been painted "with little cubes." This was credited with being the origin of the term *Cubism*.

25.7 Pablo Picasso, *Head of a Woman*, 1909. Bronze (cast); 16³⁄₁₆ × 9⅝ × 10½ in. (41.1 × 24.5 × 26.7 cm). National Gallery of Art, Washington, D.C.

Both the subject matter and the expressive possibilities of color—here limited to dark greens and browns—are subordinated to a geometric exploration of three-dimensional space. The only reminders of natural space and of the objects that occupy it are the violin and pitcher, a brief reference to the horizontal surface of a table, and a vertical architectural support on the right. Most of the picture plane, including parts of these objects, is rendered as a jumble of fragmented cubes and other solid geometric shapes. What in reality would be air space is filled up with multiple lines, planes, and geometric solids. The sense of three-dimensional form is achieved by combining shading with bold strokes of color. Despite the crisp edges of the individual shapes in Analytic Cubist pictures such as this one, the painted images lose parts of their outlines. Whereas in Impressionism edges dissolve into prominent brushstrokes, in Cubism they dissolve into shared geometric shapes. No matter how closely the forms approach dissolution, however, they never dissolve completely.

In 1909, Picasso produced the first Cubist sculpture, the bronze *Head of a Woman* (fig. **25.7**), in which he shifted the natural relationship between head and neck, creating two diagonal planes. The hair, as in Analytic Cubist paintings, is multifaceted, and the facial features are geometric rather than organic.

In 1911, two Cubist exhibitions held in Paris brought the work of avant-garde artists to the attention of the general public. The year 1911 also marked the culmination of Analytic Cubism. Although this phase of Cubism was brief, its impact on Western art was enormous. It stimulated the emergence of new and related styles, along with original techniques of image making.

Collage

Picasso's Cubist *Man with a Hat* of 1912 (fig. **25.8**) is an early example of **collage** (see box), which was a logical outgrowth of Analytic Cubism and marked the beginning of the shift to Synthetic Cubism (see p. 854). Pieces of colored paper and newspaper are pasted onto paper to form geometric representations of a head and neck; the remainder of the image is drawn in charcoal. The use of newspaper, which seems textured because of the newsprint, was a common feature of early collages. Words and letters, which are themselves abstract signs, often formed part of the overall design. Collage, like Cubism, involved disassembling objects—just as one might take apart a machine, break up a piece of writing, or even divide a single word into letters—and then rearranging (or reassembling) the parts to form a new image.

25.8 Pablo Picasso, *Man with a Hat,* after December 3, 1912. Pasted paper, charcoal, and ink; 24½ × 18⅝ in. (62.2 × 47.3 cm). Museum of Modern Art, New York (Purchase).

Collage and Assemblage

Collage (from the French word *coller,* meaning "to paste" or "to glue") developed in France from 1912. It is a technique that involves pasting lightweight materials or objects, such as newspaper and string, onto a flat surface. A technique related to collage, which developed slightly later, is **assemblage.** Heavier objects are brought together and arranged, or assembled, to form a three-dimensional image. Both techniques make use of **"found objects"** (*objets trouvés*), which are taken from everyday sources and incorporated into works of art.

Picasso's witty 1943 assemblage entitled *Bull's Head* (fig. **25.9**) is a remarkable example of his genius for synthesis. He has fused the ancient motif of the bull and the traditional medium of bronze with modern steel and plastic. He has also conflated the bull's head with African masks and effected a new spatial juxtaposition by reversing the direction of the bicycle seat and eliminating the usual space between it and the handlebars. In this work, Picasso simultaneously explores the possibilities of new media, of conflated imagery, and of the spatial shifts introduced by Cubism.

25.9 Pablo Picasso, *Bull's Head,* 1943. Assemblage of bicycle saddle and handlebars; 13¼ × 17⅛ × 7½ in. (33.7 × 43.5 × 19.1 cm). Musée Picasso, Paris. Picasso detached the seat and handlebars of a bicycle, turned the seat around, and attached it to the handlebars. The object was then cast in bronze and hung on a wall.

Synthetic Cubism

Synthetic Cubism marked a return to bright color. Whereas Analytic Cubism fragmented objects into abstract geometric forms, Synthetic Cubism arranged flat shapes of color to form objects. Picasso's *Three Musicians* (fig. **25.10**)—a clarinetist on the left, a Harlequin playing a guitar in the center, and a monk—is built up from unmodeled shapes of color arranged into tilted planes. In addition, the flat shapes—such as the dog under the table—occupy a more traditional space than those of Analytic Cubism, in which air space is filled with solid geometry. The painted shapes resemble the flat paper pasted to form a collage. Simultaneity of viewpoint is preserved—for example, in the sheet of music. It is held by the monk and turned toward the viewer, who sees both the musician and what he is reading.

25.10 Pablo Picasso, *Three Musicians,* 1921. Oil on canvas; 6 ft. 7 in. × 7 ft. 3¾ in. (2.01 × 2.23 m). Museum of Modern Art, New York (Mrs. Simon Guggenheim Fund).

Picasso's Surrealism

Another stylistic shift in Picasso's work that was influenced by Cubism has been called Surrealism. This term (see Chapter 26) literally means "above real" and denotes a truer reality than that of the visible world. In the *Girl before a Mirror* of 1932 (fig. **25.11**), Picasso aims at psychological reality. He uses the multiple viewpoint in the service of symbolism, although the precise meaning of this picture has remained elusive and has been the subject of many interpretive discussions. The girl at the left is rendered in a combined frontal and profile view, but her mirror reflection is in profile. It is also darker than the "real" girl outside the mirror, and the torsos do not match.

The device of the mirror to create multiple viewpoints is not new. Picasso was certainly familiar with Manet's *Bar at the Folies-Bergère* (see fig. 22.6) and Velázquez's *Venus with a Mirror* (see fig. 17.55) and *Las Meninas* (see fig. 17.56), all of which use mirrors to expand the viewer's range of vision. Here, however, the formal differences between the girl and her reflection suggest that outer appearances are contrasted with an inner, psychological state. One French term for *mirror* is *psyché,* which means "soul," and this provides a clue to the picture's significance. It reinforces the notion that Picasso transformed the multiple views of Cubism into multiple psychological views, which simultaneously show the girl's interior psychic reality and exterior appearance.

25.11 Pablo Picasso, *Girl before a Mirror,* 1932. Oil on canvas; 5 ft. 4 in. × 4 ft. 3¼ in. (1.62 × 1.31 m). Museum of Modern Art, New York (Gift of Mrs. Simon Guggenheim).

CONNECTIONS

See figure 22.6. Édouard Manet, *A Bar at the Folies-Bergère,* 1881–1882.

See figure 17.55. Diego Velázquez, *Venus with a Mirror (Rokeby Venus),* c. 1648.

See figure 17.56. Diego Velázquez, *Las Meninas,* 1656.

Picasso's *Guernica*

In his monumental work of 1937, *Guernica* (fig. **25.12**), Picasso combined Analytic and Synthetic Cubist forms with several traditional motifs, juxtaposing them in a new Surrealist way. The combination serves the political message of the painting—namely, Picasso's powerful protest against the brutality of war and tyranny (see caption). Consistent with its theme of death and dying, the painting is nearly devoid of color, although there is considerable tonal variation within the range of black to white. The absence of color enhances the journalistic quality of the painting, relating it to the news accounts of the bombing it protests.

Guernica is divided into three sections—a central triangle with an approximate rectangle on either side. The base of the triangle extends from the arm of the dismembered and decapitated soldier at the left to the foot of the running woman at the right. The dying horse represents the death of civilization, though it may be revived by the woman with a lamp (Liberty) rushing toward it. Another expression of hope, as well as of the light of reason, appears in the motif combining the shape of an eye with the sun's rays and a lightbulb just above the horse's head. On the right, the pose and gesture of a falling woman suggest Christ's Crucifixion. On the left, a woman holds a dead baby on her lap in a pose reminiscent of Mary supporting the dead Christ in the traditional *Pietà* scene (see fig. 14.18). Behind the woman looms the specter of the Minotaur, the monstrous tyrant of ancient Crete, whose only human qualities are the flattened face and eyes. For

CONNECTIONS

See figure 14.18.
Michelangelo, *Pietà*, 1498/9–1500.

25.12 Pablo Picasso, *Guernica*, 1937. Oil on canvas; 11 ft. 5½ in. × 25 ft. 5¾ in. (3.49 × 7.77 m). Museo Nacional Centro de Arte Reina Sofia, Madrid. From 1936 to 1939, there was a civil war between Spanish Republicans and the Fascist army of General Franco. In April 1937, Franco's Nazi allies carried out saturation bombing over the town of Guernica. Picasso painted *Guernica* to protest this atrocity. He loaned it to New York's Museum of Modern Art, stipulating that it remain there until democracy was restored in Spain. In 1981, *Guernica* was returned to Madrid.

Picasso, the Minotaur came to represent modern tyranny, as embodied by the Spanish dictator General Francisco Franco (1892–1975), who was allied with Adolf Hitler and Benito Mussolini.

These apparently disparate motifs are related by form and gesture, by their shared distortions, and by the power and content of their message. Cubist geometric shapes and sharp angles pervade the painting. Picasso's characteristic distortions of body and face emphasize the physical destruction of war. Eyes are twisted in and out of their sockets, ears and noses are slightly out of place, tongues are shaped like daggers, palms and feet are slashed. Although the integrity of the human form is maintained throughout, it is an object of attack and mutilation.

Picasso did forty-five studies for *Guernica*. The one illustrated here (fig. **25.13**) shows the dying horse and the mother with the dead child. They have been changed in the final painting, although they retain their basic character. The Cubist neck of the horse has a stronger curve in the drawing, and its protruding teeth seem to hang from the mouth. The woman howls in despair as in the painting, but in the drawing she crawls on the ground and the baby flops over like a rag doll. Picasso's spontaneous, dynamic drawing technique is evident in this study, particularly in the horse's mane and the areas of shading. The individualized anguish of the figures in the drawing becomes generalized, and thus—as with the *Demoiselles d'Avignon*—assumes mythic proportions in the final work.

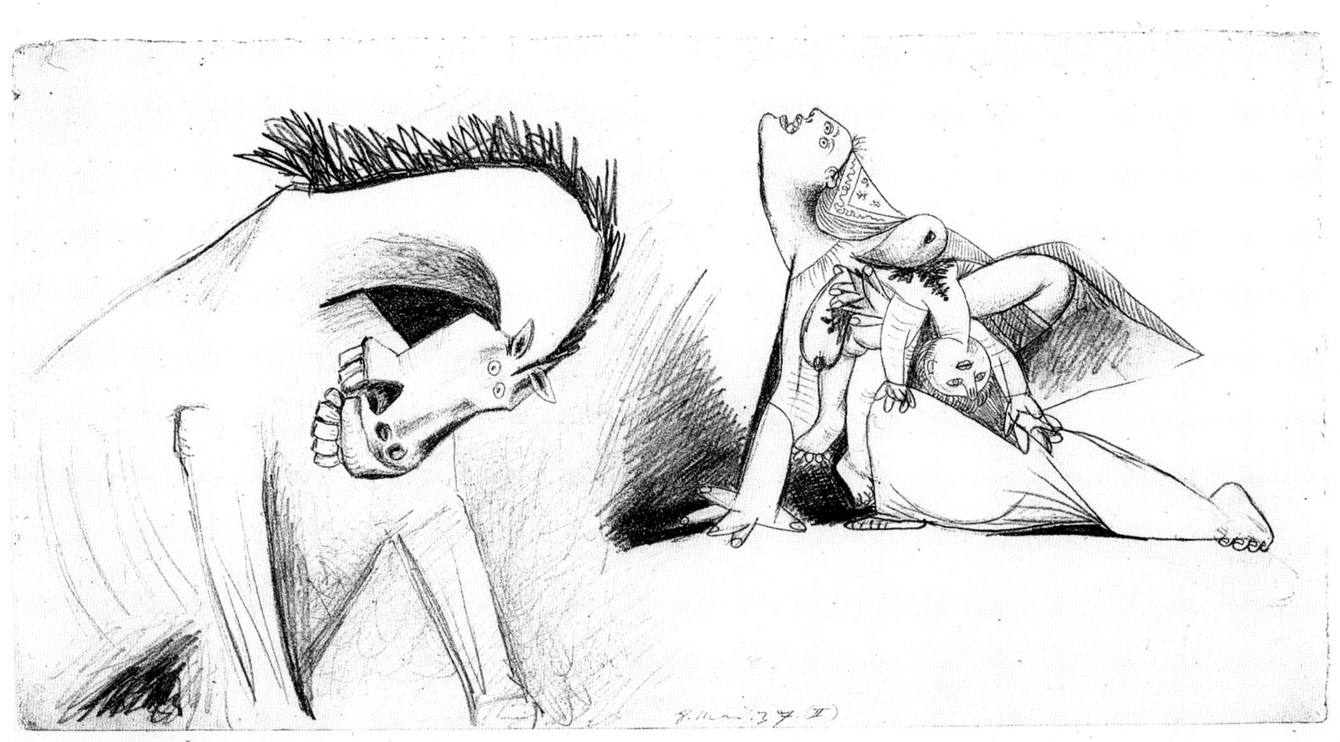

25.13 Pablo Picasso, study for *Guernica*, 1937. Pencil drawing; 9½ × 17⅞ in. (24.1 × 45.4 cm). Museo Nacional Centro de Arte Reina Sofia, Photographic Archive, Madrid, Spain.

Other Early Twentieth-Century Developments

Futurism

Related to Expressionism was the contemporary movement called Futurism, which originated in Italy. The Futurists were inspired by the dynamic energy of industry and the machine age. They argued for a complete break with the past. In February 1909, a Futurist manifesto, written by Filippo Marinetti, the editor of a literary magazine in Milan, appeared on the front page of the French newspaper *Le Figaro*. The manifesto sought to inspire in the general public an enthusiasm for a new artistic language. In all of the arts—the visual arts, music, literature, theater, and film—the old Academic traditions would be abandoned, and creative energy would be focused on the present and future. Speed, travel, technology, and dynamism would be the subjects of Futurist art.

Marinetti's language was apocalyptic in its determination to slash through the "millennial gloom" of the past. "Time and Space died yesterday," he declared. "We already live in the absolute, because we have created eternal, omnipresent speed. . . . We will destroy the museums, libraries, academies of every kind, we will fight moralism, feminism, every opportunistic or utilitarian cowardice." And later in the same tract: "We establish *Futurism,* because we want to free this land from its smelly gangrene of professors, archaeologists, . . . and antiquarians." Marinetti equated "admiring an old picture" with "pouring our sensibility into a funerary urn," and he recommended an annual "floral tribute" to the *Mona Lisa,* implying that the artistic past was dead and merited only the briefest remembrance.

Futurism was given plastic form in a 1913 sculpture by Umberto Boccioni (1882–1916) entitled *Unique Forms of Continuity in Space* (fig. **25.14**). It represents a man striding vigorously, as if with a definite goal in mind. The long diagonal from head to foot is thrust forward by the assertive angle of the bent knee. The layered surface planes, related to the fragmented planes of Analytic Cubism, convey the impression of flapping material. Organic flesh and blood are subjugated to a mechanical, robotlike appearance —a vision that corresponds to Boccioni's aims as stated in his *Technical Manifesto of Futurist Sculpture 1912.* Sculpture, he said, must "make objects live by showing their extensions in space" and by revealing the environment as part of the object.

25.14 Umberto Boccioni, *Unique Forms of Continuity in Space,* 1913. Bronze (cast 1931); 43⅞ × 34⅞ × 15¾ in. (111.2 × 88.5 × 40.0 cm). Museum of Modern Art, New York (acquired through the Lillie P. Bliss Bequest). In 1910, Boccioni wrote the *Manifesto of the Futurist Painters,* which encouraged artists to portray the speed and dynamism of contemporary life, as he himself has done in this sculpture. He fought for Italy in World War I and was killed by a fall from a horse in 1916.

25.15 Fernand Léger, *The City*, 1919. Oil on canvas; 7 ft. 7 in. × 14 ft. 9½ in. (2.31 × 4.51 m). Philadelphia Museum of Art (A. E. Gallatin Collection).

Fernand Léger's *The City*

The work of Fernand Léger (1881–1955) is more formally derived from Cubism than Boccioni's sculpture. In *The City* of 1919 (fig. **25.15**), Leger captures the cold steel surfaces of the urban landscape. Harsh forms, especially cubes and cylinders, evoke the metallic textures of industry. The jumbled girders, poles, high walls, and steps, together with the human silhouettes, create a sense of the anonymous, mechanical movement associated with the fast pace of city life. In *The City*, Léger has taken from Analytic Cubism the multiple viewpoint and superimposed solid geometry. His shapes, however, are colorful and recognizable, and there is a greater illusion of distance.

Léger described the kinship between modern art and the city as follows: "The thing that is imaged does not stay as still . . . as it formerly did. . . . A modern man registers a hundred times more sensory impressions than an 18th-century artist. . . . The condensation of the modern picture . . . its breaking up of forms, are the result of all this. It is certain that the evolution of means of locomotion, and their speed, have something to do with the new way of seeing."[3]

Piet Mondrian

In 1911, the year of the two Cubist exhibitions, Piet Mondrian (1872–1944) came to Paris from Holland. He had begun as a painter of nature but under the influence of Cubism gradually transformed his imagery to flat rectangles of color. His delicate *Amaryllis* (fig. **25.16**) exemplifies his sensitivity to nature and attention to the subtleties of surface texture. Mondrian gradually abstracted forms from nature to create flat rectangles bordered by thick, black lines. In these pictures, he plays on the tension, as well as the harmony, between vertical and horizontal. In them, he also rejects curves and diagonals altogether and expresses his belief in the purity of primary colors. According to Mondrian, chromatic purity, like the simplicity of the rectangle, had a universal character. To illustrate this, he wrote that since paintings are made of line and color, they must be liberated from the slavish imitation of nature (see the **installation** photograph in fig. 25.28).

Later, while living in New York in the early 1940s as a refugee from World War II, Mondrian painted *Broadway Boogie Woogie* (fig. **25.17**). This was one of a series of pictures that he executed in small squares and rectangles of color, which replaced the large rectangles outlined in black. The grid pattern of the New York streets, the flashing lights of Broadway, and the vertical and horizontal motion of cars and pedestrians are conveyed as flat, colorful shapes. Rapid shifts of color and their repetition recall the strong, accented rhythm of boogie-woogie, a style of piano blues. In combining musical references with the beat of city life and suggesting these qualities through color and shape, Mondrian synthesized Expressionist exuberance with Cubist order and control.

25.16 Piet Mondrian, *Red Amaryllis with Blue Background.* Watercolor on paper; 18½ × 13½ in. (47.3 × 34.2 cm). Janis Family Collection, New York. Mondrian was an Impressionist and Symbolist painter before helping to found the De Stijl movement in 1917. His spiritual attitude toward art was reflected in his belief that perfect aesthetic harmony and balance in art are derived from ethical purity and world harmony. Photo courtesy of Carroll Janis, New York. © 2006 Mondrian/Holtzman Trust c/o HCR International, Warrenton, VA, USA.

25.17 Piet Mondrian, *Broadway Boogie Woogie,* 1942–1943. Oil on canvas; 4 ft. 2 in. × 4 ft. 2 in. (1.27 × 1.27 m). The Museum of Modern Art, New York (given anonymously). © 2006 Mondrian/Holtzman Trust c/o HCR International, Warrenton, VA, USA.

The Armory Show

The burgeoning styles of the early twentieth century in western Europe did not reach the general American public until 1913. In February of that year, the Armory of the Sixty-ninth Regiment, National Guard, on Lexington Avenue between Twenty-fifth and Twenty-sixth Streets in New York, was the site of an international exhibition of modern art. A total of 1,200 exhibits, including works by Post-Impressionists, Fauves, and Cubists, as well as by American artists, filled eighteen rooms. This event marked the first widespread American exposure to the European avant-garde.

The Armory Show caused an uproar. Marcel Duchamp (1887–1968) submitted *Nude Descending a Staircase, No. 2* (fig. **25.18**), which was the most scandalous work of all. It was a humorous attack on Futurist proscriptions against traditional Academic nudity. The image has a kinetic quality consistent with the Futurist interest in speed and motion. At the same time, the figure is a combination of Cubist form and multiple images that indicate the influence of photography. She is shown at different points in her descent, so the painting resembles a series of consecutive movie stills, unframed and superimposed.

Various accounts published at the time ridiculed the *Nude*'s début in the United States. Descriptions by outraged viewers included the following: "disused golf clubs and bags," an "elevated railroad stairway in ruins after an earthquake," "a dynamited suit of Japanese armor," an "orderly heap of broken violins," an "explosion in a shingle factory," and "Rude Descending a Staircase (Rush Hour in the Subway)." Duchamp recorded his own version of the *Nude*'s place in the history of art: "My aim was a static representation of movement—a static composition of indications of various positions taken by a form in movement—with no attempt to give cinema effects through painting."[4]

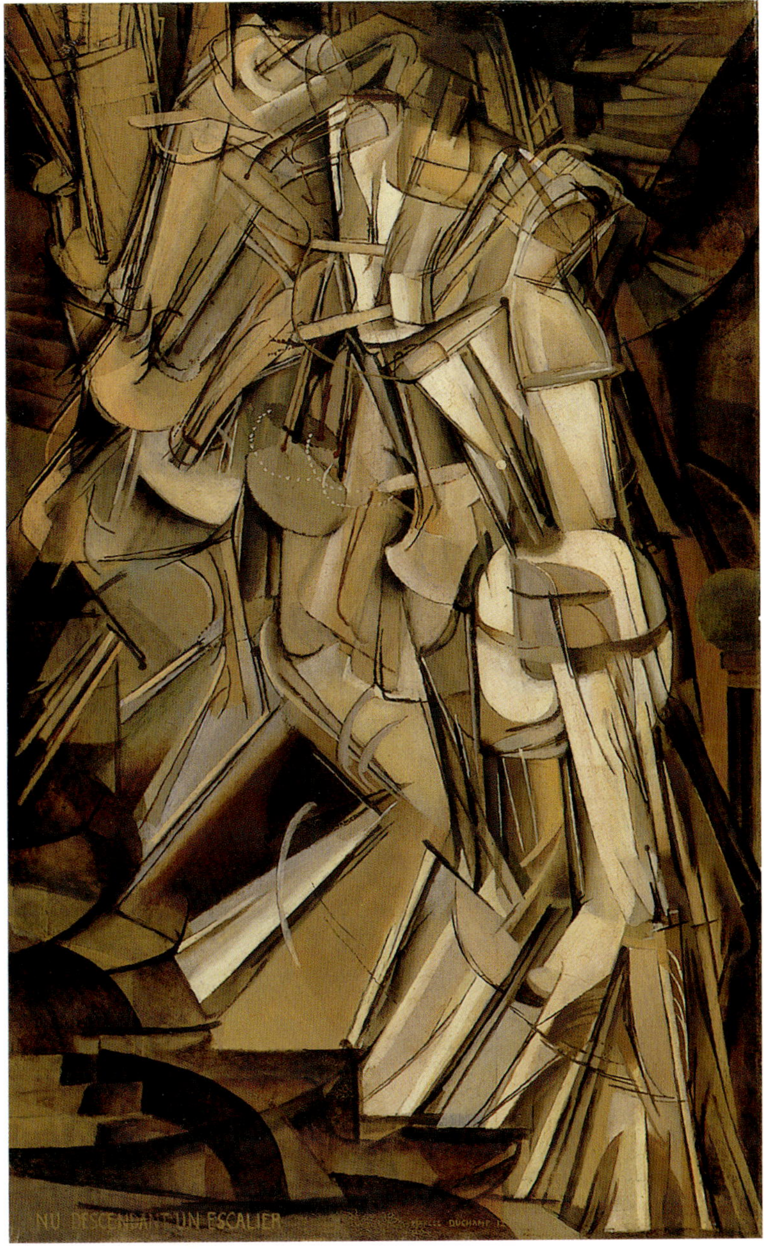

25.18 Marcel Duchamp, *Nude Descending a Staircase, No. 2*, 1912. Oil on canvas; 4 ft. 10 in. × 2 ft. 11 in. (1.47 × 0.89 m). Philadelphia Museum of Art (Louise and Walter Arensberg Collection).

The exuberance of the figures recalls the dynamic energy of jazz that also appealed to Matisse. Music appears in the subject matter of the mural—the trumpet and the drums—as well as in the rhythms of its design. The main colors are variations on the hue of rose, whereas concentric circles of yellow convey a sense of sound traveling through space. At the same time, the unmodeled character of the color allies the work with Synthetic Cubism. The green and white cotton plants in the foreground refer to the work of slaves in America and create an additional pattern superimposed over the light reds.

Kazimir Malevich and Suprematism

One of the most geometric developments that grew out of Cubism took place in Russia. Kazimir Malevich (1878–1935) was born in Kiev and in 1904 went to Moscow to study art. Although, as a student, he did not travel outside Russia, he was exposed to the European avant-garde through important collections in Moscow, and in 1908 he saw works exhibited by Cézanne, Gauguin, Matisse, and Braque. As a mature artist, Malevich combined Cubism with Futurism. He considered the proto-Cubism of Cézanne to have been rooted in village life, whereas the later development of the style was urban in character. For Malevich, it was Futurism, the more dynamic form of Cubism, that expressed the fast pace of city life.

His *Composition with the Mona Lisa* of 1914 (fig. **25.22**) is a collage composed of pasted bits of newspaper and oil paint on canvas. The structure of the composition is based on Synthetic Cubism, with the cylindrical shapes suggesting engines and other mechanical devices. Malevich literally "crossed out" the *Mona Lisa* because, he said, the new version had more value as "the face of the new art." This sentiment reflected his view that the tradition of naturalistic painting had been superseded by avant-garde abstraction.

Following his Cubist-Futurist phase, Malevich created the style he called Suprematism. His first Suprematist painting, exhibited in 1915, in St. Petersburg, Russia, consisted

25.22 Kazimir Malevich, *Composition with the Mona Lisa*, 1914. Graphite, oil, and collage on canvas; 24⅜ × 19½ in. (61.9 × 49.5 cm). State Russian Museum, St. Petersburg.

25.23 Kazimir Malevich, *Black Square,* 1929. Oil on canvas; 31¼ × 31¼ in. (79.4 × 79.4 cm). State Tretiakov Gallery, Moscow.

of a black square centered in a white background. The original became damaged, and he subsequently made several additional versions of it (fig. **25.23**). According to Malevich, the black square was an expression of the cosmic, of pure feeling, and the white was the void beyond feeling. His aim was to achieve the mystical through pure form, which embodied pure feeling, instead of depicting what is visible and natural. In his book *The Non-objective World,* Malevich summed up his philosophy of Suprematism as follows:

> Artists have always been partial to the use of the human face in their representations, for they have seen in it (the versatile, mobile, expressive mimic) the best vehicle with which to convey their feelings. The Suprematists have nevertheless abandoned the representation of the human face (and of natural objects in general) and have found new symbols with which to render direct feelings (rather than externalized reflections of feelings), for the *Suprematist does not observe and does not touch—he feels.*[6]

After the Communist Revolution of 1917, Malevich was appointed Commissar for the Preservation of Monuments and Antiquities. By the late 1920s, the Soviet government under Stalin (d. 1953) was suppressing avant-garde art and asserting state control over all the arts. Sensing that further oppression was to come, Malevich traveled in 1927 to Poland and Germany, where the Bauhaus (see p. 873) published his book in German. In 1930, he was arrested by the Soviets for artistic "deviation."

Three years later, Malevich painted his last *Self-Portrait* (fig. **25.24**), which reflects his renunciation of the "deviant" avant-garde and his return to naturalism. Ironically, he represented himself as a "Renaissance man." When he died, his white coffin was decorated with one black circle and one black square, and a white cube with a black square on it marked the place where his ashes were buried. In 1936, the Soviets confiscated his remaining pictures; they were not shown publicly again until 1977.

25.24 Kazimir Malevich, *Self-Portrait,* 1933. Oil on canvas; 28¾ × 26 in. (73.0 × 66.0 cm). State Russian Museum, St. Petersburg.

Brancusi's *Gate of the Kiss* and *Endless Column*

In 1935, the year before the Soviet confiscation of Malevich's abstract pictures, Brancusi accepted a commission for his native town of Tirgu-Jiu, in Romania. He agreed to design a peace memorial dedicated to those who had died in World War I. In its final form, the memorial consisted of three structures—*The Table of Silence, The Gate of the Kiss,* and *The Endless Column.* The central feature, *The Gate of the Kiss* (fig. **25.25**), was derived from a much earlier series of sculptures entitled *The Kiss,* of which the 1912 version is illustrated in figure **25.26.** The Cubist quality of *The Kiss* resides in its blocklike form, which Brancusi used to merge the embracing figures. The arms overlap and, as seen from the front, appear shared equally between the couple. The lips are formed into a little cube connecting the rectangular heads. As with many of Picasso's Cubist faces after 1906, these can be read simultaneously as a profile and a front view. The focal point of the face is the eye, the placement of which creates the multiple viewpoint, for it is both two eyes rendered in profile and a single eye.

In *The Gate of the Kiss,* Brancusi persists in the use of cubic form and also endows it with symbolic meaning. The lintel is decorated with incised, geometric versions of *The Kiss,* and each supporting post is decorated with four large, round "eyes." The ensemble implies that the notion of a kiss embodies love, which therefore "upholds" peace. The eyes, combined with the rectangular opening, also transform *The Gate* into a large face, which, like Janus of the ancient Roman gateways, watches those who come and those who go with equal attention.

25.26 Constantin Brancusi, *The Kiss,* 1912. Stone; 23 in. (58.4 cm) high. Philadelphia Museum of Art (Louise and Walter Arensberg Collection).

25.25 Constantin Brancusi, *The Gate of the Kiss,* 1938. Stone; 17 ft. 3½ in. × 21 ft. 7⅛ in. × 6 ft. 1½ in. (5.27 × 6.58 × 1.84 m). Public Park, Tirgu-Jiu, Romania.

The *Endless Column* (fig. **25.27**) stands alone and, like Trajan's Column (see fig. 7.34), does not function as an architectural support. Instead, it conveys an independent message, which is related to the significance of height. Rather than proclaiming the power of a single leader such as the Roman emperor (compare the column erected under Napoleon in the Place Vendôme in Paris, fig. 19.8), Brancusi's column seems to soar skyward in the manner of his *Bird in Space* (see fig. I.4). It represents the aspiration expressed by Gothic cathedral towers and, ironically, as in *The Gate of the Kiss,* the ambitious hope for peace in a world on the verge of World War II.

See figure 7.34. Trajan's Column, Rome, dedicated A.D. 113.

25.27 Constantin Brancusi, *Endless Column,* 1937. Cast iron; 96 ft. 3⅜ in. (29.35 m) high, 35⅜ in. (0.89 m) wide, 35⅜ in. (0.89 m) deep. (Formerly) Public Park, Tirgu-Jiu, Romania.

Postscript

The installation photograph in figure **25.28** illustrates the main space of the Sidney Janis Gallery in New York in the early 1980s during a landmark exhibition entitled *Brancusi + Mondrian*. Mounted nearly seventy years after the Armory Show and over fifty years after Malevich's detention for so-called "deviant" art, the exhibition conveyed the importance of the avante-garde. It also emphasized the formal and historical relationship between Brancusi and Mondrian. In the left corner, a group of highly polished bronzes by Brancusi includes two versions of *Mademoiselle Pogany*. Flanked by Mondrians are a marble and a bronze version of *Bird in Space*. Brancusi's "essences," here composed of graceful curves and rounded, volumetric shapes, are contrasted with Mondrian's pure verticals and horizontals on a flat surface. In this juxtaposition, the viewer confronts the work of two major early twentieth-century artists. Despite their apparent differences, these artists have a remarkable affinity in their pusuit of an "idea," which they render in modern, abstract form.

The art critic Sidney Geist wrote of this show that "if the century's Modernist struggle seems to have been called in question by recent developments, 'Brancusi + Mondrian' banished all doubt. . . . We have to do here with two saintly figures—for whom art was a devotion. Their lives and art evolved under the sign of inevitability."[7]

25.28 Installation view, *Brancusi + Mondrian* exhibition, December 1982–January 1983. Painting on left: Piet Mondrian, *Lozenge Composition with 8 Lines and Red/Picture No. III*, 1938. Oil on canvas; diagonal measurement 55¼ in. (140 cm). Painting on right: Piet Mondrian, *Lozenge Composition with 2 Lines*, 1931. Oil on canvas; diagonal measurement 44⅛ in. (112 cm). Photo courtesy of Carroll Janis, New York.

25.29 Frank Lloyd Wright, Robie House, Chicago, 1909. Wright's insistence on creating a total environment inspired him, sometimes against the wishes of his clients, to design the furniture and interior fixtures of his houses. In the case of the Robie House, Wright even designed outfits for Mrs. Robie to wear on formal occasions so that she would blend with his architecture.

Early Twentieth-Century Architecture

In the late nineteenth and early twentieth centuries, the most innovative developments in architecture took place in the United States. Following Louis Sullivan, who developed the skyscraper, the next major American architect was Frank Lloyd Wright (1869–1959). Wright had worked in Chicago as Sullivan's assistant before building private houses, mainly in Illinois, in the 1890s and early 1900s. But, whereas Sullivan's skyscrapers addressed the urban need to provide many offices or apartments on a relatively small area of land, Wright launched the Prairie Style, which sought to integrate architecture with the natural landscape.

Frank Lloyd Wright and the Prairie Style

In 1908, Wright wrote that "the Prairie has a beauty of its own and we should recognize and accentuate this natural beauty, its quiet level. Hence . . . sheltering overhangs, low terraces and out-reaching walls, sequestering private gardens." Wright admired Japanese architecture and its tradition of open internal spaces, which he incorporated into a series of early twentieth-century, Midwestern Prairie Style houses.

The best-known example of Wright's early Prairie Style is the Robie House of 1909 (fig. **25.29**) in south Chicago. Its horizontal emphasis, low-pitched roofs with large overhangs, and low boundary walls are related to the flat prairie landscape of the American West and Middle West. At the same time, the predominance of rectangular shapes and shifting, asymmetically arranged horizontal planes is reminiscent of Cubism.

The ground floor of the Robie House contained a playroom, garage, and other service areas. The main living area was on the second floor, and the bedrooms were on the third. The second-floor plan (fig. **25.30**) illustrates the massive central core, which doubles as a fireplace and staircase, and is the focal point of the living quarters. Around the central core, the living and dining rooms are arranged in an open plan. Verandas extend from the two main rooms. The huge cantilevered (see box, p. 870) roof on the second floor shields the windows from sunlight.

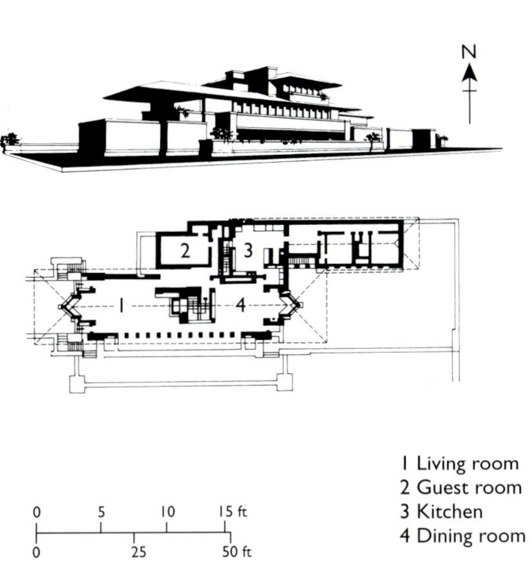

25.30 Perspective drawing and plan of the second floor of the Robie House.

Cantilever

The system of **cantilever construction** (fig. **25.31**) is one in which a horizontal architectural element, projected in space, has vertical support at one end only. Equilibrium is maintained by a support and counterbalancing weight inside the building. The cantilever requires materials with considerable tensile strength. Wright pioneered the use of **reinforced concrete** and steel girders for cantilever construction in large buildings. In a small house, wooden beams provide adequate support.

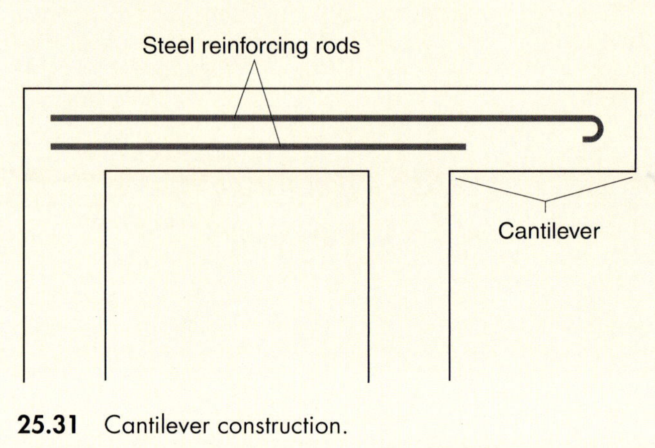

25.31 Cantilever construction.

In 1936, on a wooded site at Bear Run, Pennsylvania, Wright built a weekend house (fig. **25.32**) for the Edgar Kaufmann family that combined elements of the International Style (see below) with the Prairie Style. It is called Fallingwater because it is perched over a small waterfall. As in the Robie House, there is a large central core, composed here of local masonry. Fallingwater is surrounded by reinforced concrete terraces, which are related to the International Style. Their beige color attempts to blend with the landscape, and their cantilevered horizontals repeat the horizontals of the rocky ledges below. Although the smooth texture and light hue of the terraces actually contrast with the darker natural colors of the woods, the natural stone of the chimneys resembles the rocks in the surrounding landscape. In keeping with the Prairie Style, parts of the house are integrated with the landscape and seem to "grow" from it. Glass walls, which make nature a constant visible presence inside the house, further reinforce the association of architecture with landscape. To some extent, therefore, Fallingwater fulfills Wright's pursuit of "organic" architecture.

25.32 Frank Lloyd Wright, Fallingwater, Bear Run, Pennsylvania, 1936.

In 1938, Wright began work on his own house and office, Taliesin West (fig. **25.33**), in the Arizona foothills outside of Phoenix. Its main materials were called "desert concrete" by Wright because they consist of concrete embedded with local stones and rocks, redwood beams, and canvas awnings. As in most of his designs for private houses, Wright used squares and rectangles as his primary shapes and right angles for beams and other planar juxtapositions.

25.33 Frank Lloyd Wright, Taliesin West, Arizona, begun 1938.

International Style

From the end of World War I, a new architectural style developed in western Europe. Since it apparently originated in several countries at about the same time, it is known as the International Style.

Holland: *De Stijl* In Holland, the International Style of architecture began as a movement called *De Stijl,* of which Mondrian was a founder. The primary leader, however, was Theo van Doesburg (1883–1931), whose transformation of a cow into abstract geometric shapes is illustrated in figures I.21–I.25. Several Dutch architects, attracted by Frank Lloyd Wright's work (which had been exhibited in Germany in 1910), joined Mondrian and van Doesburg in the movement. They were idealists searching for a universal style that would satisfy human needs through mass production. The spiritual goal of world peace, they believed, would also be fostered by the "equilibrium of opposites" that was part of *De Stijl*'s credo.

Typical of this new architecture is the Schroeder House in Utrecht (fig. **25.34**), designed by Gerrit Rietveld (1888–1964). The flat roof and cantilevered balconies are similar to those in Wright's private houses. Whereas Wright emphasized horizontals, however, Rietveld preferred oppositions of horizontals and verticals derived from Cubism, which he integrated with a **skeletal construction.** There is no surface decoration to interrupt the exterior simplicity of the building. The windows and balconies, with attached rectangular panels that seem to float in midair, create a sense of tension paradoxically combined with weightlessness. Composed of predominantly white flat planes and right angles, the Schroeder House is the architectural equivalent of Mondrian's classic style (see fig. 25.28).

25.34 Gerrit Rietveld, Schroeder House, Utrecht, the Netherlands, 1923–1924. Alfred Barr, Jr., curator of New York's Museum of Modern Art, defined the International Style as follows: " . . . emphasis upon volume . . . thin planes . . . as opposed to . . . mass and solidity; . . . regularity as opposed to symmetry . . . and . . . dependence upon the intrinsic elegance of materials, perfection, and fine proportions, as opposed to applied ornament." These goals are fulfilled in the Schroeder House.

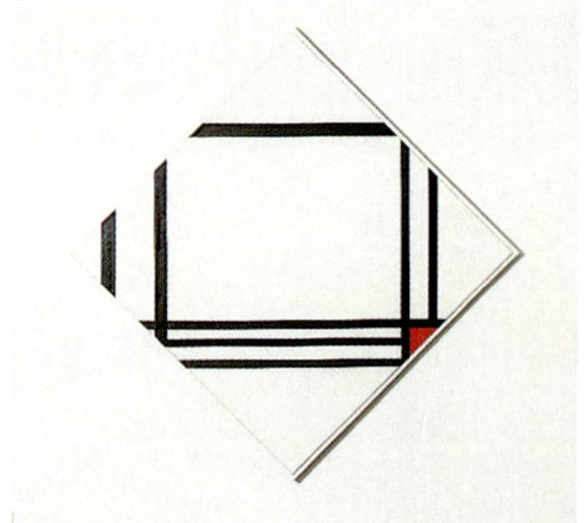

Piet Mondrian, *Lozenge Composition with 2 Lines,* 1931. Oil on canvas; 44⅛ in. (112 cm). Photo courtesy of Carroll Janis, New York. © 2006 Mondrian/Holtzman Trust, c/o HCR International, Warrenton, VA, USA.

Germany: The Bauhaus The German version of the International Style centered on the Bauhaus. In the first decade of the twentieth century, the Deutscher Werkbund ("German Craft Association") was formed. Its aim was to improve the aesthetic quality of manufactured goods and industrial architecture, to produce them more cheaply, and to make them more widely available. This produced a number of important architects and designers who had enormous international influence through the 1960s. Many who had worked together in Europe later emigrated to the United States to escape Hitler's persecutions during World War II.

The leader of this community was Walter Gropius (1883–1969), who in 1919 became the first director of the Bauhaus, in Weimar. The Bauhaus (from the German *Bau,* meaning "structure" or "building," and *Haus,* meaning "house") combined an arts-and-crafts college with a school of fine arts. Gropius believed in the integration of art and industry. With that in mind, he set out to create a new institution that would offer courses in design, architecture, and industry.

Vassily Kandinsky was a prominent member of the Bauhaus faculty from 1922, and he remained until 1933, when it was closed by the Nazis. His paintings of that period reflect the geometric angularity he espoused as part of the Russian avant-garde in Moscow at the beginning of World War I. Such forms, which were also characteristic of the Bauhaus aesthetic, can be seen, for example, in *Composition 8* (fig. **25.35**). Compared to the exuberant curvilinear forms of his Expressionist *Painting No. 201* (see fig. 24.9), this is measured, constructed, and dominated by dynamic diagonal planes. While at the Bauhaus, Kandinsky published a textbook on composition entitled *Point and Line to Plane: Contribution to the Analysis of the Pictorial Elements* (1926), in which he combined spirituality and mysticism with strict formal analysis.

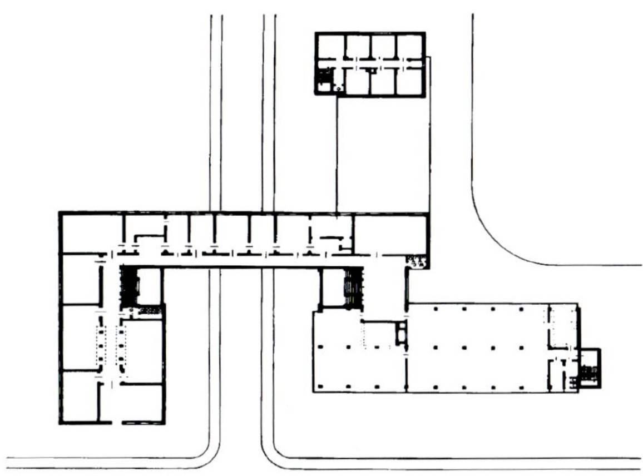

25.36 Walter Gropius, plan of the Bauhaus, Dessau, Germany, 1925–1926.

In 1926, Gropius relocated the Bauhaus from Weimar to Dessau and planned its new quarters (fig. **25.36**) according to his International Style philosophy. Three blocklike buildings contained living and working areas as well as the schools. They were linked by an elevated bridge containing offices. This differed radically from previous academic institutions, which were monumental, had a clearly marked entrance within a distinctive façade, and were usually Neoclassical in style.

25.35 Vassily Kandinsky, *Composition 8,* 1923. Oil on canvas; 55⅛ in. × 79⅛ in. (140.0 × 201.0 cm). Solomon R. Guggenheim Museum, New York.

See figure 24.9. Vassily Kandinsky, *Panel for Edwin R. Campbell No. 4,* 1914.

25.37 Walter Gropius, the Bauhaus workshop wing, Dessau, Germany, 1925–1926.

The workshop wing of the Bauhaus (fig. **25.37**) is typical of the International Style. It is entirely rectilinear, with verticals and horizontals meeting at right angles. The primary material is reinforced concrete, but, apart from two thin white bands at the top and bottom, the viewers see only sheet-glass walls from the outside. Structurally, this was a logical extension of the steel-skeleton system of construction, which, as in the Wainwright Building (see fig. 21.32), relieves the outer walls of any support function. Formal affinities with Cubism are inescapable, although Gropius, like the members of *De Stijl,* was motivated primarily by a philosophy of simplicity and harmony intended to integrate art and architecture into society. The Bauhaus exteriors, devoid of any regional identity, were an international concept translated into architectural form.

France: Le Corbusier The best-known exponent of the International Style in France during the 1920s and early 1930s was the Swiss-born architect Charles-Édouard Jeanneret, known as Le Corbusier (1887–1965). The Villa Savoye (fig. **25.38**), a weekend residence built from 1928 to 1930 at Poissy, near Paris, is the last in a series of International

25.38 Le Corbusier, Villa Savoye, Poissy-sur-Seine, France, 1928–1930. Le Corbusier believed that houses should be mass-produced. To this end, he reduced architectural components to simple forms—concrete slabs for floors, concrete pillars for vertical support, stairs linking the floors, and a flat roof. In his *Towards a New Architecture* (1931), Le Corbusier wrote: "If we eliminate from our hearts and minds all dead concepts in regard to houses . . . we shall arrive at the 'House-Machine,' the mass-production house, healthy (and morally so too) and beautiful in the same way that the working tools and instruments which accompany our existence are beautiful."

25.39 Le Corbusier, Notre-Dame-du-Haut, Ronchamp, France, 1950–1954.

Style houses by Le Corbusier. It is regarded as his masterpiece.

The Villa Savoye is a grand version of what Le Corbusier described as a "machine for living." It rests on very slender reinforced concrete pillars, which divide the second-floor windows. The second floor contains the main living area, and it is connected to the ground floor and the open terrace on the third floor by a staircase and a ramp. The driveway extends under the house and ends in a three-car carport. This part of the ground floor is deeply recessed under the second-floor overhang and contains an entrance hall and servants' quarters. All four elevations of the house are virtually identical, each having the same ribbon windows running the length of the wall.

Le Corbusier was active into his seventies, and his designs underwent a series of evolutions. In the late 1940s, he worked in a style that has come to be known as the New Brutalism, a reference to his habit of leaving the surface of concrete (still his favorite material) rough and unfinished so that it remained true to its natural texture. He also experimented with the sculptural properties inherent in the material, as in Notre-Dame-du-Haut (fig. **25.39**), a pilgrimage chapel perched on the top of a hill at Ronchamp, in eastern France. The rough concrete walls are painted white, and the roof is a huge mantle of darker concrete curving organically over the eastern wall of the chapel. Piercing the south wall are several unevenly shaped and sized windows, which are inlaid with hand-painted glass. The thickness of the wall and the small size of the windows produce an effect of focused beams of light. Between the roof and the walls is a very thin strip of clear glass, which makes the heavy roof of the chapel appear to float.

The United States The architectural principles of the International Style were brought to the United States by Bauhaus artists who were forced to leave Germany in the late 1930s. Ludwig Mies van der Rohe (1886–1969), the director of the Bauhaus from 1930, designed the glass and steel Lake Shore Drive Apartment Houses in Chicago (fig. **25.40**) with the principles of **functionalism** in mind. The influence of Cubism in their geometric repetitions is inescapable. These vertical, cubic structures, which are reminiscent of Mondrian's late paintings, inspired many similar skyscrapers throughout America's large cities.

25.40 Ludwig Mies van der Rohe, Lake Shore Drive Apartment Houses, Chicago, 1950–1952.

	Style/Period	Works of Art	Cultural/Historical Developments
		Pende Mbuya mask (**25.4**) Etoumbi mask (**25.3**)	
1900	CUBISM, FUTURISM, AND RELATED STYLES 1900–1910 	Picasso, *Gertrude Stein* (**25.1**) Picasso, *Les Demoiselles d'Avignon* (**25.2**) Laurencin, *Group of Artists* (**25.5**) Wright, Robie House (**25.29**), Chicago Braque, *Violin and Pitcher* (**25.6**) Picasso, *Head of a Woman* (**25.7**) Mondrian, *Amaryllis* (**25.16**) **Picasso, *Les Demoiselles d'Avignon***	Futurist manifesto published in *Le Figaro* (1909) 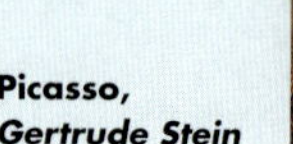 **Picasso, *Gertrude Stein*** 
1910	1910–1920  **Duchamp, *Nude Descending a Staircase, No. 2*** **Etoumbi mask, Congo**	Brancusi, *The Kiss* (**25.26**) Duchamp, *Nude Descending a Staircase, No. 2* (**25.18**) Brancusi, *Mademoiselle Pogany* (Version I) (**25.19**) Picasso, *Man with a Hat* (**25.8**) Boccioni, *Unique Forms of Continuity in Space* (**25.14**) Malevich, *Composition with the Mona Lisa* (**25.22**) Léger, *The City* (**25.15**)  **Brancusi, *Mademoiselle Pogany***	Bertrand Russell and Alfred North Whitehead, *Principia Mathematica* (1910–1913) *De Stijl* movement founded in the Netherlands (1910–1920) Two Cubist exhibitions held in Paris (1911) Gustav Mahler, *Das Lied von der Erde* (1911) Max Beerbohm, *Zuleika Dobson* (1911) J. M. Synge, *Playboy of the Western World* (1912) R. F. Scott reaches the South Pole (1912) C. G. Jung, *The Theory of Psychoanalysis* (1912) D. H. Lawrence, *Sons and Lovers* (1913) Armory Show held in New York (1913) Marcel Proust, *Remembrance of Things Past* (1913–1927) First World War (1914–1918) Margaret Sanger jailed for advocating birth control (1915) Austria, Czechoslovakia, Germany, Poland become republics (1918) Lytton Strachey, *Eminent Victorians* (1918) Willa Cather, *My Antonia* (1918) Worldwide flu epidemic kills 22 million people (1918–1920) Versailles Peace Conference (1919) Walter Gropius establishes Bauhaus in Weimar, Germany (1919) League of Nations established (1919) Sinclair Lewis, *Main Street* (1920)
1920	1920–1930	Davis, *Lucky Strike* (**25.20**) Picasso, *Three Musicians* (**25.10**) Kandinsky, *Composition 8* (**25.35**) Rietveld, Schroeder House (**25.34**), Utrecht Gropius, the Bauhaus (**25.37**), Dessau Le Corbusier, Villa Savoye (**25.38**), Poissy-sur-Seine Malevich, *Black Square* (**25.23**) 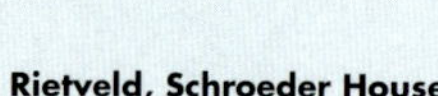 **Rietveld, Schroeder House**	Mussolini forms fascist government in Italy (1922) T. S. Eliot, *The Waste Land* (1922) James Joyce, *Ulysses* (1922) Adolf Hitler, *Mein Kampf* (1924) F. Scott Fitzgerald, *The Great Gatsby* (1925) Invention of television (1926) Vassily Kandinsky, *Point and Line to Plane* (1926) Berthold Brecht, *Threepenny Opera* (1928) Margaret Mead, *Coming of Age in Samoa* (1928) Ernest Hemingway, *A Farewell to Arms* (1929) Stock market crash on Wall Street; economic depression (1929) Museum of Modern Art opens in New York (1929) Virginia Woolf, *A Room of One's Own* (1929) Erich Maria Remarque, *All Quiet on the Western Front* (1929)
1930	1930–1940 	Picasso, *Girl before a Mirror* (**25.11**) Malevich, *Self-Portrait* (**25.24**) Douglas, *Aspects of Negro Life: From Slavery through Reconstruction* (**25.21**) Wright, Fallingwater (**25.32**), Pennsylvania Picasso, *Guernica* (**25.12–25.13**) Brancusi, *Endless Column* (**25.27**) Brancusi, *The Gate of the Kiss* (**25.25**) Wright, Taliesin West (**25.33**), Arizona **Wright, Fallingwater**	Evelyn Waugh, *Vile Bodies* (1930) Dashiell Hammett, *The Maltese Falcon* (1930) Robert Frost, *Collected Poems* (1931) Pearl S. Buck, *The Good Earth* (1931) Franklin Roosevelt introduces New Deal social and economic measures (1933) Adolf Hitler appointed German chancellor (1933) Gertrude Stein, *Autobiography of Alice B. Toklas* (1933) Development of sulfa drugs (mid-1930s) Spanish Civil War (1936–1939) World War II (1939–1945) Bauhaus artists emigrate to the United States (late 1930s)
1940	1940–1950	Mondrian, *Broadway Boogie Woogie* (**25.17**) Picasso, *Bull's Head* (**25.9**)	
1960	1950–1960	van der Rohe, Lake Shore Drive Apartment Houses (**25.40**), Chicago Le Corbusier, Notre-Dame-du-Haut (**25.39**), Ronchamp	**Picasso, *Bull's Head***

26

Dada, Surrealism, Fantasy, and the United States between the Wars

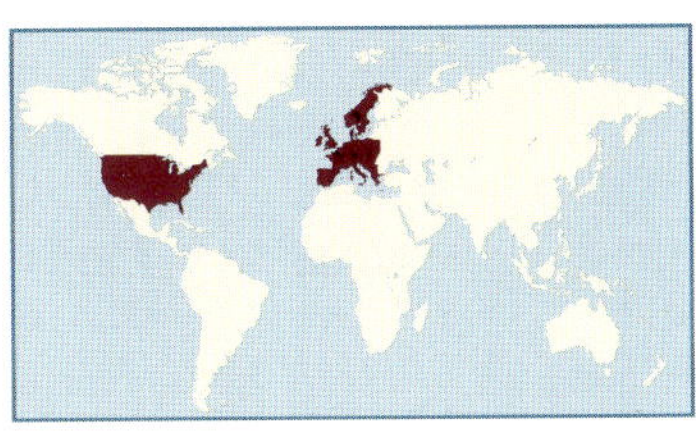

The devastation of World War I affected the arts as well as other aspects of Western civilization. For the first time in history, armies used trench warfare, barbed wire, machine guns firing along fixed lines, and chemical weapons. After treating the victims of gassing and shell shock in World War I, Freud and other medical researchers published accounts of the long-term psychological traumas of the new warfare. "The lost generation," a phrase coined by Gertrude Stein, captured the overwhelming sense of desolation experienced by the post–World War I intellectuals. In the visual arts the same pessimism and despair emerged as Dada.

Dada

The term *Dada* refers to an international artistic and literary intellectual movement that began during World War I in the relative safety of neutral Switzerland. Artists, writers, and performers gathered at the Cabaret Voltaire, a café in Zurich, for discussion, entertainment, and creative exploration (see box). Dada was thus not an artistic style in the sense of shared formal qualities that are easily recognized. Rather, it was an idea, a kind of "anti-art," predicated on a nihilist (from the Latin word *nihil,* meaning "nothing") philosophy of negation. By 1916, the term *Dada* had appeared in print—a new addition to the parade of aesthetic "manifestos" that developed in the nineteenth century. Dada lasted as a cohesive European movement until about 1920.

The Cabaret Voltaire

In February 1916, the German pacifist actor and author Hugo Ball (1886–1927) placed the following announcement in a Zurich paper:

> Cabaret Voltaire. Under this name a group of young artists and writers has formed with the object of becoming a center for artistic entertainment. The Cabaret Voltaire will be run on the principle of daily meetings where visiting artists will perform their music and poetry. The young artists of Zurich are invited to bring along their ideas and contributions.[1]

Among those who accepted Ball's invitation were Jean (Hans) Arp, the *chanteuse* Emmy Hennings, who later married Ball, and the Romanian poet Tristan Tzara. The cabaret was housed in a bar in a run-down quarter of Zurich, where poems, songs, and stories were recited and performed. Some of these were later published in the cabaret's periodical, entitled *Dada*. The movement stood for the absence of an artistic program and of rules. Dadaists rebelled against bourgeois values, which Ball referred to as "a public execution of false morality." Arp described Dada sentiments as follows:

> Revolted by the butchery of the 1914 World War, we in Zurich devoted ourselves to the arts. While the guns rumbled in the distance, we sang, painted, made collages and wrote poems with all our might. We were seeking an art based on fundamentals, to cure the madness of the age, and a new order of things that would restore the balance between heaven and hell.[2]

A feature of Dada expression was the "abstract phonetic poem," which Ball intended as a literary parallel to abstract painting and sculpture. "The next step," he wrote in his diary on March 5, 1917, "is for poetry to discard language as painting has discarded the object." One example of such poetry follows:

> gadji beri bimba glandridi laula lonni cadori
> gadjama gramma berida bimbala glandri galassassa
> laulitalomini
> Gadjama tuffm i zimzalla binban gligia wowolimai bin
> beri ban
> o katalominal rhinocerossola hopsamen laulitalomini
> hoooo gadjama
> rhinocerossola hopsamen
> bluku terullala blaulala loooo. . . .[3]

It also achieved a foothold in New York, where it flourished from about 1915 to 1923.

There are several accounts of the origin of the term *Dada.* The most widely accepted is that, when the leaders of the movement were trying to think of a name, they came upon a French-German dictionary that was opened at random to the word *Dada.* According to the 1916 manifesto, *Dada* is French for a child's wooden horse. *Da-da* are also the first two syllables spoken by children learning to talk and thus suggest a regression to early childhood. The implication was that artists wished to "start life over." Likewise, Dada's iconoclastic force challenged traditional assumptions about art and had an enormous impact on later twentieth-century **conceptual art** (see Chapter 28). Despite the despair that gave rise to Dada, however, a taste for the playful and the experimental was an important, creative, and ultimately hopeful aspect of the movement. This, in turn, is reflected in the Russian meaning of *da, da,* which is "yes, yes."

Marcel Duchamp

One of the major proponents of Dada was Marcel Duchamp (1887–1968), whose *Nude Descending a Staircase* (see fig. 25.18) had caused a sensation in the 1913 Armory Show. He shared the Dada taste for wordplay and punning, which he combined with visual images. Delighting, as children do, in nonsensical repetition, Duchamp entitled his art magazine *Wrong Rong.* The most famous instance of visual and verbal punning in Duchamp's work is *L.H.O.O.Q.* (fig. **26.1**), whose title is a bilingual pun. Read phonetically in English, the title sounds like "LOOK," which, on one level, is the artist's command to the viewer. If each letter is pronounced according to its individual sound in French, the title reads "Elle (*L*) a ch (*H*) aud (*O*) au (*O*) cul (*Q*)," meaning in English "She has a hot ass." Read backward, on the other hand, "LOOK" spells "KOOL," which counters the forward message.

When viewers do, in fact, look, they see that Duchamp has penciled a beard and mustache onto a reproduction of Leonardo's *Mona Lisa* (see fig. 14.16), turning her into a bearded lady. One might ask whether Duchamp has "defaced" the *Mona Lisa* or merely "touched her up." This question plays with the sometimes fine line between creation and destruction. (The modern expression "You have to break eggs to make an omelet" illustrates the connection between creating and destroying that was made explicit by the Dada movement.)

Duchamp called the kind of work exemplified by *L.H.O.O.Q.* a "Ready-Made-Aided." When he merely added a title to an object, he called the result a "Ready-Made."

CONNECTIONS

See figure 14.16. Leonardo da Vinci, *Mona Lisa*, c. 1503–1505.

26.1 Marcel Duchamp, replica of *L.H.O.O.Q.*, Paris, 1919, from "Boîte-en-Valise." Color reproduction of the *Mona Lisa* altered with a pencil; 7¾ × 5 in. (19.7 × 12.7 cm). Philadelphia Museum of Art (Louise and Walter Arensberg Collection). Duchamp was born in Blainville, France, the third of three sons who were all artists. In 1915, he moved to New York and in 1955 became an American citizen. After painting only twenty works, Duchamp announced his retirement in 1923 and devoted the rest of his life to chess.

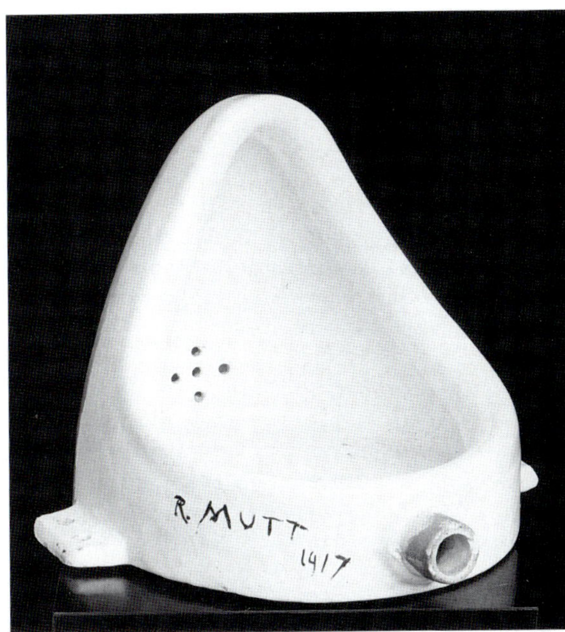

26.2 Marcel Duchamp, *Fountain (Urinal)*, 1917. Ready-made, 24 in. (61.0 cm) high. Photo courtesy of Carroll Janis, New York. Duchamp declared that it was the artist's conscious choice that made a "Ready-Made" into a work of art. In 1915, he bought a shovel in a New York hardware store and wrote on it: "In advance of a broken arm." "It was around that time," he said, "that the word 'ready-made' came to my mind. . . . Since the tubes of paint used by an artist are manufactured and ready-made products, we must conclude that all the paintings in the world are ready-made aided."[4]

Duchamp's most outrageous Ready-Made was a urinal (fig. **26.2**) that he submitted as a sculpture to a New York exhibition mounted by the Society of Independent Artists in 1917. He turned the urinal upside down, signed it "R. Mutt," and called it *Fountain*. The work was rejected by the society, and Duchamp resigned his membership.

Despite the iconoclastic qualities of his Ready-Mades and his Ready-Mades-Aided, it must be said that both *L.H.O.O.Q.* and the *Fountain* have a place in the history of art. In the former, the connection with the past is obvious, for the work reproduces a classic icon. It comments on Leonardo's homosexuality and on the sexual ambiguity of the *Mona Lisa* herself. It also reflects Duchamp's interest in creating his own alter ego as a woman, whom he named Rrose Sélavy, a pun on "c'est la vie," meaning "that's life." The *Fountain* connects the idea of a fountain and a urinating male, which in fact has been the subject of actual and painted fountains in many works of Western art.

A good example of Dada principles in a work by Duchamp is *To Be Looked At (from the Other Side of the Glass) with One Eye, Close to, for Almost an Hour* of 1918 (fig. **26.3**). A pyramidal shape (above a balance) painted on a glass surface is tilted slightly by the weight of a circle. As in *L.H.O.O.Q.*, the title is about the viewer's relationship to the work of art and its potential for shock in looking and seeing. Whereas Renaissance artists controlled the viewer's direction of sight with linear perspective, Duchamp "instructs" the observer verbally via the title. He also plays with the point of view, making it two-sided, which can be seen as a development of the Cubist simultaneous viewpoint.

The glass surface of *To Be Looked At* cracked while it was being shipped, and the cracks were allowed to remain as part of the design. This accident and Duchamp's decision to let it stand are characteristic of Dada. For the Dada artists, chance became a subject of art, just as the medium had become a subject in the late nineteenth century. In collage and assemblage, too, the medium is as prominent a feature of the image as brushstrokes were for Impressionists and Post-Impressionists. Art based on the "found object" relies on the conscious exploration of chance in finding the medium for the work. Accepting chance and using what it offers also require a degree of flexibility and spontaneity that are necessary aspects of creativity.

26.3 Marcel Duchamp, *To Be Looked At (from the Other Side of the Glass) with One Eye, Close to, for Almost an Hour*, Buenos Aires, 1918. Oil paint, silver leaf, lead wire, and magnifying lens on glass; overall height 22 in. (55.8 cm). Museum of Modern Art, New York (Katherine S. Dreier Bequest).

Jean (Hans) Arp

A quality of playfulness pervades the work of the Swiss artist Jean Arp (1887–1966), who was one of the founders of European Dada. In 1916–1917, in a famous act of Dada "chance," Arp cut up rectangles of blue, white, and gray paper and dropped them onto a surface. He then pasted them where they fell and called the result *Collage Arranged According to the Laws of Chance* (fig. **26.4**). By tilting the rectangles slightly and leaving the edges ragged, Arp animated the image and created the impression that the shapes are trying to arrange themselves.

In the cord collage *The Dancer* of 1928 (fig. **26.5**), Arp arranged a string on a flat surface. The string is equivalent to the draftsman's "line"—it defines the form and its character. By moving the string to achieve the desired shapes, Arp "played" creatively and arrived at a humorous image —a small head on a bulky torso with a circle in the center. The figure's slight tilt, the position of the left leg, and the upward curve of the right leg create a convincing impression of forward motion. The dancer literally seems to "kick up her heel," which, together with the flowing hair evoked by a single strand of string, conveys a feeling of movement through space.

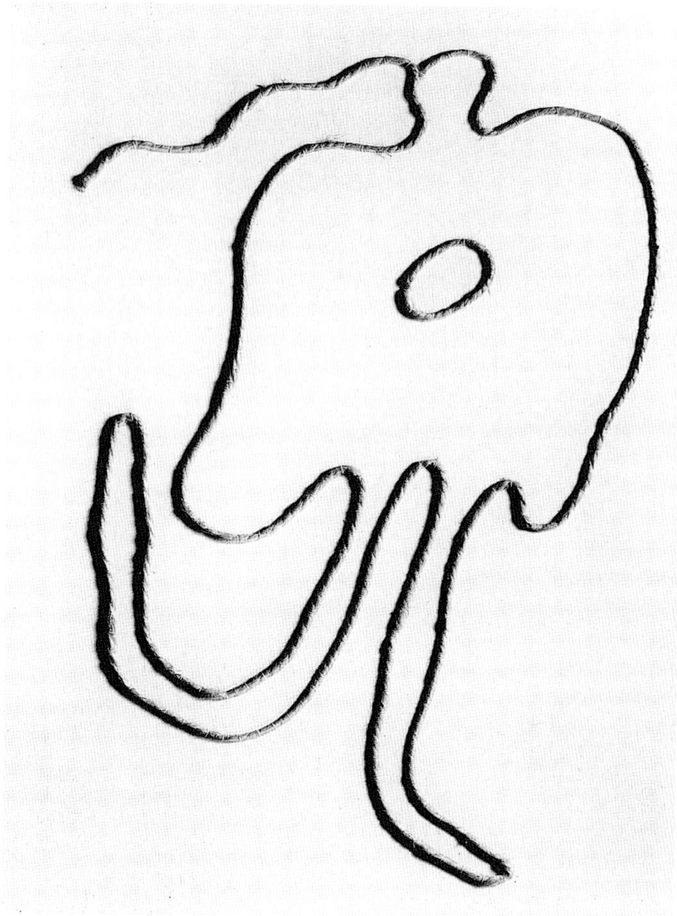

26.5 Jean (Hans) Arp, *The Dancer,* 1928. Cord collage; 20 × 15½ in. (50.8 × 39.4 cm). Photo courtesy of Carroll Janis, New York.

26.4 Jean (Hans) Arp, *Collage Arranged According to the Laws of Chance,* 1916–1917. Torn and pasted paper; 19⅛ × 13⅝ in. (48.6 × 34.6 cm). Museum of Modern Art, New York. Purchase, © 1996 Artists Rights Society (ARS). New York/VG Bild-Kunst, Bonn.

In moving the string, Arp also engaged in a form of visual free association, which was part of Dada and appealed to the interest in the spontaneous quality of chance. Dada artists and writers attempted a creative process designed to minimize the overlay of tradition and conscious control. Instead, they emphasized the expression of unconscious material through play, chance, and rapid execution. This approach was used in wordplay as well as in visual punning. The connection of both with unconscious processes had been explicated in Freud's 1911 publication *Jokes and Their Relation to the Unconscious.* Several Dada artists, including Arp, wrote poems intended to illustrate these processes (see box).

Man Ray

The American Dadaist Man Ray (1890–1976) also played with words, images, and objects, parts of which were "ready-made." His *Indestructible Object (or Object to Be Destroyed)* of 1923 (fig. **26.6**), for example, consisted of a "ready-made" metronome. He attached a photograph of a human eye to the pendulum, thereby combining the moving piece of the metronome with the eye that watches it move. The viewer is "looked at" by the metronome, which has been transformed by Man Ray's addition from a purely functional object to a work of art. The transitional state between looking and being looked at, between actual and implied motion, between utility and aesthetics is reflected in the ambivalence of the title. The object is both indestructible and intended to be destroyed. Like the European Dada artists, Man Ray played with the fine line separating creation from destruction and the mundane "found objects" of everyday life from art.

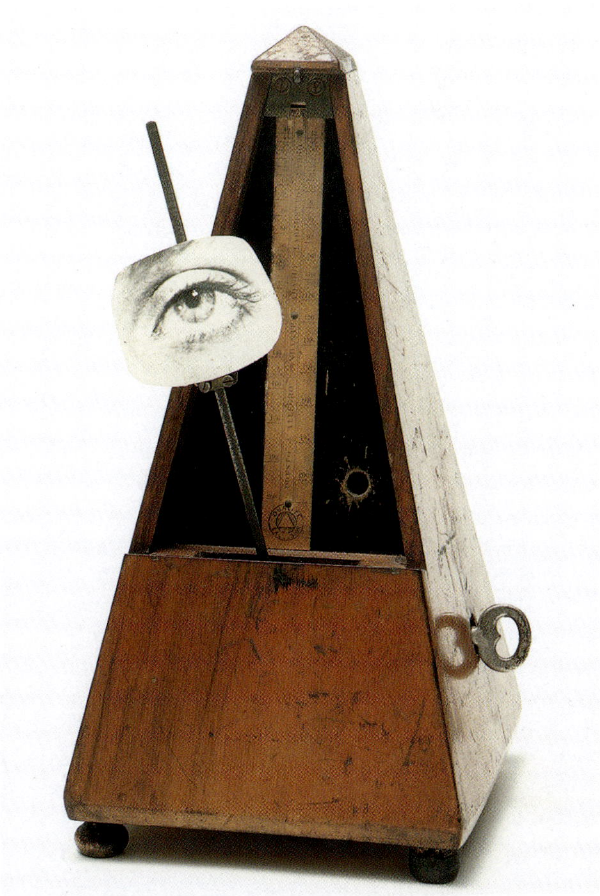

26.6 Man Ray, *Indestructible Object (or Object to Be Destroyed)*, 1964. Replica of the original of 1923. Metronome with cutout photograph of an eye on a pendulum; 8⅞ × 4⅜ × 4⅜ in. (22.5 × 11.1 × 11.1 cm). Museum of Modern Art, New York (James Thrall Soby Fund). The artist's real name was Emanuel Rudnitsky (1890–1976). His choice of the name Man Ray, although derived from his real name, illustrates the fondness for punning and word games that he shared with other Dada artists. He reportedly chose "Man" because he was male and "Ray" because of his interest in light.

Dada Poetry

Arp's efforts at Dada poetry are more comprehensible than those of Hugo Ball. He wrote several versions of a poem entitled "The Guest Expulsed," two of which follow:

The Guest Expulsed 3

Gravestones I carry on my head.
From water-bearing mortal clay
I cast offending Adam out
—To pass the time—twelve times a day.

Standing in light up to the hilt,
I leap out through my mouth perforce
And, carrying owls to Athens town,
Harness myself before my horse.

Farewell a hund- and katzen-fold.
In line with Time's polarity
I follow in disguise, lead-glazed,
The spirit of hilarity.

I mingle camphor of my own
In with the elder-pith of Time,
And into all eternity
Inwards and upwards still I climb.

The Guest Expulsed 5

Their rubber hammer strikes the sea
Down the black general so brave.
With silken braid they deck him out
As fifth wheel on the common grave.

All striped in yellow with the tides
They decorate his firmament.
The epaulette they then construct
Of June July and wet cement.

With many limbs the portrait group
They lift on to the Dadadado;
They nail their A B seizures up;
Who numbers the compartments? They do.

They dye themselves with blue-bag them
And go as rivers from the land,
With candied fruit along the stream,
An Oriflamme in every hand.[5]

Surrealism

Many members of the Dada movement also became interested in the Surrealist style that supplanted it. It was the writer André Breton who bridged the gap between Dada and Surrealism with his first *Surrealist Manifesto* of 1924 (see box). He advocated an art and literature based on Freud's psychoanalytic technique of free association as a means of exploring the imagination and entering the world of myth, fear, fantasy, and dream. The very term *surreal* connotes a higher reality—a state of being, like that depicted in Picasso's *Girl before a Mirror* (see fig. 25.11), that is more real than mere appearance.

Breton had studied medicine and, like Freud, had encountered the traumas experienced by World War I shell-shock victims. This led both Breton and Freud to recognize the power that trauma has over logical, conscious thinking. As a result, Breton wished to gain access to the unconscious mind, where, he believed, the source of creativity lay. He recommended that authors write in a state of free-floating association in order to achieve spontaneous, unedited expression. This "automatic writing" influenced European Abstract Surrealists and later, in the 1940s, had a significant impact on the Abstract Expressionists in New York City (see Chapter 27). The Surrealists' interest in gaining access to unconscious phenomena led to images that seem unreal or unlikely, as dream images often are, and to odd juxtapositions of time, place, and iconography.

André Breton's First Surrealist Manifesto

The term *Surrealist* was coined by Apollinaire to describe one of his plays. In 1924, André Breton published the first *Surrealist Manifesto,* in which he defined the term as "pure psychic automatism by which it is intended to express, either verbally or in writing, the true function of thought. Thought dictated in the absence of all control exerted by reason, and outside all aesthetic or moral preoccupations."[6]

Surrealist aims followed logically from Dada interest in spontaneous, unconscious expressions of dreams and imagination. For this development, Breton gave full credit to Sigmund Freud's *Interpretation of Dreams,* which had been published in 1899. In dreams, according to both Freud and Breton, the dreamer is not inhibited by the possibility of action and therefore gives freer reign to unconscious thoughts. "Perhaps," wrote Breton in his opening paragraph, "the imagination is on the verge of recovering its rights. If the depths of our minds conceal strange forces capable of augmenting or conquering those on the surface, it is in our greatest interest to capture them . . . and later to submit them, should the occasion arise, to the control of reason."[7]

See figure 25.11. Pablo Picasso, *Girl before a Mirror,* 1932.

Giorgio de Chirico

Breton cited Giorgio de Chirico (1888–1978), who was born in Greece of Italian parents, as the paradigm of Surrealism. De Chirico had signed the 1916 Dada manifesto and then developed an individual Surrealist style, which he termed *pittura metafisica*—"metaphysical painting." His *Place d'Italie* of 1912 (fig. **26.7**) combines a perspective construction and architectural setting reminiscent of the Italian Renaissance with an unlikely marble reclining figure in the foreground and a train in the background. Diagonal shadows are cast by the buildings, the statue, and a standing couple in the distance. One shadow, entering the picture from the left, belongs to an unseen person.

In this painting, de Chirico combines anachronistic time and place within a deceptively rational space. The reclining figure is derived from Classical sculpture and thus denotes the Greek and Roman past. The moving train, on the other hand, refers to the industrial present and the passage of time. There is an eerie, uncanny quality to this scene, reinforced by the shadows, that is typical of de Chirico. Isolation and a sense of foreboding pervade the picture space, making the viewer uneasy, as if aware of a mystery that can never be solved.

26.7 Giorgio de Chirico, *Place d'Italie,* 1912. Oil on canvas; 18½ × 22½ in. (47.0 × 57.2 cm). Collection, Dr. Emilio Jesi, Milan.

Man Ray

Among the Surrealists who had also been part of the Dada movement was Man Ray. In 1921, he moved to Paris, where he showed his paintings in the first Surrealist exhibition of 1925. He worked as a fashion and portrait photographer and as an avant-garde filmmaker. His experiments with photographic techniques included the **Rayograph**, made without a camera by placing objects on light-sensitive paper. Man Ray's most famous photograph, *Le Violon d'Ingres* (fig. **26.8**), combines Dada wordplay with Surrealist imagery. The nude recalls the odalisques of Ingres (see fig. 19.14), while the title refers to Ingres' hobby—playing the violin (which led to the French phrase *violon d'Ingres,* meaning "hobby"). By adding sound holes, Man Ray puns on the similarity between the nude's back and the shape of a violin. The combination of the nude and the holes exemplifies the dreamlike imagery of Surrealism.

Man Ray defended the art of photography and argued against those unwilling to treat it as an art form. In *Photography Can Be Art,* he wrote:

> When the automobile arrived, there were those that declared the horse to be the most perfect form of locomotion. All these attitudes result from a fear that the one will replace the other. Nothing of the kind has happened. We have simply increased our vocabulary. I see no one trying to abolish the automobile because we have the airplane.[8]

In true Dada fashion, Man Ray also published two books, *Photography Is Not Art* and *Art Is Not Photography.*

CONNECTIONS

See figure 19.14. Jean-Auguste-Dominique Ingres, *Grande Odalisque,* 1814.

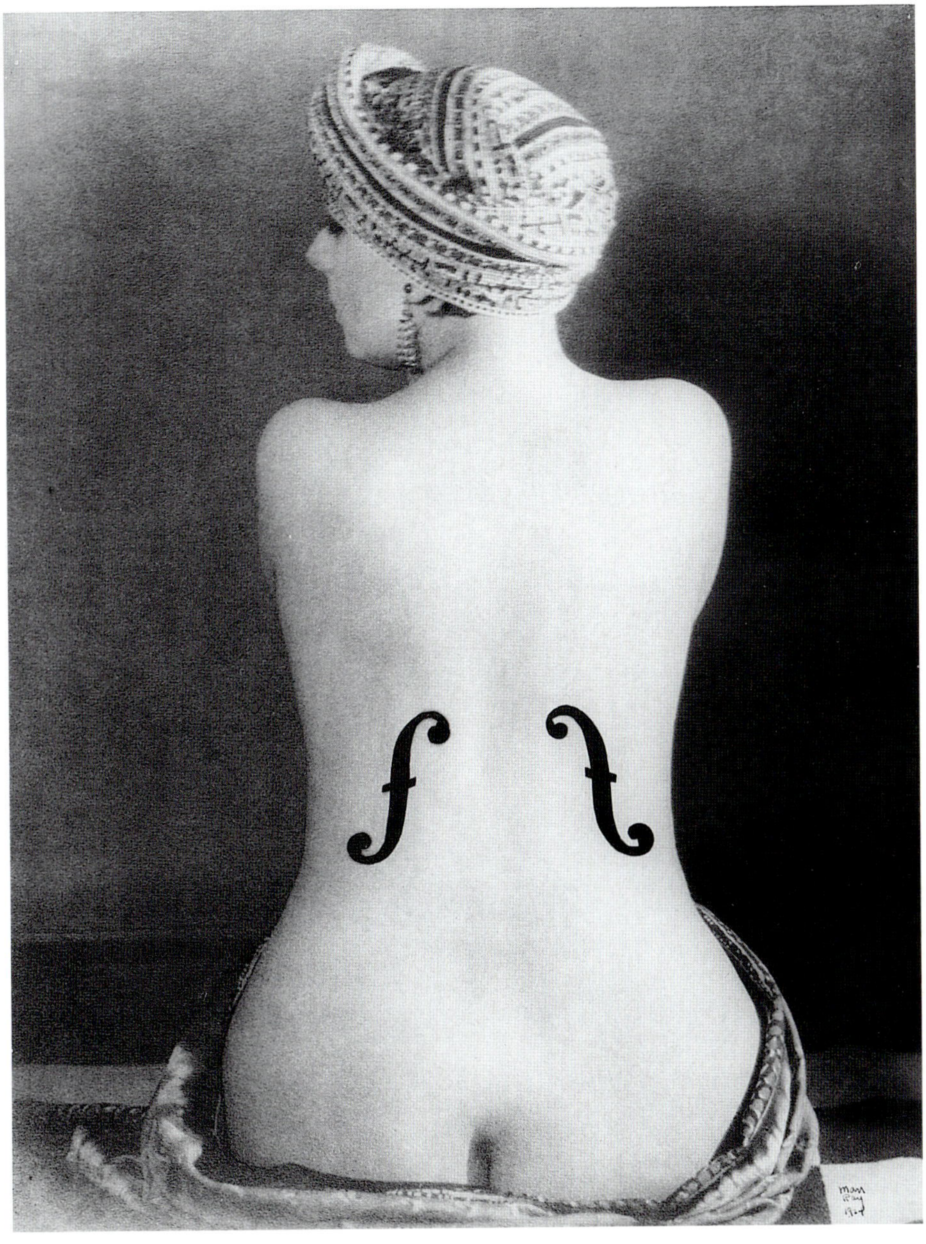

26.8 Man Ray, *Le Violon d'Ingres,* 1924. Photograph. Museé National d'Art Moderne, Centre George Pompidou.

Paul Klee

Fantasy characterizes the Surrealism of the Swiss artist Paul Klee (1879–1940), who had been a member of The Blue Rider (see p. 840). He made many pencil drawings that reveal his attraction to linear, childlike imagery as well as the influence of Surrealist "automatic writing." His *Mask of Fear* of 1932 (fig. **26.9**) reflects all of these qualities, including the recollection of a painted wooden sculpture by the Zuni carvers of the American Southwest (fig. **26.10**). Such allusions exemplify the Surrealists' search for new sources of imagery, especially those with dreamlike and mythological content. As a young man, Klee visited the folk art museum in Berlin, which had acquired the Zuni statue in 1880. In addition to formal correspondences, it is also possible that there are iconographic parallels. For the Zuni figure represents a war god and thus might have been associated in Klee's mind with the rise of the Nazi storm troopers. They, too, wore zigzag insignia reminiscent of lightning, and they aroused fear of the kind suggested by the man hidden behind the mask.

26.10 Zuni war god from Arizona or New Mexico, before 1880. Painted wood and mixed media; 30½ in. (77.5 cm). high. Museum für Volkerkunde, Berlin.

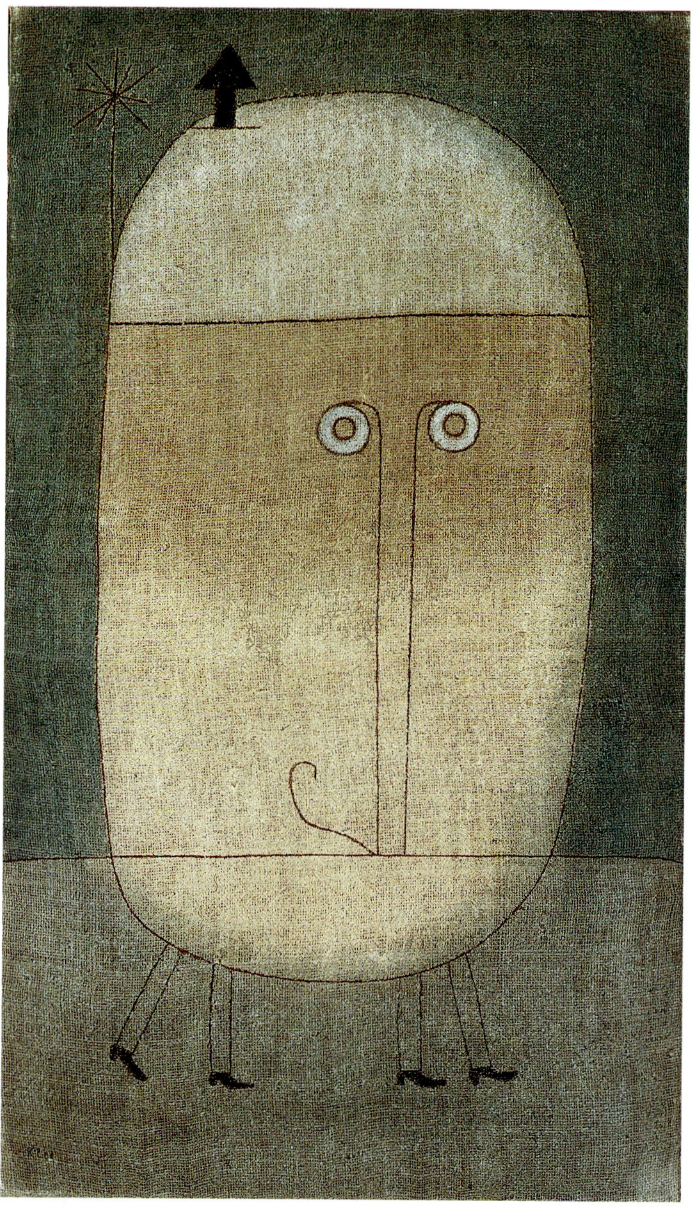

26.9 Paul Klee, *Mask of Fear,* 1932. Oil on burlap; 3 ft. 3½ in. × 1 ft. 10½ in. (1.00 × 0.57 m). Museum of Modern Art, New York (Nelson A. Rockefeller Fund). Klee described the creative process as follows: "Art does not reproduce the visible; rather, it makes visible."[9] Klee himself was enormously productive, recording a total of nearly 9,000 works.

In any event, Klee has transformed the Zuni sculpture into a flat image that plays with the boundaries between two- and three-dimensionality. The horizontal line defining the tip of the mask's nose is also the horizon line of the painting. Two pairs of legs either support the mask, whose size does not correspond naturally to theirs, or walk behind it. As a result, the viewer is startled by unlikely juxtapositions.

26.11 Salvador Dalí, *The Persistence of Memory*, 1931. Oil on canvas; 9½ in. × 13 in. (24.1 × 33.0 cm). Museum of Modern Art, New York (given anonymously).

Salvador Dalí

Salvador Dalí's (1904–1989) famous "melting clocks" in *The Persistence of Memory* (fig. **26.11**) portray the uncanny quality of certain dreams. In a stark, oddly illuminated landscape, a number of elements referring to time—watches, eggs, a dead fish, a dead tree—are juxtaposed with a single living fly and swarming ants. Displaced from an unidentified location onto the eerie landscape are two rectangular platforms at the left. The one in the foreground impossibly supports a tree, just as an impossible system of lighting produces strange color combinations.

Joan Miró

The Surrealist pictures of Joan Miró (1893–1983) are composed of imaginary motifs that are often reminiscent of childhood. His early painting *Dog Barking at the Moon* of 1926 (fig. **26.12**) depicts a colorful, toylike dog standing alone on a hill. The night sky contains a fanciful moon and another shape, which could be a bird. The most surreal form is the unsupported ladder that seems to go nowhere. As the ladder rises, its reach becomes vast, and the space between earth and sky is collapsed.

26.12 Joan Miró, *Dog Barking at the Moon*, 1926. Oil on canvas; 28¾ × 36¼ in. (73.0 × 92.1 cm). Philadelphia Museum of Art (A. E. Gallatin Collection).

Miró's later style retains biomorphic, sexually suggestive abstract forms and primary colors, but there is an increase in linear movement and complex design. The *Spanish Dancer* of 1945 (fig. **26.13**), for example, captures the rapid rhythm of Spanish dancing by juxtaposing thin curves, diagonal planes, and flat shapes that shift abruptly from one color to another. The red-and-green curve on the red-and-black shape at the lower right seems to turn in space like a dancer's torso. Two legs kick energetically to the left, while a hand is poised above the torso. Surrounding the hand is a shape with two curved points—one black, one red—which resemble breasts. At the top, the large head tilts upward as a nose and mouth (two black eyes hang from the nose) project from it to the left. Two eyes—one red, one blue—each with two black circles within it, also occupy the large head. A corresponding eye shape is lodged in the lower leg. The exuberance of Miró's dancing figure and the illusion of speed created by curved lines and shifting planes reflect his interest in Surrealist "automatic writing."

26.13 Joan Miró, *Spanish Dancer*, 1945. Oil on canvas; 4 ft. 9½ in. × 3 ft. 8⅞ in. (1.46 × 1.14 m). Fondation Beyeler, Riehen/Basle.

26.14 René Magritte, *The False Mirror,* 1928. Oil on canvas; 21¼ × 31⅞ in. (54.0 × 80.9 cm). Museum of Modern Art, New York.

See figure I.5. René Magritte, *The Betrayal of Images,* 1928.

René Magritte

The Belgian artist René Magritte (1898–1967) painted Surrealist images of a more veristic kind. Individually they are realistic, often to the point of creating an illusion. However, their context, size, or their juxtaposition of objects is unrealistic or possible only in a world of dreams. Magritte's *False Mirror* of 1928 (fig. **26.14**) depicts a large eye (from which the familiar CBS logo was derived). The black circle at the center can refer both to the pupil and to an eclipsed sun. The observer is thrown off balance by the unusual close-up view of the "eye" as well as by its unexpected character. We do not know if we are looking into the eye and seeing a reflection of the sky, or if we are inside the eye, looking past the pupil at the sky. The "mirror" is "false" because, like the "pipe" in *The Betrayal of Images* (see fig. I.5), it plays a visual trick. As puns, however, both contain truth. In *The False Mirror,* Magritte applies the simultaneous viewpoint of Cubism to clear, recognizable forms but without the Cubist use of geometric abstraction.

In *Time Transfixed* (*La Durée poignardée* in French) of 1938 (fig. **26.15**), Magritte juxtaposed two familiar objects in order to create an unfamiliar effect. Various motifs in this work are clearly depicted and easily identifiable, but their relation to each other is odd, and they convey an impression of immobility and timelessness. The clock indicates a specific hour, but the candlesticks are empty. The cold, sterile room, composed almost entirely of rectangular forms, is devoid of human figures. A steam engine has burst through the fireplace but without disrupting the wall. The shadow cast by the train is unexplained because there is no light source to account for it. The smoke, which indicates that the train is moving although it looks stationary, disappears up the chimney. *Poignardée* in the French title, literally meaning "stabbed" with a dagger or sword, expresses the "fixed," frozen quality of both the train and the time.

26.15 René Magritte, *Time Transfixed (La Durée poignardée),* 1938. Oil on canvas; 4 ft. 9⅝ in. × 3 ft. 2⅜ in. (1.46 × 0.98 m). Art Institute of Chicago (Joseph Winterbotham Collection). Freud's discovery that time does not exist in the unconscious accounts for certain unlikely condensations in dreams. The uncanniness of temporal condensation contributes to the eerie quality of this painting, as does the impossible juxtaposition of realistic objects.

26.16 Max Ernst, *The King Playing with the Queen*, 1944. Bronze (cast 1954, from original plaster); 38½ in. (97.8 cm) high, at the base 18¾ × 20½ in. (47.7 × 52.1 cm). Museum of Modern Art, New York (Gift of D. and J. de Menil).

26.17 (right) Mossi whistle, Upper Volta. Wood; 22⅜ in. (56.8 cm) high.

Sculpture Derived from Surrealism

Surrealism influenced sculptors as well as painters and photographers in Europe and America. The Surrealist interest in the literal depiction of unconscious chance and in dream images contributed to the twentieth-century break with many traditional forms and techniques.

Max Ernst

Max Ernst (1891–1976) began his artistic career as a Dadaist in Germany. He moved to France after World War I and eventually settled in the United States. *The King Playing with the Queen* (fig. **26.16**) of 1944 combines the influence of Surrealism, Cubism, a knowledge of Freud's theories, and the playful qualities of Picasso and Duchamp. A geometric king looms up from a chessboard, which is also a tabletop. His horns are related to the role of the bull as a traditional symbol of male fertility and kingship. He dominates the board by his large size and extended arms. The king is a player sitting at the table as well as a chess piece on the board. He literally "plays" with the queen, who is represented as a smaller geometric construction at the left. On the right, a few chess pieces seem detached from whatever "game" is taking place between the king and queen.

In the 1930s and 1940s, Ernst was the Surrealist most influenced by non-Western art. For example, *The King Playing with the Queen* has obvious affinities with a type of wooden whistle produced in Upper Volta, in Africa (fig. **26.17**). Its geometric head, vertical torso, and zigzag arms enclosing open space are remarkably similar to Ernst's sculpture. In addition to African sculpture, Ernst was influenced by Native American art, especially that of Arizona, where he lived from 1946 to 1953. He collected Kachina carvings made by the Hopi tribe (fig. **26.18**) and identified strongly with its mythology, envisioning himself as a shaman and describing shamanistic hallucinations in his autobiography. For Ernst, the shaman—like the artist—had highly charged sensory experiences that offered new ways of interpreting and rendering ordinary phenomena.

26.18 Max Ernst with his Kachina doll collection, 1942. Photograph by James Thrall Soby. Collection of Elaine Lustig Cohen.

Window on the World Twelve

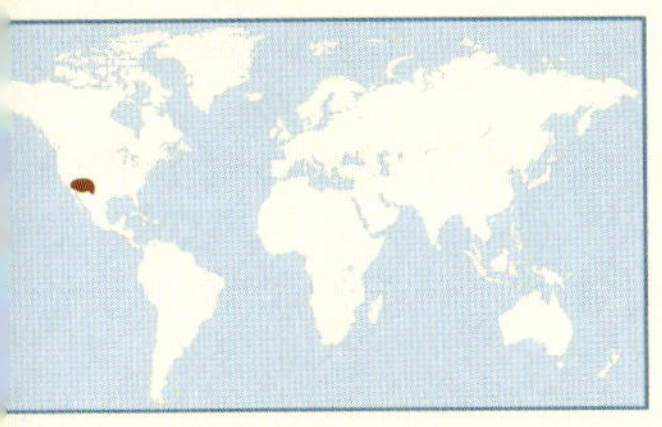

Hopi Kachinas

The Hopi Indians inhabited the American Southwest, especially Arizona, undisturbed until they were relegated to reservations in the late nineteenth century. Theirs is an agricultural society; they live in **pueblos,** which are communal houses divided into individual units made of **adobe** (mud brick). Figure **W12.1** is a diagram of a typical pueblo unit. The thick walls keep the interior cool in summer and prevent freezing in winter. The photograph in figure **W12.2** was taken in about 1929 by Ansel Adams (1902–1984), who was perhaps the leading American photographer of the Southwest. It shows a woman winnowing grain outside the Taos pueblo in New Mexico.

In Hopi villages, an open central space is a ceremonial site in which Kachinas play a major role. According to Hopi mythology, Kachinas are supernatural spirits who dwell in the mountains. They exist in three forms: as unseen spirits, as impersonations by masked men, and as carved, wooden dolls. There are over 200 such Kachinas, some of which are deceased members of the Hopi tribe. Ceremonies involving Kachinas are performed from the winter solstice to mid-July in connection with agriculture, rites of spring, and weather conditions.

W12.1 Diagram of a typical pueblo adobe unit, American Southwest.

W12.2 Ansel Adams, *Winnowing Grain, Taos Pueblo*, c. 1929. Photograph.

Each type of Kachina serves a particular function. There are runners, for example, who race with men in order to train boys in speed, and ogres, whose function is to frighten children into obedience. Clowns provide comic relief during intermissions between rites, a practice similar to the satyr plays in ancient Greece. Children are given Kachinas as presents to serve an exemplary purpose and to train them to recognize the different classes of Kachina. Although there are female Kachinas, they are always impersonated by men.

The Hopi carve Kachinas by shaping the roots of dead cottonwood trees with a chisel and saw. The finer carving is done with a penknife, and the surface is then smoothed with a rasp and sanded. Facial features are attached with glue or pins. Kachinas are painted, and the colors symbolize geographic directions or spatial orientation—blue and green represent the West or Southwest, red the South or Southeast, white the East or Northeast, black the depths, and all the colors together represent the top. Facial markings are also symbolic. For example, parallel lines under the eye denote a warrior's footprint, an inverted V over the mouth denotes an official, and phallic symbols stand for fertility.

The two Kachinas illustrated here represent Black Ogre (fig. **W12.3**) and Butterfly Maiden (fig. **W12.4**). Black Ogre wears a mask with movable jaws and prominent teeth. He has a blue crow's foot on his forehead, wears a white shirt and trousers, red leggings and moccasins, and holds a hammer and a bow. He is believed to take food from children, whom he swallows whole. Butterfly Maiden is a more benign Kachina. She wears a white mask decorated with triangles and a white robe with geometric designs, and her bare feet are yellow. Her feathered headdress is particularly elaborate. In contrast to Black Ogre, whose crow's foot between his eyes makes him seem to be frowning angrily, her expression is impassive.

W12.3 Black Ogre, Hopi Kachina. Carved cottonwood.

W12.4 Butterfly Maiden, Hopi Kachina. Carved cottonwood.

Alberto Giacometti

In the 1930s Alberto Giacometti (1901–1966) had been involved with the Surrealists in Paris, and from the 1940s he began exploring the paradoxical power of emaciated human form. The tall, thin, anti-Classical proportions of *Large Standing Woman III* (fig. **26.19**), one of his most imposing works, hark back to the rigid, standing royal figures of ancient Egypt (see fig. 3.32), which had exerted a significant influence on Giacometti's development. In figures such as this, whether large or small, Giacometti plays with the idea of extinction. His obsession with existence and nonexistence is evident in the fact that he made these sculptures as thin as they can be without collapsing. Ironically, the thinner they become, the more their presence is felt. By confronting the observer with the potential for disappearance, Giacometti arouses existential anxiety and takes the viewer to the very threshold of being. The sculpture is shown here as installed at the Sidney Janis Gallery in New York. On the wall is Mondrian's *Composition with Red, Yellow, and Blue* of 1935–1942; the juxtaposition shows the relationship of both artists to the avant-garde.

CONNECTIONS

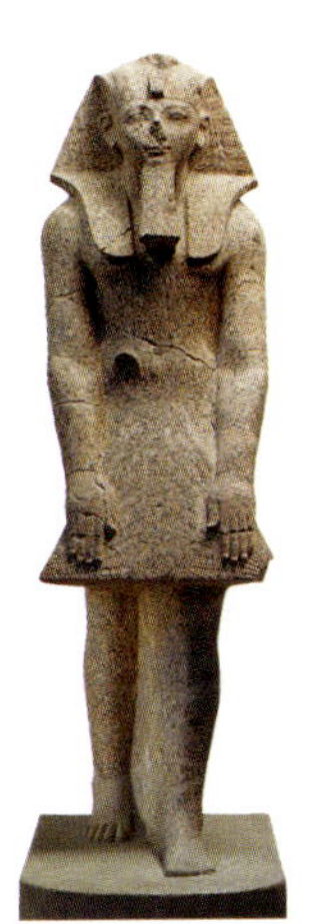

See figure 3.32. Statue of Hatshepsut as pharaoh, Eighteenth Dynasty, c. 1473–1458 B.C.

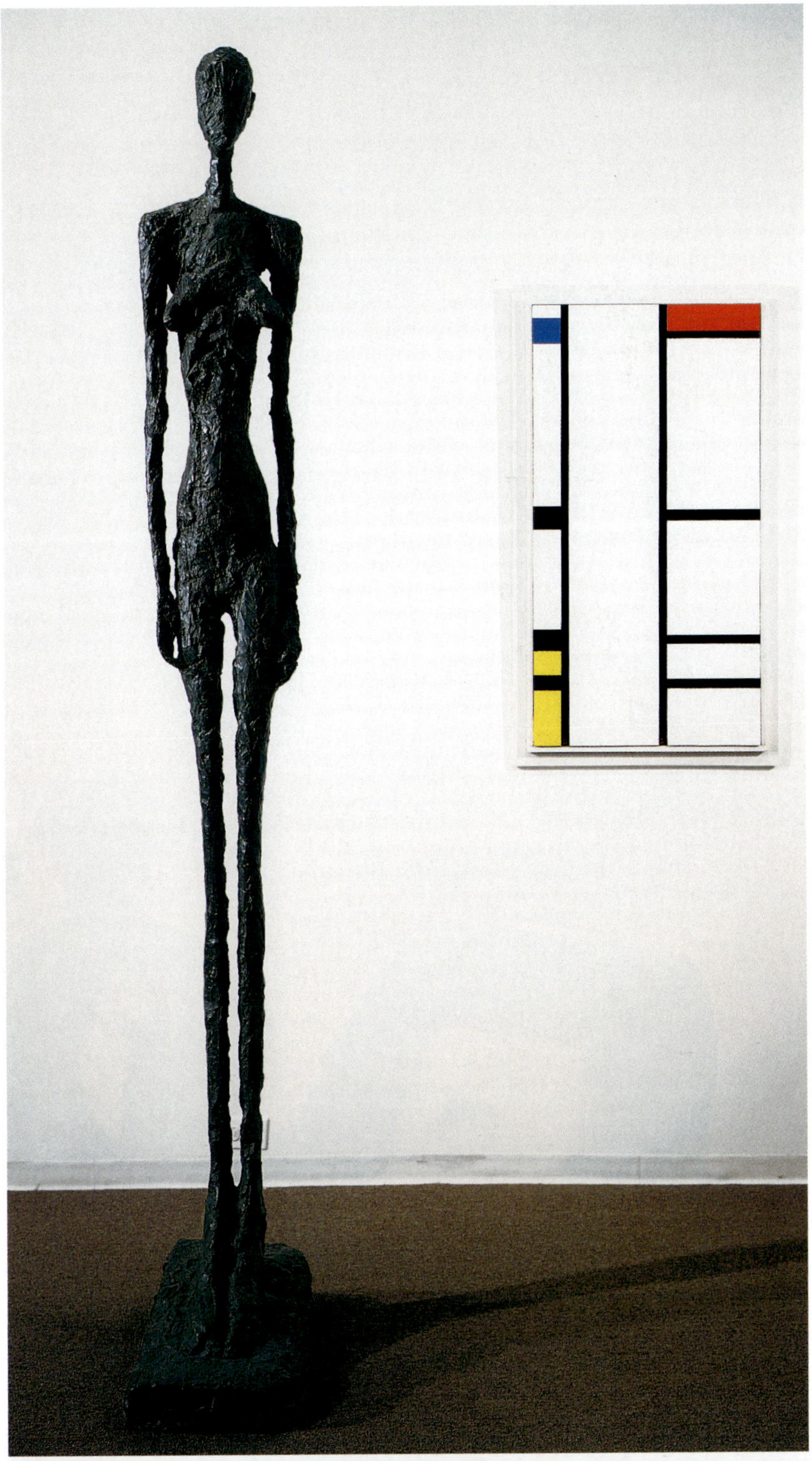

26.19 Alberto Giacometti, *Large Standing Woman III*, 1960, and Piet Mondrian, *Composition with Red, Yellow, and Blue*, 1935–1942. Giacometti: bronze; 7 ft. 8½ in. (2.35 m) high. Mondrian: oil on canvas; 3 ft. 3¼ in. × 1 ft. 8¼ in. (0.99 × 0.51 m). Photo courtesy of Carroll Janis, New York. © 2006 Artists Rights Society (ARS), New York/ADAGP, Paris. © 2006 Mondrian/Holtzman Trust, c/o HCR International, Warrenton, VA, USA. Born in Switzerland, Giacometti spent a formative period in the 1930s as a Surrealist. He met the Futurists in Italy and the Cubists in Paris, and finally developed a distinctive way of representing the human figure that has become his trademark.

Henry Moore

In contrast to Giacometti, the British sculptor Henry Moore (1898–1986) was drawn to massive, biomorphic forms. Moore's habit of collecting the chance objects of nature, such as dried wood, bone, and smooth stones from beaches, recalls the use of "found objects" in collage and assemblage. Unlike Dada and Surrealist artists, however, he used found objects as his inspiration rather than his medium, preferring the more traditional media of stone, wood, and bronze.

The motif of the reclining figure was one of Moore's favorite subjects. He related the image to the Mother Earth theme and to his fascination for the mysterious holes of nature. From the 1930s, he began making sculptures with hollowed-out spaces and openings, thereby playing with the transition between inside and outside, interior and exterior. Many of Moore's reclining figures are intended as outdoor landscape sculptures. As such, their holes permit viewers to see through the work as well as around it and thus to include the surrounding landscape in their experience of the sculpture.

Reclining Figure, in front of the main UNESCO building in Paris (fig. **26.20**), is in an architectural setting. Its curvilinear masses and open spaces contrast with the stark rectangularity of the wall. The white marble, with its pronounced grain, gleams in the natural outdoor light. Moore considered the mountainous quality of the forms and the majestic character of the upright head and torso a fitting metaphor for the noble aims of the United Nations.

In his *Helmet* series of the 1950s, Moore continued to pursue the theme of interior and exterior. *Helmet Head No. 1* (fig. **26.21**) condenses the helmet with the head in a surreal way by the eyelike forms protruding from the helmet. The inside of the helmet is occupied by a cone, leaving open spaces behind it. In this series, Moore included the idea of protective covering, which is the practical function of a helmet. But he also related the theme of protection to another favorite motif—namely, mother and child. For Moore, the helmet head is a metaphor for maternal protection, and the unformed interior figure represents the child.

26.21 Henry Moore, *Helmet Head No. 1*, 1950. Bronze; 13 in. (33.0 cm) high. Tate Gallery, London.

26.20 Henry Moore, *Reclining Figure*, 1957–1958. Roman travertine; 16 ft. 8 in. (5.08 m) long. UNESCO Building, Paris.

CONNECTIONS

See figure 14.48. Giorgione, *Sleeping Venus*, c. 1509.

Alexander Calder

From the 1930s, the American artist Alexander Calder (1898–1976) developed **mobiles,** hanging sculptures that could be set in motion by air currents. The catalyst for these works came from experiments with kinetic sculpture in Paris in the late 1920s and early 1930s. *Big Red* of 1959 (fig. **26.22**) is made from a series of curved wires arranged in a sequence of horizontal, vertical, and diagonal planes. Flat red metal shapes are attached to the wires. Because they hang from the ceiling, mobiles challenge the traditional viewpoint of sculpture. Their playful quality and the chance nature of air currents are reminiscent of Dada and Surrealism, although Calder is more abstract (in the nonfigurative sense) than many Dada and Surrealist artists. Of this mobile, Calder is quoted as having said, "I love red so much that I almost want to paint everything red."[10]

26.22 Alexander Calder, *Big Red,* 1959. Painted sheet metal and steel wire; 6 ft. 1 in. (1.88 m) high, 9 ft. 6 in. (2.90 m) wide. Whitney Museum of American Art, New York (Purchase). The playfulness of Calder's mobiles has not been lost on the toy industry. Mobiles of various figures, often activated by a wind-up motor attached to a music box, have been suspended over the cribs of generations of babies.

The United States: Regionalism and Social Realism

In spite of the variety of expression produced by the European avant-garde and exhibited in the 1913 Armory Show, art in the United States of the 1920s and 1930s was, above all, affected by economic and political events, particularly the Depression and the rise of Fascism in Europe. Two different types of response to the times, both of which had political overtones of their own, can be seen in the work of American Regionalists and Social Realists.

Painting

American Gothic (fig. **26.23**) by Grant Wood (1892–1942) reflects the Regionalists' interest in provincial America and their isolation from the European avant-garde. Although the influence of Gothic is evident in the vertical planes and the pointed arch of the farmhouse window, the figures and their environment are unmistakably those of the American Middle West. The clapboard style of domestic architecture, developed in the nineteenth century by Richard Upjohn and referred to as "Carpenter's Gothic" (see p. 724), is shown here. Wood's meticulous attention to detail and the linear quality of his forms recall the early fifteenth-century Flemish painters. All such European references, however, are subordinated to a distinctly regional American character.

Wood studied in Europe but returned to his native Iowa to paint the region with which he was most familiar. In this work, the two sober paragons of the American work ethic depicted as Iowa farmers are actually the artist's sister and dentist.

The African-American artist Jacob Lawrence (1917–2000), who was influenced by the Harlem Renaissance, dealt with

CONNECTIONS

See figure 11.19. Doorjamb statues, west façade, Chartres Cathedral, c. 1145–1170.

26.23 Grant Wood, *American Gothic*, 1930. Oil on beaverboard; 29¼ × 24½ in. (74.3 × 62.4 cm). Art Institute of Chicago (Friends of American Art Collection).

26.24 Jacob Lawrence, *Harriet Tubman Series, No. 7*, 1939–1940. **Casein** tempera on hardboard; $17\frac{1}{8} \times 12$ in. (43.5×30.5 cm). Hampton University Museum, Hampton, Virginia. From the age of ten, Lawrence lived in Harlem; in 1990, he was awarded the National Medal of Arts. This painting is from his 1939–1940 series celebrating Harriet Tubman (c. 1820–1913). She was an active abolitionist and champion of women's rights who helped southern slaves to escape to the North. From 1850 to 1860, as a "conductor" on the "underground railroad," she freed more than 300 slaves.

issues of racial inequality and social injustice. Figure **26.24** reflects the influence of European Expressionist and Cubist trends, although the subject and theme are purely American. Using a combination of flattened planes and abrupt foreshortening, Lawrence creates a powerful image of the abolitionist Harriet Tubman sawing a log. Tubman's single-minded concentration, as she fills the picture and focuses her energies on the task at hand, engages the observer directly in her activity. The geometric abstraction of certain forms, such as her raised right shoulder, contrasts with three-dimensional forms—the shaded sleeve on the right, for example—to produce shifts in tension. The result of such shifts is a formal instability that is stabilized psychologically by Tubman's evident determination.

Edward Hopper (1882–1967), also a painter of the American scene, cannot be identified strictly as either a Regionalist or a Social Realist. His work combines aspects of both styles, to which he adds an atmosphere of isolation and loneliness. His settings, whether urban or rural, are uniquely American, often containing self-absorbed human figures whose interior focus matches the still, timeless quality of their surroundings. In *Gas* of 1940 (fig. **26.25**), a lone figure stands by a gas pump, the form of which echoes his own. The road, for Hopper a symbol of travel and time, seems to continue beyond the frame. Juxtaposed with the road are the figure and station that "go nowhere," as if frozen within the space of the picture.

26.25 Edward Hopper, *Gas*, 1940. Oil on canvas; 2 ft. $2\frac{1}{4}$ in. $\times$ 3 ft. $4\frac{1}{4}$ in. (0.67×1.02 m). Museum of Modern Art, New York (Mrs. Simon Guggenheim Fund).

Photography

Photography served the aims of social documentation in America as well as in Europe. During the period of black intellectual expansion known as the Harlem Renaissance, photographers recorded the life of the black community in New York City. James Van Der Zee's (1886–1983) *Portrait of Couple, Man with Walking Stick* of 1929 (fig. **26.26**) was taken in his Lenox Avenue studio against a landscape backdrop. The couple seems self-consciously well dressed in an urban style that is slightly at odds with the scenery. Their attire places them in the 1920s at the height of the Harlem Renaissance, and their poses convey a sense of self-assurance.

Shoeshine Sign in a Southern Town of 1936 (fig. **26.27**) by Walker Evans (1903–1975) evokes the atmosphere of the Deep South in the 1930s. During the Depression, until 1937, Evans took pictures for the Resettlement Administration—later the Farm Security Administration (FSA). This organization hired photographers to illustrate rural poverty, as is suggested here by the ramshackle wall and the bare lightbulb. The necessity of earning money by shining shoes stands for the larger social picture of American life in the 1930s. At the same time, however, Evans has exploited the abstract qualities of black and white contrast and textured surfaces. The prominence of the word "SHINE" is reminiscent of early collage and reflects Evans's interest in the formal possibilities of billboards, shop signs, and posters that are part of the American landscape.

26.26 James Van Der Zee, *Portrait of Couple, Man with Walking Stick,* 1929. Silver print. James Van Der Zee Collection.

26.27 Walker Evans, *Shoeshine Sign in a Southern Town,* 1936. Gelatin-silver print; 5⅝ × 6⅝ in. (14.4 × 16.8 cm). Museum of Modern Art, New York (Stephen R. Currier Memorial Fund).

Dorothea Lange (1895–1965) also worked for the FSA, but she was less interested in formal abstraction than Evans and more committed to conveying the desired social message. Her *Migratory Cotton Picker* of 1940 (fig. **26.28**) is typical of the way in which she ennobled the poor and the working class. The man is physically attractive, but worn by laboring in the fields and toughened by the hot sun. Earth clings to his hands, the lines and veins of which create abstract patterns by virtue of the close-up viewpoint. Arizona's arid climate is portrayed in the clear, crisp sky and the precise outlines of the worker. In such images, Lange achieved her political goals by evoking sympathy for, and identification with, her subjects.

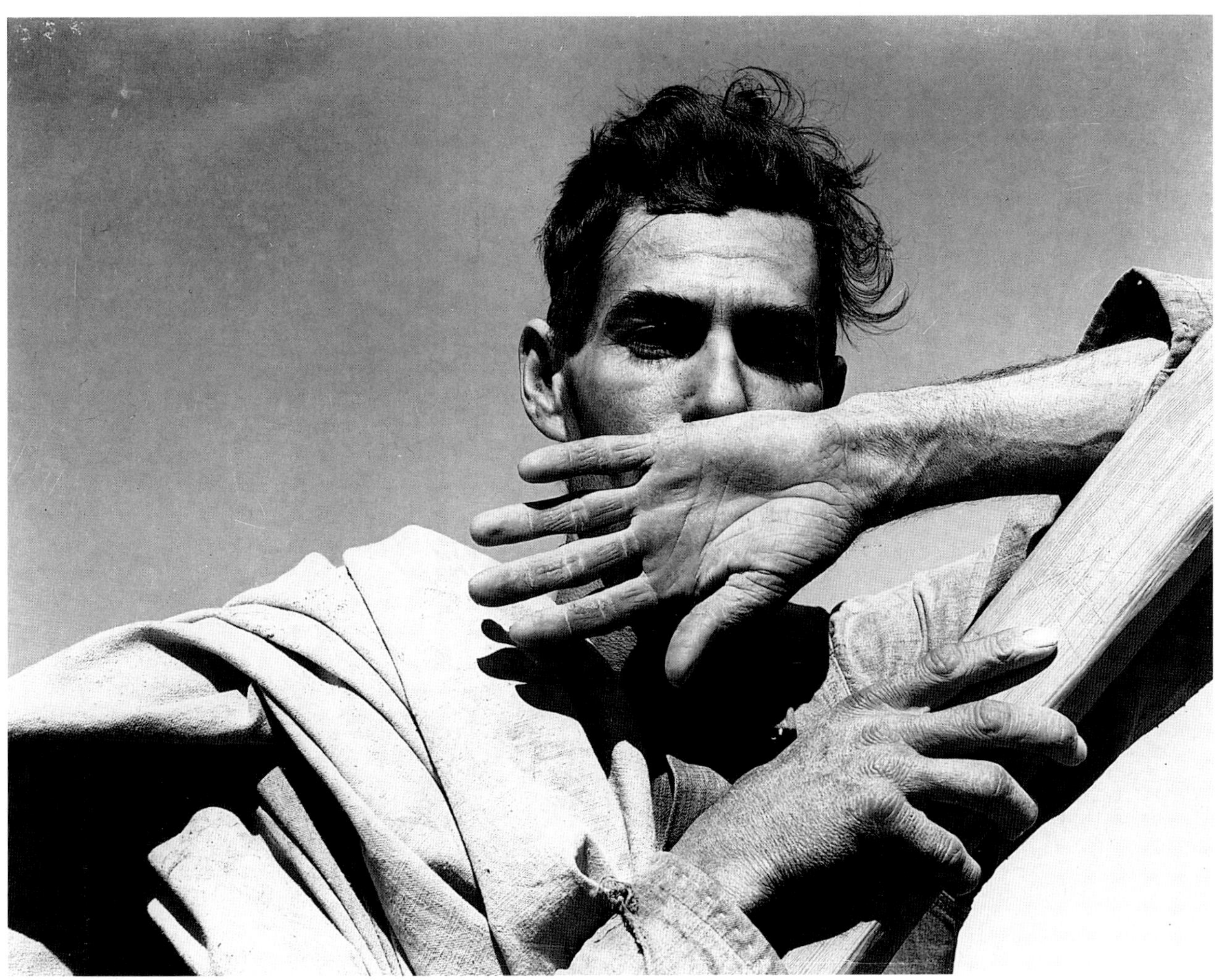

26.28 Dorothea Lange, *Migratory Cotton Picker, Eloy, Arizona,* 1940. Gelatin-silver print; 10½ × 13½ in. (26.8 × 34.3 cm). Oakland Museum.

Mexico

Diego Rivera

Another approach to social concerns can be seen in the murals of the Mexican artist Diego Rivera (1886–1957). From 1909 to 1921, he lived in Europe, where he painted in a Cubist style. On returning to Mexico, however, he renounced modernism and the avant-garde in favor of Mexican nationalism. The government commissioned him to create a series of large murals for the National Palace in Mexico City, which he used as a vehicle for depicting Mexican history. In this approach, Rivera was influenced by Social Realism.

Figure **26.29** shows the first mural in the series. At the left, the Spanish conquerors fight the native population, who perform ancient ceremonies at the far right. References to Quetzalcoatl, the pre-Columbian feathered serpent god, appear on either side of the sun, which hovers above a Mesoamerican pyramid, an alignment recalling that of the Teotihuacán pyramids of the sun and moon (see p. 349). The seated figure in front of the pyramid resembles Lenin, leaving no doubt about Rivera's political message. Rivera has thus combined a kind of historical imperative with contemporary issues, and even though he has diverged from the avant-garde, there are unmistakable Cubist forms in his imagery.

26.29 Diego Rivera, *Ancient Mexico*, from the *History of Mexico* fresco murals, 1929–1935. National Palace, Mexico City.

Frida Kahlo

Rivera's third wife, Frida Kahlo (1907–1954), shared her husband's Marxist sentiments and his Surrealist style. She joined the Communist party in the 1940s to fight Hitler and befriended Leon Trotsky, the Russian revolutionary exiled to Mexico and later assassinated.

Despite a turbulent marriage, Kahlo remained in love with Diego Rivera until her death. She shared the Surrealist interest in childhood memory and in using imagery to reveal the unconscious mind. Having suffered a serious accident as an adolescent that required repeated surgery and forced her to wear an uncomfortable back brace, Kahlo was in constant pain. This she depicted in many of her paintings, but she also portrayed the mental suffering caused by her relationship to Diego.

In figure **26.30**, Kahlo uses the Surrealist technique of painting thoughts and ideas. She depicts herself against a background of green and yellowing leaves and thorns that seem about to engulf her. The abundance of foliage, juxtaposed with the death's head in the landscape tondo on Kahlo's forehead, alludes to Mexican mythology in which life and death are seen as integral aspects of nature's continuum.

In *Marxism Will Give Health to the Sick* (fig. **26.31**), painted in the last year of her life, she depicts Karl Marx strangling a Surrealist image of Uncle Sam in the body of an eagle. At the same time, Marx is performing a "laying on of hands"—one hand with an eye embedded in the palm—thereby curing Kahlo and dispensing with her need for crutches. Formally, the released crutches create an inverted trapezoid that echoes Kahlo's wide green-and-white dress. The red plain at the right suggests the blood of her suffering, while the white dove of peace spreading its wings over the globe and fertile valleys on the left suggests a semblance of spiritual health and well-being.

26.30 Frida Kahlo, *Thinking about Death*, 1943. Oil on canvas, mounted on masonite; 17½ × 14⅓ in. (44.5 × 36.3 cm). Private collection.

26.31 Frida Kahlo, *Marxism Will Give Health to the Sick*, 1954. © Fundación Dolores Olmedo.

Toward American Abstraction

Countering the Regional and Social Realist currents of Western art between the wars was the influence of the European avant-garde. A few private New York galleries, run by dealers who understood the significance of the new styles, began to exhibit "modern" art. In 1905, the American photographer Alfred Stieglitz (1864–1946) opened the 291 Art Gallery at 291 Fifth Avenue in New York, where he exhibited work by Rodin, Cézanne, the Cubists, and Brancusi along with that by more progressive American artists. The Museum of Modern Art, under the direction of Alfred Barr, Jr., opened in 1929, the year of the stock market crash. In 1930, Stieglitz opened the American Place Gallery to exhibit abstract art. Also during this period, government support for the arts was provided by the Federal Arts Project, which operated under the aegis of Franklin Roosevelt's social programs. The Project provided employment to thousands of artists and, in doing so, granted some measure of official status to abstract art.

26.32 Alfred Stieglitz, *Equivalent,* 1923. Chloride print; 4⅝ × 3⅝ in. (11.8 × 9.2 cm). Art Institute of Chicago (Alfred Stieglitz Collection). Stieglitz was born in Hoboken, New Jersey. He organized the 1902 exhibition that led to Photo-Secession, an informal group that held exhibitions all over the world and whose objective was to gain the status of a fine art for pictorial photography. In 1903, he founded the quarterly journal *Camera Work,* which encouraged modern aesthetic principles in photography.

Alfred Stieglitz

Stieglitz's photographs straddle the concerns of American Social Realism and avant-garde abstraction. Many of his pictures document contemporary society, while others are formal studies in abstraction. In 1922, he began a series of abstract photographs entitled *Equivalent* (fig. **26.32**), in which cloud formations create various moods and textures. Stieglitz believed in what is called "straight photography," as opposed to unusual visual effects achieved, among other means, by the manipulation of negatives and chemicals.

Edward Weston

The photography of Edward Weston (1886–1958) also transformed "straight" nature pictures into abstraction. His *Two Shells* (fig. **26.33**) of 1927, for example, shows the organic character of a chambered nautilus inside another shell. Of these, Weston wrote:

> One of these two new shells when stood on end is like a magnolia blossom unfolding. The difficulty has been to make it balance on end and not cut off that important end, nor show an irrelevant base. I may have solved the problem by using another shell for the chalice. . . .[11]

By virtue of the arrangement of the two shells, as well as the close-up viewpoint, Weston's image invites free association. The shells become more than shells as a result of the suggestive metaphorical character of their forms. Weston's transformations of natural shapes into associative abstraction—like those of Stieglitz—allied him with the early twentieth-century avant-garde.

26.33 Edward Weston, *Two Shells,* 1927. Photograph.

26.34 Arthur Dove, *Goin' Fishin'*, 1925. Mixed-media collage; 19½ × 24 in. (49.5 × 61.0 cm). Phillips Collection, Washington, D.C.

Arthur Dove

Another important figure in early American abstraction was Arthur Dove (1880–1946), who lived in Europe from 1907 to 1909. He had been influenced by Kandinsky's views of the spiritual in nature and exhibited in the 1913 Armory Show. His *Goin' Fishin'* of 1925 (fig. **26.34**) is a construction of fishing poles, pieces of denim, and slabs of bark. The poles are curved, forming an arch around the flatter denim and bark, which creates a structured, architectural image. At the same time, the use of objects that are associated with fishing infuses the work with a sense of the texture of boats, workers, and bamboo. In this work, Dove "Americanizes" the collage technique by his choice of objects and by the colloquial title. He also looks forward to the work of Robert Rauschenberg in the 1950s (see p. 933).

In *Fog Horns* (fig. **26.35**), painted four years later, Dove uses circular biomorphic forms to suggest sound waves traveling through space. The shapes of sound correspond to the round openings of the horns, while their decreasing size indicates temporal distance. The pastel colors and foggy atmosphere create a mood that can be related to the mysterious, poetic quality of certain Symbolist painters. It is typical of Dove that he used the sea to convey such moods, which have a Romantic as well as a Symbolist character.

26.35 Arthur Dove, *Fog Horns*, 1929. Oil on canvas; 18 × 26 in. (45.7 × 66.0 cm). Colorado Springs Fine Arts Center.

Georgia O'Keeffe

Georgia O'Keeffe (1887–1986), who was married to Stieglitz, is difficult to place within a specific stylistic category, but it is clear that she was influenced by photography and early twentieth-century abstraction as well as by the landscape of the American Southwest. She, along with Arthur Dove and other abstractionists, had exhibited at Stieglitz's 291 in the 1920s. Her *Black and White* of 1930 (fig. **26.36**) is an abstract depiction of various textures, motion, and form without any reference to recognizable objects. By eliminating color, O'Keeffe makes use of the same tonal range that is available to the black-and-white photographer.

In her *Cow's Skull with Calico Roses* of 1931 (fig. **26.37**), O'Keeffe depicts one of the desiccated skulls found in the dry deserts of Arizona and New Mexico. The close-up view abstracts the forms. With the accent of the black vertical and the horizontal of the horns, the image evokes the Crucifixion. At the same time, the death content of O'Keeffe's subject is softened by the roses, which are still alive. This juxtaposition of living and dead forms recalls the death and resurrection themes of Christian art, as well as being a feature of the desert. It also has a Surrealist quality.

26.36 Georgia O'Keeffe, *Black and White,* 1930. Oil on canvas; 36 × 24 in. (91.4 × 61.0 cm). Collection, Whitney Museum of American Art, New York (Gift of Mr. and Mrs. R. Crosby Kemper). O'Keeffe was born in Sun Prairie, Wisconsin. In 1917, Stieglitz gave O'Keeffe her first one-woman show at 291. She married Stieglitz in 1924 and after his death in 1946 moved permanently to New Mexico, where desert objects—animal bones, rocks, flowers—became favorite motifs in her work.

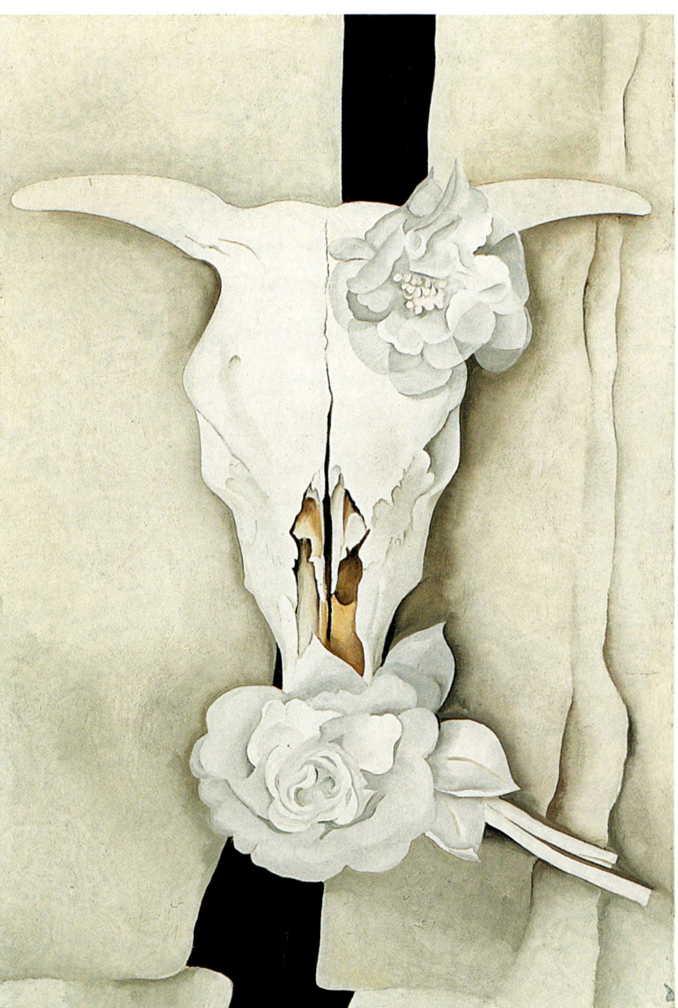

26.37 Georgia O'Keeffe, *Cow's Skull with Calico Roses,* 1931. Oil on canvas; 36 5/16 × 24 1/8 in. (92.2 × 61.3 cm). Art Institute of Chicago (Gift of Georgia O'Keeffe). In July 1931, O'Keeffe wrote from New Mexico to the art critic Henry McBride: "Attempting to paint landscape—I must think it important or I wouldn't work so hard at it—Then I see that the end of my studio is a large pile of bones—a horse's head—a cow's head—a calf's head—long bones—all sorts of funny little bones and big ones too—a beautiful ram's head has the center of the table—with a stone with a cross on it and an extra curly horn."[12]

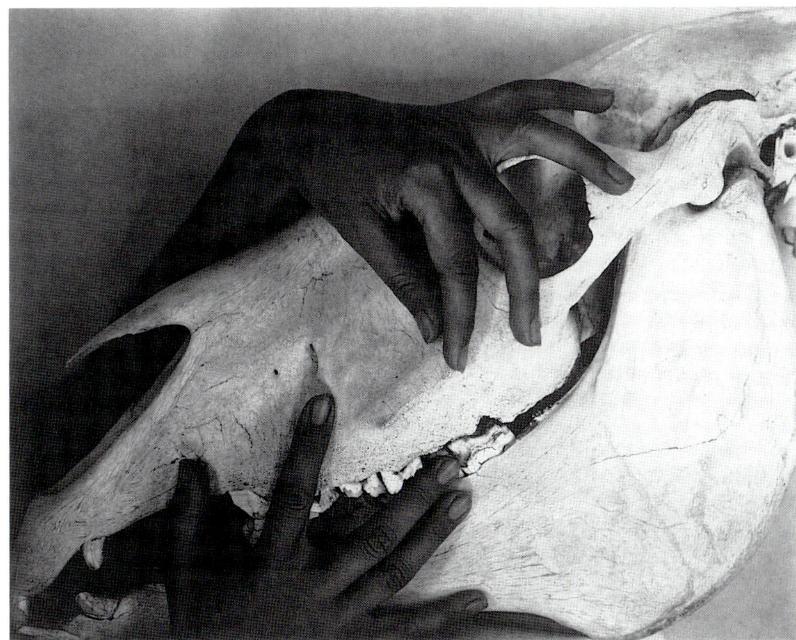

26.38 Alfred Stieglitz, *Georgia O'Keeffe: A Portrait: Hands and Bones (15)*, 1930. Silver-gelatin print, negative; 8 × 10 in. (20.3 × 25.4 cm). National Gallery of Art, Washington, D.C. (Alfred Stieglitz Collection).

Similar juxtapositions characterize Stieglitz's *Georgia O'Keeffe: A Portrait: Hands and Bones (15)* of the previous year (fig. **26.38**). In addition to the opposition of living and dead form, Stieglitz contrasts flesh with bone and soft texture with hardness. He made several "portraits" of Georgia O'Keeffe's hands—in this case, identifying them as hers by their connection with the animal skull. The close-up viewpoint, as well as the partial nature of the image, contributes to its abstraction.

Transcendental Painting

From 1938 to 1941, a unique group of avant-garde painters who were dedicated to the principles of abstraction was formed in New Mexico. These artists were inspired by the expanses of the southwestern landscape and by Kandinsky's *Concerning the Spiritual in Art.* In a brochure published by the group, they stated:

> Transcendental has been chosen as a name for this group because it best expresses its aim, which is to carry painting beyond the appearance of the physical world, through new concepts of space, color, light, and design, to imaginative realms that are idealistic and spiritual. The work does not concern itself with political, economic, or other social problems.[13]

The expression of these goals can be seen in the work of Agnes Pelton, who, like Dove, had participated in the Armory Show and exhibited at Stieglitz's gallery in New York. *The Fountains* of 1926 (fig. **26.39**) shows her use of soft color and expanding form to create an impression of otherworldly phenomena. The translucent character of the image and its flowing motion produce a mystical effect related to Transcendental notions of spirituality.

The Transcendental painters, along with Stieglitz, Dove, O'Keeffe, and other abstractionists, were among the most avant-garde artists of the early twentieth century in America. At that time, despite the Armory Show and other inroads made by the new European styles, art in the United States was still primarily conservative. It was not until the 1950s that American art finally emerged as the most innovative on an international scale.

26.39 Agnes Pelton, *The Fountains*, 1926. Oil on canvas; 36 × 31½ in. (91.4 × 80.0 cm). Collection of Georgia Riley de Havenon, New York.

American Self-Taught Painters

The United States has had a strong ongoing folk-art tradition. In the nineteenth century, folk sculpture included shop signs, carousel horses, weather vanes, ships' figureheads, carved gravestones, and cigar-store Indians. Folk art also includes quilts, embroidery, and painting, which have continued into the twenty-first century.

One of the best-known folk artists is Anna Mary Robertson (Grandma) Moses (1860–1961). She worked mainly in embroidery until she was in her seventies, when she turned to painting. Scenes such as *The Old Checkered House* of 1944 (fig. **26.40**) show the persistent appeal of styles that have not been modified by formal training.

Although Grandma Moses was self-taught, it is clear that the lively designs of embroidery provided her with a training of their own. Small patterns, particularly in the red and white squares of the house, recall those made by embroidered threads. Here they are flattened, as are the silhouetted horses, creating an impression of naiveté. But there is a convincing sense of three-dimensional space. The hills diminish in clarity as well as in size compared with the foreground forms, indicating a familiarity with both aerial and linear perspective. There is no suggestion here of the momentous international events of the period, no reference to American participation in World War II (then in its third year) or to industrialization. Instead, the scene evokes a past era of rural life, horse-drawn carriages, and soldiers of the American Civil War. The painting thus has a romantic, nostalgic quality.

26.40 Anna Mary Robertson (Grandma) Moses, *The Old Checkered House,* 1944. Oil on pressed wood; 24 × 43 in. (0.61 × 1.09 m). Seiji Togo Memorial Yasuda Kasai Museum of Art, Tokyo, Japan.

26.41 Horace Pippin, *Domino Players,* 1943. Oil on composition board; 12¾ × 22 in. (32.4 × 55.9 cm). Phillips Collection, Washington, D.C. Pippin lived in Pennsylvania. A veteran of World War I, in which he suffered a shoulder wound, he exercised his right arm by decorating cigar boxes with charcoal. In 1928, at the age of forty, he began working in oil paints, although he described himself as having been interested in pictures from his youth.

The self-taught African-American artist Horace Pippin (1888–1946) is best known for his domestic interiors, often evoking memories of his childhood. In *Domino Players* of 1943 (fig. **26.41**), he depicts three figures seated at a table playing dominoes. The two women seem intent on the game, but the boy—Pippin himself—is clearly bored. He gazes directly out of the picture, inviting viewers to identify with a child stuck in an adult setting. Behind the table, a grandmotherly figure sews a quilt. As in the work of Grandma Moses, Pippin's imagery has the appearance of folk art, emphasizing flat patterns—the dominoes, the polka-dot blouse, and the quilt. Likewise, seemingly casual details, such as the stove and the oil lamp, are reminiscent of another era.

	Style/Period	Works of Art	Cultural/Historical Developments
1900	DADA, SURREALISM, REGIONALISM, SOCIAL REALISM, AND ABSTRACTION	Hopi Black Ogre (**W12.3**) Hopi Butterfly Maiden (**W12.4**) Zuni war god (**26.10**) Mossi whistle (**26.17**)	
	1910–1920  **Duchamp, *L.H.O.O.Q.***	de Chirico, *Place d'Italie* (**26.7**) Arp, *Collage Arranged According to the Laws of Chance* (**26.4**) Duchamp, *Fountain* (*Urinal*) (**26.2**) Duchamp, *To Be Looked At* (*from the Other Side of the Glass*) *with One Eye, Close to, for Almost an Hour* (**26.3**) Duchamp, *L.H.O.O.Q.* (**26.1**) 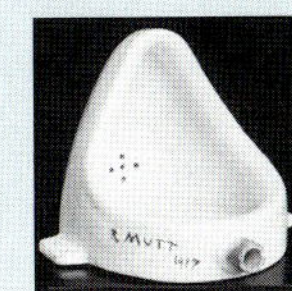 **Duchamp, *Fountain* (*Urinal*)**	World War I (1914–1918) Dada movement begins in Zurich (c. 1915) Franz Kafka, *The Metamorphosis* (1915) Harlem Renaissance (1919–1929) John Maynard Keynes, *The Economic Consequences of the Peace* (1919) Black migration to the northern U.S.A. (1920s) Gustav Holst, *The Planets* (1920) Hermann Rorschach develops the "inkblot" test (1920)
1920	1920–1930	Stieglitz, *Equivalent* (**26.32**) Man Ray, *Indestructible Object* (*or Object to Be Destroyed*) (**26.6**) Man Ray, *Le Violon d'Ingres* (**26.8**) Dove, *Goin' Fishin'* (**26.34**) Miró, *Dog Barking at the Moon* (**26.12**) Pelton, *The Fountains* (**26.39**) Weston, *Two Shells* (**26.33**) Magritte, *The False Mirror* (**26.14**) Arp, *The Dancer* (**26.5**) Dove, *Fog Horns* (**26.35**) Van Der Zee, *Portrait of Couple, Man with Walking Stick* (**26.26**) Adams, *Winnowing Grain, Taos Pueblo* (**W12.2**) Rivera, *Ancient Mexico* (**26.29**) **Man Ray, *Le Violon d'Ingres***	Revival of Ku Klux Klan in the American South (1920s) Nicola Sacco and Bartolomeo Vanzetti convicted of murder (1921) Foundation of British Broadcasting Corporation (1921) Sergei Prokofiev, *The Love for Three Oranges* (1921) John Dos Passos, *Three Soldiers* (1921) Ludwig Wittgenstein, *Tractatus Logico-Philosophicus* (1921) *Readers' Digest* founded (1922) A. E. Housman, *Last Poems* (1922) James Joyce, *Ulysses* (1922) Hermann Hesse, *Siddhartha* (1922) E. E. Cummings, *The Enormous Room* (1923) New Orleans–style jazz grows in popularity (1923) André Breton publishes first *Surrealist Manifesto* (1924) E. M. Forster, *A Passage to India* (1924) Sean O'Casey, *Juno and the Paycock* (1924) First Surrealist exhibition in Paris (1925) First edition of the *New Yorker* appears (1925) Scopes trial over teaching of evolution theory (1925) T. E. Lawrence, *The Seven Pillars of Wisdom* (1926) D. H. Lawrence, *Lady Chatterley's Lover* (1928) Jean Cocteau, *Les Enfants terribles* (1929)
1930	1930–1940  **Wood, *American Gothic***	O'Keeffe, *Black and White* (**26.36**) Wood, *American Gothic* (**26.23**) Stieglitz, *A Portrait (15)* (**26.38**) O'Keeffe, *Cow's Skull with Calico Roses* (**26.37**) Dali, *The Persistence of Memory* (**26.11**) Klee, *Mask of Fear* (**26.9**) Evans, *Shoeshine Sign in a Southern Town* (**26.27**) Magritte, *Time Transfixed* (*La Durée poignardée*) (**26.15**) Lawrence, *Harriet Tubman Series, No. 7* (**26.24**)	Social Realism in Russian art mandated by Stalin (1930s) Aldous Huxley, *Brave New World* (1932) Henry Miller, *Tropic of Cancer* (1934) George Gershwin, *Porgy and Bess* (1935) A. J. Ayer, *Language, Truth and Logic* (1936) John Steinbeck, *The Grapes of Wrath* (1939) World War II (1939–1945)
1940	1940–1950 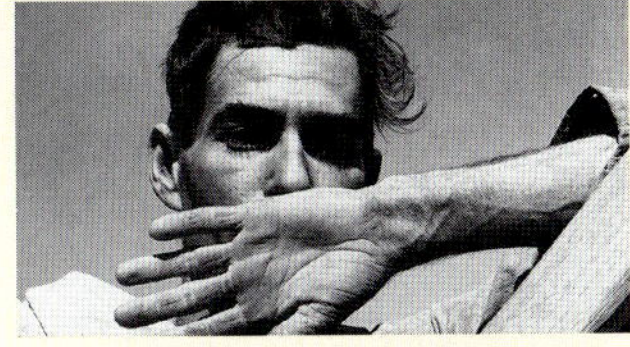 **Lange, *Migratory Cotton Picker***	Hopper, *Gas* (**26.25**) Lange, *Migratory Cotton Picker* (**26.28**) Pippin, *Domino Players* (**26.41**) Kahlo, *Thinking about Death* (**26.30**) Ernst, *The King Playing with the Queen* (**26.16**) Moses, *The Old Checkered House* (**26.40**) Miró, *Spanish Dancer* (**26.13**)	Eugene O'Neill, *Long Day's Journey into Night* (1940) Hemingway, *For Whom the Bell Tolls* (1940) Pearl Harbor attacked; United States enters war (1941) America drops atomic bombs on Japan (1945) Charles Ives wins Pulitzer Prize for Symphony No. 3 (1947) Founding of the State of Israel (1948) Birth of network television in U.S.A. (1949)
1950	1950–1960 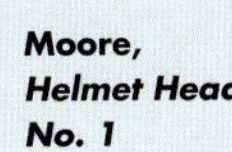 **Moore, *Helmet Head No. 1*** 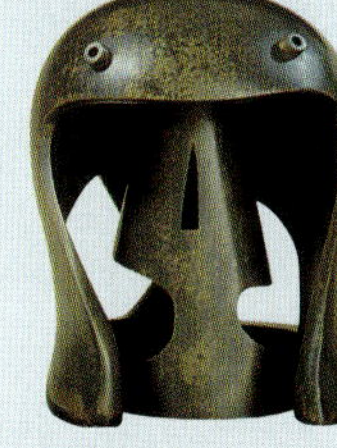	Moore, *Helmet Head No. 1* (**26.21**) Kahlo, *Marxism Will Give Health to the Sick* (**26.31**) Moore, *Reclining Figure* (**26.20**) Calder, *Big Red* (**26.22**) Giacometti, *Large Standing Woman III*, and Mondrian, *Composition with Red, Yellow, and Blue* (**26.19**)	Senator Joseph McCarthy begins Communist "witch hunt" in United States (1950) Korean War (1950–1953) *Playboy* and *TV Guide* begin publication (1953) J. R. R. Tolkien, *Lord of the Rings* (1955) Vladimir Nabokov, *Lolita* (1955) *Sputnik I* launched (1957) Creation of the European Common Market (1957) Chinua Achebe, *Things Fall Apart* (1958) New York's Guggenheim Museum opens (1959)

27

Abstract Expressionism

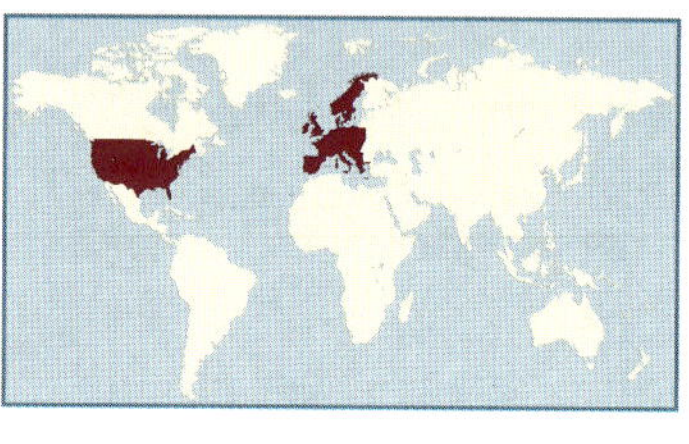

By the middle of the 1930s, the New York avant-garde was identified with abstraction, which paradoxically had emerged from the background of the more conservative Regionalism and Social Realism styles. Equally influential in the development of abstraction and the avant-garde was the influx of artists and intellectuals from overseas. In Europe during the 1930s, totalitarian leaders prevented artists from pursuing modernism on the grounds that it was degenerate and corrupted the moral fiber of the nation (see box). The waves of refugees who fled oppression and war during the last years of that decade, therefore, included many avant-garde architects, artists, musicians, and writers. By 1940, when Paris fell to the Nazis, the center of the art world had shifted to New York, whose cultural life was enriched by the émigré artists. Among the dealers and collectors who fled Europe was Peggy Guggenheim; in 1942, she opened the Art of This Century Gallery in New York, which exhibited avant-garde work.

The Teachers: Hans Hofmann and Josef Albers

Two of the most important emigrants from Germany were Hans Hofmann (1880–1966) and Josef Albers (1888–1976). They taught at the Art Students League in New York and at Black Mountain College in North Carolina, respectively, and from 1950 to 1960 Albers chaired the Department of Architecture and Design at Yale. Both Hofmann and Albers influenced a generation of American painters.

Hitler on "Degenerate Art"

On July 19, 1937, Hitler opened the first *Great German Art Exhibition* in Munich. He announced in his inaugural speech that he intended

> to clear out all the claptrap from artistic life in Germany. "Works of art" that are not capable of being understood in themselves but need some pretentious instruction book to justify their existence . . . will never again find their way to the German people. From now on, we are going to wage a merciless war of destruction against the last remaining elements of cultural disintegration.[1]

Hitler's notion of an aesthetic "clearing out" was similar to the Nazi "Final Solution," which was intended to purge Europe of Gypsies, Jews, homosexuals, the mentally sick, and liberal intellectuals. Modern music, architecture, films, and plays were declared subversive. In May 1933, "un-German" books were burned and virtually all avant-garde artists dismissed from their teaching positions. On July 20, 1937, an exhibition of over 650 works by artists such as Ernst, Kandinsky, Kirchner, Klee, and other members of the avant-garde opened, the purpose of which was to make an "example" of "degenerate art." A pamphlet accompanying the exhibition denounced the morals of certain modern artists, who were accused of viewing the world as a brothel inhabited by pimps and prostitutes. In an irony that was lost on the Nazi regime, the exhibition must have been one of the finest shows of avant-garde art that ever took place.

In June 1939, works by Gauguin, van Gogh, Braque, and Picasso were removed from German museums and auctioned to foreigners. Similar tendencies existed in other countries as well as in Germany. In France, non-French (especially Jewish) elements in the arts were eliminated by the pro-Nazi Vichy regime. In Russia, an exhibition held in Moscow in 1937 was aimed at discrediting the avant-garde.

Hofmann's *The Gate* (fig. **27.1**) is an architectural construction in paint. The intense, thickly applied color is arranged in squares and rectangles. It ranges from relatively pure hues, such as the yellow and red, to more muted greens and blues. For Hofmann, as for the Impressionists, it was the color in a picture that created light. In nature, the reverse is true; light makes color visible. In *The Gate*, edges vary from precise to textured. Everywhere, the paint is structured, combining bold, expressive color with the tectonic qualities of Cubism and related styles.

27.1 Hans Hofmann, *The Gate*, 1959–1960. Oil on canvas; 6 ft. 3⅛ in. × 4 ft. ½ in. (1.91 × 1.23 m). Solomon R. Guggenheim Museum, New York. For Hofmann, nature was the source of inspiration, and the artist's mind transformed nature into a new creation. "To me," he said, "a work is finished when all parts involved communicate themselves, so that they don't need me."[2]

27.2 Josef Albers, *Study for Homage to the Square*, 1968. Oil on masonite; 32 × 32 in. (81.3 × 81.3 cm). Photo courtesy of Carroll Janis, New York.

Albers's series of paintings entitled *Homage to the Square* (fig. **27.2**) also explores color and geometry. But his surfaces are smooth, and the medium is subordinate to the color relationships between the squares. In his investigation of light and color perception, Albers concentrated on the square because he believed that it was the shape furthest removed from nature. "Art," he said, "should not represent, but present."[3]

Abstract Expressionism: The New York School

Abstract Expressionism was a term used in 1929 by Alfred Barr, Jr. to refer to the nonfigurative and nonrepresentational paintings of Kandinsky. The style was to put the United States on the map of the international art world. In the 1950s, it was generally used to categorize the New York school of painters, which, despite its name, was actually comprised of artists from many different parts of the United States and Europe.

Nearly all the Abstract Expressionists had passed through a Surrealist phase. From this, they absorbed an interest in myths and dreams and in the effect of the unconscious on creativity. From Expressionism, they inherited an affinity for the expressive qualities of paint. This aspect emerged particularly in the so-called "Action" or "Gesture" painters of Abstract Expressionism.

Arshile Gorky

The Abstract Expressionist painter who was most instrumental in creating a transition from European Abstract Surrealism to American Abstract Expressionism was the Armenian Arshile Gorky (1904–1948). After absorbing several European styles, including Impressionism and Surrealism, he developed his own pictorial "voice" in the 1940s.

Some time between about 1926 and 1936, Gorky painted his famous work *The Artist and His Mother* (fig. **27.3**). The slightly geometric character of the faces suggests the influence of early Cubism. Flattened areas of color—the mother's lap, for example—and visible brushstrokes reveal affinities with Fauvism and Expressionism. To the left stands a rather wistful young Gorky. His more dominant mother recalls enthroned mother goddesses of antiquity (see fig. 6.8).

Gorky's painting was based on an old undated photograph of himself and his mother (fig. **27.4**). The grid (fig. **27.5**) dates to around 1936 and thus must have been made in preparation for the painting. Note that Gorky has eliminated the original pattern of his mother's dress and transformed his own coat and shoes into shapes of pure color.

Entirely different in form, though it shares the nostalgic quality of *The Artist and His Mother*, is *Garden in Sochi* of 1943 (fig. **27.6**). The third of a series depicting childhood recollections, this painting exemplifies Gorky's most characteristic innovations. Paint is applied thinly, and the colorful shapes are bounded by delicate curvilinear outlines, which create a sense of fluid motion. Both the title and the abstract biomorphic shapes suggest references to natural, organic protozoan or vegetable life. Gorky studied nature closely, sketching flowers, leaves, and grass from life before transforming the drawings into abstract forms. The suggestive, elusive identity of Gorky's shapes is reminiscent of Miró, who influenced Gorky's Surrealist phase.

Gorky related this series to a garden at Sochi on the Black Sea. He recalled porcupines and carrots and a blue rock buried in black earth with moss patches resembling fallen clouds. Village women rubbed their breasts on the rock—probably a fertility rite. Long shadows reminded the artist of the lances in the battle scenes of Uccello. Passersby tied colorful strips of clothing to a leafless tree, the fabric blowing in the wind like banners and rustling like leaves.

CONNECTIONS

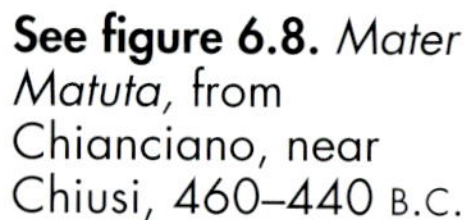

See figure 6.8. *Mater Matuta*, from Chianciano, near Chiusi, 460–440 B.C.

27.3 Arshile Gorky, *The Artist and His Mother*, c. 1926–1936. Oil on canvas; 5 ft. × 4 ft. 2 in. (1.52 × 1.27 m). Collection, Whitney Museum of American Art, New York (Gift of Julien Levy for Maro and Natasha Gorky). Gorky was born Vosdanig Manoog Adoian in Turkish Armenia and emigrated to the United States in 1920. At the height of his career, a series of misfortunes—a fire that burned most of his recent work, a cancer operation, a car crash that fractured his neck—led to his suicide in 1948.

27.4 Photographer unknown, *Arshile Gorky and His Mother,* n.d. Photograph.

27.5 Arshile Gorky, *Portrait of the Artist and His Mother,* 1926/1936. Graphite on squared paper; 24 × 19 in. (61.0 × 48.3 cm). National Gallery of Art, Washington, D.C. Ailsa Mellon Bruce Fund.

27.6 Arshile Gorky, *Garden in Sochi,* c. 1943. Oil on canvas; 31 × 39 in. (78.7 × 99.1 cm). Museum of Modern Art, New York (Acquired through the Lillie P. Bliss Bequest).

Art Critics and the Avant-Garde

Harold Rosenberg (1906–1978) and Clement Greenberg (1909–1994) were the two leading critics most closely associated with American Abstract Expressionism. In 1952, Rosenberg coined the term *Action painting* to describe the new techniques of applying paint. For American artists, he said, the canvas became "an arena in which to act—rather than . . . a space in which to reproduce. . . . What was to go on the canvas was not a picture but an event." Rather than begin a painting with a preconceived image, the Abstract Expressionists approached their canvases with the idea of doing something *to* it. "The image," wrote Rosenberg, "would be the result of this encounter."[4]

Greenberg took issue with Rosenberg's assessment on the grounds that painting thus became a private myth. Because such work did not resonate with a larger cultural audience, according to Greenberg, it could not be considered art. But he was nevertheless a staunch defender of abstraction, noting that subject matter had nothing to do with intrinsic value. "The explicit comment on a historical event offered in Picasso's *Guernica,*" he wrote in 1961, "does not make it necessarily a better or richer work than an utterly 'non-objective' painting by Mondrian."[5]

Greenberg described the shift in the artists' view of pictorial space as having "lost its 'inside' and become all 'outside.'" He surveyed this shift from the fourteenth century as follows:

> From Giotto to Courbet, the painter's first task had been to hollow out an illusion of three-dimensional space on a flat surface. One looked through this surface as through a proscenium into a stage. Modernism has rendered this stage shallower and shallower until now its backdrop has become the same as its curtain, which has now become all that the painter has left to work on.[6]

Action Painting

Just as brushstrokes are a significant aspect of Impressionism and Post-Impressionism, so the action painters developed characteristic methods of applying paint. They dripped, splattered, sprayed, rolled, and threw paint on their canvases, with the result that the final image reflects the artist's activity in the creative process (see box).

Jackson Pollock Of the "Action" or "Gesture" painters who were part of the New York school, the best-known is Jackson Pollock (1912–1956). He began as a Regionalist and turned to Surrealism in the late 1930s and early 1940s. His first paintings reflect the Regional style of his teacher, Thomas Hart Benton (1889–1975), at the Art Students League in New York. *Going West* (fig. **27.7**), which Pollock painted in the 1930s, is typical of Regionalism in that it can be identified with a specific American region. Settlers traveling in covered wagons and the stark landscape evoke the pioneering spirit of the Old West. The curves in the landscape enclose the figures, who seem to struggle through a cavernous space toward their destination. Curvilinear rhythms dominate the picture and look forward to Pollock's mature abstract style.

27.7 Jackson Pollock, *Going West,* 1934–1935. Oil on gesso ground on composition board; 15⅜ × 20⅞ in. (39.1 × 53.0 cm). Smithsonian Institution, Washington, D.C. Pollock, born in Wyoming, moved to New York in 1929. He worked for the Federal Arts Project and had his first one-man show in 1943 at Peggy Guggenheim's Art of This Century Gallery. In 1956, he died in a car accident in East Hampton, Long Island.

Guardians of the Secret (fig. **27.8**) is from Pollock's period of Surrealist abstraction. A series of thickly painted rectangles enlivened by energetic curves and zigzags recalls the spontaneous character of graffiti. The painting's linear quality is also reminiscent of graffiti and suggests the signs of a hidden and unintelligible language. The apparent spontaneity of Pollock's "signs" can be related to Surrealist automatic writing as a means of gaining access to the unconscious.

From 1947 onward, Pollock used a **drip technique** to produce his most celebrated pictures, in which he engaged his whole body in the act of painting. From cans of commercial housepainter's paint, enamel, and aluminum, Pollock dripped paint from the end of a stick or brush directly onto a canvas spread on the ground. In so doing, he achieved some of the chance effects sought by the Dada and Surrealist artists. At the same time, however, he controlled the placement of the drips and splatters through

27.8 Jackson Pollock, *Guardians of the Secret,* 1943. Oil on canvas; 4 ft. ⅜ in. × 6 ft. 3⅜ in. (1.23 × 1.91 m). San Francisco Museum of Modern Art, California (Albert M. Bender Collection, Albert M. Bender Bequest Fund Purchase). Pollock's interest in Surrealism, unconscious processes, and myth, which is apparent in this painting, led him to undertake Jungian psychoanalysis.

the motion of his arm and body (fig. 27.9a, b). He described this process as follows: "On the floor I am more at ease. I feel nearer, more a part of the painting, since this way I can walk around it, work from the four sides and literally be *in* the painting. This is akin to the Indian sand painters of the West" (see box). Pollock also declared that, when in the process of painting, he was unaware of his actions: "When I am *in* my painting, I'm not aware of what I'm doing . . . because the painting has a life of its own."[7]

27.9a Hans Namuth, *Jackson Pollock Painting*, 1950. Photograph. Center for Creative Photography, University of Arizona.

27.9b Hans Namuth, *Jackson Pollock Painting*, 1950. Color stills from a film strip. Museum of Modern Art, New York.

Navajo Sand Painting

Pollock's "Indian sand painters" were the Navajo, who led a nomadic existence in the American Southwest. They made paintings out of crushed colored rocks, which were ground to the consistency of sand. These were the sacred products of a medicine man, or shaman, who created images in order to exorcise the evil spirits of disease from a sick person. He continued to make the pictures until the patient either died or recovered. Then the image was destroyed, usually at night, and its effect dissipated.

According to Navajo belief, humans had been preceded by Holy People who created sacred images in nature. These images became a medium of communication between the human and spirit worlds. For the Navajo, sand paintings provide a means of summoning the assistance of the Holy People in order to restore the spiritual and physical balance of a sick person. Typically the patient sits inside the painting and faces east, the direction from which the Holy People enter the image. As a result, the Navajo refer to sand paintings as *iikaah*, or "the place to which gods come and from which they go."

Figure **27.10** shows a modern sand painter at work, his image not yet complete. Figure **27.11** is a sand painting of a yei god (a lesser Navajo deity). Its frontal stance, stylized, figurative character, geometric forms, and clear outlines are unlike anything in Pollock's work. Figure 27.10 also differs from Pollock's all-over drips in its flattened perspective and discrete zones of color. His interest was in energetic execution and the artist's movement around the image on the ground. It is also likely that Pollock was drawn to the shamanistic character of the medicine man and that he identified with the notion that images have curative power.

27.10 Navajo man creating a sand painting.

27.11 Yei god, sand painting, 20th century. Navajo Indian Reservation.

Pollock's *White Light* of 1954 (fig. **27.12**) eliminates all reference to recognizable objects. Lines of different widths and textures swirl through the picture space and are slashed diagonally at various points. There is an underlying chromatic organization of yellows and oranges blending with, and crisscrossed by, thick blacks and whites. The white, as indicated by the title, is what predominates, and the intensity of Pollock's light is everywhere present. His habit of trimming his finished canvases enhances their dynamic quality, for the lines appear to move rhythmically in and out of the picture, unbound by either an edge or a frame, as if self-propelled.

27.12 Jackson Pollock, *White Light,* 1954. Oil, enamel, and aluminum paint on canvas; $48\frac{1}{4} \times 38\frac{1}{4}$ in. (122.4×96.9 cm). Museum of Modern Art, New York (Sidney and Harriet Janis Collection). Pollock first exhibited paintings such as this in 1948 to a shocked public. A critic for *Time* magazine dubbed him "Jack the Dripper," but avant-garde critics came to his defense. Within a few years of his death, he was the most widely exhibited of all the artists of the New York school.

Franz Kline The dynamic energy of Pollock's monumental drip paintings is virtually unmatched, even among the Abstract Expressionist Action painters. But Franz Kline (1910–1962) achieved dynamic imagery through thick, bold strokes of paint slashing across the picture plane. He had his first one-man show in New York in 1950, by which time he had renounced figuration and begun working on his characteristic black and white canvases. *Mahoning* of 1956 (fig. **27.13**) is a typical example. Strong black diagonals are created by the wide brush of a housepainter and form a kind of "structured" calligraphy. The blacks have an (angular) architectural appearance, but they tilt, like beams about to collapse. Drips and splatters enhance the textured quality of the surface.

27.13 Franz Kline, *Mahoning,* 1956. Oil and paper collage on canvas; 6 ft. 8 in. × 8 ft. 4 in. (2.03 × 2.54 m). Whitney Museum of American Art, New York (Purchase, funds from friends of Whitney Museum of American Art).

27.14 Willem de Kooning, *Woman and Bicycle*, 1952–1953. Oil on canvas; 6 ft. 4½ in. × 4 ft. 1 in. (1.94 × 1.25 m). Collection, Whitney Museum of American Art, New York (Purchase).

Willem de Kooning De Kooning (1904–1997) was born in Rotterdam and emigrated to the United States in 1926, but did not have his first one-man show until 1948. He described his relationship to twentieth-century art as follows: "Of all movements, I like Cubism most. It had that wonderful unsure atmosphere of reflection . . . and then there is that one-man movement: Marcel Duchamp—for me a truly modern movement because it implies that each artist can do what he thinks he ought to—a movement for each person and open for everybody."[8]

In the work of Willem de Kooning, Action painting is used in the service of explicit aggression and violence. This is particularly true of the series of pictures of women that de Kooning painted in the early 1950s. Unlike Pollock and Kline, de Kooning only partially eliminated recognizable subject matter from his iconography. *Woman and Bicycle* of 1952–1953 (fig. **27.14**), for example, combines the frontal image of a large, frightening woman with aggressive brushstrokes that literally tear through the figure's outline. The anxiety created by the woman's appearance—huge staring eyes, a double set of menacing teeth, and platformlike breasts, which reveal the influence of Cubist geometry—matches the frenzy of the brushstrokes. The assault on the figure, which disintegrates into unformed paint, is also an attack on the idealized Classical image of female beauty.

27.15 Helen Frankenthaler, *The Bay,* 1963. Acrylic on canvas; 6 ft. 8¾ in. × 6 ft. 9¾ in. (2.05 × 2.12 m). Collection, Detroit Institute of Arts (Gift of Dr. and Mrs. Hilbert H. DeLawter).

Helen Frankenthaler Helen Frankenthaler (born 1928), another Action painter, used synthetic media (see box) to "stain" her canvas by pouring paint directly onto it. In 1952, she visited Pollock in his studio in the Springs, on eastern Long Island, with the critic Clement Greenberg. There she saw the effect of Pollock's paint on unprimed canvas, which revealed the staining process—a method that is basic to Color Field painting (see below). *The Bay* of 1963 (fig. **27.15**) is made of thinned paint poured on to the canvas in layers of color, engulfing the picture plane. The colors are delicate and, for the most part, pastel. The blue expands over the canvas, like water filling the recess in the yellow and green areas of color. We seem to be looking down on a body of water in a landscape.

Color Field Painting

At the opposite pole from the Action painters are the artists who applied paint in a more traditional way. This has been variously referred to as *Chromatic Abstraction* and *Color Field painting.* The latter term refers to the preference for expanses of color applied to a flat surface in contrast to the domination of line in Action painting. The imagery of Action painting is more in tune with Picasso and Expressionism. Color Field painters, by contrast, were influenced by Matisse's broad planes of color. Compared with Action paintings, Color Field imagery is typically calm and inwardly directed and is capable of evoking a meditative, even spiritual, response.

Acrylic

One of the most popular of the modern synthetic media is **acrylic,** a water-based paint. Acrylic comes in bright colors, dries quickly, and does not fade. It can be applied to paper, canvas, and board with either traditional brushes or **airbrushes.** It can be poured, dripped, and splattered. When thick, acrylic approaches the texture of oils. When thinned, it is fluid like water paint. In contrast to water paint, however, which mixes when more than one wet color is applied, acrylic can be applied in layers which do not blend even when wet. It is possible to build up several layers of paint, which retain their individual hues, and thus to create a structure of pure color—as Frankenthaler does in *The Bay* (see fig. 27.15).

Mark Rothko One of the most important Color Field artists, Mark Rothko (1903–1970) had gone through a Surrealist phase and was engaged in the search for universal symbols, which he believed were accessible through myths and dreams. His *Baptismal Scene* of 1945 (fig. **27.16**) conveys the sense of a preverbal, aquatic world. Delicate protozoan forms that elude identification swirl weightlessly in various directions, and the amoeba-like biomorphs seem to exist below the surface of consciousness. By the 1950s, Rothko had developed his most original style. Totally nonfigurative and nonrepresentational, Rothko's paintings are images of large rectangles hovering in fields of color.

In *Number 15* of 1957 (fig. **27.17**), two black-green rectangles occupy an intense, vibrant blue. Above and below the larger rectangle is a thinner bar of green. The blue background appears to be suffused into the greens and blacks, producing a shimmering, textured quality that infiltrates the overall impression of darkness. By muting the colors and blurring the edges of the rectangles, Rothko softens the potential contrast between them. He likewise mutes the observer's "attention to the "process" of painting by nearly eliminating the presence of the artist's hand.

In the absence of references to the natural world as well as to the creative process, Rothko attempted to transcend material reality. His pictures seem to have no context in time or space. The weightless quality of his rectangles is enhanced by their blurred edges and thin textures, which

27.16 Mark Rothko, *Baptismal Scene,* 1945. Watercolor; 19⅞ × 14 in. (50.4 × 35.5 cm). Whitney Museum of American Art, New York (Purchase).

27.17 Mark Rothko, *Number 15,* 1957. Oil on canvas; 103 × 116½ in. (2.62 × 2.96 m). Collection of Christopher Rothko. Rothko was born in Latvia. In 1913, his family immigrated to Portland, Oregon, and in 1923 he moved to New York.

allow the underlying blue to filter through them. Whereas Pollock's light moves exuberantly across the picture plane, weaving in and out of the colors in the form of white drips, Rothko's light is luminescent. It flickers at the edges of the rectangles and shifts mysteriously from behind and in front of them.

Rothko suffered from depression and committed suicide in 1970. He expressed his alienation from society as follows: "The unfriendliness of society to his [the artist's] activity is difficult . . . to accept. Yet this very hostility can act as a lever for true liberation. . . . The sense of community and of security depends on the familiar. Free of them, transcendental experiences become possible."[9] Rothko's striving for freedom from the familiar is evident in the absence of recognizable forms in paintings such as this one.

Ad Reinhardt Even more luminous are the late Color Field paintings of Ad (Adolph) Reinhardt (1913–1967). The longer one stares at these pictures, the stronger is the sense of light shimmering and glowing behind the paint. Reinhardt's stated intention was to avoid all association with nature. He wanted the viewer to focus on the painting as an experience in itself—distinct from other, more familiar experiences. In his series of black paintings dating from the 1960s (fig. **27.18**), Reinhardt comes close to his aim. Color is eliminated, and nine squares of dark gray and black fill the picture plane.

27.18 Adolph (Ad) Reinhardt, *Abstract Painting* (*Black*), 1965. Oil on canvas; 5 × 5 ft. (1.52 × 1.52 m). Tate Gallery, London.

27.19 Frank Stella, *Empress of India,* 1965. Metallic powder in polymer emulsion paint on canvas; 6 ft. 5 in. × 18 ft. 8 in. (1.96 × 5.69 m). Museum of Modern Art, New York (Gift of S. I. Newhouse, Jr.).

Frank Stella Frank Stella (born 1936) was trained in art during the heyday of the New York school of Abstract Expressionism, but he paints with a new vision of color and form. His early somber, largely monochrome pictures were indebted to the reductive art of Reinhardt and departed from the traditional square, rectangle, or circle. They are fitted into triangular, star-shaped, zigzag, and open rectangular frames—for example, in his *Empress of India* of 1965 (fig. **27.19**). By varying the shape of the canvas, Stella focused on presenting a picture as an object-in-itself. Within the picture, he painted stripes of flat color, separated from each other and bordered by a precise edge. This technique is sometimes referred to as Hard Edge painting.

Tahkt-i-Sulayman I of 1967 (fig. **27.20**) belongs to Stella's *Protractor Series,* in which arcs intersect as if drawn with a compass. Here, a central circle is divided into two semicircles, which are repeated symmetrically on either side by flanking semicircles. These forms are related by sweeping curves, which interlace with all three sections in a continuous, interlocking motion. The intense, bright color strips in Stella's paintings of the 1960s combine dynamic exuberance with geometric control. Since the 1960s, Stella has continued to expand his repertory of shapes, formats, colors, and textures. He has evolved from early reductive clarity to complex, often very colorful, three-dimensional wall sculptures of varying textures and materials.

27.20 Frank Stella, *Tahkt-i-Sulayman I,* 1967. Polymer and fluorescent paint on canvas; 10 ft. ¼ in. × 20 ft. 2¼ in. (3.05 × 6.15 m). Menil Collection, Houston, Texas. Stella has lived and worked in New York since 1958. The Near Eastern title of this painting indicates his interest in colorful Islamic patterns (which also influenced Matisse). The interlaced color strips reflect his study of Hiberno-Saxon designs.

Ellsworth Kelly Ellsworth Kelly (born 1923) is another leading Hard-Edge Color Field painter who works in the tradition of Josef Albers. His color is generally vibrant and arranged in large, flattened planes that sometimes seem to expand organically. In other instances—as in *Spectrum III* (fig. **27.21**)—bands of color create a sequence of visual movement through the spectrum. By aligning the colors in this way, Kelly produces a tactile effect, despite the absence of modeling. The sequential arrangement of the rich hues causes a buildup of tension that proceeds through a progression of color.

In 1990, the Sidney Janis Gallery in New York mounted an exhibition entitled *Classic Modernism: Six Generations.* Figure **27.22** is a view of the installation, with Mondrian's *Trafalgar Square* of 1939 on the left and Ellsworth Kelly's *Red, Yellow, Blue* of 1965 on the right. This juxtaposition illustrates the relationship between Kelly's pure primary colors, unframed and juxtaposed with the stark white wall of the gallery, and Mondrian's rectangles of color bounded by firm black verticals and horizontals. Kelly has enlarged the rectangles by comparison with Mondrian and liberated the color from Mondrian's black "frames." By organizing the two paintings in this way, the gallery shows Mondrian's historical role as the link between Cubism and Color Field painting.

27.21 Ellsworth Kelly, *Spectrum III*, 1967. Oil on canvas; in 13 parts; overall 9 ft. ⅝ in. × 2 ft. 9¼ in. (2.76 × 0.84 m). Collection of Anne and John Marion in Fort Worth, Texas.

27.22 Installation view of *Classic Modernism: Six Generations*. On right: Ellsworth Kelly, *Red, Yellow, Blue*, 1965. Oil on canvas; 6 ft. 10 in. × 15 ft. 5 in. (2.08 × 4.70 m). On left: Piet Mondrian, *Trafalgar Square*, 1939–1943. Oil on canvas, 57¼ × 47¼ in. (1.45 × 1.2 m). Exhibition held Nov. 15–Dec. 19, 1990, at the Sidney Janis Gallery, New York. Photo courtesy of Carroll Janis, New York. © Ellsworth Kelly. © 2006 Mondrian/Holtzman Trust c/o HCR International, Warrenton, VA, USA.

West Coast Abstraction: Richard Diebenkorn

An important group of abstract painters also developed on the West Coast. It includes Richard Diebenkorn (1922–1993), whose early landscapes were often based on views of the San Francisco Bay area, and of anonymous, isolated figures reminiscent of Hopper in mysterious, architectural settings. By the end of the 1960s, however, Diebenkorn had replaced figuration with nonfigurative abstraction, building up layers of textured geometric shapes defined by straight lines.

Diebenkorn's monumental *Ocean Park* series (1970s–1980s) suggests the open spaces of the American West and the vast expanse of the Pacific Ocean. Most of his paintings contain a dominant horizontal, suggestive of landscape. The colors of *Ocean Park No. 129* of 1984 (fig. **27.23**), for example, evoke the blue sea, while above the horizon is a narrow strip of abstract patches of color bounded by horizontals and diagonals. Despite the evident influence of Matisse and Cubism on Diebenkorn's vision, the strict geometry of the forms is relieved by the drips and paint texture, which relates his work to Abstract Expressionism.

27.23 Richard Diebenkorn, *Ocean Park No. 129,* 1984. Oil on canvas; 5 ft. 6 in. × 6 ft. 9 in. (1.68 × 2.06 m). Private collection. © Estate of Richard Diebenkorn. Courtesy Greenberg Van Doren Gallery.

Figurative Abstraction in Europe

Jean Dubuffet

During the 1950s, when American Abstract Expressionism was at its height, a more figurative kind of Expressionism developed in Europe. The French artist Jean Dubuffet (1901–1985) was fascinated by the art of non-Western cultures, of children and the insane, as well as by graffiti and the self-taught painters. He amassed a significant collection of such work, which he believed would provide a route to unconscious sources of creativity. The influence of these styles pervades his own paintings. Dubuffet's early canvases are thickly textured, dark, and often built up with granular materials such as sand. They tend to be muddy—composed mainly of browns and blacks—and to convey the rough textures of walls, doors, and pavements.

In the 1960s, Dubuffet's style changed radically, becoming more colorful and composed of lively, linear patterns. *The Reveler* of 1964 (fig. **27.24**) is a typical example of what Dubuffet called *L'Hourloupe*—his "Twenty-third period." It shows his use of animated, biomorphic form, which is generally outlined in pure hues of red and blue. The labyrinthine and doodle-like paths of line impart a quality of frenetic motion to Dubuffet's figure. This feature of his Twenty-third period is reminiscent of certain figures from Papua New Guinea (fig. **27.25**) and shows the influence of the art he collected. Dubuffet's lines also suggest the spontaneous character of Surrealist "automatic writing." Different as this style is from his early work, the scratchy quality of the lines and colored shapes maintains the emphasis on textured surfaces.

27.24 Jean Dubuffet, *The Reveler*, 1964. Oil on base of black acrylic; 6 ft. 4¼ in. × 4 ft. 3¾ in. (1.94 × 1.31 m). Dallas Museum of Art, Texas (Gift of Mr. and Mrs. James H. Clark).

27.25 Spirit figure from Wapo Creek, Papua New Guinea. Painted wood and shell; 25 in. (63.5 cm) high. Friede Collection, New York.

Francis Bacon

In England, the work of Francis Bacon (1909–1992) comprises an entirely different kind of figurative Expressionism. His *Portrait of Isabel Rawsthorne Standing in a Street in Soho* (fig. **27.26**) makes the transformation of figures into paint a subject in itself. This is reflected in Bacon's statement of 1952:

> It is in the search for the technique to trap the object at a given moment. The technique and the object become inseparable. The object is the technique and the technique is the object. Art lies in the continual struggle to come near to the sensory side of objects.[10]

When form becomes unformed color, as in the right shoe, the effect is less disturbing than in the face. There the features swivel into distortion and the mouth seems ripped open. Bacon thus confronts the viewer with a partially flayed head that is nevertheless alive and in motion. His forms simultaneously stretch and contract, are at once clear and blurred, appealing and repulsive. They are uniquely powerful in their manner of seeming to dissolve into, and emerge from, the paint itself—not through the prominent brushstrokes of Impressionism, but by the personal, determined aggression of the artist.

27.26 Francis Bacon, *Portrait of Isabel Rawsthorne Standing in a Street in Soho*, 1967. Oil on canvas; 6 ft. 6 in. × 4 ft. 10 in. (1.98 × 1.47 m). Staatliche Museen, Berlin.

Sculpture

Contemporary with the above developments in American and European painting were several sculptors whose work conveys a dynamic abstraction akin to both Abstract and Figurative Expressionism.

Isamu Noguchi

The *Kouros* (fig. **27.27**), by the Japanese-American Isamu Noguchi (1904–1988) contains biomorphic shapes like those of Miró and Gorky. Flat, protozoan forms are arranged in interlocking horizontal and vertical planes, creating a configuration that, the artist claimed, "defies gravity." Although it conforms to the principles of twentieth-century abstraction, Noguchi's figure shares a vertical stance—softened by curvilinear stylization—with the Archaic Greek *kouros* (see fig. 5.19).

Noguchi was born in Los Angeles in 1904 to an American mother and a Japanese father. He grew up in Japan and was a premedical student at Columbia University (1921–1924). He decided to become a sculptor and worked with Brancusi, whose influences can be seen in the smooth surfaces and elegant forms of the *Kouros*. In addition to sculpture, Noguchi has produced furniture and stage designs, public sculpture gardens, and playgrounds.

CONNECTIONS

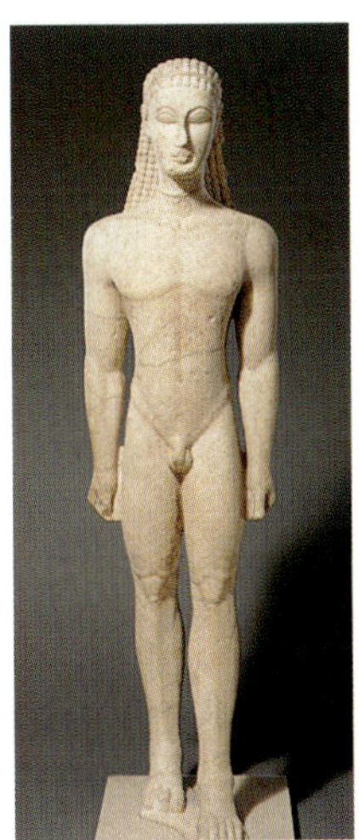

See figure 5.19.
New York Kouros, from Attica, c. 600 B.C.

27.27 Isamu Noguchi, *Kouros*, 1944–1945. Pink marble, slate base; 9 ft. 9 in. (2.97 m) high. Metropolitan Museum of Art, New York (Fletcher Fund, 1953).

David Smith

Shapes and lines combine with open space in the sculpture of David Smith (1906–1965). Smith welded iron and steel to produce a dynamic form of sculptural abstraction. His last great series of work, entitled *Cubi* (fig. **27.28**), is composed of cylinders, cubes, and solid rectangles. As both the title and the shapes indicate, Smith was influenced by Cubism. The works were intended to be installed outdoors (as in the illustration), their open spaces making it possible to experience the landscape through and around them. The surface, enlivened by variations of texture, contributes to the sense of planar motion in the individual shapes.

27.28 David Smith, *Cubi XXVII*, 1965. Polished stainless steel; 111⅜ × 87¾ × 34 in. Solomon R. Guggenheim Museum. By exchange.

Louise Nevelson

Louise Nevelson (1900–1988) made assemblages consisting of "found objects"—especially furniture parts and carpentry tools—placed inside open boxes. The boxes are piled on top of each other and arranged along a wall, much like bookshelves, so that they are seen, like paintings, from only one side. Typical of these works is *Black Wall* of 1959 (fig. **27.29**), in which the framing device of the boxes orders the assembled objects. Although originally utilitarian in nature, the objects become abstractions by virtue of their arrangement. Further abstracting the assemblage from everyday experience is the fact that the work is monochrome. As a result, the variety of shape and line takes precedence over the absence of color.

Many American Abstract Expressionists—some of whom have been illustrated in this chapter—worked beyond the 1950s, when the novelty and excitement of the style was at its height. In painting, Abstract Expressionism can be seen as a logical development of the Impressionist attention to the medium of paint. Brushstrokes became part of the critical vocabulary of Impressionism, Post-Impressionism, Fauvism, and the different forms of Expressionism. With the gestural Abstract Expressionists, paint and the way it behaved sometimes replaced narrative content entirely, emerging finally as the "subject" of painting. In sculpture as well, the texture of the medium became an increasingly significant feature of the work.

27.29 Louise Nevelson, *Black Wall*, 1959. Gilded wood; 9 ft. 4 in. × 7 ft. 1¼ in. (2.64 × 2.17 m). Tate Gallery, London.

	Style/Period	Works of Art	Cultural/Historical Developments
		Yei god, Navajo sand painting (**27.11**) Wapo Creek spirit figure (**27.25**)	
1920	ABSTRACT EXPRESSIONISM AND COLOR FIELD 1920–1940	Gorky, *The Artist and His Mother* (**27.3–27.5**) Pollock, *Going West* (**27.7**) Mondrian, *Trafalgar Square* (**27.22**)	Emigration of Bauhaus artists to the U.S.A. (late 1930s) World War II (1939–1945) *Gone with the Wind* wins Oscar for Best Picture (1939)
1940	1940–1950 **Gorky, *The Artist and His Mother***  **Arshile Gorky and His Mother**	Pollock, *Guardians of the Secret* (**27.8**) Gorky, *Garden in Sochi* (**27.6**) Noguchi, *Kouros* (**27.27**) Rothko, *Baptismal Scene* (**27.16**) 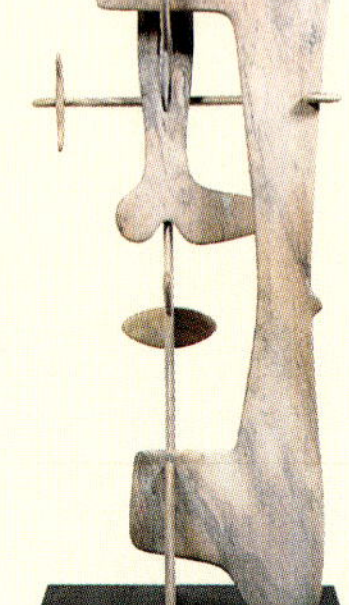 **Noguchi, *Kouros***	Graham Greene, *The Power and the Glory* (1940) Edmund Wilson, *To the Finland Station* (1940) Penicillin developed as an antibiotic (1940) Japan attacks Pearl Harbor; U.S.A. enters war (1941) Albert Camus, *L'Étranger* (1942) Aaron Copland, *Rodeo* (1942) Art of This Century art gallery opens (1942) Rodgers and Hammerstein, *Oklahoma!* (1943) Jean-Paul Sartre, *L'Être et le néant* (1943) Atomic bomb dropped on Hiroshima (1945) Establishment of United Nations (1945) Beginning of the Cold War (1945) Benjamin Britten, *Peter Grimes* (1945) India achieves independence from British rule (1947) Tennessee Williams, *A Streetcar Named Desire* (1947) Nation of Israel established (1948) Alan Paton, *Cry, The Beloved Country* (1948) People's Republic of China established (1949)
1950	1950–1960  **Pollock, *White Light***  **Hofmann, *The Gate***	Namuth, *Jackson Pollock Painting* (**27.9**) de Kooning, *Woman and Bicycle* (**27.14**) Pollock, *White Light* (**27.12**) Kline, *Mahoning* (**27.13**) Rothko, *Number 15* (**27.17**) Nevelson, *Black Wall* (**27.29**) Hofmann, *The Gate* (**27.1**)  **de Kooning, *Woman and Bicycle***  **Kelly, *Spectrum III***	Korean War (1950–1953) John Van Druten, *I Am a Camera* (1951) James Jones, *From Here to Eternity* (1951) J. D. Salinger, *Catcher in the Rye* (1951) Samuel Beckett, *Waiting for Godot* (1952) J. D. Watson and F. H. C. Crick describe the double-helix structure of DNA (1953) Arthur Miller, *A View from the Bridge* (1953) Vladimir Nabokov, *Lolita* (1955) Ingmar Bergman, *The Seventh Seal* (1956) Leonard Bernstein, *West Side Story* (1957) Boris Pasternak, *Dr. Zhivago* (1958) Truman Capote, *Breakfast at Tiffany's* (1958) Eugène Ionesco, *Rhinocéros* (1959)  **Rothko, *Number 15***
1960 1990	1960–1990  **Stella, *Tahkt-i-Sulayman I***	Frankenthaler, *The Bay* (**27.15**) Dubuffet, *The Reveler* (**27.24**) Kelly, *Red, Yellow, Blue* (**27.22**) Stella, *Empress of India* (**27.19**) Reinhardt, *Abstract Painting (Black)* (**27.18**) Smith, *Cubi XXVII* (**27.28**) Stella, *Tahkt-i-Sulayman I* (**27.20**) Kelly, *Spectrum III* (**27.21**) Bacon, *Portrait of Isabel Rawsthorne Standing in a Street in Soho* (**27.26**) Albers, *Study for Homage to the Square* (**27.2**) Diebenkorn, *Ocean Park No. 129* (**27.23**)	Harper Lee, *To Kill a Mockingbird* (1960) Construction of the Berlin Wall (1961) Joseph Heller, *Catch-22* (1961) First U.S. intervention in Vietnam (1962) James Baldwin, *Another Country* (1962) President John F. Kennedy assassinated (1963) The Beatles, "I Want to Hold Your Hand" (1964) Entire genetic code decoded (1966) Harold Pinter, *The Homecoming* (1967) Martin Luther King, Jr., assassinated (1968) James D. Watson, *The Double Helix* (1968) *Apollo II* lands on the moon (1969)

28

Pop Art, Op Art, Minimalism, and Conceptualism

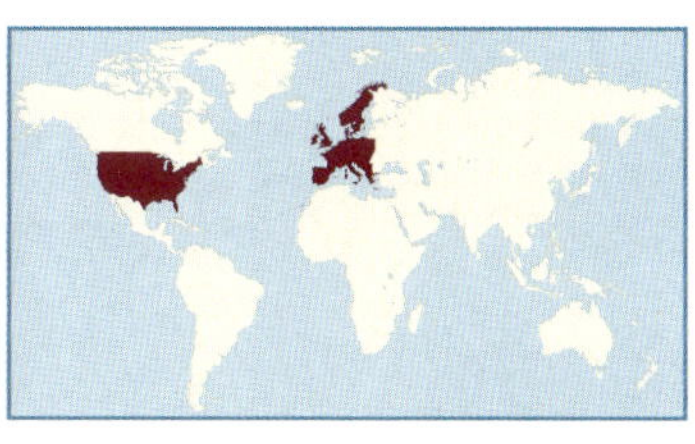

In the late 1950s and 1960s, a reaction against the nonfigurative and seemingly egocentric character of Abstract Expressionism took the form of a return to the object. The most prominent style to emerge in the United States in the 1960s was "Pop," although the origins of the style are to be found in England in the 1950s. The popular imagery of Pop Art was derived from commercial sources, the mass media, and everyday life. In contrast to Abstract Expressionist subjectivity—which viewed the work of art as a revelation of the artist's unconscious mind—the Pop artists strove for an "objectivity" embodied by an imagery of objects. What contributed to the special impact of Pop Art was the mundane character of the objects selected. As a result, Pop Art was regarded by many as an assault on accepted conventions and aesthetic standards.

Despite the 1960s emphasis on the objective "here and now," however, the artists of that period were not completely detached from historical influences or psychological expression. The elevation of everyday objects to the status of artistic imagery, for example, can be traced to the early twentieth-century taste for "found objects" and assemblage. Likewise, the widespread incorporation of letters and numbers into the iconography of Pop Art reflects the influence of the newspaper collages produced by Picasso and Braque.

Another artistic expression of the 1960s, the so-called **Happenings,** probably derived from the Dada performances at the Cabaret Voltaire in Zurich during World War I. Happenings, in which many Pop artists participated, were multimedia events that took place in specially created environments. They included painting, assemblage, television, radio, film, and artificial lighting. Improvisation and audience participation encouraged a spontaneous, ahistorical atmosphere that called for self-expression in the "here and now." Happenings were also a response to consumerism and the fact that works of art were valued as commodities. In a Happening, there is no commodity, for nothing about it—unless it is recorded or videotaped—is permanent.

Pop Art in England: Richard Hamilton

The small collage *Just what is it that makes today's homes so different, so appealing?* (fig. **28.1**), by the English artist Richard Hamilton (born 1922), was originally intended for reproduction on a poster. It can be considered a visual manifesto of what was to become the Pop Art movement. First exhibited in London in a 1956 show entitled *This Is Tomorrow,* Hamilton's collage inspired an English critic to coin the term *Pop.*

The muscleman in the middle of the modern living room is a conflation of the Classical *Spear Bearer* (see fig. 5.27) by Polykleitos and the *Medici Venus* (see fig. 13.25). The giant Tootsie Pop directed toward the woman on the couch is at once a sexual, visual, and verbal pun. Advertising references occur in the sign pointing to the vacuum hose, the Ford car emblem, and the label on the tin of ham. Mass-media imagery is explicit in the tape recorder, television set, newspaper, and movie theater. The framed cover of *Young Romance* magazine reflects popular teenage reading of the 1950s.

Despite the iconographic insistence on what was contemporary, however, Hamilton's collage contains traditional historical allusions. The image of a white-gloved Al Jolson on the billboard advertising *The Jazz Singer* recalls an earlier era of American entertainment. The old-fashioned portrait on the wall evokes an artistic past, and the silicone pinup on the couch is a plasticized version of the traditional reclining nude. Hamilton's detailed attention to the depiction of objects, especially those associated with the domestic interior, reveals his respect for fifteenth-century Flemish painters as well as his stated admiration for Duchamp.

As a guide for subsequent Pop artists, Hamilton compiled a checklist of Pop Art subject matter: "Popular (designed for a mass audience), transient (short-term solution), expendable (easily forgotten), low-cost, mass-produced, young (aimed at youth), witty, sexy, gimmicky, glamorous, big business."

CONNECTIONS

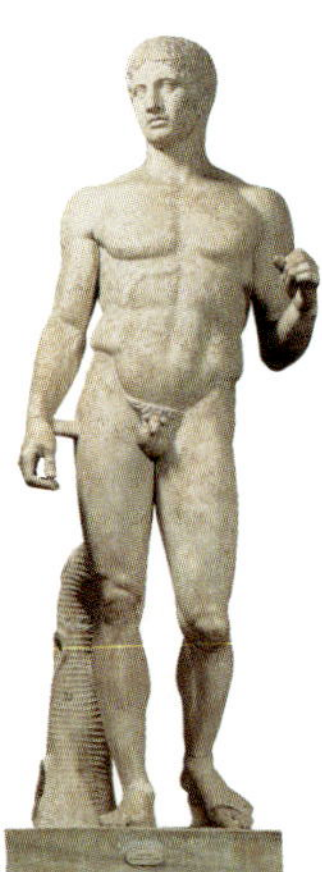

See figure 5.27. Polykleitos, *Doryphoros (Spear Bearer)*, c. 440 B.C.

See figure 13.25. *Medici Venus,* 1st century A.D.

28.1 Richard Hamilton, *Just what is it that makes today's homes so different, so appealing?*, 1956. Collage on paper; 10¼ × 9¼ in. (26.0 × 23.5 cm). Kunsthalle, Tübingen (Collection, Professor Dr. Georg Zundel).

28.2 Jasper Johns, *Three Flags*, 1958. Encaustic on canvas; 30⅞ × 45½ × 5 in. (78.4 × 115.6 × 12.7 cm). Collection, Whitney Museum of American Art, New York (Fiftieth Anniversary Gift of Gilman Foundation, Lauder Foundation, A. Alfred Taubman, anonymous donor, purchase).

Pop Art in the United States

Painting

Although Pop Art made its début in London in 1956 and continued in England throughout the 1960s, it reached its fullest development in New York. In 1962, an exhibition of the *New Realists* at the Sidney Janis Gallery gave Pop artists official status in the New York art world. Pop Art, however, was never a homogeneous style, and within this classification are many artists whose imagery and technique differ significantly. The first three artists discussed here—Jasper Johns, Larry Rivers, and Robert Rauschenberg—are actually transitional between Abstract Expressionism and Pop, for they combine textured, painterly brushwork with a return to the object.

Jasper Johns One of the constant themes of Jasper Johns (born 1930) is the boundary between everyday objects and the work of art. In the late 1950s, he chose a number of objects whose representation he explored in different ways, including the map and flag of the United States, targets, and stenciled numbers and words. In *Three Flags* of 1958 (fig. **28.2**), Johns depicts a popular image that is also a national emblem. His flags are built up with superimposed canvas strips covered with wax encaustic—a combination that creates a pronounced sense of surface texture. "Using the design of the American flag," Johns has been quoted as saying, "took care of a great deal for me because I didn't have to design it." The flag is abstract insofar as it consists of pure geometric shapes (stars and rectangles), but it is also an instantly recognizable, familiar object. The American flag has its own history, and the encaustic medium that Johns used to paint it dates back to antiquity (see Chapter 5). It thus combines the painterly qualities of Abstract Expressionism with the representation of a popular and well-known object. One question raised by Johns's treatment of this subject is "When does the flag cease to be a patriotic sign or symbol and become an artistic image?"

In Johns's painted bronze casts of cans of Ballantine Ale (fig. **28.3**), he retains the painterly texture of the *Three Flags*. As a Pop artist, Johns deals with themes of commercialism and repeated imagery versus the unique work of art. In this case, he draws commercial objects into the realm of art but, in contrast to Duchamp (see Chapter 26), Johns makes the artist's presence visible in the artistic process. In repeating the ale cans, Johns has created an imposing pair of cylinders. The more we look at them, the more we have the impression that they are standing up and looking back at us. Each label thus takes on the quality of a face.

28.3 Jasper Johns, *Painted Bronze (Ale Cans)*, 1960. Painted bronze; 5½ × 8 × 4¾ in. (14.0 × 20.3 × 12.1 cm). Museum Ludwig, Cologne.

Larry Rivers Larry Rivers (1923–2002) studied with Hans Hofmann (see Chapter 27) and never lost his sense of painterly texture. His *Portrait of Frank O'Hara* (fig. **28.4**) combines words with the poet's image. The picture is co-signed "Rivers" above "O'Hara" near the figure's shoulder on the right, signifying that the work is a collaborative effort of painter and poet. As such, the portrait recalls Dada combinations of words and pictures, and other forms of multimedia experimentation.

28.4 Larry Rivers, *Portrait of Frank O'Hara,* 1961. Oil on canvas; 36 × 36 in. (91.4 × 91.4 cm). Private collection. Photo Maggie Nimkin. Rivers worked as a professional saxophonist before taking up painting in 1945. His portrait of Frank O'Hara (1926–1966), a post–World War II poet, playwright, and art critic, reveals his interest in diverse expressive media. O'Hara himself worked as a curator at the Museum of Modern Art, New York, and his poems depict mental states of consciousness in a style reminiscent of Abstract Expressionism.

Robert Rauschenberg Robert Rauschenberg (born 1925) was as liberal in his choice of imagery as Johns was frugal. His sculptures and "combines"—descendants of Duchamp's Ready-Mades and Picasso's assemblages—include stuffed animals, quilts, pillows, and rubber tires. His paintings contain images from a wide variety of sources, such as newspapers, television, billboards, and old masters.

The **silkscreen** print of 1964, *Retroactive I* (fig. **28.5**), is an arrangement of cutouts resembling a collage. It illustrates the artist's expressed wish to "unfocus" the mind of the viewer by presenting simultaneous images that are open to multiple interpretations. The newspaper imagery evokes current events, reflecting the contemporary emphasis of Pop Art. A returning astronaut parachutes to earth in the upper left frame, while in the center President Kennedy, who had been assassinated the previous year, extends his finger as if to underline a point. The frame at the lower right reveals a historical thread behind Rauschenberg's "current events" iconography. It contains a blowup of a stroboscopic photograph of a takeoff on Duchamp's *Nude Descending a Staircase* (see fig. 25.18); at the same time, it is strongly reminiscent of Masaccio's *Expulsion of Adam and Eve* of c. 1425 (see fig. 13.24).

Despite the presence of media images in this print, Rauschenberg seems to have covered it with a thin veil of paint. Brushstrokes and drips running down the picture's surface are particularly apparent at the top. The dripping motion of paint parallels the fall of the astronaut: one drip lands humorously in a glass of liquid embedded in the green patch on the right. More hidden, or "veiled," is the iconographic parallel between the falling paint, the astronaut, and the "Fall of Man." Kennedy's "mythic" character is implied by his formal similarity to the Christ of Michelangelo's *Last Judgment* (see fig. 14.27) and to God in his *Creation of Adam* (see fig. 14.23).

CONNECTIONS

See figure 14.27. Michelangelo, *Last Judgment*, detail: figure of Christ, 1534–1541.

See figure 14.23. Michelangelo, *Creation of Adam*, c. 1510.

28.5 Robert Rauschenberg, *Retroactive I*, 1964. Silkscreen print with oil on canvas; 7 × 5 ft. (2.13 × 1.52 m). Wadsworth Athenaeum, Hartford, Connecticut (Gift of Susan Morse Hilles).

Andy Warhol Andy Warhol (1928–1987) was the chief example of the Pop Art lifestyle as well as the creator of highly individual works of art. With his flair for multimedia events and self-promotion, Warhol turned himself into a work of Pop Art and became the central figure of a controversial cult. One of his most characteristic works, *Campbell's Soup I* (*Tomato*) of 1968 (fig. **28.6**), illustrates his taste for commercial images. The clear precision of his forms and the absence of any visible reference to paint texture intensify the confrontation with the object represented—with the object as object. Warhol's famous assertion "I want to be a machine" expresses his obsession with mass production and his personal identification with the mechanical, mindless, repetitive qualities of mass consumption.

Warhol's iconography is wide-ranging. In addition to labels advertising products, he created works that monumentalize commercial American icons. These include Coca-Cola bottles, Brillo and Heinz boxes, comic books, matchbook covers, green stamps, dollar bills, and so forth. He also produced portraits of iconic American heroes and heroines—John F. Kennedy, Jackie Kennedy, Marilyn Monroe, Elvis Presley, Elizabeth Taylor, Marlon Brando, and Troy Donahue. Icons have a mythic quality, and Warhol did a myth series that included Superman, Howdy Doody, Mickey Mouse, Uncle Sam, Dracula, and the Wicked Witch of Oz.

28.6 Andy Warhol, *Campbell's Soup I* (*Tomato*), 1968. One from a portfolio of screenprints on paper; 35 × 23 in. (88.9 × 59.4 cm). The Andy Warhol Foundation, Inc./ Art Resource, NY. © 2006 Andy Warhol Foundation for the Visual Arts/ ARS, NY/TM Licensed by Campbell's Soup Co. All rights reserved.

In *Elvis I and II* (fig. **28.7**), Warhol depicts an icon of American pop culture in the traditional diptych format. He juxtaposes a monochrome pair of images with a colored pair, creating the impression of photographic repetition. Elvis is shown in an aggressive stance with his gun drawn, transforming the conventional cowboy image into that of a pop star.

28.7 Andy Warhol, *Elvis I and II*, 1964. Synthetic polymer paint and silkscreen ink on canvas, aluminum paint and silkscreen on canvas; each panel 82 × 82 in. (2.08 × 2.08 m). Copyright The Andy Warhol Foundation, Inc./Art Resource, New York.

Roy Lichtenstein Popular American reading matter of the 1940s and 1950s included comic books. These provided the source for some of the best-known images of Roy Lichtenstein (1923–1997). He monumentalized the flat, clear comic-book drawings with "balloons" containing dialogue. *Torpedo . . . Los!* (fig. **28.8**) is a blowup inspired by a war comic, illustrating a U-boat captain launching a torpedo. The impression of violence is enhanced by the close-up of the figure's open mouth and scarred cheek. The absence of shading, except for some rudimentary hatching, and the clear, outlined forms replicate the character of comic-book imagery.

In addition to comic books, Lichtenstein became inspired by the work of previous artists—Picasso, Matisse, Mondrian, and others—and he painted versions of their pictures. He also did a series of paintings in which he made "objects" out of brushstrokes (fig. **28.9**), which are implicit comments on the "objectlessness" of many Abstract Expressionist works. As with his comic-book imagery, Lichtenstein enlarges the brushstrokes along with their drips and splatters, indicating in solid black the indentations in the paint made by the bristles of the brush. But the flattening of the paint eliminates the natural texture of such a brushstroke. The background is composed of hundreds of Ben Day dots, which identify the surface of commercially printed paper and render the image static.

28.8 Roy Lichtenstein, *Torpedo . . . Los!*, 1963. Oil on canvas; 5 ft. 8 in. × 6 ft. 8 in. (1.73 × 2.03 m). Estate of Roy Lichtenstein.

By isolating the brushstroke, Lichtenstein "objectifies" it. At the same time, he retains the dynamic movement and gestural expressiveness of the Action painters. In this combination of techniques, he creates a synthesis of the Pop Art taste for objects with the Abstract Expressionist transformation of medium into content. The title of the painting illustrated here, *Little Big Picture,* refers to the battle of 1876 in which General George Armstrong Custer made his famous "last stand" against the Sioux—the Battle of Little Bighorn. Lichtenstein thus links the cultural struggles that made American history with conflicting styles of American art.

28.9 Roy Lichtenstein, *Little Big Picture,* 1965. Oil and synthetic polymer on canvas; 5 ft. 8 in. × 6 ft. 8 in. (1.73 × 2.03 m). Whitney Museum of American Art, New York (Purchase, Friends of Whitney Museum of American Art).

28.10 Richard Lindner, *Rock-Rock,* 1966–1967. Oil on canvas; 5 ft. 10 in. × 5 ft. (1.78 × 1.52 m). Dallas Museum of Fine Arts (Gift of Mr. and Mrs. James H. Clark).

Richard Lindner Richard Lindner (1901–1978) was born in Hamburg, Germany, and emigrated to the United States in 1941. His mechanical figures are somewhat reminiscent of Léger's volumetric Cubism, but his bright colors and metallic and shiny leather surfaces have affinities with Pop Art. *Rock-Rock* of 1966–1967 (fig. **28.10**) has an electric quality that recalls the blinking lights and tinny sounds of pinball machines as well as the dynamic energy of rock music. It depicts the rock star in a frontal pose, as a cultural icon of ambiguous gender. The dark glasses enhance the anonymity of the figure, while the background diagonals radiate in the manner of a halo. Bisecting the composition is the electric guitar, which has become a hallmark of the rock movement. It is also a formal reminder of Man Ray's Surrealist photograph *Le Violon d'Ingres* (see fig. 26.8), in which the violin is conflated with the back of the nude woman. In *Rock-Rock,* the guitar merges with the torso of the rock star—it curves around the collar, and the holes at the right resemble buttons. The figure seems literally to "wear" the guitar, which, in the end, *is* its identity.

R. B. Kitaj An entirely different atmosphere pervades the Pop Art of R. B. Kitaj (1932–1997), an American artist who lived and worked in London. His *Juan de la Cruz* of 1967 (fig. **28.11**) depicts a black American, Sergeant Cross, as a soldier during the Vietnam War. Through the window to his right, a nude Saint Teresa (see caption) wearing high heels is ordered to walk the plank by two thugs in the guise of Counter-Reformation Inquisitors. Kitaj relates the abuses of the Inquisition to various forms of twentieth-century discrimination by juxtaposing different cultural allusions. For example, the woman's nudity accentuates her victimization by the two men, the black sergeant fights for a country that discriminates against his people, while the Hispanic title of the painting merges another American minority with the Spanish martyr. Formally, too, Kitaj's arrangement of slightly textured patches of color recalls the juxtapositions of collage.

28.11 R. B. Kitaj, *Juan de la Cruz,* 1967. Oil on canvas; 6 ft. × 5 ft. (1.83 × 1.52 m). Astrup Fearnley Collection, Oslo. Kitaj was born in Cleveland, Ohio. After World War II, he became preoccupied with his Jewish heritage and the Holocaust. His interest in Saint Teresa, originally a Jew, and in Saint John of the Cross, who was rumored to have been Jewish, is related to Kitaj's sense of his own cultural identity. Although she became a Christian mystic, Saint Teresa was accused by the Inquisition of having relapsed. Saint John of the Cross was her protégé and a mystic poet.

28.12 (right) Tom Wesselmann, *Great American Nude No. 57*, 1964. Synthetic polymer on composition board; 4 ft. × 5 ft. 5 in. (1.22 × 1.65 m). Whitney Museum of American Art, New York (Purchase).

CONNECTIONS

See figure 14.52. Titian, *Venus of Urbino* (detail), c. 1538.

Tom Wesselmann The *Great American Nude* series by Tom Wesselmann (1931–2004) combines Hollywood pinups with the traditional reclining nude. In *No. 57* (fig. **28.12**), the nude is a symbol of American vulgarity. She lies on a leopard skin, and two stars on the back wall evoke the American flag. She is faceless except for her open mouth, and her body bears the suntan traces of a bathing suit. Her pose is related to figures such as Titian's *Venus of Urbino* (see fig. 14.52) and Manet's *Olympia* (see fig. 21.26), but Wesselmann's surfaces are unmodeled, though they appear to have volume. The partly drawn curtain opens onto a distant landscape, and the oranges and flowers refer to the woman's traditional role as a fertile earth goddess. This metaphor is reinforced by the formal parallels between the mouth, nipples, and interior of the flowers. In this work, Wesselmann combines three-dimensional forms with flattened geometric abstractions, the interior bedroom with exterior landscape, and intimacy with universal themes.

Wayne Thiebaud Born in 1920, the West Coast artist Wayne Thiebaud arranges objects in a self-consciously ordered manner. Although identified with Pop Art, he, like Larry Rivers, emphasizes the texture of paint. In the 1960s, Thiebaud focused on cafeteria-style food arrangements, but his content in the following decades includes a wide range of objects, portraits, and atmospheric images of cloud formations and landscape.

His *Thirteen Books* of 1992 (fig. **28.13**) depicts a neat pile of books, which has a constructed, architectural quality that is enhanced by the oblique angle. Each book functions as an individual structural element that contributes to the effect of the whole and creates the impression of a rectangular column. The textured edges of the books and the bright colors of their spines contrast with the stark white background. The titles are blurred and unreadable, thereby suggesting the hidden, secret content of the proverbial "closed book."

To the right of the stack, there is no distinction between the surface supporting the books and the background. This leaves the viewer uncertain of their exact placement in space—they seem to float in a plane of white. At the left, on the other hand, the books cast a gray, trapezoidal shadow edged in orange, which identifies a source of light and confirms the presence of a supporting surface. The predominance of white is characteristic of the artist's paintings of objects. White was of particular interest to Thiebaud as it combines all the colors of the visible spectrum, as well as simultaneously absorbing and reflecting light.

28.13 Wayne Thiebaud, *Thirteen Books*, 1992. Oil on panel; 13 × 10 in. (33.0 × 25.4 cm). Allan Stone Gallery, New York.

Sculpture

Generally included among the leading New York Pop artists are the sculptors Claes Oldenburg (born 1929) and George Segal (1924–2000). Although both can be considered Pop artists in the sense that their subject matter is derived from everyday objects and mass media, their work is distinctive in maintaining a sense of the textural reality of their materials.

Claes Oldenburg Oldenburg has produced an enormous, innovative body of imagery, ranging from clothing, light switches, food displays, and furniture sets to tea bags. *Soft Switches* (fig. **28.14**) is one of his "soft" vinyl sculptures, which amuses us because it is unexpected. We expect a light switch to be a hard, solid object which we can flick on or off. Here, however, the switches sag like a pair of shoes poking through a pouch. Oldenburg also creates "ghosts," or ghost versions of his sculptures, which are devoid of color and usually made of canvas (fig. **28.15**). These sculptures are not only startling because of their material, but also because of their size. We expect light switches to be small, almost unnoticeable, and purely functional household fixtures. But these are imposing, and they announce their presence, insisting on being noticed. In so doing, the switches reflect the characteristic Pop Art taste for monumentalizing everyday objects and the style's introduction of a new body of subject matter.

Oldenburg's giant *Clothespin* of 1976 in Philadelphia (fig. **28.16**) is also an enlargement of an everyday household object. The clothespin has an anthropomorphic quality, resembling a tall man standing with his legs apart, as if striding forward. The wire spring suggests an arm, and the curved top with its two circular openings, a head and face. Despite the hard texture of this work, Oldenburg manages to arouse a tactile response by association with actual clothespins. Pressing together the "legs," for example, would cause the spring to open up the spaces at the center of the "head." The tactile urge aroused by the clothespin, together with its anthropomorphic character, reflects Oldenburg's talent for conveying paradox and metaphor. The clothespin thus assumes the quality of a visual pun, which is reminiscent of Picasso's *Bull's Head* (see fig. 25.9) and of the unlikely, surprising juxtapositions of the Surrealist aesthetic that were calculated to raise the consciousness of the viewer.

28.14 Claes Oldenburg, *Soft Switches*, 1964. Vinyl with Dacron and canvas; 47 × 47 × 3¼ in. (119.4 × 119.4 × 8.3 cm). Nelson-Atkins Museum, Kansas City, Missouri (Chapin family in memory of Chapin Buckwalter, 65-29).

28.15 Claes Oldenburg, *Soft Light Switches—Ghost Version*, 1971 version of a 1964 original. Canvas filled with kapok, gesso, and pencil; 47 × 47 × 12 in. (121.9 × 121.9 × 30.5 cm). Collection of Claes Oldenburg and Coosje van Bruggen, New York, on loan to the Museum für Moderne Kunst, Frankfurt.

28.16 Claes Oldenburg, *Clothespin,* Central Square, Philadelphia, 1976. Cor-Ten and stainless steel; 45 ft. × 6 ft. 3¾ in. × 4 ft. ⅓ in. (13.72 × 1.92 × 1.32 m). This is one of several "projects for colossal monuments," based on everyday objects, which Oldenburg proposed for various cities. Others include a giant *Teddy Bear* for New York, a *Drainpipe* for Toronto, and a *Lipstick* for London (presented to Yale University in 1969). Oldenburg says that he has always been "fascinated by the values attached to size."

28.17 George Segal, *Chance Meeting,* 1989. Plaster, paint, aluminum post, and metal sign; 10 ft. 3 in. × 3 ft. 5 in. × 4 ft. 7 in. (3.12 × 1.04 × 1.40 m). Photo courtesy of Carroll Janis, New York. Segal wrapped the subject's body in gauze bandages dipped in wet plaster. Once the plaster hardened, he cut it off in sections, which he then reassembled. His effigies, the descendants of Egyptian mummies and Roman death masks, were usually in unpainted white plaster, but sometimes in gray or color. Segal's subjects, however, were alive when the cast was made and were often depicted in the course of some activity.

28.18 George Segal, *Cinema,* 1963. Plaster, illuminated Plexiglas, and metal; 118 × 96 × 30 in. (299.7 × 243.8 × 76.2 cm). Albright-Knox Art Gallery, Buffalo (Gift of Seymour H. Knox, 1964).

George Segal The sculptures of George Segal differ from Oldenburg's in that they are literally "figurative." Segal creates environments in which he places figures, singly or in groups, that convey a sense of isolation or self-absorption. In *Chance Meeting* (fig. **28.17**), three life-sized pedestrians encounter each other by a one-way street sign. Their otherworldliness is emphasized by Segal's "mummification" of living figures (see caption) and the impression that they do not communicate. Their light, textured surfaces create a paradoxical impression of emotional coldness for, although they have been molded from living people, they seem ghostly and alien.

In *Cinema* (fig. **28.18**), which was Segal's favorite work, he has also created a ghostly figure. In contrast to *Chance Meeting,* this figure is alone, placing an *R* on the neon billboard. His anonymous whiteness is accentuated by the glare of the white light in front of him. The red letters of "CINEMA" reflect the Pop Art use of commercial letters and numbers, and the influence of advertising. By juxtaposing a human form with the electric sign, Segal shows the way in which technology overwhelms humanity as well as its isolating effects.

28.19 Marisol Escobar, *The Last Supper* (installed at the Sidney Janis Gallery), 1982. Wood, brownstone, plaster, paint, and charcoal; 10 ft. 1 in. × 29 ft. 10 in. × 5 ft. 7 in. (3.07 × 9.09 × 1.70 m). Photo courtesy of Carroll Janis, New York.

Marisol Escobar Marisol Escobar's (born 1930) brand of Pop Art combines Cubist-inspired blocks of wood with figuration. In her monumental sculptural installation of *The Last Supper* (fig. **28.19**), she re-creates Leonardo's fresco (see fig. 14.14) in a modern idiom. The architectural setting replicates the Leonardo, with four rectangular panels on either side that recede toward a back wall, a triple window, and a curved pediment. The apostles, like Leonardo's, are arranged in four groups of three, with corresponding poses. An image of Marisol herself sits opposite the scene, playing the role of viewer as well as being the artist. As viewer, Marisol contemplates the past, which she appropriates.

Niki de Saint-Phalle Niki de Saint-Phalle (1930–2002) was born in Paris, grew up in New York, and returned to Paris in 1951. There she began painting and making combinations of reliefs and assemblages, using toys as a primary medium. She was originally part of the French *nouveaux réalistes,* a group of artists that was formed in 1960. In New York, these artists were termed the New Realists, which was also the title of the exhibition held in 1962 at the Sidney Janis Gallery.

De Saint-Phalle's most characteristic works are her so-called *Nanas,* which are polyester sculptures of large women. Generally, as with her *Black Venus* of 1965–1967 (fig. **28.20**), the *Nanas* are painted in bright, unshaded colors that are reminiscent of folk imagery. The torso of this figure looks inflated, ironically even more so than the beach ball, which seems to be losing its air. De Saint-Phalle's *Venus* shares exaggerated breasts and hips with the Paleolithic *Venus of Willendorf* (see fig. 1.1), but the head is small by comparison, a device that has a Mannerist quality. The figure also seems engaged in an energetic dance movement, which, together with its "blackness," allies it with the exuberance and modernism of jazz.

28.20 Niki de Saint-Phalle, *Black Venus,* 1965–1967. Painted polyester; 110 × 35 × 24 in. (279.4 × 88.5 × 61.0 cm). Whitney Museum of American Art, New York (Gift of Howard and Jean Lipman Foundation).

CONNECTIONS

See figure 1.1. *Venus of Willendorf,* c. 25,000–21,000 B.C.

28.21 Bridget Riley, *Aubade (Dawn)*, 1975. Acrylic on linen; 6 ft. 10 in. × 8 ft. 11½ in. (2.08 × 2.73 m). Private collection.

Op Art

Another artistic movement that flourished during the 1960s has been called Optical, or Op, Art. In 1965, the Museum of Modern Art contributed to the vogue for the style by including it in an exhibition entitled *The Responsive Eye*. Op Art is akin to Pop Art in rhyme only, for the recognizable object is totally eliminated from Op Art in favor of geometric abstraction, and the experience of it is exclusively retinal. The Op artists produced kinetic effects (that is, illusions of movement), using arrangements of color, lines, and shapes, or some combination of these elements.

In *Aubade (Dawn)* of 1975 (fig. **28.21**), by the British painter Bridget Riley (born 1931), there are evident affinities with Albers and the Color Field painters. Riley has arranged pinks, greens, and blues in undulating vertical curves of varying widths, evoking the vibrancy of dawn itself. The changing width of each line, combined with the changing hues, makes her picture plane seem to pulsate with movement. Riley's work generally relies on two effects—producing a hallucinatory illusion of movement (as here), or encouraging the viewer to focus on a particular area before using secondary shapes and patterns to intrude and disturb the original perception. Riley's early Op Art pictures were in black and white and shades of gray. In the mid-1960s, she turned to color compositions such as this one.

Minimalism

Sculptures of the 1960s "objectless" movement were called "minimal," or "primary," structures because they were direct statements of solid geometric form. In contrast to the personalized process of Abstract Expressionism, Minimalism, like Color Field painting, eliminates all sense of the artist's role in the work, leaving only the medium for viewers to contemplate. There is no reference to narrative or to nature, and little content beyond the medium. The impersonal character of Minimalist sculptures is intended to convey the idea that a work of art is a pure object having only shape and texture in relation to space.

Donald Judd

Untitled (fig. **28.22**) by Donald Judd (1928–1994) is a set of rectangular "boxes" derived from the solid geometric shapes of David Smith's *Cubi* series (see fig. 27.28) and the "minimal" simplicity of Ad Reinhardt (see fig. 27.18). Judd's boxes, however, do not stand on a pedestal. Instead, they

28.22 Donald Judd, *Untitled*, 1967. Green lacquer on galvanized iron; each unit 9 × 40 × 31 in. (22.9 × 101.6 × 78.7 cm). Museum of Modern Art, New York. Helen Achen Bequest and gift of Joseph A. Helman.

hang from the wall, thereby involving the immediate environment in the viewer's experience of them. They are made of galvanized iron and painted with green lacquer, reflecting the Minimalist preference for industrial materials. Judd has arranged the boxes vertically, with each one placed exactly above another at regular intervals, to create a harmonious balance. The shadows cast on the wall, which vary according to the interior lighting, participate in the design. They break the monotony of the repeated modules by forming trapezoids between each box, and between the lowest box and the floor. The shadows also emphasize the vertical character of the boxes' alignment by linking them visually and creating the impression of a modern, nonstructural pilaster.

Dan Flavin

Light was the primary medium of the Minimalist fluorescent sculptures of Dan Flavin (1933–1996). As store-bought objects transformed into "art" by virtue of the artist's intervention, they can be related to Duchamp's Ready-Mades. Flavin defines interior architectural spaces with tubes of fluorescent lights arranged in geometric patterns or shapes. Light spreads from the tubes and infiltrates the environment, creating an installation within an available space. The technological character of the medium and its impersonal geometry is typical of the Minimalist aesthetic. Sometimes, as in *Untitled (in Honor of Harold Joachim)* (fig. **28.23**), the color combinations are unexpected. Flavin's merging of light and color, dependent as it is on technology and twentieth-century nonrepresentation, nevertheless has a spiritual quality that ironically allies his work with stained-glass windows and the play of light and color inside Gothic cathedrals (see fig. 11.33).

Flavin described this work as a "corner installation . . . intended to be beautiful, to produce the color mix of a lovely illusion. . . . [He] did not expect the change from the slightly blue daylight tint on the red rose pink near the paired tubes to the light yellow midway between tubes and the wall juncture to yellow amber over the corner itself."[1]

CONNECTIONS

See figure 11.33. Nave, Reims Cathedral, 1211–c. 1290.

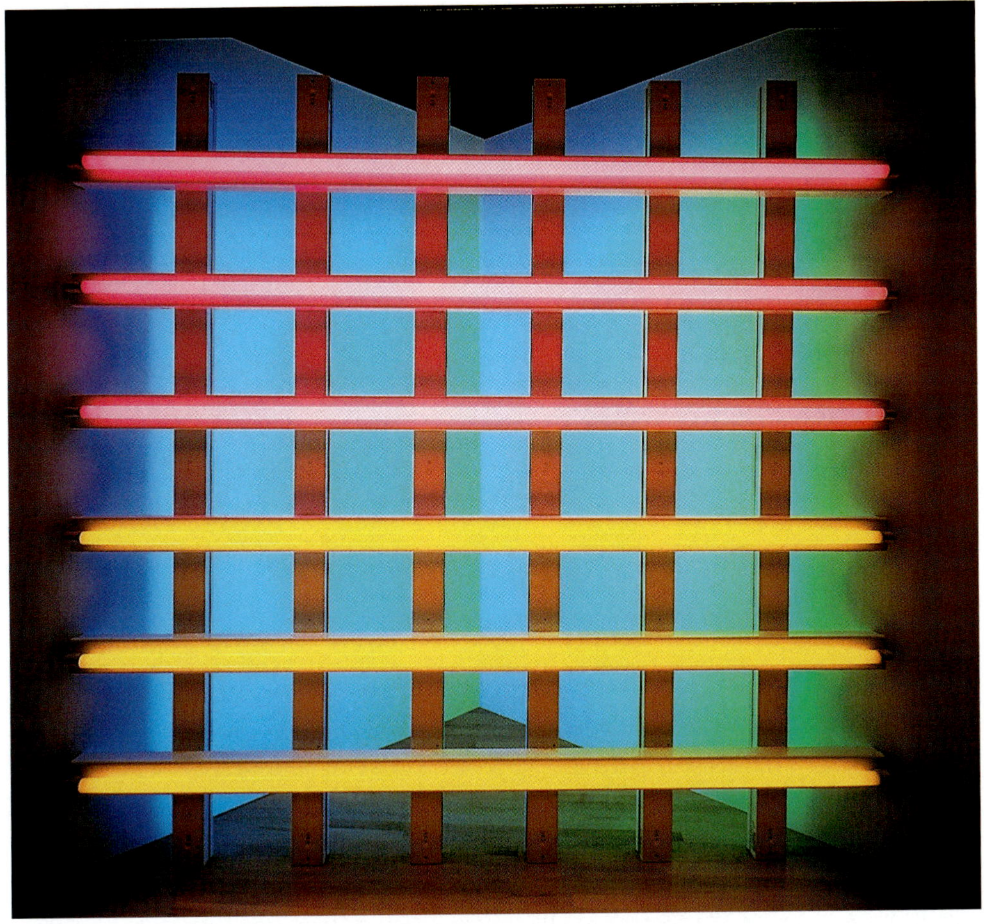

28.23 Dan Flavin, *Untitled (in Honor of Harold Joachim)*, 1977. Fluorescent light fixtures with pink, blue, green, and yellow tubes; 8 ft. (2.44 m) square across the corner. Courtesy, Dia Center for the Arts, New York.

Agnes Martin

The early work of Agnes Martin (1912–2004) was an inspiration to the Minimalists, but she developed in a more painterly direction. She was born in Saskatchewan, Canada, and moved to the United States in the 1930s. Her first one-woman show was held at the Betty Parsons Gallery in New York City. Martin's early allover grid paintings consist of grids penciled by hand that criss-crossed the canvas, which appear, like Minimalist sculpture, to "minimalize" the presence of the artist. In contrast to the Minimalists, however, she fills the picture with glowing color that seems to radiate from an inner mental landscape projected beneath the material surface of the finished work. In so doing, she reveals affinities with the vast—because conceptually vast—pictorial spaces of Ad Reinhardt and Mark Rothko.

From 1967 to 1974, Martin took a "sabbatical" from painting and traveled through Canada and the American West, finally settling into an isolated existence in New Mexico. When she returned to painting in the 1970s, her work had changed, progressing even further beyond the material world—possibly influenced by her interest in Far Eastern philosophy. *Untitled #9* (fig. **28.24**) is an example of her work in 1990. The allover grid has been replaced by gray horizontal bands that potentially extend beyond the confines of the frame. Their geometry and the fact that the grays lighten as they rise present an image that combines the structure of architecture with the changing, cyclical quality of nature.

The following excerpts from Martin's writings were selected to accompany her exhibition of 1992–1993 at the Whitney Museum of American Art in New York:

> I didn't paint the plane
> I just drew this horizontal line
> Then I found out about all the other lines
> But I realized what I liked was the horizontal line
>
> Art restimulates inspirations and awakens sensibilities
> That's the function of art
>
> Any thing is a mirror.
> There are two endless directions. In and out.[2]

28.24 Agnes Martin, *Untitled #9*, 1990. Synthetic polymer and graphite on canvas; 6 × 6 ft. (1.83 × 1.83 m). Whitney Museum of American Art, New York (Gift of the American Art Foundation 92.60).

28.25 Eva Hesse, *Metronomic Irregularity I*, 1966. Painted wood, sculpmetal, and cotton-covered wire; 12 × 18 × 1 in. (30.5 × 45.7 × 2.5 cm). Collection, Robert Smithson, New York. © The Estate of Eva Hesse. Museum Wiesbaden.

Eva Hesse

The American sculptor Eva Hesse (1936–1970) took Minimalism in a new direction by consciously "writing" her autobiography into her work. As a result, she is sometimes referred to as a Post-Minimalist. She was born a Jew in Hamburg, Germany, and was taken to Amsterdam to escape Nazi persecution. After a few traumatic years, she went with her family to New York, where her mother killed herself. Hesse's psychological difficulties and sense of abandonment found expression in an art that was rooted in the forms and materials of Minimalism. She studied at the Yale School of Art, where she came under the influence of Josef Albers, and after graduation returned to Germany. She had her first solo exhibition in Düsseldorf in 1965, and, by the time of her own early death at the age of thirty-four, she had produced an influential body of work.

Hesse's *Metronomic Irregularity I* of 1966 (fig. **28.25**), the first in a series of three, explores the relationship of line to plane in a literal way. The surfaces of the rectangles are inscribed with a grid pattern; there is a small hole in the corner of each square of the grid. White cotton-covered wires are threaded from holes in one rectangle through holes in another. Formally, Hesse has juxtaposed actual, three-dimensional lines (the threads) with the flat planes of the two vertical plaques. The space between them participates in the image, creating a nonrepresentational triptych in which medium and content converge. From an autobiographical point of view, one can read the threads as attachments, binding together the plaques across a space, as a metaphor for Hesse's fear of separation and abandonment, and also as links between her two identities, German and American. Her lifelong sense of anxiety is perhaps reflected in the frantic, though lyrical, quality of the connecting threads.

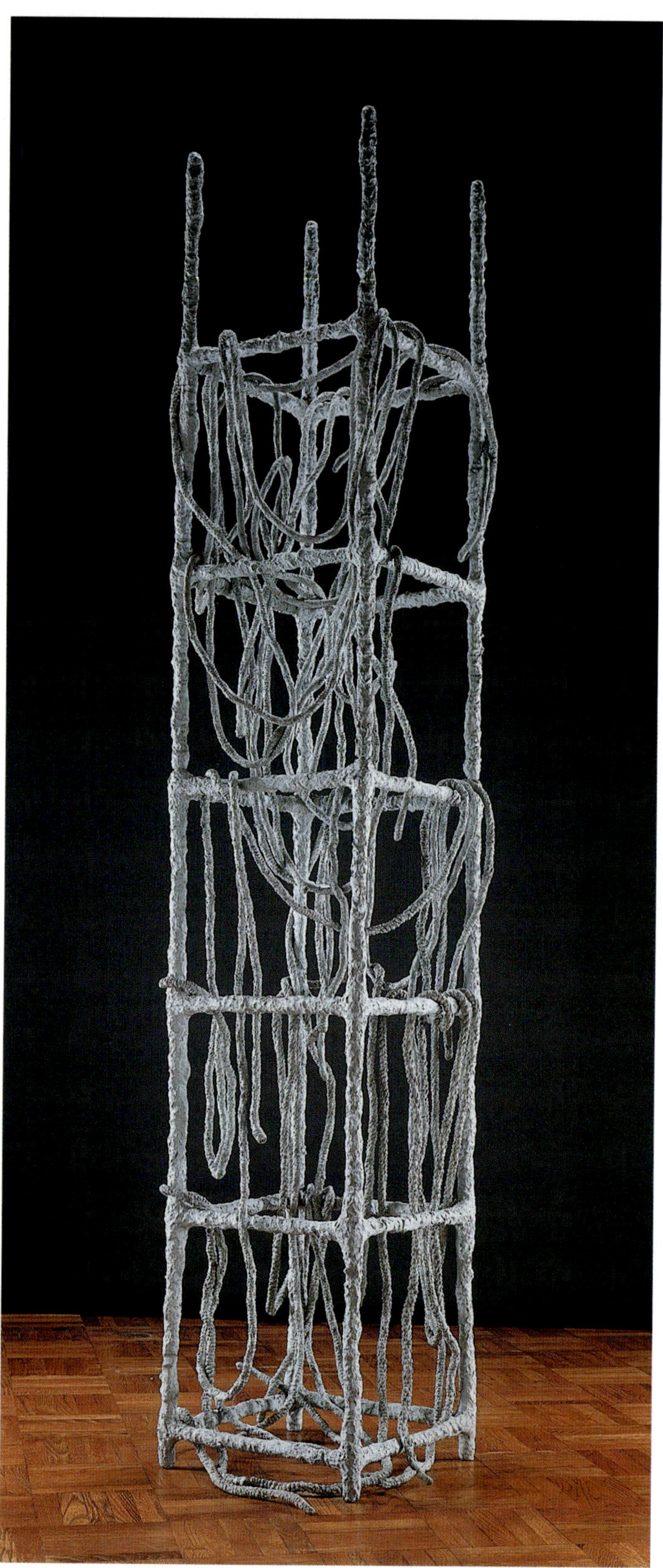

28.26 Eva Hesse, *Laocoön,* 1966. Acrylic paint, cloth-covered cord, wire, and papier-mâché over plastic plumber's pipe; 120 × 24 × 24 in. (304.8 × 61.0 × 61.0 cm). Allen Memorial Art Museum, Oberlin College, Ohio. Fund for Contemporary Art and gift of the artist and the Fischbach Gallery, 1970.

A similar aesthetic informs Hesse's *Laocoön* of the same year (fig. **28.26**). This work, too, although not part of a series, evolved in stages. A vertical armature of plastic pipes—a combination ladder and scaffold—is wrapped in cloth. Cloth-covered cords are intertwined around the open cubes, animating their spaces.

Hesse's sense of irony and identification with the work is clear from its title, which refers to the second-century-B.C. Hellenistic sculpture *Laocoön and His Two Sons* (see fig. 5.75). Hesse's cords bind her armature just as, in the Greek statue, the snakes bind and connect the figures. But Laocoön's snakes are also the messengers and instruments of his death. Just as the snakes envelop and kill the Trojan seer and his two sons, so the cords seem both to connect and to strangle Hesse's structure. The structure is herself, uncannily prefiguring her own death from a brain tumor four years later. "My life and art," she said, "have not been separated. They have been together."[3]

CONNECTIONS

See figure 5.75. *Laocoön and His Two Sons.*

Action Sculpture: Joseph Beuys

The German artist Joseph Beuys (1921–1986), like Eva Hesse, was significantly affected by World War II, although in an entirely different way. He flew a Stuka for the Luftwaffe and was shot down by the Russians in 1943. This led Beuys to construct an autobiographical myth that continually informed his art and has become a staple of art-world mythology. According to Beuys, he was rescued by Tartars (a Mongolian people of central Asia) and wrapped in animal fat and felt, which kept him alive. Beuys viewed this event as a kind of resurrection through which he identified with Christ. Influenced by German Romanticism and Germanic myth, and impelled to atone for the German atrocities in the war, Beuys was drawn to mysticism and spirituality, and projected the self-image of a shaman on an international scale. As such, he set out to cure the social, economic, and political ills of the world. To this purpose he dedicated thousands of drawings, sculptures, and, above all, a series of carefully choreographed so-called "action sculptures" with moving figures and music, conceived of as neither happenings nor performances, but containing elements of both.

Like Marc, Beuys believed in the spirituality of animals and, like Kandinsky, in the spiritual in art (see Chapter 24). As a shaman, he experimented with the boundary between human and animal, just as politically he worked toward peace among nations and cultures by crossing borders and merging boundaries. On July 20, 1964 (the anniversary of the unsuccessful attempt on Hitler's life), for example, Beuys staged a performance in the cathedral at Aachen, where Charlemagne (see Chapter 9) had his court in the ninth century. Disrupted by Neo-Nazi students, Beuys became even more politically engaged, founding several leftist groups, including the predecessor to the Green party.

Individual works of sculpture such as the *Fat Chair* (a chair wrapped in fat) and *Ur-Sled* (composed of an orange box, ribbon, and fat), both of 1964, were inspired by his rescue. Other materials that were relics from his war experiences were batteries and transistors, and these, like the fat, assumed the quality of religious icons for Beuys.

The Pack of 1969 (fig. **28.27**) creates the impression of a sculpture in the process of becoming. It shows twenty sleds emerging from the back of a Volkswagen bus. Each sled carries a felt blanket roll, fat, and a flashlight, all elements Beuys associated with his rescue by the Tartars in a Russian snowstorm. Their nomadic form of transportation is juxtaposed with the vehicle (*wagen*) of the "civilized" German people (*volk*), which is a reference to World War II. The arrangement and forms of the sleds animate them; they resemble enlarged insectlike creatures pouring forth from the bus and rushing to a scene of rescue. Their runners resemble legs, their flashlights, eyes, and their blanket rolls, bodies.

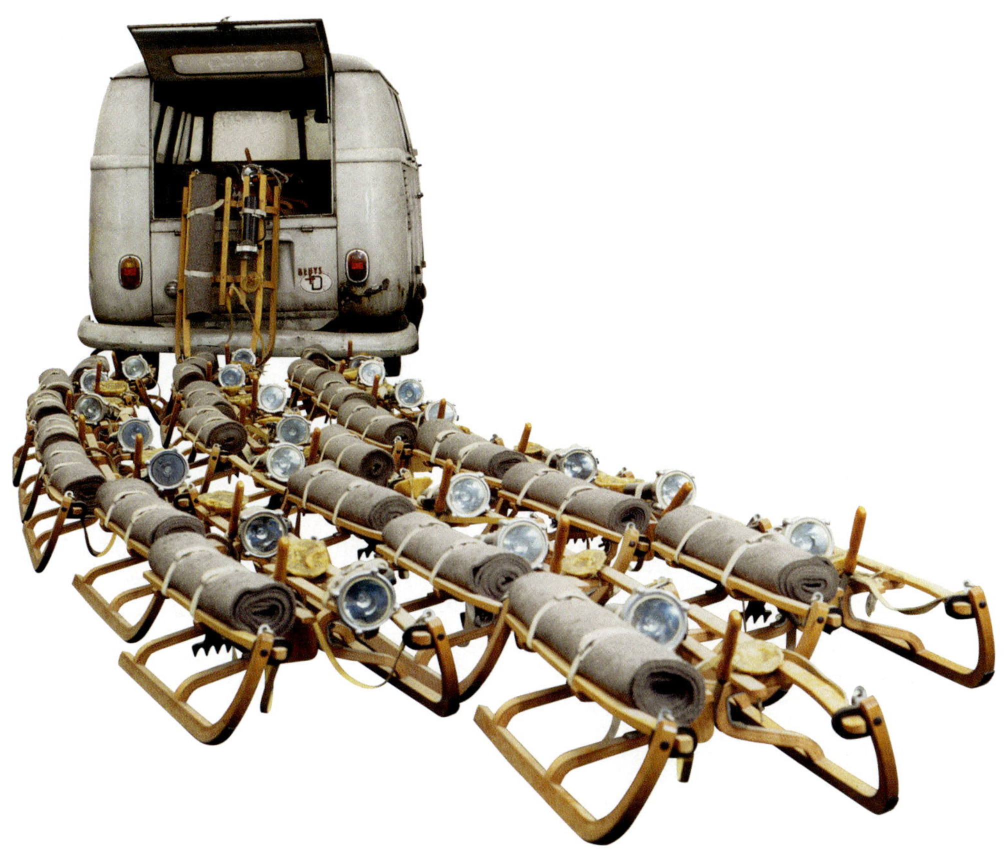

28.27 Joseph Beuys, *The Pack*, 1969. Volkswagen bus with twenty sleds, felt, fat, and flashlights. Neue Gallery, Staatliche Museen, Kassel.

28.28 and **28.29** Joseph Beuys, *Coyote, I Like America and America Likes Me*, two views of a week-long sequence, 1974. Action sculpture. New York.

In 1973, Beuys became seriously ill and once again associated his recovery with Christ's Resurrection. After that, he lectured passionately about art and the state of the world, writing and drawing on a blackboard before audiences. In 1974, Beuys performed one of his most famous action sculptures, *Coyote, I Like America and America Likes Me* (figs. **28.28** and **28.29**). He arrived in New York and was taken, wrapped in felt, by ambulance to the René Block Gallery. For a week, he and a live coyote performed the sculpture on the floor of the gallery, which had a pile of felt for the coyote to sit on. Fifty copies of the *Wall Street Journal* were placed on the floor every day as a sign of the financial values overwhelming modern culture. Beuys himself was wrapped up in a tentlike felt blanket with a Tartar's crook emerging from the top. As he moved, the coyote moved, and vice versa. Tied together by their gazes, at once uniting them and signifying their mutual suspicion, Beuys and the coyote engaged in a dance calculated, shamanlike, to blur the boundaries between man and animal.

Many meanings have been read into this performance, most based on Beuys's autobiographical myth. The Tartar's felt that kept him alive protects him from the wild animal, while the crook has associations with Christ as the Good Shepherd. To celebrate the plane crash and subsequent rescue at the Eurasian border of two continents, Beuys tries to bridge the borders of human and animal, of the Native American worship of the coyote and the white man's fear and hatred of it, and of modern commercial society and the values of a less technological age.

The aesthetic quality of the action sculpture is in the planned and unplanned movements and positions of the two performers, and the lighting and setting as captured by the camera. Figure 28.28 shows the coyote gazing fixedly at the triangular felt "tent," with the crook protruding at the top in the manner of a Native American tepee. Backlit from the window at the left, the coyote and the tent create stark silhouettes against the back wall. Both are static, frozen in space. In figure 28.29, the close-up camera angle captures the simultaneity of movement as both figures now turn in space, and the diagonal of the coyote's head and neck parallels that of the crook. The nature of the relationship, Beuys seems to be saying, moves dynamically from enmity, to suspicious contemplation and mutual assessment, to harmony. Such was his program for the world.

Conceptualism: Joseph Kosuth

For Beuys, thinking about art was creative, and therefore the idea itself was a work of art. In that view, he had affinities with the Conceptual artists of the 1960s, who wanted to extend Minimalism so that even the materials of art would be eliminated, leaving only the idea, or concept, of the art. Like Duchamp and the Dadaists, for the Conceptualists the mental concept takes precedence over the object. This is also related to the Minimalist rejection of the object as a consumer product. Although the term itself was coined in the 1960s, Conceptual art attained official status through the 1970 exhibition at the Museum of Modern Art, New York. The show's title—*Information*—reflected the emphasis of Conceptual art on language and text, rather than on imagery.

Some Conceptual works combine objects with text, and others, such as Joseph Kosuth's (born 1945) *Art as Idea as Idea* of 1966 (fig. **28.30**), consist only of text. The "text" in this instance is composed of five dictionary definitions of the noun *painting*. Definition numbers 4 and 5, which are marked "Obs.," or "obsolete," describe the term in its most painterly ("colors laid on") and pictorial ("vivid image") sense. Their "obsolescence," therefore, is consistent with the takeover by the idea and with the presumed demise of the object. At the same time, however, Kosuth presents the text as a photographic enlargement within a pictorial field. As a result, the text is as much an "object" as it is the expression of an idea.

See figure I.5. René Magritte, *The Betrayal of Images*, 1928.

The dichotomy of words and pictures, which Magritte portrayed in *The Betrayal of Images* (see fig. I.5), is a subtext of Kosuth's *Art as Idea as Idea*. Due to the flat, empty space between Magritte's "pipe" and his written words, the artist "pictures" the developmental and conceptual space between words and pictures—children "read" pictures and objects before they read words. And animals, like the ancient Greek horse who neighed at the painted horse of Zeuxis and the birds who tried to eat his painted grapes, read images but not words. Conceptual art makes images of words by arranging ideas conveyed through words on a pictorial surface.

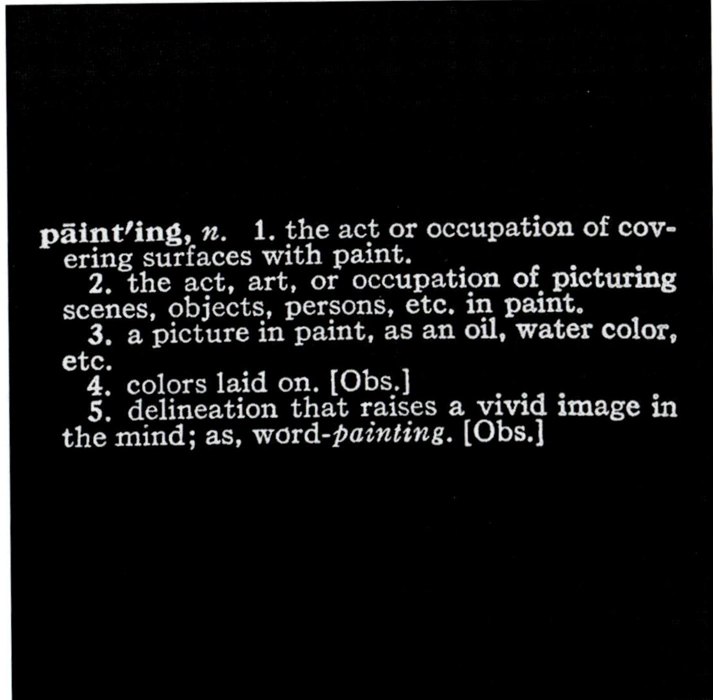

28.30 Joseph Kosuth, *Art as Idea as Idea*, 1966. Mounted photostat; 4 × 4 ft. (1.22 × 1.22 m).

The 1960s was a decade of social and political upheaval both in the United States and in western Europe. It culminated in the Paris riots of May 1968, campus takeovers by college students, and radical changes in educational curricula. The burgeoning women's movement, advances in civil rights—especially in the United States—and, above all, the Vietnam War contributed to the cultural turmoil. In the arts, these currents were expressed in the "here and now" character of the Happenings and other types of artistic performances, in the protests against commercialism implied by some Pop Art, in the withdrawal from figuration by the Minimalists, and in the exaltation of the idea by the Conceptualists.

The contradictory aspect of the 1960s, in which two generations clashed over social and political issues, was reflected in the arts. On the one hand, Pop artists imposed the "object" by making it a central image, and, on the other hand, they protested against the abuses of materialism and the profit motives of industry. Minimalists avoided the "figurative" object in favor of geometric form but used industrial materials to do so. In the next and final chapter, we shall see that it is in the nature of art to evolve dynamically by continually responding to the past, while also "pushing the envelope" into the future.

	Style/Period	Works of Art	Cultural/Historical Developments
1950	POP ART, OP ART, MINIMALISM, AND CONCEPTUALISM 1950–1960	Hamilton, *Just what is it that makes today's homes so different, so appealing?* (**28.1**) Johns, *Three Flags* (**28.2**)	Fidel Castro becomes premier of Cuba (1959) Charles de Gaulle proclaimed president of Fifth Republic (1959)
1960	1960–1970  **Johns, *Three Flags***  **Lichtenstein, *Little Big Picture***	Johns, *Painted Bronze (Ale Cans)* (**28.3**) Rivers, *Portrait of Frank O'Hara* (**28.4**) Warhol, *Elvis I and II* (**28.7**) Segal, *Cinema* (**28.18**) Lichtenstein, *Torpedo . . . Los!* (**28.8**) Rauschenberg, *Retroactive I* (**28.5**) Wesselmann, *Great American Nude No. 57* (**28.12**) Lichtenstein, *Little Big Picture* (**28.9**) de Saint-Phalle, *Black Venus* (**28.20**) Hesse, *Metronomic Irregularity I* (**28.25**) Hesse, *Laocoön* (**28.26**) Kosuth, *Art as Idea as Idea* (**28.30**) Lindner, *Rock-Rock* (**28.10**) Oldenburg, *Soft Switches* (**28.14**) Judd, *Untitled* (**28.22**) Kitaj, *Juan de la Cruz* (**28.11**) Warhol, *Campbell's Soup I (Tomato)* (**28.6**) Beuys, *The Pack* (**28.27**)  **Warhol, *Cambell's Soup I***	Cuban missile crisis (1962) Rachel Carson, *Silent Spring;* start of environmentalist movement (1962) Edward Albee, *Who's Afraid of Virginia Woolf?* (1962) Mary McCarthy, *The Group* (1963) Betty Friedan's *Feminine Mystique* launches the women's movement (1963) John Le Carré, *The Spy Who Came in from the Cold* (1963) Assassination of President John F. Kennedy (1963) Civil rights bill bans discrimination in voting, jobs, etc. (1964) *Autobiography of Malcolm X* (1964) First rock musical, *Hair* (1967) Assassination of Martin Luther King, Jr. (1968) John Updike, *Couples* (1968) Joe Orton, *Loot* (1968) Philip Roth, *Portnoy's Complaint* (1969) Music festival at Woodstock, New York, attracts half a million people (1969) *Apollo II* lands on the moon (1969) Student riots in United States and Europe (late 1960s) Gay liberation movement begins (late 1960s)
1970	1970–1980  **Flavin, *Untitled***	Oldenburg, *Soft Light Switches—Ghost Version* (**28.15**) Beuys, *Coyote* (**28.28–28.29**) Riley, *Aubade (Dawn)* (**28.21**) Oldenburg, *Clothespin* (**28.16**) Flavin, *Untitled (in Honor of Harold Joachim)* (**28.23**) 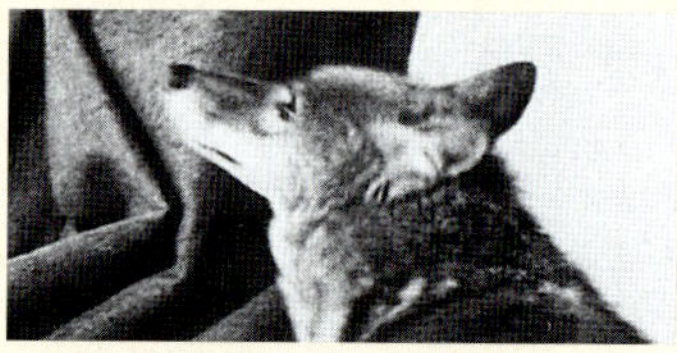 **Beuys, *Coyote***	Sylvia Plath, *The Bell Jar* (1971) *Grease* (Tom Moore, director) (1972) U.S. Supreme Court legalizes abortion (1973) End of Vietnam War (1973) DNA recombined for the first time; birth of genetic engineering (1973) Nixon resigns U.S. presidency after Watergate scandal (1974) Aleksandr Solzhenitsyn, *The Gulag Archipelago* (1974) Saul Bellow, *Humboldt's Gift* (1976) Alex Haley, *Roots* (1976) David Mamet, *American Buffalo* (1977) Woody Allen, *Annie Hall* (1977) Mother Teresa wins Nobel Peace Prize (1979) William Styron, *Sophie's Choice* (1979)
1990	1980–1990 	Marisol, *The Last Supper* (**28.19**) Segal, *Chance Meeting* (**28.17**) Martin, *Untitled #9* (**28.24**) Thiebaud, *Thirteen Books* (**28.13**) **Thiebaud, *Thirteen Books***	 **Warhol, *Elvis I and II***

29

Innovation, Continuity, and Globalization

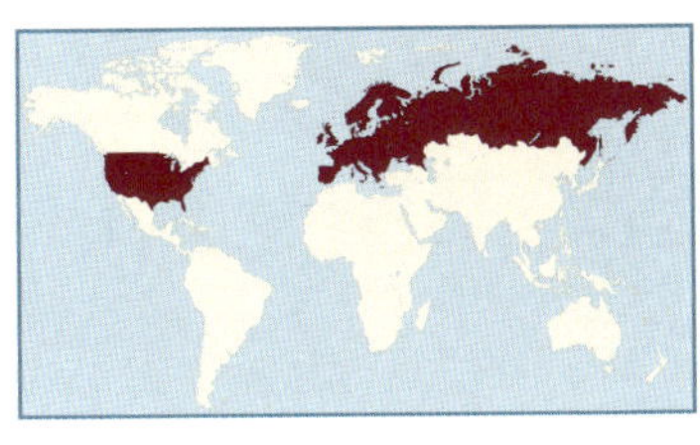

As we respond to contemporary art, our sense of historical perspective inevitably diminishes. The more recent the development or style, the more necessary the passage of time before one can properly evaluate a work of art and assess whether or not it will endure. Accordingly, of all the chapters in this survey, this one is the most subject to revision.

Continuing Controversy: Government Funding of the Arts

The difficulty in assessing the artistic value of a work of one's own time was reflected in the 1927 trial over whether Brancusi's *Bird in Space* (see fig. I.4) was "art." More recently, from 1989 to 1990, controversial works have raised First Amendment issues of censorship in the United States. The work of two photographers, Andres Serrano (born 1950) and Robert Mapplethorpe (1946–1989), provoked heated national debates over the degree to which freedom of speech in the visual arts should be guaranteed by the Constitution. Both Serrano and Mapplethorpe tested the limits of convention and propriety, and challenged traditional taboos—Serrano in regard to religion, Mapplethorpe in regard to sexuality. Since both artists had been funded, directly or indirectly, by the National Endowment for the Arts (NEA), questions were raised about government funding for the arts in general.

See figure I.4. Constantin Brancusi, *Bird in Space*, 1928.

Andres Serrano

In the 1980s, Serrano (see p. 975) made a series of color photographs (Cibachromes) dealing with Catholic imagery and, in some cases, used body fluids as both subject matter and symbol. For example, he filled with blood a Plexiglas container in the shape of a cross and photographed it against a dazzling sky. He photographed a transparent cross filled with milk, which was immersed in a vat of blood, thereby creating a sharp contrast of red and white. In these images, Serrano evokes traditional Christian iconography, making the "Blood of the Cross" into a concrete form. The reference to milk evokes associations with the Virgin Mary's role as both the mother of Christ and the maternal intercessor for all Christians. More controversial was the artist's photograph of his own semen in the form of an illuminated streak against a dark background. Such content reflects Serrano's interest in the life forces that are normally contained within the body and hidden from view.

The work that ultimately caused a furor and brought Serrano into the limelight was his photograph of a Crucifixion set against a red background and lit up as if by a flash of soft, yellow light. The latter turned out to have been the artist's urine, which he had saved up and into which he had immersed a plastic Crucifix. By calling the work *Piss Christ,* Serrano left viewers in no doubt about the nature of his media.

Piss Christ was included in a group exhibition of 1989—*Awards in the Visual Arts 7*—which had been arranged by the Southeastern Center for Contemporary Art (SECCA), in Winston-Salem, North Carolina. Serrano was one of ten artists chosen from 599 entries and was awarded a $15,000 grant. The show ran in the Los Angeles County Museum and in the Carnegie-Mellon University Art Gallery in Pittsburgh without incident. But after it closed at the Museum of Fine Arts in Richmond, Virginia, a letter of protest was published on Palm Sunday in the *Richmond Dispatch Times.* The author of the letter accused the museum of promoting "hatred and intolerance" and asked whether Christianity had "become fair game in our society for any kind of blasphemy and slander."

Piss Christ then came to the attention of the Reverend Wildmon, who had founded the National Federation of Decency (later renamed the American Family Association). Wildmon objected to Serrano *and* the NEA, and exhorted his supporters to write to Congress and the NEA, which they did by the thousands. Wildmon referred to the work as "hate-filled, bigoted, anti-Christian, and obscene art." In response, factions of the art world organized an Art Emergency Day—August 26, 1989.

Wildmon's vilification of the NEA was endorsed by Senators Alfonse D'Amato (R-NY) and Jesse Helms (R-NC), the evangelist Pat Robertson, and army colonel Oliver North. Of Serrano, Helms declared: "He is not an artist, he is a jerk. Let him be a jerk on his own time and with his own resources. Do not dishonor our Lord."[1]

Robert Mapplethorpe

In 1989, federal funding also went to Mapplethorpe, whose subject matter ranges from flowers, to portraits, to nude studies, to frankly homosexual and sadomasochistic acts. From December 9, 1988, to January 29, 1989, Mapplethorpe exhibited 175 photographs at the Philadelphia Institute of Contemporary Art. Funded by the NEA, the show was entitled *Robert Mapplethorpe: The Perfect Image*. It included three portfolios—the 1978 X-Portfolio depicting some homosexual and sadomasochistic scenes, the 1978 Y-Portfolio depicting flowers, and the 1981 Z-Portfolio of black men, mainly shown in Classical poses. From February 25 to April 9, 1989, the show was held in Chicago, where it was well attended.

Problems for Mapplethorpe began in Washington, D.C., in the midst of the Serrano controversy. Senator Helms cited the Mapplethorpe grant as another example of irresponsible NEA funding, whereupon the exhibition of photographs at the Corcoran Gallery (scheduled to open July 1, 1989) was canceled by the director. The works were shown instead in an alternative space—the Washington Project for the Arts. Subsequent scheduled stops at the Wadsworth Athenaeum, in Hartford, Connecticut, and at the University Art Museum in Berkeley, California, were quite successful.

Meanwhile, a five-year moratorium on funding for the SECCA was proposed by the Senate. NEA funding was cut by $45,000, equivalent to the $15,000 grant to Serrano and the $30,000 grant to Philadelphia for the Mapplethorpe exhibition. Congress also approved a one-year ban on government grants to artists who depict obscene or perverse subjects, or who exploit children for sexual purposes, provided that their work has no "serious literary, artistic, political, or scientific value."

Robert Mapplethorpe: The Perfect Image hit a new and unprecedented snag on the way to Cincinnati, Ohio. Dennis Barrie, director of the Contemporary Arts Center in that city, had decided—over local protests—that the show would go on. It was scheduled to open on April 6 and to run until May 27, 1990. But, bowing to propriety, Barrie planned to segregate the X-Portfolio in a separate room and to exclude visitors under the age of eighteen. In addition, a notice posted outside the X-rated area served as a warning that sexually explicit photographs were on view.

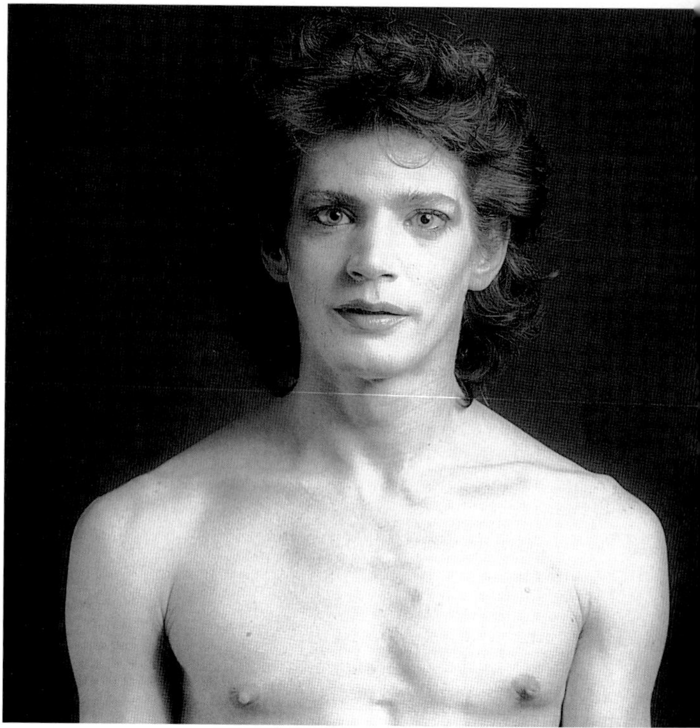

29.1 Robert Mapplethorpe, *Self-Portrait*, 1980. Unique gelatin silver print; 30 × 30 in. (76.2 × 76.2 cm). Collection, Howard and Suzanne Feldman.

In Washington, the first Bush administration took a stand against censorship and supported the NEA. Performers and arts administrators lobbied Congress on behalf of First Amendment protection for the arts. But in Cincinnati, there was a flurry over "moral values." The Cincinnati Citizens for Community Values mounted vigorous opposition to the show. Editorials and caricatures flooded the press. In the March 24 edition of the *Cincinnati Enquirer*, three medical doctors argued against the show on the grounds that it was an attack on civilized society. Local law-enforcement officials declared Mapplethorpe's pictures "criminally obscene." The chief of police warned, "There are no raving Neanderthals running amok in the streets of Cincinnati."[2] Cincinnati was, after all, the headquarters of the National Coalition against Pornography and was noteworthy for the absence of peep shows, X-rated movies, adult bookstores, and the like.

The city also had its art lovers, for membership in the Contemporary Arts Center rose by 40 percent. A poll published by the *Cincinnati Post* on April 13 indicated that 59 percent of those questioned were in favor of the show, 39 percent were opposed to it, and 3 percent had no opinion. Three days later, *Newsweek* published Mapplethorpe's 1980 *Self-Portrait* (fig. **29.1**) with the caption "Eye of the Storm." Although this photograph is not as graphic as some from the X-Portfolio, it clearly reveals Mapplethorpe's identification with homosexual themes. Here, he represents himself partly as a transvestite, partly as an androgynous, male–female figure. He plays with the boundaries of gender and with the limits of sexual identity. The image itself is beautifully printed, and, as with all his black-and-white photographs, the forms are imbued with a soft, silver glow.

On April 7, an Ohio grand jury indicted the Arts Center and its director on obscenity charges. These focused on five pictures showing homosexual acts and on two pictures of children with their genitals exposed. The following day, a federal district judge ruled that the exhibition could not be shut down, pending the outcome of the trial. The director, Dennis Barrie, pleaded not guilty, and the trial began on September 24 before a jury of four men and four women, none of whom was particularly interested in art.

The art world, including prominent museum directors, came out in force to testify for the defense. The position of the defense resembled that of the modernists in the 1927 Brancusi trial—namely, that works in museums, like works made by artists, are, by definition, ART. And, they further argued, artistic statements made by artists are protected by the First Amendment. At one point, the prosecutor asked the jury to consider whether the offending photographs were "van Goghs," as if that were the ultimate criterion. The irony of that question, rhetorical as it may have been, lies in the fact that van Gogh's paintings were not considered ART by the prevailing taste of his own generation and that van Gogh lived in poverty because no one would buy his pictures. Recourse to the example of van Gogh is thus a risky business when arguing the cause of aesthetic judgment.

After five days of testimony, the judge instructed the jury on the legal test for obscenity: "That the average person applying contemporary community standards would find that the picture, taken as a whole, appeals to prurient interest in sex, that the picture depicts or describes sexual conduct in a patently offensive way and that the picture, taken as a whole, lacks serious literary, artistic, political, or scientific value." The jury deliberated for two hours and on October 5 acquitted both the museum and Barrie. When the jurors were interviewed later, one stated: "We learned that art doesn't have to be pretty."

When the Mapplethorpe show closed in Cincinnati, it traveled to Boston's Institute of Contemporary Art, where it was exhibited without incident.

In 1999, Mayor Giuliani of New York City sued to close the Brooklyn Museum over an exhibit of young British artists entitled *Sensation*. In that case, the mayor had not seen the show, but he professed outrage at a painting of the Virgin with a small lump of dried elephant dung on one breast. Unfortunately, the impulsiveness of the mayor's rush to judgment exposed his own lack of contextual knowledge, for in parts of Africa—where the artist had been raised—elephant dung was endowed with magic properties. Whatever the aesthetic value of the work turns out to be, it was neither pornographic nor an offense in the context of the history of Christian art. In any case, the media attention given to the uproar and the money spent on lawyers show that debates over censorship of the arts, as well as government funding, are likely to continue. The controversies over such works of art, some of which challenge convention, tradition, and even propriety, are evidence of the continuing power of images.

Performance

Gilbert and George

Two English performing artists, Gilbert (Proesch, born 1943) and George (Passmore, born 1942), created a series of performances related to the "happenings" of the 1960s and became their own works of art. Figure **29.2** illustrates a 1969 performance of their much-repeated piece, *Singing Sculptures,* in which they mimed in slow motion to a recording of an old English music-hall song while standing on a low platform. They gilded their faces and hands and wore business suits. Their only props were Gilbert's cane and George's gloves. This and similar performances raised the issue of the boundary between artists and their work. By describing themselves as "living sculptures," Gilbert and George explored the ambiguous transitional space between living and nonliving, and between illusion and reality.

29.2 Gilbert and George, *Singing Sculptures,* 1971.

29.3 Laurie Anderson, *Nerve Bible Tour,* 1995. Photo: Adriana Friere.

Laurie Anderson

The multimedia performance art of Laurie Anderson (born 1947) uses photography, video, film, and music. Her message, which is typically delivered in spoken narrative, is political and social. Figure **29.3** is a still from the *Nerve Bible Tour* in July 1995 at the Park Theater in Union City, New Jersey. Anderson describes her performances as being "about a collaboration between people and technology." Like Gilbert and George, she participates as an actor in her own work of art. In so doing, she explores the boundary between artist and art, subject and object, and the natural and the technological worlds.

Return to Realism

With the development of photography in the nineteenth century, artists found a new medium for capturing a likeness. Many painters and sculptors used photographs to decrease the posing time of their sitters. In the late 1960s, the popularity of photography, its relationship to Pop Art, and the belief that it permits an objective record of reality led to the development of Super Realism.

Chuck Close

In his 1968 study for *Self-Portrait* (fig. **29.4**), Chuck Close (born 1940) used a grid to convert a photographic image—in this case a black-and-white passport-style close-up of his own head—into a painting. The final picture conveys a sense of rugged monumentality. Because the face is frontal and seen from slightly below the chin, the nose and cigarette are foreshortened. At the same time, there is an interplay between the curvilinear strands of the hair and the textures of the flesh. Up to 1970, it was Close's habit to paint mainly in black and white, as here, and to use an airbrush to create a smooth surface. The result is a work that resembles a photographic enlargement and, in a sense, forms a transition between painting and photography.

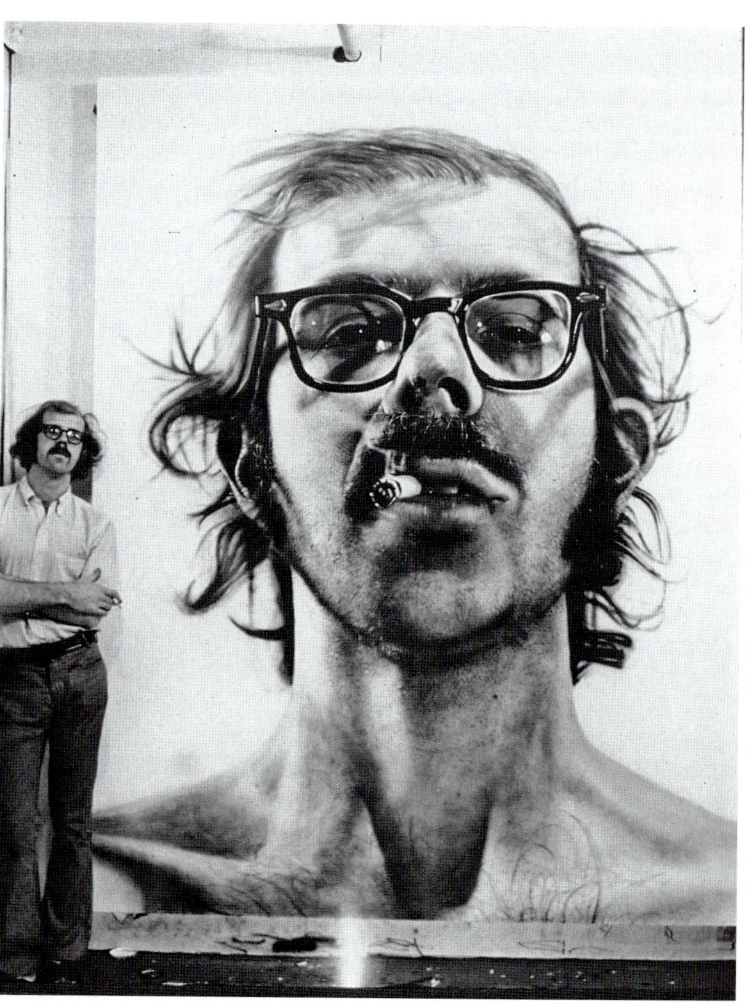

29.4 Chuck Close, *Self-Portrait,* 1968. Acrylic on canvas; 9 × 7 ft. (2.74 × 2.13 m). Photo Kenny Lester, courtesy of the Pace Gallery, New York. The grid used to transfer this image from a photograph to a painting consisted of 567 squares ruled on a piece of paper measuring 14 × 11 inches (35.6 × 27.9 cm). The photographic data in each small square were enlarged to fill squares of approximately 16 square inches (103 cm^2).

29.5 Chuck Close, *Self-Portrait*, 1997. Oil on canvas; 8 ft. 6 in. × 7 ft. (2.59 × 2.13 m). Pace Wildenstein Gallery, New York.

For the past thirty years, Close has been creating portraits of art-world figures. He is the first artist in the history of art to produce a large body of work consisting of portraits of other artists, appropriating them for a new brand of iconography. Figure **29.5** is an example of his more recent work, his *Self-Portrait* as a close-up, still based in photography but painstakingly painted, colored square by colored square. Combining the crystalline structure of Cubism with the illusion of a computer-derived image, and assembling the building blocks of paint as if each were a mosaic *tessera,* Close creates a head that emerges in a blaze of light and color from the black edge of the picture plane.

Richard Estes

One of the most prominent Super Realist painters is Richard Estes (born 1936). His oil paintings resemble color photographs, although they are on a larger scale and are more crisply defined than a photograph of similar size would be. His *Williamsburg Bridge* of 1987 (fig. **29.6**) combines an urban landscape with the reflections of steel, chrome, and glass. Divided by the strong vertical accent of the red subway car, the painting is an optical play between the interior on the left and the exterior, visible through the window of the car, on the right. The self-absorption of the subway riders contrasts with the moving cars and distant city skyline on the right. As in the Renaissance, Estes's illusionistic effects are enhanced by the use of linear perspective.

29.6 Richard Estes, *Williamsburg Bridge*, 1987. Oil on canvas; 3 ft. × 5 ft. 6 in. (0.91 × 1.68 m). Courtesy, Allan Stone Gallery, New York. Estes assembles color photographs and re-creates the scene with brushes and oil on canvas. "The incorporation of the photograph into the means of painting," he wrote, "is the direct way in which the media have affected the type of painting. That's what makes New Realism new."[3]

Duane Hanson

The Super Realist sculptures of the American artist Duane Hanson (1925–1996) are striking for their illusionism. Whereas no one would mistake Gilbert and George for actual sculptures or Close's portraits for the figures themselves, Hanson's sculptures are often taken for real people. As in the allover white plaster figures of George Segal, Hanson's sculptures are created directly from the models themselves. His convincing *trompe-l'oeil* illusionism is reminiscent of ancient Greek legends about the artist Daedalos, who reportedly rivaled the gods by making living sculptures. In clothing his figures, Hanson also evokes Ovid's tale of Pygmalion, the sculptor who dressed and attended to his statue of Galatea as if she were a real woman.

Combined with a contemporary aesthetic and dependence on modern materials, Hanson's *The Cowboy* of 1995 (fig. **29.7**) assumes a traditional *contrapposto* pose. Like Donatello's *David* (see fig. 13.29), despite an entirely different characterization, the *Cowboy* is meditative, gazing downward and forming a closed space within the boundaries of the sculpture. He holds a bridle in his right hand—David holds Goliath's sword—and wears the costume of a canonical American cowboy. His hat, checked shirt, suede vest, dungarees, and leather boots identify the type, whereas the "five o'clock shadow" and the chest hair contribute to the illusion that he is also a specific individual.

CONNECTIONS

See figure 13.29. Donatello, *David,* c. 1430–1440.

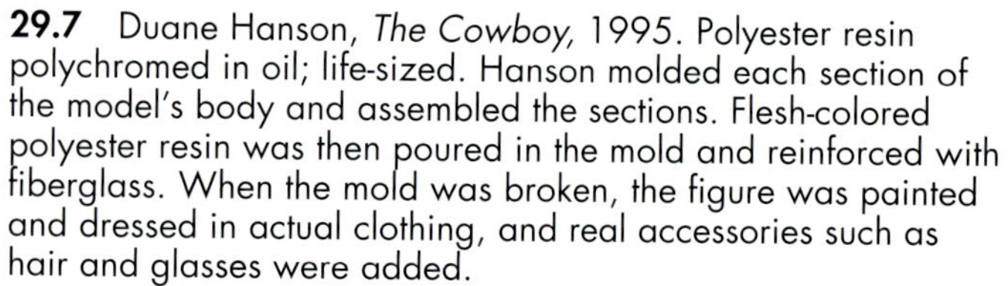

29.7 Duane Hanson, *The Cowboy,* 1995. Polyester resin polychromed in oil; life-sized. Hanson molded each section of the model's body and assembled the sections. Flesh-colored polyester resin was then poured in the mold and reinforced with fiberglass. When the mold was broken, the figure was painted and dressed in actual clothing, and real accessories such as hair and glasses were added.

29.8 Ron Mueck, *Mask II,* 2001. Mixed media; 30⅜ × 33½ in. (77.2 × 85.1 cm). Photo courtesy James Cohan Gallery. Mueck began his career working for children's television and then went into advertising and film. He turned from photographing objects to making the object, rather than the photograph, the end product.

Ron Mueck and Constantin Brancusi

More recent examples of Super Realism can be seen in works by the Australian-born Ron Mueck (born 1958), who now lives in London. His intriguing *Mask II* of 2001 (fig. **29.8**), like Hanson's sculptures, is made of modern materials such as fiberglass resin. *Mask II* also seems uncannily alive, despite the absence of a body. The head lies sideways; the eyes are closed, and the lips are parted. The head thus appears to be sleeping, with the slight creases in the forehead suggesting mental activity—as if the figure were dreaming.

In this work, Mueck continues the theme of partial form that characterized the human figures of Rodin and Brancusi (see Chapters 22 and 25). Brancusi produced several versions in bronze and marble of *Sleeping Muse,* which also shows a detached head lying sideways, with closed eyes and an open mouth. But *Sleeping Muse I* (fig. **29.9**) has an abstract, curvilinear quality and a smooth contour that create an impression of elegance. As with *Bird in Space* (see fig. I.4), Brancusi has captured the essence of a figure—in this case, a detached head replicating the detachment of sleep. Mueck's head, in contrast, is very much present by virtue of its "in your face" realism.

29.9 Constantin Brancusi, *Sleeping Muse I,* 1909–1910. Marble; 6¾ × 10⅞ × 8⅜ in. (17.2 × 27.6 × 21.2 cm). Hirshhorn Museum and Sculpture Garden, Smithsonian Institution, Washington, D.C. (Gift of Joseph H. Hirshhorn, 1966, 66.610).

Developments in Architecture

Estes's Super Realist painting of the Guggenheim Museum (fig. **29.10**) illustrates the exterior of Frank Lloyd Wright's impressive building in New York City. Its purpose was to house the Guggenheim collection and to provide space for exhibitions of twentieth-century art.

The Guggenheim Museum, New York

Built between 1956 and 1959, somewhat earlier than the other works in this chapter, the Guggenheim embodies the climax of Wright's interest in curvilinear form. Its most distinctive feature is the large inverted cone, which encloses a six-story ramp coiling around a hollow interior. Natural light enters through a flat skylight. Viewers inside the Guggenheim Museum look at paintings and sculptures as they walk down the ramp, so that they are always slightly tilted in relation to the works of art.

Despite a design that is frankly inconvenient for viewing art, the Guggenheim is itself a monumental work of art. Unlike Wright's Prairie Style architecture (see Chapter 25), it cannot be said to blend into its surroundings. Located on Fifth Avenue directly across from Central Park, the spiral cone can be conceived of organically as growing upward and outward, toward the sky, like the trees opposite. Most observers, however, experience the museum in relation to the neighboring rectangular buildings, which generally tend to become smaller toward the top. These formal anomalies between the Guggenheim and its architectural environment were, for a while, a source of considerable controversy.

29.10 Richard Estes, *Solomon R. Guggenheim Museum,* 1979. Oil on canvas; 2 ft. 7⅛ in. × 4 ft. 7⅛ in. (0.79 × 1.40 m). Solomon R. Guggenheim Museum, New York.

Guggenheim Museum Installations: Jenny Holzer and Matthew Barney

The interior of the Guggenheim Museum has provided a unique context for many innovative installation exhibitions devoted to a single artist. In 1989, for example, Jenny Holzer (born 1950) installed a program lasting 105 minutes and consisting of some 330 verbal messages conveyed through vivid colored lights (fig. **29.11**). The view shown here looks toward the skylight at the top of the inverted cone.

Holzer is a Conceptual artist who uses the power of words and texts—carved in stone or signed in neon lights—and combines them with impressive visual form. Among her groups of messages are *Laments, Truisms, Inflammatory Essays, The Living Series,* and *The Survival Series,* all of which were represented in the Guggenheim installation. She used the circular format of the ramp in a unique way, aligning its spiraling plane with the viewer's sequential reading of texts. Below the skylight on the ground floor of the museum, Holzer arranged in a circle seventeen red granite benches inscribed with verbal messages. She thus juxtaposed the age-old tradition of inscribing texts in stone with the more transitory electronic media of the modern era.

In 2003, the Guggenheim Museum became the site of a complex installation by Matthew Barney (born 1967) entitled *The Cremaster Cycle.* This was an elaborate

29.11 Jenny Holzer, *Untitled* (selections from *Truisms, Inflammatory Essays, The Living Series, The Survival Series, Under a Rock, Laments,* and *Mother and Child Text*), 1989–1990. Temporary installation with extended helical tricolor LED electronic display signboard. Installed at the Solomon R. Guggenheim Museum, New York. Commissioned by the Guggenheim Museum. Partial gift of the artist, 1989.

29.12 Matthew Barney, *Cremaster 4: The Loughton Candidate*, 1994. Color photograph, 19½ × 17⅝ in. (49.5 × 45.3 cm). © 1994 Matthew Barney. Photo: Michael James O'Brien. Courtesy Gladstone Gallery.

combination of sculptures, drawings, still photographs, videos, and music that drew on a wide range of media and iconographic sources. Media ranged from film to Astroturf, and imagery from myth and surreal fantasy to biogenetics. The term *cremaster* refers to the muscle of the testicles and reflects the artist's preoccupation with sexuality and anatomy. The cycle has five parts, adding up to an epic display of imagery that encompasses the history of the human race.

Barney created a number of sculptures depicting mutating species and shifting genders. Nearly all his work is based in the human figure and is influenced by issues in modern biology. Figure **29.12** is a video still from *Cremaster 4*. A male figure, formally dressed in a white coat, is represented against a blue-plaid background. The head, like certain facial configurations of Picasso, is arresting because it distorts and disrupts our expectations of how a face should look. It attacks our narcissism by challenging Classical idealization and threatens our sense of being human. The pointed ears assume an animal quality, whereas the curls recall old-fashioned hair styles for men. At the same time, the folds of flesh in the forehead and the flattened nose seem in the very process of mutating into some unknown and unknowable future species.

The Whitney Museum

Less than a mile away from the Guggenheim Museum is the Whitney Museum of American Art (fig. **29.13**). This was designed by the German architect Marcel Breuer (1902–1981) in a style inspired by the stark rectangularity of the Bauhaus (see Chapter 25). The floors are cantilevered out toward Madison Avenue like a chest with its drawers pulled out at increasing distances. The only features that interrupt the wall surfaces are the slightly projecting trapezoidal windows. Inside and out, the museum is constructed of concrete and dark gray granite blocks, which correspond to its stark, angular character.

In contrast to the Guggenheim, the Whitney is well conceived for viewing works of art. The floors are horizontal rather than slanted, and the galleries are ample and flexible, with ceilings that can support mobile wall partitions. Both buildings, however, have thick, massive walls, in contrast to the earlier International Style developed at the Bauhaus.

29.13 Marcel Breuer, Whitney Museum of American Art, New York, 1966. Breuer was one of the first graduates of the Bauhaus. He became chairman of its carpentry department and designed his celebrated S-shaped chairs in aluminum, plywood, and steel tubing. In 1936, he emigrated to the United States, where he taught at Harvard under Gropius and established an architectural practice that was responsible for, among other things, the UNESCO building in Paris.

The Geodesic Dome: R. Buckminster Fuller

One of the more interesting personalities of twentieth-century design, R. Buckminster Fuller (1895–1983), was a philosopher, poet, architect, and engineer, as well as a cult figure among American college students. His architecture expresses his belief that the world's problems can be solved through technology. One of his first designs (1927–1928) was a house that he called Dymaxion, a name conflating "dynamic" and "maximum." These reflect key concepts for Fuller, who wanted to achieve the maximum output with the minimum energy consumption. The Dymaxion house was a prefabricated, factory-assembled structure that hung from a central mast and cost no more than a car to build. A later invention was a three-wheeled Dymaxion car (1933), but, like the house, it was never produced commercially.

Fuller is best known for the principle of structural design that led to the invention of the **geodesic dome.** It is composed of polyhedral units (from the Greek words *poly,* meaning "many," and *hedron,* meaning "side")—usually either tetrahedrons (four-sided figures) or octahedrons (eight-sided figures). The units are assembled in the shape of a sphere.

The geodesic dome offers four main advantages. First, because it is a sphere, it encloses the maximum volume per unit of surface area. Second, the strength of the framework increases logarithmically in proportion to its size. This fulfills Fuller's aim of combining units to create a greater strength than the units have individually. Third, the dome can be constructed of any material at low cost. And fourth, it is easy to build. Apart from purely functional structures like greenhouses and hangars, however, the geodesic dome has been used very little. Fuller's design for the American Pavilion at the Montreal Expo of 1967 (fig. **29.14**) reveals both its utility and its curious aesthetic attraction. (The architectural principle underlying the geodesic dome is shared by a class of carbon molecules, named "fullerenes" after Buckminster Fuller. They were discovered in the late 1980s and possess unique qualities of stability and symmetry.)

29.14 R. Buckminster Fuller, American Pavilion, Expo '67, Montreal, 1967. Fuller was descended from eight generations of New England lawyers and ministers. He was expelled from Harvard twice, served in the U.S. Navy in World War I, and worked in the construction business. In 1959, he became a professor of design science at Southern Illinois University. Fuller's abiding interest in education is revealed by his belief that all children are born geniuses. "It is my conviction from having watched a great many babies grow up," he said, "that all of humanity is born a genius and then becomes de-geniused very rapidly by unfavourable circumstances and by the frustration of all their extraordinary built-in capabilities."[4]

Post-Modern Architecture

Fuller's architectural ideas remained isolated from the stylistic mainstream of the late twentieth century. Post-Modernism, on the other hand, has developed into a widespread movement. Post-Modern architecture is eclectic. It combines different styles from the past to produce a new vision, which is enhanced, but not determined, by modern technology. Post-Modernism rejects the International Style philosophy that "form follows function" and juxtaposes traditional architectural features without regard for their historical contexts.

Charles Moore A good example of Post-Modernism is Charles Moore's (born 1925) Piazza d'Italia (fig. **29.15**)—Italy Square—in New Orleans. In this illustration, the piazza is shown at night, illuminated by colored neon lights. The lights define space and accentuate architectural form—an effect that relates the piazza to Flavin's sculptures. Color conforms to each particular architectural element; the central entablature and its round arch are green, and the supporting Corinthian columns are red. Curved colonnades on either side are alternately red and yellow, and the inner Corinthian capitals are predominantly blue. The pool of water reflects the lights in broad patches of color.

Piazza d'Italia is a Post-Modern rearrangement of Classical, Renaissance, and Baroque architectural forms, enlivened by the light and color possibilities of twentieth-century technology. Whereas Flavin's light sculptures are designed for interiors and are intimate in scale, those in the Piazza d'Italia contribute to its expansive relationship with the surrounding area.

29.15 Charles W. Moore and William Hersey, Piazza d'Italia, New Orleans, 1978–1979. The piazza was built to celebrate the contributions made to New Orleans by Italian immigrants. Its eclecticism is characteristic of the Post-Modern style.

29.16 Michael Graves, Public Services Building, Portland, Oregon, 1980–1982.

Michael Graves The massive, blocklike Post-Modern buildings of Michael Graves (born 1934) assimilate elements of Cubism and Classical architecture. His striking Public Services Building (fig. **29.16**) in Portland, Oregon, built from 1980 to 1982, also uses color as a significant architectural feature. He defined the stepped base in green and the upper cube in a cream color. Planned mainly for offices, the Public Services Building is decorated on the exterior with multiple square windows piercing the wall surfaces. The side most visible in figure 29.16 incorporates two sets of six dark verticals accented like fluted pilasters against a glass rectangle. Capping these are projecting, inverted trapezoidal blocks that are a visual—not structural—equivalent of Classical capitals. Above these is a large, flat, inverted trapezoid enclosing horizontal strips of windows separated by dark cream-colored horizontal sections.

Complaints that the building is not "environmentally correct"—that is, that it does not conform to the surrounding architecture—ignore the fact that it is "color coded" with the blue sky and green trees. It looms upward from a green base, with the cream block framed above and below by green. Since green combines cream with blue, the building is unified with its natural, if not with its architectural, surroundings. Architecturally it is an amalgam of the Mesopotamian ziggurat, the Egyptian pylon, the Greek temple, and the contemporary American office building. In the original model for the building, Graves had planned to add a group of small structures, inspired by Greek temples and Renaissance churches. Their function would have been to enclose the machinery used to run the building, but they were eliminated from the final version.

I. M. Pei: The Louvre Pyramid

Glass and steel form the prevailing aesthetic in I. M. Pei's (born 1917) Louvre Pyramid (fig. **29.17**). In 1983, the French government commissioned Pei to redesign parts of the Louvre in Paris. Completed in 1988, the pyramid includes an underground complex of reception areas, retail stores, conference rooms, information desks, and other facilities, all located below the vast courtyard. To serve as a shelter, skylight, and museum entrance for the underground area, Pei built a large glass pyramid between the wings of the sixteenth-century building.

Paris had not witnessed such architectural controversy since the construction of the Eiffel Tower in 1889. Not only was the architect not a Frenchman, but the imposing façade of the Louvre, former residence of French kings, was to be blocked by a pyramid—and a glass one at that. Pei's Pyramid has an undeniable presence, with transparent glass that allows a fairly clear view of the buildings beyond. Broad expanses of water around the Pyramid create a reflective interplay with the glass, literally mirroring the old in the new. The view shown here illustrates the dramatic possibilities of the Pyramid as a pure geometric form juxtaposed with a Baroque environment.

CONNECTIONS

See figure 3.12.
Pyramids at Giza, Egypt, c. 2551–2472 B.C.

29.17 I. M. Pei, Louvre Pyramid, Paris, 1988. The pyramid is 65 feet (19.81 m) high at its apex and 108 feet (32.92 m) wide; it contains 105 tons (107,000 kg) of glass.

29.18a, b Richard Rogers, Lloyd's Building, London, 1986. Rogers wrote that "esthetically one can do what one likes with technology . . . but we ignore it at our peril. To our practice, its natural functionalism has an intrinsic beauty." In the Lloyd's Building, Rogers has fulfilled his philosophical view of uniting technology with aesthetic appeal.

Richard Rogers: The Lloyd's Building

By 1977, Lloyd's of London, the international insurance market, needed new quarters. In addition to accommodating the more than five thousand people who use the building every day, the new Lloyd's had to adapt to the technological changes, principally in communications, that were revolutionizing the insurance and other financial markets.

Richard Rogers (born 1933), who was given the commission, is an English architect who had been jointly responsible for the Pompidou Centre in Paris in the 1970s. The irregular, triangular space that Rogers had to work with in London was large, but not large enough to accommodate all of the underwriting staff on one floor. Rogers solved the problem in two ways. First, he created an *atrium*—the original central court of Etruscan and Roman houses—and wrapped all the floors around it. The *atrium,* an architectural feature that was widely revived in the 1970s, is a rectangle rising the entire height of the building (twelve floors) and culminating in a barrel-vaulted, glass and steel roof (fig. **29.18**). The three lower floors form galleries around the *atrium*. Together, they make up the approximately 115,000 square feet (10,700 m^2) where underwriters sit and negotiate terms with brokers. This solution visually unified the working areas of the building and illuminated them from above.

Second, Rogers left the *atrium* space as flexible and open as possible by housing all the ancillary services—air-conditioning ducts, elevators, staircases, toilet facilities, and so forth—in satellite towers built apart from the main structure. At the top of the towers are boxlike "plant rooms," which dominate distant views of the building. Each room is three stories high and contains elevator motors, tanks, and an air-handling plant. On the roofs, bright yellow cradles for carrying maintenance crews are suspended from blue cranes.

Rogers's system (see fig. **29.19**) has the advantage of ensuring the greatest flexibility of space on each floor. On the ground floor, the only structural elements that interrupt the working space are eight concrete columns supporting the galleries, and the escalator block that links the basement and the underwriting floors. Since the mechanical services are located in the towers, they can be replaced or upgraded without disturbing the main floors.

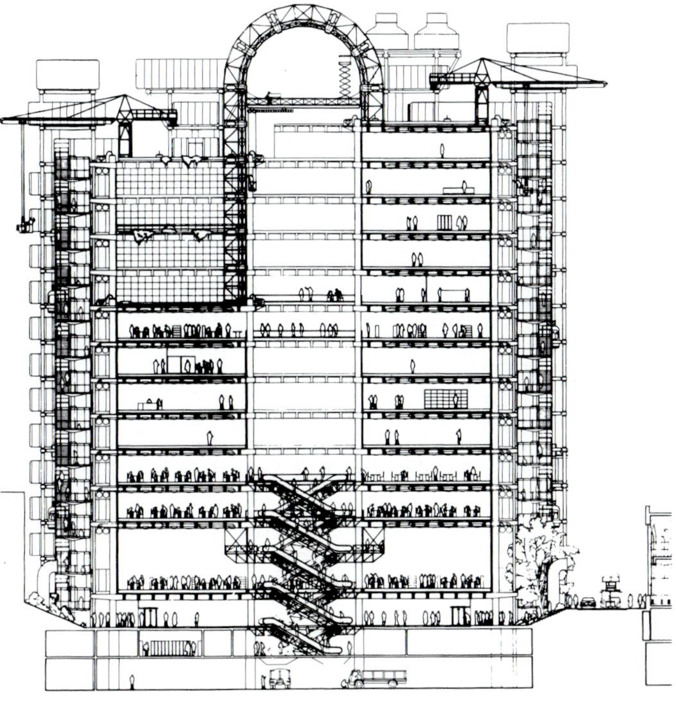

29.19 Schematic section of the Lloyd's Building.

Frank Gehry: The Solomon R. Guggenheim Museum Bilbao

In 1997, the Solomon R. Guggenheim Museum Bilbao opened in Bilbao, on the Bay of Biscay, in Spanish Basque country (fig. **29.20**). The architect, Frank Gehry (born 1929), originally from Toronto, Canada, came to the United States in 1974, living and working mainly in Los Angeles. He is known for his ability to integrate striking new forms into existing spaces. In the 1980s, for example, he assisted in the placement of a giant pair of binoculars by Oldenburg at the entrance to the city of Venice, in California. In 1990, Gehry completed the Frederick R. Weisman Museum in Minneapolis (fig. **29.21**), which shows his interest in merging sculptural with architectural form, animating the building so that it seems to grow and expand upward from its site.

29.20 Frank O. Gehry, Solomon R. Guggenheim Museum Bilbao, Bilbao, Spain, 1993–1997. The museum is 257,000 square feet (24,290 m^2), with 112,000 square feet (10,560 m^2) of gallery space, and stands on the site of an old factory and parking lot. Its construction was part of an urban renewal project for Bilbao and cost $100 million.

29.21 Frank O. Gehry, Frederick R. Weisman Museum, Minneapolis, Minnesota, finished 1990.

The Bilbao Guggenheim, begun in 1993, is situated by the Nervión River, across from a bridge and a thriving port, and surrounded by a water garden. Its striking curvilinear roof forms, referred to as a "metallic flower," are made of titanium, which is durable in the salty atmosphere of Bilbao, and the main structural elements are of limestone-covered blocks. The complexity of the design and its unusual variety of shapes is clear from the plan in figure **29.22**, which shows the way in which the building seems to transform itself as one viewpoint succeeds another. The otherwise prohibitive cost of such a building was mitigated by a three-dimensional computer program known as

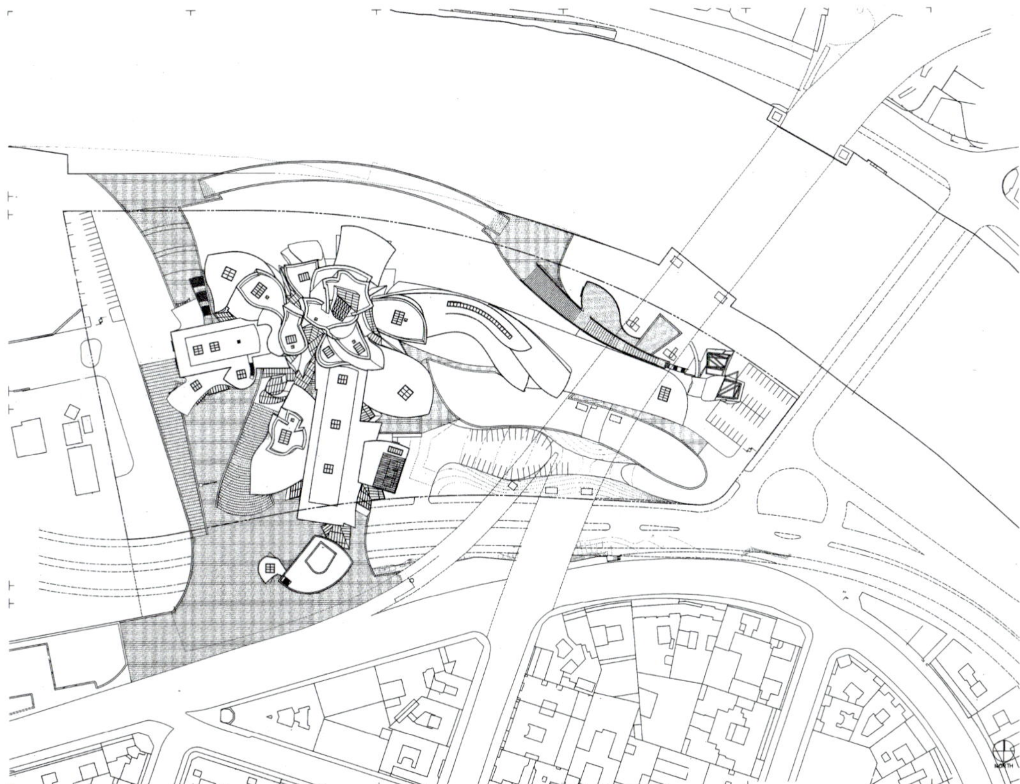

29.22 Frank O. Gehry, plan of the Solomon R. Guggenheim Museum Bilbao, finished 1997.

29.23 Computer-generated Catia image used for the Solomon R. Guggenheim Museum Bilbao, finished 1997.

Catia, designed in France for aerospace projects. Figure **29.23** is a computer image generated by digital mapping of paper and wood models that saved the architect time and reduced expenses by virtually building the museum prior to its actual construction. Gehry described the computer as his "interpreter."

The interior of the museum consists of a large *atrium,* 165 feet (50.29 m) high, which is illuminated by light from windows in the roof. The style of the galleries varies from traditional to boat-shaped (fig. **29.24**), the latter with no columns to interrupt the viewing of installation pieces. All the galleries surround the *atrium* and are accessed by a glass elevator, a system of bridges, and towers containing stairs.

Note the monumental rolled-steel sculpture by the Minimalist Richard Serra (born 1939), which dominates the interior space. The simplified curved planes correspond formally to Gehry's broad, curvilinear architectural spaces. Both the sculpture and the building are united in an expansive, flowing motion. In 2005, Serra installed seven additional sculptures inside the Bilbao Guggenheim, where their curved walls and massive, often claustrophobic interiors also contrast with the open spaces of the building.

29.24 Interior gallery, Solomon R. Guggenheim Museum Bilbao.

Environmental Art

All works of art affect the environment in some way. In its broadest sense, the environment encompasses any indoor or outdoor space. Today, the term tends to refer more to the outdoors—the rural and urban landscape—than to indoor spaces. Four recent artists whose work has had a startling, though usually temporary, impact on the natural environment are Robert Smithson (1938–1973), the Christos (both born 1935), and Andy Goldsworthy (born 1956). The environmental works of Nancy Holt (born 1938), on the other hand, are intended to be permanent.

Robert Smithson

Robert Smithson's *Spiral Jetty* (fig. **29.25**), a huge, single spiral that jutted 400 yards (366 m) out into the Great Salt Lake of Utah, is his best-known "earthwork." As an isolated form, set against a background—in this case, water—*Spiral Jetty* was rooted in 1960s Minimalism, but its concept and actuality are related to the gesture painting of Abstract Expressionism. The philosophy of Smithson's earthworks, however, which is extensively described in his writings, has many levels of meaning. In some of his gallery exhibits, he placed rocks and earth—reflecting his interest in the natural landscape—in boxes and bins indoors (the "non-site," in Smithson's terminology). Crystals, in particular, appealed to him as examples of the earth's geometry, and he used them, along with earth, as an artistic medium.

Ecology, as one might expect, was one of Smithson's primary concerns. *Spiral Jetty* and his other earthworks are all degradable and will eventually succumb to the natural elements. Smithson's interest in the earth has a primeval character. He was inspired by the Neolithic stone structures of Great Britain and their mythic association with the land. Although he created his own earthworks with modern construction equipment, his affinity for the prehistoric earth mounds of the United States and Mexico also influenced the shape of his monuments and their integration with the landscape.

29.25 Robert Smithson, *Spiral Jetty,* Great Salt Lake, Utah, 1970. Rock, salt crystals, earth, and algae; coil 1,500 ft. (457.20 m) long, approx. 15 ft. (4.57 m) wide. Financed by two art galleries, Smithson took a twenty-year lease on 10 acres (4 ha) of land. He hired a contractor to bulldoze some 6,000 tons of earth. The resulting spiral consists of black rock, earth, and salt crystals. The algae inside the spiral change the water's color to red. Smithson wrote an essay on this work, and photographed and filmed it from a helicopter. The Jetty was, for a time, under water but is now becoming visible again.

Nancy Holt

Architectural and sculptural ideas merge in Nancy Holt's approach to environmental art. She was introduced to the subject by her late husband, Robert Smithson, and, after his death, continued to pursue an independent career. Her *Stone Enclosure: Rock Rings* of 1977–1978 (fig. **29.26**) is located in the landscape of Western Washington University (Bellingham, Washington). It is constructed of two concentric rings of stone, which are pierced by arches and twelve circular openings at eye level. Like Stonehenge (see figs. 1.22 and 1.26), *Stone Enclosure* rises abruptly from a green expanse and is related to the sky—what Holt calls the "dead center of the universe." The round holes are connected diagonally by lines of sight corresponding to the directions of the compass. The plane of the structure evokes the antiquity of ideas connecting the circle with divine form. By virtue of the formal association to Stonehenge and other Neolithic cromlechs, and to the later development of arch construction, *Stone Enclosure* embodies the continued existence of the past in the present.

CONNECTIONS

See figure 1.26. The inside ring of Stonehenge.

29.26 Nancy Holt, *Stone Enclosure: Rock Rings,* Western Washington University, 1977–1978. Brown Mountain stone; outer ring 40 ft. (12.19 m) diameter, inner ring 20 ft. (6.10 m) diameter, height of ring walls 10 ft. (3.05 m).

Andy Goldsworthy

For the British artist Andy Goldsworthy (born 1956), nature is the primary medium. He creates dazzling works by arranging foliage, stones, and twigs on the earth's surface. He also forms snow and ice into temporary sculptures, which he photographs in their natural setting before they disappear. He has had exhibitions in Europe and Japan, and is scheduled to have a one-man show at the National Gallery in Washington, D.C. Goldsworthy's main themes involve the changing character of nature, its sense of process and energy. In the sculpture illustrated in figure **29.27**, he has created a starlike burst of icicles radiating from a central point and balanced on natural rock. The variations in the icicles emit different degrees of translucency. This was created in Scotland and photographed in January 1987.

29.27
Andy Goldsworthy,
Icicles
thick ends dipped in snow then water
held until frozen to the work
pouring on water until solid
occasionally using forked sticks as support until stuck
a tense moment when taking them away
breathing on the stick first to release it
sun catching the work for a dangerous half hour
but always intensely cold.
1987. © Andy Goldsworthy.
Courtesy Galerie Lelong, New York.

Christo and Jeanne-Claude

Another approach to shaping the environment can be seen in the work of Christo and Jeanne-Claude. They create a sense of mystery by "wrapping up" buildings or sections of landscape, paradoxically covering something from view while accentuating its external contour. Among the structures they have "wrapped" are the Kunsthalle in Berne (1968) and the Pont-Neuf, the oldest bridge in Paris (1985). They have surrounded eleven islands in Biscayne Bay, Florida, with over 6 million square feet (560,000 m^2) of pink fabric (*Surrounded Islands*) and have run a white fabric fence (*Running Fence*) 24½ miles (39 km) long and 18 feet (5.49 m) high through two California counties.

Christo and Jeanne-Claude's work is sometimes referred to as Conceptual art, which emphasizes its relation to an idea or a concept. This is not, however, the case because the artists actually realize the concept. Unlike artists who intend their works to last, Christo and Jeanne-Claude always remove their projects from their sites, leaving the environment intact. The temporary nature of their large-scale works is part of their aesthetic identity. The continued existence of the work depends on film, photographs, drawings, and models. It endures as a series of visual concepts, temporarily realized on a monumental scale. Another feature distinguishes Christo and Jeanne-Claude from many artists—a unique view of patronage. They accept no financial sponsorship or commissions for large-scale projects and personally provide the funding for construction. Money is raised by selling drawings, collages, and scale models for the projects, as well as early work from the 1950s and 1960s.

Figures **29.28** and **29.29** illustrate sections of the blue and yellow *Umbrellas* in Japan and California, respectively. Their placement is related to their environment. The blue umbrellas are close together, reflecting the limited space of Japan, and the yellow umbrellas are farther apart, whimsically spread out in harmony with the vast California landscape. Blue is consistent with the water that fertilizes the Japanese rice fields, while the yellow echoes the blond grass and brown hills of the dry valley in which the California umbrellas were located. As freestanding, dynamic forms, the umbrellas have a sculptural quality. They define space and interact with it, casting shadows and swaying with the wind. Each umbrella was the size of a small studio apartment.

29.28 and **29.29** Christo and Jeanne-Claude, *The Umbrellas*, Japan–U.S.A., 1984–1991. Nylon and aluminum. Photos Wolfgang Volz, Christo. **29.28:** detail of 1,340 blue umbrellas in Ibraki, Japan. **29.29:** detail of 1,760 yellow umbrellas in California, U.S.A. *Umbrellas* ran 12 miles (19 km) in length in Japan and 18 miles (29 km) in California. Height of each umbrella, including the base, was 19 feet 8¼ inches (6.00 m), diameter was 28 feet 5 inches (8.66 m), weight without base was 448 pounds (203 kg). The fabric area was about 638 square feet (59.27 m^2). At sunrise on October 9, 1991, 1,880 workers opened 3,100 umbrellas in Ibraki, Japan, and in California. The project, which cost the artists $20 million, was dismantled eighteen days after the umbrellas were opened, and the aluminum was recycled. Christo was born in communist Bulgaria but escaped and settled in Paris in 1958, where he met Jeanne-Claude. They moved to New York in 1964 and have lived there ever since, although their projects have taken them around the world.

29.30 Christo and Jeanne-Claude, *Wrapped Reichstag*, Berlin, 1971–1995. Photos Wolfgang Volz, Christo. The wrapping was carried out in 1995 by 90 climbers and 120 installation workers, and 10 German companies manufactured the equipment. The wrapping material consisted of 1,076,000 square feet (99,963.67 m^2) of woven polypropylene fabric with an aluminum surface and 51,181 feet (15,599.97 m) of blue polypropylene rope, 1¼ inches (3.18 cm) thick.

On June 24, 1995, Christo and Jeanne-Claude completed the wrapping of the Reichstag in Berlin (fig. **29.30**). They had spent twenty-four years and made fifty-four trips to Germany in their efforts to obtain permission for the project, which was denied three times—in 1977, 1981, and 1987. The building itself was originally designed in 1894. In 1933, soon after Hitler became chancellor, it was set on fire. The Reichstag was destroyed again in 1945, during the Battle of Berlin, and later restored. In 1990, following the reunification of Germany, the seat of German government moved from Bonn to Berlin, and the Reichstag was occupied by the Bundestag, the lower house of the German parliament. Permission for the "wrapping" was finally granted in February 1994, after members of the Bundestag debated the issue and voted 292 in favor, 223 against, with 9 abstentions.

The *Wrapped Reichstag* was a silver-gray architectural specter, which is shown here surrounded by crowds of visitors. The vertical folds of the silvery fabric are reminiscent of Classical draperies. The fabric is held against the building with blue ropes, which accent the Reichstag's structural elements and create a sense of expanding, organic form. Two weeks from the day of its completion, on July 7, the "wrapped" Reichstag was unwrapped, and the aluminum and steel were recycled.

In 1980, Christo and Jeanne-Claude proposed a two-week project entitled *The Gates, Project for Central Park, New York City* (fig. **29.31**). As is often the case, the project

29.31 Christo, *The Gates, Project for Central Park, New York City,* 2003 (in two parts). Pencil, pastel, wax crayon, technical data, fabric sample, and aerial photograph; 15 × 96 in. (0.38 × 2.44 m) and 42 × 96 in. (1.07 × 2.44 m).

initially met with vigorous local resistance. A 185-page report by the Parks Department rejected the idea. Eventually, however, New York's Mayor Bloomberg supported the project, which became a reality in February 2005.

Christo and Jeanne-Claude envisioned steel gates with rectangles of saffron fabric extending from the top of each gate to some 6 feet over the ground. In 1979, the first drawing was entitled *Ten Thousand Gates;* in 2005, there were 7,500 gates. The gates were 12 feet tall in 1979; they were 16 feet tall in 2005. In 1979, the thin steel poles were considered only as a means of suspending fabric panels, while in 2005 the poles were made of a thick saffron-colored vinyl and had a commanding profile, 5 inches × 5 inches. They were no longer simply structural, but an important part of the sculpture. The top of the fabric panel in 1979 was attached by loops to a horizontal steel cable; in 2005, the upper parts of the fabric panels were secured inside the bottom part of the horizontal pole in a "sail tunnel."

The view in figure **29.32** shows the *Gates* as it was realized in Central Park for a two-week period. The wind is blowing, creating a variety of shapes and rhythms in the flowing fabric. There is also variety in the color—ranging from orange and saffron to yellow, depending on the light. The movement of the *Gates* is repeated in the visitors strolling through the walkways, whereas the skyscrapers surrounding the park create a backdrop of patterned, static vertical stone.

29.32 Christo and Jeanne-Claude, *The Gates*, Central Park, New York City, 1979–2005. © Christo 2005. Photo: Wolfgang Volz.

29.33 Valerie Jaudon, *Long Division,* 23rd Street Station, IRT Subway Line, New York, 1988. Painted steel; 12 × 60 ft. (3.66 × 18.29 m). Photo courtesy of Carroll Janis, New York.

Urban Environment

The urban environment has also been influenced by artistic "projects." *Long Division* of 1988 (fig. **29.33**) by Valerie Jaudon (born 1945) is a painted steel barrier commissioned by the Metropolitan Transportation Authority in New York City. Located in the 23rd Street subway station, *Long Division* is an "open wall" enlivened by curves and diagonals that seem to dance across the vertical bars. The surrounding neon lights and broad areas of color create a sharp contrast to the dark accents of the barrier.

A recent development in painting that has been inspired by an aspect of the modern urban environment are works with imagery derived from graffiti. Graffiti—which are visual statements and often a personal affirmation—and public reactions to them call into question the boundary between the creative and destructive impulses.

CARBON/OXYGEN of 1984 (fig. **29.34**) by Jean-Michel Basquiat (1960–1988) conveys the frenetic pace and mortal dangers of the city in a harsh, linear style derived from graffiti. The child-like drawing of the buildings is ironically contrasted with scenes of explosion and death. Various methods of transportation—cars, planes, and rocket ships—create a sense of speed and of the technology that pollutes the environment. The black face at the center of the picture stares blankly at the viewer as if warning of threatened destruction. The title implicitly poses the question whether we are going to poison the air we breathe or ensure that it remains clean.

29.34 Jean-Michel Basquiat, *CARBON/OXYGEN,* 1984. Acrylic, oilstick, and silkscreen on canvas; 66 × 60 in. (167.6 × 152.4 cm). Private collection, Switzerland. Courtesy, Robert Miller Gallery, New York.

Another modern expression of the urban environment in works of art is reflected in Andres Serrano's (born 1950) series of thirty photographs entitled *Nomads.* These large Cibachromes represent the homeless of America's cities. Although the title of the series refers to the figures of nomads who wander the city streets, the photographs do not show the suffering, poverty, or anonymity of the figures. Instead, as in *Sir Leonard* (fig. **29.35**), Serrano disrupts expectations by ennobling and individualizing his subjects. He also monumentalizes them by combining a close-up viewpoint with an enlarged scale. Sir Leonard, for example, is relatively well groomed. His beard and mustache are neatly trimmed, and he wears a felt hat, a jacket, and woolen gloves. The only suggestions of his homelessness (contradicted by the epithet "Sir") are the torn fabric by his white scarf and the fact that he wears two jackets and two scarves.

He also displays a belt buckle as if it were a medal; it appears to have been taken from a pair of jeans, for it is inscribed "IN DENIM WE TRUST" and "QUALITY GARMENTS FOR QUALITY PEOPLE." The former is a pun on the United States currency inscription "IN GOD WE TRUST," an ironic allusion to Sir Leonard's indigence. At the same time, the central image on the buckle is a relief of the famous fourth-century-B.C. Etruscan bronze statue *Wounded Chimera* (see fig. 6.3), a creature having the body of a lion and a serpent's tail. A goat's head emerges from the Chimera's back. In the detail on the belt buckle, Serrano associates Sir Leonard with the mythic Greek hero Bellerophon, who rode the winged horse Pegasus and slew the Chimera.

CONNECTIONS

See figure 6.3. *Wounded Chimera,* Arezzo, second quarter of the 4th century B.C.

29.35 Andres Serrano, *Nomads (Sir Leonard),* 1990. Cibachrome print, edition of four; 60 × 49½ in. (1.52 × 1.26 m).

Feminist Art

Although women artists for centuries have made significant contributions to the history of Western art, the iconography of feminism per se is a phenomenon of the twentieth and twenty-first centuries.

Judy Chicago: *The Dinner Party*

In 1979, Judy Chicago (née Cohen; born 1939) created her monumental installation *The Dinner Party* (fig. **29.36**) with the assistance of hundreds of female coworkers. The result is a triangular feminist version of *The Last Supper* (see fig. 14.14) with strong diagonals that are reminiscent of Tintoretto's *Last Supper* (see fig. 15.15). We saw in Marisol's *Last Supper* (see fig. 28.19) that the artist introduced herself as both viewer and participant in the work. Here, on the other hand, Jesus and his apostles have been replaced by the place settings of thirty-nine distinguished women such as Queen Hatshepsut of Egypt, the American painter Georgia O'Keeffe, and the British author Virginia Woolf. The settings are designed to commemorate the achievements of such women even though the women themselves are not actually represented. The plates are decorated with designs that are intentionally vaginal because, according to the artist, that was the one feature all the women at the table had in common.

Thirty-nine is three times the number of Jesus plus his twelve apostles. The tiled floor contains 999 names of famous women not referred to in the place settings. Traditional female crafts, such as embroidery, appliqué, needlepoint, painting on china, and so forth, are used for details. In part, this is to emphasize the value of these skills, which feminists believe to have been undervalued by a male-dominated society.

The artist established a foundation to send *The Dinner Party* on tour and later published a monograph on it that included the biographies of the women it celebrated. Despite the originality of Chicago's conception and the new iconographic content of her piece, the work would have less impact without its historical relevance. For although the triangle can be read as a female symbol, it also refers to the Trinity and is thus rooted in Christian art and culture. Likewise, the numerical regularity and symmetry of the design links the formal arrangement of *The Dinner Party* with Leonardo's *Last Supper*.

29.36 Judy Chicago, *The Dinner Party*, 1974–1979. Mixed media; 48 ft. × 42 ft. × 3 ft. (14.63 m × 12.80 m × 0.91 m). © Judy Chicago, 1979. Collection of The Brooklyn Museum of Art, Gift of The Elizabeth A. Sackler Foundation. Photo: © Donald Woodman. In 1970 at Valencia, California, Chicago cofounded the first feminist art program in the United States. This involved the collection of historical data about female artists and other consciousness-raising activities, including *Womanhouse* (1972), a project in which Chicago and others renovated a disused house and filled it with mixed-media constructions on the theme of traditional female roles.

CONNECTIONS

See figure 14.14. Leonardo da Vinci, *Last Supper*, c. 1495–1498.

CONNECTIONS

See figure 15.15. Jacopo Tintoretto, *Last Supper*, 1592–1594.

Body Art: Kiki Smith

A recent development, particularly in sculpture, that is derived from the feminist movement is so-called Body Art. In general, Body Art signals a return to the interest in the human form, which in some artists focuses primarily on the female body.

The Body Art of Kiki Smith (born 1954) challenges viewers by refusing to be "pretty." Smith has developed an iconography of body parts, in particular those that reveal the interior functions of the female. There is a political significance for Smith in the metaphor of the body and the "body politic," with the hidden body systems as signs of hidden social issues. She has been engaged with contemporary controversies over AIDS, gender, race, and battered women.

Smith was born in Germany to American parents; her father and sister were artists. When her parents died, she made death masks of them, as well as of her grandmother when she died. In 1976, Smith came to New York, studied *Gray's Anatomy* in 1979, and in 1985 trained as an emergency medical technician. Among her works are her mother's feet cast in glass, a bronze womb, hanging heads and hands, and veins, arteries, and body fluids preserved in jars. In these subjects, Smith evokes both the embalming practices of ancient Egypt and the severed body parts of Brancusi.

Smith's *Mary Magdalene* of 1994 (fig. **29.37**) is a traditional Christian subject rendered in a new light. The bronze body is covered with incised lines, except for the smooth breasts and navel area. The lines are reminiscent of the Magdalene's hair, grown long after the Crucifixion as penance for her sins. As such, the figure represents the penitent Magdalene, like that depicted by Donatello (see fig. 13.58) and other Renaissance artists. The long hair, combined with the ankle chain, endows the figure with a subhuman quality, which places her at the borderline between human and animal, saint and sinner, chastity and lust.

Smith has related this sculpture to French folktales about the Magdalene's life after Jesus's death. According to these stories, Mary Magdalene lived in the wilderness for seven years. When, on one occasion, she happened to catch sight of her reflection in a pool, she was punished for her narcissism and condemned to do further penance. Her flowing tears created the seven rivers of Provence, in the south of France.

CONNECTIONS

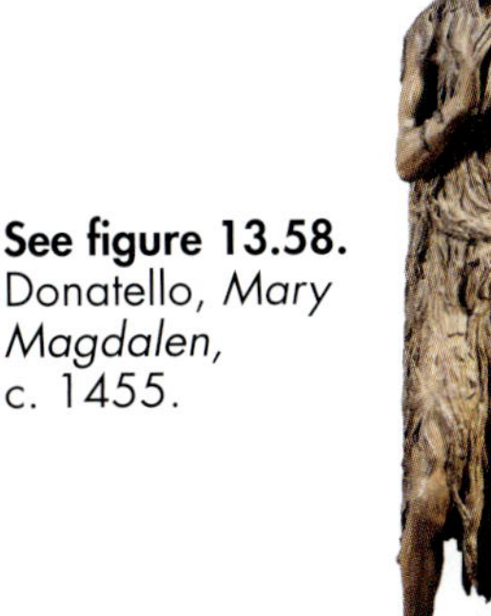

See figure 13.58. Donatello, *Mary Magdalen*, c. 1455.

29.37 (right) Kiki Smith, *Mary Magdalene*, 1994. Silicon bronze and forged steel, edition 2 of 3; 59⅞ × 20½ × 21⅝ in. (152.1 × 52.1 × 54.9 cm).

Maya Ying Lin: *The Women's Table*

On October 1, 1993, Yale University dedicated *The Women's Table* (fig. **29.38**) by Maya Ying Lin (born 1959). Juxtaposed here with the more traditional campus architecture, the *Table* memorializes Yale's decision to admit women. Designed as a place for students to meet, talk, and read, the *Table* is also a "fountain." A smooth swirl of water slides across the tabletop and echoes the curvilinear shape of the green granite spiral. This, in turn, is supported by an irregular triangular base made of black granite, on which students can sit. The smooth texture of the granite and its sleek, elegant forms are reminiscent of the high polish and "essential" forms achieved by Brancusi. Lin also has affinities with the outdoor sculptures and taste for varieties of stone that are characteristic of Noguchi's work.

Carved into the top of the *Table* is a spiral, which records the numbers of females attending Yale (fig. **29.39**). At the center of the spiral are about three rings of zeros. The last zero is followed by the number 13, which corresponds to the year 1873, when thirteen women were enrolled in the School of Fine Arts. Carved to the side of the spiral are the decades from 1870 to 1990, indicating the number of female students in any single year. As the spiral expands, the number of women increases, and its open-ended design looks forward to the growing future of women on the Yale campus.

29.38 Maya Ying Lin, *The Women's Table*, Yale University, New Haven, Connecticut, 1993. Green granite on black granite base; 30 in. (76.2 cm) high, 10 × 15 ft. (3.05 × 4.57 m) in diameter.

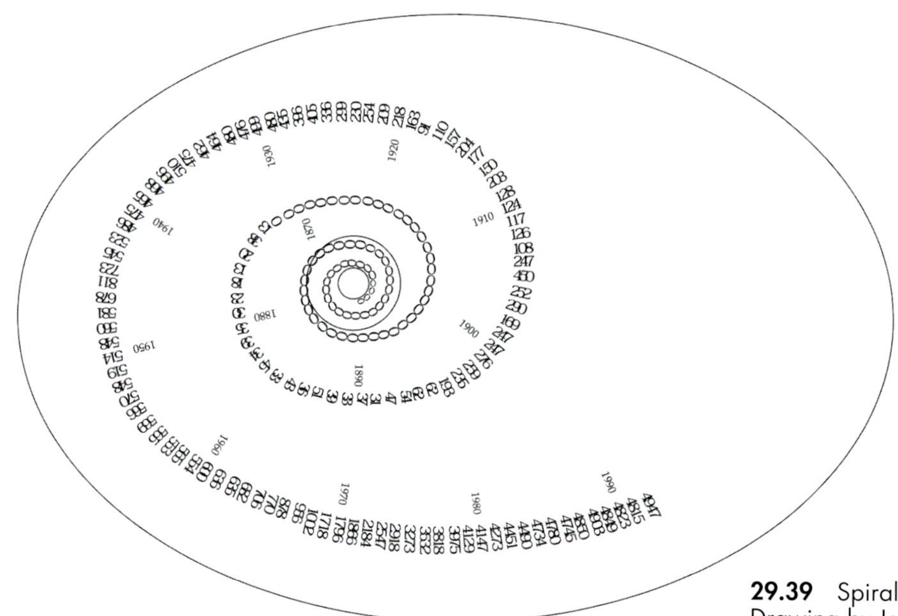

29.39 Spiral diagram of *The Women's Table*, fig. 29.38. Drawing by Ian Hunt.

Plus ça change . . .

At times, history seems to repeat itself. The French expression *Plus ça change, plus c'est la même chose* ("The more things change, the more they remain the same") well describes this historical paradox. In the visual arts, it is possible to witness this phenomenon unfolding before our very eyes. Themes persist, styles change and are revived. New themes appear, old themes reappear. The media of art also persist; artists still use bronze and marble, fresco, oil paint, encaustic, and stained glass. Nevertheless, modern technology is constantly expanding the media available to artists as well as introducing new subjects and inspiring stylistic developments. This can be illustrated by four trends of the early twentieth century that continue to emerge in contemporary art—Expressionism, the preeminence of the object, the rejection of the object by Conceptual artists, and Surrealism. Technology has also influenced artistic media, and this has given rise to new art forms—among them, video and digital art—although similar themes continue to be represented.

Bob Thompson and the Renaissance

The African-American artist Bob Thompson (1937–1966) died in Rome before the age of thirty. His powerful images, which heralded a promising artistic future, reflect some of the ways in which artists assimilate the past and rework it. Thompson's *Crucifixion* of 1963–1964 (fig. **29.40**) shows the influence of Symbolist color (see Chapter 23) combined with Renaissance iconography and the racial turmoil of the American civil rights movement of the 1960s. He was influenced by monumental Italian Renaissance painters such as Masaccio and Piero della Francesca, and by the sixteenth-century Northern humanist artists Bruegel and Cranach.

Thompson's *Crucifixion* was inspired by Cranach's *Crucifixion* (see fig. 16.19)—in the arrangement of the figures and in the iconography. The foreshortened red, crucified Jesus on the right corresponds to Cranach's placement of the same figure; the swirling sky, also similar to Cranach's, alludes to nature's ominous response to the death of Jesus. Thompson's Jesus, shown in three-quarter view, is the artist's self-portrait. The yellow figure—the good thief (on Jesus's right)—is seen in front view. The unrepentant thief, depicted in orange, is on Jesus's left (as well as ours) and is turned away from the viewer, which accentuates his anonymity. The blue, red-haired Mary resembles Thompson's Caucasian wife who, as in the Cranach, seems to be conversing with Saint John. The "colored" people in the painting reflect both Thompson's interest in contemporary racial issues and the correlation between his personal artistic identity as a man of color and of colors.

CONNECTIONS

See figure 16.19. Lucas Cranach the Elder, *Crucifixion*, 1503.

29.40 Bob Thompson, *Crucifixion*, 1963–1964. Oil on canvas; 5 × 4 ft. (1.52 × 1.22 m). Private collection. Photo Maggie Nimkin.

Bruce Nauman and Marcel Duchamp

Another example of artistic appropriation in the 1960s can be seen in the work of Bruce Nauman (born 1941), for whom figuration is part of a more general return to the object. His wide range of media includes neon lighting, holography, video, and audio effects, as well as the more traditional forms of painting and sculpture. He has filmed himself in a variety of performance sequences, using dance, music, and language. His attraction to the object is consistent with Dada, especially the multimedia of Man Ray and the wordplay of Duchamp. "My interest in Duchamp," Nauman has said, "has to do with his use of objects to stand for ideas. I like Man Ray better: there's less 'tied-upness' in his work, more unreasonableness."[5]

Nauman's relationship to Duchamp is evident in his *Self-Portrait as a Fountain* (fig. **29.41**). Illuminated from the right by an eerie green light and from the left by a yellow light, he emerges from a dark background reminiscent of Caravaggio's tenebrism (see Chapter 17). Nauman reflects the twentieth-century trend in which the artist is present in his own work. He spouts water from his mouth, holding up his hands as if to balance himself.

Echoing the visual pun of Duchamp's *Urinal* (see fig. 26.2), Nauman himself is the ready-made in this photograph, which has been "aided" by the artist's action. In addition to visual punning, Nauman is fascinated by philosophical and literary language as well as wordplay—especially of certain modern French writers. He is quoted as saying, "I think the point where language starts to break down as a useful tool for communication is the same edge where poetry or art occurs. . . . If you only deal with what is known, you'll have redundancy; on the other hand, if you only deal with the unknown, you cannot communicate at all. There's always some combination of the two, and it is how they touch each other that makes communication interesting."[6]

29.41 Bruce Nauman, *Self-Portrait as a Fountain,* 1966–1970. Photograph; 19¾ × 22¾ in. (50.2 × 57.8 cm). Leo Castelli, New York.

CONNECTIONS

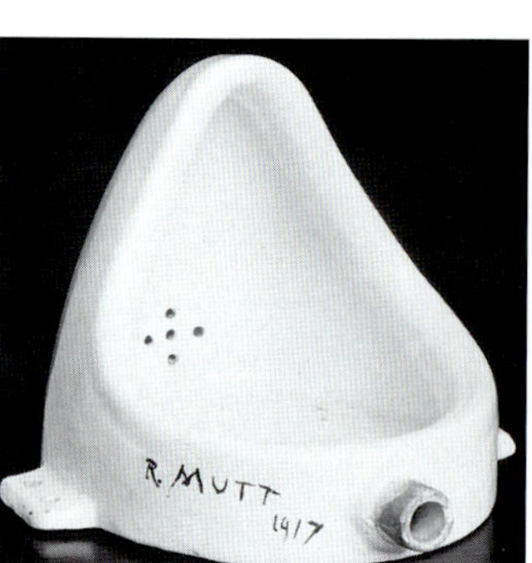

See figure 26.2. Marcel Duchamp, *Fountain (Urinal),* 1917.

Susan Rothenberg

In a striking break with the geometric abstraction of the late 1960s and early 1970s, the animal imagery of Susan Rothenberg (born 1945), like the work of Nauman, marks a partial return to figuration. This is exemplified in her paintings of horses, which have been a subject of Western art since the Paleolithic era. Rothenberg's *IXI* of 1976–1977 (fig. **29.42**) is figurative, but the impasto character of the paint, from which the horse literally seems to emerge, has an Expressionist quality. The paint's rich texture, together with the horse's submersion in it, creates the impression that the paint and the horse are one and the same. The two asymmetrical black diagonals enhance the movement of the horse, while the white verticals restrain it. By this dynamic balance, Rothenberg achieves a unique simultaneity of arrest and motion.

29.42 Susan Rothenberg, *IXI*, 1976–1977. Vinyl emulsion and acrylic on canvas; 6 ft. 6⅛ in. × 8 ft. 8 in. (1.98 × 2.64 m). Hirshhorn Museum and Sculpture Garden, Smithsonian Institution (Joseph H. Hirshhorn Purchase Fund, 1990). Rothenberg is married to Bruce Nauman; they live on a ranch in northern New Mexico, where horses continue to be a large part of Rothenberg's life (although she has not painted one since 1979).

Memorial Art: Anselm Kiefer and Maya Ying Lin

Anselm Kiefer Anselm Kiefer (born 1945), a prominent German Neo-Expressionist and a student of Joseph Beuys, creates powerful canvases using aggressive lines and harsh textures. His *To the Unknown Painter* of 1983 (fig. **29.43**) protests the Fascist persecution of artists in Europe and tyranny of all kinds. It also evokes one of the primary impulses to make art—namely, the wish to keep alive the memory of the deceased. The somber colors, jagged surface texture, and dynamic energy of the brushwork evoke the devastation and chaos of war. From beneath the scorched picture plane a large, rectangular structure comes into focus, looming upward to memorialize those who stand for the forces of creativity and to defeat the forces of war and destruction. The image seems to be engaged in its own process of becoming, as if literally forming itself from the formlessness of what has been destroyed.

29.43 Anselm Kiefer, *To the Unknown Painter,* 1983. Oil, emulsion, woodcut, shellac, latex, and straw on canvas; 9 ft. 2 in. × 9 ft. 2 in. (2.79 × 2.79 m). Carnegie Museum of Art, Pittsburgh (Richard M. Scaife Fund and A. W. Mellon Acquisition Endowment Fund, 83.53).

Maya Ying Lin Some eleven years before the dedication of *The Women's Table,* when Maya Lin was still a student at the Yale School of Architecture, she won the commission to design a memorial to those who died in the Vietnam War. Known as the *Vietnam Veterans Memorial* (fig. **29.44**), the work is a more understated form of protest than Kiefer's. On two wings of polished granite, each 246 feet (74.99 m) long, seventy slabs display the names of every American killed in the war. A total of 58,183 names are inscribed in the order of their deaths. Viewers become engaged in reading the names as the reflective nature of the wall mirrors the world of the living. In this work, therefore, it is the name of the deceased, rather than the image or likeness, that conveys immortality.

29.44 Maya Ying Lin, *Vietnam Veterans Memorial,* the Mall, Washington, D.C., 1981–1983. Polished granite.

29.45 Jeff Koons, *New Hoover Convertibles, Green, Blue; New Hoover Convertibles, Green, Blue; Double-Decker,* 1981–1987. Vacuum cleaners, Plexiglas, fluorescent lights; 22 units overall, 9 ft. 8 in. × 3 ft. 5 in. × 2 ft. 4 in. (2.95 × 1.04 × 0.71 m). Collection, Whitney Museum of American Art, New York (Purchase, funds from Sondra and Charles Gilman, Jr., Foundation/Painting and Sculpture Committee).

Jeff Koons: Return to the Object

The "objects" of Jeff Koons (born 1955), sometimes dismissed as kitsch, are clearly derived from Duchamp's Ready-Mades. They are also related to Oldenburg's Pop Art iconography of everyday household objects and Flavin's neon-light sculptures. They lack the Expressionist attraction to the material textures of paint and the traditional media of sculpture. His *New Hoover Convertibles, Green, Blue; New Hoover Convertibles, Green, Blue; Double-Decker* of 1981–1987 (fig. **29.45**), for example, consists of four vacuum cleaners in Plexiglas cases illuminated by fluorescent lights. Koons enshrines the vacuums, revealing them as icons of our technological society. His title is a kind of verbal collage, juxtaposing the brand of vacuum (Hoover) with the formality of color (blue and green) and allusions to modern transportation (convertible—as in cars—and double-decker—as in buses).

Nancy Graves

The influence of Dada and Surrealism, in which content and objects are often playfully infused with ideas, can be seen in *Morphose* (fig. **29.46**) by Nancy Graves (1940–1995). Her linear abstractions of natural form are reminiscent of Calder's witty mobiles. The central part is a turbine rotor from a ship, which integrates the "object" into a sculptural assemblage, as Picasso did in his *Bull's Head* of 1943 (see fig. 25.9). Anthropomorphic quality is created by Graves in a series of visual metaphors—a ball for the head, sardines for hair, bronze bananas for fingers. At the same time, however, the sculpture as a whole resembles a sea animal rotating slowly in space. Graves's title is itself a kind of Surrealist pun, suggesting the words *metamorphosis, anthropomorphism,* and *metaphor.* All are related to the Greek word *morphe,* meaning "shape" or "form," which is a foundation of every work of art.

CONNECTIONS

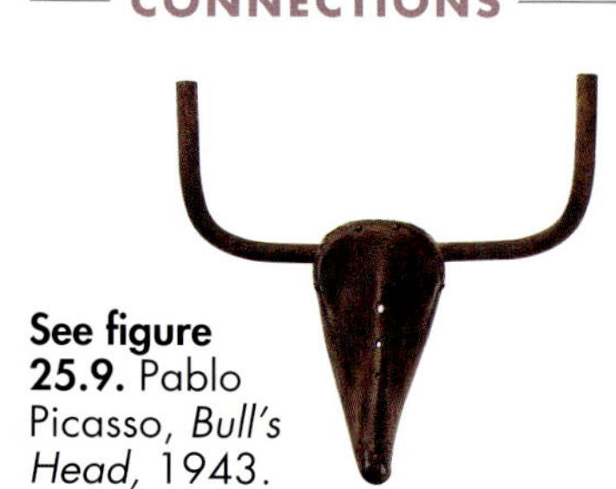

See figure 25.9. Pablo Picasso, *Bull's Head,* 1943.

29.46 Nancy Graves, *Morphose,* 1986. Bronze and copper with polychrome patina and baked enamel; 4 ft. 6 in. × 3 ft. 3 in. × 3 ft. 3 in. (1.37 × 0.99 × 0.99 m). Courtesy, M. Knoedler & Co., Inc. Among Graves's earlier works are a series of freestanding abstract forms based on the objects and rituals of Native Americans and other tribal societies. From the late 1970s, she began adding three-dimensional *objets trouvés* to her paintings and surface colors to her sculptures.

Mark Tansey

In *Action Painting II* (fig. **29.47**), Mark Tansey (born 1949) uses conceptual appropriation to create a visual pun combining Abstract Expressionist Action painting with Realism. This large, monochromatic canvas shows a group of eerily static, self-consciously posing male and female artists painting a rocket launch. Here, the "action" is the explosive burst of fire and smoke billowing from the tail of the rocket and its sharp, vertical thrust into space. Echoing the rocket's vertical is the flagpole at the left. The fluttering Stars and Stripes denotes the Americanness of the event. Art history itself is also a subject of the picture, for the artist draws on the theme of paintings within paintings and recalls Courbet's *Studio* (see fig. 21.5). But whereas Courbet's artist is shown painting a calm landscape, Tansey's artists depict an explosive technological event that extends the notion of nature and reality beyond the planet Earth.

CONNECTIONS

See figure 21.5. Gustave Courbet, *Interior of My Studio*, detail: center section, 1855.

29.47 Mark Tansey, *Action Painting II*, 1984. Oil on canvas; 76 × 110 in. (193.0 × 279.4 cm).

Cindy Sherman

The theme of innovation and continuity is expressed literally in some of the work of Cindy Sherman (born 1954). Her medium is photography and she is her own model. She has photographed herself in various guises from fashion model to cadaver. In an early series of black-and-white photographs, she showed herself as if in stills from gangster movies. Her *Untitled* of 1989 (fig. **29.48**) is a photograph of herself as Raphael's *Fornarina* (fig. **29.49**). In what is apparently a satire on its Renaissance inspiration, Sherman attaches a pair of false breasts and shows herself as pregnant. Her left hand replicates the traditional gesture signifying both modesty and seduction (cf. figs. 13.24, 13.25, 13.57). With her right hand she holds up the heavy mesh drapery resembling a household curtain, which contrasts with Raphael's lighter, more diaphanous material. This gesture recalls that of Arnolfini's bride (see fig. 13.67). Instead of the orderly, embroidered headscarf of the Fornarina, Sherman wears a ragged cloth. In such transformations of the Renaissance work, Sherman creates a pregnant, housewifely replacement of Raphael's idealized, Classical muse.

The Fornarina ("baker's wife" in Italian) was reputed to have been one of Raphael's mistresses, a reading that is reinforced by the background leaves of laurel, myrtle, and quince. All are attributes of Venus and therefore associated with love. This work is also one of Raphael's very few signed paintings—the neatly jeweled armband is inscribed "Raphael of Urbino," suggesting his possession of the woman. Cindy Sherman, on the other hand, wears a garter on her arm, as if to declare her independence from men. At the same time, however, she plays on various aspects of the woman's role in society, including the sense that she is weighed down by childbearing and household chores. Sherman's humor lies in her visual punning and in the fine line between aspects of her own role, which shifts between artist and model, self and other.

29.48 Cindy Sherman, *Untitled,* 1989. Color photograph, 5 ft. 1½ in. × 4 ft. ¼ in. (1.56 × 1.22 m). Metro Pictures, New York. One of Sherman's best-known projects of the late 1970s was a series of black-and-white film stills, in which she dressed as a stereotypical female character—the heroine, the ingénue, the vamp—in grade-B Hollywood movies.

29.49 Raphael, *La Fornarina,* c. 1518. Oil on panel; 33½ × 23½ in. (85.1 × 59.7 cm). Galleria Nazionale (Palazzo Barberini), Rome.

29.50 Yasumasa Morimura, *Self-Portrait (Actress)/White Marilyn*, 1996. Ilfochrome and acrylic sheet; $37\frac{1}{4} \times 47\frac{1}{4}$ in. (94.6 × 120.0 cm). Courtesy Luhring Augustine Gallery, New York.

Yasumasa Morimura

The Post-Modern Japanese artist Yasumasa Morimura (born 1951) remakes European paintings, using himself as the model. He also photographs himself as movie stars, regardless of whether the actual person is male or female. He thus crosses the boundaries of race, gender, and nationality, and uses computers to make digital alterations to the original photograph.

In *Self-Portrait (Actress)/White Marilyn* (fig. **29.50**), Morimura shows himself in three provocative poses, all in imitation of Marilyn Monroe, who is self-consciously aware of being looked at by an audience. "She" stands in silver high-heels on large cylindrical pedestals, her blowing white skirt based on a scene from *The Seven Year Itch*. We also recognize Marilyn Monroe's signature dyed blonde hair and prominent red lipstick, and yet the face is the narrow face of the artist, rather than hers.

Video Art: Nam June Paik, Bill Viola, and Shirin Neshat

The medium of video has offered artists new ways of conveying old, as well as contemporary, themes. One of the leading exponents of video art was the Korean-born composer, performer, and visual artist Nam June Paik (1932-2006). He studied philosophy, aesthetics, and music at the University of Tokyo and in 1956 went to Munich to study music. In Germany, Paik met the avant-garde musician John Cage and worked with Joseph Beuys. In the late 1960s, Paik began to create video sculptures consisting of television monitors arranged in significant shapes and projecting specific, controlled images. He developed a philosophy of cybernetics (the study of communication processes) that he translated into works, merging the transitory character of performance art with the durability of the created object. In a pamphlet entitled *Manifestos* of 1966, Paik wrote: "As the Happening is the fusion of various arts, so cybernetics is the exploitation of boundary regions between and across various existing sciences."[7]

In *TV Buddha* of 1974 (fig. **29.51**), Paik plays with the border between spiritual meditation and the technology of the machine age. Sometimes referred to as the "Zen Master of Video," Paik juxtaposes the religious leader with the new religion of the masses—the TV set. The Buddha sits in a traditional pose and sees himself on the screen, a metaphor, like Picasso's *Girl before a Mirror* (see fig. 25.11), in which the reflection is an instrument of self-contemplation. The rotundity of both the TV set and the Buddha accentuates the narcissistic pun—are we seeing the ideal selflessness of Buddhism or the mindlessness of one who is "glued to the television"? *TV Buddha* exemplifies Paik's assertion that "cybernated art is very important, but art for cybernetic life is more important, and the latter need not be cybernated."[8]

In 1996, inspired by a trip to Denmark, Paik produced the *Robot* series—portraits of six famous Danes. Figure **29.52** is *Hamlet Robot*, composed of radios, televisions, and laser-disc players. Paik's *Hamlet*, like Shakespeare's, is a man who would be king but bows his crowned head as if weighed down by despair. The artist conveys Hamlet's proverbial ambivalence by the contrast of the lowered right arm holding the staff of rule with the raised left arm. The skull of Yorick posed on Hamlet's left hand is reminiscent of the warnings inherent in *vanitas* iconography, and its juxtaposition with Hamlet's head seems to foreshadow his tragic end. "The Buddhists also say," according to Paik, that "karma is samsara. Relationship is metempsychosis. We are in open circuits."[9]

29.51 Nam June Paik, *TV Buddha*, 1974. Video installation with statue. Stedelijk Museum, Amsterdam.

29.52 Nam June Paik, *Hamlet Robot*, 1996. 2 radios, 24 TVs, transformer, 2 laser-disc players, laser discs, crown, scepter, sword, and skull; 12 ft. 1 in. × 7 ft. 4⅕ in. × 2 ft. 7⅞ in. (3.66 × 2.24 × 0.81 m).

The same year that Paik created *Hamlet Robot* out of radios and television monitors, Bill Viola (born 1951) presented his video installation *The Crossing*. Using sound as well as video, Viola combined the ancient dualism of fire and water with modern media. He projected two sequences, one on either side of a screen, in which a man is consumed and destroyed by the elemental power of nature. Influenced by Eastern religions (including Buddhism and Islam) and interested in the relationship of light and color to form, Viola shows a rapid evolution (a crossing over) from human to nonhuman—and implicitly from physicality to spirituality—as his man disappears into fire or water.

Both sequences are shown simultaneously and begin with a man walking toward the viewer. In the fire sequence (fig. **29.53**), a votive candle at the man's feet becomes a raging fire (accompanied by a roar) and swallows him up. The same sequence occurs on the opposite side of the screen, but with water (fig. **29.54**). At first a few drops fall on the man, but then they become a flood and, also accompanied by a roar, engulf him. In contrast to traditional works, found in nearly every culture, that represent various religious and mythical accounts of human creation, Viola reverses the process and undoes the creation of human form. His man thus stands for humanity as a whole, which is destroyed by the elemental forces of fire and water.

In the context of twentieth- and twenty-first-century art history, Viola's video can also be seen as a metaphor for the dissolution of the figure with the rise of abstraction. He begins with figuration—the man—which dissolves into images of unformed light and color. By projecting the sequences onto opposite sides of a screen, Viola creates an anxiety in viewers who cannot apprehend both at once. They must either watch first one sequence and then the other or move back and forth between the two. Thus there is always something happening that the viewer cannot see. The resulting anxiety echoes the panic that results from contemplating one's own physical dissolution.

29.53 Bill Viola, *The Crossing*, fire still, 1996. Video installation, first edition. Collection Solomon R. Guggenheim Museum, New York.

29.54 Bill Viola, *The Crossing*, water still, 1996. Video installation, first edition. Collection Solomon R. Guggenheim Museum, New York.

29.55 Shirin Neshat, *Rapture*, production still of women, 1999. Video. Barbara Gladstone Gallery, New York.

The Iranian-born artist Shirin Neshat (born 1957), like Nam June Paik, combines Eastern and Western themes. Like Viola, she projects videos, but her sequences face each other so that viewers can stand between them and turn from side to side to see them. The shifts required of viewers replicate the social and gender-based oppositions of Neshat's native Iran. They also reinforce the sense of difference between East and West, while at the same time calling for their reconciliation.

The impressive stills of *Rapture* (figs. **29.55** and **29.56**) show a group of women on the beach approaching the ocean and a group of men walking on top of a walled hill overlooking the ocean. Neither group connects with the other, reflecting the gender divide between men and women as well as between the Islamic custom of covering women and allowing men to wear Western dress. In these scenes, the men are more differentiated, even though seen in back view, for they wear white shirts and black pants, and their heads are uncovered. The women, on the other hand, are seen from a greater distance and are mere silhouettes.

In subsequent scenes, the women board a boat and sail away as if into freedom, although their boat is without a sail, a rudder, or a motor. The women are thus left to the mercy of the elements. The men remain on land and are confined by the wall. Here, therefore, Neshat deals with political and religious boundaries, especially as they affect the roles of men and women in contemporary society.

Having entered the twenty-first century, we are presented with a proliferation of artistic styles and expanding definitions of what constitutes art. The pace of technological change, particularly in communications and the media, spawns new concepts and styles at an increasing rate. Tastes and styles continue to change, and it will be for future generations to look back at our era and to separate the permanent from the impermanent. How long a work of art must endure for it to claim a place in the artistic canon is a matter of dispute. The little *Venus of Willendorf* has existed for over 25,000 years, the Sistine ceiling for over 450. And yet some of the modern art discussed in this chapter is intentionally transitory. Performance art, for example, lasts no longer than the performance itself, except in memory or on film.

In this survey we have considered some of the artists whose works have stood the test of time. Artists, the "children" of preceding generations of artists, are influenced by their predecessors. This survey will have fulfilled its purpose if readers are affected by some of the best of what has survived.

29.56 Shirin Neshat, *Rapture*, production still of men, 1999. Video. Barbara Gladstone Gallery, New York.

	Style/Period	Works of Art	Cultural/Historical Developments
		Raphael, *La Fornarina* (**29.49**) Brancusi, *Sleeping Muse I* (**29.9**)	**Fuller, American Pavilion**
1960	INNOVATION AND CONTINUITY 1960–1970	Thompson, *Crucifixion* (**29.40**) Nauman, *Self-Portrait as a Fountain* (**29.41**) Breuer, Whitney Museum of American Art (**29.13**), New York Fuller, American Pavilion (**29.14**), Montreal Close, *Self-Portrait* (**29.4**) Gilbert and George, *Singing Sculptures* (**29.2**)	 **Paik, *Hamlet Robot***
1970	1970–1980  **Estes, *Solomon R. Guggenheim Museum***	Smithson, *Spiral Jetty* (**29.25**) Paik, *TV Buddha* (**29.51**) Chicago, *The Dinner Party* (**29.36**) Rothenberg, *IXI* (**29.42**) Holt, *Stone Enclosure: Rock Rings* (**29.26**) Moore and Hersey, Piazza d'Italia (**29.15**), New Orleans Estes, *Solomon R. Guggenheim Museum* (**29.10**)	**Smithson, *Spiral Jetty***
1980	1980–1990 **Goldsworthy, *Icicles***  **Pei, Louvre Pyramid**	M. Graves, Public Services Building (**29.16**), Portland, Oregon Mapplethorpe, *Self-Portrait* (**29.1**) Lin, *Vietnam Veterans Memorial* (**29.44**) Koons, *New Hoover Convertibles* (**29.45**) Kiefer, *To the Unknown Painter* (**29.43**) Basquiat, *CARBON/OXYGEN* (**29.34**) Tansey, *Action Painting II* (**29.47**) Christo and Jeanne-Claude, *The Umbrellas* (**29.28–29.29**) N. Graves, *Morphose* (**29.46**) Rogers, Lloyd's Building (**29.18**), London Estes, *Williamsburg Bridge* (**29.6**) Goldsworthy, *Icicles* (**29.27**) Pei, Louvre Pyramid (**29.17**), Paris Jaudon, *Long Division* (**29.33**) Sherman, *Untitled* (**29.48**) Holzer, Guggenheim Museum installation (**29.11**)	Norman Mailer, *The Executioner's Song* (1980) Tom Wolfe, *The Right Stuff* (1980) Ronald Reagan elected president of the United States (1980) Thomas Keneally, *Schindler's List* (1982) First patient receives permanent artificial heart (1982) Alice Walker, *The Color Purple* (1983) David Mamet, *Glengarry Glen Ross* (1984) Milan Kundera, *The Unbearable Lightness of Being* (1984) Early stages of AIDS epidemic in the United States (mid-1980s) Toni Morrison, *Beloved* (1988) Communist governments in eastern Europe fall (1989) **Gehry, Solomon R. Guggenheim Museum Bilbao**
1990 2000	1990–2005  **Close, *Self-Portrait***  **Christo, *The Gates***	Gehry, Frederick R. Weisman Museum (**29.21**), Minneapolis Serrano, *Nomads (Sir Leonard)* (**29.35**) Lin, *The Women's Table* (**29.38–29.39**) Barney, *Cremaster 4* (**29.12**) Smith, *Mary Magdalene* (**29.37**) Anderson, *Nerve Bible Tour* (**29.3**) Christo and Jeanne-Claude, *Wrapped Reichstag* (**29.30**) Hanson, *The Cowboy* (**29.7**) Paik, *Hamlet Robot* (**29.52**) Viola, *The Crossing* (**29.53–29.54**) Morimura, *Self-Portrait (Actress)/White Marilyn* (**29.50**) Close, *Self-Portrait* (**29.5**) Gehry, Solomon R. Guggenheim Museum Bilbao (**29.20, 29.22–29.24**) Neshat, *Rapture* (**29.55–29.56**) Mueck, *Mask II* (**29.8**) Christo and Jeanne-Claude, *The Gates* (**29.31–29.32**)	August Wilson, *The Piano Lesson* (1990) Apartheid ends in South Africa; Nelson Mandela freed (1990) Iraq invades Kuwait; Operation Desert Shield (1990–1991) Dissolution of the U.S.S.R. (1992) Bill Clinton elected president of the United States (1992) North American Free Trade Agreement takes effect (1994) Federal office building in Oklahoma City bombed (1995) George W. Bush elected president of the United States (2000) Islamic fundamentalists fly planes into the World Trade Center in New York and the Pentagon in Washington, D.C. (2001) United States invades Iraq and topples the government of Saddam Hussein (2003) Pope John Paul II dies; Benedict XVI elected new pope (2005)

Notes

Introduction

1. Cited by Martha Joukowsky, *A Complete Manual of Field Archaeology: Tools and Techniques of Field Work for Archaeologists* (Englewood Cliffs, N.J., 1980), p. 1.

Chapter 12

1. Cited by Laurie M. Schneider, ed., *Giotto in Perspective* (Englewood Cliffs, N.J., 1974), p. 29.
2. Dante, *Purgatory* II.91–95, in Millard Meiss, *Painting in Florence and Siena after the Black Death* (Princeton, 1951), p. 5.
3. Cited by Linnea H. Wren and David J. Wren, eds., *Perspectives on Western Art,* 2 vols. (New York, 1987–1994), I, p. 270.
4. Cited *ibid.,* pp. 274–277.

Chapter 13

1. Cited by Linnea H. Wren and David J. Wren, eds., *Perspectives on Western Art,* 2 vols. (New York, 1987–1994), II, p. 33.
2. Cited *ibid.,* pp. 36–37.
3. Marsilio Ficino, *Commentary on Plato's Symposium on Love,* trans. Jayne Sears, 2nd rev. ed. (Dallas, 1985), pp. 53–54; cited by Wren and Wren, pp. 35–37.

Chapter 14

1. Giorgio Vasari, *Lives of the Most Eminent Painters, Sculptors, and Architects,* trans. Gaston du C. de Vere, 3 vols. (New York, 1979), II, p. 800.
2. *Ibid.*

Chapter 15

1. John Ashbery, *Selected Poems* (New York, 1985), p. 188.
2. In Elizabeth B. G. Holt, ed., *Literary Sources of Art History: An Anthology of Texts from Theophilus to Goethe* (Princeton, 1947), pp. 245 ff.
3. Giorgio Vasari, *Lives of the Most Eminent Painters, Sculptors, and Architects,* trans. Gaston du C. de Vere, 3 vols. (New York, 1979), II, p. 1045.
4. Cited by Linnea H. Wren and David J. Wren, eds., *Perspectives on Western Art,* 2 vols. (New York, 1987–1994), II, pp. 77–78.

Chapter 16

1. Cited by Linnea H. Wren and David J. Wren, eds., *Perspectives on Western Art,* 2 vols. (New York, 1987–1994), II, p. 105.
2. Cited *ibid.,* p. 109.
3. W. H. Auden, *Collected Poems,* ed. Edward Mendelson (London, 1976), p. 146.
4. Saint Bridget, *Revelations* IV; cited by James Snyder, *Northern Renaissance Art: Painting, Sculpture, the Graphic Arts from 1350 to 1575* (New York, 1985), pp. 149–150.

Chapter 17

1. Cited by Linnea H. Wren and David J. Wren, eds., *Perspectives on Western Art,* 2 vols. (New York, 1987–1994), II, p. 126.
2. Giovanni Pietro Bellori, *The Lives of Annibale and Agostino Carracci,* trans. Catherine Enggass (University Park, Pa., 1968), p. 33.
3. Karel van Mander, *Het Schilder-boeck* (Haarlem, 1604); cited by Howard Hibbard, *Caravaggio* (New York, 1983), p. 344.

Chapter 19

1. Cited by William Howard Adams, *Jefferson's Monticello* (New York, 1983), p. 16.

Chapter 20

1. Edmund Burke, "Philosophical Enquiry into the Origin of Our Ideas of the Sublime and Beautiful," in *The Works of the Right Honorable Edmund Burke,* 9th ed., 12 vols. (Boston, 1889), I, pp. 110–111, 130.

Chapter 21

1. Julia Margaret Cameron, *Annals of My Glass House* (Claremont, Calif., 1996).

Chapter 22

1. See Bradford R. Collins, ed., *Twelve Views of Manet's Bar* (Princeton, 1996).
2. James Baldwin, in an introduction at the opening of Beauford Delaney's exhibition at the Gallery Lambert, Paris, December 4, 1964.
3. Henry Miller, *Remember to Remember* (New York, 1941); repr. in *Air-conditioned Nightmare,* 2 vols. (New York, 1945–1947), II.
4. James McNeill Whistler, letter to Henri Fantin-Latour, 1867; cited by Stanley Weintraub, *Whistler: A Biography* (New York, 1974), p. 124.

Chapter 23

1. Cited by W. H. Auden, ed., *Van Gogh: A Self-Portrait—Letters Revealing His Life as a Painter* (New York, 1989), p. 15.
2. Vincent van Gogh, letter 554, reprinted from *The Complete Letters of Vincent van Gogh, with Reproductions of All the Drawings in the Correspondence,* 3 vols. (Boston, 1991), III, p. 86.
3. Paul Gauguin, in *L'Écho de Paris,* February 23, 1891; cited by Daniel Guérin, ed., *The Writings of a Savage: Paul Gauguin* (New York, 1990), p. 48.
4. Paul Gauguin, in *L'Écho de Paris,* May 13, 1895; cited by Guérin, p. 109.
5. Cited by Arne Eggum, *Symbols and Images,* exh. cat. (Washington, D.C.: National Gallery, 1978), p. 391.

Chapter 24

1. Wallace Stevens, *Collected Poems* (New York, 1954), pp. 165–184.
2. Ernst Kirchner, cited by Leopold Reidmeister, *Das Ursprüngtische und die Moderne* (Berlin, 1964), no. 92; also cited by William Rubin, ed., *"Primitivism" in 20th-Century Art,* 2 vols. (New York, 1984), II, p. 373.
3. Emil Nolde, *Jahre der Kampf;* cited by Donald E. Gordon, "German Expressionism," in Rubin, II, p. 383, as trans. in Herschel B. Chipp, *Theories of Modern Art: A Source Book by Artists and Critics* (Berkeley, 1968), pp. 150–151.
4. Vassily Kandinsky, "Der Blaue Reiter (Rück blick)," *Das Kunstblatt* (1930), as trans. in *Kandinsky, Complete Writings on Art,* ed. Kenneth C. Lindsay and Peter Vergo, 2 vols. (Boston, 1982), II, p. 746; cited by Robert Goldwater, *Primitivism in Modern Art,* rev. ed. (New York, 1967), p. 127, and also cited by Rubin, II, p. 375.
5. Franz Marc, in *Auguste Macke, Franz Marc: Briefwechsel* (Cologne, 1964), pp. 39–41; also cited by Rubin, II, p. 375.
6. Henri Matisse, cited by D. H. Kahnweiler, *Juan Gris, sa vie, son oevre, ses écrits* (Paris, 1946), pp. 155–156; also cited by Rubin, I, p. 216.
7. Pablo Picasso, *La Tête obsidienne;* in André Malraux, *Picasso's Mask,* trans. June Guicharnaud and Jacques Guicharnaud (New York, 1976), p. 18; also cited by Rubin, I, p. 255.
8. Georges Braque, cited by Dora Vallier, "Braque, la peinture et nous," *Cahiers d'art* 29, nos. 1–2 (Oct. 1954): 14; also cited by Rubin, I, p. 307.

Chapter 25

1. Gertrude Stein, *Camera Work* (Aug. 1912): 29–30.
2. Guillaume Apollinaire, "Du Sujet dans la peinture moderne," *Les Soirées de Paris* no. 1 (Feb. 1912): 1–4.
3. Fernand Léger, *Contemporary Achievements in Painting* (Paris, 1914); cited by Edward F. Fry, *Cubism* (New York, 1978), pp. 135–139.
4. From an interview with James Johnson Sweeney, in "Eleven Europeans in America," *Bulletin of the Museum of Modern Art* [New York] 13, nos. 4–5 (1946): 19–21.
5. From the *New York Evening Sun* (1913); cited by Milton W. Brown, *The Story of the Armory Show* (New York, 1963), p. 113.
6. Kazimir S. Malevich, *The World as Non-objectivity: Unpublished Writings 1922–25,* ed. Troels Andersen, trans. Xenia Glowacki-Prus and Edmund T. Little (Copenhagen, 1976).
7. Sidney Geist, in *Artforum* (Feb. 1983): 69.

Chapter 26

1. Cited by Hans Richter, *Dada: Art and Anti-Art,* trans. David Britt (London, 1965), p. 16.
2. Hans Arp, *Dadaland: Zürcher Erinnerungen aus der Zeit des Ersten Weltkrieges* (Zurich, 1948).
3. Cited by Richter, p. 42.
4. Cited *ibid.,* p. 89.
5. Cited *ibid.,* pp. 38, 52–53.
6. Cited by Patrick Waldberg, *Surrealism* (London, 1966), p. 11.
7. Cited *ibid.,* p. 66.
8. Man Ray, "Photography Can Be Art," in *Man Ray: Photographs* (New York, 1982), p. 34.

9. Paul Klee, "Creative Credo," originally published as *Schöpferische Konfession,* ed. K. Edschmid (Berlin, 1920); cited by Herschel B. Chipp, *Theories of Modern Art: A Source Book by Artists and Critics* (Berkeley, 1968), p. 182.
10. Cited by Jean Lipman, with Margaret Aspinwall, *Alexander Calder and His Magical Mobiles* (New York, 1981), p. 53.
11. Cited by Nancy Newhall, ed., *Edward Weston, the Flame of Recognition: His Photographs, Accompanied by Excerpts from the Daybooks and Letters* (New York, 1975), p. 23.
12. Georgia O'Keeffe, letter to Henry McBride, July 1931; cited by Jack Cowart, Juan Hamilton, and Sarah Greenough, eds., *Georgia O'Keeffe: Art and Letters* (Washington, D.C., 1987), p. 203.
13. Cited by Alfred Morang, *Transcendental Painting* (Santa Fe: American Foundation for Transcendental Painting, 1940).

Chapter 27

1. Cited by Willibald Sauerländer, "Un-German Activities," *New York Review of Books,* Apr. 7, 1994.
2. Cited by Herschel B. Chipp, *Theories of Modern Art: A Source Book by Artists and Critics* (Berkeley, 1968).
3. Excerpt from a transcript of an artists' session held in New York, 1948; cited by Chipp, p. 564.
4. Harold Rosenberg, "Getting inside the Canvas," *Art News* (New York) (Dec. 1952): 22–23; repr. in Harold Rosenberg, *The Tradition of the New* (New York, 1959); cited by Chipp, p. 580.
5. Clement Greenberg, "Abstract Representation, and So Forth," in *Art and Culture: Critical Essays* (Boston, 1961), pp. 133–138; cited by Chipp, p. 579.
6. Greenberg, pp. 137–138; cited by Chipp, p. 580.
7. Jackson Pollock, in *Arts and Architecture* 61 (Feb. 1944): 193; cited by Chipp, p. 546.
8. Willem de Kooning, from the symposium "What Abstract Art Means to Me," held at the Museum of Modern Art, New York, 1951.
9. Mark Rothko, "The Romantics Were Prompted," *Possibilities I* (New York) (Winter 1947/48): 84.
10. Francis Bacon, *Statements, 1952–1955,* in *Time* (1952, 1953); cited by Chipp, p. 620.

Chapter 28

1. Cited by Brydon Smith, *Dan Flavin, Fluorescent Light, etc. from Dan Flavin,* exh. cat. (Ottawa: National Gallery of Canada, 1969), p. 206.
2. Cited by Barbara Haskell, *Agnes Martin,* exh. cat. (New York: Whitney Museum of American Art, 1992), pp. 16, 17, 24.
3. Cited by Lucy Lippard, *Eva Hesse* (New York, 1976), p. 5.

Chapter 29

1. Jesse Helms, in *Art in America* (Sept. 1989): 39.
2. Cited in *Newsweek,* Apr. 16, 1990, p. 27.
3. Cited by Linda Chase and Tom McBurnett, "Tom Blackwell," in "The Photo-Realists: Twelve Interviews," *Art in America* (Nov.–Dec. 1972): 76.
4. Cited in the *New York Times,* July 3, 1983.
5. Cited in Robert Storr, *Bruce Nauman,* exh. cat. (New York: Museum of Modern Art, 1995), p. 59.
6. *Ibid.,* p. 55.
7. Nam June Paik, in *Manifestos* (New York, 1966).
8. *Ibid.*
9. *Ibid.*

Glossary

Abacus: the flat slab that forms the topmost unit of a Doric **column** and on which the **architrave** rests.
Abhaya: see ***mudrā***.
Abstract: in painting and sculpture, having a generalized or essential form with only a symbolic resemblance to natural objects.
Abutment: the part of a building intended to receive and counteract the **thrust**, or pressure, exerted by **vaults** and **arches.**
Academy: (a) the gymnasium near Athens where Plato taught; (b) from the eighteenth century, the cultural and artistic establishment and the standards that they represent.
Acanthus: a Mediterranean plant with prickly leaves, supposedly the source of foliage-like ornamentation on Corinthian **columns.**
Achromatic: free of color.
Acrylic: a fast-drying, water-based synthetic paint **medium.**
Aedicule: (a) a small building used as a shrine; (b) a **niche** designed to hold a statue. Both types are formed by two **columns** or **pilasters** supporting a **gable** or **pediment.**
Aerial (or **atmospheric**) **perspective:** a technique for creating the illusion of distance by the use of less distinct contours and a reduction in color **intensity.**
Aesthetic: the theory and vocabulary of an individual artistic style.
Aesthetics: the philosophy and science of art and artistic phenomena.
Agora: the open space in an ancient Greek town used as a marketplace or for general meetings.
Airbrush: a device for applying a fine spray of paint or other substance by means of compressed air.
Aisle: a passageway flanking a central area (e.g., the corridors flanking the **nave** of a **basilica** or **cathedral**).
Alabaster: a dense variety of fine-textured gypsum, usually white and translucent, but sometimes gray, red, yellow, or banded, used for carving on a small scale.
Allegory: the expression (artistic, oral, or written) of a generalized moral statement or truth by means of symbolic actions or figures.
Altar: (a) any structure used as a place of sacrifice or worship; (b) a tablelike structure used in a Christian church to celebrate the **Eucharist.**
Altarpiece: a painted or sculpted work of art designed to stand above or behind an **altar.**
Āmalaka: a **finial** in the shape of a notched ring (derived from a fruit) atop a northern-style Hindu temple's ***shikhara.***
Ambulatory: a **vaulted** passageway, usually surrounding the **apse** or **choir** of a church.
Amphitheater: an oval or circular space surrounded by rising tiers of seats, as used by the ancient Greeks and Romans for plays and other spectacles.
Amphora: an ancient Greek two-handled vessel for storing grain, honey, oil, or wine.
Analogous hues: hues containing a common color, though in different proportions.
Aṇḍa: the **dome** of a Buddhist **stupa,** its egg shape symbolizing the arc of the heavens.
Aniconic: depicting a figure, usually a deity, symbolically instead of anthropomorphically.
Annular: ring-shaped, as in an annular **barrel vault.**
Apocalypse: (a) a name for the last book of the New Testament, generally known as the Revelation of Saint John the Divine; (b) a prophetic revelation.
Apostle: in Christian terminology, one of the twelve followers, or disciples, chosen by Christ to spread his Gospel; also used more loosely to include early missionaries such as Saint Paul.
Apotropaion: an object or device designed to avert, or turn aside, evil.
Apsaras: celestial dancers seen in south and southeast Asian religious art.
Apse: a projecting part of a building (especially a church), usually semicircular and topped by a half-**dome** or **vault.**
Aquatint: a **print** from a metal **plate** on which certain areas have been "stopped out" to prevent the action of the acid.
Aqueduct: a man-made conduit for transporting water.
Arabesque: literally meaning "in the Arabian fashion," an intricate pattern of **interlaced** or knotted lines consisting of stylized floral, foliage, and other **motifs.**
Arcade: a **gallery** formed by a series of **arches** with supporting **columns** or **piers**, either freestanding or blind (i.e., attached to a wall).
Arch: a curved architectural member, generally consisting of wedge-shaped blocks (**voussoirs**), which is used to span an opening; it transmits the downward pressure laterally.
Archaeometry: a branch of archaeology that dates objects through the use of various techniques such as amino-acid and **radiocarbon dating.**
Architrave: the lowest unit of an **entablature,** resting directly on the **capital** of a **column.**
Archivolt: the ornamental band or **molding** surrounding the **tympanum** of a Romanesque or Gothic church.
Arena: the central area in a Roman **amphitheater** where gladiatorial spectacles took place.
Armature: (a) a metal framework for a **stained-glass** window; (b) a fixed, inner framework supporting a sculpture made of a flexible material.
Arriccio: the rough first coat of plaster in a **fresco.**
Assemblage: a group of **three-dimensional** objects brought together to form a work of art.
Asymmetrical: characterized by asymmetry, or lack of **balance,** in the arrangement of parts or components.
Atmospheric perspective: see **aerial perspective.**
Atrium: (a) an open courtyard leading to, or within, a house or other building, usually surrounded on three or more sides by a **colonnade;** (b) in a modern building, a rectangular space off which other rooms open.
Attic: in Classical architecture, a low story placed above the main **entablature.**
Attribute: an object closely identified with, and thought of as belonging to, a specific individual —particularly, in art, a deity or saint.
Avant-garde: literally the "advanced guard," a term used to denote innovators or nontraditionalists in a particular field.
Axis: an imaginary straight line passing through the center of a figure, form, or structure and about which that figure is imagined to rotate.
Axonometric projection: the depiction on a single **plane** of a **three-dimensional** object by placing it at an angle to the **picture plane** so that three faces are visible.
Balance: an aesthetically pleasing equilibrium in the combination or arrangement of elements.
Baldacchino: a canopy or canopylike structure above an **altar** or throne.
Balustrade: a series of balusters, or upright **pillars,** supporting a rail (as along the edge of a balcony or bridge).
Baptistery: a building, usually round or polygonal, used for Christian baptismal services.
Barrel (or **tunnel**) **vault:** a semicylindrical **vault,** with parallel **abutments** and an identical **cross section** throughout, covering an oblong space.
Base: (a) that on which something rests; (b) the lowest part of a wall or **column** considered as a separate architectural feature.
Basilica: (a) in Roman architecture, an oblong building used for tribunals and other public functions; (b) in Christian architecture, an early church with similar features to the Roman prototype.
Bas-relief: see **low relief.**
Bay: a unit of space in a building, usually defined by **piers, vaults,** or other elements in a structural system.
Beaverboard: a type of fiberboard used for partitions and ceilings.
Bhūmi (literally "earth"): the stacked ridges that horizontally segment a northern-style Hindu temple's ***shikhara.***
Bhūmisparsha: see ***mudrā.***
Binder, binding medium: a substance used in paint and other **media** to bind particles of **pigment** together and enable them to adhere to the **support.**
Biomorphic: derived from or representing the forms of living things rather than **abstract** shapes.
Bister, bistre: a brown **medium** made from the soot of burnt wood.
Black-figure: describing a style of Greek pottery painting of the sixth century B.C., in which the decoration is black on a red background.
Blind niche: see **niche.**
Bodhisattva: one of many enlightened Buddhist deities who delay their own nirvana in order to help mortals attain enlightenment.
Book of Hours: a prayer book, intended for lay use, containing the devotions, or acts of worship, for the hours of the Roman Catholic Church (i.e., the times appointed for prayer, such as Matins and Vespers).
Broken pediment: a **pediment** in which the **cornice** is discontinuous or interrupted by another element.
Bronze: a metal alloy composed of copper mixed with tin.
Buon fresco: see **fresco.**
Burin: a metal tool with a sharp point to incise designs on pottery and **etching plates,** for example.
Burr: in **etching,** the rough ridge left projecting above the surface of an engraved **plate** where the design has been incised.
Bust: a sculptural or pictorial representation of the upper part of the human figure, including the head and neck (and sometimes part of the shoulders and chest).
Buttress: an external architectural support that counteracts the lateral thrust of an **arch** or wall.
Caduceus: the symbol of a herald or physician, consisting of a staff with two snakes twined around it and two wings at the top.
Calligraphy: handwriting designed to be beautiful; **calligraphic** writing or drawing can be expressive as well as beautiful.
Camera obscura: a dark enclosure or box into which light is admitted through a small hole, enabling images to be projected onto a wall or screen placed opposite that hole; the forerunner of the photographic camera.
Campanile: Italian for bell tower, usually freestanding, but built near a church.
Canon: a set of rules, principles, or standards used to establish scales or **proportions.**
Canopic: relating to the city of Canopus in ancient Egypt.

Canopic jar: a vessel in which ancient Egyptians preserved the viscera of the dead.
Cantilever: a long, low architectural support that enables a **cantilevered** element such as an eave or a **cornice** to project horizontally without vertical support at the far end.
Capital: the decorated top of a **column** or **pilaster**, providing a transition from the **shaft** to the **entablature.**
Caricature: a representation in art or literature that distorts, exaggerates, or oversimplifies certain features.
Cartonnage: layers of linen or papyrus glued together and usually coated with **stucco.**
Cartoon: (a) a full-scale preparatory drawing for a painting; (b) in more modern usage, a comical or satirical drawing.
Cartouche: an oval or **scroll**-shaped design or ornament, usually containing an inscription, a heraldic device, or (as in Egypt) a ruler's name.
Carving: creating an image by removing material from an original material.
Caryatid: a supporting **column** in **post-and-lintel** construction carved to represent a human or animal figure.
Casein: a light-colored, protein-based substance derived from milk, used in the making of paint, adhesives, etc.
Casting: a process in which liquefied material, usually metal, is formed by being poured into a mold; the mold is removed when the material has solidified, leaving a **cast** object in the shape of the mold.
Castrum (pl. ***castra***): an ancient Roman fortress; a Roman encampment.
Catacomb: an underground complex of passageways and **vaults,** such as those used by Jews and early Christians to bury their dead.
Cathedral: the principal church of a diocese (the ecclesiastical district supervised by a bishop).
Cella: the main inner room of a temple, often containing the cult image of the deity.
Centering: the temporary wooden framework used in the construction of **arches, vaults,** and **domes.**
Centrally planned: radiating from a central point.
Ceramics: (a) the art of making objects from clay or other substances (such as **enamel** and porcelain) that require **firing** at high temperatures; (b) the objects themselves.
***Chaitya* arch:** a splayed, horsehoe-shaped curve derived from the profile of a **barrel-vaulted *chaitya* hall;** used to frame doors, windows, and gables, and as a decorative motif in early south Asian architecture.
***Chaitya* hall:** a U-shaped Buddhist structural or rock-cut chamber for congregational worship centered on a **stupa.**
Chancel: that part of a Christian church, reserved for the clergy and choir, in which the **altar** is placed.
Chapter house: a meeting place for the discussion of business in a **cathedral** or **monastery.**
Château: French word for a castle or large country house.
Chattra: a royal parasol crowning the **dome *(aṇḍa)*** of a Buddhist **stupa,** symbolically honoring the Buddha.
Chaurī: a royal fly-whisk, symbolically honoring the Buddha.
Chevet: French term for the east end of a Gothic church, comprising the **choir, ambulatory,** and **radiating chapels.**
Chiaroscuro: the subtle gradation of light and shadow used to create the effect of **three-dimensionality.**
Chinoiserie: a Western style popular in the eighteenth century, reflecting Chinese **motifs** or qualities.
Choir: part of a Christian church, near the **altar,** set aside for those chanting the services; usually part of the **chancel.**
Chroma: see **intensity.**
Chromatic: colored or pertaining to color.
Chryselephantine: consisting of, or decorated with, gold and ivory.
Circumambulate: to walk around something, especially an object of worship or veneration.
Circus: in ancient Rome, an oblong space, surrounded by seats, used for chariot races, games, and other spectacles.
Cire-perdue: see **lost-wax bronze casting.**
Citadel: a fortress or other fortified area placed in an elevated or commanding position.
Clerestory: the upper part of the main outer wall of a building (especially a church), located above an adjoining roof and admitting light through a row of windows.
Cloisonné: a multicolored surface made by pouring **enamels** into compartments outlined by bent wire fillets, or strips.
Cloister: in a **monastery,** a covered passage or **ambulatory,** usually with one side walled and the other open to a courtyard.
Close: an enclosed space, or precinct, usually next to a building such as a **cathedral** or castle.
Cluster (or **compound**) **pier:** a **pier** composed of a group, or cluster, of **engaged column** shafts, often used in Gothic architecture.
Codex (pl. **codices**): sheets of **parchment** or **vellum** bound together—the precursor of the modern book.
Coffer, coffering: a recessed geometrical panel in a ceiling.
Collage: a work of art formed by pasting fragments of printed matter, cloth, and other materials (occasionally **three-dimensional**) to a flat surface.
Colonnade: a series of **columns** set at regular intervals, usually supporting **arches** or an **entablature.**
Colonnette: a small, slender **column,** usually grouped with others to form **cluster piers.**
Color wheel: a circular, two-dimensional model illustrating the relationships of the various **hues.**
Column: a cylindrical support, usually with three parts—**base, shaft,** and **capital.**
Complementary colors: hues that lie directly opposite each other on the **color wheel.**
Compluvium (pl. ***compluvia***): a square opening in the roof of a Roman ***atrium*** through which rain fell into an ***impluvium.***
Composition: the arrangement of **formal elements** in a work of art.
Compound pier: see **cluster pier.**
Conceptual art: art in which the idea is more important than the **form** or **style.**
Cone mosaic: a surface decorated by pressing pieces (usually colored and of conical shape) of stone or baked clay into damp plaster.
Content: the themes or ideas in a work of art, as distinct from its **form.**
Contour: a line representing the outline of a figure or form.
Contrapposto (or **counterpoise**): a stance of the human body in which one leg bears the weight, while the other is relaxed, creating an **asymmetry** in the hip-shoulder **axis.**
Contrast: an abrupt change, such as that created by the juxtaposition of dissimilar colors, objects, etc.
Convention: a custom, practice, or principle that is generally recognized and accepted.
Corbeling: brick or masonry **courses,** each projecting beyond, and supported by, the one below it; the meeting of two corbels would create an **arch** or **vault.**
Corinthian: see **Order.**
Cornice: the projecting horizontal unit, usually molded, that surmounts an **arch** or wall; the topmost member of a Classical **entablature.**
Counterpoise: see ***contrapposto.***
Courses: horizontal layers of brick or masonry in a wall.
Crayon: a stick for drawing formed from powdered **pigment** mixed with wax.
Crenellated: having a series of indentations, like those in a battlement.
Cromlech: a prehistoric monument consisting of a circle of **monoliths.**
Crosshatching: a pattern of superimposed parallel lines (**hatching**) on a two-dimensional surface used to create shadows and suggest **three-dimensionality.**
Crossing: the area in a Christian church where the **transepts** intersect the **nave.**
Cross section: a diagram showing a building cut by a vertical **plane,** usually at right angles to an **axis.**
Cross vault: see **groin vault.**
Cruciform: shaped or arranged like a cross.
Crypt: a chamber or **vault** beneath the main body of a church.
Cuneiform: a form of writing consisting of wedge-shaped characters, used in ancient Mesopotamia.
Cupola: a small, domed structure crowning a roof or **dome,** usually added to provide interior lighting.
Curvilinear: composed of, or bounded by, curved lines.
Cyclopaean masonry: stone construction using large, irregular blocks without mortar.
Cylinder seal: a small cylinder of stone or other material engraved in **intaglio** on its outer surface and used (especially in Mesopotamia) to roll an impression on wet clay.
Daguerreotype: mid-nineteenth-century photographic process for **fixing** positive images on silver-coated metal **plates.**
Decussis: the Latin numeral ten (X).
Deësis: a tripartite **icon** in the Byzantine tradition, usually showing Christ enthroned between the Virgin Mary and Saint John the Baptist.
Dendrochronology: a science using the annual rings of trees to determine the chronological order and dates of historical events.
Dharmachakra: see ***mudrā.***
Dhyāna: see ***mudrā.***
Diorite: a type of dark (black or gray) crystalline rock.
Diptych: a writing tablet or work of art consisting of two panels side by side and connected by hinges.
Dolmen: a prehistoric structure consisting of two or more **megaliths** capped with a horizontal slab.
Dome: a **vaulted** (frequently hemispherical) roof or ceiling, erected on a circular **base,** which may be envisaged as the result of rotating an **arch** through 180 degrees about a central **axis.**
Doric: see **Order.**
Dressed stone: blocks of stone that have been cut and shaped to fit in a particular place for a particular purpose.
Drip technique: a painting technique in which paint is dripped from a brush or stick onto a horizontal canvas or other **ground.**
Drum: (a) one of the cylindrical blocks of stone from which the **shaft** of a **column** is made; (b) the circular or polygonal wall of a building surmounted by a **dome** or **cupola.**
Drypoint: an **engraving** in which the image is scratched directly into the surface of a metal **plate** with a pointed instrument.
Earthenware: pottery that has been either air-dried or **fired** at a relatively low temperature.
Easel: a frame for supporting a canvas or wooden panel.
Echinus: in the **Doric Order,** the rounded **molding** between the **necking** and the ***abacus.***
Edition: a batch of **prints** made from a single **plate** or print form.
Egg and dart: a decorative **molding** consisting of alternating oval (egg) and downward-pointing (dart) elements.
Elevation: an architectural diagram showing the exterior (or, less often, interior) surface of a building as if projected onto a vertical **plane.**
Emulsion: a light-sensitive chemical coating used to transfer photographic images onto metal **plates** or other surfaces.

Enamel: a vitreous coating applied by heat fusion to the surface of metal, glass, or pottery. See also ***cloisonné.***

Encaustic: a painting technique in which **pigment** is mixed with a **binder** of hot wax and fixed by heat after application.

Engaged (half-) column: a **column,** decorative in purpose, that is attached to a supporting wall.

Engraving: (a) the process of incising an image on a hard material, such as wood, stone, or a copper **plate;** (b) a **print** or impression made by such a process.

Entablature: the portion of a Classical architectural **Order** above the **capital** of a **column.**

Entasis: the slight bulging of a **Doric column,** which is at its greatest about one third of the distance from the **base.**

Etching: (a) a printmaking process in which an impression is taken from a metal **plate** on which the image has been etched, or eaten away by acid; (b) a **print** produced by such a process.

Etching ground: a resinous, acid-resistant substance used to cover a copper **plate** before an image is etched on it.

Eucharist: (a) the Christian sacrament of Holy Communion, commemorating the Last Supper; (b) the consecrated bread and wine used at the sacrament.

Evil eye: a malicious glance which, in superstitious belief, is thought to be capable of causing material harm.

Façade: the front or "face" of a building.

Facing: an outer covering or sheathing.

Faïence: earthenware or pottery decorated with brightly colored **glazes** (originally from Faenza, a city in northern Italy).

Fantasy: imagery that is derived solely from the imagination.

Figura serpentinata: a snakelike twisting of the body, typical of Mannerist art.

Figurative: representing the likeness of a recognizable human (or animal) figure.

Finial: a small decorative element at the top of an architectural member such as a **gable** or pinnacle, or of a smaller object such as a **bronze** vessel.

Fire (verb): to prepare (especially **ceramics**) by baking in a kiln or otherwise applying heat.

Fixing: the use of a chemical process to make an image (a photograph, for example) more permanent.

Fleur-de-lis: (a) a white iris, the royal emblem of France; (b) a **stylized** representation of an iris, common in artistic design and heraldry.

Flutes, fluting: a series of vertical grooves used to decorate the **shafts** of **columns** in Classical architecture.

Flying buttress, or **flyer:** a **buttress** in the form of a strut or open half-**arch.**

Foreground: the area of a picture, usually at the bottom of the **picture plane,** that appears nearest to the viewer.

Foreshortening: the use of **perspective** to represent a single object extending back in space at an angle to the **picture plane.**

Form: the overall plan or structure of a work of art.

Formal analysis: analysis of a work of art to determine how its integral parts, or **formal elements,** are combined to produce the overall **style** and effect.

Formal elements: the elements of **style** (line, shape, color, etc.) used by an artist in the **composition** of a work of art.

Formalism: the doctrine or practice of strict adherence to **stylized** shapes or other external **forms.**

Forum: the civic center of an ancient Roman city, containing temple, marketplace, and official buildings.

Found object (or ***objet trouvé***): an object not originally intended as a work of art, but presented as one.

Fresco: a technique (also known as ***buon fresco***) of painting on the plaster surface of a wall or ceiling while it is still damp, so that the **pigments** become fused with the plaster as it dries.

Fresco secco: a variant technique of **fresco** painting in which the paint is applied to dry plaster; this is often combined with ***buon fresco,*** or "true" fresco painting.

Frieze: (a) the central section of the **entablature** in the Classical **Orders;** (b) any horizontal decorative band.

Functionalism: a philosophy of design (in architecture, for example) holding that **form** should be consistent with material, structure, and use.

Gable (or **pitched**) **roof:** a roof formed by the intersection of two **planes** sloping down from a central beam.

Gallery: the second story of a church, placed over the side **aisles** and below the **clerestory.**

Garbha griha (literally "womb chamber"): a small, cubical **sanctuary** that is the sacred core of a Hindu temple.

Genre: a category of art representing scenes of everyday life.

Geodesic dome: a **dome**-shaped framework consisting of small, interlocking polygonal units.

Geometric: (a) based on mathematical shapes such as the circle, square, or rectangle; (b) a **style** of Greek pottery made between c. 900 and 700 B.C., characterized by geometric decoration.

Gesso: a white coating made of chalk, plaster, and **size** that is spread over a surface to make it more receptive to paint.

Gilding: a decorative coating made of gold leaf or simulated gold; objects to which gilding has been applied are **gilded** or **gilt.**

Glaze: (a) in **oil painting,** a layer of translucent paint or varnish, sometimes applied over another color or **ground,** so that light passing through it is reflected back by the lower surface and modified by the glaze; (b) in pottery, a material applied in a thin layer that, when **fired,** fuses with the surface to produce a glossy, nonporous effect.

Glyptic art: the art of carving or **engraving,** especially on small objects such as seals or precious stones.

Gospel: one of the first four books of the New Testament, which recounts the life of Christ.

Gouache: an opaque, water-soluble painting **medium.**

Greek cross: a cross in which all four arms are of equal length.

Grisaille: a **monochromatic** painting (usually in shades of black and gray, to simulate stone sculpture).

Groin (or **cross-**) **vault:** the ceiling configuration formed by the intersection of two **barrel vaults.**

Ground: in painting, the prepared surface of the **support** to which the paint is applied.

Ground plan: a plan of the ground floor of a building, seen from above (as distinguished from an **elevation**).

Guilds: organizations of craftsmen, such as those that flourished in the Middle Ages and Renaissance.

Half-column: see **engaged column.**

Halo: a circle or disk of golden light surrounding the head of a holy figure.

Happening: an event in which artists give an unrehearsed performance, sometimes with the participation of the audience.

Harmikā: a square platform surmounting the **dome** of a Buddhist **stupa.**

Hatching: close parallel lines used in drawings and prints to create the effect of shadow on **three-dimensional** forms. See also **cross-hatching.**

Hierarchical proportion or **scale:** the representation of more important figures as larger than less important ones.

Hieroglyphic: written in a script (especially in ancient Egypt) whose characters are pictorial representations of objects.

Highlight: in painting, an area of high **value** color.

High relief: relief sculpture in which the figures project substantially (e.g., more than half of their natural depth) from the background surface.

Hôtel: in eighteenth-century France, a city mansion belonging to a person of rank.

Hue: a pure color with a specific wavelength.

Hydria: an ancient Greek or Roman water jar.

Hypostyle: a hall with a roof supported by rows of **columns.**

Icon: a sacred image representing Christ, the Virgin Mary, or some other holy person.

Iconography: the analysis of works of art through the study of the meanings of symbols and images in the context of the contemporary culture.

Iconology: the study of the meaning or content of a larger **program** to which individual works of art belong.

Idealized, idealization: the representation of objects and figures according to ideal standards of beauty rather than to real life.

Ideograph: a written symbol standing for a concept, usually formed by combining **pictographs.**

Ignudi (pl.): nude figures (in Italian).

Illuminated manuscript: see **manuscript.**

Illusionism, illusionistic: a type of art in which the objects are intended to appear real.

Impasto: the thick application of paint, usually **oil** or **acrylic,** to a canvas or panel.

Impost block: a block between a **capital** of a **column** and the **springing** of an **arch.**

Impluvium (pl. ***impluvia***): a basin or cistern in the ***atrium*** of a Roman house to collect rainwater falling through the ***compluvium.***

Incise: to cut designs or letters into a hard surface with a sharp instrument.

Incised relief: see **sunken relief.**

Inlay: to decorate a surface by inserting pieces of a different material (e.g., to inlay a panel with contrasting wood).

Installation: a **three-dimensional** environment or ensemble of objects, presented as a work of art.

Insula (pl. ***insulae***): an ancient Roman building or group of buildings standing together and forming an apartment block.

Intaglio: a printmaking process in which lines are incised into the surface of a **plate** or **print** form (e.g., **engraving** and **etching**).

Intensity: the degree of purity of a color; also known as **chroma** or **saturation.**

Interlace: a form of decoration composed of strips or ribbons that are intertwined, usually symmetrically about a longitudinal **axis.**

Ionic: see **Order.**

Isocephaly, isocephalic: the horizontal alignment of the heads of all the figures in a composition.

Isometric projection: an architectural diagram combining a **ground plan** of a building with a view from an exterior point above and slightly to one side.

Ithyphallic: an image having an erect or prominent phallus.

Jambs: the upright surfaces forming the sides of a doorway or window, often decorated with sculptures in Romanesque and Gothic churches.

Japonisme: the Japanese aesthetic as absorbed by the West in the latter part of the nineteenth century.

Jatakā: a tale recounting an incident in one of the Buddha's lives, frequently depicted in Buddhist art.

Keystone: the wedge-shaped stone at the center of an **arch, rib,** or **vault** that is inserted last, locking the other stones into place.

Kiln: an oven used to bake (or **fire**) clay.
Kondō: the main hall of a Japanese Buddhist temple, where religious images are kept.
Kore (pl. ***korai***): Greek word for maiden; an Archaic Greek statue of a standing female, usually clothed.
Kouros (pl. ***kouroi***): Greek word for young man; an Archaic Greek statue of a standing nude youth.
Krater: a wide-mouthed bowl for mixing wine and water in ancient Greece.
Kufic: an early form of Arabic script in which letters are relatively uncursive; used later for headings and formal inscriptions.
Kylix: an ancient Greek drinking cup with a wide, shallow bowl.
Lamassu (pl.): in Assyrian art, figures of bulls or lions with wings and human heads.
Lancet: a tall narrow, arched window without **tracery.**
Landscape: a pictorial representation of natural scenery.
Lantern: the structure crowning a **dome** or tower, often used to admit light to the interior.
Lapis lazuli: a semiprecious blue stone; used to prepare the blue **pigment** known as ultramarine.
Lares and **penates:** (a) in ancient Rome, the tutelary gods of the household; (b) figuratively, one's most valued household possessions.
Latin cross: a cross in which the vertical arm is longer than the horizontal arm, through the midpoint of which it passes.
Leaf and dart: a decorative design consisting of alternating leaf- and dart-shaped elements.
Lekythos (or ***lecythus***): an ancient Greek vessel with a long, narrow neck, used primarily for pouring oil.
Linear: a style in which lines are used to depict figures with precise, fully indicated outlines.
Linear (or **scientific**) **perspective:** a mathematical system devised during the Renaissance to create the illusion of depth in a two-dimensional image, through the use of straight lines converging toward a **vanishing point** in the distance.
Lintel: the horizontal cross beam spanning an opening in the **post-and-lintel** system.
Lithography: a printmaking process in which the printing surface is a smooth stone or **plate** on which an image is drawn with a **crayon** or some other oily substance.
Load-bearing construction: a system of construction in which solid forms are superimposed on one another to form a tapering structure.
Loggia: a roofed **gallery** open on one or more sides, often with **arches** or **columns.**
Longitudinal section: an architectural diagram giving an inside view of a building intersected by a vertical **plane** from front to back.
Lost-wax bronze casting (also called ***cire-perdue***): a technique for **casting bronze** and other metals.
Low relief (also known as **bas-relief**): **relief** sculpture in which figures and forms project only slightly from the background **plane.**
Luminism: an American nineteenth-century art style emphasizing the effect of light on **landcape.**
Lunette: (a) a semicircular area formed by the intersection of a wall and a **vault;** (b) a painting, **relief** sculpture, or window of the same shape.
Machtkunst: art used in the service of a military or other authority; literally, "power art" in German.
Magus (pl. **Magi**): in the New Testament, one of the three wise men who traveled from the East to pay homage to the infant Christ.
Mandala: a cosmic diagram in Asian art.
Mandapa: a northern-style Hindu temple's assembly hall.
Mandorla: an oval or almond-shaped aureola, or radiance, surrounding the body of a holy person.
Manuscript: a handwritten book produced in the Middle Ages or Renaissance. If it has painted illustrations, it is known as an **illuminated manuscript.**
Martyrium: a church or other structure built over the tomb or relics of a martyr.
Masonite: a type of fiberboard used in insulation and paneling.
Mastaba: a rectangular burial monument in ancient Egypt.
Mausoleum (pl. **mausolea**): an elaborate tomb (named for Mausolos, a fourth-century-B.C. ruler commemorated by a magnificent tomb at Halikarnassos).
Meander pattern: a fret or key pattern originating in the Greek **Geometric** period.
Medium (pl. **media**): (a) the material with which an artist works (e.g., watercolor on paper); (b) the liquid substance in which **pigment** is suspended, such as oil or water.
Megalith: a large, undressed stone used in the construction of prehistoric monuments.
Megaron: Greek for "large room"; used principally to denote a rectangular hall, usually supported by **columns** and fronted by a porch, traditional in ancient Greece since Mycenaean times.
Memento mori: an image, often in the form of a skull, to remind the living of the inevitability of death.
Menhir: a prehistoric **monolith** standing alone or grouped with other stones.
Metonym: an allusion to a subject through the representation of something related to it or a part of it.
Metope: the square area, often decorated with **relief** sculpture, between the **triglyphs** of a **Doric frieze.**
Mezzanine: in architecture, an intermediate, low-ceilinged story between two main stories.
Mezzotint: a method of **engraving** by burnishing parts of a roughened surface to produce an effect of light and shade.
Mihrāb: a niche, often highly ornamented, in the center of a ***qibla*** wall, toward which prayer is directed in an Islamic **mosque.**
Minaret: a tall, slender tower attached to a **mosque,** from which the *muezzin* calls the Muslim faithful to prayer.
Minbar: a **pulpit** from which a Muslim (Islamic) ***imam*** addresses a congregation in a ***jāmi'*** **mosque.**
Miniature: a representation executed on a much smaller scale than the original object.
Mithuna: a loving couple, symbolizing unity, in ancient south Asian art.
Mobile: a delicately balanced sculpture with movable parts that are set in motion by air currents or mechanical propulsion.
Modeling: (a) in two-dimensional art, the use of **value** to suggest light and shadow, and thus create the effect of mass and weight; (b) in sculpture, the creation of **form** by manipulating a pliable material such as clay.
Module: a unit of measurement on which the **proportions** of a building or work of art are based.
Molding: a continuous contoured surface, either recessed or projecting, used for decorative effect on an architectural surface.
Monastery: a religious establishment housing a community of people living in accordance with religious vows.
Monochromatic: having a color scheme based on shades of black and white, or on **values** of a single **hue.**
Monolith: a large block of stone that is all in one piece (i.e., not composed of smaller blocks), used in **megalithic** structures.
Monumental: being, or appearing to be, larger than life-sized.
Mosaic: the use of small pieces of glass, stone, or tile ***(tesserae),*** or pebbles to create an image on a flat surface such as a floor, wall, or ceiling.
Mosque: an Islamic (Muslim) house of worship of two main types: the ***masjid,*** used for daily prayer by individuals or small groups; and the ***jāmi',*** used for large-scale congregational prayer on the Friday sabbath and on holidays.
Motif: a recurrent element or theme in a work of art.
Mudrā: a symbolic hand gesture, usually made by a deity, in Hindu or Buddhist art. Common Buddhist ***mudrās*** include ***abhaya mudrā*** (right hand raised, palm outward and vertical), meaning "fear not"; ***dhyāna mudrā*** (hands in lap, one resting on the other, palms up, thumb tips touching), signifying meditation; ***Dharmachakra mudrā*** (hands at chest level, palms out, thumb and forefinger of each forming a circle), representing the beginning of Buddhist teaching; and ***bhumisparsha mudrā*** (left hand in lap, right hand reaching down, palm in and vertical, to ground level), symbolizing Shakyamuni Buddha's calling the earth to bear witness at the moment of his enlightenment.
Mural: a painting on a wall, usually on a large scale and in **fresco.**
Naive art: art created by artists with no formal training.
Naos: the inner **sanctuary** of an ancient Greek temple.
Narthex: a porch or vestibule in early Christian churches.
Naturalism, naturalistic: a style of art seeking to represent objects as they actually appear in nature.
Nave: in **basilicas** and churches, the long, narrow central area used to house the congregation.
Necking: a groove or **molding** at the top of a **column** or **pilaster** forming the transition from **shaft** to **capital.**
Necropolis (pl. **necropoleis**): an ancient or prehistoric burial ground (literally "City of the Dead").
Nemes: a head cloth worn by the pharaohs of ancient Egypt.
Neutral: lacking color; white, gray, or black.
Niche: a hollow or recess in a wall or other architectural element, often containing a statue; a **blind niche** is a very shallow recess.
Nike: a winged statue representing Nike, the goddess of victory.
Nonrepresentational (or **nonfigurative**): not representing any known object in nature.
Obelisk: a tall, four-sided stone, usually **monolithic,** that tapers toward the top and is capped by a **pyramidion.**
Objet trouvé: see **found object.**
Obverse: the side of a coin or medal considered to be the front and that bears the main image.
Oculus: a round opening in a wall or at the apex of a **dome.**
Oenochoe: an ancient Greek wine jug.
Oil paint: a slow-drying and flexible paint formed by mixing **pigments** with the **medium** of oil.
One-point perspective: a **perspective** system involving a single **vanishing point.**
Opisthodomos (or ***opisthodome***): a back chamber, especially the part of the ***naos*** of a temple farthest from the entrance.
Orant: standing with outstretched arms as if in prayer.
Orchestra: in an ancient Greek theater, a circular space used by the chorus.
Order: one of the architectural systems **(Corinthian, Ionic, Doric)** used by the Greeks and Romans to decorate and define the **post-and-lintel** system of construction.
Organic: having the quality of living matter.
Orthogonals: the converging lines that meet at the **vanishing point** in the system of **linear perspective.**
Pagoda: a multistoried Buddhist **reliquary** tower, tapering toward the top and characterized by projecting eaves.

Painterly: in painting, using the quality of color and **texture,** rather than line, to define form.
Palette: (a) the range of colors used by an artist; (b) an oval or rectangular tablet used to hold and mix the **pigments.**
Palette knife: a knife with a flat, flexible blade and no cutting edge, used to mix and spread paint.
Papyrus: (a) a plant found in ancient Egypt and neighboring countries; (b) a paperlike writing material made from the pith of the plant.
Parapet: (a) a wall or rampart to protect soldiers; (b) a low wall or railing built for the safety of people at the edge of a balcony, roof, or other steep place.
Parchment: a paperlike material made from bleached and stretched animal hides, used in the Middle Ages for **manuscripts.**
Pastel: a **crayon** made of ground **pigments** and a gum **binder,** used as a drawing **medium.**
Patina: (a) the colored surface, often green, that forms on **bronze** and copper either naturally (as a result of oxidation) or artificially (through treatment with acid); (b) in general, the surface appearance of old objects.
Patron: the person or group that commissions a work of art from an artist.
Pedestal: the **base** of a **column,** statue, vase, or other upright work of art.
Pediment: (a) in Classical architecture, the triangular section at the end of a **gable roof,** often decorated with sculpture; (b) a triangular feature placed as a decoration over doors and windows.
Pendentive: in a domed building, an inwardly curving triangular section of the **vaulting** that provides a transition from the round **base** of the **dome** to the supporting **piers.**
Peplos: in ancient Greece, a woolen outer garment worn by women, wrapped in folds about the body.
Peripteral: surrounded by a row of **columns** or **peristyle.**
Peristyle: a **colonnade** surrounding a structure; in Roman houses, the courtyard surrounded by **columns.**
Perspective: the illusion of depth in a two-dimensional work of art.
Pictograph: a written symbol derived from a **representational** image.
Picture plane: the flat surface of a drawing or painting.
Picture stone: in Viking art, an upright boulder with images **incised** on it.
Piece-molding: a complex technique for shaping pottery, metal, or glass objects between an inner core and an outer mold; especially suited to elaborate decoration.
Pier: a vertical support used to bear loads in an **arched** or **vaulted** structure.
Pietà: an image of the Virgin Mary holding and mourning over the dead Christ.
Pigment: a powdered substance that is used to give color to paints, inks, and dyes.
Pilaster: a flattened, rectangular version of a **column,** sometimes **load-bearing,** but often purely decorative.
Pillar: a large vertical architectural element, usually freestanding and **load-bearing.**
Pitched roof: see **gable roof.**
Plane: a surface on which a straight line joining any two of its points lies on that surface; in general, a flat surface.
Plate: (a) in **engraving** and **etching,** a flat piece of metal into which the image to be printed is cut; (b) in photography, a sheet of glass, metal, etc., coated with a light-sensitive **emulsion.**
Plinth: (a) in Classical architecture, a square slab immediately below the circular **base** of a **column;** (b) a square block serving as a base for a statue, vase, etc.
Podium: (a) the masonry forming the **base** of a temple; (b) a raised platform or **pedestal.**
Polychrome: consisting of several colors.
Polyptych: a painting or **relief,** usually an **altarpiece,** composed of more than three sections.
Portal: the doorway of a church and the architectural composition surrounding it.
Portico: (a) a **colonnade;** (b) a porch with a roof supported by **columns,** usually at the entrance to a building.
Portrait: a visual representation of a specific person, a likeness.
Portraiture: the art of making portraits.
Postament: (a) a **pedestal** or **base;** (b) a frame of **molding** for a **relief.**
Post-and-lintel construction: an architectural system in which upright members, or posts, support horizontal members, or **lintels.**
Prana: the fullness of life-giving breath that appears to animate some south and southeast Asian sculpture.
Predella: the lower part of an **altarpiece,** often decorated with small scenes that are related to the subject of the main panel.
Primary color: the pure **hues**—blue, red, yellow—from which all other colors can in theory be mixed.
Print: a work of art produced by one of the printmaking processes—**engraving, etching,** and **woodcut.**
Print matrix: an image-bearing surface to which ink is applied before a **print** is taken from it.
Program: the arrangement of a series of images into a coherent whole.
Pronaos: the vestibule of a Greek temple in front of the ***cella*** or ***naos.***
Proportion: the relation of one part to another, and of parts to the whole, with respect to size, height, and width.
Propylaeum (pl. **propylaea**): (a) an entrance to a temple or other enclosure; (b) the entry gate at the western end of the Acropolis, in Athens.
Protome (or **protoma**): a representation of the head and neck of an animal, often used as an architectural feature.
Provenience: origin, derivation; the act of coming from a particular source.
Psalter: a copy of the Book of Psalms in the Old Testament, often illuminated.
Pseudoperipteral: appearing to have a **peristyle,** though some of the **columns** may be **engaged columns** or **pilasters.**
Pulpit: in church architecture, an elevated stand, surrounded by a **parapet** and often richly decorated, from which the preacher addresses the congregation.
Putto (pl. ***putti***): a chubby male infant, often naked and sometimes depicted as a Cupid, popular in Renaissance art.
Pylon: a pair of truncated, pyramidal towers flanking the entrance to an Egyptian temple.
Pyramidion: a small pyramid, as at the top of an **obelisk.**
Qibla: a wall inside the prayer hall of a **mosque** that is oriented toward Mecca and is, therefore, the focus of worship.
Quadrant (or **half-barrel**) **vaulting:** vaulting whose arc is one-quarter of a circle, or 90 degrees.
Quatrefoil: an ornamental "four-leaf clover" shape —i.e., with four lobes radiating from a common center.
Radiating chapels: chapels placed around the **ambulatory** (and sometimes the **transepts**) of a medieval church.
Radiocarbon dating: a method of dating prehistoric objects based on the rate of degeneration of radioactive carbon in organic materials.
Rayograph: an image made by placing an object directly on light-sensitive paper, using a technique developed by Man Ray.
Realism, realistic: attempting to portray objects from everyday life as they actually are; not to be confused with the nineteenth-century movement called Realism.
Rebus: the representation of words and syllables by pictures or symbols, the names of which sound the same as the intended words or syllables.
Rectilinear: consisting of, bounded by, or moving in, a straight line or lines.
Red-figure: describing a style of Greek pottery painting of the sixth or fifth century B.C., in which the decoration is red on a black background.
Refectory: a dining hall in a **monastery** or other similar institution.
Register: a range or row, especially when one of a series.
Reinforced concrete: concrete strengthened by embedding an internal structure of wire mesh or rods.
Relief: (a) a mode of sculpture in which an image is developed outward **(high** or **low relief)** or inward **(sunken relief)** from a basic **plane;** (b) a printmaking process in which the areas not to be printed are carved away, leaving the desired image projecting from the **plate.**
Reliquary: a casket or container for sacred relics.
Repoussé: in metalwork, decorated with patterns in **relief** made by hammering on the reverse side.
Representational: representing natural objects in recognizable form.
Reverse: the side of a coin or medal considered to be the back; opposite of **obverse.**
Rhyton: an ancient drinking vessel usually shaped like an animal or part of an animal (typically, the head).
Rib: an **arched** diagonal element in a **vault** system that defines and supports a **ribbed vault.**
Ribbed vault: a **vault** constructed of **arched** diagonal **ribs,** with a **web** of lighter masonry in between.
Romanticize: to glamorize or portray in a romantic, as opposed to a **realistic,** manner.
Roof comb: an ornamental architectural crest on top of a Maya temple.
Rosette: circular stylization of a rose.
Rose window: a large, circular window decorated with **stained glass** and **tracery.**
Rosin: a crumbly resin used in making varnishes and lacquers.
Rotunda: a circular building, usually covered by a **dome.**
Rune stone: in Viking art, an upright boulder with characters of the runic alphabet inscribed on it.
Rusticate: to give a rustic appearance to masonry blocks by roughening their surface and beveling their edges so that the joints are indented.
Sahn: an enclosed courtyard in an Islamic **mosque,** used for prayer when the interior is full.
Salon: (a) a large reception room in an elegant private house; (b) an officially sponsored exhibition of works of art.
Sanctuary: (a) the most holy part of a place of worship, the inner sanctum; (b) the part of a Christian church containing the **altar.**
Sarcophagus: a stone coffin, sometimes decorated with a **relief** sculpture.
Sarsen: a large sandstone block used in prehistoric monuments.
Saturation: see **intensity.**
Satyr: an ancient woodland deity with the legs, tail, and horns of a goat (or horse), and the head and torso of a man.
Schematic: diagrammatic and generalized rather than specifically relating to an individual object.
Scientific perspective: see **linear perspective.**
Screen wall: a nonsupporting wall, often pierced by windows.
Scriptorium (pl. **scriptoria**): the room (or rooms) in a **monastery** in which **manuscripts** were produced.
Scroll: (a) a length of writing material, such as **papyrus** or **parchment,** rolled up into a

cylinder; (b) a curved **molding** resembling a scroll (e.g., the **volute** of an **Ionic** or **Corinthian capital**).

Sculptured wall motif: the conception of a building as a massive block of stone with openings and spaces carved out of it.

Sculpture in the round: freestanding sculptural figures carved or modeled in **three dimensions.**

Secondary colors: hues produced by combining two **primary colors.**

Section: a diagrammatic representation of a building intersected by a vertical **plane.**

Serapaeum: a building or shrine sacred to the Egyptian god Serapis.

Serekh: a rectangular outline containing the name of a king in the Early Dynastic period of ancient Egypt.

Seriation: a technique for determining a chronology by studying a particular type or **style** and analyzing the increase or decrease in its popularity.

Sfumato: the definition of form by delicate gradations of light and shadow.

Shading: decreases in the **value** or **intensity** of colors to imitate the fall of shadow when light strikes an object.

Shaft: the vertical, cylindrical part of a **column** that supports the **entablature.**

Shikhara: (literally "mountain peak"), a northern-style Hindu temple tower surmounting a ***garbha griha,*** typically curved inward toward the top, with vertical lobes and horizontal segments ***(bhūmi),*** and crowned by ***āmalaka.***

Sibyl: a prophetess of the ancient, pre-Christian world.

Silhouette: the outline of an object, usually filled in with black or some other uniform color.

Silkscreen: a printmaking process in which **pigment** is forced through the mesh of a silkscreen, parts of which have been masked to make them impervious.

Size, sizing: a mixture of glue or resin that is used to make a **ground** such as canvas less porous so that paint will not be absorbed into it.

Skeletal (or **steel-frame**) **construction:** a method of construction in which the walls are supported at ground level by a steel frame consisting of vertical and horizontal members.

Skene: in a Greek theater, the stone structure behind the ***orchestra*** that served as a backdrop or stage wall.

Slip: in **ceramics,** a mixture of clay and water used (a) as a decorative finish or (b) to attach different parts of an object (e.g., handles to the body of a vessel).

Spacer: a small peg or ball used to separate metal, pottery, or glass objects from other objects during processes such as **casting, firing,** and mold-blowing.

Spandrel: the triangular area between (a) the side of an **arch** and the right angle that encloses it or (b) two adjacent arches.

Sphinx: in ancient Egypt, a creature with the body of a lion and the head of a human, an animal, or a bird.

Spolia: materials taken from an earlier building for re-use in a new one.

Springing: (a) the architectural member of an **arch** that is the first to curve inward from the vertical; (b) the point at which this curvature begins.

Squinch: a small single **arch,** or a series of concentric **corbeled** arches, set diagonally across the upper inside corner of a square building to facilitate the transition to a round **dome** or other circular superstructure.

Stained glass: windows composed of pieces of colored glass held in place by strips of lead.

State: one of the successive printed stages of a **print,** distinguished from other stages by the greater or lesser amount of work carried out on the image.

Steel-frame construction: see **skeletal construction.**

Stele: an upright stone slab or **pillar,** usually carved or inscribed for commemorative purposes.

Step pyramid: a pyramid constructed of **mastaba** forms of successively decreasing size.

Stereobate: a substructure or foundation of masonry visible above ground level.

Stigmata (pl.): marks resembling the wounds on the crucified body of Christ (from *stigma,* "a mark" or "scar").

Still life: a picture consisting principally of inanimate objects such as fruit, flowers, or pottery.

Stratigraphy: a technique for determining a chronology by studying the relative locations of layers of material in an archaeological site.

Stringcourses: decorative horizontal bands on a building.

Stucco: (a) a type of cement used to coat the walls of a building; (b) a fine plaster used for **moldings** and other architectural decorations.

Stupa: in Buddhist architecture, a **dome**-shaped or rounded structure made of brick, earth, or stone, containing the relic of a Buddha or other honored individual.

Style: in the visual arts, a manner of execution that is characteristic of an individual, a school, a period, or some other identifiable group.

Stylization: the distortion of a **representational** image to conform to certain artistic **conventions** or to emphasize particular qualities.

Stylobate: the top step of a **stereobate,** forming a foundation for a **column, peristyle,** temple, or other structure.

Stylus: a pointed instrument used in antiquity for writing on clay, wax, **papyrus,** and **parchment;** a pointed metal instrument used to scratch an image on the **plate** used to produce an **etching.**

Sunken (or **incised**) **relief:** a style of **relief** sculpture in which the image is recessed into the surface.

Support: in painting, the surface to which the **pigment** is applied.

Suspension bridge: a bridge in which the roadway is suspended from two or more steel cables, which usually pass over towers and are then anchored at their ends.

Symmetria: Greek for **symmetry.**

Symmetry: the aesthetic balance that is achieved when parts of an object are arranged about a real or imaginary central line, or **axis,** so that the parts on one side correspond in some respect (shape, size, color) with those on the other.

Symposium: (a) a drinking party; (b) a social gathering at which there is a free exchange of ideas.

Synthesis: the combination of parts or elements to form a coherent, more complex whole.

Taberna: part of a Roman building fronting on a street and serving as a shop.

Talud-tablero: an architectural **style** typical of Teotihuacán sacred structures in which paired elements—a sloping **base** (the ***talud***) supporting a vertical ***tablero*** (often decorated with sculpture or painting)—are stacked, sometimes to great heights.

Tectonic: of, or pertaining to, building or construction.

Tell: an archaeological term for a mound composed of the remains of successive settlements in the Near East.

Tempera: a fast-drying, water-based painting **medium** made with egg yolk, often used in **fresco** and panel painting.

Tenebrism: a style of painting used by Caravaggio and his followers in which most objects are in shadow, while a few are brightly illuminated.

Tenon: a projecting member in a block of stone or other building material that fits into a groove or hole to form a joint.

Tensile strength: the internal strength of a material that enables it to support itself without rupturing.

Terra-cotta: (a) an **earthenware** material, with or without a **glaze;** (b) an object made of this material.

Tertiary color: a **hue** produced by combining a **primary color** and a **secondary color.**

Tessera (pl. ***tesserae***): a small piece of colored glass, marble, or stone used in a **mosaic.**

Texture: the visual or tactile surface quality of an object.

Tholos: (a) a circular tomb of beehive shape approached by a long, horizontal passage; (b) in Classical times, a round building modeled on ancient tombs.

Three-dimensional: having height, width, and depth.

Thrust: the lateral force exerted by an **arch, dome,** or **vault,** which must be counteracted by some form of **buttressing.**

Tondo: (a) a circular painting; (b) a medallion with **relief** sculpture.

Toraṇa: a ritual gateway in Buddhist architecture.

Trabeated: constructed according to the **post-and-lintel** method.

Tracery: a decorative, **interlaced** design (as in the stonework in Gothic windows).

Transept: a cross arm in a Christian church, placed at right angles to the **nave.**

Transverse rib: a **rib** in a **vault** that crosses the **nave** or **aisle** at right angles to the **axis** of the building.

Travertine: a hard limestone used as a building material by the Etruscans and Romans.

Tribhaṅga: in Buddhist art, the "three bends posture," in which the head, chest, and lower portion of the body are angled instead of being aligned vertically.

Tribune: (a) the **apse** of a **basilica** or basilican church; (b) a **gallery** in a Romanesque or Gothic church.

Triforium: in Gothic architecture, part of the **nave** wall above the **arcade** and below the **clerestory.**

Triglyph: in a **Doric frieze,** the rectangular area between the **metopes,** decorated with three vertical grooves (glyphs).

Trilithon: an ancient monument consisting of two vertical **megaliths** supporting a third as a **lintel.**

Trilobed: having three rounded projections.

Triptych: an **altarpiece** or painting consisting of one central panel and two wings.

Trompe l'oeil: **illusionistic** painting that "deceives the eye" with its appearance of reality.

Trumeau: in Romanesque and Gothic architecture, the central post supporting the **lintel** in a double doorway.

Truss construction: a system of construction in which the architectural members (such as bars and beams) are combined, often in triangles, to form a rigid framework.

Tufa: a porous, volcanic rock that hardens on exposure to air, used as a building material.

Tumulus (pl. **tumuli**): an artificial mound, typically found over a grave.

Tunnel vault: see **barrel vault.**

Tympanum: a **lunette** over the doorway of a church, often decorated with sculpture.

Type: a person or object serving as a prefiguration or symbolic representation, usually of something in the future.

Typology: the Christian theory of **types,** in which characters and events in the New Testament (i.e., after the birth of Jesus) are prefigured by counterparts in the Old Testament.

Underpainting: a preliminary painting, subsequently covered by the final layer(s) of paint.

Uraeus (pl. **uraei**): a **stylized** representation of an asp, often included on the headdress of ancient rulers.

Urṇā: in Buddhist art, a whorl of hair or protuberance between the eyebrows of a Buddha or other honored individual.

Ushṇīsha: a **conventional** identifying topknot of hair on an image of Shakyamuni Buddha, symbolic of his wisdom.
Value: the degree of lightness (high value) or darkness (low value) in a **hue.**
Vanishing point: in the **linear perspective** system, the point at which the **orthogonals,** if extended, would intersect.
Vanitas: a category of painting, often a **still life,** the theme of which is the transitory nature of earthly things and the inevitability of death.
Vault, vaulting: a roof or ceiling of masonry constructed on the **arch** principle; see also **barrel vault, groin vault, quadrant vaulting, ribbed vault.**
Vedikā: a railing marking off sacred space in south Asian architecture, often found surrounding a Buddhist **stupa** or encircling the **axis**-pillar atop its **dome *(aṇḍa).***
Vehicle: a term often used interchangeably with **medium** to mean the liquid in which **pigments** are suspended but not dissolved and which, as it dries, binds the color to the surface of the painting.
Vellum: a cream-colored, smooth surface for painting or writing, prepared from calfskin.
Veranda: a **pillared** porch preceding an interior chamber, common in Hindu temples and Buddhist ***chaitya*** **halls.**
Verisimilitude: the quality of appearing real or truthful.
Vihāra: Buddhist monks' living quarters, either an individual cell or a space for communal activity.
Villa: (a) in antiquity and the Renaissance, a large country house; (b) in modern times, a detached house in the country or suburbs.
Visible spectrum: the colors, visible to the human eye, that are produced when white light is dispersed by a prism.
Vitreous: related to, derived from, or consisting of glass.
Volute: in the Ionic **order**, the spiral **scroll motif** decorating the **capital.**
Voussoir: one of the individual, wedge-shaped blocks of stone that make up an **arch.**
Wash: a thin, translucent coat of paint (e.g., in **watercolor**).
Watercolor: (a) paint made of **pigments** suspended in water; (b) a painting executed in this **medium.**
Wattle and daub: a technique of wall construction using woven branches or twigs plastered with clay or mud.
Web: in Gothic architecture, the portion of a **ribbed vault** between the **ribs.**
Westwork: from the German ***Westwerk,*** the western front of a church, containing an entrance and vestibule below, a chapel or **gallery** above, and flanked by two towers.
White-ground: describing a style of Greek pottery painting of the fifth century B.C., in which the decoration is usually black on a white background.
Wing: a side panel of an **altarpiece** or screen.
Woodcut: a **relief** printmaking process in which an image is carved on the surface of a wooden block by cutting away those parts that are not to be printed.
Yaksha, yakshī: indigenous south Asian fertility deities, respectively male and female, later assimilated into Buddhist art.
Ziggurat: a trapezoidal stepped structure representing a mountain in ancient Mesopotamia.

Suggestions for Further Reading

General

Adams, Laurie. *Art on Trial: From Whistler to Rothko.* New York: Walker, 1976.

———. *Art and Psychoanalysis.* New York: HarperCollins, 1993.

———. *The Methodologies of Art: An Introduction.* New York: HarperCollins, 1996.

———. *Looking at Art.* Englewood Cliffs, N.J.: Prentice-Hall, 2002.

———. *World Views: Topics in Non-Western Art.* New York: McGraw-Hill, 2004.

Arntzen, Etta, and Robert Rainwater. *Guide to the Literature of Art History.* Chicago: American Library Association, 1980.

Barasch, Moshe. *Theories of Art: From Plato to Winckelmann.* New York: New York University Press, 1985.

———. *Modern Theories of Art,* I: *From Winckelmann to Baudelaire.* New York: New York University Press, 1990.

Baxandall, Michael. *Patterns of Intention: On the Historical Explanation of Pictures.* New Haven: Yale University Press, 1985.

Bois, Yve-Alain. *Painting as Model.* Cambridge, Mass.: MIT Press, 1990.

Broude, Norma, and Mary D. Garrard, eds. *Feminism and Art History: Questioning the Litany.* New York: Harper & Row, 1982.

———, eds. *The Expanding Discourse: Feminism and Art History.* New York: HarperCollins, 1992.

Bryson, Norman. *Vision and Painting: The Logic of the Gaze.* New Haven: Yale University Press, 1983.

———. *Vision and Painting.* New Haven: Yale University Press, 1987.

———, et al., eds. *Visual Theory: Painting and Interpretation.* New York: Cambridge University Press, 1991.

Cahn, Walter. *Masterpieces: Chapters on the History of an Idea.* Princeton: Princeton University Press, 1979.

Carrier, David. *Principles of Art History Writing.* University Park, Pa.: Pennsylvania State University Press, 1991.

Chadwick, Whitney. *Women, Art, and Society.* 3rd ed. New York: Thames & Hudson, 2002.

Chicago, Judy, and Miriam Schapiro. In *Anonymous Was a Woman.* Valencia, Calif.: Feminist Art Program, California Institute of the Arts, 1974.

Chilvers, Ian, and Harold Osborne, eds. *The Oxford Dictionary of Art.* New York: Oxford University Press, 1988.

Clark, Kenneth M. *The Nude: A Study in Ideal Form.* Garden City, N.Y.: Doubleday, 1959.

Clark, Toby. *Art and Propaganda in the Twentieth Century: The Political Image in the Age of Mass Culture.* New York: Abrams, 1997.

Derrida, Jacques. *The Truth in Painting.* Trans. Geoff Bennington and Ian McLeod. Chicago: University of Chicago Press, 1987.

Ehresmann, Donald L. *Architecture: A Bibliographic Guide to Basic Reference Works, Histories, and Handbooks.* Littleton, Col.: Libraries Unlimited, 1984.

———. *Fine Arts: A Bibliographic Guide to Basic Reference Works, Histories, and Handbooks.* 3rd ed. Englewood, Col.: Libraries Unlimited, 1990.

Eliade, Mircea. *A History of Religious Ideas.* Trans. Willard R. Trask. 3 vols. Chicago: University of Chicago Press, 1978.

Elsen, Albert E. *The Purposes of Art: An Introduction to the History and Appreciation of Art.* 4th ed. New York: Holt, Rinehart & Winston, 1981.

Encyclopedia of World Art. 17 vols. New York: McGraw-Hill, 1959–1987.

Fine, Elsa Honig. *Women and Art.* Montclair, N.J.: Allanheld & Schram, 1978.

Flynn, Tom. *The Body in Three Dimensions.* New York: Abrams, 1998.

Freedberg, David. *The Power of Images: Studies in the History and Theory of Response.* Chicago: University of Chicago Press, 1989.

Gedo, Mary Mathews. *Looking at Art from the Inside Out: The Psychoiconographic Approach to Modern Art.* New York: Cambridge University Press, 1994.

Getlein, Mark. *Gilbert's Living with Art.* 7th ed. New York: McGraw-Hill, 2005.

Gombrich, Ernst. *Art and Illusion: A Study in the Psychology of Pictorial Representation* (1960). Millennium ed., with new preface by author. Princeton: Princeton University Press, 2000.

———. *The Image and the Eye: Further Studies in the Psychology of Pictorial Representation.* Ithaca, N.Y.: Cornell University Press, 1982.

———. *Meditations on a Hobby Horse, and Other Essays on the Theory of Art* (1963). 4th ed. Oxford: Phaidon, 1985.

———. *Shadows: The Depiction of Cast Shadows in Western Art.* London: National Gallery, 1995.

Hall, James. *Illustrated Dictionary of Symbols in Eastern and Western Art.* New York: HarperCollins, 1994.

———. *Dictionary of Subjects and Symbols in Art.* Rev. ed. London: Murray, 1996.

Harris, Ann Sutherland, and Linda Nochlin. *Women Artists, 1550–1950.* Los Angeles: Los Angeles County Museum of Art; New York: Random House, 1976.

Harrison, Charles, and Paul Wood, eds. *Art in Theory, 1900–1990: An Anthology of Changing Ideas.* Cambridge, Mass.: Blackwell, 1993.

Hauser, Arnold. *The Philosophy of Art History.* New York: Knopf, 1958.

———. *The Social History of Art.* 3rd ed. 4 vols. New York: Routledge, 1999.

Hedges, Elaine, and Ingrid Wendt. *In Her Own Image: Women Working in the Arts.* New York: McGraw-Hill, 1980.

Heller, Nancy G. *Women Artists: An Illustrated History.* 4th ed. New York: Abbeville, 2003.

Hess, Thomas B., and Elizabeth C. Baker, eds. *Art and Sexual Politics: Women's Liberation, Women Artists, and Art History.* New York: Macmillan, 1973.

Hinz, Berthold. *Art in the Third Reich.* Trans. Robert Kimber and Rita Kimber. New York: Pantheon, 1979.

Holt, Elizabeth Gilmore, ed. *A Documentary History of Art.* 2 vols. Princeton: Princeton University Press, 1981.

Kemp, Martin. *The Science of Art: Optical Themes in Western Art from Brunelleschi to Seurat.* New Haven: Yale University Press, 1990.

Kleinbauer, W. Eugene. *Modern Perspectives in Western Art History: An Anthology of Twentieth-Century Writings on the Visual Arts* (1971). Toronto: University of Toronto Press, 1989.

Kleinbauer, W. Eugene, and Thomas P. Slavens. *Research Guide to Western Art History.* Chicago: American Library Association, 1982.

Kostof, Spiro. *The Architect: Chapters in the History of the Profession* (1977). Berkeley: University of California Press, 2000.

———. *A History of Architecture: Settings and Rituals* (1985). 2nd ed. Rev. Greg Castillo. New York: Oxford University Press, 1995.

Kris, Ernst, and Otto Kurz. *Legend, Myth, and Magic in the Image of the Artist: An Historical Experiment.* New Haven: Yale University Press, 1979.

Kultermann, Udo. *The History of Art History.* New York: Abaris, 1993.

Lever, Jill, and John Harris. *The Illustrated Dictionary of Architecture, 800–1914.* 2nd ed. Boston: Faber & Faber, 1993.

Levine, Lawrence W. *Highbrow/Lowbrow: The Emergence of Cultural Hierarchy in America.* Cambridge, Mass.: Harvard University Press, 1988.

McCoubrey, John W. *American Art, 1700–1960: Sources and Documents.* Englewood Cliffs, N.J.: Prentice-Hall, 1965.

Mayer, Ralph. *The Artist's Handbook of Materials and Techniques.* 5th ed. New York: Viking, 1991.

———. *The HarperCollins Dictionary of Art Terms and Techniques.* 2nd ed. New York: HarperCollins, 1991.

Mitchell, W. J. T. *Picture Theory: Essays on Verbal and Visual Representation.* Chicago: University of Chicago Press, 1994.

Munsterberg, Hugo. *A History of Women Artists.* New York: Potter, 1975.

Murray, Peter, and Linda Murray. *The Penguin Dictionary of Art and Artists.* 7th ed., rev. New York: Penguin, 1997.

Nochlin, Linda. *Women, Art, and Power: And Other Essays.* New York: Harper & Row, 1988.

Ocvirk, Otto G., et al. *Art Fundamentals: Theory and Practice.* 10th ed. New York: McGraw-Hill, 2005.

Panofsky, Erwin. *Meaning in the Visual Arts: Papers in and on Art History.* Garden City, N.Y.: Doubleday, 1955.

———. *Idea: A Concept in Art Theory.* Columbia: University of South Carolina Press, 1968.

———. *Perspective as Symbolic Form.* New York: Zone Books, 1991.

Parker, Rozsika, and Griselda Pollock. *Old Mistresses: Women, Art, and Ideology.* New York: Pantheon, 1982.

Penny, Nicholas. *The Materials of Sculpture.* New Haven: Yale University Press, 1993.

Petersen, Karen, and J. J. Wilson. *Women Artists: Recognition and Reappraisal from the Early Middle Ages to the Twentieth Century.* New York: Harper & Row, 1976.

Pollock, Griselda. *Vision and Difference: Femininity, Feminism and Histories of Art* (1988). London: Routledge, 2003.

Praz, Mario, *Mnemosyne: The Principle between Literature and the Visual Arts.* Princeton: Princeton University Press, 1970.

Pultz, John. *The Body and the Lens: Photography 1839 to the Present.* New York: Abrams, 1995.

Reid, Jane Davidson, ed. *The Oxford Guide to Classical Mythology in the Arts, 1330–1990s.* 2 vols. New York: Oxford University Press, 1993.

Roth, Leland M. *Understanding Architecture: Its Elements, History, and Meaning.* New York: HarperCollins, 1993.

Saxl, Fritz. *A Heritage of Images: A Selection of Lectures.* Harmondsworth: Penguin, 1970.

Schiller, Gertrud. *Iconography of Christian Art.* Trans. Janet Seligman. 2 vols. Greenwich, Conn.: New York Graphic Society, 1971.

Scully, Vincent. *Architecture: The Natural and the Man-Made.* New York: St. Martin's, 1991.

Sporre, Dennis J. *The Creative Impulse: An Introduction to the Arts.* 7th ed. Upper Saddle River, N.J.: Prentice-Hall, 2005.

Stephenson, Jonathan. *The Materials and Techniques of Painting* (1989). New York: Thames & Hudson, 1993.

Summerson, John. *The Classical Language of Architecture* (1963). Cambridge, Mass.: MIT Press, 1984.

Trachtenberg, Marvin, and Isabelle Hyman. *Architecture, from Pre-History to Postmodernity.* 2nd ed. New York: Abrams, 2002.

Van Keuren, Frances. *Guide to Research in Classical Art and Mythology.* Chicago: American Library Association, 1991.

Verhelst, Wilbert. *Sculpture: Tools, Materials, and Techniques.* 2nd ed. Englewood Cliffs, N.J.: Prentice-Hall, 1988.

Watkin, David. *The Rise of Architectural History.* Chicago: University of Chicago Press, 1983.

Westermann, Mariët. *A Worldly Art: The Dutch Republic, 1585–1718.* New York: Abrams, 1996.

Williams, Raymond. *Culture and Society, 1780–1950* (1958). New York: Harper & Row, 1966.

———. *The Sociology of Culture.* New York: Schocken, 1982.

Winternitz, Emanuel. *Musical Instruments and Their Symbolism in Western Art.* New York: Norton, 1967.

Wittkower, Rudolf. *Allegory and the Migration of Symbols.* London: Thames & Hudson, 1977.

———. *Sculpture.* New York: Harper & Row, 1977.

Wittkower, Rudolf, and Margot Wittkower. *Born under Saturn: The Character and Conduct of Artists, a Documented History from Antiquity to the French Revolution* (1963). New York: Norton, 1969.

Wodehouse, Lawrence, and Marian Moffett. *A History of Western Architecture.* Mountain View, Calif.: Mayfield, 1989.

Wolff, Janet. *The Social Production of Art.* 2nd ed. New York: New York University Press, 1993.

Wölfflin, Heinrich. *Principles of Art History: The Problem of the Development of Style in Later Art* (1932). Trans. M. D. Hottinger. New York: Dover, 1956.

———. *Classic Art: An Introduction to the Italian Renaissance* (1952). 5th ed. Trans. Peter Murray and Linda Murray. London: Phaidon, 1994.

———. *The Sense of Form in Art: A Comparative Psychological Study.* Trans. Alice Muehsam and Norma A. Shettan. New York: Chelsea, 1958.

Wollheim, Richard. *Art and Its Objects: With Six Supplementary Essays* (1980). 2nd ed. New York: Cambridge University Press, 1992.

———. *Painting as an Art.* Princeton: Princeton University Press, 1987.

Wren, Linnea H., and David J. Wren, eds. *Perspectives on Western Art.* 2 vols. New York: HarperCollins, 1987–1994.

Yates, Frances A. *The Art of Memory* (1966). London: Routledge, 1999.

The Art of Prehistory

Amiet, Pierre, ed. *Art in the Ancient World: A Handbook of Styles and Forms.* Trans. Valerie Bynner. New York: Rizzoli, 1981.

Bandi, Hans-Georg, and Henri Breuil. *The Art of the Stone Age: Forty Thousand Years of Rock Art.* 2nd ed. Trans. Ann E. Keep. London: Methuen, 1970.

Bataille, Georges, *Lascaux; or, The Birth of Art: Prehistoric Painting.* Trans. Austryn Wainhouse. Lausanne: Skira, 1955.

Breuil, Henri. *Four Hundred Centuries of Cave Art* (1952). Trans. Mary E. Boyle. New York: Hacker, 1979.

Castleden, Rodney. *The Making of Stonehenge.* London: Routledge, 1993.

Chauvet, Jean-Marie, Eliette Brunel Deschamps, and Christian Hillaire. *Dawn of Art: The Chauvet Cave, the Oldest Known Paintings in the World.* Trans. Paul G. Bahn. New York: Abrams, 1996.

Chippindale, Christopher. *Stonehenge Complete.* Exp. ed. London: Thames & Hudson, 2004.

Clottes, Jean, and Jean Courtin. *The Cave beneath the Sea: Paleolithic Images at Cosquer.* New York: Abrams, 1996.

Finegan, Jack. *Light from the Ancient Past.* 2 vols. 2nd ed. Princeton: Princeton University Press, 1974.

Gimbutas, Marija. *The Gods and Goddesses of Old Europe, 7000–3500 B.C.: Myths, Legends, and Cult Images.* Berkeley: University of California Press, 1974.

Graziosi, Paolo. *Paleolithic Art.* New York: McGraw-Hill, 1960.

James, Edwin O. *From Cave to Cathedral: Temples and Shrines of Prehistoric, Classical, and Early Christian Times.* London: Thames & Hudson, 1965.

Leroi-Gourhan, André. *Treasures of Prehistoric Art.* New York: Abrams, 1967.

———. *The Dawn of European Art: An Introduction to Paleolithic Cave Painting.* New York: Cambridge University Press, 1982.

Powell, T. G. E. *Prehistoric Art.* New York: Praeger, 1966.

Ruspoli, Mario. *The Cave of Lascaux: The Final Photographs.* New York: Abrams, 1987.

Sieveking, Ann. *The Cave Artists.* London: Thames & Hudson, 1979.

Sandars, N. K. *Prehistoric Art in Europe.* 2nd ed. Pelican History of Art. New Haven: Yale University Press, 1985.

Twohig, Elizabeth Shee. *The Megalithic Art of Western Europe.* New York: Oxford University Press, 1981.

Wainwright, Geoffrey. *The Henge Monuments: Ceremony and Society in Prehistoric Britain.* London: Thames & Hudson, 1989.

The Ancient Near East

Akurgal, Ekrem. *The Art of the Hittites.* New York: Abrams, 1962.

Bottéro, Jean. *Mesopotamia: Writing, Reasoning, and the Gods.* Trans. Zainab Bahrani and Marc Van De Mieroop. Chicago: University of Chicago Press, 1992.

Collon, Dominique. *First Impressions: Cylinder Seals in the Ancient Near East.* London: British Museum Press, 1987.

Crawford, Harriet. *Sumer and the Sumerians.* 2nd ed. New York: Cambridge University Press, 2004.

Ferrier, R. W., ed. *The Arts of Persia.* New Haven: Yale University Press, 1989.

Frankfort, Henri. *The Art and Architecture of the Ancient Orient.* 5th ed. Pelican History of Art. New Haven: Yale University Press, 1996.

Ghirshman, Roman. *The Arts of Ancient Iran from Its Origins to the Time of Alexander the Great.* Trans. Stuart Gilbert and James Emmons. New York: Golden Press, 1962.

Gilgamesh: Translated from the Sîn-leqi-unninnī Version. Trans. James Gardner and John Maier. New York: Knopf, 1984.

Groenewegen-Frankfort, H. A. *Arrest and Movement: An Essay on Space and Time in the Representational Art of the Ancient Near East.* Cambridge, Mass.: Belknap Press, 1987.

Groenewegen-Frankfort, H. A., and Bernard Ashmole. *Art of the Ancient World: Painting, Pottery, Sculpture, Architecture from Egypt, Mesopotamia, Crete, Greece, and Rome.* New York: Abrams, 1972.

Harper, Prudence, Joan Aruz, and Françoise Tallon, eds. *The Royal City of Susa: Ancient Near Eastern Treasures in the Louvre.* New York: Metropolitan Museum of Art, 1992.

Kramer, Samuel Noah. *The Sumerians: Their History, Culture, and Character.* Chicago: University of Chicago Press, 1963.

———. *History Begins at Sumer: Thirty-nine Firsts in Man's Recorded History.* 3rd rev. ed. Philadelphia: University of Pennsylvania Press, 1981.

Leick, Gwendolyn. *A Dictionary of Ancient Near Eastern Architecture.* New York: Routledge, 1988.

Lloyd, Seton. *The Archaeology of Mesopotamia: From the Old Stone Age to the Persian Conquest* (1978). Rev. ed. London: Thames & Hudson, 1984.

Lloyd, Seton, and Hans W. Müller. *Ancient Architecture: Mesopotamia, Egypt, Crete.* New York: Electa/Rizzoli, 1986.

Mellaart, James. *The Earliest Civilizations of the Near East.* New York: McGraw-Hill, 1965.

———. *Çatal Hüyük: A Neolithic Town in Anatolia.* New York: McGraw-Hill, 1967.

Moortgat, Anton. *The Art of Ancient Mesopotamia.* Trans. Judith Filson. New York: Phaidon, 1969.

Moscati, Sabatino, ed. *The Phoenicians* (1988). New York: Rizzoli, 1999.

Muscarella, Oscar W. *Bronze and Iron: Ancient Near Eastern Artifacts in the Metropolitan Museum of Art.* New York: Metropolitan Museum of Art, 1988.

Oates, Joan. *Babylon.* Rev. ed. London: Thames & Hudson, 1986.

Oppenheim, A. Leo. *Ancient Mesopotamia: Portrait of a Dead Civilization.* Rev. ed. Chicago: University of Chicago Press, 1977.

Parrot, André. *The Arts of Assyria.* Trans. Stuart Gilbert and James Emmons. New York: Golden Press, 1961.

———. *Sumer: The Dawn of Art.* Trans. Stuart Gilbert and James Emmons. New York: Golden Press, 1961.

Porada, Edith, and Robert H. Dyson. *The Art of Ancient Iran: Pre-Islamic Cultures.* Rev. ed. New York: Greystone Press, 1967.

Reade, Julian. *Mesopotamia.* 2nd ed. London: British Museum Press, 2000.

Roux, Georges. *Ancient Iraq.* 3rd ed. New York: Penguin, 1992.

Saggs, Henry W. F. *The Greatness That Was Babylon: A Survey of the Ancient Civilization of the Tigris-Euphrates Valley.* Rev. ed. London: Sidgwick & Jackson, 1988.

Woolley, Leonard. *The Art of the Middle East, Including Persia, Mesopotamia, and Palestine.* New York: Crown, 1961.

———. *The Development of Sumerian Art.* Westport, Conn.: Greenwood Press, 1981.

Ancient Egypt

Aldred, Cyril. *Akhenaten and Nefertiti.* New York: Viking Press, 1973.

———. *Egyptian Art in the Days of the Pharaohs, 3100–320 B.C.* New York: Oxford University Press, 1980.

Andrews, Carol. *Ancient Egyptian Jewelry.* New York: Abrams, 1991.

Badawy, Alexander. *A History of Egyptian Architecture.* 3 vols. Berkeley: University of California Press, 1954–68.

Brier, Bob. *Egyptian Mummies: Unraveling the Secrets of an Ancient Art.* New York: Morrow, 1994.

Davis, Whitney. *The Canonical Tradition in Ancient Egyptian Art.* New York: Cambridge University Press, 1989.

Doxiadis, Euphrosyne. *The Mysterious Fayum Portraits: Faces from Ancient Egypt.* New York: Abrams, 1995.

Edwards, I. E. S. *The Pyramids of Egypt.* Rev. ed. New York: Penguin, 1991.

El Mahdy, Christine, ed. *The World of the Pharaohs: A Complete Guide to Ancient Egypt.* London: Thames & Hudson, 1990.

The Egyptian Book of the Dead: The Book of Going Forth by Day, Being the Papyrus of Ani (Royal Scribe of the Divine Offerings). Trans. Raymond O. Faulkner. San Francisco: Chronicle, 1994.

Gardiner, Alan H. *Egypt of the Pharaohs.* Oxford: Oxford University Press, 1978.

Hayes, William C. *The Scepter of Egypt: A Background for the Study of the Egyptian Antiquities in the Metropolitan Museum of Art.* 2 vols. Cambridge, Mass.: Harvard University Press, 1960.

James, T. G. H. *Egyptian Painting and Drawing in the British Museum.* London: British Museum Press, 1985.

James, T. G. H., and W. V. Davies. *Egyptian Sculpture.* Cambridge, Mass.: Harvard University Press, 1983.

Lange, Kurt, and Max Hirmer. *Egypt: Architecture, Sculpture, Painting in Three Thousand Years.* 4th ed. London: Phaidon, 1968.

Lurker, Manfred. *The Gods and Symbols of Ancient Egypt: An Illustrated Dictionary.* Rev. ed. Trans. Barbara Cummings. New York: Thames & Hudson, 1982.

Martin, Geoffrey T. *The Hidden Tombs of Memphis: New Discoveries from the Time of Tutankhamun and Ramesses the Great.* London: Thames & Hudson, 1991.

Panofsky, Erwin. *Tomb Sculpture: Four Lectures on Its Changing Aspects from Ancient Egypt to Bernini.* Foreword by Martin Warnke. New York: Abrams, 1992.

Priese, Karl-Heinz. *The Gold of Meroë.* New York: Metropolitan Museum of Art, 1993.

Redford, Donald B. *Akhenaten: The Heretic King.* Princeton: Princeton University Press, 1984.

Reeves, Nicholas. *The Complete Tutankhamun: The King, the Tomb, the Royal Treasure.* New York: Thames & Hudson, 1990.

Robins, Gay. *Women in Ancient Egypt.* Cambridge, Mass.: Harvard University Press, 1993.

———. *Proportion and Style in Ancient Egyptian Art.* Austin: University of Texas Press, 1994.

Schäfer, Heinrich. *Principles of Egyptian Art.* Rev. ed. Trans. John Baines. Oxford: Griffith Institute, 1986.

Smith, William Stevenson, and William Kelly Simpson. *The Art and Architecture of Ancient Egypt.* Rev. ed. New Haven: Yale University Press, 1988.

Strouhal, Eugen. *Life of the Ancient Egyptians.* Trans. Deryck Viney. Norman: University of Oklahoma Press, 1992.

Taylor, John H. *Egypt and Nubia.* London: British Museum Press, 1991.

Walker, Susan, and Morris Bierbrier. *Ancient Faces: Mummy Portraits from Roman Egypt.* 2nd ed. London: British Museum Press, 2000.

Wilkinson, Charles K. *Egyptian Wall Paintings: The Metropolitan Museum of Art's Collection of Facsimiles.* New York: Metropolitan Museum of Art, 1983.

Wilkinson, Richard H. *Reading Egyptian Art: A Hieroglyphic Guide to Ancient Egyptian Painting and Sculpture.* New York: Thames & Hudson, 1992.

Woldering, Irmgard. *Gods, Men and Pharaohs: The Glory of Egyptian Art.* Trans. Ann E. Keep. New York: Abrams, 1967.

Wolff, Walther. *The Origins of Western Art: Egypt, Mesopotamia, the Aegean.* New York: Universe, 1989.

The Aegean

Barber, R. L. N. *The Cyclades in the Bronze Age.* Iowa City: University of Iowa Press, 1987.

Boardman, John. *Pre-Classical: From Crete to Archaic Greece.* Harmondsworth: Penguin, 1978.

Chadwick, John. *The Mycenaean World.* Cambridge, Eng.: Cambridge University Press, 1976.

Doumas, Christos. *The Wall-Paintings of Thera.* Trans. Alex Doumas. Athens: Thera Foundation, 1992.

Getz-Preziosi, Pat. *Sculptors of the Cyclades: Individual and Tradition in the Third Millennium* B.C. Ann Arbor: University of Michigan Press, 1987.

Graham, J. Walter. *The Palaces of Crete.* Rev. ed. Princeton: Princeton University Press, 1987.

Hampe, Roland, and Erika Simon. *The Birth of Greek Art from the Mycenaean to the Archaic Period.* New York: Oxford University Press, 1981.

Higgins, Reynold A. *Minoan and Mycenaean Art.* New rev. ed. London: Thames & Hudson, 1997.

Hood, Sinclair. *The Arts in Prehistoric Greece.* Pelican History of Art. Harmondsworth: Penguin, 1978.

———. *The Minoans: The Story of Bronze Age Crete.* New York: Praeger, 1981.

Hurwit, Jeffrey M. *The Art and Culture of Early Greece, 1100–480* B.C. Ithaca, N.Y.: Cornell University Press, 1985.

Immerwahr, Sara A. *Aegean Painting in the Bronze Age.* University Park: Pennsylvania State University Press, 1990.

Jenkins, Ian. *The Parthenon Frieze.* Austin: University of Texas Press, 1994.

McDonald, William. *Progress into the Past: The Rediscovery of Mycenaean Civilization.* 2nd ed. Bloomington: Indiana University Press, 1990.

Marinatos, Spyridon N., and Max Hirmer. *Crete and Mycenae.* Trans. John Boardman. New York: Abrams, 1960.

Morgan, Catherine. *Athletes and Oracles: The Transformation of Olympia and Delphi in the Eighth Century* B.C. Cambridge, Eng.: Cambridge University Press, 1990.

Morgan, Lyvia. *The Miniature Wall Paintings of Thera: A Study in Aegean Culture and Iconography.* Cambridge, Eng.: Cambridge University Press, 1988.

Mylonas, George E. *Mycenae and the Mycenaean Age.* Princeton: Princeton University Press, 1966.

Nilsson, Martin P. *The Minoan-Mycenaean Religion and Its Survival in Greek Religion.* 2nd rev. ed. New York: Biblo and Tannen, 1971.

Palmer, Leonard R. *Mycenaeans and Minoans: Aegean Prehistory in the Light of the Linear B Tablets.* 2nd rev. ed. Westport, Conn.: Greenwood Press, 1980.

Renfrew, Colin. *The Emergence of Civilisation: The Cyclades and the Aegean in the Third Millennium* B.C. London: Methuen, 1972.

Willetts, R. F. *The Civilization of Ancient Crete.* Berkeley: University of California Press, 1977.

The Art of Ancient Greece

Arafat, K. W. *Classical Zeus: A Study in Art and Literature.* Oxford: Clarendon, 1990.

Ashmole, Bernard. *Architect and Sculptor in Classical Greece.* New York: New York University Press, 1972.

Beazley, John D. *Attic Red-Figure Vase-Painters.* 2nd ed. 3 vols. New York: Hacker, 1984.

———. *The Development of the Attic Black-Figure.* Rev. ed. Berkeley: University of California Press, 1986.

Biers, William. *The Archaeology of Greece: An Introduction.* 2nd ed. Ithaca, N.Y.: Cornell University Press, 1996.

Boardman, John. *Greek Art.* New rev. ed. New York: Thames & Hudson, 1985.

———. *The Parthenon and Its Sculptures.* Austin: University of Texas Press, 1985.

———. *Athenian Red-Figure Vases, the Classical Period: A Handbook.* New York: Thames & Hudson, 1989.

———. *Athenian Black-Figure Vases: A Handbook.* Corrected ed. New York: Thames & Hudson, 1991.

———. *Athenian Red-Figure Vases, the Archaic Period: A Handbook.* New York: Thames & Hudson, 1991.

———. *Greek Sculpture, the Archaic Period: A Handbook.* New York: Thames & Hudson, 1991.

———. *Greek Sculpture, the Classical Period: A Handbook.* New York: Thames & Hudson, 1991.

Brilliant, Richard. *Arts of the Ancient Greeks.* New York: McGraw-Hill, 1973.

Camp, John M. *The Athenian Agora: Excavations in the Heart of Classical Athens.* Updated ed. New York: Thames & Hudson, 1992.

Carpenter, Rhys. *The Esthetic Basis of the Greek Art of the Fifth and Fourth Centuries* B.C. Bloomington: Indiana University Press, 1959.

———. *Greek Sculpture: A Critical Review.* Chicago: University of Chicago Press, 1960.

———. *The Architects of the Parthenon.* Baltimore: Penguin, 1970.

Carpenter, Thomas H. *Art and Myth in Ancient Greece: A Handbook.* New York: Thames & Hudson, 1991.

Chitham, Robert. *The Classical Orders of Architecture.* 2nd ed. New York: Rizzoli, 2005.

Cook, Robert M. *Greek Art: Its Development, Character, and Influence.* New York: Farrar, Straus, Giroux, 1973.

Coulton, J. J. *Ancient Greek Architects at Work: Problems of Structure and Design.* Ithaca, N.Y.: Cornell University Press, 1977.

Dinsmoor, William B. *The Architecture of Ancient Greece.* 3rd ed. New York: Norton, 1975.

Francis, Eric David. *Image and Idea in Fifth-Century Greece: Art and Literature after the Persian Wars.* London: Routledge, 1990.

Havelock, Christine M. *Hellenistic Art: The Art of the Classical World from the Death of Alexander the Great to the Battle of Actium.* 2nd ed. New York: Norton, 1981.

Kampen, Natalie Boymel. *Sexuality in Ancient Art: Near East, Egypt, Greece, and Italy.* Cambridge: Cambridge University Press, 1996.

Koloski-Ostrow, Ann Olga, and Claire L. Lyons, eds. *Naked Truths: Women, Sexuality, and Gender in Classical Art and Archaeology.* London: Routledge, 1997.

Kraay, Colin M., and Max Hirmer. *Greek Coins.* New York: Abrams, 1966.

Lawrence, A. W. *Greek Architecture.* 5th ed. Pelican History of Art. New Haven: Yale University Press, 1996.

Onians, John. *Art and Thought in the Hellenistic Age: The Greek World View, 350–50* B.C. London: Thames & Hudson, 1979.

———. *Bearers of Meaning: The Classical Orders in Antiquity, the Middle Ages, and the Renaissance.* Princeton: Princeton University Press, 1988.

Papaioannou, Kostas. *The Art of Greece.* Trans. I. Mark Paris. New York: Abrams, 1989.

Pedley, John Griffiths. *Greek Art and Archaeology.* 2nd ed. New York: Abrams, 1998.

Pollitt, J. J. *The Art of Greece, 1400–31* B.C.*: Sources and Documents.* Englewood Cliffs, N.J.: Prentice-Hall, 1965.

———. *Art and Experience in Classical Greece.* Cambridge, Eng.: Cambridge University Press, 1972.

———. *The Ancient View of Greek Art: Criticism, History, and Terminology.* New Haven: Yale University Press, 1974.

———. *Art in the Hellenistic Age.* Cambridge, Eng.: Cambridge University Press, 1986.

Richter, Gisela M. A. *Archaic Greek Art against Its Historical Background: A Survey.* New York: Oxford University Press, 1949.

———. *Kouroi.* 3rd ed. New York: Phaidon, 1970.

———. *The Sculpture and Sculptors of the Greeks.* 4th ed., rev. New Haven: Yale University Press, 1970.

———. *A Handbook of Greek Art.* 9th ed. New York: Da Capo, 1987.

Ridgway, Brunilde Sismondo. *The Severe Style in Greek Sculpture.* Princeton: Princeton University Press, 1970.

———. *Fifth-Century Styles in Greek Sculpture.* Princeton: Princeton University Press, 1981.

Ridgway, Brunilde Sismondo. *Hellenistic Sculpture, I.* Madison: University of Wisconsin Press, 1990.

——— *The Archaic Style in Greek Sculpture.* 2nd ed. Chicago: Ares, 1993.

———. *Hellenistic Sculpture, II.* Madison: University of Wisconsin Press, 2000.

Robertson, Martin. *A History of Greek Art.* 2 vols. London: Cambridge University Press, 1975.

Roes, Anna. *Greek Geometric Art, Its Symbolism and Its Origin.* London: Oxford University Press, 1933.

Schefold, Karl. *Myth and Legend in Early Greek Art.* Trans. Audrey Hicks. New York: Abrams, 1966.

———. *Gods and Heroes in Late Archaic Greek Art.* Trans. Alan Griffiths. New York: Cambridge University Press, 1992.

Schmidt, Evamaria. *The Great Altar of Pergamon.* Trans. Lena Jaeck. Boston: Boston Book and Art Shop, 1965.

Scully, Vincent. *The Earth, the Temple, and the Gods: Greek Sacred Architecture.* Rev. ed. New Haven: Yale University Press, 1979.

Smith, R. R. R. *Hellenistic Sculpture: A Handbook.* New York: Thames & Hudson, 1991.

Stewart, Andrew. *Greek Sculpture: An Exploration.* New Haven: Yale University Press, 1990.

———. *Art, Desire, and the Body in Ancient Greece.* Cambridge, Eng.: Cambridge University Press, 1997.

Stobart, J. C. *The Glory That Was Greece.* 4th ed. New York: Praeger, 1984.

Vermeule, Emily. *Greece in the Bronze Age.* Chicago: University of Chicago Press, 1972.

———. *Aspects of Death in Early Greek Art and Poetry.* Berkeley: University of California Press, 1979.

Webster, T. B. L. *The Art of Greece: The Age of Hellenism.* New York: Crown, 1966.

Whitley, James. *Style and Society in Dark Age Greece: The Changing Face of a Pre-literate Society, 1100–700 B.C.* Cambridge, Eng.: Cambridge University Press, 1991.

The Art of the Etruscans

Bloch, Raymond. *Etruscan Art.* Greenwich, Conn.: New York Graphic Society, 1965.

Boëthius, Axel. *Etruscan and Early Roman Architecture.* 2nd integrated ed. Rev. by Roger Ling and Tom Rasmussen. New York: Penguin, 1978.

Bonfante, Larissa, ed. *Etruscan Life and Afterlife: A Handbook of Etruscan Studies.* Detroit: Wayne State University Press, 1986.

———. *Etruscan: Reading the Past.* Berkeley: University of California Press/British Museum, 1990.

———. *Etruscan Mirrors.* New York: Metropolitan Museum of Art, 1997.

Brendel, Otto J. *Etruscan Art.* 2nd ed. New Haven: Yale University Press, 1995.

Buranelli, Francesco. *The Etruscans: Legacy of a Lost Civilization from the Vatican Museums.* Memphis, Tenn.: Lithograph, 1992.

de Grummond, Nancy Thomson, ed. *A Guide to Etruscan Mirrors.* Tallahassee Archaeological News, 1982.

Harris, William Vernon. *Rome in Etruria and Umbria.* Oxford: Clarendon, 1971.

Macnamara, Ellen. *Everyday Life of the Etruscans.* Cambridge, Mass.: Harvard University Press, 1991.

Mansuelli, Guido Achille. *The Art of Etruria and Early Rome.* Trans. C. E. Ellis. New York: Crown, 1964.

Pallottino, Massimo. *Etruscan Painting.* Trans. M. E. Stanley and Stuart Gilbert. Geneva: Skira, 1952.

Richardson, Emeline H. *The Etruscans, Their Art and Civilization.* Chicago: University of Chicago Press, 1964.

Spivey, Nigel, and Simon Stoddart. *Etruscan Italy: An Archaeological History.* London: Batsford, 1992.

Sprenger, Maja, Gilda Bartoloni, and Max Hirmer. *The Etruscans: Their History, Art, and Architecture.* Trans. Robert Erich Wolf. New York: Abrams, 1983.

Steingräber, Stephan, ed. *Etruscan Painting: Catalogue Raisonné of Etruscan Wall Paintings.* Trans. Mary Blair and Brian Phillips. New York: Johnson Reprint, 1986.

Ward-Perkins, J. B. *Roman Architecture* (1974). Milan/London: Electa/Phaidon, 2003.

Ancient Rome

Andreae, Bernard. *The Art of Rome.* Trans. Robert Erich Wolf. New York: Abrams, 1977.

Bianchi Bandinelli, Ranuccio. *Rome, the Center of Power, 500 B.C. to A.D. 200.* Trans. Peter Green. New York: Braziller, 1970.

———. *Rome, the Late Empire: Roman Art, A.D. 200–400.* Trans. Peter Green. New York: Braziller, 1971.

Brendel, Otto J. *Prolegomena to the Study of Roman Art.* New Haven: Yale University Press, 1979.

Brilliant, Richard. *Roman Art from the Republic to Constantine.* London: Phaidon, 1974.

———. *Pompeii A.D. 79: The Treasure of Rediscovery.* New York: Potter, 1979.

D'Ambra, Eve. *Roman Art.* New York: Cambridge University Press, 1998.

Feder, Theodore H. *Great Treasures of Pompeii and Herculaneum.* New York: Abbeville, 1978.

Goldscheider, Ludwig. *Roman Portraits.* New York: Oxford University Press, 1940.

Guillaud, Jacqueline, and Maurice Guillaud. *Frescoes in the Time of Pompeii.* New York: Potter, 1990.

Hanfmann, George M. A. *Roman Art: A Modern Survey of the Art of Imperial Rome* (1964). New York: Norton, 1975.

Heintze, Helga von. *Roman Art* (1972). New York: Universe, 1990.

Henig, Martin, ed. *Handbook of Roman Art: A Comprehensive Survey of All the Arts of the Roman World.* Ithaca, N.Y.: Cornell University Press, 1983.

Jenkyns, Richard., ed. *The Legacy of Rome: A New Appraisal.* New York: Oxford University Press, 1992.

Krautheimer, Richard. *Rome: Profile of a City, 312–1308* (1980). Princeton: Princeton University Press, 2000.

Ling, Roger. *Roman Painting.* New York: Cambridge University Press, 1991.

MacDonald, William L. *The Architecture of the Roman Empire: An Introductory Study* (1965). Rev. ed. New Haven: Yale University Press, 1982.

———. *The Pantheon: Design, Meaning, and Progeny* (1976). Cambridge, Mass.: Harvard University Press, 2002.

Pollitt, J. J. *The Art of Rome c. 753 B.C.–A.D. 337: Sources and Documents.* New York: Cambridge University Press, 1983.

Ramage, Nancy H., and Andrew Ramage. *The Cambridge Illustrated History of Roman Art.* Cambridge: Cambridge University Press, 1991.

———. *Roman Art: Romulus to Constantine.* 4th ed. Upper Saddle River, N.J.: Prentice-Hall, 2005.

Robertson, Donald S. *Greek and Roman Architecture.* 2nd ed. Cambridge, Eng.: Cambridge University Press, 1969.

Sear, Frank. *Roman Architecture.* Rev. ed. London: Batsford, 1989.

Strong, Donald E. *Roman Imperial Sculpture: An Introduction to the Commemorative and Decorative Sculpture of the Roman Empire down to the Death of Constantine.* London: Tiranti, 1961.

———. *Roman Art.* 2nd ed. Pelican History of Art. New Haven: Yale University Press, 1995.

Vermeule, Cornelius. *European Art and the Classical Past.* Cambridge, Mass.: Harvard University Press, 1964.

Vitruvius. *The Ten Books on Architecture.* Trans. Morris Hicky Morgan. Reprint of 1914 edition. New York: Dover, 1960.

Ward-Perkins, John B. *Roman Architecture* (1976). New York: Electa/Rizzoli, 1988.

———. *Roman Imperial Architecture* (1981). New Haven: Yale University Press, 1994.

Wells, Colin M. *The Roman Empire.* 2nd ed. Cambridge, Mass.: Harvard University Press, 1995.

Wheeler, Mortimer. *Roman Art and Architecture* (1964). New York: Thames & Hudson, 1985.

Wilkinson, L. P. *The Roman Experience.* New York: Knopf, 1974.

Zanker, Paul. *The Power of Images in the Age of Augustus.* Trans. Alan Shapiro. Ann Arbor: University of Michigan Press, 1988.

Early Christian and Byzantine Art

Age of Spirituality: Late Antique and Early Christian Art, Third to Seventh Century. New York: Metropolitan Museum of Art, 1979.

Beckwith, John. *The Art of Constantinople: An Introduction to Byzantine Art (330–1453).* 2nd ed. New York: Phaidon, 1968.

———. *Early Christian and Byzantine Art.* 2nd ed. New York: Penguin, 1979.

Boyd, Susan A. *Byzantine Art.* Chicago: University of Chicago Press, 1979

Christe, Yves, et al. *Art of the Christian World, A.D. 200–1500: A Handbook of Styles and Forms.* New York: Rizzoli, 1982.

Demus, Otto. *Byzantine Art and the West.* New York: New York University Press, 1970.

———. *Byzantine Mosaic Decoration: Aspects of Monumental Art in Byzantium.* New Rochelle, N.Y.: Caratzas, 1976.

Ferguson, George W. *Signs and Symbols in Christian Art.* New York: Oxford University Press, 1967.

Gough, Michael. *The Origins of Christian Art.* London: Thames & Hudson, 1973.

Grabar, André. *Byzantium: Byzantine Art in the Middle Ages.* Trans. B. Forster. London: Methuen, 1966.

———. *The Beginnings of Christian Art, 200–395.* Trans. Stuart Gilbert and James Emmons. London: Thames & Hudson, 1967.

———. *The Golden Age of Justinian, from the Death of Theodosius to the Rise of Islam.* Trans. Stuart Gilbert and James Emmons. New York: Odyssey, 1967.

———. *Christian Iconography: A Study of Its Origins* (1968). London: Henley, Routledge & Kegan Paul, 1980.

Kitzinger, Ernst. *Byzantine Art in the Making: Main Lines of Stylistic Development in Mediterranean Art, 3rd–7th Century.* Cambridge, Mass.: Harvard University Press, 1980.

Krautheimer, Richard. *Studies in Early Christian, Medieval, and Renaissance Art.* New York: New York University Press, 1969.

———. *Early Christian and Byzantine Architecture.* 4th ed. Pelican History of Art. New York: Penguin, 1986.

Lane Fox, Robin. *Pagans and Christians* (1987). San Francisco: Harper San Francisco, 1995.

Lowrie, Walter. *Art in the Early Church* (1947). New York: Norton, 1969.

Mainstone, Rowland J. *Hagia Sophia: Architecture, Structure, and Liturgy of Justinian's Great Church.* London: Thames & Hudson, 1988.

Mango, Cyril. *Byzantine Architecture.* New York: Rizzoli, 1985.

———. *The Art of the Byzantine Empire, 312–1453: Sources and Documents* (1972). Toronto: University of Toronto Press, 1986.

Mancinelli, Fabrizio. *Catacombs and Basilicas: The Early Christians in Rome.* Trans. Carol Wasserman. Florence: Scala, 1981.
Mathew, Gervase. *Byzantine Aesthetics.* London: Murray, 1963.
Mathews, Thomas. *Byzantium: From Antiquity to the Renaissance.* New York: Abrams, 1998.
Morey, Charles Rufus. *Early Christian Art: An Outline of the Evolution of Style and Iconography in Sculpture and Painting from Antiquity to the Eighth Century.* 2nd ed. Princeton: Princeton University Press, 1953.
Oakeshott, Walter. *The Mosaics of Rome: From the Third to the Fourteenth Centuries.* London: Thames & Hudson, 1967.
Rice, David T. *The Appreciation of Byzantine Art.* London: Oxford University Press, 1972.
Schapiro, Meyer. *Late Antique, Early Christian, and Mediaeval Art.* New York: Braziller, 1979.
Stevenson, James. *The Catacombs: Rediscovered Monuments of Early Christianity.* London: Thames & Hudson, 1978.
Volbach, Wolfgang, and Max Hirmer. *Early Christian Art.* Trans. Christopher Ligota. New York: Abrams, 1962.
von Simson, Otto G. *Sacred Fortress: Byzantine Art and Statecraft in Ravenna.* Princeton: Princeton University Press, 1987.
Weitzmann, Kurt. *Studies in Classical and Byzantine Manuscript Illustration.* Chicago: University of Chicago Press, 1971.
———. *Art in the Medieval West and Its Contacts with Byzantium.* London: Variorum, 1982.
———, et al. *The Icon.* New York: Knopf, 1982.

The Early Middle Ages

Aldhouse-Green, Miranda. *Celtic Art.* New York: Sterling, 1997.
Alexander, Jonathan J. G. *Medieval Illuminators and Their Methods of Work.* New Haven: Yale University Press, 1992.
Atil, Esin. *Art of the Arab World.* Washington, D.C.: Smithsonian Institution, 1975.
Backes, Magnus, and Regine Dölling. *Art of the Dark Ages.* Trans. F. Garvie. New York: Abrams, 1971.
Backhouse, Janet, ed. *The Lindisfarne Gospels.* Oxford: Phaidon, 1981.
Backhouse, Janet, D. H. Turner, and Leslie Webster. *The Golden Age of Anglo-Saxon Art, 966–1066.* Bloomington: Indiana University Press, 1984.
Barasch, Moshe. *Gestures of Despair in Medieval and Early Renaissance Art.* New York: New York University Press, 1976.
Basing, Patricia. *Trades and Crafts in Medieval Manuscripts.* London: The British Library, 1990.
Beckwith, John. *Early Medieval Art: Carolingian, Ottonian, Romanesque* (1969). New York: Oxford University Press, 1985.
Blair, Sheila S., and Jonathan M. Bloom. *The Art and Architecture of Islam, 1250–1800.* New Haven: Yale University Press, 1994.
Braunfels, Wolfgang. *Monasteries of Western Europe: The Architecture of the Orders.* Trans. Alastair Laing. London: Thames & Hudson, 1972.
Brown, Peter, ed. *The Book of Kells.* New York: Knopf, 1980.
Calkins, Robert G. *Illuminated Books of the Middle Ages.* Ithaca, N.Y.: Cornell University Press, 1983.
Conant, Kenneth John. *Carolingian and Romanesque Architecture, 800 to 1200.* 4th ed. Pelican History of Art. New Haven: Yale University Press, 1993.
Davis-Weyer, Caecilia, ed. *Early Medieval Art, 300–1150: Sources and Documents* (1971). Toronto: University of Toronto Press, 1986.
Diebold, William J. *Word and Image: An Introduction to Early Medieval Art.* Boulder, Col.: Westview, 2000.
Dodwell, C. R. *The Pictorial Arts of the West, 800–1200.* Pelican History of Art. New Haven: Yale University Press, 1993.
Ettinghausen, Richard. *Arab Painting.* Geneva: Skira, 1977.
Ettinghausen, Richard, and Oleg Grabar. *The Art and Architecture of Islam, 650–1250.* New York: Penguin, 1987.
Fernie, Eric. *The Architecture of the Anglo-Saxons.* London: Batsford, 1983.
Finlay, Ian. *Celtic Art: An Introduction.* London: Faber, 1973.
Frishman, Martin, and Hasan-Uddin Khan, eds. *The Mosque: History, Architectural Development and Regional Diversity.* London: Thames & Hudson, 2002.
Grabar, André, and Carl Nordenfalk. *Early Medieval Painting from the Fourth to the Eleventh Century: Mosaics and Mural Paintings.* New York: Skira, 1957.
Grabar, Oleg. *The Formation of Islamic Art.* Rev. and enl. ed. New York: Yale University Press, 1983.
Grant, Michael. *The Dawn of the Middle Ages, A.D. 476–814.* New York: McGraw-Hill, 1981.
Grube, Ernst J. *Architecture of the Islamic World: Its History and Social Meaning* (1978). Ed. George Michell. New York: Thames & Hudson, 1984.
Henderson, George. *From Durrow to Kells: The Insular Gospel-Books, 650–800.* London: Thames & Hudson, 1987.
———. *Early Medieval* (1972). Toronto: University of Toronto Press, 1993.
Henry, Françoise. *Irish Art in the Early Christian Period, to 800 A.D.* Ithaca, N.Y.: Cornell University Press, 1965.
———. *Irish Art during the Viking Invasions, 800–1020 A.D.* Ithaca, N.Y.: Cornell University Press, 1967.
Hinks, Roger P. *Carolingian Art: A Study of Early Medieval Painting and Sculpture in Western Europe* (1935). Ann Arbor: University of Michigan Press, 1966.
Horn, Walter W., and Ernest Born. *Plan of Saint Gall: A Study of the Architecture and Economy of and Life in a Paradigmatic Carolingian Monastery.* 3 vols. Berkeley: University of California Press, 1979.
Hubert, Jean, Jean Porcher, and W. F. Volbach. *Europe of the Invasions.* Trans. Stuart Gilbert and James Emmons. New York: Braziller, 1969.
———. *The Carolingian Renaissance.* New York: Braziller, 1970.
Irwin, Robert. *Islamic Art in Context: Art, Architecture, and the Literary World.* New York: Abrams, 1997.
Kendrick, Thomas D. *Anglo-Saxon Art to A.D. 900* (1938). New York: Barnes & Noble, 1972.
Kidson, Peter. *The Medieval World.* New York: McGraw-Hill, 1967.
Kitzinger, Ernst. *Early Medieval Art in the British Museum.* Rev. ed. Bloomington: Indiana University Press, 1983.
Laing, Lloyd, and Jennifer Laing. *Art of the Celts.* New York: Thames & Hudson, 1992.
Lasko, Peter. *Ars Sacra, 800–1200.* 2nd ed. Pelican History of Art. New Haven: Yale University Press, 1994.
Martindale, Andrew. *The Rise of the Artist in the Middle Ages and Early Renaissance.* New York: McGraw-Hill, 1972.
Megaw, Ruth, and Vincent Megaw. *Celtic Art: From Its Beginnings to the Book of Kells.* Rev. and exp. ed. New York: Thames & Hudson, 2001.
Mütherich, Florentine, and Joachim E. Gaehde. *Carolingian Painting.* New York: Braziller, 1976.
Nordenfalk, Carl. *Celtic and Anglo-Saxon Painting: Book Illumination in the British Isles, 600–800.* New York: Braziller, 1977.
———. *Early Medieval Book Illumination.* New York: Rizzoli, 1988.
Pächt, Otto. *The Rise of Pictorial Narrative in Twelfth-Century England.* Oxford: Clarendon, 1962.
———. *Book Illumination in the Middle Ages: An Introduction.* London: Miller, 1986.
Panofsky, Erwin. *Tomb Sculpture: Four Lectures on Its Changing Aspects from Ancient Egypt to Bernini* (1964). New York: Abrams, 1992.
Papadopoulo, Alexandre. *Islam and Muslim Art.* Trans. Robert Erich Wolf. New York: Abrams, 1979.
Pevsner, Nikolaus. *An Outline of European Architecture.* 7th ed. Baltimore: Penguin, 1970.
———. *Islamic Art.* London: Thames & Hudson, 1975.
Richardson, Hilary, and John Scarry. *An Introduction to Irish High Crosses.* Dublin: Mercier, 1990.
Rickert, Margaret. *Painting in Britain: The Middle Ages.* 2nd ed. Pelican History of Art. Harmondsworth: Penguin, 1965.
Saalman, Howard. *Medieval Architecture: European Architecture, 600–1200.* New York: Braziller, 1962.
Schimmel, Annemarie. *Calligraphy and Islamic Culture.* New York: New York University Press, 1984.
Snyder, James. *Medieval Art: Painting, Sculpture, Architecture, 4th–14th Century.* New York: Harry N. Abrams, 1989.
Stokstad, Marilyn. *Medieval Art.* 2nd ed. Boulder, Col.: New York: Westview, 2004.
Tasker, Edward G. *Encyclopedia of Medieval Church Art.* Ed. John Beaumont. London: Batsford, 1993.
Verzone, Paolo. *The Art of Europe: The Dark Ages from Theodoric to Charlemagne.* New York: Crown, 1968.
Ward, Rachel. *Islamic Metalwork.* New York: Thames & Hudson, 1993.
Wilson, David M. *Anglo-Saxon Art: From the Seventh Century to the Norman Conquest.* London: Thames & Hudson, 1984.
Wilson, David M., and Ole Klindt-Jensen. *Viking Art.* 2nd ed. Minneapolis: University of Minnesota Press, 1980.
Wormald, Francis. *Collected Writings.* Vol. I: *Studies in Medieval Art from the Sixth to the Twelfth Centuries.* New York: Oxford University Press, 1984–1988.
Zarnecki, George. *Art of the Medieval World: Architecture, Sculpture, Painting, the Sacred Arts.* New York: Abrams, 1975.

Romanesque Art

Busch, Harald, and Bernd Lohse, eds. *Romanesque Sculpture.* Trans. Peter Gorge. London: Batsford, 1962.
Cahn, Walter. *Romanesque Bible Illumination.* Ithaca, N.Y.: Cornell University Press, 1982.
Clapham, Alfred W. *Romanesque Architecture in Western Europe.* Oxford: Clarendon, 1959.
Demus, Otto. *Romanesque Mural Painting.* New York: Abrams, 1970.
Evans, Joan. *Art in Medieval France, 987–1498* (1963). Oxford: Clarendon, 1969.
Focillon, Henri. *The Art of the West in the Middle Ages.* Ed. Jean Bony. Trans. Donald King. 2 vols. Ithaca, N.Y.: Cornell University Press, 1980.
Forsyth, Ilene H. *The Throne of Wisdom: Wood Sculptures of the Madonna in Romanesque France.* Princeton: Princeton University Press, 1972.
Gibbs-Smith, Charles H. *The Bayeux Tapestry.* London: Phaidon, 1973.
Grabar, André, and Carl Nordenfalk. *Romanesque Painting from the Eleventh to the Thirteenth Century: Mural Painting.* Trans. Stuart Gilbert. New York: Skira, 1958.
Grape, Wolfgang. *The Bayeux Tapestry: Monument to a Norman Triumph.* New York: Prestel, 1994.

Hearn, Millard F. *Romanesque Sculpture: The Revival of Monumental Stone Sculpture in the Eleventh and Twelfth Centuries.* Ithaca, N.Y.: Cornell University Press, 1981.
Holt, Elizabeth G. *A Documentary History of Art.* 3 vols. Princeton: Princeton University Press, 1981–1986.
Jacobs, Michael. *Northern Spain: The Road to Santiago de Compostela.* San Francisco: Chronicle, 1991.
Kennedy, Hugh. *Crusader Castles.* Cambridge: Cambridge University Press, 1994.
Kubach, Hans E. *Romanesque Architecture.* New York: Electa/Rizzoli, 1988.
Künstler, Gustav. *Romanesque Art in Europe.* Greenwich, Conn.: New York Graphic Society, 1968.
Little, Bryan D. G. *Architecture in Norman Britain.* London: Batsford, 1985.
Mâle, Émile. *Religious Art in France, the Twelfth Century: A Study of the Origins of Medieval Iconography.* Bollingen Series, 90:1. Princeton: Princeton University Press, 1978.
———. *Art and Artists of the Middle Ages.* Redding Ridge, Conn.: Black Swan, 1986.
Nichols, Stephen G., Jr. *Romanesque Signs: Early Medieval Narrative and Iconography.* New Haven: Yale University Press, 1983.
Petzold, Andreas. *Romanesque Art.* New York: Abrams, 1995.
Platt, Colin. *The Architecture of Medieval Britain: A Social History.* New Haven: Yale University Press, 1990.
Radding, Charles M., and William W. Clark. *Medieval Architecture, Medieval Learning: Builders and Masters in the Age of Romanesque and Gothic.* New Haven: Yale University Press, 1992.
Saxl, Fritz. *English Sculptures of the 12th Century.* Ed. Hanns Swarzenski. London: Faber & Faber, 1954.
Schapiro, Meyer. *Romanesque Art: Selected Papers.* New York: Braziller, 1977.
———. *The Romanesque Sculpture of Moissac.* New York: Braziller, 1985.
Stoddard, Whitney S. *Art and Architecture in Medieval France: Medieval Architecture, Sculpture, Stained Glass, Manuscripts, the Art of the Church Treasuries.* New York: Harper & Row, 1972.
Swarzenski, Hanns. *Monuments of Romanesque Art: The Art of Church Treasures in North-Western Europe.* 2nd ed. Chicago: University of Chicago Press, 1974.
Tate, Robert B., and Marcus Tate. *The Pilgrim Route to Santiago.* Oxford: Phaidon, 1987.
The Year 1200. 2 vols. New York: Metropolitan Museum of Art, 1970.
Thompson, Daniel V. *The Materials and Techniques of Medieval Painting.* New York: Dover, 1956.
Zarnecki, George. *Romanesque Art.* New York: Universe, 1971.
Zarnecki, George, Janet Holt, and Tristram Holland. *English Romanesque Art, 1066–1200.* London: Weidenfeld & Nicolson, 1984.

Gothic Art

Alexander, Jonathan J. G., and Paul Binski, eds. *Age of Chivalry: Art in Plantagenet England, 1200–1400.* London: Royal Academy of Arts, 1987.
Andrews, Francis B. *The Mediaeval Builder and His Methods.* Mineola, N.Y.: Dover, 1999.
Armi, C. Edson. *The "Headmaster" of Chartres and the Origins of "Gothic" Sculpture.* University Park: Pennsylvania State University Press, 1994.
Aubert, Marcel. *Gothic Cathedrals of France and Their Treasures.* Trans. Lionel Kochan and Miriam Kochan. London: Kaye, 1959.
———. *The Art of the High Gothic Era.* Trans. Peter Gorge. New York: Crown, 1965.
Blum, Pamela Z. *Early Gothic Saint-Denis: Restorations and Survivals.* Berkeley: University of California Press, 1992.
Bony, Jean. *The English Decorated Style: Gothic Architecture Transformed, 1250–1350.* Ithaca, N.Y.: Cornell University Press, 1979.
———. *French Gothic Architecture of the Twelfth and Thirteenth Centuries.* Berkeley: University of California Press, 1983.
Bowie, Theodore, ed. *The Sketchbook of Villard de Honnecourt* (1959). Westport, Conn.: Greenwood, 1982.
Branner, Robert. *St. Louis and the Court Style in Gothic Architecture.* London: Zwemmer, 1965.
———. *Chartres Cathedral.* New York: Norton, 1969.
Brieger, Peter H. *English Art, 1216–1307.* Oxford: Clarendon, 1957.
Camille, Michael. *The Gothic Idol: Ideology and Image-Making in Medieval Art.* New York: Cambridge University Press, 1989.
———. *Gothic Art: Glorious Visions.* New York: Abrams, 1996.
Erlande-Brandenburg, Alain. *Gothic Art.* Trans. I. Mark Paris. New York: Abrams, 1989.
Favier, Jean. *The World of Chartres.* Trans. F. Garvie. New York: Abrams, 1990.
Frankl, Paul. *Gothic Architecture.* Rev. ed. Paul Crossley. Pelican History of Art. New Haven: Yale University Press, 2000.
Frisch, Teresa G. *Gothic Art, 1140–c.1450: Sources and Documents* (1971). Toronto: University of Toronto, 1987.
Gerson, Paula Lieber, ed. *Abbot Suger and Saint-Denis: A Symposium.* New York: Metropolitan Museum of Art, 1986.
Grodecki, Louis. *Gothic Architecture* (1976). Trans. I. Mark Paris. New York: Electa/Rizzoli, 1985.
Grodecki, Louis, and Catherine Brisac. *Gothic Stained Glass, 1200–1300.* Ithaca, N.Y.: Cornell University Press, 1985.
Henderson, George D. S. *Gothic.* Baltimore: Penguin, 1967.
———. *Chartres.* Baltimore: Penguin, 1968.
Jantzen, Hans. *High Gothic: The Classic Cathedrals of Chartres, Reims, Amiens* (1962). Trans. James Palmes. Princeton: Princeton University Press, 1984.
Katzenellenbogen, Adolf. *The Sculptural Programs of Chartres Cathedral: Christ, Mary, Ecclesia* (1959). New York: Norton, 1964.
Lord, Carla. *Royal French Patronage of Art in the Fourteenth Century: An Annotated Bibliography.* Boston: Hall, 1985.
Mâle, Émile. *The Gothic Image: Religious Art in France of the Thirteenth Century.* New York: Harper & Row, 1972.
———. *Religious Art in France, the Thirteenth Century: A Study of Medieval Iconography and Its Sources.* Princeton: Princeton University Press, 1984.
———. *Religious Art in France, the Late Middle Ages: A Study of Medieval Iconography and Its Sources.* Princeton: Princeton University Press, 1986.
Martindale, Andrew. *Gothic Art* (1967). New York: Thames & Hudson, 1985.
Meulen, Jan van der. *Chartres: Sources and Literary Interpretation: A Critical Bibliography.* Boston: Hall, 1989.
Panofsky, Erwin, and Gerda Panofsky-Soergel. eds. *Abbot Suger on the Abbey Church of St.-Denis and Its Art Treasures.* 2nd ed. Princeton: Princeton University Press, 1979.
Panofsky, Erwin. *Gothic Architecture and Scholasticism.* New York: World, 1957.
Pevsner, Nikolaus, and Priscilla Metcalf. *The Cathedrals of England.* 2 vols. Harmondsworth: Viking, 1985.
Pope-Hennessy, John. *Italian Gothic Sculpture.* 3rd ed. Oxford: Phaidon, 1986.
Sandler, Lucy Freeman. *Gothic Manuscripts, 1285–1385.* A Survey of Manuscripts Illuminated in the British Isles 5. 2 vols. London: Miller, 1986.
Sauerländer, Willibald. *Gothic Sculpture in France, 1140–1270.* Trans. Janet Sondheimer. New York: Abrams, 1972.
Swaan, Wim. *The Gothic Cathedral* (1969). London: Ferndale, 1981.
Voelkle, William. *The Stavelot Triptych: Mosan Art and the Legend of the True Cross.* New York: Pierpont Morgan Library, 1980.
von Simson, Otto G. *The Gothic Cathedral: Origins of Gothic Architecture and the Medieval Concept of Order.* 3rd ed. Princeton: Princeton University Press, 1988.
Watson, Percy. *Building the Medieval Cathedrals.* Cambridge: Cambridge University Press, 1976.
Wieck, Roger S. *Time Sanctified: The Book of Hours in Medieval Art and Life.* 2nd ed. New York: Braziller, 2001.
Williamson, Paul. *Gothic Sculpture, 1140–1300.* New Haven: Yale University Press, 1995.
Wilson, Christopher. *The Gothic Cathedral: The Architecture of the Great Church, 1130–1530.* Rev. ed. New York: Thames & Hudson, 2000.

Precursors of the Renaissance

Barasch, Moshe. *Giotto and the Language of Gesture.* Cambridge: Cambridge University Press, 1987.
Barolsky, Paul. *Giotto's Father and the Family of Vasari's Lives.* University Park, Pa.: Pennsylvania State University Press, 1992.
Baxandall, Michael. *Giotto and the Orators: Humanist Observers of Painting in Italy and the Discovery of Pictorial Composition, 1350–1450.* Oxford: Oxford University Press, 1971.
Bomford, David. *Italian Painting before 1400.* London: National Gallery Publications, 1989.
Borsook, Eve. *The Mural Painters of Tuscany: From Cimabue to Andrea del Sarto.* 2nd ed. New York: Oxford University Press, 1980.
Borsook, Eve, and Fiorella Superbi Gioffredi. *Italian Altarpieces 1250–1550: Function and Design.* Oxford: Clarendon, 1994.
Burckhardt, Jacob. *The Civilization of the Renaissance in Italy.* New York: Modern Library, 2002.
Campbell, Lorne. *Renaissance Portraits: European Portrait-Painting in the 14th, 15th, and 16th Centuries.* New Haven: Yale University Press, 1990.
Cennini, Cennino. *The Craftsman's Handbook (Il Libro dell'Arte)* (1954). Trans. Daniel V. Thompson, Jr. New York: Dover, 1954.
Chiellini, Monica. *Cimabue.* Trans. Lisa Pelletti. Florence: Scala, 1988.
Cole, Bruce. *Giotto and Florentine Painting, 1280–1375.* New York: Harper & Row, 1976.
———. *Sienese Painting: From Its Origins to the 15th Century.* New York: Harper & Row, 1980.
———. *The Renaissance Artist at Work: From Pisano to Titian.* New York: Harper & Row, 1983.
Davis, Howard McP. *Gravity in the Paintings of Giotto* (1971). 1971. Reprinted in Schneider, 1974.
Maginnis, Hayden B. J. *Painting in the Age of Giotto: A Historical Reevaluation.* University Park, Pa.: Pennsylvania State University Press, 1997.
Martindale, Andrew. *The Rise of the Artist in the Middle Ages and Early Renaissance.* New York: McGraw-Hill, 1972.
———. *Simone Martini.* New York: New York University Press, 1988.
Meiss, Millard. *French Painting in the Time of Jean de Berry: The Late Fourteenth Century and the Patronage of the Duke.* 2nd ed. New York: Braziller, 1969.
———. *Painting in Florence and Siena after the Black Death: The Arts, Religion, and Society in the Mid-Fourteenth Century* (1951). Princeton: Princeton University Press, 1978.

Meiss, Millard, and Elizabeth H. Beatson. *The "Belles Heures" of Jean, Duke of Berry: The Cloisters, the Metropolitan Museum of Art.* New York: Braziller, 1974.

Moskowitz, Anita Fiderer. *The Sculpture of Andrea and Nino Pisano.* Cambridge: Cambridge University Press, 1986.

Rosenberg, Charles M., ed. *Art and Politics in Late Medieval and Early Renaissance Italy, 1250–1500.* Notre Dame, Ind.: University of Notre Dame Press, 1990.

Schneider, Laurie M., ed. *Giotto in Perspective.* Englewood Cliffs, N.J.: Prentice-Hall, 1974.

Smart, Alastair. *The Dawn of Italian Painting, 1250–1400.* Ithaca, N.Y.: Cornell University Press, 1978.

Stubblebine, James H., ed. *Giotto: The Arena Chapel Frescoes.* New York: Norton, 1969.

———. *Ducento Painting: An Annotated Bibliography.* Boston: Hall, 1983.

———. *Assisi and the Rise of Vernacular Art.* New York: Harper & Row, 1985.

Vasari, Giorgio. *The Lives of the Most Eminent Painters, Sculptors and Architects.* Trans. Gaston du C. de Vere. New York: Abrams, 1979.

White, John. *Duccio: Tuscan Art and the Medieval Workshop.* New York: Thames & Hudson, 1979.

———. *The Birth and Rebirth of Pictorial Space.* 3rd ed. Cambridge, Mass.: Belknap, 1987.

The Early Renaissance

Adams, Laurie Schneider. *Key Monuments of the Italian Renaissance.* Boulder, Col.: Westview, 2000.

———. *Italian Renaissance Art.* Boulder, Col.: Westview, 2001.

Alazard, Jean. *The Florentine Portrait.* New York: Schocken, 1968.

Alberti, Leon Battista. *Ten Books on Architecture* (1955). Ed. J. Rykwert. Trans. J. Leoni. New York: Transatlantic Arts, 1966.

———. *On Painting* (1966). Trans J. R. Spencer. Rev. ed. Westport, Conn.: Greenwood, 1976.

Ames-Lewis, Francis. *Drawing in Early Renaissance Italy.* Rev. ed. New Haven: Yale University Press, 2000.

Antal, Frederick. *Florentine Painting and Its Social Background: The Bourgeois Republic before Cosimo de' Medici's Advent to Power, Fourteenth and Early Fifteenth Centuries* (1948). Cambridge, Mass.: Belknap, 1986.

Barolsky, Paul. *Infinite Jest: Wit and Humor in Italian Renaissance Art.* Columbia: University of Missouri Press, 1978.

———. *Walter Pater's Renaissance.* University Park, Pa.: Pennsylvania State University Press, 1987.

Baxandall, Michael. *Painting and Experience in Fifteenth-Century Italy.* 2nd ed. Oxford: Oxford University Press, 1988.

Beck, James. *Italian Renaissance Painting.* New York: Harper & Row, 1981.

Bennett, Bonnie A., and David G. Wilkins. *Donatello.* Oxford: Phaidon, 1984.

Berenson, Bernard. *Italian Painters of the Renaissance.* 2 vols. London: Phaidon, 1968.

———. *Italian Pictures of the Renaissance: Florentine School.* 3 vols. London: Phaidon, 1968.

———. *The Drawings of the Florentine Painters* (1938). 3 vols. Chicago: University of Chicago Press, 1973.

———. *The Italian Painters of the Renaissance.* Ithaca, N.Y.: Cornell University Press, 1980.

Blunt, Anthony. *Artistic Theory in Italy, 1450–1600.* New York: Oxford University Press, 1994.

Bober, Phyllis P., and Ruth O. Rubinstein. *Renaissance Artists and Antique Sculpture: A Handbook of Sources.* New York: Oxford University Press, 1986.

Borsook, Eve. *The Mural Painters of Tuscany: From Cimabue to Andrea del Sarto.* 2nd ed. New York: Oxford University Press, 1980.

Butterfield, Andrew. *The Sculptures of Andrea del Verrocchio.* New Haven: Yale University Press, 1997.

Chastel, André. *The Studios and Styles of the Italian Renaissance.* New York: Odyssey, 1966.

Christiansen, Keith. *Gentile da Fabriano.* Ithaca, N.Y.: Cornell University Press, 1982.

———, Laurence B. Kanter, and Carl Brandon Strehle, eds. *Painting in Renaissance Siena, 1420–1500.* New York: Metropolitan Museum of Art, 1988.

Clark, Kenneth. *The Art of Humanism.* London: Murray, 1983.

Cole, Alison. *Virtue and Magnificence: Art of the Italian Renaissance Courts.* New York: Abrams, 1995.

d'Ancona, Mirella L. *The Garden of the Renaissance: Botanical Symbolism in Italian Painting.* Florence: Olschki, 1977.

Edgerton, Samuel Y., Jr. *The Renaissance Rediscovery of Linear Perspective.* New York: Harper & Row, 1976.

Gilbert, Creighton E., ed. *Renaissance Art.* New York: Harper & Row, 1973.

———, ed. *Italian Art, 1400–1500. Sources and Documents.* Englewood Cliffs, N.J.: Prentice-Hall, 1980.

Goffen, Rona, ed. *Masaccio's Trinity.* Cambridge: Cambridge University Press, 1998.

Goldthwaite, Richard A. *The Building of Renaissance Florence: An Economic and Social History.* Baltimore: Johns Hopkins University Press, 1982.

Gombrich, Ernst H. *The Heritage of Apelles: Studies in the Art of the Renaissance.* Ithaca, N.Y.: Cornell University Press, 1976.

———. *Norm and Form: Studies in the Art of the Renaissance.* 4th ed. Chicago: University of Chicago Press, 1985.

———. *Symbolic Images* (1972). 3rd ed. Chicago: University of Chicago Press, 1985.

———. *New Light on Old Masters* (1986). London: Phaidon, 2000.

Greenstein, Jack M. *Mantegna and Painting as Historical Narrative.* Chicago: University of Chicago Press, 1992.

Grendler, Pl. *Schooling in Renaissance Italy: Literacy and Learning, 1300–1600.* Baltimore: Johns Hopkins University Press, 1989.

Hale, J. R. *Artists and Warfare in the Renaissance.* New Haven: Yale University Press, 1990.

Harbison, Craig. *The Mirror of the Artist: Northern Renaissance Art in Its Historical Context.* New York: Abrams, 1995.

Hartt, Frederick. *A History of Italian Renaissance Art.* 5th ed. New York: Abrams, 2003.

Heydenreich, Ludwig H., and Paul Davies. *Architecture in Italy, 1400–1600.* New Haven: Yale University Press, 1996.

Hibbert, Christopher. *The House of Medici: Its Rise and Fall.* New York: Morrow Quill, 1980.

Hind, Arthur M. *History of Engraving and Etching.* 3rd ed., rev. Boston: Houghton Mifflin, 1923.

Horster, Marita. *Andrea del Castagno.* Ithaca, N.Y.: Cornell University Press, 1980.

Jacks, Philip. *The Antiquarian and the Myth of Antiquity: The Origins of Rome in Renaissance Thought.* Cambridge: Cambridge University Press, 1993.

Janson, Horst W. *The Sculpture of Donatello* (1957). Princeton: Princeton University Press, 1963.

Kemp, Martin. *Behind the Picture: Art and Evidence in the Italian Renaissance.* New Haven: Yale University Press, 1997.

Kent, Dale. *Cosimo de'Medici and the Florentine Renaissance.* New Haven: Yale University Press, 2000.

Krautheimer, Richard, and Trude Krautheimer-Hess. *Lorenzo Ghiberti.* Princeton: Princeton University Press, 1982.

Lavin, Marilyn A. *Piero della Francesca: The Flagellation* (1972). Chicago: University of Chicago Press, 1990.

Lee, Rensselaer W. *Ut Pictura Poesis: The Humanistic Theory of Painting.* New York: Norton, 1967.

Lightbown, Ronald. *Sandro Botticelli.* 2 vols. Berkeley: University of California Press, 1978.

Lowrey, Bates. *Renaissance Architecture.* New York: Braziller, 1962.

Machiavelli, Niccolò. *Florentine Histories.* Trans. Laura F. Banfield and Harvey C. Mansfield, Jr. Princeton: Princeton University Press, 1988.

Murray, Peter. *Renaissance Architecture.* New York: Rizzoli, 1985.

Panofsky, Erwin. *Renaissance and Renascences in Western Art.* New York: Harper & Row, 1972.

———. *Studies in Iconology: Humanistic Themes in the Art of the Renaissance.* New York: Harper & Row, 1972.

Panofsky, Erwin, and Dora Panofsky. *Pandora's Box: The Changing Aspects of a Mythical Symbol.* 2nd ed., rev. New York: Harper & Row, 1965.

Pater, Walter. *The Renaissance: Studies in Art and Poetry* (1893). Ed. Donald L. Hill. Berkeley: University of California Press, 1980.

Pope-Hennessy, John. *The Portrait in the Renaissance* (1963). Princeton: Princeton University Press, 1979.

———. *An Introduction to Italian Sculpture.* 4th ed. 3 vols. London: Phaidon, 1996.

Prager, Frank D., and Gustina Scaglia. *Brunelleschi: Studies of His Technology and Inventions.* Cambridge, Mass.: MIT Press, 1970.

Rabil, Albert, Jr. *Renaissance Humanism: Foundations, Forms, and Legacy.* 3 vols. Philadelphia: University of Pennsylvania Press, 1988.

Rosenberg, Charles M. *The Este Monuments and Urban Developments in Renaissance Ferrara.* Cambridge: Cambridge University Press, 1997.

Ruggiero, Guido. *Violence in Early Renaissance Venice.* New Brunswick, N.J.: Rutgers University Press, 1980.

Saxl, Fritz. *A Heritage of Images: A Selection of Lectures.* Ed. Hugh Honour and John Fleming. Harmondsworth: Penguin, 1970.

Seidel, Linda. *Jan van Eyck's Arnolfini Portrait: Stories of an Icon.* Cambridge: Cambridge University Press, 1993.

Seymour, Charles, Jr. *The Sculpture of Verrocchio.* Greenwich, Conn.: New York Graphic Society, 1971.

Seznec, Jean. *The Survival of the Pagan Gods: The Mythological Tradition and Its Place in Renaissance Humanism and Art.* Trans. Barbara F. Sessions. Princeton: Princeton University Press, 1995.

Thomson, David. *Renaissance Architecture: Critics, Patrons, Luxury.* Manchester: Manchester University Press, 1993.

Turner, A. Richard. *Renaissance Florence: The Invention of a New Art.* New York: Abrams, 1997.

Valentiner, W. R. *Studies of Italian Renaissance Sculpture.* London: Phaidon, 1950.

Wackernagel, Martin. *The World of the Florentine Renaissance Artist: Projects and Patrons, Workshop and Art Market.* Trans. Alison Luchs. Princeton: Princeton University Press, 1981.

Weiss, Roberto. *The Renaissance Discovery of Classical Antiquity.* 2nd ed. Oxford: Blackwell, 1988.

Wind, Edgar. *Pagan Mysteries in the Renaissance.* Rev. and enl. ed. Oxford: Oxford University Press, 1980.

Wittkower, Rudolf. *Idea and Image: Studies in the Italian Renaissance.* New York: Thames & Hudson, 1982.

———. *Architectural Principles in the Age of Humanism.* 4th ed. New York: St. Martin's, 1988.

Wölfflin, Heinrich. *Renaissance and Baroque.* Trans. Kathrin Simon. Ithaca, N.Y.: Cornell University Press, 1966.

———. *Classic Art: An Introduction to the Italian Renaissance.* Trans. L. and P. Murray. 5th ed. London: Phaidon, 1994.

Woods-Marsden, Joanna. *The Gonzaga of Mantua and Pisanello's Arthurian Frescoes.* Princeton: Princeton University Press, 1988.

The High Renaissance in Italy

Ackerman, James S. *The Architecture of Michelangelo.* 2nd ed. Chicago: University of Chicago Press, 1986.

Barolsky, Paul. *Michelangelo's Nose: A Myth and Its Maker.* University Park, Pa.: Pennsylvania State University Press, 1990.

———. *Why Mona Lisa Smiles and Other Tales by Vasari.* University Park, Pa.: Pennsylvania State University Press, 1991.

Brown, David Alan. *Leonardo's Last Supper: The Restoration.* Washington, D.C.: National Gallery of Art, 1983.

Brown, Patricia Fortini. *Venetian Narrative Painting in the Age of Carpaccio.* New Haven: Yale University Press, 1988.

———. *Art and Life in Renaissance Venice.* New York: Abrams, 1997.

Castiglione, Baldesar. *The Book of the Courtier* (1528). Rev. ed. Trans. G. Bull. Baltimore: Penguin, 1976.

Chastel, André. *The Sack of Rome, 1527.* Trans. Beth Archer. Princeton: Princeton University Press, 1983.

Clark, Kenneth M. *Leonardo da Vinci.* New York: Penguin, 1993.

Collins, Bradley I. *Leonardo, Psychoanalysis and Art History: A Critical Study of Psychobiographical Approaches to Leonardo da Vinci.* Evanston, Ill.: Northwestern University Press, 1997.

de Tolnay, Charles. *Michelangelo.* 2nd rev. ed. 5 vols. Princeton: Princeton University Press, 1969–1971.

Eissler, K. R. *Leonardo da Vinci: Psychoanalytic Notes on the Enigma.* New York: International Universities Press, 1961.

Fischel, Oskar. *Raphael.* Trans. B. Rackham. 2 vols. London: Spring Books, 1964.

Freedberg, Sydney J. *Painting of the High Renaissance in Rome and Florence.* Rev. ed. 2 vols. New York: Hacker, 1985.

———. *Painting in Italy, 1500–1600.* 3rd ed. Pelican History of Art. New Haven: Yale University Press, 1993.

Gilbert, Creighton E. *Michelangelo: On and Off the Sistine Ceiling.* New York: Braziller, 1994.

Goffen, Rona. *Piety and Patronage in Renaissance Venice: Bellini, Titian, and the Franciscans.* New Haven: Yale University Press, 1986.

———. *Giovanni Bellini.* New Haven: Yale University Press, 1989.

———, ed. *Titian's "Venus of Urbino."* Cambridge: Cambridge University Press, 1997.

———. *Titian's Women.* New Haven: Yale University Press, 1997.

Hall, Marcia, ed. *Raphael's "School of Athens."* New York: Cambridge University Press, 1997.

Heydenreich, Ludwig H. *Leonardo: The Last Supper.* London: Allen Lane, 1974.

Hibbard, Howard. *Michelangelo.* 2nd ed. New York: Harper & Row, 1985.

Humfrey, Peter. *Painting in Renaissance Venice.* New Haven: Yale University Press, 1995.

Huse, Norbert, and Wolfgang Wolters. *The Art of Renaissance Venice: Architecture, Sculpture, and Painting, 1460–1590.* Trans. E. Jephcott. Chicago: University of Chicago Press, 1990.

Kemp, Martin, ed. *Leonardo on Painting: An Anthology of Writings.* Trans. Martin Kemp and Margaret Walker. New Haven: Yale University Press, 1989.

Leonardo da Vinci. *The Notebooks.* Trans. Edward MacCurdy. 2 vols. New York: Braziller, 1958.

Levey, Michael. *High Renaissance.* Harmondsworth: Penguin, 1975.

Murray, Linda. *The High Renaissance and Mannerism: Italy, the North, and Spain, 1500–1600.* New York: Oxford University Press, 1977.

Panofsky, Erwin. *Problems in Titian, Mostly Iconographic.* New York: New York University Press, 1969.

Partridge, Loren. *The Art of Renaissance Rome, 1400–1600.* New York: Abrams, 1996.

Partridge, Loren, and Randolph Starn. *A Renaissance Likeness: Art and Culture in Raphael's Julius II.* Berkeley: University of California Press, 1980.

Pedretti, Carlo. *Leonardo da Vinci on Painting: A Lost Book.* Berkeley: University of California Press, 1964.

———. *Leonardo: Studies for the Last Supper from the Royal Library at Windsor Castle.* Ivrea: Olivetti, 1983.

Pope-Hennessy, John. *Raphael.* New York: New York University Press, 1970.

———. *Italian High Renaissance and Baroque Sculpture.* 3rd ed. New York: Phaidon, 1986.

Riess, Jonathan B. *The Renaissance Antichrist: Luca Signorelli's Orvieto Frescoes.* Princeton: Princeton University Press, 1995.

Robertson, Giles. *Giovanni Bellini.* New York: Hacker, 1981.

Rosand, David. *Titian.* New York: Abrams, 1978.

———. *Painting in Cinquecento Venice: Titian, Veronese, Tintoretto.* Rev. ed. New Haven: Yale University Press, 1997.

Ruggiero, Guido. *The Boundaries of Eros: Sex Crime and Sexuality in Renaissance Venice.* New York: Oxford University Press, 1985.

———. *Binding Passions: Tales of Magic, Marriage, and Power at the End of the Renaissance.* New York: Oxford University Press, 1993.

Saslow, James M. *Ganymede in the Renaissance: Homosexuality in Art and Society.* New Haven: Yale University Press, 1986.

———. *The Poetry of Michelangelo: An Annotated Translation.* New Haven: Yale University Press, 1991.

Settis, Salvatore. *Giorgione's Tempest: Interpreting the Hidden Subject.* Chicago: University of Chicago Press, 1990.

Steinberg, Leo. *Leonardo's Incessant Last Supper.* New York: Zone Books, 2001.

Tafuri, Manfredo. *Venice and the Renaissance.* Trans. Jessica Levine. Cambridge, Mass.: MIT Press, 1989.

Turner, A. Richard. *Inventing Leonardo.* Berkeley: University of California Press, 1993.

Vasari, Giorgio. *Vasari on Technique.* Trans. Louise S. Maclehose. New York: Dover, 1960.

Wethey, Harold E. *The Paintings of Titian.* 3 vols. London: Phaidon, 1969–.

Wilde, Johannes. *Venetian Art from Bellini to Titian.* Oxford: Clarendon, 1981.

Mannerism and the Later Sixteenth Century in Italy

Ackerman, James S. *Palladio.* London: Penguin, 1991.

Cellini, Benvenuto. *Autobiography.* Trans. J. A. Symonds. Ed. John Pope-Hennessy. London: Phaidon, 1960.

Cochrane, Eric. *Florence in the Forgotten Centuries, 1527–1800: A History of Florence and the Florentines in the Age of the Grand Dukes.* Chicago: University of Chicago Press, 1973.

Cox-Rearick, Janet. *The Drawings of Pontormo: A Catalogue Raisonné with Notes on the Paintings.* Rev. ed. 2 vols. New York: Hacker, 1981.

———. *Dynasty and Destiny in Medici Art: Pontormo, Leo X, and the Two Cosimos.* Princeton: Princeton University Press, 1984.

———. *Bronzino's Chapel of Eleonora in the Palazzo Vecchio.* Berkeley: University of California Press, 1993.

Freedberg, Sidney J. *Parmigianino: His Works in Painting.* Cambridge, Mass.: Harvard University Press, 1950.

Hauser, Arnold. *Mannerism: The Crisis of the Renaissance and the Origin of Modern Art.* Cambridge, Mass.: Belknap, 1986.

Holt, Elizabeth Gilmore, ed. *A Documentary History of Art.* Vol. 2: *Michelangelo and the Mannerists, the Baroque and the Eighteenth Century.* Princeton: Princeton University Press, 1981.

Pope-Hennessy, John. *Cellini.* London: Macmillan, 1985.

Shearman, John K. G. *Mannerism* (1967). Harmondsworth: Penguin, 1977.

Smythe, Craig Hugh. *Mannerism and Maniera.* 2nd ed. Vienna: IRSA, 1992.

Tomlinson, Janis. *From El Greco to Goya: Painting in Spain, 1561–1828.* New York: Abrams, 1997.

Würtenberger, Franzsepp. *Mannerism: The European Style of the Sixteenth Century.* New York: Holt, Rinehart & Winston, 1963.

Sixteenth-Century Painting and Printmaking in Northern Europe

Benesch, Otto. *The Art of the Renaissance in Northern Europe: Its Relation to the Contemporary Spiritual and Intellectual Movements.* Rev. ed. London: Phaidon, 1965.

———. *German Painting, from Dürer to Holbein.* Trans. H. S. B. Harrison. Geneva: Skira, 1966.

Chastel, André. *The Age of Humanism: Europe, 1480–1530.* Trans. Katherine Delavenay and E. M. Gwyer. New York: McGraw-Hill, 1964.

Cuttler, Charles D. *Northern Painting from Pucelle to Bruegel, Fourteenth, Fifteenth, and Sixteenth Centuries.* Fort Worth: Holt, Rinehart & Winston, 1991.

Davies, Martin. *Rogier van der Weyden: An Essay with a Critical Catalogue of Paintings Assigned to Him and to Robert Campin.* New York: Phaidon, 1972.

Friedländer, Max J. *Early Netherlandish Painting.* 14 vols. Trans. Heinz Norden. New York: Praeger, 1967–1976.

———. *From Van Eyck to Bruegel.* Trans. Marguerite Kay. 3rd ed. New York: Phaidon, 1969.

Fuchs, Rudolf H. *Dutch Painting.* New York: Oxford University Press, 1978.

Gilbert, Creighton E. *History of Renaissance Art: Painting, Sculpture, Architecture throughout Europe.* New York: Abrams, 1973.

Harbison, Craig. *The Mirror of the Artist: Northern Renaissance Art in Its Historical Context.* New York: Abrams, 1995.

Hayum, Andrée. *The Isenheim Altarpiece: God's Medicine and the Painter's Vision.* Princeton: Princeton University Press, 1989.

Hind, Arthur M. *A History of Engraving and Etching from the Fifteenth Century to the Year 1914.* 3rd rev. ed. New York: Dover, 1963.

———. *An Introduction to a History of Woodcut: With a Detailed Survey of Work Done in the Fifteenth Century.* New York: Dover, 1963.

Koerner, Joseph Leo. *The Moment of Self-Portraiture in German Renaissance Art.* Chicago: University of Chicago Press, 1993.

Lane, Barbara G. *The Altar and the Altarpiece: Sacramental Themes in Early Netherlandish Painting.* New York: Harper & Row, 1984.

Melion, Walter S. *Shaping the Netherlandish Canon: Karel van Mander's Schilder-boeck.* Chicago: University of Chicago Press, 1991.

Mellinkoff, Ruth. *The Devil at Isenheim: Reflections of Popular Belief in Grünewald's Altarpiece.* Berkeley: University of California Press, 1988.

Panofsky, Erwin. *Early Netherlandish Painting: Its Origin and Character* (1958). 2 vols. New York: Harper & Row, 1971.

———. *Life and Art of Albrecht Dürer.* Princeton: Princeton University Press, 2005.

Pevsner, Nikolaus, and Michael Meier. *Grünewald.* New York: Abrams, 1958.

Philip, Lotte Brand. *The Ghent Altarpiece and the Art of Jan van Eyck.* Princeton: Princeton University Press, 1971.

Snyder, James. *Northern Renaissance Art: Painting, Sculpture, the Graphic Arts from 1350 to 1575.* 2nd ed. Upper Saddle River, N.J.: Prentice-Hall, 2005.

Stechow, Wolfgang. *Northern Renaissance Art, 1400–1600: Sources and Documents* (1966). Evanston, Ill.: Northwestern University Press, 1989.

The Baroque Style in Western Europe

Adams, Laurie Schneider. *Key Monuments of the Baroque.* Boulder, Col.: Westview, 2000.

Alpers, Svetlana. *The Art of Describing: Dutch Art in the Seventeenth Century.* Chicago: University of Chicago Press, 1983.

———. *Rembrandt's Enterprise: The Studio and the Market.* Chicago: University of Chicago Press, 1988.

———. *The Making of Rubens.* New Haven: Yale University Press, 1995.

Avery, Charles. *Bernini, Genius of the Baroque.* London: Thames & Hudson, 1997.

Bazin, Germain. *Baroque and Rococo.* New York: Thames & Hudson, 1985.

Berger, Robert W. *Versailles: The Chateau of Louis XIV.* University Park, Pa.: Pennsylvania State University Press, 1985.

———. *The Palace of the Sun: The Louvre of Louis XIV.* University Park, Pa.: Pennsylvania State University Press, 1993.

Blunt, Anthony. *Art and Architecture in France, 1500–1700.* 5th ed. New Haven: Yale University Press, 1999.

Blunt, Anthony, et al. *Baroque and Rococo: Architecture and Decoration.* New York: Harper & Row, 1982.

Brown, Christopher. *Scenes of Everyday Life: Dutch Genre Painting of the Seventeenth Century.* London: Faber & Faber, 1984.

Brown, Jonathan. *Velázquez: Painter and Courtier.* New Haven: Yale University Press, 1986.

———. *The Golden Age of Painting in Spain.* New Haven: Yale University Press, 1991.

Carrier, David. *Poussin's Paintings: A Study in Art-Historical Methodology.* University Park, Pa.: Pennsylvania State University Press, 1993.

Clark, Kenneth. *Rembrandt and the Italian Renaissance* (1966). New York: Norton, 1968.

Domínguez Ortiz, Antonio, Alfonso E. Pérez Sánchez, and Julián Gállego. *Velázquez.* New York: Metropolitan Museum of Art, 1989.

Enggass, Robert, and Jonathan Brown. *Italy and Spain, 1600–1750: Sources and Documents.* Englewood Cliffs, N.J.: Prentice-Hall, 1970.

Friedländler, Walter F. *Caravaggio Studies* (1955). New York: Schocken, 1969.

Garrard, Mary D. *Artemisia Gentileschi: The Image of the Female Hero in Italian Baroque Art.* Princeton: Princeton University Press, 1989.

Gerson, Horst. *Rembrandt Paintings.* Trans. Heinz Norden. Ed. Gary Schwartz. New York: Reynal, 1968.

Goldscheider, Ludwig, ed. *Vermeer, the Paintings: Complete Edition.* 2nd ed. London: Phaidon, 1967.

Grimm, Claus. *Frans Hals: The Complete Work.* Trans. Jürgen Riehle. New York: Abrams, 1990.

Haak, Bob. *The Golden Age: Dutch Painters of the Seventeenth Century.* Trans. Elizabeth-Willems-Treeman. New York: Abrams, 1984.

Haskell, Francis. *Patrons and Painters: A Study in the Relations between Italian Art and Society in the Age of the Baroque.* Rev. and enl. ed. New Haven: Yale University Press, 1980.

Haverkamp-Begemann, E. *Rembrandt: The Nightwatch.* Princeton: Princeton University Press, 1982.

Held, Julius, and Donald Posner. *Seventeenth- and Eighteenth-Century Art.* New York: Abrams, 1974.

Hibbard, Howard. *Bernini.* Baltimore: Penguin, 1966.

———. *Caravaggio.* New York: Harper & Row, 1983.

Hill, G. F., and Graham Pollard. *Renaissance Medals from the Samuel H. Kress Collection at the National Gallery of Art.* London: Phaidon, 1967.

Kahr, Madlyn M. *Dutch Painting in the Seventeenth Century.* 2nd ed. New York: HarperCollins, 1993.

Kitson, Michael. *The Age of Baroque.* London: Hamlyn, 1976.

Koning, Hans. *The World of Vermeer, 1632–1765.* New York: Time-Life, 1967.

Martin, John R. *Baroque.* New York: Harper & Row, 1977.

Minor, Vernon Hyde. *Baroque and Rococo: Art and Culture.* New York: Abrams, 1999.

Moir, Alfred. *The Italian Followers of Caravaggio.* 2 vols. Cambridge, Mass.: Harvard University Press, 1967.

———. *Anthony van Dyck.* New York: Abrams, 1994.

Montagu, Jennifer. *Roman Baroque Sculpture: The Industry of Art.* New Haven: Yale University Press, 1989.

Nicolson, Benedict. *The International Caravaggesque Movement: Lists of Pictures by Caravaggio and His Followers throughout Europe from 1590 to 1650.* Oxford: Phaidon, 1979.

Norberg-Schulz, Christian. *Late Baroque and Rococo Architecture.* New York: Rizzoli, 1985.

———. *Baroque Architecture.* New York: Rizzoli, 1986.

Orso, Steven N. *Velázquez, Los Borrachos, and Painting at the Court of Philip IV.* Cambridge: Cambridge University Press, 1993.

Powell, Nicolas. *From Baroque to Rococo: An Introduction to Austrian and German Architecture from 1580 to 1790.* London: Faber, 1959.

Rosenberg, Jakob. *Rembrandt: Life and Work.* Rev. ed. Ithaca, N.Y.: Cornell University Press, 1980.

Rosenberg, Jakob, Seymour Slive, and E. H. ter Kuile. *Dutch Art and Architecture, 1600 to 1800.* 3rd ed. Pelican History of Art. New York: Penguin, 1977.

Schama, Simon. *The Embarrassment of Riches: An Interpretation of Dutch Culture in the Golden Age* (1987). New York: Vintage, 1997.

Schwartz, Gary. *Rembrandt, His Life, His Paintings.* New York: Penguin, 1991.

Scribner, Charles, III. *Peter Paul Rubens.* New York: Abrams, 1989.

———. *Gianlorenzo Bernini.* New York: Abrams, 1991.

Slive, Seymour. *Rembrandt and His Critics, 1630–1730.* New York: Hacker, 1988.

———, ed. *Frans Hals.* Munich: Prestel, 1989.

Snow, Edward. *A Study of Vermeer.* Rev. and enl. ed. Berkeley: University of California Press, 1994.

Stechow, Wolfgang. *Dutch Landscape Painting of the Seventeenth Century.* 3rd ed. Oxford: Phaidon, 1981.

Strong, Roy. *Van Dyck: Charles I on Horseback.* New York: Viking, 1972.

Sutton, Peter C. *The Age of Rubens.* Boston: Museum of Fine Arts, 1993.

Varriano, John. *Italian Baroque and Rococo Architecture.* New York: Oxford University Press, 1986.

Wallace, Robert. *The World of Bernini, 1598–1680.* New York: Time-Life, 1970.

Waterhouse, Ellis K. *Roman Baroque Painting.* Oxford: Phaidon, 1976.

Wedgwood, C. V. *The World of Rubens, 1577–1640.* New York: Time-Life, 1967.

Welu, James A., and Pieter Biesboer, eds. *Judith Leyster: A Dutch Master and Her World.* New Haven: Yale University Press, 1993.

Wheelock, Arthur K., Jr. *Jan Vermeer.* New York: Abrams, 1988.

Wheeler, Arthur K., Jr., Susan J. Barnes, and Julius S. Held. *Anthony Van Dyck.* Washington, D.C.: National Gallery of Art, 1990.

White, Christopher. *Rembrandt.* London: Thames & Hudson, 1984.

———. *Peter Paul Rubens: Man and Artist.* New Haven: Yale University Press, 1987.

Wittkower, Rudolf. *Bernini: The Sculptor of the Roman Baroque.* 4th ed. London: Phaidon, 1997.

———. *Art and Architecture in Italy, 1600–1750.* 6th ed. 3 vols. Pelican History of Art. New Haven: Yale University Press, 1999.

Wright, Christopher. *The French Painters of the Seventeenth Century.* Boston: Little, Brown, 1985.

Rococo and the Eighteenth Century

Abrams, Ann Uhry. *The Valiant Hero: Benjamin West and Grand-Style History Painting.* Washington, D.C.: Smithsonian Institute, 1985.

Alpers, Svetlana, and Michael Baxandall. *Tiepolo and the Pictorial Intelligence.* New Haven: Yale University Press, 1994.

Antal, Frederick. *Hogarth and His Place in European Art.* London: Routledge & Kegan Paul, 1962.

Bryson, Norman. *Word and Image: French Painting of the Ancien Régime.* Cambridge: Cambridge University Press, 1981.

Burke, Joseph. *English Art, 1714–1800.* Oxford: Clarendon, 1976.

Châtelet, Albert, and Jacques Thuillier. *French Painting, from Le Nain to Fragonard.* Trans. James Emmons. Geneva: Skira, 1964.

Conisbee, Philip. *Painting in Eighteenth-Century France.* Ithaca, N.Y.: Cornell University Press, 1981.

Crow, Thomas E. *Painters and Public Life in Eighteenth-Century Paris.* New Haven: Yale University Press, 1985.

Duncan, Carol. *The Pursuit of Pleasure: The Rococo Revival in French Romantic Art.* New York: Garland, 1976.

Frankenstein, Alfred Victor. *The World of Copley, 1738–1815.* New York: Time-Life, 1970.

Grasselli, Margaret Morgan, and Pierre Rosenberg. *Watteau, 1684–1721.* Washington, D.C.: National Gallery of Art, 1984.

Hitchcock, Henry R. *Rococo Architecture in Southern Germany.* London: Phaidon, 1968.

Kalnein, Karl Wend Graf, and Michael Levey. *Art and Architecture of the Eighteenth Century in France.* Harmondsworth: Penguin, 1972.

Kimball, Fiske. *The Creation of the Rococo Decorative Style* (1943). New York: Dover, 1980.

Levey, Michael. *Rococo to Revolution: Major Trends in Eighteenth-Century Painting.* New York: Oxford University Press, 1977.

———. *Painting in Eighteenth-Century Venice.* 3rd ed. New Haven: Yale University Press, 1994.

Manners and Morals: Hogarth and British Painting, 1700–1760. London, Tate Gallery, 1987.

Minguet, J. Philippe. *Esthétique du Rococo.* Paris: Vrin, 1966.

Palladio, Andrea. *The Four Books of Architecture.* 1738. Reprint of the Isaac Ware edition. New York: Dover, 1965.

Paulson, Ronald. *The Art of Hogarth.* London: Phaidon, 1975.

Pignatti, Terisio. *The Age of Rococo.* Trans. Lorna Andrade. London: Cassell, 1988.

Posner, Donald. *Watteau: A Lady at Her Toilet.* New York: Viking, 1973.

Rosenberg, Pierre. *Chardin, 1699–1779.* Ed. Sally W. Goodfellow. Trans. Emilie P. Kadish and Ursula Korneitchouk. Cleveland: Cleveland Museum of Art, 1979.

Rosenblum, Robert. *Transformations in Late Eighteenth-Century Art* (1967). Princeton: Princeton University Press, 1970.

Snodin, Michael. *Rococo: Art and Design in Hogarth's England.* London: Trefoil Books/Victoria and Albert Museum, 1984.

Summerson, John. *The Architecture of the Eighteenth Century.* New York: Thames & Hudson, 1986.

Wittkower, Rudolf. *Palladio and Palladianism* (1974). New York: Thames & Hudson, 1983.

Neoclassicism: The Late Eighteenth and Early Nineteenth Centuries

Arnason, H. H. *The Sculptures of Houdon.* London: Phaidon, 1975.

Boime, Albert. *Art in an Age of Revolution, 1750–1800.* Chicago: University of Chicago Press, 1987.

———. *Art in an Age of Bonapartism, 1800–1815* (1990). Chicago: University of Chicago Press, 1993.

Bryson, Norman. *Tradition and Desire: From David to Delacroix.* New York: Cambridge University Press, 1984.

Burchard, John, and Albert Bush-Brown. *The Architecture of America: A Social and Cultural History.* Boston: Little, Brown, 1966.

Cooper, Wendy A. *Classical Taste in America, 1800–1840.* Baltimore: Baltimore Museum of Art, 1993.

Eitner, Lorenz. *Neoclassicism and Romanticism, 1750–1850: An Anthology of Sources and Documents.* New York: Harper & Row, 1989.

———. *An Outline of Nineteenth-Century European Painting: From David through Cézanne.* 2 vols. New York: HarperCollins, 1996.

Elsen, Albert E. *Rodin.* New York: Museum of Modern Art, 1963.

———. *Auguste Rodin: Readings on His Life and Work.* Englewood Cliffs, N.J.: Prentice-Hall, 1965.

Friedländer, Walter F. *David to Delacroix* (1952). Trans. Robert Goldwater. Cambridge, Mass.: Harvard University Press, 1980.

Honour, Hugh. *Neo-Classicism.* Harmondsworth: Penguin, 1987.

Irwin, David. *English Neoclassical Art: Studies in Inspiration and Taste.* London: Faber & Faber, 1966.

Jaffe, Irma B. *Trumbull: The Declaration of Independence.* New York: Viking, 1976.

Lindsay, Jack. *Death of the Hero: French Painting from David to Delacroix.* London: Studio, 1960.

McLaughlin, Jack. *Jefferson and Monticello: The Biography of a Builder.* New York: Holt, 1988.

Middleton, Robin, and David Watkin. *Neoclassical and 19th-Century Architecture.* 2 vols. New York: Electa/Rizzoli, 1987.

Nanteuil, L. de. *Jacques-Louis David.* New York: Abrams, 1985.

Novotny, Fritz. *Painting and Sculpture in Europe, 1780–1880.* Pelican History of Art. Harmondsworth: Penguin, 1980.

Roberts, Warren E. *Jacques-Louis David, Revolutionary Artist: Art, Politics, and the French Revolution.* Chapel Hill: University of North Carolina Press, 1989.

Rosenblum, Robert. *Transformations in Late Eighteenth-Century Art.* Princeton: Princeton University Press, 1970.

———. *Jean-Auguste-Dominique Ingres* (1967). New York: Abrams, 1985.

Roworth, Wendy Wassyng, ed. *Angelica Kauffmann: A Continental Artist in Georgian England.* London: Reaktion, 1992.

Rykwert, Joseph, and Anne Rykwert. *Robert and James Adam: The Men and the Style.* New York: Electa/Rizzoli, 1985.

Stillman, Damie. *English Neo-classical Architecture.* 2 vols. London: Zwemmer, 1988.

Vaughan, Will, and Helen Weston, eds. *Jacques-Louis David's "Marat."* New York: Cambridge University Press, 1999.

Romanticism: The Late Eighteenth and Early Nineteenth Centuries

Athanassoglou-Kallmyer, Nina M. *Eugène Delacroix: Prints, Politics, and Satire, 1814–1822.* New Haven: Yale University Press, 1991.

Bindman, David. *William Blake: His Art and Times.* New Haven: Yale Center for British Art, 1982.

Born, Wolfgang. *American Landscape Painting: An Interpretation.* New Haven: Yale University Press, 1948.

Börsch-Supan, Helmut. *Caspar-David Friedrich.* 2nd ed. New York: te Neues, 1990.

Brion, Marcel. *Art of the Romantic Era: Romanticism, Classicism, Realism.* New York: Praeger, 1966.

Clark, Kenneth. *The Romantic Rebellion: Romantic versus Classic Art.* New York: Harper & Row, 1973.

Clay, Jean. *Romanticism.* Trans. Daniel Wheeler and Craig Owen. New York: Vendome, 1981.

Courthion, Pierre. *Romanticism.* Trans. Stuart Gilbert. Geneva: Skira, 1961.

Eitner, Lorenz. *Géricault's "Raft of the Medusa."* London: Phaidon, 1972.

———. *Géricault: His Life and Work.* London: Orbis, 1983.

Faxon, Alicia Craig. *Dante Gabriel Rossetti.* New York: Abbeville, 1989.

Gage, John. *J. M. W. Turner: A Wonderful Range of Mind.* New Haven: Yale University Press, 1987.

Harris, Enriqueta. *Goya.* Rev. ed. London: Phaidon, 1994.

Hilton, Timothy. *Pre-Raphaelites.* New York: Abrams, 1971.

Honour, Hugh. *Romanticism.* New York: Harper & Row, 1979.

Jobert, Barthélémy. *Delacroix.* Princeton: Princeton University Press, 1998.

Kroeber, Karl. *British Romantic Art.* Berkeley: University of California Press, 1986.

Licht, Fred. *Goya: The Origins of the Modern Temper in Art.* New York: Harper & Row, 1983.

López-Rey, José. *Goya's Caprichos: Beauty, Reason and Caricature.* 2 vols. Princeton: Princeton University Press, 1953.

Mendelowitz, Daniel M. *A History of American Art.* 2nd ed. New York: Holt, Rinehart & Winston, 1970.

Murphy, Alexandra R. *Jean-François Millet.* Boston: Museum of Fine Arts, 1984.

Nochlin, Linda. *The Body in Pieces: The Fragment as a Metaphor of Modernity.* London: Thames & Hudson, 1994.

Parry, Ellwood C., III. *The Art of Thomas Cole: Ambition and Imagination.* Newark, Del.: University of Delaware Press, 1988.

Pérez Sánchez, Alfonso E., and Eleanor A. Sayre. *Goya and the Spirit of Enlightenment.* Boston: Museum of Fine Arts, 1989.

Powell, Earl A. *Thomas Cole.* New York: Abrams, 1990.

Praz, Mario. *The Romantic Agony.* New York: Oxford University Press, 1983.

The Pre-Raphaelites. London: Tate Gallery, 1984.

Prideaux, Tom. *The World of Delacroix, 1798–1863.* New York: Time-Life, 1966.

Raine, Kathleen. *William Blake.* New York: Oxford University Press, 1970.

Rosenblum, Robert, and Horst W. Janson. *Nineteenth-Century Art.* Rev. ed. New York: Abrams, 2005.

Truettner, William H., and Alan Wallach, eds. *Thomas Cole: Landscape into History.* New Haven: Yale University Press, 1994.

Vaughan, William. *German Romantic Painting.* New Haven: Yale University Press, 1980.

———. *Romanticism and Art.* New York: Thames & Hudson, 1994.

Walker, John. *John Constable.* New York: Abrams, 1991.

Wilton, Andrew. *Turner and the Sublime.* Chicago: University of Chicago Press, 1981.

———. *Turner in His Time.* New York: Abrams, 1987.

Wolf, Bryan Jay. *Romantic Re-vision: Culture and Consciousness in Nineteenth-Century American Painting and Literature.* Chicago: University of Chicago Press, 1982.

Nineteenth-Century Realism

Ashton, Dore. *Rosa Bonheur: A Life and a Legend.* New York: Viking, 1981.

Barger, M. Susan, and William B. White. *The Daguerreotype: Nineteenth-Century Technology and Modern Science* (1991). Baltimore: Johns Hopkins University Press, 2000.

Boime, Albert. *A Social History of Modern Art.* 3 vols. Chicago: University of Chicago Press, 1987–2004.

Cachin, Françoise, Charles S. Moffet, and Michel Melot, eds. *Manet, 1832–1883.* New York: Metropolitan Museum of Art, 1983.

Carrier, David. *High Art: Charles Baudelaire and the Origins of Modernist Painting.* University Park, Pa.: Pennsylvania State University Press, 1996.

Clark, T. J. *The Absolute Bourgeois: Artists and Politics in France, 1848–1851* (1973). Berkeley: University of California Press, 1999.

———. *Image of the People: Gustave Courbet and the 1848 Revolution* (1973). Berkeley: University of California Press, 1999.

Eisenman, Stephen F. *Nineteenth-Century Art: A Critical History.* 2nd ed. New York: Thames & Hudson, 2002.

Elsen, Albert. *Rodin.* New York: Museum of Modern Art, 1963.

Farwell, Beatrice. *Manet and the Nude: A Study of Iconography in the Second Empire.* New York: Garland, 1981.

Fried, Michael. *Courbet's Realism.* Chicago: University of Chicago Press, 1990.

Gosling, Nigel. *Nadar.* New York: Knopf, 1976.

Hamilton, George H. *Manet and His Critics* (1954). New Haven: Yale University Press, 1986.

Homer, William Innes. *Thomas Eakins: His Life and Art.* New York: Abbeville, 1992.

Isaacson, Joel. *Manet: Le Déjeuner sur l'Herbe.* New York: Viking, 1972.

Janson, H. W. *Nineteenth-Century Sculpture.* New York: Abrams, 1985.

Johns, Elizabeth. *Thomas Eakins: The Heroism of Modern Life.* Princeton: Princeton University Press, 1983.

Krell, Alan. *Manet and the Painters of Contemporary Life.* London: Thames & Hudson, 1996.

Lindsay, Jack. *Gustave Courbet: His Life and Art.* New York: State Mutual Reprints, 1981.

McKean, John. *Crystal Palace: Joseph Paxton and Charles Fox.* London: Phaidon, 1994.

Maison, K. E. *Honoré Daumier: Catalogue Raisonné of the Paintings, Watercolours, and Drawings.* 2 vols. Greenwich, Conn.: New York Graphic Society, 1968.

Meredith, Roy. *Mr. Lincoln's Camera Man, Mathew B. Brady.* 2nd rev. ed. New York: Dover, 1974.

Needham, Gerald. *Nineteenth-Century Realist Art.* New York: Harper & Row, 1988.

Newhall, Beaumont. *The History of Photography: From 1839 to the Present.* 5th ed. New York: Museum of Modern Art, 1999.

Nicolson, Benedict. *Courbet: The Studio of the Painter.* New York: Viking, 1973.

Nochlin, Linda. *Realism and Tradition in Art, 1848–1900: Sources and Documents.* Englewood Cliffs, N.J.: Prentice-Hall, 1966.

———. *Realism.* Harmondsworth: Penguin, 1971.

———. *Gustave Courbet: A Study of Style and Society.* New York: Garland, 1976.

Novak, Barbara. *American Painting of the Nineteenth Century.* 2nd ed. New York: Harper & Row, 1979.

O'Gorman, James F. *Three American Architects: Richardson, Sullivan, and Wright, 1865–1915.* Chicago: University of Chicago Press, 1991.

Passeron, Roger. *Daumier.* Trans. Helga Harrison. New York: Rizzoli, 1981.

Reff, Theodore. *Manet, Olympia.* New York: Viking, 1977.

Schneider, Pierre. *The World of Manet, 1832–1883.* New York: Time-Life, 1968.

Sullivan, Louis. *The Autobiography of an Idea.* New York: Dover, 1956.

Touissaint, Hélène. *Gustave Courbet, 1819–1877.* London: Arts Council of Great Britain, 1978.

Tucker, Paul H., ed. *Manet's Le Déjeuner sur l'Herbe.* New York: Cambridge University Press, 1998.

Weisberg, Gabriel P., ed. *The European Realist Tradition.* Bloomington: Indiana University Press, 1982.

Nineteenth-Century Impressionism

Bell, Quentin. *Ruskin.* New York: Braziller, 1978.

Boggs, Jean Sutherland, et al. *Degas.* Exh. cat. New York: Metropolitan Museum of Art, 1988.

Clark, T. J. *The Painting of Modern Life: Paris in the Art of Manet and His Followers.* Rev. ed. Princeton: Princeton University Press, 1984.

Gerdts, William H. *American Impressionism.* 2nd ed. New York: Abbeville, 2001.

Guth, Christine. *Art of Edo Japan: The Artist and the City 1615–1868.* New York: Abrams, 1996.

Hanson, Anne Coffin. *Manet and the Modern Tradition.* New Haven: Yale University Press, 1977.

Hanson, Lawrence. *Renoir: The Man, the Painter, and His World.* London: Frewin, 1972.

Herbert, Robert L. *Impressionism: Art, Leisure and Parisian Society.* New Haven: Yale University Press, 1988.

Higonnet, Anne. *Berthe Morisot's Images of Women.* Cambridge, Mass.: Harvard University Press, 1992.

Kelder, Diane. *The French Impressionists and Their Century.* New York: Praeger, 1970.

Kendall, Richard. *Degas: Beyond Impressionism.* London: National Gallery Publications, 1996.

Locke, Nancy. *Manet and the Family Romance.* Princeton: Princeton University Press, 2001.

Mathews, Nancy Mowll. *Mary Cassatt.* New York: Abrams, 1987.

Nochlin, Linda. *Impressionism and Post-Impressionism, 1874–1904: Sources and Documents.* Englewood Cliffs, N.J.: Prentice-Hall, 1966.

Pissarro, Joachim. *Camille Pissarro.* New York: Abrams, 1993.

Pool, Phoebe. *Impressionism.* New York: Praeger, 1967.

Prideaux, Tom. *The World of Whistler, 1834–1903.* New York: Time-Life, 1970.

Rewald, John. *The History of Impressionism.* 4th rev. ed. New York: Museum of Modern Art, 1973.

———. *Studies in Impressionism.* New York: Abrams, 1986.

Rouart, Denis. *Renoir.* New York: Skira/Rizzoli, 1985.

Smith, Paul. *Impressionism: Beneath the Surface.* New York: Abrams, 1995.

Spate, Virginia. *Claude Monet: Life and Work.* New York: Rizzoli, 1992.

Tucker, Paul Hayes. *Claude Monet: Life and Art.* New Haven: Yale University Press, 1995.

Walker, John. *James McNeill Whistler.* New York: Abrams, 1987.

Post-Impressionism and the Late Nineteenth Century

Andersen, Wayne. *Gauguin's Paradise Lost.* New York: Viking, 1971.

Badt, Kurt. *The Art of Cézanne.* Trans. Sheila Ann Ogilvie. Berkeley: University of California Press, 1965.

Champigneulle, Bernard. *Rodin.* Trans. J. Maxwell Brownjohn. New York: Thames & Hudson, 1986.

Collins, Bradley, Jr. *Van Gogh and Gauguin: Electric Arguments and Utopian Dreams.* Boulder, Col.: Westview, 2001.

d'Alleva, Anne. *Arts of the Pacific Islands.* New York: Abrams, 1998.

Denvir, Bernard. *Toulouse-Lautrec.* New York: Thames & Hudson, 1991.

———. *Post-Impressionism.* New York: Thames & Hudson, 1992.

Edvard Munch: Symbols and Images. Washington, D.C.: National Gallery of Art, 1978.

Eggum, Arne. *Edvard Munch: Paintings, Sketches, and Studies.* Trans. Ragnar Christophersen. London: Thames & Hudson, 1984.

Eisenman, Stephen F. *Gauguin's Skirt.* London: Thames & Hudson, 1997.

Geist, Sidney. *Interpreting Cézanne.* Cambridge, Mass.: Harvard University Press, 1988.

Gogh, Vincent van. *The Complete Letters of Vincent van Gogh.* 2nd ed. Trans. J. van Gogh-Bonger and C. de Dood. 3 vols. Boston: Little, Brown, 1978.

Goldwater, Robert. *Paul Gauguin.* New York: Abrams, 1972.

Gordon, Robert, and Andrew Forge. *Degas.* New York: Abrams, 1988.

Gowing, Lawrence, ed. *Cézanne: The Early Years, 1859–72.* New York: Abrams, 1988.

Hamilton, George H. *Painting and Sculpture in Europe, 1880–1940.* 6th ed. Pelican History of Art. New Haven: Yale University Press, 1993.

Heller, Reinhold. *Edvard Munch: The Scream.* New York: Viking, 1972.

Holt, Elizabeth Gilmore, ed. *The Expanding World of Art, 1874–1902.* New Haven: Yale University Press, 1988.

Huisman, Philippe, and M. G. Dortu. *Toulouse-Lautrec.* Garden City, N.Y.: Doubleday, 1973.

Jullian, Philippe. *The Symbolists.* 2nd ed. New York: Dutton, 1977.

Mainardi, Patricia. *The End of the Salon: Art and the State in the Early Third Republic.* Cambridge, Eng.: Cambridge University Press, 1993.

Pickvance, Ronald. *Van Gogh in Arles.* New York: Metropolitan Museum of Art, 1984.

———. *Van Gogh in Saint-Rémy and Auvers.* New York: Metropolitan Museum of Art, 1986.

Post-Impressionism: Cross-Currents in European and American Painting, 1880–1906. Washington, D.C.: National Gallery of Art, 1980.

Rewald, John. *Post-Impressionism: From Van Gogh to Gauguin.* 3rd ed. New York: Museum of Modern Art, 1978.

———. *Studies in Post-Impressionism.* New York: Abrams, 1986.

Rubin, William, ed. *Cézanne, the Late Work: Essays.* New York: Museum of Modern Art, 1977.

Russell, John. *Seurat.* New York: Praeger, 1965.

Schapiro, Meyer. *Vincent van Gogh.* New York: Abrams, 2003.

———. *Paul Cézanne.* New York: Abrams, 2004.

Shiff, Richard. *Cézanne and the End of Impressionism: A Study of the Theory, Technique, and Critical Evaluation of Modern Art.* Chicago: University of Chicago Press, 1984.

Smith, Paul. *Seurat and the Avant-Garde.* New Haven: Yale University Press, 1997.

Stang, Ragna. *Edvard Munch: The Man and His Art.* Trans. Geoffrey Culverwell. New York: Abbeville, 1988.

Thomson, Belinda, *Gauguin.* New York: Thames & Hudson, 1987.

Thomson, Richard, et al. *Toulouse-Lautrec.* New Haven: Yale University Press, 1991.

Wood, Mara-Helen, ed. *Edvard Munch: The Frieze of Life.* London: National Gallery Publications, 1992.

Turn of the Century: Early Picasso, Fauvism, Expressionism, and Matisse

Arnason, Hjorvardur H. *History of Modern Art: Painting, Sculpture, Architecture, Photography.* 5th ed. Upper Saddle River, N.J.: Prentice-Hall, 2004.

Barr, Alfred H., Jr. *Matisse, His Art and His Public* (1951). New York: Arno, 1966.

Bascom, William Russell. *African Art in Cultural Perspective: An Introduction.* New York: Norton, 1973.

Ben-Amos, Paula G. *The Art of Benin.* 2nd rev. ed. London: British Museum, 1995.

Berlo, Janet, and Lee A. Wilson. *Arts of Africa, Oceania, and the Americas: Selected Readings.* Englewood Cliffs, N.J.: Prentice-Hall, 1993.

Blier, Suzanne Preston. *The Royal Arts of Africa: The Majesty of Form.* New York: Abrams, 1998.

Chipp, Herschel B. *Theories of Modern Art: A Source Book by Artists and Critics.* Berkeley: University of California Press, 1968.

Duncan, Alastair. *Art Nouveau.* London: Thames & Hudson, 1994.

Duthuit, Georges. *The Fauvist Painters.* Trans. Ralph Manheim. New York: Wittenborn, Schultz, 1950.

Elderfield, John. *The Cut-Outs of Henri Matisse.* New York: Braziller, 1978.

Flam, Jack D. *Matisse: The Man and His Art, 1869–1918.* Ithaca, N.Y.: Cornell University Press, 1986.

———. *Matisse on Art.* Rev. ed. Berkeley: University of California Press, 1995.

___. *Matisse and Picasso: The Story of Their Rivalry and Friendship.* Cambridge, Mass.: Westview, 2003.

Gordon, Donald E. *Expressionism: Art and Idea.* New Haven: Yale University Press, 1987.

Hahl-Koch, Jelena. *Kandinsky.* Trans. Karin Brown et al. New York: Rizzoli, 1993.

Herbert, James D. *Fauve Painting: The Making of Cultural Politics.* New Haven: Yale University Press, 1992.

Kerchache, Jacques, Jean-Louis Paudrat, and Lucien Stéphan. *Art of Africa.* Trans. Marjolijn de Jager. New York: Abrams, 1993.

Lloyd, Jill. *German Expressionism: Primitivism and Modernity.* New Haven: Yale University Press, 1991.

Magnin, André, and Jacques Soulillou. *Contemporary Art of Africa.* New York: Abrams, 1996.

Messer, Thomas M. *Vasily Kandinsky.* New York: Abrams, 1997.

Myers, Bernard Samuel. *The German Expressionists: A Generation in Revolt.* New York: Praeger, 1956.

Perani, Judith, and Fred T. Smith. *The Visual Arts of Africa: Gender, Power, and Life Cycle Rituals.* Upper Saddle River, N.J.: Prentice-Hall, 1998.

Prelinger, Elizabeth. *Käthe Kollwitz.* Washington, D.C.: Yale University Press/National Gallery of Art, 1992.

Richardson, John. *A Life of Picasso.* I: *1881–1906.* New York: Random House, 1991.

Rubin, William, ed. *"Primitivism" in 20th Century Art.* 2 vols. New York: The Museum of Modern Art, 1984.

Russell, John. *The World of Matisse, 1869–1954.* New York: Time-Life, 1969.
Schmutzler, Robert. *Art Nouveau.* Trans. Edouard Roditi. New York: Abrams, 1962.
Schneider, Pierre. *Matisse.* Trans. M. Taylor and B. S. Romer. New York: Rizzoli, 1984.
Steinberg, Leo. *Other Criteria: Confrontations with Twentieth-Century Art* (1972). New York: Oxford University Press, 1975.
Taylor, Brandon. *Avant-Garde and After: Rethinking Art Now.* New York: Abrams, 1995.
Vogt, Paul. *Expressionism: German Painting, 1905–1920.* Trans. Antony Vivis. New York: Abrams, 1980.

Cubism, Futurism, and Related Twentieth-Century Styles

Ashton, Dore. *Twentieth-Century Artists on Art.* New York: Pantheon, 1985.
Barr, Alfred H., Jr. *Picasso: Fifty Years of His Art* (1946). New York: Museum of Modern Art, 1974.
———. *Cubism and Abstract Art: Painting, Sculpture, Constructions, Photography, Architecture, Industrial Art, Theatre, Films, Posters, Typography* (1936). Cambridge, Mass.: Belknap, 1986.
Bayer, Herbert, Walter Gropius, and Ise Gropius. *Bauhaus, 1919–1928* (1938). New York: Museum of Modern Art, 1975.
Blake, Peter. *Frank Lloyd Wright, Architecture and Space.* Baltimore: Penguin, 1964.
Brown, Milton. *The Story of the Armory Show: The 1913 Exhibition That Changed American Art.* 2nd ed. New York: Abbeville, 1988.
Chipp, Herschel B. *Picasso's Guernica: History, Transformations, Meanings.* Berkeley: University of California Press, 1988.
Cooper, Douglas. *The Cubist Epoch* (1970). Oxford: Phaidon, 1976.
Cowling, Elizabeth, and John Golding. *Picasso: Sculptor/Painter.* London: Tate Gallery, 1994.
Curtis, William J. R. *Le Corbusier: Ideas and Forms.* New York: Rizzoli, 1986.
Doesburg, Theo van. *Principles of Neo-Plastic Art.* Trans. Janet Seligman. Greenwich, Conn.: New York Graphic Society, 1968.
Elsen, Albert E. *Origins of Modern Sculpture: Pioneers and Premises.* New York: Braziller, 1974.
Fry, Edward F. *Cubism.* New York: Oxford University Press, 1978.
Geist, Sidney. *Brancusi: The Sculpture and Drawings.* New York: Abrams, 1975.
———. *Brancusi: The Kiss.* New York: Harper & Row, 1978.
Golding, John. *Cubism: A History and an Analysis, 1907–1914.* 3rd ed. Cambridge, Mass.: Harvard University Press, 1988.
Gray, Camilla. *The Russian Experiment in Art, 1863–1922.* Rev. and enl. ed. New York: Thames & Hudson, 1986.
Green, Christopher, ed. *Picasso's Les Demoiselles d'Avignon.* Cambridge, Eng.: Cambridge University Press, 2001.
Harrison, Charles, Francis Frascina, and Gill Perry. *Primitivism, Cubism, Abstraction: The Early Twentieth Century.* New Haven: Yale University Press, 1993.
Hilton, Timothy. *Picasso* (1975). New York: Thames & Hudson, 1985.
Hultén, Pontus. *Futurism and Futurisms.* New York: Abbeville, 1986.
Hunter, Sam, and John Jacobus. *American Art of the Twentieth Century: Painting, Sculpture, Architecture.* New York: Abrams, 1973.
Hunter, Sam, John Jacobus, and Daniel Wheeler. *Modern Art.* 3rd ed. Upper Saddle River, N.J.: Prentice-Hall, 2005.
Jaffé, Hans L. C. *De Stijl, 1917–1931: The Dutch Contribution to Modern Art.* Cambridge, Mass.: Belknap, 1986.
Kuenzli, Rudolf, and Francis M. Naumann. *Marcel Duchamp: Artist of the Century.* Cambridge, Mass.: MIT Press, 1989.
Larkin, David, and Bruce Brooks Pfeiffer, eds. *Frank Lloyd Wright: The Masterworks.* New York: Rizzoli, 1993.
Lodder, Christina. *Russian Constructivism.* New Haven: Yale University Press, 1983.
Mondrian, Piet C. *Plastic Art and Pure Plastic Art, 1937, and Other Essays, 1941–1943.* New York: Wittenborn, Schultz, 1951.
Overy, Paul. *De Stijl.* New York: Thames & Hudson, 1991.
Pfeiffer, Bruce Brooks, and Gerald Nordland, eds. *Frank Lloyd Wright in the Realm of Ideas.* Carbondale: Southern Illinois University Press, 1988.
Read, Herbert. *A Concise History of Modern Painting* (1959). 3rd ed. New York: Praeger, 1975.
Richardson, John. *A Life of Picasso.* II: *1907–1917.* New York: Random House, 1996.
Rosenblum, Robert. *Cubism and Twentieth-Century Art.* Rev. ed. New York: Abrams, 2001.
Rubin, William, ed. *Pablo Picasso: A Retrospective.* New York: Museum of Modern Art, 1980.
———. *Picasso and Braque: Pioneering Cubism.* New York: Museum of Modern Art, 1989.
Schiff, Gert, ed. *Picasso in Perspective.* Englewood Cliffs, N.J.: Prentice-Hall, 1976.
Silver, Kenneth E. *Esprit de Corps: The Art of the Parisian Avant-Garde and the First World War, 1914–1925.* Princeton: Princeton University Press, 1989.
Taylor, Joshua C. *Futurism.* New York: Museum of Modern Art, 1961.
Tisdall, Caroline, and Angelo Bozzolla. *Futurism.* New York: Oxford University Press, 1978.
Tomkins, Calvin. *Duchamp: A Biography* (1996). New York: Holt, 1998.
Weiss, Jeffrey S. *The Popular Culture of Modern Art: Picasso, Duchamp, and Avant-Gardism.* New Haven: Yale University Press, 1994.
Whitford, Frank. *Bauhaus.* London: Thames & Hudson, 1984.
Wilkin, Karen. *Georges Braque.* New York: Abbeville, 1991.
Wright, Frank Lloyd. *American Architecture.* Ed. E. Kaufmann. New York: Horizon, 1955.
Zhadova, Larissa A. *Malevich: Suprematism and Revolution in Russian Art, 1910–1930.* Trans. Alexander Lieven. London: Thames & Hudson, 1982.

Dada, Surrealism, Fantasy, and the United States between the Wars

Alexandrian, Sarane. *Surrealist Art* (1970). Trans. Gordon Clough. London: Thames & Hudson, 1985.
Arp, Hans. *Arp on Arp: Poems, Essays, Memories.* Ed. Marcel Jean. New York: Viking, 1972.
Baigell, Matthew. *The American Scene: American Painting of the 1930's.* New York: Praeger, 1974.
Barr, Alfred H., Jr., ed. *Fantastic Art, Dada, Surrealism* (1936). New York: Arno, 1969.
Bearden, Romare, and Harry Henderson. *A History of African-American Artists: From 1792 to the Present.* New York: Pantheon, 1993.
Dachy, Marc. *The Dada Movement, 1915–1923.* Trans. Michael Taylor. New York: Skira/Rizzoli, 1990.
Davidson, Abraham A. *Early American Modernist Painting, 1910–1935.* New York: Harper & Row, 1981.
Eldredge, Charles C. *Georgia O'Keeffe.* New York: Abrams, 1991.
Foucault, Michel. *This Is Not a Pipe.* Trans. J. Harkness. Berkeley: University of California Press, 1983.
Franciscono, Marcel. *Paul Klee: His Work and Thought.* Chicago: University of Chicago Press, 1991.
Herrera, Hayden. *Frida Kahlo: The Paintings.* New York: HarperCollins, 1991.
Homer, William Innes. *Alfred Stieglitz and the American Avant-Garde.* Boston: New York Graphic Society, 1977.
Lane, John R., and Susan C. Larsen, eds. *Abstract Painting and Sculpture in America, 1927–1944.* Pittsburgh: Pittsburgh Museum of Art, Carnegie Institute, 1984.
Levin, Gail. *Edward Hopper: An Intimate Biography.* New York: Knopf, 1995.
Lippard, Lucy R., ed. *Surrealists on Art.* Englewood Cliffs, N.J.: Prentice-Hall. 1970.
Lynes, Barbara Buhler. *O'Keeffe, Stieglitz, and the Critics, 1916–1929* (1989). Chicago: University of Chicago Press, 1991.
Masheck, Joseph, ed. *Marcel Duchamp in Perspective* (1975). Cambridge, Mass.: Da Capo, 2002.
Norman, Dorothy. *Alfred Stieglitz, an American Seer* (1973). New York: Aperture, 1990.
Picon, Gaëtan. *Surrealists and Surrealism, 1919–1939.* Trans. James Emmons. New York: Rizzoli, 1977.
Powell, Richard J. *Black Art and Culture in the Twentieth Century.* London: Thames & Hudson, 1997.
Richter, Hans. *Dada: Art and Anti-Art.* New York: Abrams, 1965.
Rubin, William S. *Dada and Surrealist Art.* New York: Abrams, 1968.
Russell, John. *Max Ernst: Life and Work.* New York: Abrams, 1967.
Schwarz, Arturo. *Man Ray: The Rigour of Imagination.* New York: Rizzoli, 1977.
———, ed. *The Complete Works of Marcel Duchamp.* 3rd ed. 2 vols. London: Greenridge, 1997.
Stich, Sidra. *Anxious Visions: Surrealist Art.* New York: Abbeville, 1990.
Sylvester, David. *Magritte: The Silence of the World.* New York: Abrams, 1992.
Waldberg, Patrick. *Surrealism.* New York: Oxford University Press, 1978.
Wheat, Ellen Harkins. *Jacob Lawrence: American Painter.* Seattle: University of Washington Press, 1986.

Abstract Expressionism

Albright, Thomas. *Art in the San Francisco Bay Area, 1945–1980.* Berkeley: University of California Press, 1985.
Alloway, Lawrence. *Topics in American Art since 1945.* New York: Norton, 1975.
Ashton, Dore. *American Art since 1945.* New York: Oxford University Press, 1982.
———. *About Rothko* (1983). Cambridge, Mass.: Da Capo, 2003.
Barron, Stephanie, ed. *Degenerate Art: The Fate of the Avant-Garde in Nazi Germany.* Los Angeles: Los Angeles County Museum of Art, 1991.
Doss, Erika. *Benton, Pollock, and the Politics of Modernism: From Regionalism to Abstract Expressionism.* Chicago: University of Chicago Press, 1991.
Francis, Richard H. *Jasper Johns.* New York: Abbeville, 1984.
Frasina, Frances, ed. *Pollock and After: The Critical Debate.* 2nd ed. New York: Routledge, 2000.
Geldzahler, Henry. *New York Painting and Sculpture: 1940–1970.* New York: Dutton, 1969.
Gordon, John. *Louise Nevelson.* New York: Praeger, 1967.
Greenberg, Clement. *Art and Culture: Critical Essays* (1961). Boston: Beacon, 1965.
Guberman, Sidney. *Frank Stella: An Illustrated Biography.* New York: Rizzoli, 1995.
Herbert, Robert L, ed. *Modern Artist on Art: Ten Unabridged Essays.* 2nd ed. Mineola, N.Y.: Dover, 2000.

Hertz, Richard. *Theories of Contemporary Art.* 2nd ed. Englewood Cliffs, N.J.: Prentice-Hall, 1993.
Hess, Thomas B. *Willem de Kooning.* Exh. cat. New York: Museum of Modern Art, 1968.
Howell, John, ed. *Breakthroughs: Avant-Garde Artists in Europe and America, 1950–1990.* New York: Rizzoli, 1991.
Hughes, Robert. *The Shock of the New.* 2nd ed. New York: McGraw-Hill, 1991.
Hunter, Sam. *An American Renaissance: Painting and Sculpture since 1940.* New York: Abbeville, 1986.
Johnson, Ellen H. *Modern Art and the Object: A Century of Changing Attitudes.* New York: Harper & Row, 1976.
———, ed. *American Artists on Art: From 1940 to 1980.* New York: Harper & Row, 1982.
Krauss, Rosalind E. *The Originality of the Avant-Garde and Other Modernist Myths.* Cambridge, Mass.: MIT Press, 1985.
———. *Passages in Modern Sculpture.* Cambridge, Mass.: MIT Press, 1989.
Lipman, Jean. *Calder's Universe.* Philadelphia and London: Running Press, 1989.
Lucie-Smith, Edward. *Movements in Art since 1945.* New ed. London: Thames & Hudson, 2001.
O'Connor, Francis V. *Jackson Pollock.* New York: Museum of Modern Art, 1967.
Reinhardt, Ad. *Art-as-Art: The Selected Writings of Ad Reinhardt* (1975). Ed. Barbara Rose. Berkeley: University of California Press, 1991.
Rose, Barbara. *Frankenthaler.* New York: Abrams, 1971.
———. *American Art since 1960.* Rev. ed. New York: Praeger, 1975.
———. *Jackson Pollock: Drawing into Painting.* New York: Museum of Modern Art, 1980.
Rosenberg, Harold. *Art on the Edge: Creators and Situations.* New York: Macmillan, 1975.
———. *The De-Definition of Art: Action Art to Pop to Earthworks.* Chicago: University of Chicago Press, 1983.
———. *The Tradition of the New.* New York: Da Capo, 1994.
Rosenblum, Robert. *Frank Stella.* Harmondsworth: Penguin, 1971.
Russell, John. *The Meanings of Modern Art.* Rev. ed. New York: Icon, 1989.
Sandler, Irving. *The Triumph of American Painting: A History of Abstract Expressionism.* New York: Harper & Row, 1970.
———. *American Art of the 1960s.* New York: Harper & Row, 1988.
Selz, Peter. *Art in Our Times: A Pictorial History, 1890–1980.* New York: Abrams, 1981.
Smith, David. *David Smith—Sculpture and Writing* (1968). Ed. Cleve Gray. New York: Thames & Hudson, 1988.
Tomkins, Calvin. *The Scene: Reports on Post-Modern Art.* New York: Viking, 1976.
Waldman, Diane. *Mark Rothko, 1903–1970: A Retrospective.* New York: Abrams, 1978.
Wheeler, Daniel. *Art since Mid-Century: 1945 to the Present.* New York: Vendome, 1991.

Pop Art, Op Art, Minimalism, and Conceptualism

Alloway, Lawrence. *American Pop Art.* New York: Collier, 1974.
———. *Robert Rauschenberg.* Washington, D.C.: Smithsonian Institution, 1976.
Baker, Kenneth. *Minimalism: Art of Circumstance.* New York: Abbeville, 1988.
Battcock, Gregory, ed. *Minimal Art: A Critical Anthology* (1968). Berkeley: University of California Press, 1995.
Bourdon, David. *Warhol.* New York: Abrams, 1989.
Crichton, Michael. *Jasper Johns.* Rev. & exp. ed. New York: Whitney Museum/Abrams, 1994.
Crow, Thomas. *The Rise of the Sixties: American and European Art in the Era of Dissent, 1955–69.* London: Laurence King, 2005.
Frith, Simon, and Howard Horne. *Art into Pop.* London: Methuen, 1987.
Geldzahler, Henry, and Robert Rosenblum. *Andy Warhol: Portraits of the Seventies and Eighties.* London: Anthony d'Offay Gallery/Thames & Hudson, 1993.
Goodyear, Frank H., Jr. *Contemporary American Realism since 1960.* Boston: New York Graphic Society, 1981.
Lippard, Lucy R. *Six Years: The Dematerialization of the Art Object from 1966 to 1972.* New York: Praeger, 1973.
———. *Pop Art.* New York: Thames & Hudson, 1985.
———. *Mixed Blessings: New Art in a Multicultural America.* New York: Pantheon, 1990.
Livingstone, Marco. *Pop Art: A Continuing History.* New York: Abrams, 1990.
Lucie-Smith, Edward. *Art in the Seventies.* Ithaca, N.Y.: Cornell University Press, 1980.
———. *Art in the Eighties.* New York: Phaidon, 1990.
———. *American Art Now.* New York: William Morrow, 1985.
McShine, Kynaston, ed. *Andy Warhol: A Retrospective.* New York: Museum of Modern Art, 1989.
Meyer, Ursula. *Conceptual Art.* New York: Dutton, 1972.
Rose, Barbara. *Claes Oldenberg.* New York: Museum of Modern Art, 1970.
Russell, John, and Suzi Gablik. *Pop Art Redefined.* London: Thames & Hudson, 1969.
Varnedoe, Kirk. *Jasper Johns: A Retrospective.* New York: Museum of Modern Art, 1996.
Varnedoe, Kirk, and Adam Gopnik, eds. *Modern Art and Popular Culture: Readings in High and Low.* New York: Museum of Modern Art, 1990.
Warhol, Andy. *America.* New York: Harper & Row, 1985.

Innovation, Continuity, and Globalization

Alloway, Lawrence. *Christo.* New York: Abrams, 1969.
Auping, Michael. *Susan Rothenberg: Paintings and Drawings.* New York: Rizzoli, 1992.
Baal-Teshuva, Jacob, ed. *Christo: The Reichstag and Urban Projects.* Munich: Prestel, 1993.
Barents, Els. *Cindy Sherman.* Munich: Schirmer/Mosel, 1982.
Barrette, Bill. *Eva Hesse Sculpture: Catalogue Raisonné.* New York: Timken, 1989.
Battcock, Gregory. *Super Realism: A Critical Anthology.* New York: Dutton, 1975.
Beardsley, John. *Earthworks and Beyond: Contemporary Art in the Landscape.* 3rd ed. New York: Abbeville, 1998.
Bourdon, David. *Christo.* New York: Abrams, 1972.
Bruggen, Coosje van. *Bruce Nauman.* New York: Rizzoli, 1988.
Carmean, E. A., Jr., et al. *The Sculpture of Nancy Graves: A Catalogue Raisonné with Essays.* New York: Hudson Hills, 1987.
Carrier, David. *The Aesthete in the City: The Philosophy and Practice of American Abstract Painting in the 1980s.* University Park, Pa.: Pennsylvania State University Press, 1994.
Chicago, Judy. *The Dinner Party: A Symbol of Our Heritage.* Garden City, N.Y.: Anchor/Doubleday, 1979.
———. *The Birth Project.* Garden City, N.Y.: Doubleday, 1985.
Cruz, Amanda, Elizabeth A. T. Smith, and Amelia Jones. *Cindy Sherman: Retrospective.* London: Thames & Hudson, 1997.
Danto, Arthur C. *History Portraits/Cindy Sherman.* New York: Rizzoli, 1991.
Flam, Jack, ed. *Robert Smithson: The Collected Writings.* Berkeley: University of California Press, 1996.
Frank, Peter, and Michael McKenzie. *New, Used, and Improved: Art for the Eighties.* New York: Abbeville, 1987.
Gilmour, John C. *Fire on the Earth: Anselm Kiefer and the Postmodern World.* Philadelphia: Temple University Press, 1990.
Godfrey, Tony. *The New Image: Painting in the 1980s.* New York: Abbeville, 1986.
Goldberg, RoseLee. *Performance Art: From Futurism to the Present.* Rev. ed. New York: Thames & Hudson, 2001.
Haskell, Barbara. *Agnes Martin.* New York: Whitney Museum of American Art, 1992.
Henri, Adrian. *Total Art: Environments, Happenings, and Performances.* New York: Praeger, 1974.
Hobbs, Robert. *Robert Smithson: Sculpture.* Ithaca, N.Y.: Cornell University Press, 1981.
Hobbs, Robert, Wendy Steiner, and Marcia Tucker. *Andres Serrano: Works 1983–1993.* Philadelphia: Institute of Contemporary Art, University of Pennsylvania, 1994.
Hunter, Sam. *Valerie Jaudon: New Masters.* Exh. cat. Berlin: Amerika Haus, 1983.
Koons, Jeff. *The Jeff Koons Handbook.* New York: Rizzoli, 1992.
Laporte, Dominique G. *Christo.* Trans. Abby Pollak. New York: Pantheon, 1986.
Lippard, Lucy R. *Eva Hesse.* New York: New York University Press, 1976.
Marshall, Richard, et al. *Robert Mapplethorpe.* New York: Whitney Museum of American Art, 1988.
———. *Jean-Michel Basquiat.* New York: Whitney Museum of American Art, 1992.
Meyer, Ursula, ed. *Conceptual Art.* New York: Dutton, 1971.
Ratcliff, Carter. *Komar and Melamid.* New York: Abbeville, 1988.
Rosen, Randy, and Catherine C. Brawer, eds. *Making Their Mark: Women Artists Move into the Mainstream, 1970–85.* New York: Abbeville, 1989.
Sandler, Irving. *Art of the Postmodern Era: From the Late 1960s to the Early 1990s.* New York: HarperCollins, 1996.
Smithson, Robert. *The Writings of Robert Smithson: Essays with Illustrations.* Ed. Nancy Holt. New York: New York University Press, 1975.
Stachelhaus, Heiner. *Joseph Beuys.* Trans. David Britt. New York: Abbeville, 1991.
Storr, Robert. *Chuck Close.* New York: Museum of Modern Art, 1998.
Tisdall, Caroline. *Joseph Beuys.* New York: Solomon R. Guggenheim Museum, 1979.
Vaizey, Marina. *Christo.* New York: Rizzoli, 1990.
Wolf, Jahn. *The Art of Gilbert and George; or, An Aesthetic of Existence.* Trans. David Britt. London: Thames & Hudson, 1989.

African Art

Bascom, William Russell. *African Art in Cultural Perspective.* New York: Norton, 1980.
Ben-Amos, Paula G. *The Art of Benin.* 2nd rev. ed. London: British Museum Press, 1995.
Berlo, Janet Catherine, and Lee Anne Wilson, eds. *Arts of Africa, Oceania, and the Americas: Selected Readings.* Englewood Cliffs, N.J.: Prentice-Hall, 1993.
Blier, Suzanne Preston. *The Royal Arts of Africa: The Majesty of Form.* New York: Abrams, 1998.
Kerchache, Jacques, Jean-Louis Paudrat, and Lucien Stéphan. *Art of Africa.* Trans. Marjolijn de Jager. New York: Abrams, 1993.
Magnin, André, and Jacques Soulillou, eds. *Contemporary Art of Africa.* New York: Abrams, 1996.

Perani, Judith, and Fred T. Smith. *The Visual Arts of Africa: Gender, Power, and Life Cycle Rituals.* Upper Saddle River, N.J.: Prentice-Hall, 1998.

Buddhist Art

Bechert, Heinz, and Richard Gombrich, eds. *The World of Buddhism.* London: Thames & Hudson, 1991.
Fisher, Robert E. *Buddhist Art and Architecture.* New York: Thames & Hudson, 1993.
Rowland, Benjamin. *The Evolution of the Buddha Image* (1963). New York: Arno, 1976.
Seckel, Dietrich. *Art of Buddhism.* Trans. Ann E. Keep. New York: Crown, 1964.
Zwalf, W., ed. *Buddhism: Art and Faith.* New York: Macmillan, 1985.

Chinese Art

The Arts of China. 3 vols. Tokyo: Kodansha, 1968–1970.
Barnhart, Richard M., James Cahill, Wu Hung, Yang Xin, Nie Chongzheng, and Lang Shaojun. *Three Thousand Years of Chinese Painting.* New Haven: Yale University Press, 1997.
Confucius. *Analects.* Ed. Bradley Smith and Wan-go Weng. In Bradley Smith and Wan-go Weng. *China: A History in Art.* New York: Doubleday, 1973.
Laozi. *Daode jing.* Ed. Wing-tsit Chan. In Wing-tsit Chan. *A Source Book in Chinese Philosophy.* Princeton: Princeton University Press, 1969.
Loehr, Max. *The Great Painters of China.* New York: Harper & Row, 1980.
Rawson, Jessica, ed. *The British Museum Book of Chinese Art.* New York: Thames & Hudson, 1993.
Sickman, Laurence C. S., and Alexander Soper. *Art and Architecture of China.* Pelican History of Art. Harmondsworth: Penguin, 1971.
Speiser, Werner. *The Art of China: Spirit and Society.* Trans. George Lawrence. New York: Crown, 1961.
Treasures from the Bronze Age of China. Exh. cat. New York: Metropolitan Museum of Art, 1980.
Tregear, Mary. *Chinese Art.* Rev. ed. New York: Thames & Hudson, 1997.
Vainker, S. J. *Chinese Pottery and Porcelain: From Prehistory to the Present.* London: British Museum Press, 1991.

Far Eastern Art (General)

Bussagli, Mario. *Oriental Architecture.* Trans. John Shepley. 2 vols. New York: Electa/Rizzoli, 1989.
Lee, Sherman E. *A History of Far Eastern Art.* 5th ed. New York: Abrams, 1994.
Louis-Frédéric. *The Temples and Sculpture of Southeast Asia.* Trans. Arnold Rosin. London: Thames & Hudson, 1965.
Martynov, Anatoliĭ I. *The Ancient Art of Northern Asia.* Urbana: University of Illinois Press, 1991.

Indian Art

Asher, Catherine B. *Architecture of Mughal India.* New York: Cambridge University Press, 1992.
Basham, Arthur Llewellyn. *The Wonder That Was India.* London: Sidgwick & Jackson, 1987.
Behl, Benoy K. *The Ajanta Caves: Artistic Wonder of Ancient Buddhist India.* New York: Abrams, 1998.
Brown, Percy. *Indian Architecture.* 6th repr. ed. Bombay: Taraporevala, 1976.
Coomaraswamy, Ananda K. *History of Indian and Indonesian Art.* New York: Dover, 1965.
Craven, Roy C. *Indian Art: A Concise History.* Rev. ed. New York: Thames & Hudson, 1997.
Dallapiccola, Anna L., and Stephanie Zingel-Avé Lallemant, eds. *The Stúpa: Its Religious, Historical, and Architectural Significance.* Wiesbaden: Steiner, 1979.
Goetz, Hermann. *The Art of India: Five Thousand Years of Indian Art.* 2nd ed. New York: Crown, 1964.
Harle, James C. *The Art and Architecture of the Indian Subcontinent.* 2nd ed. Pelican History of Art. Harmondsworth: Penguin, 1987.
Huntington, Susan L., and John C. Huntington. *The Art of Ancient India: Buddhist, Hindu, Jain.* New Haven: Yale University Press, 1994.
Lannoy, Richard. *The Speaking Tree: A Study of Indian Culture and Society.* New York: Oxford University Press, 1974.
Meister, Michael W., and M. A. Dhaky, eds. *Encyclopaedia of Indian Temple Architecture.* Philadelphia: University of Pennsylvania Press, 1983.
Michell, George. *The Hindu Temple: An Introduction to Its Meaning and Forms.* Chicago: University of Chicago Press, 1988.
———. *The Penguin Guide to the Monuments of India.* 2 vols. New York: Viking, 1989.
Nou, Jean-Louis, Amina Okada, and M.C. Joshi. *Taj Mahal.* New York: Abbeville, 1993.
Rowland, Benjamin. *Art and Architecture of India: Buddhist, Hindu, Jain.* Pelican History of Art. Harmondsworth: Penguin, 1977.
Sivaramamurti, Calambur. *The Art of India.* New York: Abrams, 1977.
Soundara Rajan, K. V. *Indian Temple Styles: The Personality of Hindu Architecture.* New Delhi: Munshiram Manoharlal, 1972.
Volwahsen, Andreas. *Living Architecture: Indian.* Trans. Ann E. Keep. New York: Grosset & Dunlap, 1969.
Weiner, Sheila L. *Ajaṇṭā: Its Place in Buddhist Art.* Berkeley: University of California Press, 1977.
Zimmer, Heinrich. *Myths and Symbols in Indian Art and Civilization* (1946). Princeton: Princeton University Press, 1992.

Japanese Art

Akiyama, Terukazu. *Japanese Painting.* Treasures of Asia. Geneva: Skira, 1977.
Mason, Penelope. *History of Japanese Art.* 2nd ed. Upper Saddle River, N.J.: Prentice-Hall, 2005.
Paine, Robert T., and Alexander Soper. *The Art and Architecture of Japan.* 3rd ed. Pelican History of Art. Harmondsworth: Penguin, 1981.
Stanley-Baker, Joan. *Japanese Art.* Rev. and exp. ed. New York: Thames & Hudson, 2000.
Yoshikawa, Itsuji. *Major Themes in Japanese Art.* Trans. Armins Nikovskis. New York: Weatherhill, 1976.

Japanese Woodblock Prints

Andō, Hiroshige. *One Hundred Famous Views of Edo* (1986). New York: Braziller/Brooklyn Museum, 1992.
Chibbert, David. *The History of Japanese Printing and Book Illustration.* New York: Kodansha, 1977.
Lane, Richard. *Images from the Floating World: The Japanese Print, Including an Illustrated Dictionary of Ukiyo-e.* New York: Putnam, 1978.
Amy Newland and Chris Uhlenbeck, eds. *Ukiyo-e: The Art of Japanese Woodblock Prints.* New York: Smithmark, 1994.

Mesoamerican and South Pacific Art

Blocker, H. Gene. *The Aesthetics of Primitive Art.* Lanham, Md.: University Press of America, 1994.
Caruana, Wally. *Aboriginal Art.* 2nd ed. New York: Thames & Hudson, 2003.
Coe, Michael D. *The Maya.* 5th ed. New York: Thames & Hudson, 1993.
Coote, Jeremy, and Anthony Shelton, eds. *Anthropology, Art, and Aesthetics.* New York: Oxford University Press, 1992.
Corbin, George A. *Native Arts of North America, Africa, and the South Pacific: An Introduction.* New York: Harper & Row, 1988.
Kubler, George. *The Art and Architecture of Ancient America: The Mexican, Maya, and Andean Peoples.* 3rd ed. Pelican History of Art. New Haven: Yale University Press, 1990.
Mexico: Splendors of Thirty Centuries. New York: Metropolitan Museum of Art, 1990.
Miller, Mary Ellen. *The Art of Mesoamerica: From Olmec to Aztec.* 3rd ed. New York: Thames & Hudson, 2001.
Pasztory, Esther. *Pre-Columbian Art.* New York: Cambridge University Press, 1998.
Spinden, Herbert J. *A Study of Maya Art, Its Subject Matter and Historical Development* (1913). New York: Dover, 1975.
Stone-Miller, Rebecca. *The Art of the Andes from Chavín to Inca.* 2nd ed. New York: Thames & Hudson, 2002.
Townsend, Richard. *The Ancient Americas: Art from Sacred Landscapes.* Chicago: Art Institute of Chicago, 1992.

Native American Art

Corbin, George A. *Native Arts of North America, Africa, and the South Pacific: An Introduction.* New York: Harper & Row, 1988.
Feest, Christian F. *Native Arts of North America.* Rev. ed. London: Thames & Hudson, 1992.
Hunt, Mary Austin. *Taos Pueblo* (1930). Photographed by Ansel Adams and described by Mary Austin. Boston: New York Graphic Society, 1977.
Whiteford, Andrew. *North American Indian Arts.* New York: Golden Press, 1970.

Oceanic Art

Barrow, Terence. *The Art of Tahiti and the Neighbouring Society, Austral and Cook Islands.* New York: Thames & Hudson, 1979.
Corbin, George A. *Native Arts of North America, Africa, and the South Pacific: An Introduction.* New York: Harper & Row, 1988.
Hanson, Allan, and Louise Hanson, eds. *Art and Identity in Oceania.* Honolulu: University of Hawaii Press, 1990.

Persian Painting and Miniatures

Binyon, Laurence, J. V. S. Wilkinson, and Basil Gray. *Persian Miniature Painting* (1931). New York: Dover, 1971.
Canby, Sheila R., ed. *Persian Masters: Five Centuries of Painting.* Bombay: Marg, 1990.
———. *Persian Painting.* New York: Thames & Hudson, 1993.
Titley, Norah M. *Persian Miniature Painting and Its Influence on the Arts of Turkey and India: The British Library Collections.* Austin: University of Texas Press, 1984.

Literary Acknowledgments

Ch. 15, p. 585 John Ashbery, " Self-portrait in a Convex Mirror." Reprinted by permission of Georges Borchardt, Inc., for the author.

Ch. 16, p. 613 W. H. Auden, "Musée des Beaux-Arts" (1938), from W. H. *Auden: Collected Poems.* Copyright " 1940, 1952, and renewed 1968 by W. H. Auden. Reprinted by permission of Random House, Inc. and Faber & Faber, Ltd.

Ch. 24, p. 831 Wallace Stevens, "The Man with the Blue Guitar" (1937), from *Collected Poems.* Copyright " 1936 by Wallace Stevens and renewed 1964 by Holly Stevens. Reprinted by permission of Alfred A. Knopf, Inc., and Faber & Faber, Ltd.

Ch. 25, p. 865 Kazimir Malevich, from *The World as Non-objectivity: Unpublished Writings, 1922–25,* ed. Troels Andersen, trans. Xenia Glowacki-Prus. English translation copyright © 1976 Borgens Vorlag, Valby, Denmark.

Ch. 27, p. 910 Clement Greenberg, "Abstract, Representation, and So Forth," from *Art and Culture* (1961), pp. 133–38. Reprinted by permission of Beacon Press.

Ch. 28, p. 944 Agnes Martin, selections in Barbara Haskell, Agnes Martin (New York: Whitney Museum of American Art, (1992). Reprinted by permission of Pace Wildenstein for the artist.

Acknowledgments

Many of the line drawings in this book have been specially drawn by Taurus Graphics, Kidlington, and the maps have been rendered or re-rendered by Patti Isaacs of Parrot Graphics. McGraw-Hill is grateful to all who have allowed their plans and diagrams to be reproduced. Every effort has been made to contact the copyright holders, but should there be any errors or omissions, they would be pleased to insert the appropriate acknowledgement in any subsequent edition of this publication.

12.5 John McKenna illustration and design.

13.6 From Peter Murray, *Renaissance Architecture.* New York: Harry N. Abrams, 1975. " Electra Archive, Milan, Italy.

17.3 From Lawrence Wodehouse and Marian Moffett, *A History of Western Architecture.* Mountain View, CA: Mayfield Publishing, 1989.

17.5, 19.18, 19.19 From Werner Blaser, *Drawings of Great Buildings.* Basel, Switzerland: Birkhäuser Verlag AG. 1983. © Werner Blaser.

21.8, 25.31 John McKenna illustration and design.

Picture Credits

I.1 Amsterdam, Van Gogh Museum (Vincent van Gogh Foundation)
I.2 © Daniel Schwartz/Lookat, Zurich
I.3 © akg-images/Jean-Louis Nou
I.4 The Museum of Modern Art, New York. Given anonymously. Digital Image © The Museum of Modern Art/Licensed by SCALA/Art Resource, NY. © 2006 Artists Rights Society (ARS), New York/ADAGP, Paris
I.5 Photograph © 2006 Museum Associates/LACMA. © 2006 C. Herscovici, Brussels/Artists Rights Society (ARS), New York
I.6 Osterreichische Nationalbibliothek, Vienna
I.7 Erich Lessing/Art Resource, NY
I.8 Image © 2006 Board of Trustees, National Gallery of Art, Washington, DC, Paul Mellon Collection, National Gallery of Art, Washington, DC. 1983.1.46
I.9 Réunion des Musées Nationaux/Art Resource, NY
I.10 Artothek
I.11 The Museum of Modern Art, New York. Digital Image © The Museum of Modern Art/Licensed by SCALA/Art Resource, NY. © 2006 Artists Rights Society (ARS), New York/ProLitteris, Zurich
I.14 © 2006 Estate of Alexander Calder/Artists Rights Society (ARS), New York
I.21, I.22, I.24, I.25 The Museum of Modern Art, New York. Purchase. Digital Image © The Museum of Modern Art/Licensed by SCALA/Art Resource, NY. © 2006 Artists Rights Society (ARS), New York/Beeldrecht, Amsterdam
I.23 The Museum of Modern Art, New York. Gift of Nelly van Doesburg. Digital Image © The Museum of Modern Art/Licensed by SCALA/Art Resource, NY. © 2006 Artists Rights Society (ARS), New York/Beeldrecht, Amsterdam
12.1, 12.6, 12.7, 12.8, 12.9, 12.10, 12.11, 12.12, 12.13, 12.17, 12.18, 12.19, 12.20, 12.21, 12.24, 12.25 Scala/Art Resource, NY
12.2 Alinari/Art Resource, NY
12.3 Galleria degli Uffizi, Florence, Italy/Bridgeman Art Library
12.4, 12.14 © Canali Photobank
12.15a From John White, Duccio, published by Thames & Hudson Ltd./By permission of Thames & Hudson Ltd., London
12.15b Quattrone, Florence
12.16 From John White, Duccio, published by Thames & Hudson Ltd./By permission of Thames & Hudson Ltd., London
12.22 Santa Croce, Florence, Italy/Bridgeman Art Library
12.23 Nicolo Orsi Battaglini/Art Resource, NY
12.26, 12.27 © Paul M.R. Maeyaert
12.28 Erich Lessing/Art Resource, NY
12.29, 12.30 Giraudon/Art Resource, NY
13.1, 13.31 © Canali Photobank
13.2, 13.3, 13.4, 13.7, 13.10, 13.11, 13.12, 13.13, 13.15, 13.16, 13.20, 13.21, 13.23, 13.24, 13.26, 13.27, 13.29, 13.30, 13.35, 13.39, 13.40, 13.41, 13.42, 13.43, 13.45a, b, 13.47, 13.48, 13.49, 13.50, 13.51, 13.53, 13.54, 13.57, 13.58, 13.62, 13.64, 13.69, 13.72, 13.73 Scala/Art Resource, NY
13.9, 13.25, 13.28, 13.33, 13.37, 13.38, 13.44b Alinari/Art Resource, NY
13.14 Drawing by Thomas Czarnowski, New York
13.17 Nimatallah/Art Resource, NY
13.18, 13.19 © The Trustees of The British Museum
13.22 Quattrone, Florence
13.32 Image © 2006 Board of Trustees, National Gallery of Art, Washington, DC, Samuel H. Kress Collection. 1957.14.658.b
13.36 Image © 2006 Board of Trustees, National Gallery of Art, Washington, DC, Widener Collection. 1942.9.8. (604)/PA
13.44a, 13.67 Erich Lessing/Art Resource, NY
13.46, 13.52 © Canali Photobank, Milan, on licence of the Ministero dei Beni Culturali di Arezzo
13.55 Réunion des Musées Nationaux/Art Resource, NY
13.56, 13.59, 13.66, 13.68 © National Gallery, London
13.60, 13.61 The Metropolitan Museum of Art, The Cloisters Collection, 1956 (56.70). Photograph © 1996 The Metropolitan Museum of Art
13.63, 13.65 © Paul M.R. Maeyaert/© St. Baafskathedraal Gent
13.70 Museum of Fine Arts, Boston. Gift of Mr. and Mrs. Henry Lee Higginson, 93.153. Photograph © 2006 Museum of Fine Arts, Boston
13.71a, b The Metropolitan Museum of Art, Bequest of Benjamin Altman, 1913 (14.40.626). Photograph © 1981 The Metropolitan Museum of Art
Connection picture p. 483 Timothy McCarthy/Art Resource, NY
W7.1 The Palace Museum, Beijing
W7.2 Scala/Art Resource, NY
14.1, 14.5, 14.12, 14.14, 14.18, 14.19, 14.22, 14.29, 14.31, 14.32, 14.37, 14.42, 14.46, 14.47, 14.51, 14.52 Scala/Art Resource, NY
14.2 Bridgeman-Giraudon/Art Resource, NY
14.3, 14.33 © Canali Photobank
14.7 © The Trustees of The British Museum
14.10 Photo by James Morris, London. Courtesy of Axiom, London
14.11 The Royal Collection © 2006, Her Majesty Queen Elizabeth II
14.13 © akg-images
14.15, 14.30 Erich Lessing/Art Resource, NY
14.16, 14.39, 14.49 Réunion des Musées Nationaux/Art Resource, NY
14.17 Staatliche Graphische Sammlung, Munich, Kupferstichkabinett
14.20, 14.21, 14.23, 14.24, 14.25, 14.27, 14.28, 14.34, 14.35, 14.36, 14.38 Photo Vatican Museums/A. Bracchetti - P. Zigrossi © 2000
14.26 © akg-images/Rabatti-Domingie
14.40, 14.44 © National Gallery, London
14.41a Image © 2006 Board of Trustees, National Gallery of Art, Washington, DC, Samuel H. Kress Collection, 1957.14.737.a
14.41b Image © 2006 Board of Trustees, National Gallery of Art, Washington, DC, Samuel H. Kress Collection, 1957.14.737.b
14.43 Cameraphoto/Art Resource, NY
14.45 Copyright The Frick Collection, New York
14.48 Courtesy Staatliche Kunstsammlungen Dresden. Gemäldegalerie Alte Meister. Photo: H.-P. Klut
14.50 © akg-images/Cameraphoto
14.53 Isabella Stewart Gardner Museum, Boston/Bridgeman Art Library
Connection on p. 552 Scala/Art Resource, NY
15.1, 15.3, 15.5, 15.6, 15.8a, b, 15.13, 15.14, 15.15, 15.17, 15.20, 15.25 Scala/Art Resource, NY
15.2, 15.7 Erich Lessing/Art Resource, NY
15.4 © National Gallery, London
15.9 Alinari/Art Resource, NY
15.10 Milwaukee Art Museum, Layton Art Collection, Gift of the Family of Mrs. Fred Vogel, Jr
15.12 © Canali Photobank
15.16 The Metropolitan Museum of Art, Gift of Mr. and Mrs. Charles Wrightsman, 1978 (1978.416). Photograph © 2003 The Metropolitan Museum of Art
15.18 Lauros-Giraudon/Art Resource, NY
15.21 © Angelo Hornak Library
15.24 RIBA Library Photographs Collection
16.1, 16.2, 16.9 Erich Lessing/Art Resource, NY
16.3, 16.4, 16.5, 16.10, 16.18, 16.22 Scala/Art Resource, NY
16.6 © akg-images
16.7, 16.8 Bildarchiv Preussischer Kulturbesitz/Art Resource, NY
16.11 Artothek/Blauel/Gnamm
16.12 The Metropolitan Museum of Art. Gift of Junius S. Morgan, 1919. (19.73.209)
16.13 The Metropolitan Museum of Art. Harris Brisbane Dick Fund, 1943. (43.106.1)
16.14, 16.16 Giraudon/Art Resource, NY
16.15 © Musée d'Unterlinden, Colmar, France. Photo: O. Zimmermann
16.17, 16.19 Artothek
16.20 City of Bristol Museum and Art Gallery, England/Bridgeman Art Library
16.21 Bridgeman Art Library
17.1, 17.4, 17.18a, b, 17.19a, b, 17.21, 17.22, 17.23, 17.24, 17.25, 17.26, 17.27, 17.29, 17.30, 17.52, 17.53 Scala/Art Resource, NY
17.2, 17.43 Bildarchiv Preussischer Kulturbesitz/Art Resource, NY
17.6 © Achim Bednorz Architekturfotografie
17.7 Alinari/Art Resource, NY
17.8 © Achim Bednorz Architekturfotografie
17.10, 17.54 Erich Lessing/Art Resource, NY
17.11 © akg-images/Erich Lessing
17.12 Fotomas Index UK
17.13, 17.14, 17.15, 17.48 Réunion des Musées Nationaux/Art Resource, NY
17.17 © Angelo Hornak Library
17.20 © akg-images/Pirozzi
17.28 © akg-images/Rabatti-Domingie
17.31 The Detroit Institute of Arts, Gift of Mr. Leslie H. Green. Photograph © 1984 The Detroit Institute of Arts
17.32 The Metropolitan Museum of Art, Gift of Harry Payne Bingham, 1937 (37.162). Photograph © 1983 The Metropolitan Museum of Art
17.33, 17.35, 17.37, 17.39, 17.50, 17.55 © National Gallery, London
17.34 Peter Willi/Bridgeman Art Library
17.36 Stadelsches Kunstinstitut, Frankfurt. Photo: Artothek
17.38, 17.41, 17.42 Rijksmuseum, Amsterdam
17.40 Staatliche Museen Kassel, Gemäldegalerie Alte Meister
17.44 Museum the Rembrandt House, Amsterdam
17.45 Reproduced by permission of Trustees of the Wallace Collection, London
17.46 Philadelphia Museum of Art, John G. Johnson Collection
17.47 Stadelsches Kunstinstitut, Frankfurt and Artothek-Blauel/Gnamm
17.49 Photograph © Mauritshuis, The Hague. Royal Cabinet of Paintings Mauritshuis The Hague
17.51 Kunsthistorisches Museum, Vienna
17.56 © Oronoz
17.57 Image © 2006 Board of Trustees, National Gallery of Art, Washington, DC, Ailsa Mellon Bruce Fund. 1963.5.1. (1905)/PA
17.58 Reproduced by permission of the Trustees of the Wallace Collection, London
17.59 Courtesy the Board of Trustees of the Walker Art Gallery, National Museums Liverpool
W8.1 Victoria and Albert Museum, London/Art Resource, NY
W8.2 Freer Gallery of Art and Arthur M. Sackler Gallery, Smithsonian Institution, Washington DC. Purchase. F1942.15a
W8.3 © akg-images/Jean-Louis Nou
18.1 Victoria and Albert Museum, London/Art Resource, NY

18.2, 18.15, 18.16 Scala/Art Resource, NY
18.3, 18.12 © National Gallery, London
18.4, 18.5, 18.8 Réunion des Musées Nationaux/Art Resource, NY
18.6 Image © 2006 Board of Trustees, National Gallery of Art, Washington, DC, Chester Dale Collection. 1943.7.2
18.7 By the kind permission of the Trustees of the Wallace Collection, London
18.9 Museum of Fine Arts, Boston. The Forsyth Wickes Collection, 65.2655. Photograph © 2006 Museum of Fine Arts, Boston
18.10 © akg-images
18.11 Image © 2006 Board of Trustees, National Gallery of Art, Washington, DC, Andrew W. Mellon Collection. 1937.1.92
18.13 HIP/Art Resource, NY
18.14 © akg-images/Erich Lessing
18.17, 18.19 Erich Lessing/Art Resource, NY
18.20 John Bethell/Bridgeman Art Library
18.22, 18.23 A. F. Kersting, London
18.24 The National Museum of Fine Art, Stockholm. Photo: Hans Thorwid
18.25 Réunion des Musées Nationaux/Art Resource, NY
18.26 Virginia Museum of Fine Arts, Richmond, Virginia. The Adolph D. and Wilkins C. Williams Fund. Photo Katherine Wetzel. © Virginia Museum of Fine Arts
18.27 Museum of Fine Arts, Boston. Gift of Joseph W., William B., and Edward H.R. Revere, 30.781 Photograph © 2006 Museum of Fine Arts, Boston
18.28 National Gallery of Canada, Ottawa (Gift of the Duke of Westminster, 1918)
19.1 The Metropolitan Museum of Art, Bequest of Benjamin Altman, 1913 (14.40.687). Photograph © 1990 The Metropolitan Museum of Art
19.2, 19.3, 19.10, 19.11, 19.13, 19.14 Réunion des Musées Nationaux/Art Resource, NY
19.4 The Metropolitan Museum of Art, Catharine Lorillard Wolfe Collection, Wolfe Fund, 1931 (31.45). Photograph © 1995 The Metropolitan Museum of Art
19.5 Musées Royaux des Beaux-Arts de Belgique, Museum of Modern Art, Bruxelles Inv. 3260 Ekta nr MD019 © MRBAB/KMSKB (Photo Cussac)
19.6 Réunion des Musées Nationaux/Art Resource, NY
19.7 A. F. Kersting, London
19.8 © Paul M.R. Maeyaert
19.9 Scala/Art Resource, NY
19.12 © photo Musée de l'Armée, Paris
19.15 Museum of Fine Arts, Boston, George Nixon Black Fund. (inv. 34.129). Photograph © 2006 Museum of Fine Arts, Boston
19.16 Art Resource, NY
19.18 Laurie Schneider Adams
19.20 M. Freeman/Bruce Coleman, Inc.
19.21 Architect of the Capitol, Washington DC. Photo: National Graphic Center, Falls Church, VA
19.22 National Museum of American Art, Washington DC/Art Resource, NY
19.23 Library of Congress
20.1 © akg-images/Jürgen Raible
20.2 Leo Sorel, New York
20.3 © Angelo Hornak Library
20.4 Bridgeman-Giraudon/Art Resource, NY
20.5 © The Trustees of The British Museum
20.6, 20.8, 20.9, 20.10, 20.11, 20.12, 20.13 Réunion des Musées Nationaux/Art Resource, NY
20.7 Giraudon/Art Resource, NY
20.14, 20.15 © Oronoz
20.16, 20.18 All rights reserved. © Museo Nacional del Prado - Madrid
20.17 Erich Lessing/Art Resource, NY
20.19 Staatliche Kunstsammlungen, Dresden
20.20 The Metropolitan Museum of Art, Bequest of Mary Stillman Harkness, 1950 (50.145.8). Photograph © 1992 The Metropolitan Museum of Art
20.21 © The Cleveland Museum of Art, 2001, Bequest of John L. Severance, 1942.647
20.22 The Metropolitan Museum of Art, Gift of Mrs. Russell Sage, 1908 (08.228). Photograph © 1995 The Metropolitan Museum of Art
20.23 Museum of Fine Arts, Boston. Bequest of Henry Lee Shattuck in memory of the late Ralph W. Gray, 1971.154. Photograph © 2006 Museum of Fine Arts, Boston
20.24 Amon Carter Museum, Fort Worth, Texas 1966.1
20.25 Image © 2006 Board of Trustees, National Gallery of Art, Washington, DC, Paul Mellon Collection. 1965.16.347
20.26 Image © 2006 Board of Trustees, National Gallery of Art, Washington, DC, Gift of Edgar William and Bernice Chrysler Garbisch. 1980.62.15
21.1, 21.4, 21.25, 21.26 Réunion des Musées Nationaux/Art Resource, NY
21.2 The Metropolitan Museum of Art, Gift of Cornelius Vanderbilt, 1887 (87.25). Photograph © 1997 The Metropolitan Museum of Art
21.3 Staatliche Kunstsammlungen Dresden
21.5 Giraudon/Art Resource, NY
21.6 The Metropolitan Museum of Art, Bequest of Mrs. H. O. Havermeyer, 1929. The H. O. Havermeyer Collection (29.100.129). Photograph © 1985 The Metropolitan Museum of Art
21.7 The Walters Art Museum, Baltimore
21.9, 21.15 © akg-images
21.10, 21.14, 21.30 Bibliothèque Nationale de France, Paris
21.11 Courtesy George Eastman House, Rochester, NY
21.12 Harry Ransom Humanities Research Center, The University of Texas at Austin, Gernsheim Collection
21.13 © Bettmann/Corbis
21.16 National Museum of Photography, Film & Television/Science & Society Picture Library
21.17, 21.18 Library of Congress, Washington, DC
21.19 The Museum of Modern Art, New York. New Purchase. Photograph © 2006 The Museum of Modern Art, New York/Art Resource, NY
21.20 Tate Gallery, London/Art Resource, NY
21.21 Private collection
21.22 The Metropolitan Museum of Art, Rogers Fund, 1923 (23.94). Photograph © 1999 The Metropolitan Museum of Art
21.23 The Metropolitan Museum of Art, Fletcher Fund, 1924 (24.108). Photograph © 1999 The Metropolitan Museum of Art
21.24 Philadelphia Museum of Art, Purchased with the W. P. Wilstach Fund, 1899
21.27 Victoria and Albert Museum, London/Art Resource, NY
21.28 Three Lions/Hulton Archives/Getty Images
21.29 National Park Service/Richard Frear
21.31 A. F. Kersting, London
21.32 Marvin Trachtenberg
22.1 La Documentation francaise/Interphotothèque. Photo: Andre Guyomard/Air France
22.2 Spectrum Colour Library, London
22.4 Bibliothèque Nationale de France, Paris
22.5, 22.7, 22.8, 22.15, 22.16, 22.23 Réunion des Musées Nationaux/Art Resource, NY
22.6 The Samuel Courtauld Trust, Courtauld Institute of Art Gallery, London
22.9 Museum of Fine Arts, Boston. Gift of Mr. and Mrs. John McAndrew, 69.49. Photograph © 2006 Museum of Fine Arts, Boston
22.10 Sterling and Francine Clark Art Institute, Williamstown, Massachusetts, USA
22.11 Bridgeman-Giraudon/Art Resource, NY
22.12 Eadweard Muybridge Collection, Kingston Museum
22.13 Image © 2006 Board of Trustees, National Gallery of Art, Washington, DC, Chester Dale Collection. 1963.10.94. (1758)/PA
22.14 Philadelphia Museum of Art, The Louis E. Stern Collection, 1963. Photo: Lynn Rosenthal
22.17 The Metropolitan Museum of Art, Purchased with special contributions and purchase funds given or bequeathed by friends of the Museum, 1967 (67.241). Photograph © 1989 The Metropolitan Museum of Art
22.18 Denver Art Museum Collection. Funds from the Helen Dill bequest, 1935.14. © Denver Art Museum 2006
22.19 Image © 2006 Board of Trustees, National Gallery of Art, Washington, DC, Chester Dale Collection. 1963.10.179
22.20 Fondation Beyeler, Riehen/Basel
22.21 Image © 2006 Board of Trustees, National Gallery of Art, Washington, DC, Ailsa Mellon Bruce Fund. 1970.17.58
22.22 William Hood Dunwoody Fund, The Minneapolis Institute of Arts
22.24 Musée Rodin, Paris S.788 Photo: A. Rzepka
22.25 Giraudon/Art Resource, NY
22.26 The Museum of Modern Art, New York. Digital Image © The Museum of Modern Art/Licensed by SCALA/Art Resource, NY
22.27 © Estate of the Artist, Courtesy of Michael Rosenfeld Gallery, New York
22.28 Image © 2006 Board of Trustees, National Gallery of Art, Washington, DC, Gift of W. L. and May T. Mellon Foundation. 1943.13.1
22.29 Museum of Fine Arts, Boston. Gift of Mary Louisa Boit, Julia Overing Boit, Jane Hubbard Boit, and Florence D. Boit in memory of their father, Edward Darley Boit, 19.124. Photograph © 2006 Museum of Fine Arts, Boston
22.30 The Detroit Institute of Arts, Gift of Dexter M. Ferry, Jr. Photograph © 1988 The Detroit Institute of Arts
22.31 from Punch, December 7, 1878, p. 254, Reproduced with the permission of Punch, Ltd
W9.1 Private Collection
W9.2, W9.3, W9.5 Victoria and Albert Museum, London/Art Resource, NY
W9.4, W9.9 © The Trustees of The British Museum
W9.6 Private Collection
W9.7 The Bridgeman Art Library
W9.8 © Réunion des Musées Nationaux/Art Resource, NY
W9.10 The Whitworth Art Gallery, The University of Manchester
23.1 Image © 2006 Board of Trustees, National Gallery of Art, Washington, DC, Chester Dale Collection. 1963.10.221
23.2 The Metropolitan Museum of Art, Harris Brisbane Dick Fund, 1932 (32.88.12). Photograph © 1996 The Metropolitan Museum of Art
23.3 The Foundation E.G. Buhrle Collection, Zurich
23.4, 23.14, 23.19, 23.24 Réunion des Musées Nationaux/Art Resource, NY
23.5 By kind permission of the Provost and Fellows of King's College, Cambridge, England. Keynes Collection. Photo © Fitzwilliam Museum University of Cambridge, England
23.6 Philadelphia Museum of Art, Purchased with the W. P. Wilstach Fund, 1937. Photo: Graydon Wood
23.7 Scala/Art Resource, NY
23.8 The Art Institute of Chicago, Helen Birch Bartlett Memorial Collection, 1926.224. Photography © The Art Institute of Chicago
23.9 The Metropolitan Museum of Art. Bequest of Miss Adelaide Milton de Groot, 1967 (67.187.35). Photograph © 1989 The Metropolitan Museum of Art
23.10 The Art Institute of Chicago, Helen Birch Bartlett Memorial Collection, 1926.224. Photography © The Art Institute of Chicago
23.11, 23.12, 23.18 Amsterdam, Van Gogh Museum (Vincent van Gogh Foundation)
23.13 The Brooklyn Museum of Art/The Bridgeman Art Library
23.15, 23.16 Amsterdam, Van Gogh Museum (Vincent van Gogh Foundation)

23.17 The Museum of Modern Art, New York. Acquired through the Lillie P. Bliss Bequest. Digital Image © The Museum of Modern Art/Licensed by SCALA/Art Resource, NY
23.20 Albright-Knox Art Gallery, Buffalo, New York. General Purchase Funds, 1946
23.21 Image © 2006 Board of Trustees, National Gallery of Art, Washington, DC, Chester Dale Collection. 1963.10.150 (1814)/PA
23.22 The Samuel Courtauld Trust, Courtauld Institute of Art Gallery, London
23.23, 23.30, 23.31 Erich Lessing/Art Resource, NY
23.25 © Oslo National Gallery, 2006. Photographer: J. Lathion. M 514. © 2006 The Munch Museum/The Munch-Ellingsen Group/Artists Rights Society (ARS), New York
23.26 Museum of Fine Arts, Boston. Ernest Wadsworth Longfellow Fund, 59.301. Photograph © 2006 Museum of Fine Arts, Boston. © 2006 The Munch Museum/The Munch-Ellingsen Group/Artists Rights Society (ARS), New York
23.27 Princeton University Library. Aubrey Beardsley Collection. Manuscripts Division. Department of Rare Books and Special Collections, Princeton University Library
23.28 Martin Charles, London
23.29 © Art on File/Corbis
23.32 The Museum of Modern Art, New York, NY. Gift of Nelson A. Rockefeller. (252.1954). Digital Image © The Museum of Modern Art/Licensed by SCALA/Art Resource, NY
W10.1 © David T. Horwell Photography
W10.2 Réunion des Musées Nationaux/Art Resource, NY
24.1 The Art Institute of Chicago, Helen Birch Bartlett Memorial Collection, 1926.253. Photography © The Art Institute of Chicago. © 2006 Estate of Pablo Picasso/Artists Rights Society (ARS), New York
24.2 Albright Knox Art Gallery, Buffalo, NY. Gift of Seymour H. Knox, 1927. © 2006 Succession H. Matisse, Paris/Artists Rights Society (ARS), New York
24.3 Statens Museum for Kunst, Copenhagen. © 2006 Succession H. Matisse, Paris/Artists Rights Society (ARS), New York
24.4 San Francisco Museum of Modern Art. Bequest of Elise S. Haas. Photography: Ben Blackwell. © 2006 Succession H. Matisse, Paris/Artists Rights Society (ARS), New York
24.5 The Museum of Modern Art, New York. Purchase. Digital Image © The Museum of Modern Art/Licensed by SCALA/Art Resource, NY. © by Dr. Wolfgang & Ingeborg Henze-Ketterer, Wichtrach/Bern
24.6 Ludwig Museum, Cologne/Rheinisches Bildarchiv, Cologne © by Dr. Wolfgang & Ingeborg Henze-Ketterer, Wichtrach/Bern
24.7 The Nelson-Atkins Museum of Art, Kansas City, Missouri, (Gift of the Friends of Art). © Nolde-Stiftung Seebüll
24.8 © Nolde-Stiftung Seebull. Photo: Ralph Kleinhempel, Hamburg
24.9 The Museum of Modern Art, New York. Nelson A. Rockefeller Fund (by exchange). Digital Image © The Museum of Modern Art/Licensed by SCALA/Art Resource, NY. © 2006 Artists Rights Society (ARS), New York/ADAGP, Paris
24.10 Solomon R. Guggenheim Museum, New York, Gift, 1941. Photograph by David Heald © The Solomon R. Guggenheim Foundation, New York. © The Solomon R. Guggenheim Foundation, New York (FN 41.283). © 2006 Artists Rights Society (ARS), New York/ADAGP, Paris
24.11 Collection Walker Art Center, Minneapolis, Gift of the T. B. Walker Foundation, Gilbert Walker Fund, 1942
24.12 © The Trustees of The British Museum. © 2006 Artists Rights Society (ARS), New York/VG Bild-Kunst, Bonn
24.13 Scala/Art Resource, NY. © 2006 Succession H. Matisse, Paris/Artists Rights Society (ARS), New York
24.14 The Museum of Modern Art, New York. Gift of Nelson A. Rockefeller in honor of Alfred H. Barr, Jr. Digital Image © The Museum of Modern Art/Licensed by SCALA/Art Resource, NY. © 2006 Succession H. Matisse, Paris/Artists Rights Society (ARS), New York
24.15 The Museum of Modern Art, New York. Mrs. Simon Guggenheim Fund. Digital Image © The Museum of Modern Art/Licensed by SCALA/Art Resource, NY. © 2006 Succession H. Matisse, Paris/Artists Rights Society (ARS), New York
24.16 Art Gallery of Ontario, Toronto. © 2006 Succession H. Matisse, Paris/Artists Rights Society (ARS), New York
24.17 Private collection, formerly Collection Henri Matisse
24.18 Musée National d'Art Moderne, Centre Georges Pompidou, France, RMN/Art Resource, NY. © 2006 Succession H. Matisse, Paris/Artists Rights Society (ARS), New York
24.19 The Museum of Modern Art, New York. The Louis E. Stern Collection. Digital Image © The Museum of Modern Art/Licensed by SCALA/Art Resource, NY. © 2006 Succession H. Matisse, Paris/Artists Rights Society (ARS), New York
W11.1 © abm - archives barbier-mueller - Studio Ferrazzini-Bouchet, Genève
W11.2 Photo: Ursula Held, Ecublens
W11.3, W11.4, W11.5 © The Trustees of The British Museum
W11.6 Bildarchiv Preussischer Kulturbesitz/Art Resource, NY
25.1 The Metropolitan Museum of Art. Bequest of Gertrude Stein, 1947 (47.106). Photograph © 1996 The Metropolitan Museum of Art. © 2006 Estate of Pablo Picasso/Artists Rights Society (ARS), New York
25.2 The Museum of Modern Art, New York. Acquired through the Lillie P. Bliss Bequest. Digital Image © The Museum of Modern Art/Licensed by SCALA/Art Resource, NY © 2006 Estate of Pablo Picasso/Artists Rights Society (ARS), New York
25.3 © abm - archives barbier-mueller - Studio Ferrazzini-Bouchet, Genève
25.4 © Africa-Museum Tervuren, Belgium. (Photo R. Asselberghs)
25.5 The Baltimore Museum of Art, The Cone Collection, formed by Dr. Claribel Cone and Miss Etta Cone of Baltimore, Maryland (BMA 1950.215). © 2006 Artists Rights Society (ARS), New York/ADAGP, Paris
25.6 Oeffentliche Kunstsammlung Basel, Kunstmuseum, Gift of Raoul La Roche, 1952. Photo: Oeffentliche Kunstsammlung Basel, Martin Bühler/© 2006 Artists Rights Society (ARS), New York/ADAGP, Paris
25.7 Image © 2006 Board of Trustees, National Gallery of Art, Washington, DC, Patrons' Permanent Fund and Gift of Mitchell P. Rales. 2002.1.1/SC. © 2006 Estate of Pablo Picasso/Artists Rights Society (ARS), New York
25.8 The Museum of Modern Art, New York. Purchase. Digital Image © The Museum of Modern Art/Licensed by SCALA/Art Resource, NY. © 2006 Estate of Pablo Picasso/Artists Rights Society (ARS), New York
25.9 Réunion des Musées Nationaux/Art Resource, NY. © 2006 Estate of Pablo Picasso/Artists Rights Society (ARS), New York. Photo: Beatrice Hatala
25.10 The Museum of Modern Art, New York. Mrs. Simon Guggenheim Fund. Digital Image © The Museum of Modern Art/Licensed by SCALA/Art Resource, NY. © 2006 Estate of Pablo Picasso/Artists Rights Society (ARS), New York
25.11 The Museum of Modern Art, New York (Gift of Mrs. Simon Guggenheim). Digital Image © The Museum of Modern Art/Licensed by SCALA/Art Resource, NY. © 2006 Estate of Pablo Picasso/Artists Rights Society (ARS), New York
25.12, 25.13 Museo Nacional Centro de Arte Reina Sofia, Photographic Archive, Madrid, Spain. © 2006 Estate of Pablo Picasso/Artists Rights Society (ARS), New York
25.14 The Museum of Modern Art, New York. Acquired through the Lillie P. Bliss Bequest. Digital Image © The Museum of Modern Art/Licensed by SCALA/Art Resource, NY
25.15 Philadelphia Museum of Art: A. E. Gallatin Collection, 1950. © 2006 Artists Rights Society (ARS), New York/ADAGP, Paris
25.16 Photo courtesy of Carroll Janis, New York. © 2006 Mondrian/Holtzman Trust c/o HCR International Warrenton VA USA
25.17 The Museum of Modern Art, New York. Given anonymously. (73.1943). Digital Image © The Museum of Modern Art/Licensed by SCALA/Art Resource, NY. © 2006 Mondrian/Holtzman Trust c/o HCR International Warrenton VA USA
25.18 Philadelphia Museum of Art: Louise and Walter Arensberg Collection, 1950. © 2006 Artists Rights Society (ARS), New York/ADAGP, Paris/Succession Marcel Duchamp
25.19a Private Collection. Courtesy Acquavella Galleries. © 2006 Artists Rights Society (ARS), New York/ADAGP, Paris
25.19b The Museum of Modern Art, New York. Acquired through the Lillie P. Bliss Bequest. Digital Image © The Museum of Modern Art/Licensed by SCALA/Art Resource, NY. © 2006 Artists Rights Society (ARS), New York/ADAGP, Paris
25.20 The Museum of Modern Art, New York. Gift of the American Tobacco Company, Inc. Digital Image © The Museum of Modern Art/Licensed by SCALA/Art Resource, NY. Art © Estate of Stuart Davis/Licensed by VAGA, New York, NY
25.21 Schomburg Center, The New York Public Library/Art Resource, NY
25.22, 25.24 State Russian Museum, St. Petersburg, Russia/www.bridgeman.co.uk
25.23 State Tretiakov Gallery, Moscow
25.25 The Art Archive. © 2006 Artists Rights Society (ARS), New York/ADAGP, Paris
25.26 Philadelphia Museum of Art, Louise and Walter Arensberg Collection, 1950. © 2006 Artists Rights Society (ARS), New York/ADAGP, Paris
25.27 Photo by permission of Sidney Geist. © 2006 Artists Rights Society (ARS), New York/ADAGP, Paris
25.28 Photo courtesy of Carroll Janis, New York. © 2006 Mondrian/Holtzman Trust c/o HCR International Warrenton VA USA. © 2006 Artists Rights Society (ARS), New York/ADAGP, Paris
25.29, 25.33 Ezra Stoller © Esto. All rights reserved
25.32 © Scott Francis/Esto
25.34 Centraal Museum, Utrecht
25.35 Solomon R. Guggenheim Museum, New York, Gift, 1937. 37.262. Photograph by David Heald © The Solomon R. Guggenheim Foundation, New York. © 2006 Artists Rights Society (ARS), New York/ADAGP, Paris
25.37 © Architectural Association Photograph/Petra Hagen Hodgson
25.38 Anthony Scibilia/Art Resource, NY
25.39 Erich Lessing/Art Resource, NY
25.40 © Angelo Hornak/Corbis
26.1 Philadelphia Museum of Art, Louise and Walter Arensberg Collection, 1950. © 2006 Artists Rights Society (ARS), New York/ADAGP, Paris/Succession Marcel Duchamp

26.2 Photo courtesy of Carroll Janis, New York. © 2006 Artists Rights Society (ARS), New York/ADAGP, Paris/Succession Marcel Duchamp

26.3 The Museum of Modern Art, New York, Katherine S. Dreier Bequest. Digital Image © The Museum of Modern Art/Licensed by SCALA/Art Resource, NY. © 2006 Artists Rights Society (ARS), New York/ADAGP, Paris/Succession Marcel Duchamp

26.4 The Museum of Modern Art, New York. Purchase. (457.1937). Digital Image © The Museum of Modern Art/Licensed by SCALA/Art Resource, NY. © 2006 Artists Rights Society (ARS), New York/VG Bild-Kunst, Bonn

26.5 Photo courtesy of Carroll Janis, New York. © 2006 Artists Rights Society (ARS), New York/VG Bild-Kunst, Bonn

26.6 The Museum of Modern Art, New York, James Thrall Soby Fund. Digital Image © The Museum of Modern Art/Licensed by SCALA/Art Resource, NY. © 2006 Man Ray Trust/© 2006 Artists Rights Society (ARS), New York/ADAGP, Paris

26.7 Scala/Art Resource, NY. © 2006 Artists Rights Society (ARS), New York/SIAE, Rome

26.8 Musée National d'Art Moderne, Centre Georges Pompidou, Inv.: AM 1993-117. © CNAC/MNAM/Dist. Réunion des Musées Nationaux/Art Resource, NY. © 2006 Man Ray Trust/Artists Rights Society (ARS), New York/ADAGP, Paris

26.9 The Museum of Modern Art, New York, Nelson A. Rockefeller Fund. Digital Image © The Museum of Modern Art/Licensed by SCALA/Art Resource, NY. © 2006 Artists Rights Society (ARS), New York/VG Bild-Kunst, Bonn

26.10 Bildarchiv Preussischer Kulturbesitz/Art Resource, NY

26.11 The Museum of Modern Art, New York. Given anonymously. Digital Image © The Museum of Modern Art/Licensed by SCALA/Art Resource, NY. © 2006 Salvador Dali, Gala-Salvador Dali Foundation/Artists Rights Society (ARS), New York

26.12 Philadelphia Museum of Art, A. E. Gallatin Collection, 1952. © 2006 Successió Miró/Artists Rights Society (ARS), New York/ADAGP, Paris

26.13 Fondation Beyeler, Riehen/Basel. © 2006 Successió Miró/Artists Rights Society (ARS), New York/ADAGP, Paris

26.14 The Museum of Modern Art, New York. Purchase. Digital Image © The Museum of Modern Art/Licensed by SCALA/Art Resource, NY. © 2006 C. Herscovici, Brussels/Artists Rights Society (ARS), New York

26.15 The Art Institute of Chicago, Joseph Winterbotham Collection, 1970.426. Photography © The Art Institute of Chicago. © 2006 C. Herscovici, Brussels/Artists Rights Society (ARS), New York

26.16 The Museum of Modern Art, New York, Gift of D. and J. de Menil. Digital Image © The Museum of Modern Art/Licensed by SCALA/Art Resource, NY. © 2006 Artists Rights Society (ARS), New York/ADAGP, Paris

26.17 Private collection

26.18 Photo by James Thrall Soby, 1942. Collection of Elaine Lustig Cohen, New York

26.19 Photo courtesy of Carroll Janis, New York. © 2006 Artists Rights Society (ARS), New York/ADAGP, Paris © 2006 Mondrian/Holtzman Trust, c/o HCR International Warrenton VA USA

26.20 Photo courtesy of David Finn. Reproduced by permission of the Henry Moore Foundation

26.21 Tate Gallery,London/Art Resource, NY. The work illustrated has been reproduced by permission of the Henry Moore Foundation

26.22 Whitney Museum of American Art, New York. Purchase, with funds from the Friends of the Whitney Museum of American Art, and exchange. 61.46. Photograph © 2006: Whitney Museum of American Art. Photography by Sandak, Inc./G. K. Hall & Company. © 2006 Estate of Alexander Calder/Artists Rights Society (ARS), New York

26.23 The Art Institute of Chicago, Friends of American Art Collection. 1930.934. Photograph by Bob Hashimoto. Photography © The Art Institute of Chicago

26.24 Hampton University Museum, Hampton, Virginia. © 2006 The Jacob and Gwendolyn Lawrence Foundation, Seattle/Artists Rights Society (ARS), New York

26.25 The Museum of Modern Art, New York, Mrs. Simon Guggenheim Fund. Digital Image © The Museum of Modern Art/Licensed by SCALA/Art Resource, NY

26.26 James VanDerZee Collection. © Donna Mussenden VanDerZee

26.27 The Museum of Modern Art, New York, Stephen R. Currier Memorial Fund. Digital Image © The Museum of Modern Art/Licensed by SCALA/Art Resource, NY./ © Walker Evans Archive, The Metropolitan Museum of Art

26.28 The Oakland Museum of California, City of Oakland. Gift of Paul S. Taylor. A87.137.40059-3. © The Dorothea Lange Collection

26.29 Bob Schalkwijk/Art Resource, NY/© 2006 Banco de Mexico Diego Rivera & Frida Kahlo Museums Trust. Av. Cinco de Mayo No. 2, Col. Centro, Del. Cauahtémoc 06059, Mexico, D. F. and Instituto Nacional de Bellas Artes Y Litteratura

26.30 CENIDIAP/INBA. Biblioteca de las Artes, CENART (México). © 2006 Banco de Mexico Diego Rivera & Frida Kahlo Museums Trust. Av. Cinco de Mayo No.2, Col. Centro, Del. Cauahtémoc 06059, Mexico, D. F. and Instituto Nacional de Bellas Artes Y Litteratura

26.31 Bob Schalkwijk/Art Resource, NY. © 2006 Banco de Mexico Diego Rivera & Frida Kahlo Museums Trust. Av. Cinco de Mayo No. 2, Col. Centro, Del. Cauahtémoc 06059, Mexico, D. F. and Instituto Nacional de Bellas Artes Y Litteratura

26.32 The Art Institute of Chicago, Alfred Stieglitz Collection, 1949.795. Photography © The Art Institute of Chicago

26.33 Collection Center for Creative Photography, The University of Arizona. © 1981 Arizona Board of Regents

26.34 Acquired 1937, The Phillips Collection, Washington, DC

26.35 Colorado Springs Fine Arts Center, Anonymous Gift

26.36 Whitney Museum of American Art, New York. 50th Anniversary Gift of Mr. and Mrs. R. Crosby Kemper, (81.9). Photograph by Malcolm Varon, NYC © 1987: Whitney Museum of Art, New York. © 2006 The Georgia O'Keeffe Foundation/Artists Rights Society (ARS), New York

26.37 The Art Institute of Chicago, Alfred Stieglitz Collection, gift of Georgia O'Keeffe. 1947.712. Photography © The Art Institute of Chicago. © 2006 The Georgia O'Keeffe Foundation/Artists Rights Society (ARS), New York

26.38 Image © 2006 Board of Trustees, National Gallery of Art, Washington, DC, Alfred Stieglitz Collection. 1980.70.242.(D-1569)/PH

26.39 Collection of Georgia Riley de Havenon, New York. Photo courtesy of the author

26.40 Seiji Togo Memorial Sompo Japan Museum of Art. Copyright © 1996, Grandma Moses Properties Co., New York

26.41 Acquired 1943. The Phillips Collection, Washington, D.C

W12.2 Corbis Images, Trustees of the Ansel Adams Publishing Rights Trust. All rights reserved

W12.3 Courtesy of Museum of Northern Arizona Photo Archives (98-09-01) (E5000db). Photo: Tony Marinella

W12.4 Courtesy of Museum of Northern Arizona Photo Archives (98-09-02) (E5000db). Photo: Tony Marinella

27.1 Solomon R. Guggenheim Museum, New York, Gift. 62.1620. Photograph by David Heald © The Solomon R. Guggenheim Foundation, New York. © 2006 Estate of Hans Hofmann/Artists Rights Society (ARS), New York

27.2 Photo courtesy of Carroll Janis, New York. © 2006 The Josef and Anni Albers Foundation/Artists Rights Society (ARS), New York

27.3 Whitney Museum of American Art, New York. Gift of Julien Levy for Maro and Natasha Gorky in memory of their father 50.17. Photograph © 2006: Whitney Museum of American Art. © 2006 Estate of Arshile Gorky/Artists Rights Society (ARS), New York

27.4 Courtesy of the Arshile Gorky Estate

27.5 Image © 2006 Board of Trustees, National Gallery of Art, Washington, DC, Ailsa Mellon Bruce Fund. 1979.13.4. © 2006 Estate of Arshile Gorky/Artists Rights Society (ARS), New York

27.6 The Museum of Modern Art, New York, Acquired through the Lillie P. Bliss Bequest. Digital Image © The Museum of Modern Art/Licensed by SCALA/Art Resource, NY. © 2006 Estate of Arshile Gorky/Artists Rights Society (ARS), New York

27.7 Bridgeman Art Library. © 2006 The Pollock-Krasner Foundation/Artists Rights Society (ARS), New York

27.8 Albert M. Bender Collection, Albert M. Bender Bequest Fund Purchase, San Francisco Museum of Modern Art, 45.1308. Photo: Ben Blackwell. © 2006 The Pollock-Krasner Foundation/Artists Rights Society (ARS), New York

27.9a © 1991 Hans Namuth Estate. Courtesy Center for Creative Photography, University of Arizona. © Estate of Hans Namuth. © 2006 The Pollock-Krasner Foundation/Artists Rights Society (ARS), New York

27.9b © Estate of Hans Namuth. © 2006. Pollock-Krasner House and Study Center, East Hampton, NY. © 2006 The Pollock-Krasner Foundation/Artists Rights Society (ARS), New York

27.10 Michal Heron/Woodfin Camp & Associates

27.11 © Buddy Mays/Corbis

27.12 The Museum of Modern Art, New York. The Sidney and Harriet Janis Collection. Digital Image © The Museum of Modern Art/Licensed by SCALA/Art Resource, NY. © 2006 The Pollock-Krasner Foundation/Artists Rights Society (ARS), New York

27.13 Whitney Museum of American Art, New York. Purchase, with funds from friends of Whitney Museum of American Art 57.10. Photograph © 2004: Whitney Museum of American Art. © 2006 The Franz Kline Estate/Artists Rights Society (ARS), New York

27.14 Whitney Museum of American Art, New York. Purchase. 55.35. Photograph © 2004: Whitney Museum of American Art. © 2006 The Willem de Kooning Foundation/Artists Rights Society (ARS), New York

27.15 The Detroit Institute of Arts, Founders Society Purchase with funds from Dr. and Mrs. Hilbert H. DeLawter. Photograph © 1991 Detroit Institute of Arts. © 2006 Helen Frankenthaler

27.16 Whitney Museum of American Art, New York. Purchase. 46.12. Photograph © 2006: Whitney Museum of American Art. Photograph by Geoffrey Clements. © 2006 Kate Rothko Prizel & Christopher Rothko/Artists Rights Society (ARS), New York
27.17 © 1998 Kate Rothko Prizel & Christopher Rothko/Artists Rights Society (ARS), New York
27.18 Tate Gallery, London/Art Resource, NY © 2006 Estate of Ad Reinhardt/Artists Rights Society (ARS), New York
27.19 The Museum of Modern Art, New York. Gift of S. I. Newhouse, Jr. Digital Image © The Museum of Modern Art/Licensed by SCALA/Art Resource, NY. © 2006 Frank Stella/Artists Rights Society (ARS), New York
27.20 The Menil Collection, Houston. Photo: Hickey-Robinson. © 2006 Frank Stella/Artists Rights Society (ARS), New York
27.21 Collection of Anne and John Marion in Fort Worth, Texas. Digital Image © The Museum of Modern Art/Licensed by SCALA/Art Resource, NY. © Ellsworth Kelly
27.22 Photo courtesy of Carroll Janis, New York. © Ellsworth Kelly. © 2006 Mondrian/Holtzman Trust c/o HCR International Warrenton VA USA
27.23 © Estate of Richard Diebenkorn. Courtesy Greenberg Van Doren Gallery
27.24 Dallas Museum of Art. Gift of Mr. and Mrs. James H. Clark. © 2006, Dallas Museum of Art. All rights reserved. © 2006 Artists Rights Society (ARS), New York/ADAGP, Paris
27.25 Friede Collection, New York
27.26 Bildarchiv Preussischer Kulturbesitz/Art Resource, NY. © 2006 The Estate of Francis Bacon, ARS, New York/DACS, London
27.27 The Metropolitan Museum of Art, Fletcher Fund, 1953. (53.87 a-i). Photograph © 1995 The Metropolitan Museum of Art. © 2006 The Isamu Noguchi Foundation and Garden Museum, New York/Artists Rights
27.28 Solomon R. Guggenheim Museum, By exchange. 67.1862. Photograph by David Heald © The Solomon R. Guggenheim Foundation, New York. Art © Estate of David Smith/Licensed by VAGA, New York, NY
27.29 Tate Gallery, London/Art Resource, NY. © 2006 Estate of Louise Nevelson/Artists Rights Society (ARS), New York
28.1 Kunsthalle, Tübingen, Collection Zundel. © 2006 Artists Rights Society (ARS), New York/DACS, London
28.2 Whitney Museum of American Art, New York. 50th Anniversary Gift of the Gilman Foundation, Inc., The Lauder Foundation, A. Alfred Taubman, an anonymous donor, and purchase. 80.32. Photograph © 2006: Whitney Museum of American Art. Art © Jasper Johns/Licensed by VAGA, New York, NY
28.3 Museum Ludwig, Cologne. Art © Jasper Johns/Licensed by VAGA, New York, NY
28.4 Photo: Maggie Nimkin. Art © Estate of Larry Rivers/Licensed by VAGA, New York, NY
28.5 Wadsworth Atheneum, Hartford, Gift of Susan Morse Hilles. Art © Robert Rauschenberg/Licensed by VAGA, New York, NY
28.6 The Andy Warhol Foundation, Inc./Art Resource, NY - © 2006 Andy Warhol Foundation for the Visual Arts/ARS, NY/TM Licensed by Campbell's Soup Co. All rights reserved
28.7 The Andy Warhol Foundation, Inc./Art Resource, NY. © 2006 Andy Warhol Foundation for the Visual Arts/Artists Rights Society (ARS), New York
28.8 © Estate of Roy Lichtenstein
28.9 Purchase with funds from the Friends of the Whitney Museum of American Art 66.2. Photograph © 2006: Whitney Museum of American Art/© Estate of Roy Lichtenstein
28.10 Dallas Museum of Art. Gift of Mr. and Mrs. James H. Clark. Photo: © 2006, Dallas Museum of Art. All rights reserved/© 2006 Artists Rights Society (ARS), New York/ADAGP, Paris
28.11 Astrup Fearnley Collection, Oslo. © R. B. Kitaj, courtesy, Marlborough Gallery, New York
28.12 Whitney Museum of American Art, New York. Purchase, with funds from the Friends of the Whitney Museum of American Art. 65.10. Photograph Copyright © 2006: Whitney Museum of American Art. Art © Estate of Tom Wesselmann/Licensed by VAGA, New York, NY
28.13 Photo Courtesy of Allan Stone Gallery, New York City. Art © Wayne Thiebaud/Licensed by VAGA, New York, NY
28.14 The Nelson-Atkins Museum of Art, Kansas City, Missouri. Gift of the Chapin Family in memory of Susan Chapin Buckwalter. 65-29. Photo: Robert Newcombe. © 2006 Claes Oldenburg and Coosje van Bruggen
28.15 Museum für Moderne Kunst, Frankfurt am Main Foto: Rudolf Nagel, Frankfurt/Main. © 2006 Claes Oldenburg and Coosje van Bruggen
28.16 © 2006 Claes Oldenburg and Coosje van Bruggen
28.17 Art © The George and Helen Segal Foundation/Licensed by VAGA, New York, NY
28.18 Albright-Knox Gallery, Buffalo. Gift of Seymour H. Knox. 1964. Photo courtesy of Carroll Janis, New York. Art © The George and Helen Segal Foundation/Licensed by VAGA, New York, NY
28.19 Photo courtesy of Carroll Janis, New York. Art © Marisol/Licensed by VAGA, New York, NY
28.20 Whitney Museum of American Art, New York. Gift of Howard and Jean Lipman Foundation, Inc. 68.73. Photography by Sandak, Inc./Division of Macmillan Publishing Company. © 2006 Artists Rights Society (ARS), New York/ADAGP, Paris
28.21 © 2006 Bridget Riley. All rights reserved. Courtesy Karsten Schubert, London
28.22 The Museum of Modern Art, New York, Helen Achen Bequest and gift of Joseph A. Helman. Digital Image © The Museum of Modern Art/Licensed by SCALA/Art Resource, NY. Art © Estate of Donald Judd/Licensed by VAGA, New York, NY
28.23 Courtesy Dia Center of the Arts, New York. © 2006 Estate of Dan Flavin/Artists Rights Society (ARS), New York
28.24 Whitney Museum of American Art, New York. Gift of the American Art Foundation 92.60. Photograph © 2006: Whitney Museum of American Art. © Agnes Martin, courtesy Pace Wildenstein, New York
28.25 Museum Wiesbaden. © The Estate of Eva Hesse. Hauser & Wirth, Zürich
28.26 Allen Memorial Art Museum, Oberlin College, Ohio. Fund for Contemporary Art and gift of the artist and the Fischbach Gallery, 1970. © The Estate of Eva Hesse. Courtesy Galerie Hauser & Wirth, Zurich
28.27 © Neue Gallery, Staatliche Museen Kassel, Germany. Photo: Ute Brunzel. © 2006 Artists Rights Society (ARS), New York/VG Bild-Kunst, Bonn
28.28 © 2006 Artists Rights Society (ARS), New York/VG Bild-Kunst, Bonn. Photo: courtesy Robert Violette, London
28.29 © 2006 Artists Rights Society (ARS), New York/VG Bild-Kunst, Bonn. Photo: courtesy Robert Violette, London
28.30 © 2006 Joseph Kosuth/Artists Rights Society (ARS), New York
29.1 © Copyright The Robert Mapplethorpe Foundation. Courtesy Art + Commerce Anthology
29.2 Courtesy Sonnabend Gallery, New York
29.3 Courtesy of Canal Street Communications, Inc.
29.4, 29.5 Photograph by Ellen Page Wilson, courtesy of Pace Wildenstein Gallery/© 2006 Chuck Close
29.6 Photo: courtesy Allan Stone Gallery, NY. © Richard Estes. Courtesy Marlborough Gallery
29.7 © 2006 Photo and permission courtesy of Mrs. Duane Hanson. Art © Estate of Duane Hanson/Licensed by VAGA, New York, NY
29.8 Photo: courtesy James Cohan Gallery
29.9 Hirshhorn Museum and Sculpture Garden, Smithsonian Institution, Gift of Joseph H. Hirshhorn, 1966 (HMSG 66.610). Photo: Lee Stalsworth. © 2006 Artists Rights Society (ARS), New York/ADAGP, Paris
29.10 Solomon R. Guggenheim Museum, New York. Purchased with the aid of funds from the National Endowment for the Arts, in Washington DC, a Federal Agency matching funds contributed by Mr. and Mrs. Barrie M. Damson, 1979. 79.2552. Photograph by David Heald © The Solomon R. Guggenheim Foundation, New York. © Richard Estes, courtesy, Marlborough Gallery, New York
29.11 Solomon R. Guggenheim Museum, New York. Partial gift of the artist, 1989. 89.3626. Photograph by David Heald © The Solomon R. Guggenheim Foundation, New York. © 2006 Jenny Holzer/Artists Rights Society (ARS), New York
29.12 © 1994 Matthew Barney. Photo: Michael James O'Brien. Courtesy Gladstone Gallery
29.13 Ezra Stoller © Esto. All rights reserved
29.14 Architectural Association, London/Gardner/Halls
29.15 © Norman McGrath
29.16 © Architectural Association, Photograph/Tom Clark
29.17 Sautereau/Cosmos/Woodfin Camp and Associates
29.18a Richard Bryant/Arcaid, London
29.18b © Grant Smith/Corbis
29.20 © FMGB Guggenheim Bilbao Museoa, 2006. Photographer David Heald. All rights reserved. Partial or total reproduction prohibited. © TAMCB, Guggenheim Bilbao Museoa, 2006
29.21 Photo courtesy Frederick R. Weisman Museum, Minneapolis
29.22 Courtesy Gehry Partners, LLP. © 2006 Frank G. Gehry
29.23, 29.24 Photo: Erika Barahona Ede © FMGB Guggenheim Bilbao Museoa. Bilbao, © 1997. All rights reserved. Total or partial reproduction is prohibited
29.25 Estate of Robert Smithson, Courtesy James Cohan Gallery, New York. Collection: DIA Center for the Arts, New York. Photo by Gianfranco Gorgoni. Art © Estate of Robert Smithson/Licensed by VAGA, New York, NY
29.26 Funding from the Virginia Wright Fund, the National Endowment for the Arts, Washington State Arts Commission. Western Washington University Art Fund and the artist's contributions. Collection of Western Washington University, Bellingham, Washington. Photo courtesy of the artist. Art © Nancy Holt/Licensed by VAGA, New York, NY
29.27 © Andy Goldsworthy. Courtesy Galerie Lelong, New York
29.28 © Christo 1991. Photo: Wolfgang Volz
29.29 © Christo 1991. Photo: Wolfgang Volz
29.30 © 1995 Christo and Jeanne-Claude. Photo: Wolfgang Volz
29.31 © Christo 2003. Photo: Wolfgang Volz
29.32 © Christo 2005. Photo: Wolfgang Volz
29.33 Photo courtesy of Carroll Janis, New York. Art © Valerie Jaudon/Licensed by VAGA, New York, NY

29.34 Courtesy, Robert Miller Gallery, New York. © 2006 The Estate of Jean-Michel Basquiat/ADAGP, Paris/ARS, New York

29.35 Courtesy of the Paula Cooper Gallery, New York

29.36 © Judy Chicago, 1979. Collection of the Brooklyn Museum of Art, Gift of The Elizabeth A. Sackler Foundation. Photo: © Donald Woodman

29.37 Photograph by Herbert Lotz, courtesy Pace Wildenstein, New York. © Kiki Smith, courtesy PaceWildenstein, New York

29.38 Photo: courtesy Yale Office of Public Affairs

29.39 Drawing by Ian Hunt

29.40 Photo Maggie Nimkin

29.41 Courtesy Sperone Westwater, New York. © 2006 Bruce Nauman/Artists Rights Society (ARS), New York

29.42 Hirshhorn Museum and Sculpture Garden, Smithsonian Institution, Joseph H. Hirshhorn Purchase Fund, 1990/Photo: Lee Stalsworth. © 2006 Susan Rothenberg/Artists Rights Society (ARS), New York

29.43 Carnegie Museum of Art, Pittsburgh; Richard M. Scaife Fund and A. W. Mellon Acquisition Endowment Fund, 83.53. © Anselm Kiefer. Courtesy Gagosian Gallery, New York

29.44 D. P. Hershkowitz/Bruce Coleman, Inc.

29.45 Whitney Museum of American Art, New York. Purchase, with funds from The Sondra and Charles Gilman, Jr. Foundation, Inc., and the Painting and Sculpture Committee 89.30a-v. Photograph © 2006: Whitney Museum of American Art. © Jeff Koons

29.46 Courtesy M. Knoedler & Co., Inc. Art © Nancy Graves Foundation/Licensed by VAGA, New York, NY

29.47 Courtesy Gagosian Gallery, New York. © Mark Tansey

29.48 Courtesy of the Artist and Metro Pictures, New York

29.49 Scala/Art Resource, NY

29.50 Courtesy of the artist and Luhring Augustine, New York

29.51 Courtesy Nam June Paik and Stedelijk Museum, Amsterdam

29.52 Courtesy Nam June Paik

29.53, 29.54 Bill Viola, The Crossing, 1996, video/sound installation, consists of two pictures one of fire and one of water. Collection: Edition 1, Collection of the Solomon R. Guggenheim Museum, New York, gift of The Bohen Foundation. Edition 2, Collection of Pamela and Richard Kramlich, San Francisco. Edition 3, Dallas Museum of Art, Texas. Photo: Kira Perov

29.55, 29.56 © 1999 Shirin Neshat. Photo: Larry Barns. Courtesy Gladstone Gallery

Index

Page numbers in **boldface** refer to illustrations.

D

E

F

Q

R

T

Y

Z